MW01201931

Virtualizing Hadoop

VMware Press is the official publisher of VMware books and training materials, which provide guidance on the critical topics facing today's IT professionals and students. VMware virtualization and cloud infrastructure technologies simplify IT complexity and streamline operations, helping organizations of all kinds and sizes to become more agile, efficient, and profitable.

VMware Press provides proven, technically accurate information that will help you achieve your goals for customizing, building, and maintaining a virtual environment—from the data center to mobile devices to the public, private, and hybrid cloud.

With books, certification and study guides, video training, and learning tools produced by world-class architects and IT experts, VMware Press helps you master a diverse range of topics on virtualization and cloud computing and is the official source of reference materials for preparing for the VMware Certified Professional certifications.

VMware Press is also pleased to have localization partners that can publish its products into more than 42 languages, including, but not limited to, Chinese (Simplified), Chinese (Traditional), French, German, Greek, Hindi, Japanese, Korean, Polish, Russian, and Spanish.

For more information about VMware Press, please visit **vmwarepress.com**.

vmware® PRESS

vmwarepress.com

Complete list of products • User Group Info • Articles • Newsletters

VMware® Press is a publishing alliance between Pearson and VMware, and is the official publisher of VMware books and training materials that provide guidance for the critical topics facing today's technology professionals and students.

With books, eBooks, certification study guides, video training, and learning tools produced by world-class architects and IT experts, VMware Press helps IT professionals master a diverse range of topics on virtualization and cloud computing, and is the official source of reference materials for preparing for the VMware certification exams.

Make sure to connect with us!
vmwarepress.com

vmware® | PEARSON IT CERTIFICATION | Safari® Books Online

ALWAYS LEARNING

PEARSON

Virtualizing Hadoop

HOW TO INSTALL, DEPLOY, AND OPTIMIZE HADOOP IN A VIRTUALIZED ARCHITECTURE

George J. Trujillo, Jr.
Charles Kim
Steven Jones
Rommel Garcia
Justin Murray

vmware® PRESS

New York • Boston • Indianapolis • San Francisco
Toronto • Montreal • London • Munich • Paris • Madrid
Capetown • Sydney • Tokyo • Singapore • Mexico City

Virtualizing Hadoop

Copyright © 2016 VMware, Inc.

Published by Pearson Education, Inc.

Publishing as VMware Press

All rights reserved. Printed in the United States of America. This publication is protected by copyright, and permission must be obtained from the publisher prior to any prohibited reproduction, storage in a retrieval system, or transmission in any form or by any means, electronic, mechanical, photocopying, recording, or likewise.

ISBN-10: 0-13-381102-6

ISBN-13: 978-0-13-381102-5

Library of Congress Control Number: 2015938462

Printed in the United States of America

First Printing: July 2015

All terms mentioned in this book that are known to be trademarks or service marks have been appropriately capitalized. The publisher cannot attest to the accuracy of this information. Use of a term in this book should not be regarded as affecting the validity of any trademark or service mark.

VMware terms are trademarks or registered trademarks of VMware in the United States, other countries, or both.

Warning and Disclaimer

Every effort has been made to make this book as complete and as accurate as possible, but no warranty or fitness is implied. The information provided is on an "as is" basis. The authors, VMware Press, VMware, and the publisher shall have neither liability nor responsibility to any person or entity with respect to any loss or damages arising from the information contained in this book.

The opinions expressed in this book belong to the author and are not necessarily those of VMware.

Special Sales

For information about buying this title in bulk quantities, or for special sales opportunities (which may include electronic versions; custom cover designs; and content particular to your business, training goals, marketing focus, or branding interests), please contact our corporate sales department at corpsales@pearsoned.com or (800) 382-3419.

For government sales inquiries, please contact

governmentsales@pearsoned.com

For questions about sales outside the U.S., please contact

international@pearsoned.com

PUBLISHER
Paul Boger

ASSOCIATE PUBLISHER
David Dusthimer

EXECUTIVE EDITOR
Mary Beth Ray

VMWARE PRESS PROGRAM MANAGER
Karl Childs

DEVELOPMENT EDITOR
Ellie Bru

MANAGING EDITOR
Sandra Schroeder

SENIOR PROJECT EDITOR
Tonya Simpson

COPY EDITOR
Barbara Hacha

PROOFREADER
The Wordsmithery LLC

INDEXER
Tim Wright

EDITORIAL ASSISTANT
Vanessa Evans

COVER DESIGNER
Chuti Prasertsith

COMPOSITOR
Trina Wurst

We Want to Hear from You!

As the reader of this book, *you* are our most important critic and commentator. We value your opinion and want to know what we're doing right, what we could do better, what areas you'd like to see us publish in, and any other words of wisdom you're willing to pass our way.

We welcome your comments. You can email or write us directly to let us know what you did or didn't like about this book—as well as what we can do to make our books better.

Please note that we cannot help you with technical problems related to the topic of this book.

When you write, please be sure to include this book's title and author as well as your name, email address, and phone number. We will carefully review your comments and share them with the author and editors who worked on the book.

Email: VMwarePress@vmware.com

Mail: VMware Press
ATTN: Reader Feedback
800 East 96th Street
Indianapolis, IN 46240 USA

Reader Services

Visit our website at www.pearsonitcertification.com/title/9780133811025 and register this book for convenient access to any updates, downloads, or errata that might be available for this book.

The inspiration of this book is to share knowledge and insight with others. So my dedication is to the people closest to me who have taught me so much. To my mother, for teaching me to never give up, to take responsibility and action for solving your own problems, and the incredible power of unconditional love. To my stepfather, Bob, for showing me the value of never compromising your character or values, and there is not a mountain you cannot climb. To my wife, Karen, for showing me the importance of a gentle heart. To my son, Cole, for helping me see the beauty of the world in a whole new light. To my daughter, Madison, for helping me understand the importance of opening your heart. To my son, Gage, for showing me it doesn't hurt to slow down and enjoy the world around you. I just hope you all have been able to learn a fraction of the things from me that you have all taught me. I thank God every day for the incredible gift of having you all in my life.
—George J. Trujillo, Jr.

I dedicate this book to my father, who passed away to be with the Lord earlier this year.
—Charles Kim

This book is dedicated to my amazingly talented coauthors whom I greatly respect. To my wife, Kay, and awesome two red-headed daughters, Bethany and Rebekah, who patiently listened to Hadoop stories. And an amazing and talented VMware education team that always demonstrates excellence.
—Steven Jones

I dedicate this book to my beloved wife, Elizabeth, and our two beautiful children, Mila and Braden. They fill my life with plenty of joy and inspiration. Thank goodness, I married an English major.
—Rommel Garcia

I dedicate this book to my wife, Chris, with all my love. Thank you for your inspiration
—Justin Murray

About the Authors

George J. Trujillo, Jr. is an experienced corporate executive with exceptional communication skills. He is an expert in change management with strong leadership skills, critical thinking, and data-driven decisions. George is an internationally recognized data architect, leader, and speaker in big data and cloud solutions. His background includes Big Data Architecture, Hadoop (Hortonworks, Cloudera), data governance, schema design, metadata management, security, NoSQL, and BI. He has many industry recognitions, including Oracle Recognized Double ACE, Sun Ambassador for Sun Microsystem's Application Middleware Platform, VMware Recognized vExpert, VMware Certified Instructor, MySQL's Socrates Award, and MySQL Certified DBA. His leadership in the user community includes Independent Oracle Users Group (IOUG) board of directors, president of IOUG Cloud SIG, chair for RMOUG Big Data SIG, president of RMOUG Cloud SIG, Oracle Fusion Council and Oracle Beta Leadership Council, IOUG's Elected to "Oracles of Oracle" circle, and master presenter for the IOUG's Master Series. His many job positions have included vice president of big data architecture in the financial services industry, master principal big data specialist at Hortonworks, tier one data specialist for VMware Center of Excellence, and CEO for professional services and training organization.

Charles Kim is the president of Viscosity North America, a niche consulting organization specializing in big data, Oracle Exadata/RAC, and virtualization. Charles is an architect in Hadoop/big data, Linux infrastructure, cloud, virtualization, engineered systems, and Oracle clustering technologies. Charles is an author with Oracle Press, Pearson, and APress in Oracle, Hadoop, and Linux technology stacks. He holds certifications in Oracle, VMware, Red Hat Linux, and Microsoft and has more than 23 years of IT experience on mission- and business-critical systems.

Charles presents regularly at VMworld, Oracle OpenWorld, IOUG, and various local/regional user group conferences. He is an Oracle ACE director, VMware vExpert, Oracle Certified DBA, Certified Exadata Specialist, and a Certified RAC Expert. Charles's books include the following:

- *Oracle Database 11g New Features for DBA and Developers*
- *Linux Recipes for Oracle DBAs*
- *Oracle Data Guard 11g Handbook*
- *Virtualizing Business Critical Oracle Databases: Database as a Service*
- *Oracle ASM 12c Pocket Reference Guide*
- *Expert Exadata Handbook*

Charles is the president of the Cloud Computing (and Virtualization) SIG for the Independent Oracle User Group. Charles blogs regularly at the DBAExpert.com/ blog site.

His LinkedIn profile is http://www.linkedin.com/in/chkim.

His Twitter tag is @racdba

Steven Jones is a 16-year veteran of technical training with experience in UNIX, networking, database technology, virtualization, and big data. Steven works at VMware as a VMware Certified Instructor; VCA; VCP 4, 5, 6; and vExpert 2014, 2015. He is a coauthor of *Virtualize Oracle Business Critical Databases: Database Infrastructure as a Service*, by Charles Kim, George Trujillo, Steven Jones, and Sudhir Balasubramanian 2014 iBooks. He was a speaker for VMworld 2013 Virtualizing Mission Critical Oracle RAC with vC Ops, San Francisco and Barcelona, and a co-speaker worldwide for VMware Education SDDC Intensive Workshop. Steven seeks to bring innovation, analogy, and narrative to understanding and mastering information technology as a service.

Rommel Garcia is a senior solutions engineer at Hortonworks, a leading open source company driving the adoption of Hadoop. Rommel has spent the past few years focusing on the design, installation, and deployment of large-scale Hadoop ecosystems. He has helped organizations implement security best practices and guidelines for Hadoop platforms. He has performance tuned Hadoop clusters ranging from fast-growing startups to Fortune 100 organizations. Rommel is a nationally recognized speaker at Hadoop and big data conferences. He is also well known for his expertise in performance tuning Java applications and middle-tier platforms. He has a BS in electronics engineering and an MS degree in computer science. Rommel resides in Atlanta with his wife, Elizabeth, and his children, Mila and Braden.

Justin Murray is a senior technical marketing architect at VMware. He holds a BA and a post-graduate diploma in computer science from University College Cork in Ireland. Justin has worked in software engineering, technical training, and consulting in various companies in the UK and the United States. Since 2007, he has been working with VMware's partner companies to validate and optimize big data and other next-generation application workloads on VMware vSphere.

Contributor

Leonid Fedotov has been in the IT industry for the past 25 years. He graduated with a master of electrical engineering from Moscow State Technical University, Moscow, Russia. Earlier in his career he was a software engineer (Assembly, Pascal, C), and then in 1993, he switched to UNIX systems administration. In 1997, he also started to learn Oracle administration and development and worked as a UNIX systems administrator and Oracle DBA for about 15 years. In 2011 he was introduced to the Hadoop world and worked as a support engineer and later as a Hadoop platform systems architect and security architect. He is an author of several Hadoop-related books, published in the iBook store at Apple.

About the Technical Editor

Erin Cizina has more than 15 years of experience as a technical writer and reviewer. She has worked on a variety of hardware and software products for IBM, VMware, NetApp, and Hitachi, most recently working on the Big Data Extensions product. Her areas of expertise include cloud-based technologies, virtualization, data protection, disaster recovery, and IT project management. She earned her project management (PMP) certification in 2009.

Acknowledgments

George J. Trujillo, Jr.:

To my wife, Karen, who has provided the strength and stability for our family while allowing me to pursue so many ventures and opportunities. I never could have accomplished half of what I've done in my life without your wisdom and support. You have always helped make the impossible seem possible. Thank you for believing in me.

Charles Kim:

I thank my wonderful wife, Melissa, who always supported my career aspirations no matter how crazy they seemed. I also would like to thank my three precious sons: Isaiah, Jeremiah, and Noah, for always making me smile.

Many thanks go out to Ellie Bru for coordinating the book to completion.

Rommel Garcia:

I'd like to thank my wife, Elizabeth, for her support, which provided me confidence and strength that allowed me to enjoy the journey of my profession and attain achievement.

A big thanks to all developers of the Hadoop platform and their continued effort to push Hadoop further.

Thanks to George Trujillo for being an excellent mentor. He provided different perspectives that helped me write several chapters of this book in an interesting way.

Many thanks to Ellie Bru, Tonya Simpson, and Erin Cizina for providing extensive reviews and feedback on the book. Special thanks to Mary Beth Ray and her team at Pearson for providing all the help I needed, particularly for making the writing experience as smooth as possible.

Justin Murray:

I want to first thank my wife, Chris, for her love, inspiration, and support.

I also want to thank my colleagues at VMware, the team at VMware Press, and Pearson who have helped make this book a reality.

Contents at a Glance

Contents

Foreword

Have you ever been caught up in a compelling or fascinating idea? There are two key words in this book: virtualization and Hadoop. We think no matter which one you are familiar with, you will be interested in finding answers to the questions combining these two words, such as, "Can I virtualize Hadoop," "Why virtualize Hadoop," and "How to virtualize Hadoop." These are key questions to define a strategy of running Hadoop effectively in an enterprise. The authors of this book want to help others understand how these two words can be brought together successfully for the delivery of enterprise data platforms.

Hadoop is no longer optional for organizations, especially large enterprises. Hadoop is a technology that enables organizations to capture insights from high-scale and highly variable data in an affordable way. More and more organizations are building innovative data-driven businesses with Hadoop. Those that are not using Hadoop are thinking hard about how to use it. An important factor in success is understanding how to merge the three worlds of developing great software solutions, managing infrastructure platforms for the enterprise, and generating rapid/quality insights from data science.

Hadoop usage in an organization often starts from a Proof of Concept (PoC) project in a business department. The strategy of running Hadoop is simple: Just choose the most convenient resource you can get. It could be physical servers outside of central IT, VMs created by the IT department, or even VMs in a public cloud. Time to business generated insight is the key at this stage. This means that Hadoop projects often start with the goal of providing business insight or data monetization at accelerated rates. Then the project must grow to answer many "how-to" questions about software development and management.

An organization must define a strategy of running Hadoop when it starts putting the first use case into production. It's very common that the number of servers for Hadoop grows quickly to hundreds. We also often see that more departments line up requesting Hadoop clusters when they see examples of success. The IT department becomes responsible for operating Hadoop clusters efficiently and satisfying the requirements from business departments. A good strategy should reduce costs, ensure high availability and business continuity, improve agility, and get a company to business insight generation faster with quality results. This is where the beauty of two ideas, Hadoop and virtualization, come together.

Virtualization has been widely adopted in enterprises. It has been proven that virtualization helps enterprises reduce IT expenses while greatly boosting efficiency and agility. Many enterprises have decided to virtualize all their applications; however, a lot of myths exist around running Hadoop on virtualization. Someone says "virtualization adds significant overhead," "Hadoop distribution vendors don't support virtual implementations,"

"Hadoop requires local disk but virtualization uses shared storages," and so on. These are misunderstandings to virtualizing Hadoop. Enterprises will find that the virtual infrastructure can be the best place to run Hadoop in most cases. We are now seeing Hadoop vendors acknowledge that a virtualized Hadoop cluster is a viable solution and must be supported across all customers if they prefer virtual machines.

The authors of this book are specialists in big data infrastructure, VMware software, and data architecture, with years of industry experience in building enterprise data solutions. In this book, you can learn the knowledge, experience, and observations of virtualization and Hadoop. It will help you to answer the questions about virtualizing Hadoop. Virtualizing Hadoop will help you begin a journey with good answers to important questions that determine success or failure.

—Bo Dong, Senior Product Line Manager at VMware

Preface

A key objective around Hadoop and big data is being able to get insight faster with a higher degree of accuracy with less risk. Business, government, schools, and science are all looking at leveraging data-driven decisions around big data and fast data. Organizations are also looking at ways to reduce the cost of working with data as well as how to improve the efficiency for processing data. This requires a platform that can rapidly provision new clusters for development, testing, and proof of concept or proof of value projects. A platform running Hadoop must have the agility and flexibility to absorb the rapid changes of the ecosystems around big data, the changing rates and volumes of evolving applications, and the evolving frameworks and products around Hadoop. Virtualization and cloud platforms offer additional choices in achieving the speed, flexibility, and agility needed for Hadoop platforms, as well as the elasticity needed for constantly evolving workloads. Virtualization is not required for a cloud platform; however, virtualization often is a key component.

This book is about helping readers understand the choices and considerations around virtualizing Hadoop platforms. *Virtualizing Hadoop* brings together a group of authors who have spent a large part of their careers designing and building optimized data platforms. The chapters are organized into a flow that will help with the ingestion of big data and Hadoop concepts, fundamentals of virtualization, and the virtualization of Hadoop. Virtualization can offer faster time to market-based decisions with faster deployments on a highly adaptable platform. This book shows you how to accomplish this.

Part I is for anyone new to Hadoop. This section takes you through an understanding of the big data challenge, driving factors for Hadoop, introductory concepts of Hadoop, and then a detailed understanding of YARN, HDFS, Tez, Map Reduce, the data ingestion frameworks, the provisioning/management/monitoring frameworks, and the data processing and transformation frameworks. An emphasis is placed on understanding Hadoop SQL engines and understanding key areas around multitenancy for a Hadoop ecosystem.

Part II is for individuals who are knowledgeable in Hadoop but need to understand virtualization. The chapters are "Virtualization Fundamentals" and "Best Practices for Virtualizing Hadoop."

Part III brings the concepts of Hadoop and virtualization together. The final chapters look at the choices around virtualizing Hadoop, key factors in virtualizing master nodes, and virtualizing worker (data) nodes in a private cloud. There are sections on installing Linux, installing Hadoop, setting up your provisioning tool (Big Data Extensions) correctly, and getting all your technical prerequisites in place for generating your first Hadoop cluster on VMware.

A lot of organizations are asking the question, "Can we virtualize Hadoop?" The simple answer is to stay with physical servers. However, in a lot of environments, using physical servers is not the automatic correct answer. Today more new servers are being put on virtual servers versus physical servers. This trend is not changing. The reason is with current hypervisors, virtual servers offer a number of advantages over physical servers. Being able to create new Hadoop clusters for development and testing on demand offers significant advantages. However, with these advantages are things to be considered, such as the runtime characteristics of Hadoop in a virtual infrastructure, virtual topology awareness of Hadoop, the complexity of running Hadoop in a virtual infrastructure, and providing elastic Hadoop services. As Hadoop continues to grow in popularity, more organizations are going to be looking at two key questions. The first is whether they should virtualize Hadoop and, if so, to what level. Virtualization is also a natural stepping stone to the cloud. The second question is whether they should be deploying Hadoop in the cloud. This book addresses both questions. The virtualization of Hadoop might not be an either/or situation but a blended solution.

The goal of this book is to share knowledge on virtualizing Hadoop, as well as to address key areas around Hadoop SQL engines, multitenancy, security, and enterprise operability. With *Virtualizing Hadoop*, someone can learn the fundamentals of big data, cultural changes required for organizational transformation, Hadoop, and key factors in deploying Hadoop in a private cloud with key best practices highlighted for successful implementations.

Motivation for Writing This Book

Hadoop and big data ecosystems are growing at an amazing rate. This has created a number of challenges for organizations, which include how to build a solid, flexible, and agile platform that can also deliver the speed necessary to allow organizations to get to business insight faster, fail faster to get to business value, and be able to deliver big data platforms that can meet the use cases that organizations need to address. Virtual and cloud enterprise platforms offer more functionality and can provide the platform glue for a number of frameworks and products that need to work together. The motivation for writing this book is to show readers the options and the pros and cons of virtualizing Hadoop. Over the next few years, more Hadoop platforms are going to be virtualized and/or offered in the cloud. A key goal is to provide readers with one book that can introduce Hadoop to virtualization experts, introduce virtualization to Hadoop experts, and then discuss the considerations for virtualizing Hadoop. So we looked at who was building some of the biggest Hadoop clusters in the world, who specialized in Hadoop deployments and virtualization infrastructures, and who was an industry leader in deploying data platforms and an expert in virtual data infrastructures; that is how this group of authors got together. One other criteria for all the authors and contributing editors were individuals who were knowledge experts but also believed in giving back to the user community.

Prerequisites

Readers should have a fundamental background in technical infrastructures and data platforms. This book is designed for Hadoop administrators, virtual administrators, Linux administrators, architects, managers, and developers who need to understand the fundamentals of virtualizing Hadoop.

Who Should Read This Book

This book is designed for the reader who needs to think out of the box and understand the advantages and disadvantages of different choices around virtualizing Hadoop.

How to Use This Book

This book is split into 15 chapters:

- **Chapter 1, "Understanding the Big Data World":** This chapter discusses the driving factors around Hadoop and big data. An emphasis is placed on data challenges traditional platforms are looking at and how the Hadoop ecosystem addresses them. The chapter wraps up by taking a look at the critical role organizational transformation plays in the success of Hadoop platforms.

- **Chapter 2, "Hadoop Fundamental Concepts":** This chapter helps you understand that Hadoop is not a single entity. A Hadoop distribution is made up of several frameworks and products. A Hadoop platform is designed to support different types of configurations to address use cases. Hadoop distributions are discussed. The chapter ends by looking at the different roles in a Hadoop environment.

- **Chapter 3, "YARN and HDFS":** YARN and HDFS make up the two core frameworks of Hadoop. YARN addresses resource management for all the processing, and HDFS manages the storage and the input/output. This is an excellent chapter for understanding the core functionality and features of the two core frameworks that set the foundation for a Hadoop platform.

- **Chapter 4, "The Modern Data Platform":** This chapter discusses design considerations for an enterprise data platform that needs to address the data challenges of today. Data movement and the organization of data in a Hadoop platform are covered.

- **Chapter 5, "Data Ingestion":** A key factor in any large enterprise data platform is data ingestion. This chapter looks at some of the key frameworks for ingesting data into a Hadoop platform.

- **Chapter 6, "Hadoop SQL Engines":** One of the biggest challenges organizations face when working with Hadoop is defining a SQL engine strategy to meet SLAs. This chapter discusses key factors and capabilities of the different SQL engines.

- **Chapter 7, "Multitenancy in Hadoop":** Multitenancy is another important area in Hadoop. This chapter looks at multitenancy from a security, data isolation, and scheduling viewpoint.

- **Chapter 8, "Virtualization Fundamentals":** This chapter looks at the key features and functionality of virtualization. Terminology, concepts, and capabilities of virtualization are covered.

- **Chapter 9, "Best Practices for Virtualizing Hadoop":** The virtual infrastructure must be set up properly. This chapter looks at best practices, guidelines, and key metrics to understand from a virtualization infrastructure.

- **Chapter 10, "Virtualizing Hadoop":** This chapter answers the question of how you manage and bring together several different frameworks and products that need to work together as one system. The benefits of virtualizing Hadoop as well as considerations are covered here. The chapter ends with a discussion of different paths to virtualizing Hadoop.

- **Chapter 11, "Virtualizing Hadoop Master Servers":** One goal of configuring the Hadoop master daemons is high availability. This chapter discusses considerations and options for virtualizing the master daemons of a Hadoop cluster.

- **Chapter 12, "Virtualizing the Hadoop Worker Nodes":** This chapter focuses on the different deployment models for virtualizing the Hadoop worker (compute and storage) daemons.

- **Chapter 13, "Deploying Hadoop as a Service in the Private Cloud":** This chapter looks at the steps in configuring Hadoop as a service.

- **Chapter 14, "Understanding the Installation of Hadoop":** Many management tools can automate the installation of Hadoop clusters, such as Ambari, Cloudera Manager, and VMware Big Data Extensions. This chapter explains a manual installation of Hadoop so readers can understand what happens underneath the covers of a Hadoop installation.

- **Chapter 15, "Configuring Linux for Hadoop":** Hadoop can run on Linux and Windows platforms. This chapter focuses on best practices and guidelines for configuring Linux for a Hadoop environment.

- **Appendix A, "Hadoop Cluster Creation: A Prerequisite Checklist":** This appendix covers the best practices and guidelines for creating Hadoop clusters.

- **Appendix B, "Big Data/Hadoop on VMware vSphere Reference Materials":** This appendix lists references used to create the book.

## Chapter 1

Understanding the Big Data World

*The intelligent TIR infrastructure—the Internet of Things—
will connect everyone and everything in a seamless network.
People, machines, natural resources, production lines, logistics
networks, consumption habits, recycling flows, and virtually
every other aspect of economic and social life will be connected via
sensors and software to the TIR platform, continually feeding
Big Data to every node—businesses, homes, vehicles, etc.—
moment to moment in real time. The Big Data, in turn, will be
analyzed with advanced analytics, transformed into predictive
algorithms, and programmed into automated systems, to improve
thermodynamic efficiencies, dramatically increase productivity,
and reduce the marginal cost of producing and delivering a full
range of goods and services to near zero across the entire economy.*

—Jeremy Rifkin

Big data has become the solution of choice for data disruption occurring today. Social
media, sensors, GPS, Renaissance Place ID (RPID), clickstream, server logs, and so on are
generating massive volumes of data to be looked at. Personalization and the omni-channel
experience is increasing the need to make business decisions faster. A perfect storm of data
is occurring in the business world. Organizations are looking at big data platforms to help
them define strategies to not only ride out the storm but also to leverage their knowledge
of data to gain a competitive advantage.

The Data Revolution

There have been multiple global changes that are so significant they are referred to as revolutions. Everyone has different categories and levels. One list of top global changes include the First (industrial), Second (technology/Internet), Third (renewable energy), and Fourth (data). The way organizations collect, use, manage, and leverage data is changing how organizations make decisions as well as changing our lives in ways beyond our imagination.

Hadoop's capability to store all kinds of data from different sources at extremely large volume, cost effectively, enables predictive analytics, correlation, and business insight to go to new levels. Organizations want to know how products and services fit into the emotional lives of customers (digital personalization). Understanding human behavior in more detail helps organizations understand price levels that create action in customers, the triggers that create the actions and responses, products that a customer is going to buy in the future, and why they will buy them. Sensors exist in just about everything, and being able to process the large volumes of data coming from sensors that go in cars, toasters, soda machines, jet engines, and even kids clothes are redefining how people look at their products, competition, and customers. Organizations want more detail and need to understand "thick" and "thin" data. Thick data helps someone understand the triggers, intentions, meanings, context, and development of an action a person or organization may take. Thin data provides details on the action or the facts that occurred, which focuses more on causation. Data warehouses have been doing this for years—the concept is not new. The dramatically low cost of local disks being used around distributed highly parallel systems, thus allowing organizations to store extremely large volumes of detailed data, is the catalyst for this new data environment.

We've had highly parallel systems and distributed platforms for years. Hadoop software makes it easier to store large volumes of data cost effectively, ingest incredibly high rates of data, and work easily with data of all types, including semi-structured and unstructured data. Hadoop is also considered a next generation Extract, Transform, and Load (ETL) and data retention platform. Hadoop can be used as an ETL off-load optimization from Enterprise Data Warehouse (EDW) because of the lower cost per TB. Data can be stored much longer in a Hadoop cluster versus an EDW due to the much lower total cost of ownership.

Hadoop enables organizations to look at thick and thin data in great detail and manage extremely large-scale data cost effectively. This enables organizations to be able to ask questions they could never ask before. It is important to understand that Hadoop is not a new type of data warehouse. There is overlap in function and objectives, however; Hadoop and data warehouses were designed from the ground up to solve different types of problems. It's good to note that all the skills and expertise of existing data experts can be leveraged in Hadoop because it's still about solving business problems with data. Hadoop software distributions and NoSQL databases offer new ways of solving today's data challenges. As a Hadoop environment matures the data flows between relational databases and data warehouses, and Hadoop will increase. We discuss the differences between Hadoop and EDWs in more detail later.

Customers are sending tremendous amounts of detail through their social media activities, clickstream activity on websites, email, and cell phones. This digital information can provide incredible insights into the patterns and behaviors of individuals and groups. Digital personalization is about deeper understanding and then being able to provide customized services around value choices that are relevant and dynamic across all digital channels (computer, smart phone, tablet, watch, and so on). Combining this digital information with a history of a customer's transactions and external data about other customers or groups with similar characteristics provides tremendous clarity into the likely next actions of a customer or group. Someone who understands a customer's likely next actions not only has the capability of influencing the next action but can also influence the drivers of that action. This can provide a distinct competitive advantage.

The digital revolution is taking the business world through a tremendous transformation that demands competitive organizations make accurate business decisions faster than their competition. The digital revolution has flattened out global competition. Organizations are faced with new aggressive competition that can allow small organizations to compete against large organizations in the digital space. Customers have ever-increasing expectations across the different digital channels they use. The future industry leaders will be the organizations that can adapt and make business decisions faster than their competition with higher accuracy and confidence and with less risk. This transformation will impact everyone's personal environment and how they interact in that environment. Every organization must understand its customers better and to be forward thinking by understanding their customers' next best steps. This requires better and faster analytics.

A store that sells expensive scotch or wine might learn through external data that their high-profile customers visit their store more often when the cigar store or cheese store has sales or introduces new products. Car sensors collect data points around how a car is used and how the car responds to this usage related to where a car is. This information can influence the next generation of car, highway, traffic light design, and neighborhood and city design. Combining data from hospitals and social media, as well as historical patterns, can allow the identification of virus outbreaks from a few weeks down to a few days and even a few hours. It now becomes very clear why analysts are predicting that as much as 80% of the data an organization needs to look at will be generated external to a business unit or group. The great magnifier is being able to also correlate internal data with external data sources to increase the insight and accuracy of the analytics.

Organizations can have hundreds or thousands of different relational databases, operational data stores, and enterprise data warehouses. Data arrives from clickstream, application servers, machines, social media, GPS, RFID, and the like in ever increasing numbers. The new enterprise data platform that organizations will use to solve these data challenges is big data. This chapter introduces the driving force behind big data and how big data is the right solution at the right time.

Traditional Data Systems

Traditional data systems, such as relational databases and data warehouses, have been the primary way businesses and organizations have stored and analyzed their data for the past 30 to 40 years. Although other data stores and technologies exist, the major percentage of business data can be found in these traditional systems. Traditional systems are designed from the ground up to work with data that has primarily been structured data. Characteristics of structured data include the following:

- Clearly defined fields organized in records. Records are usually stored in tables. Fields have names, and relationships are defined between different fields.

- Schema-on-write that requires data be validated against a schema before it can be written to disk. A significant amount of requirements analysis, design, and effort up front can be involved in putting the data in clearly defined structured formats. This can increase the time before business value can be realized from the data.

- A design to get data from the disk and load the data into memory to be processed by applications. This is an extremely inefficient architecture when processing large volumes of data this way. The data is extremely large and the programs are small. The big component must move to the small component for processing.

- The use of Structured Query Language (SQL) for managing and accessing the data.

- Relational and warehouse database systems that often read data in 8k or 16k block sizes. These block sizes load data into memory, and then the data are processed by applications. When processing large volumes of data, reading the data in these block sizes is extremely inefficient.

- Organizations today contain large volumes of information that is not actionable or being leveraged for the information it contains.

- An order management system is designed to take orders. A web application is designed for operational efficiency. A customer system is designed to manage information on customers. Data from these systems usually reside in separate data silos. However, bringing this information together and correlating with other data can help establish detailed patterns on customers.

- In a number of traditional siloed environments data scientists can spend 80% of their time looking for the right data and 20% of the time doing analytics. A data-driven environment must have data scientists spending a lot more time doing analytics.

Every year organizations need to store more and more detailed information for longer periods of time. Increased regulation in areas such as health and finance are significantly increasing storage volumes. Expensive shared storage systems often store this data because of the critical nature of the information. Shared storage arrays provide features such as striping (for performance) and mirroring (for availability). Managing the volume and cost of this data growth within these traditional systems is usually a stress point for IT organizations. Examples of data often stored in structured form include Enterprise Resource Planning (ERP), Customer Resource Management (CRM), financial, retail, and customer information.

Atomicity, Consistency, Isolation, Durability (ACID) compliant systems and the strategy around them are still important for running the business. A number of these systems were built over the years and support business decisions that run an organization today. Relational databases and data warehouses can store petabytes (PB) of information. However, these systems were not designed from the ground up to address a number of today's data challenges. The cost, required speed, and complexity of using these traditional systems to address these new data challenges would be extremely high.

Semi-Structured and Unstructured Data

Semi-structured data does not conform to the organized form of structured data but contains tags, markers, or some method for organizing the data. Unstructured data usually does not have a predefined data model or order. Examples of unstructured data include Voice over IP (VoIP), social media data structures (Twitter, Facebook), application server logs, video, audio, messaging data, RFID, GPS coordinates, machine sensors, and so on. This unstructured data is completely dwarfing the volume of structured data being generated. Organizations are finding that this unstructured data that is usually generated externally is just as critical as the structured internal data being stored in relational databases. External data about your products and services can be just as important as the data you collect. Every time you use social media or use a smart device, you might be broadcasting the information shown in Table 1.1, or more. In fact, smartphones are generating massive volumes of data that telecommunication companies have to deal with.

Table 1.1   Social Media Data That Can Be Used to Establish Patterns

Environment	Personal
What you are doing?	What do you think?
Where you are going?	How do you feel?
Where are you?	What do you like and not like?
Where have you been?	What are your driving patterns?
What neighborhood are you in?	What are your purchasing patterns?
What store you are visiting?	
Are you at work?	
Are you on vacation?	
What products are you looking at?	
What road are you on?	

This information can be correlated with other sources of data, and with a high degree of accuracy, which can predict some of the information shown in Table 1.2.

Table 1.2   Examples of Patterns Derived from Social Media

Health	Money	Personal	Infrastructure
Detection of diseases or outbreaks	Questionable trading practices	Is someone a safe driver?	Is a machine component wearing out or likely to break?
Activity and growth patterns	Credit card fraud	Is someone having an affair?	Designing roads to reflect traffic patterns and activity in different areas
Probability of a heart attack or stroke	Identify process failures and security breaches	Who you will vote for	Activity and growth patterns
Are you an alcoholic?	How money is spent	Products in your home	Identify process failures and security breaches
The outbreak of a virus	How much money you make	Are you likely to commit a crime?	Driving patterns in a city
	Purchase patterns	What you do for relaxation	A good place to put a store or business
	Products you are likely to buy	How you use a website	Brand loyalty and why people switch brands

Health	Money	Personal	Infrastructure
	Probability of loan default	Products you are likely to buy	
	Brand loyalty and why people switch brands	Type of people you associate with	
		Activities you enjoy	

In a very competitive world, people realize they need to use this information and mine it for the "business insight" it contains. In some ways, business insight or insight generation might be a better term than big data because insight is one of the key goals for a big data platform. This type of data is raising the minimum bar for the level of information an organization needs to make competitive business decisions.

Causation and Correlation

Storing large volumes of data on shared storage systems is very expensive. So for most of the critical data we have talked about, companies have not had the capability to save it, organize it, and analyze it or leverage its benefits because of the storage costs. We have lived in a world of causation. With causation, detailed information is filtered, aggregated, averaged, and then used to try to figure out what "caused" the results. After the data has been processed this way, most of the golden secrets of the data have been stripped away. The original detailed records can provide much more insight than aggregated and filtered data. The ever increasing volume of data, the unstoppable velocity of the data that is being generated in the world, and the complexity of working with unstructured data as well as the costs have kept organizations from leveraging the details of the data. This impacts the capability to make good business decisions in an ever-changing competitive environment.

When you look at large corporations, it is typical to see hundreds and even thousands of relational databases of different types and multiple data warehouses. Organizations must be able to analyze together the data from databases, data warehouses, application servers, machine sensors, social media, and so on. Data can be organized into repositories that can store data of all kinds, of different types, and from different sources in data refineries and data lakes. This data can be correlated using more data points for increased business value. By processing data from different sources into a single source, organizations can do a lot more descriptive and predictive analytics. Organizations are not only wanting to predict with high degrees of accuracy but also to reduce the risk in the predictions.

Organizations want to centralize a lot of their data for improved analytics and to reduce the cost of data movement. These centralized data repositories are referred to differently, such as data refineries and data lakes.

- A data refinery is a repository that can ingest, process, and transform disparate polystructured data into usable formats for analytics. A data refinery is analogous to an oil refinery. With an oil refinery, it is understood how to make gasoline and kerosene from oil. A data refinery is a little more rigid in the data it accepts for analytics. There is an emphasis in making sure garbage data does not enter the data refinery. A data refinery can work with extremely large datasets of any format cost effectively.

- A data lake is a new concept where structured, semi-structured, and unstructured data can be pooled into one single repository where business users can interact with it in multiple ways for analytical purposes. A data lake is an enterprise data platform that uses different types of software, such as Hadoop and NoSQL. A data lake can run applications of different runtime characteristics. A water lake does not have rigid boundaries. The shoreline of a lake can change over a period of time. A data lake is designed with similar flexibility to support new types of data and combinations of data so it can be analyzed for new sources of insight. This does not mean that a data lake should allow any data inside it, so it turns into a swamp. Control must be maintained to ensure that quality data or data with the potential of new insights is stored in the data lake. The data lake should not enable itself to be flooded with just any type of data.

Data Challenges

They say that necessity is the mother of all invention. That definitely holds true for data. Banks, governments, insurance firms, manufacturing companies, health institutions, and retail companies all realized the issues of working with these large volumes of data. Yet, it was the Internet companies that were forced to solve it. Organizations such as Google, Yahoo!, Facebook, and eBay were ingesting massive volumes of data that were increasing in size and velocity every day, and to stay in business they had to solve this data problem. Google wanted to be able to rank the Internet. It knew the data volume was large and would grow larger every day. It went to the traditional database and storage vendors and saw that the costs of using their software licenses and storage technology was so prohibitive they could not even be considered. So Google realized it needed a new technology and a new way of addressing the data challenges.

Back to the Basics

Google realized that if it wanted to be able to rank the Internet, it had to design a new way of solving the problem. It started with looking at what was needed:

- Inexpensive storage that could store massive amounts of data cost effectively

- To scale cost effectively as the data volume continued to increase

- To analyze these large data volumes very fast

- To be able to correlate semi-structured and unstructured data with existing structured data

- To work with unstructured data that had many forms that could change frequently; for example, data structures from organizations such as Twitter can change regularly

Google also identified the problems:

- The traditional storage vendor solutions were too expensive.

- When processing very large volumes of data at the level of hundreds of terabytes and petabytes, technologies based on "shared block-level storage" were too slow and couldn't scale cost effectively. Relational databases and data warehouses were not designed for the new level of scale of data ingestion, storage, and processing that was required. Today's data scale requires a high-performance super-computer platform that could scale at cost.

- The processing model of relational databases that read data in 8k and 16k increments and then loaded the data into memory to be accessed by software programs was too inefficient for working with large volumes of data.

- The traditional relational database and data warehouse software licenses were too expensive for the scale of data Google needed.

- The architecture and processing models of relational databases and data warehouses were designed to handle transactions for a world that existed 30 to 40 years ago. These architectures and processing models were not designed to process the semi-structured and unstructured data coming from social media, machine sensors, GPS coordinates, and RFID. Solutions to address these challenges are so expensive that organizations wanted another choice.

- Reducing business data latency was needed. Business data latency is the differential between the time when data is stored to the time when the data can be analyzed to solve business problems.

- Google needed a large single data repository to store all the data. Walk into any large organization and it typically has thousands of relational databases along with a number of different data warehouse and business analysis solutions. All these data platforms stored their data in their own independent silos. The data needed to be correlated and analyzed with different datasets to maximize business value. Moving data across data silos is expensive, requires lots of resources, and significantly slows down the time to business insight.

The solution criteria follows:

- Inexpensive storage. The most inexpensive storage is local storage from off-the-shelf disks.

- A data platform that could handle large volumes of data and be linearly scalable at cost and performance.

- A highly parallel processing model that was highly distributed to access and compute the data very fast.

- A data repository that could break down the silos and store structured, semi-structured, and unstructured data to make it easy to correlate and analyze the data together.

The key whitepapers that were the genesis for the solution follow. These are still recommended readings because they lay down the foundation for the processing and storage of Hadoop. These articles are also insightful because they define the business drivers and technical challenges Google wanted to solve.

- Google's article on MapReduce: "Simplified Data Processing on Large Clusters." http://static.googleusercontent.com/media/research.google.com/en/us/archive/ mapreduce-osdi04.pdf

- Yahoo!'s article on the Hadoop Distributed File System: http://dl.acm.org/ citation.cfm?id=1914427

- Google's "Bigtable: A Distributed Storage System for Structured Data": http:// static.googleusercontent.com/media/research.google.com/en/us/archive/ bigtable-osdi06.pdf.

- Yahoo!'s white paper, "The Hadoop Distributed File System Whitepaper" by Shvachko, Kuang, Radia, and Chansler. Published in the proceedings of the 2010 IEEE 26th Symposium on Mass Storage Systems and Technologies (MSST).

Solving the Data Problem

Necessity may be the mother of all invention, but for something to be created and grow, it needs a culture and environment that can support, nurture, and provide the nutrients. Look at the Italian Renaissance period, which was a great period in the history of art. Why? During the Renaissance period, in a very condensed area in Europe, there were artists who started studying at childhood, often as young as seven years old. They would learn as apprentices to other great artists, with kings and nobility paying for their works. During the Renaissance period, great artists flourished because a culture existed that allowed individuals with talent to spend their entire lives studying and working with other great artists.

During the industrial revolution there was a great need for stronger materials to grow larger buildings in condensed areas, for faster and more efficient transportation, and to be able to create products quickly for fast-growing populations. During the industrial revolution, steel manufacturing and transportation grew almost overnight. The Italian Renaissance, the industrial revolution, and Hadoop all grew from the need, demand, and culture that could promote their growth. Today's current data challenges have created a demand for a new platform, and open source is a culture that can provide tremendous innovation by leveraging great talent from around the world in collaborative efforts. The capability to store, process, and analyze information at ever faster rates will change how businesses, organizations, and governments run; how people think; and change the very nature of the world created around us.

The Necessity and Environment for Solving the Data Problem

The environment that solved the problem turned out to be Silicon Valley in California, and the culture was open source. In Silicon Valley, a number of Internet companies had to solve the same problem to stay in business, but they needed to be able to share and exchange ideas with other smart people who could add the additional components. Silicon Valley is unique in that it has a large number of startup and Internet companies that by their nature are innovative, believe in open source, and have a large amount of cross-pollination in a very condensed area. Open source is a culture of exchanging ideas and writing software from individuals and companies around the world. Larger proprietary companies might have hundreds or thousands of engineers and customers, but open source has tens of thousands to millions of individuals who can write software and download and test software.

Individuals from Google, Yahoo!, and the open source community created a solution for the data problem called Hadoop. Hadoop was created for a very important reason—survival. The Internet companies needed to solve this data problem to stay in business and be able to grow.

Giving the Data Problem a Name

The data problem is being able to store large amounts of data cost effectively (volume), with large ingestion rates (velocity), with data that can be of different types and structures (variety). This data must be able to provide value (veracity) to an organization. This type of data is referred to as *big data*. These are the Vs of big data. Yet big data is not just volume, velocity, or variety. Big data is the name given to a data context or environment when the data environment is too difficult to work with, too slow, or too expensive for traditional relational databases and data warehouses to solve.

What's the Deal with Big Data?

Across the board, industry analyst firms consistently report almost unimaginable numbers on the growth of data. The traditional data in relational databases and data warehouses are growing at incredible rates. The growth of traditional data is by itself a significant challenge for organizations to solve. The cost of storing just the traditional data growth on expensive storage arrays is strangling the budgets of IT departments.

The big news, though, is that VoIP, social media, and machine data are growing at almost exponential rates and are completely dwarfing the data growth of traditional systems. Most organizations are learning that this data is just as critical to making business decisions as traditional data. This nontraditional data is usually semi-structured and unstructured data. Examples include web logs, mobile web, clickstream, spatial and GPS coordinates, sensor data, RFID, video, audio, and image data.

Big data from an industry perspective:

- All the industry analysts and pundits are making predictions of massive growth of the big data market. In every company we walk into, one of their top priorities involves using predictive analytics to better understand their customers, themselves, and their industry.

- Opportunities for vendors will exist at all levels of the big data technology stack, including infrastructure, software, and services.

- Organizations that have begun to embrace big data technology and approaches are demonstrating that they can gain a competitive advantage by being able to take action based on timely, relevant, complete, and accurate information rather than guesswork.

Data becomes big data when the volume, velocity, and/or variety of data gets to the point where it is too difficult or too expensive for traditional systems to handle. Big data is not when the data reaches a certain volume or velocity of data ingestion or type of data. However, it is the exponential data growth that is the driving factor of the data revolution.

Open Source

Open source is a community and culture designed around crowd sourcing to solve problems. Many of the most innovative individuals who work for companies or themselves help to design and create open source software. It is created under open source license structures that can make the software free and the source code available to anyone. Be aware that there are different types of open source licensing. The open source culture provides an environment that allows rapid innovation, software to be free, and hardware that is relatively inexpensive because open source uses commodity x86 hardware. MySQL,

Linux, Apache HTTP Server, Ganglia, Nagios, Tomcat, Java, Python, and JavaScript are all growing significantly in large organizations. An example of the rapid innovation is that proprietary vendors often come out with a major new release every two to three years. However, Hadoop recently had three new major releases in a year.

The ecosystem around Hadoop is innovating just as fast. For example, frameworks such as Spark, Storm, and Kafka are significantly increasing the capabilities around Hadoop. Open source solutions can be very innovative because the source can be generated from sources all around the world and from different organizations. There is increasing participation from large vendor companies as well, and software teams in large organizations also generate open source software. Large companies, such as EMC, HP, Hitachi, Oracle, VMware, and IBM are now offering solutions around big data. The innovation being driven by open source is completely changing the landscape of the software industry. In looking at Hadoop and big data, we see that open source is now defining platforms and ecosystems, not just software frameworks or tools.

Why Traditional Systems Have Difficulty with Big Data

The reason traditional systems have a problem with big data is that they were not designed for it.

- **Problem—Schema-On-Write:** Traditional systems are schema-on-write. Schema-on-write requires the data to be validated when it is written. This means that a lot of work must be done before new data sources can be analyzed. Here is an example: Suppose a company wants to start analyzing a new source of data from unstructured or semi-structured sources. A company will usually spend months (3–6 months) designing schemas and so on to store the data in a data warehouse. That is 3 to 6 months that the company cannot use the data to make business decisions. Then when the data warehouse design is completed 6 months later, often the data has changed again. If you look at data structures from social media, they change on a regular basis. The schema-on-write environment is too slow and rigid to deal with the dynamics of semi-structured and unstructured data environments that are changing over a period of time. The other problem with unstructured data is that traditional systems usually use Large Object Byte (LOB) types to handle unstructured data, which is often very inconvenient and difficult to work with.

- **Solution—Schema-On-Read:** Hadoop systems are schema-on-read, which means any data can be written to the storage system immediately. Data are not validated until they are read. This enables Hadoop systems to load any type of data and begin analyzing it quickly. Hadoop systems have extremely short business latency compared to traditional systems. Traditional systems require schema-on-write, which was designed more than 50 years ago. A lot of companies need real-time processing of data and customer models generated in hours or days versus weeks or months. The Internet of Things (IoT) is accelerating the data streams coming from different types of devices and physical objects, and digital personalization is accelerating the need to be able to make real-time decisions. Schema-on-read gives Hadoop a tremendous advantage over traditional systems in an area that matters most, that of being able to analyze the data faster to make business decisions. When working with complex data structures that are semi-structured or unstructured, schema-on-read enables data to be accessed much faster than schema-on-write systems.

- **Problem—Cost of Storage:** Traditional systems use shared storage. As organizations start to ingest larger volumes of data, shared storage is cost prohibitive.

- **Solution—Local Storage:** Hadoop can use the Hadoop Distributed File System (HDFS), a distributed file system that leverages local disks on commodity servers. Shared storage is about $1.20/GB, whereas local storage is about $.04/GB. Hadoop's HDFS creates three replicas by default for high availability. So at 12 cents per GB, it is still a fraction of the cost of traditional shared storage.

- **Problem—Cost of Proprietary Hardware:** Large proprietary hardware solutions can be cost prohibitive when deployed to process extremely large volumes of data. Organizations are spending millions of dollars in hardware and software licensing costs while supporting large data environments. Organizations are often growing their hardware in million dollar increments to handle the increasing data. New technology in traditional vendor systems that can grow to petabyte scale and good performance are extremely expensive.

- **Solution—Commodity Hardware:** It is possible to build a high-performance super-computer environment using Hadoop. One customer was looking at a proprietary hardware vendor for a solution. The hardware vendor's solution was $1.2 million in hardware costs and $3 million in software licensing. The Hadoop solution for the same processing power was $400,000 for hardware, the software was free, and the support costs were included. Because data volumes would be constantly increasing, the proprietary solution would have grown in $500k and $1 million dollar increments, whereas the Hadoop solution would grow in $10,000 and $100,000 increments.

- **Problem—Complexity:** When you look at any traditional proprietary solution, it is full of extremely complex silos of system administrators, DBAs, application server teams, storage teams, and network teams. Often there is one DBA for every 40 to 50 database servers. Anyone running traditional systems knows that complex systems fail in complex ways.

- **Solution—Simplicity:** Because Hadoop uses commodity hardware and follows the "shared-nothing" architecture, it is a platform that one person can understand very easily. Numerous organizations running Hadoop have one administrator for every 1,000 data nodes. With commodity hardware, one person can understand the entire technology stack.

- **Problem—Causation:** Because data is so expensive to store in traditional systems, data is filtered and aggregated, and large volumes are thrown out because of the cost of storage. Minimizing the data to be analyzed reduces the accuracy and confidence of the results. Not only are accuracy and confidence to the resulting data affected, but it also limits an organization's ability to identify business opportunities. Atomic data can yield more insights into the data than aggregated data.

- **Solution—Correlation:** Because of the relatively low cost of storage of Hadoop, the detailed records are stored in Hadoop's storage system HDFS. Traditional data can then be analyzed with nontraditional data in Hadoop to find correlation points that can provide much higher accuracy of data analysis. We are moving to a world of correlation because the accuracy and confidence of the results are factors higher than traditional systems. Organizations are seeing big data as transformational. Companies building predictive models for their customers would spend weeks or months building new profiles. Now these same companies are building new profiles and models in a few days. One company would have a data load take 20 hours to complete, which is not ideal. They went to Hadoop and the time for the data load went from 20 hours to 3 hours.

- **Problem—Bringing Data to the Programs:** In relational databases and data warehouses, data are loaded from shared storage elsewhere in the datacenter. The data must go over wires and through switches that have bandwidth limitations before programs can process the data. For many types of analytics that process 10s, 100s, and 1000s of terabytes, the capability of the computational side to process data greatly exceeds the storage bandwidth available.

- **Solution—Bringing Programs to the Data:** With Hadoop, the programs are moved to where the data is. Hadoop data is spread across all the disks on the local servers that make up the Hadoop cluster, often in 64MB or 128MB block increments. Individual programs, one for every block, runs in parallel (up to the number of available map slots, more on this later) across the cluster, delivering a very high level of parallelization and Input/Output Operations per Second (IOPS). This means Hadoop systems can process extremely large volumes of data much faster than traditional systems and at a fraction of the cost because of the architecture model. Moving the programs (small component) to the data (large component) is an architecture that supports the extremely fast processing of large volumes of data.

Successfully leveraging big data is transforming how organizations are analyzing data and making business decisions. The "value" of the results of big data has most companies racing to build Hadoop solutions to do data analysis. Often, customers bring in consulting firms and want to "out Hadoop" their competitors. Hadoop is not just a transformation technology; it has become the strategic difference between success and failure in today's modern analytics world.

Hadoop's Framework Architecture

Hadoop is a software solution where all the components are designed from the ground up to be an extremely parallel high-performance platform that can store large volumes of information cost effectively. It handles very large ingestion rates; easily works with structured, semi-structured, and unstructured data; eliminates the business data latency problem; is extremely low cost in relation to traditional systems; has a very low entry cost point; and is linearly scalable in cost effective increments.

A Hadoop distribution is made of a number of separate frameworks that are designed to work together. The frameworks are extensible as well as the Hadoop framework platform. Hadoop has evolved to support fast data as well as big data. Big data was initially about large batch processing of data. Now organizations also need to make business decisions real time or near real time as the data arrives. Fast data involves the capability to act on the data as it arrives. Hadoop's flexible framework architecture supports the processing of data with different run-time characteristics.

NoSQL Databases

NoSQL databases were also designed from the ground up to be able to work with very large datasets of different types and to perform very fast analysis of that data. Traditional databases were designed to store relational records and handle transactions. NoSQL databases are nonrelational. When records need to be analyzed, it is the columns that contain the important information. NoSQL databases may mean data is accessed in the following ways:

- Without SQL using APIs ("No" SQL).
- With SQL or other access methods ("Not only" SQL).

When using Apache Hive (Hadoop framework) to run SQL in NoSQL databases, those queries are converted to MapReduce(2) and run as a batch operation to process large volumes of data in parallel. APIs can also be used to access the data in NoSQL to process interactive and real-time queries.

Popular NoSQL databases include HBase, Accumulo, MongoDB, and Cassandra. They are databases designed to provide very fast analysis of column data. Accumulo is a NoSQL database designed by the National Security Agency (NSA) of the United States, so it has additional security features currently not available in HBase.

NoSQL databases have different characteristics and features. For example, they can be key-value based, column based, document based, or graph based. Each NoSQL database can emphasize different areas of the Cap Theorem (Brewer Theorem). The Cap Theorem states that a database can excel in only two of the following areas: consistency (all data nodes see same data at the same time), availability (every request for data will get a response of success or failure), and partition tolerance (the data platform will continue to run even if parts of the system are not available). NoSQL databases are often indexed by key but not all support secondary indexes. Data in NoSQL databases is usually distributed across local disks across different servers. Fan-out queries are used to access the data. With NoSQL systems supporting eventual consistency, the data can be stored in separate geographical locations. NoSQL is discussed in more detail in Chapter 2, "Hadoop Fundamental Concepts."

RDBMS systems enforce schemas, are ACID compliant, and support the relational model. NoSQL databases are less structured (nonrelational). Tables can be schema free (a schema can be different in each row), are often open source, and can be distributed horizontally in a cluster. Some NoSQL databases are evolving to support ACID. There are Apache projects such as Phoenix, which has a relational database layer over HBase. Schema tables can be very flexible for even simple schemas such as an order table that stores addresses from different countries that require different formats. A number of customers start looking at NoSQL when they need to work with a lot of unstructured or semi-structured data or when they are having performance or data ingestion issues because of the volume or velocity of the data.

In-Memory Frameworks

Fast data is driving the adoption of in-memory distributed data systems. Frameworks such as Apache Spark and Cloudera's Impala offer in-memory distributed datasets that are spread across the Hadoop cluster. Apache Drill and Hortonworks Tez are additional frameworks emerging as additional solutions for fast data.

The Modern Data Architecture

Existing data architectures are being pushed to the breaking point with the large amount of data, velocity of data ingestion, and variety of data they need to process and store. Industry analysts are predicting that up to 80% of the new data will be semi-structured and unstructured (video, pictures, audio, documents, emails, and so on) data coming from clickstream, sentiment/social media, machine sensors, server logs, RFID, and GPS (geographic). There are more than 3ZB in 2013, and predictions of 40ZB by 2020 are not considered underestimates.

The Modern Data Architecture (MDA) adds Hadoop to existing enterprise data platforms to solve this data pressure problem. A Hadoop cluster can be used as a combination ingestion, storage, and compute grid. Hadoop, NoSQL, and in-memory solutions are becoming the new data components that make up a big data platform. The data landscape for enterprises is evolving to support relational databases, enterprise data warehouses, NoSQL databases, in-memory, and Hadoop. Organizations are blending these solutions to leverage what each platform does extremely well.

Organizing data into a single data source or just a few data sources allows a richer set of questions to be asked of the data. Being able to add additional correlation sources increases the confidence and reduces the risk of the results of the questions. Different names are associated with these single source platforms. Some popular names are data refinery, enterprise data hub, and data lake. Each of these platforms is similar. They all use Hadoop, NoSQL, and different Apache frameworks for delivering data solutions. Data refinery, data lake, and enterprise data hubs are used by different organizations to refer to single-source big data platforms that leverage a Hadoop software distribution. The terms are cross-pollinating with new variations, and new terms are rising as well, such as a marshal data yard. What they have in common is the ingestion of data from all types of data sources, with rapid data movement and the flexibility of quickly working with schema-less data being used with schema-on-read capability.

Data warehouses are considered more rigid with schema-on-write, ACID compliance, and much less data movement. Data warehouses usually transform the data before entry using well-defined formats. Big data platforms load the data in first and then, based on the analytics and data usage, transform the data as needed. This is important to understand. Data analysts and scientists often spend 80% of their time looking at the data and 20% analyzing it. A big data platform can significantly change this ratio, allowing data insight to occur faster. We introduced data refinery and data lake, but we thought we should describe all the definitions together. All these assume centralizing the data into a single source; there is just emphasis on different areas.

- A big data refinery is a data platform that can store, transform, and process polystructured data sources. Refining the data creates new insights leveraging all different types of data sources. A data refinery controls more tightly what data can be ingested inside it.

- A *data lake* is one way to store and process data in its native format. A data lake is a single place to land all data and do analysis regardless of toolset. Putting data from different sources together allows data mashups and correlation to occur. A data lake has more flexibility in allowing new types of data in for exploration, but this does not mean any data can go inside it so that it gets swamped and loses veracity. The term *data lake* is more popular with the Hortonworks distribution, but it is a concept and is not tied to any distribution.

- An enterprise data hub, also referred to as a data lake, is a big data platform leveraging Hadoop. An enterprise data hub is a concept where Hadoop is the central data platform with data flowing in and out of other data platforms in a hublike architecture. The enterprise data hub is more popular with the Cloudera distribution; again, it is a concept that does not have to be tied to a distribution.

- A data marshal yard describes a big data platform with the emphasis on the data movement—similar to a railroad marshal yard where trains are moving in and out of a central location.

It is incredibly painful, inefficient, and expensive for organizations to have data take a lot of hops when it goes from being stored, transformed, and then analyzed. The data lake can be used as a data ingestion, analytics, and/or compute grid. The data lake can absorb a lot of the ETL processing done by data warehouses and be used to offload data from a data warehouse. This enables a data warehouse to be right-sized and stay at a fixed size. If a data warehouse can store data for only 6 months and the volume of data keeps growing, moving the data to a data lake reduces growth pressure on the data warehouse. Letting the big data platform handle the data ingestion also frees up a lot of compute cycles to be used for analytics and not data ingestion.

A data lake enables business units to land data once in a single place. Backups, analytics, joins, security, downstream reporting, data science, and data ingestion can all be performed in one system. Hadoop's distributed file system enables it to easily store data in any form, so it can be stored in its raw data form. Hadoop is a schema-on-read platform, so a schema does not need to be applied to new data right away. Data can be integrated when it is needed. Data lakes enable data science to go to a new level with data mashups allowing for a 720° view of a customer. A 360° view of the customer is an old term that refers to having a complete view of the customer. A 720° view refers to an additional 360° view of the customer using unstructured and semi-structured data. This allows cross-silo and cross-channel analysis. Businesses such as banks, credit card companies, insurance, retail, health care, financial services, telcos, gaming, and Internet companies all need this capability.

Organizational Transformation

Transforming an organization is very difficult. Transformation includes bringing in vendors and external consultants that recommend different software, tools, and methods for building a big data environment. Internal employees must learn new approaches and new technologies. Business units must find the right use cases and be able to ask questions they want to ask and what insights they are looking to get to address business challenges. Business units must have confidence that moving their data into a big data platform is the right thing to do. Companies must learn how to become learning organizations and adapt to the rate of innovation in open source. Data analysts and data scientists must be found who have the skill to be able to ask the right questions of the data to find new insights. Finding the right blend of open and closed software is important. Working on minimizing the political, territorial, and technical silos built over years around data takes time. At the same time, there is a war on talent with organizations competing for the small group of qualified talent. The skilled talent is not coming anywhere close to keeping up with demand. Competing in today's digital environment requires a company to use data as a corporate asset and a competitive advantage.

Successful data-driven IT organizations need teams that have the skills and ability equivalent to being able to build and change a plane while flying it. Hadoop is maturing and evolving quickly, which is demonstrating the power of open source innovation. Everyone understands that change is required, but most are not prepared for the speed of this change. This is challenging organizations to be able to absorb and adapt to this rate of change. Success with Hadoop requires a new way of thinking as well as a sense of urgency. Organizations now want the capability of batch processing and interactive and real-time queries with their big data platforms. This requires building the right combination of software frameworks, tools, in-memory software, distributed search, and NoSQL databases around Hadoop, and leveraging the existing software from proprietary software firms.

Organizations need to greatly reduce data silos and centralize data more efficiently for better correlation and analytics. The analytical systems that maximize business value are data repositories that allow data from multiple sources of different types to be correlated to find new data patterns that provide significantly increased accuracy. The world of relational databases and data warehouses that require deleting, ignoring, aggregating, and summarizing data because of the high costs of storage is a losing formula for descriptive and predictive analytics. It is the detailed data that contains the golden information (insights) for success. Big data platforms bring together a number of very important components required for fast and accurate analytics. These components include low-cost storage, schema-on-read, linearly scalable platforms, super-computer platforms that leverage a large number of spinning disks using commodity hardware, and highly parallelized processing frameworks. Hadoop is a platform that enables the secret sauce of all these important components to come together into a single data repository.

The following contain some of the key goals around big data:

- Be able to make business decisions faster than your competition with a higher degree of confidence and less risk.

- Increase the type and number of questions you can ask of your data for more business insight and value.

- Increase the level of efficiency and competitiveness of an organization.

- Create an environment that provides new business insight through data.

Saving money by using commodity hardware is also important, but making sure the business results are achieved should be a higher priority. A key area of being successful with big data is transforming into a learning organization. Time needs to be invested in educating the business units on what big data is and how it benefits the business unit as well as the organization. Most companies do not do this well, and they end up dragging the business unit across the finish line. More importantly, it can significantly delay projects and keep the benefits of realizing the benefits of big data by months and even years. There is a lot to big data platforms such as Hadoop, NoSQL, and the ecosystem surrounding them. The technical teams have to be educated. The problem with this is that the traditional training that organizations use does not always build the right type of knowledge, skill, understanding, and expertise needed by the internal teams. Look at the evolution and growth of big data and the skill set that needs to be created versus looking at what training classes your teams can take. Using traditional training classes is not always the optimized method. Look at how you need to build the skills within your internal organization as well as how quickly the technology around big data is growing.

Industry Transformation

Hadoop has so much energy and momentum that it has the potential to transform the industry around it. Similar to the Unix days of the AIX, Solaris, HP-UX, and Dynix operating systems, open-source Linux became a standard to which many organizations moved, eliminating many of the different versions of Unix. Industry leaders such as GE, Hortonworks, IBM, Infosys, Pivotal, SAS, Altiscale, Capgemini, CenturyLink, PLDT, Splunk, Teradata, VMware, Wandisco, EMC, and Verizon have created an industry association named the Open Data Platform (ODP). ODP will work directly with Apache Software Foundation projects with the goal of creating a standardized version of Hadoop, beginning with Apache Hadoop 2.6. This group's goal is to create a tested reference version of Apache Hadoop that will be built directly from the open-source Apache projects. This will make it much easier for software companies to certify their products and software vendors to validate their products on a standardized version of Hadoop. The core of Apache Hadoop 2.6 includes HDFS, YARN, and Ambari. Not all Hadoop distributions will join ODP. Cloudera and MapR have decided not to join at this time. ODP will start standardizing on Hadoop but might expand to other areas of the big data ecosystem. It's too early to understand the potential of ODP or the industry ramifications, but it's clear that Hadoop has the capability to transform the industry around it.

Summary

The data volume, velocity, variety, and need to perform analytics on data from multiple different sources are disrupting business. Big data solutions such as Hadoop, in-memory, distributed search, and NoSQL are solutions for addressing the data disruption. The level of data disruption requires organizations to change not only how they make business decisions but how they build their IT organizations. The level of speed, volume, and rate of change in technology requires organizations to be able to respond and adapt quickly.

Don't get wrapped up in the technology of big data. Focus on business goals as well as data strategies and objectives. Remember, it's all about the data. Big data is an addition to the overall enterprise that provides additional capabilities but also has the capability to leverage existing resources and platforms. An important goal is to be a solutions and speed-driven organization, not just a data-driven organization. Speed does not mean sacrificing quality or flexibility. Use big data platforms to significantly improve the efficiency of how your company works with data, with a key goal of being able to make business decisions faster with more accuracy and confidence and with less risk.

## Chapter 2

Hadoop Fundamental Concepts

Without big data analytics, companies are blind and deaf,
wandering out onto the Web like deer on a freeway.

—Geoffrey Moore

The goal of this chapter is to introduce the main components of a Hadoop cluster. It is important that someone new to Hadoop get an overall understanding of what Hadoop is and its major components before looking at Hadoop in detail. We introduce a number of Hadoop distributions. At the end of this chapter you will understand the main Hadoop software processes and Hadoop hardware profiles. We finish the chapter with the different roles needed in a Hadoop environment.

Types of Data in Hadoop

Hadoop can store data of different types from lots of different sources. Let's start by taking a look at some of the different types of data being loaded into Hadoop. The following list shows some examples of data that organizations want to move into Hadoop. Large volumes of data and unstructured data are strong candidates for Hadoop platforms.

- **Clickstream data** is the stream of clicks someone performs when visiting a website. This information can be used for path optimization, next product to buy analysis, customer segmentation, and gaining insight into customers in general. Clickstream is used to measure visitors' activity and their behavior in the website. Organizations want to be able to quickly identify the intent of website visitors and dynamically adjust the interfaces to influence and trigger customer actions. Clickstream data is key to digital personalization across different channels (smartphones, computers, tablets, email, catalog, TV, radio, smoke signals, and so on).

- **Sentiment data** from social media, combined with text from server logs and customer data, can be used to understand how to influence behavior on a website. Online retailers can reduce bounce rates and improve sales. Sentiment data enables organizations to respond to user sentiments, positive and negative, from their customers and their competitors. On social media, customers also discuss what products they would like to have as well as products they don't like. This information is important for measuring brand loyalty and brand recognition.

- **Sensor/machine** information is detailed information on parts and components and environmental conditions with these parts. This information can be used to improve design, reduce failures, and provide notice when components may be wearing out and about to break. Refrigerators, cars, jet engines, washing machines, soda fountain machines, and just about anything that has components that can break can have their sensor data analyzed for predictive maintenance.

- **Geographic data** from global positioning systems, radio-frequency identification (RFID), cellular phones, and tablets all provide information on the locations of people and objects, where they are moving, what time they are moving, and the volume of the movement. This can be used to design highways, off ramps, stop signs, neighborhoods, cities, and rapid transit systems. This information can be used to determine the best routes and which drivers have the most unsafe or safe behavior. Geographic information can be used to determine where to put cell towers, which customers to give bandwidth during high activity, what billboards to dynamically put up on a highway, or how much to charge someone for car insurance. Software such as OnStar tracks the actions of drivers and where they are. OnStar is used for automatic crash response, stolen vehicles, vehicle diagnostics, and the like. This information can then be used to identify patterns in these events. Stores are also looking at using Wi-Fi in cell phones to track someone's movement in a store to improve store layouts. RFID is being used in hospitals, manufacturing plants, offices, and shopping malls to optimize layout designs.

- **Server logs** collect detailed information about customers logging in to websites. It might be important to see when people log in, where they log in from, and how long they stay logged in, and what external events, such as sales advertising, commercials, radio advertisement, weather, holidays, and other activities, impact when someone logs in to a website. Monitoring and analyzing server logs is one of the first steps in security forensics. Server logs can also be mined to determine patterns that identify future component failures from server machines or software environments. Server logs can help identify patterns that identify the beginning of a problem before the problem creates downtime.

- **Unstructured data** (text, video, pictures, and so on) can track activities and behaviors and identify patterns. Newer security methods are tracking patterns on video to identify activities that are likely to happen. This can be used to anticipate criminal activity, traffic issues, violence patterns, or movement in individuals to identify responses to visual cues. Facial recognition in malls, airports, and city streets can be used to find lost children, repeat customers, and potential criminal movement.

Use Cases

Hadoop is transforming the way organizations do business. Organizations are making faster and faster decisions with high rates of accuracy. Mathematical models are used to predict outbreaks of viruses, epidemics, and infectious diseases. Being able to identify these situations quickly can have a large impact on public health responses. Correlating internal data with social media has greatly improved the accuracy and reduced the time frame for discovery. Outbreak discovery time frames have been reduced from weeks to days.

An online marketing firm had one of its key reports for online marketing programs take 5 days. It moved the data from an IBM mainframe to a Hadoop cluster, let Hadoop process the data, and then moved the aggregated data back into the mainframe for the analysis. The time needed to do market analysis for ad campaigns was reduced from 5 days to 5 hours. These types of changes are transformational to an organization.

Retail organizations are performing log analysis, website optimization, and customer loyalty programs by using brand and sentiment analysis and market basket analysis. Dynamic pricing, website real-time customization, and product recommendations are the results of this analysis. The finance industry is using big data for fraud pattern detection and to perform analyses for corruption, bribery, risk modeling, and trade analytics. This enables them to improve their customer risk evaluation and fraud detection, as well as to design programs for real-time up sell and cross-marketing offers. Energy is doing analyses of grid failure, soil analytics, predictive mechanical failure, chemical analysis, and smart meters to name a few. Manufacturing is performing supply chain analysis, customer churn analysis, and part replacement, as well as layout and design of manufacturing plants and factories. Telecommunication firms use big data information for customer profiling, cell tower analysis, optimizing customer experience, monitoring equipment status, and network analysis. This improves hardware maintenance, product recommendations, and location-based advertising. Health care uses electronic medical records (EMR) and RFID to perform hospital design, patient treatment, clinical decision support, clinical trial analysis, and real-time instrument and patient monitoring and analysis. Government is using big data for areas such as threat identification, government program analysis, and person-of-interest discovery. It's the power of the data that is disrupting business and the IT industry.

Understanding the right use cases is important for getting started with big data. What questions do you want to ask of the data, what business problems are you looking to solve, and what business insights are you searching for? Focus early on how to do analytics of the new data. Strive to be a fact-driven organization.

What Is Hadoop?

When you look at a building, what you see depends on the view that you are looking from. A building can viewed from different angles and perspectives. Great West Life has a set of buildings in southeast Denver that look cylindrical if you look from one side and square if you look from another side, as shown in Figure 2.1. A building can be viewed from a structural, electrical, plumbing, or functional perspective. To think like an architect is to use these perspectives to grasp the essential essence of a "building" that is both functional and beautiful.

Figure 2.1   Great West Life buildings, Denver, CO.

Hadoop must be looked at from several perspectives to understand its design and elegance. Let's start with purpose. Hadoop was architected to be a horizontally scalable data platform for storing and processing very large datasets extremely fast. Hadoop was designed to scale cost effectively using commodity hardware and local disks. Multiple copies of data are stored across the disks of local servers to allow highly parallelized operations and high availability. Simply put, all that is required to store more data, generate more IOPS, or do more processing is to add more individual servers. Each new server adds more parallel processing capability (CPU and memory), more IOPS, and more storage capacity. There is no need for expensive specialized proprietary hardware or costly storage area networks. This also greatly reduces the complexity required to run a Hadoop distributed cluster. Because commodity hardware is used, it is possible for one person to understand the entire hardware stack.

Hadoop is an open source distribution designed from the ground up to address the challenges of big data. As an open source Apache project, it has the wisdom of the crowd to help the best ideas win, and it is rapidly evolving in features and functionality. Open source brings together the expertise of organizations such as Google, Facebook, Yahoo!, LinkedIn, UC Berkeley, eBay, Hortonworks, Cloudera, MapR, Pivotal, RedHat, IBM, HP, Intel, WanDisco, Microsoft, Teradata, and VMware, to name a few. The global open source community brings a lot of expertise in the largest Hadoop and HPC environments in the world, along with expertise in hardware, CPU cores, memory, and hardware and software engineering. Open source code is available for anyone to review.

Open source gets massive amounts of downloads and testing that proprietary systems cannot compare against. This open source innovation and community of users is driving the next generation of data platform innovation through Hadoop. Open source is also enterprise grade and extremely well tested. Open source can have thousands of organizations as well as millions of individuals testing alpha and beta releases. Here is one example: Hortonworks Data Platform (HDP) 2.0 went generally available (GA) in October 2013. HDP 2.0 ran on clusters with thousands of nodes in production environments for 10 months before the distribution went GA. Another example is the Falcon framework, which was introduced in HDP 2.1 in April 2014. InMobi was developing and using Falcon for years before it turned over to the Apache foundation and had the open source community make it enterprise grade and take it through open source testing and patching.

A Hadoop distribution is made up of several software frameworks that each has a different purpose and role, as shown in Figure 2.2. Hadoop and the individual frameworks are designed to be extensible. Think of a Hadoop distribution as a symphony. A symphony is a standard ensemble made up of different sections, such as strings, woodwinds, brass, and percussion instruments. A Hadoop platform has standard frameworks that are part of a distribution. An orchestra may add different sections, such as a piano, celesta, keyboard, or electric instruments. Similarly, a Hadoop distribution may add additional frameworks, such as Storm, Spark, Kafka, and Giraph. A big data environment can also have different types of NoSQL databases, such as HBase, Accumulo, Cassandra, MongoDB, and CouchDB. Over time, an orchestra might grow into the additional sections and keep them as part of the ensemble. Changing the sections can change how the music sounds. In the same way, Hadoop distributions may make additional frameworks or NoSQL databases as part of their future distributions. If an orchestra is not properly built for the type of music it wants to play, it will not sound well. The same holds true for a Hadoop distribution that must be designed and built properly to be an enterprise data platform that meets the use cases of the organization.

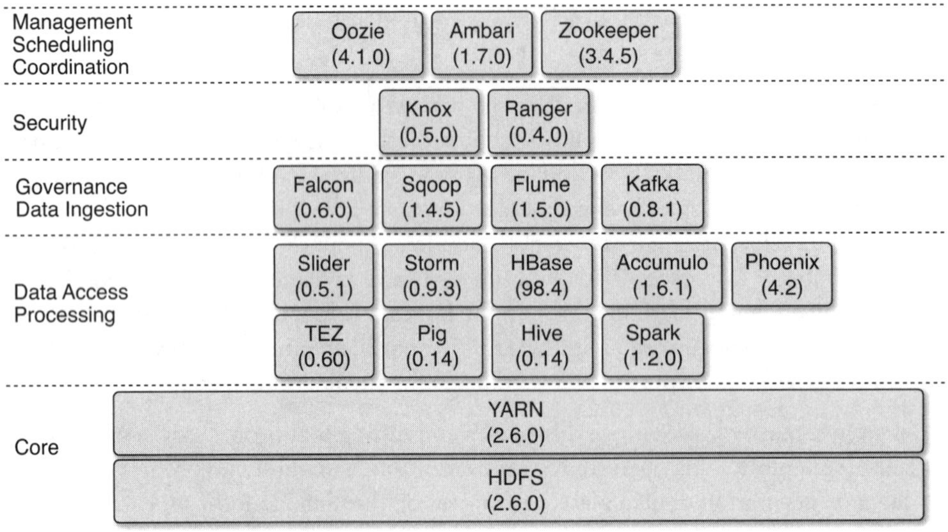

Management Scheduling Coordination	Oozie (4.1.0)	Ambari (1.7.0)	Zookeeper (3.4.5)		
Security		Knox (0.5.0)	Ranger (0.4.0)		
Governance Data Ingestion	Falcon (0.6.0)	Sqoop (1.4.5)	Flume (1.5.0)	Kafka (0.8.1)	
Data Access Processing	Slider (0.5.1)	Storm (0.9.3)	HBase (98.4)	Accumulo (1.6.1)	Phoenix (4.2)
	TEZ (0.60)	Pig (0.14)	Hive (0.14)	Spark (1.2.0)	
Core	YARN (2.6.0)				
	HDFS (2.6.0)				

Figure 2.2 HDP 2.2 (Hadoop 2.4.0): A Hadoop distribution is made up of frameworks.

Understanding Hadoop requires learning the different frameworks and understanding how each framework fits into an essential purpose for this "building" or "orchestra" we call the Hadoop platform infrastructure. To understand a new release of Hadoop, you must understand how Hadoop's form and function are improved by the new features of each framework component. Hadoop's initial design focused on large batch processing (Hadoop 1). As more and more data was stored in Hadoop data repositories and data lakes, customers wanted the capability to have interactive and real-time queries and data caching, and the capability to perform insert, update, and delete operations. Hadoop can now be used to analyze many types of data, with different runtime characteristics with different types of SLAs, all in the same Hadoop cluster. This flexibility is accomplished by the addition of frameworks that store, move, consume, and produce deep insight into data largely untouched before Hadoop. Software frameworks such as Impala (Cloudera), Tez

(Hortonworks), and Spark enable interactive and real-time query capabilities in Hadoop. The Hive framework will support insert, update, and delete operations with Hive .14. The point is that Hadoop is evolving to support more and more functionality. Hadoop is moving past being just a batch-processing system. NoSQL databases also provide real-time query capability.

There are so many Hadoop frameworks out there that organizations are having a hard time grasping the differences. Organizations want to make sure that they use the right tool for the right job, and this is somewhat due to the maturity of the framework. For instance, a lot of people think that MapReduce is dead, but it's a proven batch-oriented data processing framework that scales to the petabytes level. There are datasets so big they can't fit into memory and need to be batch processed, and that's where MapReduce fits the bill. Tez, on the other hand, was designed from the ground up to run DAG pipelines in memory particularly for Hive. With the release of HDP 2.2, Pig can now also run on Tez to make ETL processing a lot faster. Spark gives you the benefit of extremely efficient coding and reusing resilient distributed datasets across its components; these are two very attractive features and processing all happens in memory. The Spark community made it possible to integrate with Hive, where SQL query can be intermixed with Spark's API programming model. For example, you can write a line of code in Spark ML that calls out a Hive query, which returns a resilient distributed dataset (RDD) that can then be plugged in to Spark ML for mathematical calculations. As of the writing of this book, Hive can run on MapReduce and Tez. But the community is aggressively building Hive on Spark integration, which is slated for 2015.

To help establish a formal definition and some computer science terms regarding Hadoop, consider the words from hadoop.apache.org:

> The Apache Hadoop project develops open-source software for reliable, scalable, distributed computing.

> The Apache Hadoop software library is a framework that allows for the distributed processing of large data sets across clusters of computers using simple programming models. It is designed to scale up from single servers to thousands of machines, each offering local computation and storage. Rather than rely on hardware to deliver high-availability, the library itself is designed to detect and handle failures at the application layer, so delivering a highly available service on top of a cluster of computers, each of which may be prone to failures.

A Hadoop software distribution is made up of different frameworks. Following is the definition of a software framework from wikipedia.org:

> In computer programming, a software framework is an abstraction in which software providing generic functionality can be selectively changed by additional user-written

code, thus providing application-specific software. A software framework is a universal, reusable software platform to develop applications, products and solutions. Software frameworks include support programs, compilers, code libraries, tool sets, and application programming interfaces (APIs) that bring together all the different components to enable development of a project or solution.

Frameworks contain key distinguishing features that separate them from normal libraries:

- inversion of control: In a framework, unlike in libraries or normal user applications, the overall program's flow of control is not dictated by the caller, but by the framework.

- default behavior: A framework has a default behavior. This default behavior must be some useful behavior and not a series of no-ops.

- extensibility: A framework can be extended by the user usually by selective overriding or specialized by user code to provide specific functionality.

- non-modifiable framework code: The framework code, in general, is not supposed to be modified, excepting extensibility. Users can extend the framework, but should not modify its code.

You might ask why the formality? It is important for your future growth to understand some of the formal vocabulary of Hadoop and big data. Hadoop is a software distribution made up of different software frameworks that are each designed to be extensible. The main daemons for Hadoop frameworks are Java applications that run in JVMs. There are also separate frameworks that are not part of a standard distribution that can be added to Hadoop to add additional functionality. Popular open source frameworks can be added to new Hadoop distributions.

The beauty of using Java for these core essentials is write once and run everywhere! Java enables portability that invites everyone to join the party. Already the current release of Hadoop is a single merged Java code set for both Linux and Windows. There are three types of Hadoop processes:

- **Master servers:** Primary management daemons coordinate with slave servers.

- **Slave servers:** Responsible for all data storage and computational activities. I/O operations occur on the data nodes where the slave server processes run.

- **Clients:** Responsible for launching applications.

Knowing the daemons, files, and commands of Hadoop gives you a vital perspective in day-to-day management of your Hadoop deployment. At the same time, there are management tools that can perform the provisioning, monitoring, and management of the Hadoop cluster. Ambari is an open source management framework. Serengeti is an open source management project. Cloudera Manager is available with the Cloudera Distribution of Hadoop. There are also management and provisioning tools being developed by independent companies. Everyone understands that for Hadoop to grow in the market, it must be easy to use. The management tools for Hadoop greatly simplify the management of a Hadoop cluster. Operations that used to take a few hours to a few days and required a lot of in-depth skill can now be performed with the click of a button. It is very strongly recommended that you go through Hadoop administration training to learn administration fundamentals and how these Hadoop management tools can greatly simplify that management of a Hadoop cluster.

This book focuses on the Hadoop platform from a technology and a framework perspective. Be aware that big data platforms need to be "all about the data." A car has tires, an ignition, brakes, leather seats, and maybe even a cool stereo system. However, the purpose of a car is to get you from one place to another safely. Hadoop has all kinds of cool frameworks similar to a car having a lot of cool components. These components include multi-petabyte distributed storage framework (HDFS), highly parallel computation framework (MapReduce2), distributed in memory data sets (RDD), SQL interface (Hive), and so on.

It can be exciting for an organization to get excited about all the Hadoop components that combine to create a high-performance super-computer platform. However, do not lose sight of the key goal of Hadoop, which is to increase the competitive advantage of an organization so it can make more accurate business decisions faster. Data analytics is a critical factor in the success of a Hadoop platform. All the data in the world does no good if it is not actionable. Organizations need to build expertise and advanced analytical skills in the silos of an organization, in the business units, at the department level, and at the application level. An organization must create a unified data management strategy and implement it properly. IT operations must build a production class Hadoop infrastructure that can handle the growth of the cluster and optimize Hadoop at scale. Data governance is critical for the management of the data in a cluster and to make the data consumable. Data lifecycle management, lineage, and impact analysis are all very important parts of a data governance solution. Security must be addressed at all the different levels as well. Another ingredient to the secret sauce for Hadoop is finding the right tools to ask the right questions. Again, it's $E=mc^2$ (being balanced), but the balance, coordination, and collaboration must also exist across the business units, management, infrastructure teams, data scientists and analysts, application developers, and users.

Hadoop Distributions

There are a number of different distributions of Hadoop. Some of the key distributions are shown in the following list. Each distribution seeks to add value to customers by giving support, extra tools, optimization, additional features, or specialized attention to particular problems. Each Hadoop distribution vendor selects the version level of each framework they want to put into their distribution. The Hadoop vendors often add patches and enhancements to their distributions and add additional frameworks and products they want to be part of their distributions.

- Open Source Apache Hadoop distribution from the Apache Software Foundation is also available for download. This release is more leading edge.

- The Hortonworks Data Platform (HDP) is 100% open source, and every line of code developed is contributed back to Apache Hadoop.

- The Cloudera Distribution Including Apache Hadoop (CDH) offers an open core distribution along with a number of frameworks that can be purchased, such as Cloudera Search, Impala, Cloudera Navigator, and Cloudera Manager.

- MapR's distribution of Hadoop supports Network Attached Storage (NAS). MapR added optimization for different frameworks and added additional functionality.

- Pivotal HD's distribution of Hadoop includes a number of Pivotal software products such as HAWQ (SQL engine), GemFire, XD (analytics), Big Data Extensions, and USS (storage abstraction). BDE is part of VMware Sphere. Pivotal supports building one physical platform to support multiple virtual clusters as well as Platform as a Service (PaaS) using Hadoop and RabbitMQ.

- IBM InfoSphere BigInsights is built on the Apache Hadoop distribution and includes visualization and exploration, advanced analytics, security, and administration.

Hadoop Frameworks

Each Hadoop distribution has advantages the distribution vendors have provided with their selection of how their distributions are created. The Hortonworks Data Platform (HDP) was selected for this book because it is an enterprise distribution of Hadoop and is 100% open source and free. Hortonworks contributes 100% of its code back to Apache Hadoop. The Hortonworks founding strategy is on innovating the core (Hadoop, YARN, Stringer, Tez, Knox, Falcon) and allowing the Hadoop ecosystem to easily adopt and extend its platforms. This allows large hardware and software organizations like Microsoft, Teradata, SAS, SAP, and so on to let Hortonworks focus on the foundation, and software vendors can add enhancements for their own products and services. This is how Linux (open source) began to dominate the Unix operating system market. AIX, HP-UX, and Solaris were all outstanding products, but letting organizations such as RedHat and SUSE focus on the core allowed organizations such as IBM and HP to reduce their research and development costs for operating systems by up to 75%. Then IBM, HP, and other organizations contributed more resources to Linux to help accelerate the process of it being an enterprise-grade operating system. By HDP putting all its emphasis on the core foundation, we are seeing HDP become one of the market leaders and we are seeing tremendous innovation of Hadoop being accelerated by the largest organizations in the world. At the same time, other distributions are contributing to Hadoop, adding additional frameworks and software that are driving innovation around Hadoop.

The Hadoop ecosystem is growing by leaps and bounds every day. Cloud and hosting solutions are provided by Amazon, Microsoft, AT&T, Rackspace, CSC, HP, and the like. Each year we see more organizations looking at hosting Hadoop and Hadoop as a service. One architecture platform being looked at is Hadoop as a shared service with a data lake. Data organizations such as Teradata, SAP, Vertica, Microsoft (SQL Server), IBM, Oracle, and SAS are integrating their products and services into Hadoop or providing connectors. Infrastructure organizations, such as Microsoft, RedHat, HP, and Netapp, are all deeply involved in Hadoop. One large area of competition is the analytics side of Hadoop with SAP, PowerPivot, SAS, Datameer, Talend, IBM, Microstrategy, and so on all looking to be the solution for analytics with Hadoop.

Because HDP focuses on an open source distribution coordinated to maintain that "building essence," if you know HDP you can learn the advantages and disadvantages of other distributions. HDP frameworks are broken into different categories: Core, Common, Scheduling/Security/Data Lifecycle Management, as well as management (provisioning, management, and monitoring). We introduce the key frameworks and then discuss the frameworks in detail in following chapters. Not all frameworks listed are part of the HDP default distribution. Cassandra is not part of HDP but can be used as the NoSQL database of choice instead of HBase or Accumulo. Ganglia and Nagios functionality will be integrated into Ambari in a future release. The point of Figure 2.3 is to show examples of the different types of frameworks, NoSQL databases, and software that can be part of a Hadoop ecosystem. A number of frameworks can be installed with a Hadoop distribution. Additional software like Kerberos can be part of a Hadoop distribution to provide authentication. A Hadoop installation can also install different NoSQL databases, such as Cassandra, as well as additional frameworks that are not part of a distribution, such as Giraph. Different machine learning libraries can be installed, such as Mahout.

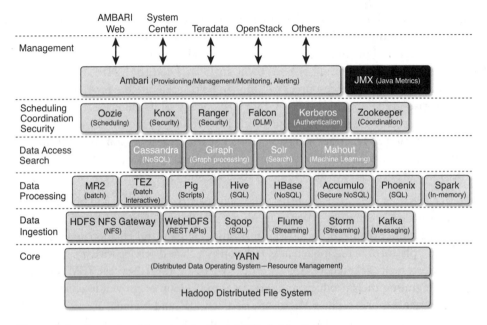

Figure 2.3 Example of frameworks in an HDP distribution.

The foundation of Hadoop is the two core frameworks YARN and HDFS. These two frameworks deal with processing and storage. YARN, which stands for Yet Another Resource Negotiator, is the foundation for distributed processing in Hadoop. YARN can be considered a distributed data operating system because it is responsible for controlling the allocation of compute resources across a Hadoop platform. YARN greatly increases the scale out capability of Hadoop by allowing applications with different runtime characteristics to run with a single resource management model for the distributed cluster.

Different computational frameworks and resource management solutions are available in Hadoop. This book focuses only on YARN. Without a single resource management model it was not possible to control how applications with different runtime characteristics used hardware resources. This often required separate clusters for Hadoop, NoSQL, Spark, and so on. Users did not want large batch processes to take away resources from other processes that need to return data near time. YARN allows different frameworks, such as Hadoop, NoSQL, and Spark, to run under a single resource management model if desired. A number of frameworks are on the roadmap to be certified with YARN in upcoming releases.

- Hadoop clusters can scale to 5,000+ nodes with the potential scalability to 10,000+ node clusters.

- The goal of YARN is to support different types of workloads, such as batch and interactive queries, streaming, graphing data, in-memory processing, messaging systems, streaming video, columnar databases, and so on in the same cluster. You can think of YARN as a highly scalable and distributed data operating system that supports workloads with different runtime characteristics. YARN also supports multitenancy.

The sweet spot (price/performance) for hardware is constantly changing. A few years ago data nodes had 24GB, 48GB, and 64GB RAM data nodes. Today it is common to see 256GB RAM with 12 CPUs, 12 4TB disks, and a 10GB NIC for a data node. As the hardware sweet spot changes, we will see this impact the design and layout of clusters. A customer might want to manage fewer data nodes and look at larger configurations that use 40GB NICs. The goal is to always try to balance the memory, CPU, storage, and networking, and minimize bottlenecks as a cluster grows horizontally over time.

The Hadoop Distributed File System (HDFS) is a distributed file system that spreads data blocks across the storage defined for the Hadoop cluster. Data is usually distributed in 64MB or 128MB–1GB block sizes. The data has three replicas (default) for high availability. The Hadoop Distributed File System (HDFS) is a distributed file system that spreads blocks for a file across multiple disks on separate servers. Spreading the blocks across the disks enables HDFS to leverage the throughput and IOPS that all the disks can generate. Each block has three replicas (default) for high availability. HDFS can work with different types of storage, but for performance, local disks are recommended. Just a Bunch of Disks (JBOD) minimizes the overhead that can occur with RAID, SAN, and NFS systems.

Let's move beyond the core framework. Following is a high-level summary of the common frameworks and software components that make up HDP:

- **Tez:** A data processing framework that optimizes batch processing while also providing interactive query capability for Hadoop. Note: Tez is not available with all Hadoop vendor distributions.

- **MapReduce(2):** An execution framework that can process large amounts of data in parallel. MapReduce was initially designed for large batch processing of text data. MapReduce(2) runs under YARN.

- **Hive:** A data warehouse infrastructure than runs on top of Hadoop. Hive supports SQL queries, star schemas, partitioning, join optimizations, caching of data, and so on. Abstract table definitions map to underlying data in HDFS that can be stored in formats such as text, XML, JSON, and binary. Hive translates the SQL into a MapReduce or Tez job.

- **Pig:** A scripting language for processing Hadoop data in parallel. The pig script gets converted into a MapReduce or Tez job.

- **HBase:** A NoSQL columnar database for providing extremely fast scanning of column data for analytics.

- **Accumulo:** A NoSQL columnar database that uses a key/value distributed data platform supporting cell level security.

- **Scoop:** A tool used to transfer data between SQL platforms and Hadoop.

- **Flume:** A tool for ingesting streaming data into Hadoop.

- **WebHDFS:** A protocol that supports HDFS operations from outside the HDFS cluster using REST API interfaces.

- **Oozie:** A workflow manager and scheduler.

- **Zookeeper:** A coordinator infrastructure used for high availability and HBase.

- **Knox:** A single point gateway for Hadoop authentication and access.

- **Falcon:** A Data Lifecycle Management (DLM) tool for Hadoop.

- **Storm:** A library for object-relational mapping that supports real-time stream processing.

- **Mahout:** A machine learning library that supports recommendation, clustering, classification, and frequent data mining.

- **Ganglia:** An open source system for collecting real-time metrics. Ganglia functionality is part of Ambari. Each Hadoop distribution has its own method for monitoring and alerts.

- **Nagios:** An open source system for managing alerts. Nagios functionality is part of Ambari. Each Hadoop distribution has its own method for monitoring and alerts.

- **Ambari:** An open source management interface for installing, monitoring, and managing a Hadoop cluster. Ambari has also been selected as the Hadoop management interface for OpenStack.

- **Giraph:** A graphing framework that is currently not part of the default HDP distribution but can be added separately.

- **Spark:** A cluster computing framework that supports in-memory processing for iterative and interactive analytics. Spark currently is not part of the default HDP distribution but can be added separately.

- **Hue:** A web interface that contains a file browser for HDFS; a job browser for YARN; an HBase browser; query editors for Hive, Pig, and Sqoop; and a Zookeeper browser. Hue is not part of the default HDP distribution but can be added separately.

- **Kafka:** A message queuing framework built by LinkedIn that handles a massive amount of real-time data traffic. Commonly paired with Storm to provide a streaming application for Hadoop.

- **Phoenix:** Originally developed by SalesForce.com out of the need to query HBase data via SQL for query performance. It is possible to query 1 trillion rows of data in HBase in less than 10 seconds.

- **Solr:** Indexes massive amount of files and provides full text search indexing.

- **Ranger:** Formerly XA Secure, acquired by Hortonworks, who then donated it to Apache. It provides and applies data access policies to all data in Hadoop easily via a browser.

- **Slider:** A new framework built on top of YARN specifically for long-running applications or jobs in YARN.

- **Cascading:** A framework that enables a developer to create complex data pipelines. It runs on top of Tez.

This large array of common frameworks and software components coordinated together enables a platform architect to craft a solution that maintains the essence of the "orchestra" called Hadoop while determining the right frameworks to work in unison to play wonderful data music for any given enterprise. Hadoop is extensible, so if additional functionality is needed for different types of data, applications, or usage, different frameworks can be added.

NoSQL Databases

Relational databases and data warehouses are necessary to run corporate businesses. They were designed for specific functionality in which they excel. Hadoop was not designed to replace them. Hadoop adds additional capabilities and features that together with relational databases and data warehouses are defining the next evolution of enterprise data platforms.

Relational databases are based on the relational model, provide online transaction processing (OLTP), schema-on-write, and SQL. Data warehouses are based on the relational model and support online analytical processing (OLAP). Data warehouses are designed to optimize data analysis, reporting, and data mining. Data is extracted, transformed, and loaded (ETL) from other data sources to load data for a data warehouse. However, today's data environment demands innovations that are faster, extremely scalable, scale cost effectively, and work easily with structured, semi-structured, and unstructured data. Hadoop and NoSQL databases are designed to work easily with structured, unstructured, and semi-structured data. Hadoop, along with relational databases and data warehouses, increases the strategies and capabilities of leveraging data to increase the accuracy and speed of business decisions. Hadoop plays an important role in the modern data architecture. Organizations that can leverage the capabilities of relational databases, data warehouses, Hadoop, and all the data sources available will have a competitive advantage.

When accessing big data, there is a demand for databases that are unrelational and that are designed to work with semi-structured, unstructured, and structured data. A nonrelational database provides a flexible data model, layout, and format. Predefined schemas are not required for NoSQL databases. NoSQL databases have traditionally been nonrelational databases that are distributed and designed to scale to very large sizes. NoSQL databases are designed to address the challenges of big data.

What Is NoSQL?

NoSQL is a database management system that has characteristics and capabilities that can address big data in ways that traditional databases were not designed for. NoSQL means nonrelational. NoSQL solutions usually have the following features or characteristics:

- Scalability of big data (100s of TBs to PBs). Horizontal scalability with x64 commodity hardware.

- Schema-on-read (versus traditional databases schema-on-write) makes it much easier to work with semi-structured and unstructured data.

- Data spread out using distributed file systems that use replicas for high availability.

- High availability and self-healing capability.

- Connectivity can include SQL, Thrift, REST, JavaScript, APIs, and so on.

As of the writing of this book, here is the Wikipedia definition of NoSQL:

> A NoSQL database provides a mechanism for storage and retrieval of data that employs less constrained consistency models than traditional relational databases. Motivations for this approach include simplicity of design, horizontal scaling, and finer control over availability. NoSQL databases are often highly optimized key–value stores intended for simple retrieval and appending operations, with the goal

being significant performance benefits in terms of latency and throughput. NoSQL databases are finding significant and growing industry use in big data and real-time web applications. NoSQL systems are also referred to as "Not only SQL" to emphasize that they may in fact allow SQL-like query languages to be used.

The term *NoSQL* is more of an approach or way to address data management versus being a rigid definition. Different types of NoSQL databases exist, and they often share certain characteristics but are optimized for specific types of data, which then require different capabilities and features. NoSQL may mean Not only SQL, or it may mean "No" SQL. A No SQL database may use APIs or JavaScript to access data versus traditional SQL. NoSQL datastores may be optimized for key/value, columnar, document-oriented, XML, graph, and object data structures. NoSQL databases are very scalable, have high availability, and provide a high level of parallelization for processing large volumes of data quickly. NoSQL solutions are evolving constantly.

There are many differences among NoSQL databases, including the following:

- Scale (smaller scale—MongoDB and Hypertable)
- Pricing
- Management complexity
- Features such as data center replication (Cassandra)
- Fast writes (Cassandra)
- Languages (C++, Java)
- Fine-grained security (Accumulo)
- Real-time analytics (HBase, Accumulo, Cassandra)
- BigTable-based (HBase, Accumulo, Cassandra, Hypertable)
- Graph database (Neo4j—supports nodes and relationships)
- Protocols (HTTP/REST, JSON over HTTP, memcached, proprietary)
- Support of the relational model (VoltDB)
- Licensing (Apache, GPL, BSD)
- Bidirectional replication (CouchDB)
- Document oriented (ElasticSearch)
- In-memory (Redis)

A number of the NoSQL databases can point to Google's BigTable design as their parent source, including HBase, Cassandra, Hypertable, and Accumulo. Bigtable is a distributed storage system designed for structured data with extremely high scalability. Characteristics of Google BigTable include the following:

- Designed to support massive scalability of tens to hundreds of petabytes

- Intended to move the programs to the data versus relational databases that move the data to the programs (memory)

- Sorts data using row keys

- Designed to be deployed in a clustered environment using x64 commodity hardware

- Supports compression algorithms

- Distributes data across local disk drives on commodity hardware supporting massive levels of IOPS

- Supports replicas of data for high availability

- Uses a parallel execution framework such as Map Reduce or something similar for extremely high parallelization capabilities

- NoSQL databases that support a row key, column key and a timestamp; for example:

  (row:string, column:string, time:int64)-> string

Tables based on BigTable are a distributed persistent multidimensional stored map. Column keys are stored in sets called column families. Data stored in a column family is usually of the same time frame. Column families store their data physically together, supporting fast column access and high rates of compression. Column families were designed for extremely fast access of column data without having the overhead of reading rows as in a relational table. Access control, as well as disk and memory processing, are handled at the column-family level. Cells can store multiple values in a cell using timestamps, which are 64-bit integers that can store time in microseconds. Tables enable single-row transactions on data stored with a single row key. Values are stored in the map as an uninterpreted array of bytes.

The two primary NoSQL databases supported by the Hortonworks Data Platform (HDP) are HBase and Accumulo:

- **HBase:** (Columnar)—Designed for optimized scanning of column data.

- **Accumulo:** Key/value datastore that can maintain data consistency at the petabyte level, read and write in near real time, and contains cell-level security. Accumulo was developed at the National Security Agency.

Following are examples of other NoSQL databases available in the marketplace:

- **Cassandra:** A real-time datastore that is highly scalable. Uses a peer-peer distributed system and supports datacenter replication. Supports primary and secondary databases. It is key oriented using column families and has CSQL as the SQL language.

- **MongoDB (document-oriented):** A highly scalable database that runs MapReduce jobs using JavaScript. A document store that does not run natively on HDFS.

- **CouchDB (document-oriented):** A highly scalable database that can survive just about anything. Uses JavaScript to access data.

- **Terracotta:** Uses an in-memory data management approach to deliver fast, highly scalable systems.

- **Voldemort:** A distributed data store using a key/value distributed storage system.

- **MarkLogic:** A highly scalable XML-based database management system.

- **Neo3J (graph-oriented):** A graph database that enables you to access your data in the form of a graph. Gives you fast access to information associated with nodes and relationships.

- **VMware vFabric GemFire (object entries):** A distributed data grid database that uses key/value pairs for in-memory data management.

- **Redis:** An in-memory database using a key/value data cache. String-oriented keys can be hashes, lists, or sets. The entire data set is cached in memory with disk persistence. Highly scalable.

- **Riak:** A distributed database using a key/value data cache. A text-oriented, scalable system based on Amazon's Dynamo.

NoSQL databases are not designed to replace the traditional RDBMS or data warehouses. It's important to understand that Hadoop is not a database, it is a data platform. Relational databases and data warehouses have a foundation of the relational model, use schema-on-write, and have features, tools, and ecosystems focused for types of operations different than Hadoop or NoSQL databases. It is not that there cannot be overlap between relational databases, data warehouses, Hadoop, and NoSQL databases, especially as Hadoop and NoSQL evolve. But each was designed for a specific core purpose. NoSQL databases are becoming part of the enterprise data platform for organizations and providing functionality that traditional systems do not handle well, either because of the size, complexity of data, or the volume of data being absorbed.

NoSQL is a natural product of the new innovation surrounding big data and adds to the arsenal of getting greater and greater value from big data platforms. Some NoSQL databases can be part of a Hadoop platform (HBase) or can be set up as a separate cluster.

Previously, it was believed that you could have speed, reliability, and price, but not all three at the same time. Hadoop changes that because with Hadoop you can have speed, reliability, and price (commodity hardware) at the same time.

The CAP Theorem says that for distributed databases you can have consistency, availability, and partition (CAP) tolerance, but not all three at the same time. Choosing a NoSQL database requires choosing what the CAP priorities are. If the data is distributed and replicated, and nodes or networks between the nodes go down, a decision must be made between data consistency (having the current version of the data) or availability. NoSQL databases can address this with an eventual consistency model (Cassandra). Eventual consistency means a DataNode is always available to handle data requests, but at a point in time the data may be inconsistent but still relatively accurate. NoSQL databases choose their priority for CAP tolerance. Neo4j is consistent and available. HBase and Accumulo are consistent and partition tolerant. CouchDB is available and partition tolerant.

Choosing the correct NoSQL database requires understanding factors such as the requirements, SLAs (latency), initial size and growth projections, costs, feature/functionality, and concurrency. It's also important to understand that NoSQL databases have their defaults and may have the capability of changing their priorities for CAP. It is also important to understand the roadmap of these NoSQL databases because they are evolving quickly.

A Hadoop Cluster

A Hadoop cluster is made up of a number of daemons and software processes that work together to provide a complete solution to meet today's data needs. The Hadoop master and worker daemons all run as Java processes in their individual JVMs. Like any high-performance computing environment, tuning of the JVMs and their garbage collection is important.

As in the symphony, the conductor seeks to coordinate a series of very specialized instruments played by professionals at the top of their craft, all surrendered to the greater purpose of a perfect musical experience. In the end, it's the music that makes a symphony work. All the complexity being explored is a servant of that musical outcome. We embrace this complexity, the discipline, and this coordination to achieve highs of data insight and value never possible before Hadoop. So let's meet the players. Figure 2.4 is a listing of software processes and components of a typical Hadoop cluster.

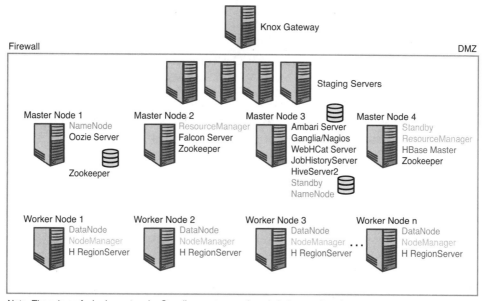

Figure 2.4 Software processes and components of a typical Hadoop cluster.

Master servers manage the Hadoop services/frameworks. DataNode servers handle all the HDFS storage activity. NodeManager servers handle all the computational tasks. Traditionally, each worker (data) node runs one DataNode process and one NodeManager process. An HBase RegionServer process runs if HBase is running on the Hadoop cluster. Client processes launch the applications. Examples include the Hadoop, Pig, and Hive clients. Third-party software can also be running on the client nodes. Master servers and slave servers are daemons that stay up and running all the time. A client process runs until the job it initiated is complete, but newer architectures supported by virtualization enable these functions to be separated into different virtual machines on the same physical host. This enables secure multitenancy and more effective elasticity.

- A Hadoop cluster should not share network traffic unless sufficient network bandwidth has been configured. A firewall usually exists to protect the Hadoop cluster.

- A Knox Gateway may be used for authentication for the Hadoop clusters in a data center. The Knox Gateway would typically run in a DMZ zone. Its sole purpose is to protect Hadoop clusters at the network layer. It integrates with SSO frameworks such as SiteMinder. The Apache community is actively pursuing other security frameworks that will integrate with Knox to simplify management of user authentication.

- A Falcon server manages Data Lifecycle Management (DLM) and Data Lineage.

- An Active Directory (AD) or Lightweight Directory Access Protocol (LDAP) server may be used to manage directory services for users. It can be integrated with Knox.

- Gateway, edge, and/or staging servers run in a Hadoop cluster to facilitate access to the Hadoop cluster and to provide ETL services. These servers can contain Hadoop clients, Flume agents, Sqoop clients, and HDFS NFS clients.

- An Ambari and Ganglia agent will run on each node being monitored.

Master servers manage the framework for which they are responsible. The master servers include the following:

- **NameNode:** Responsible for all I/O and storage metadata.

- **ResourceManager:** The scheduler responsible for all processing.

- **Zookeeper processes:** Provides coordination service.

- **Standby NameNode:** Provides failover capability for the NameNode.

- **Secondary NameNode:** Cleans out the edit logs of the NameNodes metadata if a Standby NameNode is not used. The cluster can have a Standby NameNode (HA) or a Secondary NameNode (clean edit.log) but not both. If there is a Standby NameNode, it will clean the edit.log, so a Secondary NameNode is not needed.

- **Backup NameNode:** Similar to the Secondary NameNode but it receives journal streams of file system edits from the NameNode as opposed to downloading fsimage/edit files. This stream is persisted to disk and to memory immediately.

- **Secondary ResourceManager:** Provides failover capability for the ResourceManager.

- **Ozzie server:** Schedules jobs and manages the workflow of jobs submitted.

- **HiveServer2:** Provides the JDBC/ODBC interface for Hive queries.

- **HBase Master(s):** Manages the HBase environment.

- **Ambari server:** Used for provisioning, managing, and monitoring a Hadoop cluster.

- **Ganglia server:** Manages the Ganglia environment that collects.

- **Nagios server:** Collects information for alerts.

- **JobHistoryServer:** Collects and manages job history for MapReduce jobs.

- **WebHCatServer:** Processes HTTP requests for running YARN applications such as MapReduce, Hive, and Pig, as well as HCatalog DDL commands.

All data is stored on the worker nodes (slave servers). Typically, data processing occurs on the worker nodes. The worker node servers are also referred to as slave servers or DataNodes. DataNode is the term most commonly used. A slave server can contain a DataNode, NodeManager, or both.

Slave servers include the following:

- **DataNodes:** Handle all I/O locally on their own nodes. These are slave servers for the name nodes.

- **NodeManagers:** Manage all YARN processes running on their slave servers. These are slave servers for the ResourceManager.

- **HBase region servers:** Responsible for all local processing of HBase applications. These are slave servers for the HBase masters. These processes run on the DataNodes.

- **Different frameworks such as Storm, Kafka, Spark, Accumulo, Cassandra:** These frameworks can have different processes that may be running in the Hadoop cluster or in a different cluster. Each framework has separate processes for its operations.

Clients run the applications in the cluster.

- Hadoop client launches Tez and MapReduce applications.

- Pig client launches Pig scripts. Converts to Tez or MapReduce.

- Hive client launches Hive SQL statements. Converts to Tez or MapReduce.

A Hadoop cluster must be able to handle large data transfers in and out of the cluster. Edge or Management servers can be set up to launch data ingestion jobs that are multihomed with internal and external network cards. This server must be configured to store or process the necessary volume or velocity of data. Multiple 10GB network cards might be necessary for these servers.

Hadoop Software Processes

The Hortonworks Data Platform (HDP) is an open source software distribution. The only cost for the software is in the support costs because the software is free. Open source MySQL database servers can be used for the metadata repositories. The Apache HTTP server can be leveraged to serve web services and content for Hadoop. Who does not like free software, especially for enterprise-class software? Hadoop has become an enticing platform for the Fortune 500 customers. Table 2.1 outlines the software requirements needed by Hadoop.

Table 2.1 Hadoop Software Requirements

Category	Software
64-bit operating systems	Red Hat Enterprise Linux (RHEL) 5.x or 6.x
	CentOS 5.x or 6.x
	Oracle Linux 5.x or 6.x
	Windows 2008 R2 or Windows Server 2012 R2
	Ubuntu
	SLES 11, SP1
Java	Oracle JDK 1.7 or OpenJDK 7 is recommended.
	(The Oracle JDK 1.6.0_31 is no longer supported.)
Utilities	yum, rpm, wget, curl, scp, ssh, python
Automation tools	Puppet, Chef (not required but helpful), Serengeti (helpful)

The Hadoop software processes can be spread across different servers or can run on a single server or in a single virtual machine (VM). The Hortonworks Sandbox is a full-blown Hadoop cluster running on a single VM and is available for download from http://hortonworks.com/products/hortonworks-sandbox/. The Sandbox VM can be VMware, VirtualBox, or Hyper-V. Hadoop master processes can all run on a single machine or be spread across multiple machines. If it is a small cluster (fewer than 20 DataNodes) the master servers can run on one or two nodes dependent on the workload and whether the environment is a development, test, or production environment. As the Hadoop cluster gets larger or moves into production, it is recommended to have the server processes spread across multiple nodes. The goal is to not have any of the daemons and server processes competing for resources. The HDP sandbox is a great way to get introduced to the latest Hadoop distribution and is packed with tutorials that you can get up and running in 5 minutes.

The following list outlines the organization of the Hadoop processes:

- HDFS framework processes include the NameNode(s) (master) and the DataNodes (slaves). NameNode high availability is recommended for production environments. The availability of the NameNode and other master daemons can be further increased by running them in virtual machines that are protected by VMware HA or FT technologies.

- YARN framework processes include the ResourceManager (master) and the NodeManagers running on a set of slave servers. A standby ResourceManager is recommended for production environments. Every YARN job that starts up will have its own Application Master that will run on one of the slave servers. The Application Master is responsible for job life-cycle management.

- HBase can have multiple HBase Masters. Only one HBase Master is primary, and the other HBase Masters run in standby mode. An HBase RegionServer runs on each DataNode containing HBase data.

- The zookeeper processes manage the coordination services of the cluster and enable High Availability (HA) for services such as NameNode, ResourceManager, and HBase.

- Services such as Ambari, Oozie, and HiveServer2 all have a relational database that is their metadata repository. The relational databases can be Oracle, Postgres, or MySQL. These databases must be backed up and have a recovery solution for each one. It is recommended that you pick one relational database product to simplify the backup and disaster recovery solution for the metadata repositories.

- The monitoring infrastructure is made up of the Ambari server, Ganglia server, Nagios server, and their related agents.

- Additional servers, such as the WebHCat server (REST APIs), HiveServer2 (JDBC/ODBC), Falcon Server, and Ozzie Server, can be spread across the master servers.

- The Gateway, Edge, and/or Staging servers can stage the data and launch data ingestion or applications. These are the access servers from outside the Hadoop cluster.

- A Hadoop cluster generates a lot of internal networking activity, so it is recommended that you not share network traffic with anything outside the Hadoop cluster. A firewall is recommended for the Hadoop cluster. A Knox Gateway provides perimeter security for Hadoop. Kerberos is a standard for providing authentication. An LDAP or AD server is used to provide directory services for users. Think of Knox as the point of entry for all access to the Hadoop cluster with security in place. After a request is authenticated and passed down to the cluster, Kerberos applies authentication at the Hadoop service layer. Both Knox and Kerberos have the capability to integrate with LDAP/AD.

- Each Hadoop daemon has an embedded Netty application server. This enables each daemon to have a web interface. Each daemon can have its information accessed through a defined port using a web user interface.

Hadoop Hardware Profiles

A Hadoop cluster has a relatively low hardware cost by using commodity x64 hardware that can scale horizontally to a super computer. A Hadoop cluster should be designed from the perspective of building a massively parallel super computer. A Hadoop cluster can be purchased with a small capitalization expenditure (CAPEX) and run under a greatly reduced operational expenditure (OPEX) when compared to proprietary vertically scalable platforms. Hadoop is not simple, but after it is up and running it is fault tolerant and self-healing. A Hadoop cluster is not simple either, but after it is up and running you can expect to have one administrator for every 1,000 to 2,000 nodes.

A few years ago, a slave server could have had the hardware profile shown in Table 2.2 because of the price/performance sweet spot of hardware at that time. A typical guess-timate is to give 70% of disk to HDFS and 30% to software, log files, and intermediate data generated by mappers. It is not necessary to split the disk between HDFS and temp data (generated by both map and reduce tasks). But software and log files might be on a different disk or location.

Table 2.2   Older DataNode Hardware Profile (from a Few Years Ago; No Longer Applicable)

Hardware	Software
Two Xeon Quad Cores @ 2.x GHz	Red Hat Enterprise Linux 5.1
24GB RAM	Sun JDK v1.6
Four 1TB SATA drives	
Two network	

Table 2.3 reflects the trend in hardware profiles based on the changing of the price/performance sweet spot for hardware. Dell, HP, IBM, Cisco, Quanta, SuperMicro, and the hardware vendors offering Hadoop appliances all offer similar profiles. Whether using Xeon, Dual Ivy Bridge, and so on, the fastest and latest cores have significantly increased prices. Companies will consider not using the most current cores and use the price saving on more memory, storage, or slave servers. Hadoop hardware is consistently purchased around the sweet spot of price/performance. The key is to get quality commodity hardware.

A distribution of hard disk for a DataNode is still around 70% of disk to HDFS and 30% to software, log files, Tez spill files, and intermediate data generated by mappers. The hardware profile can change if there is an increased emphasis on performance or storage. Profiles for master nodes are impacted depending on the number of Hadoop master processes that are running on a single server. DataNode profiles can change if running

HBase regions servers, or HBase, Storm, and the like on YARN. If virtualizing Hadoop, the hardware profile will change so multiple VMs can run on each ESXi host.

With the price of SSDs dropping, we can expect to see more blended storage solutions. Expect hardware profiles to constantly evolve as Hadoop distributions introduce new components with each release, as well as hardware components evolving. For hardware purchases, you also need to consider the data center costs around space, power, cooling, and so on. Tables 2.3 and 2.4 show the typical hardware profiles for Master Servers and DataNodes, respectively.

Table 2.3   Typical Hardware Profile for Master Server

Hardware	Software
Four 12 Xeon Dual/Quad Cores @ 2.x GHz	Red Hat Enterprise Linux 6.5
64–256GB RAM	Oracle/Open JDK v1.7
Four 1TB or 2TB SAS/SATA drives, RAID10+	
Include one spare disk	
Two 1G bonded NICs or two drives, RAI (older profile)	
Enterprise server configuration will include additional power supplies and the like to minimize single points of failure.	

Table 2.4   Typical Hardware Profile for Slave Server (DataNode)

Hardware	Software
Two processors with 10–12 Xeon Dual/Quad Cores @ 2.x GHz	Red Hat Enterprise Linux 6.5
64–256GB RAM	Oracle/Open JDK v1.7
Ten 10–20 SATA drive	vSphere 5.5
Two 1G Bonded NICs or 1x 6.5x GH	

Hadoop offers a "shared nothing" architecture. Data is stored locally across a number of distributed servers. The processing occurs on the local NodeManager servers. I/O workloads run in parallel across the DataNodes. Each DataNode has its own independent CPU, memory, storage, and networking. Master processes can be spread across different master nodes for service high availability and performance. It is important to separate the processing of master and slave servers. If a slave server goes down, a new process will be started on a different slave server using one of the block replicas to complete the job.

As mentioned, Hadoop is designed to run on low-cost x64 commodity hardware. Hadoop vendors sell Hadoop appliances. Some appliances have enterprise features that are great for protecting tier-one databases. Hadoop master servers can leverage these enterprise grade features. However, a lot of the enterprise grade features in more expensive Hadoop appliances are not leveraged by the Hadoop DataNodes.

Hadoop is very resilient against node and disk failures. Losing a node or disk is barely noticed in a medium or large cluster. Be careful about equating CPU cores and disk spindles to throughput. Memory and network bandwidth will also impact throughput. Look at the projected growth and understand how the hardware design is impacted by future growth. For master servers, enterprise features such as dual power supplies (ideally with each using a different Power Distribution Unit [PDU]) and Dual-InLine Memory Module (DIMM) sparing along with RAID for disk protection are recommended. DIMM sparing requires twice the amount of memory. For example, with DIMM sparing, 128GB of memory is set up as two mirrored 64GB of memory.

Master server nodes can use commodity hardware; however, an enterprise-grade server with RAID 10 is recommended. The design of an enterprise-grade server is to minimize the probability of failure. The DataNode servers are recommended to use a commodity-grade server. Remember, commodity does not mean cheap and of low quality. The current price/performance for hardware has both Master and DataNode servers ranging from 128GB to 256GB being the midrange of memory and CPUs ranging from 8 to 12 cores. Master nodes often have 1TB to 2TB drives, and DataNodes have 3TB to 4TB drives. The hardware vendors all offer similar profiles for a Hadoop cluster. Consider the role of the Master and DataNodes in terms of the hardware profile, support agreements, and management required for each.

One of the keys to a Hadoop cluster is to understand the formula $E=mc^2$. This is an old Greek philosophy that means to find happiness in life, one must have balance. This balance formula applies not only to energy and life but also to a Hadoop cluster. A cluster must be properly balanced across the disk/network to schedulable cores (leveraging threads) and memory to minimize bottlenecks. The processing capability of the memory and CPU needs the right level of storage and network bandwidth. Parity-based RAID is not recommended. RAID 10 (mirroring and striping) is recommended for master servers where high availability is the priority. The Hadoop environment provides high availability for slave servers, so slave servers must be configured for performance.

The cost of the CPU, memory, storage, and networking must also be balanced with the processing capability, the throughput, and the reliability of the platform. Because a Hadoop cluster grows horizontally with the addition of slave servers and their disks, the cluster must remain reliable, efficient, flexible, and cost effective as it grows. Design for balance in the following areas:

- Overall Hadoop cluster

- Slave servers

- CPU and memory with disk I/O and network

- Management/Staging/Edge nodes

The master server's hardware profile needs to focus on availability first and performance second. From a best practices perspective regarding the hardware profile for a master server, you should consider the following:

- Dual power supplies.

- Dual network cards. Dual-GbE cards are recommended. Hadoop will leverage full duplex. As the price goes down, 10GB network cards can be used and should be considered for future proofing.

- RAID 10 (RAID1+0) to protect against disk failure. Enterprise-grade NFS servers can be used as well. RAID 1 can be used for mirroring the master data.

- Disk drives should be a minimum of 7200RPM. SATA-II drives offer better pricing, but NL-SAS drives have better throughput.

- A server should be configured with a minimum of 12-port controllers. Modern 8-port controllers are plenty, as long as the ports are 6GB/s.

- For memory, the priority should be on advanced protection versus performance optimization. Error correcting code (ECC) memory is recommended. The NameNode stores metadata on each directory, file, and block in memory. 64GB of RAM can support approximately 100 million files. The NameNode doesn't require a lot of memory. Typically, 1PB of data is represented in NameNode memory as 1GB of metadata. However, a common configuration often runs additional processes on the NameNode.

- 2.x GHz memory chips are standard. As previously mentioned, there is often quite a price jump for the most current and fastest chips. NameNodes and ResourceManagers do a lot of communicating with their slave processes. Larger clusters might need to consider 16 to 24 cores. Each DataNode increases the scalability of the cluster but also requires the master servers to communicate with a larger number of slave servers.

The DataNode hardware profile needs to focus on performance. HDFS and YARN will address high availability for the DataNodes. From a best practices perspective, the hardware profile for a DataNode should consider the following:

- If dual network cards are used, they should be configured for performance with link aggregation. Dual-GbE cards are recommended. Hadoop will leverage full duplex. As the price goes down, 10GB network cards can be used and should be considered for future proofing. 10GB NICs become more important if there are a higher number of cores and memory.

- Local disks (JBOD) are recommended. HDFS takes care of data availability. RAID is not recommended for the DataNodes. RAID increases cost, complexity, and performance overhead. The strength of the DataNodes are in their numbers, so all disks in the box must be utilized for HDFS storage.

- Disk drives should be a minimum of 7200 RPM. SATA-II drives offer better pricing, but NL-SAS drives have better throughput. Power requirements are proportional to the number of disks. Add more and larger disks for storage. Data nodes use Hadoop software and replication for self healing. Purchase disks with good mean time between failure (MTBF) statistics. SATA is good for a storage dense cluster, NL-SAS for balanced cluster, and SSD for high performance.

- HDFS uses replication to protect the data (default of three replicas). For every 1TB of data, 3TBs of storage is required. Intermediate data (covered later) used in MapReduce may require 1TB to 5TB of storage for the intermediate data and the logs. Having three replicas is very typical for production clusters but varies on other environments. For instance, disaster recovery might not need three replicas but instead two, whereas a DEV cluster might require only one. Storage profiles for disaster recovery are normally dense.

- Memory should put the priority on performance optimization. ECC memory is recommended. The memory used for streaming jobs must be considered.

Because Hadoop clusters scale horizontally, the hardware profiles match close to the price/performance cost of hardware for that year. A few years ago Hadoop clusters had memory profiles for data nodes ranged from 24GB to 48GB. Today, 64GB to 96GB profiles are more popular. As customers look to build data lakes and run applications with different runtime characteristics, many customers are looking at 128GB to 256GB hardware profiles. If running additional frameworks on the Hadoop cluster, such as Spark, Giraph, or Storm, the memory requirements will increase. Each framework has different requirements. For example, a set of machines with very high RAM in the cluster might be specific for Spark for in-memory processing requiring increased memory, whereas Storm for stream processing would require more CPU cores.

Remember that commodity hardware does not mean poor quality hardware. Buy quality commodity hardware, which provides ECC memory, and quality CPU cores, disk drives, and network cards with low failure rates. Hardware vendors provide hardware compatibility lists based on recommended reference architectures. Take the following into consideration when purchasing hardware:

- Number of DataNodes

- Storage considerations per DataNode: number of disks, size of disks, mean time between failures (MTBF), and the replication cost of disk failure

- Compute power per node (sockets, cores, clock speed)

- Memory per DataNode

- Network throughput (speed of ports)

Rack topologies are very popular for Hadoop clusters. Balance needs to be maintained as the cluster grows and more racks are added. A small cluster has 3 racks or fewer. A medium cluster has between 3 and 30 racks. Anything above 30 racks is considered a large cluster. Minimize the probability of rack failure in the design by using multiple power supplies, dual ToR (Top of Rack) switches, and dual aggregation switches. Having bonded links between Core, ToR, and aggregation switches is recommended. Hot spares should be available for the master nodes. Be careful about making the Hadoop cluster too complex. Complexity can generate its own type of failure.

The following is a list of guidelines to consider when configuring Hadoop in a rack topology:

- Master server processes should be spread across different racks. It is important to ensure that the frameworks with HA capability have the primary and standby server processes on separate racks.

- A load balancer should be considered to spread the workload for data loading and ETL across different staging/edge/gateway servers in the different racks.

- HA configurations should separate primary processes from standby processes across different racks. High availability is handled separately for different processes and framework, such as NameNode, ResourceManager, Oozie, HBase, Storm, and so on.

- Understand the data center requirements to determine the sizing for the ToR and aggregation switches.

- Rack configurations should have built-in redundancies to minimize the probability of a rack failure.

- Hadoop will always try to maintain the default number of replicas for each block (the default is three). If a rack goes down, Hadoop will try to create new replicas of the blocks that were lost on the other racks. This is why it might be better to have three or four racks than two big ones. You want your rack platform to be resilient. The more racks you have and the more DataNodes you have, the better your Hadoop cluster can handle hardware failure.

Figure 2.5 shows an example of a topology with two racks.

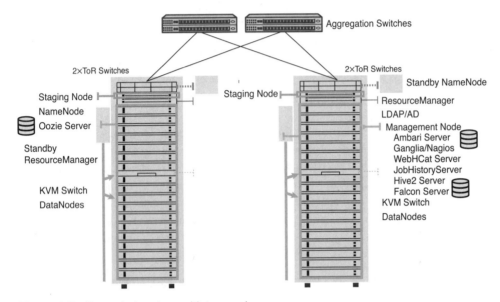

Figure 2.5   Example topology with two racks.

Hardware vendors offer a number of solutions for Hadoop. A lot of the discussion of cluster confirmations occurs around the slave servers because this is where most of the work occurs. A few years ago, DataNodes were often configured with 24GB to 48GB of memory. The CPU, storage, and memory were configured for that amount of memory. Recently, DataNodes had 48GB to 64GB of memory. Today, 96GB to 256GB of memory configurations are being considered. Because Hadoop grows horizontally, hardware is often purchased around the sweet spot of price versus performance.

The solutions are often offered in a performance, balanced, or storage emphasized solution. Examples of the different solutions include the following:

- The performance platforms often come with 256GB of memory with 1TB to 2TB drives.

- A balanced solution often has 128MB of memory.

- A storage solution will often go with 4TB disk drives.

Table 2.5 shows some sample configurations from different hardware vendors. Popular platforms include IBM's X3650 M4 BD, Cisco's C240, HP's DL380, Dell's R720, Super-Micro 6027R, and Quanta OpenRack. Most of the hardware vendors have publicly listed recommended configurations. The different vendors offer similar configurations. The hardware decision often comes down to options, support costs, relationships, and platform costs. Be aware that hardware vendors have models and appliances designed for Hadoop. Different models can support up to 26 disks, which would see an increase of cores up to 20 to 24.

Table 2.5 Examples of the Three Common Profiles for DataNodes

	Performance	Balanced	Storage
Processor	Dual Ivy Bridge	Dual Ivy Bridge	Dual Ivy Bridge
Cores per Processor	10 to 12	8	8
Disk	12 x 1 TB, + 2 x 300GB	12 x 2TB	12 x 4TB
Memory	256GB	128GB	128GB
Network	2 x 10GbE	2 x 10GbE	2 x 10GbE

There is no magic formula for choosing hardware; however, there are key factors to consider. Any hardware profile needs to balance the processing capability of the CPUs and memory with the throughput of the storage and network. Fast CPUs and a lot of memory will be underutilized if the storage and network cannot handle the throughput and bottlenecks that occur. On the flip side, lots of storage and network bandwidth does not help if the CPU and memory cannot drive enough throughput. As we've said, it's all about $E=mc^2$.

Remember there are master and DataNodes that have different runtime requirements. Disks can range from 12 to 24 disks with 1TB to 4TB of storage. CPUs can run with two to four sockets with quad, hex, and octo cores, usually with 2.xGHz. Be aware with the fastest GHz chips, the cost and the power and heat consumption increase significantly. Master nodes are likely to have fewer disks (4–6) with smaller sizes (1TB–2TB). DataNodes usually have more disks (6–24) with larger sizes (3TB–4TB). Two-socket configurations tend to be more popular to meet the sweet spot of price versus performance. A four-socket configuration requires more memory, storage, and networking bandwidth to keep the system balanced, thus completely changing the price and performance considerations.

What makes the hardware profile more challenging is understanding the type of processing that will run on the hardware. ETL, data transformations, indexing, data mining, compression, encryption, batch processing, and interactive queries generate different workloads. Frameworks like Tez, Flume, Sqoop, Elastic Search, Solr, HDFS commands, WebHDFS, Storm, Kafka, and so on also put different workloads on a Hadoop cluster. So decisions such as whether to run a federated NameNode configuration, whether to separate the Hadoop cluster from the NoSQL platform, and how to handle future growth all need to be considered. What helps is understanding that YARN is the distributed data operating system that can be configured to allocate resources of different workloads. What is also difficult is that customers building a Hadoop cluster often do not know the workloads required for the Hadoop cluster or how fast new types of data from different sources may be loaded into Hadoop.

IT operations are very experienced with understanding the runtime characteristics of database, web, app, LDAP, AD, and similar servers where blades and SAN storage were common. Hadoop has different runtime characteristics than a number of different software environments. With Hadoop, rack topologies and JBOD are common. The reason is that the Hadoop software (HDFS and YARN) addresses scalability, high availability, and resource management. Getting help from your hardware vendor and Hadoop distribution vendor is critical in designing the right hardware profile.

Larger enterprise companies standardize with a specific vendor for hardware and can acquire high performance Dell/IBM/HP/Oracle servers and the like for relatively low cost. You should standardize server configurations for your Hadoop cluster. Deploying servers with the same configuration for CPU and memory can simplify provisioning and maintenance efforts. With virtualization in the equation, cold and hot spare servers can be architected for scalability, reliability, and an even higher level of availability.

Roles in the Hadoop Environment

One of the success factors for Hadoop projects is the successful integration of software and hardware teams. With proprietary vertical scalable systems there were large technical silos around software applications, storage, networking, and the OS. Each silo had a tremendous amount of required proprietary knowledge and technical expertise. With commodity hardware it is possible for someone to understand the entire technology stack. With relational databases, it is common for one DBA to manage 30 to 50 database servers, dependent on the type of system and complexity. With Hadoop, it is a common goal to have one administrator for every 1,000 to 2,000 slave servers. However, it takes time for the knowledge and automation to mature to this level of administration.

Another factor for success is a well-trained technical team around Hadoop. Here is a list of the possible roles in a Hadoop environment.

Platform Architect

- Understands the physical requirements and is deeply involved in the design of the Hadoop cluster.

- Works with the infrastructure teams to make sure the right hardware and software are purchased.

- Has strong understanding of x64 hardware, operating systems, storage, and networking.

- Can help with tuning the Hadoop platform and addressing the challenges of Hadoop at scale.

Systems Architect

- Designs the Hadoop cluster architecture and is involved with best practices around configuration and management.

- Provides architectural management for the entire project.

- Is involved in proof of concept projects and performance tuning.

- Is able to design performance tests and make decisions about performance and capacity planning.

Project Manager

- Manages the project plan.

- Understands the project design and scope and manages statuses and updates.

- Provides guidance with all the infrastructure teams.

Data Engineer

- Understands use cases and the data movement for data ingestion and extraction.

- Is able to work with ETL tools and determine best ingestion methods.

- Has strong technical skills for areas such as Pig, Hive, Java, Python, Flume, WebHDFS, Sqoop, HDFS NFS, Storm, and Kafka.

- Understands data architecture, schema design, and the lambda architecture.

- Understands workflow and is able to assist with the scheduling of data movement.

- Is able to work with a scheduler such as Oozie.

- Understands data retention, ETL strategies, and archiving.

- Is able to assist with the data movement between external sources, data warehouses, and relational databases.

- Understands data formats such as JSON, XML, ORC files, and so on.

- Is knowledgeable about Thrift (an interface definition language and binary communication protocol) and Avro (a remote procedure call and data serialization framework).

Developer

- Develops Hadoop applications.

- Is able to provide design and development techniques for Hadoop clusters.

- Has strong programming skills around Java, Hive, Pig, Python, JavaScript.

- Is knowledgeable about Thrift and Avro.

Data Scientist

- Is able to work with business units for the creation of use cases.

- Has a strong math and statistics background.

- Is able to use programming languages such as R and/or Python to write algorithms to prove use cases.

- Understands data and the collection of data from different sources.

- Is able to convince business units of the accuracy of the algorithms around use cases.

- Has a strong background in computer science and applications.

- Provides expertise in mathematics, analytics, statistics, and modeling.

- Has the ability to find patterns in the data and choose the write models for the data.

- Has the communication skills to be able to explain and convince others that their approach is the best one for the problem to be solved.

- Has programming skills to test the algorithms and models they develop.

- Has the ability to look at data from different sources and find different ways the data can provide insight.

Hadoop Administrator

- Possesses strong OS skills in Linux.

- Has Windows Server skills if Hadoop is running on Windows.

- Has strong scripting skills in Shell, Awk, and/or Python.

- Has strong skills in automation using tools such as Puppet or Chef.

- Has strong knowledge skills in system management, performance tuning, capacity planning, LDAP/AD/Directory Services, disaster recovery skills, and trouble-shooting around x64 platforms, including storage and networking.

vAdministrators

- Hadoop administrators that understand enterprise virtual infrastructures.

Cloud Administrators

- Administrators with skills in cloud infrastructure, deployments, and orchestration.

Summary

Hadoop enables an organization to set up centralized data sources for multiple uses. NoSQL, in-memory datasets, and distributed search are often important components of a big data platform. Hadoop is the central data source and is the next evolution of high performance computing. No other platform out there manages its infrastructure easily, self heals, and could scale 1:1000 for operating the cluster using commodity hardware. Hadoop is a data platform with a goal of accelerating business insight generation faster and at lower cost.

Hadoop greatly reduces the cost of managing terabytes to petabytes of data and provides a distributed processing framework to finish the tasks as fast as it can by utilizing commodity hardware. It essentially is a Swiss army knife for big data projects because of the vast array of data access tools it exposes to various users—analysts, data scientists, and many more. Batch processing in Hadoop is old news but still important. The advent of interactive and real-time data processing is now a reality and critical for organizations. Fast data that allows decisions near-real time can be just as important as big data capabilities. A Hadoop cluster can be purchased with a small CAPEX and run under a greatly reduced OPEX when compared to proprietary vertically scalable platforms.

A Hadoop cluster is made up of a number of master and slave software processes that work together to deliver a massively parallel super-computer platform that can support batch processes as well as interactive queries. Master processes manage the infrastructure of their framework. Different frameworks in a Hadoop distribution work together to deliver a complete platform. All the user data resides on the DataNodes. The programs move to the data in a Hadoop cluster, so that is why all the processing and I/O for data operations occurs on the DataNodes. In later chapters we cover virtualizing Hadoop and Hadoop as a service.

## Chapter 3

YARN and HDFS

Those people who develop the ability to continuously acquire new and better forms of knowledge that they can apply to their work and to their lives will be the movers and shakers in our society for the indefinite future.

—Brian Tracy

We've seen that a Hadoop distribution is made up of multiple frameworks. Hadoop is constantly evolving, and new frameworks are constantly being added to Hadoop distributions. Succeeding with Hadoop requires big data teams to stay up to speed and use the better forms of the evolving frameworks to apply to their Hadoop ecosystems. We introduced the core frameworks of YARN and HDFS in the previous chapter. In this chapter, we look at YARN and HDFS in more detail. Because these are the two core frameworks, it is important that you understand them well.

A Hadoop Cluster Is Distributed

As we have seen in Chapter 2, "Hadoop Fundamental Concepts," and in Figure 3.1, a Hadoop cluster is made up of software frameworks with processes that may be distributed across different servers (physical or virtual). Also, the master and slave daemon processes usually are configured to run on separate physical servers or virtual machines. The database icons in Figure 3.1 with the master servers represent metadata repositories for the Oozie server, Ambari server (with HDP), and Hive server.

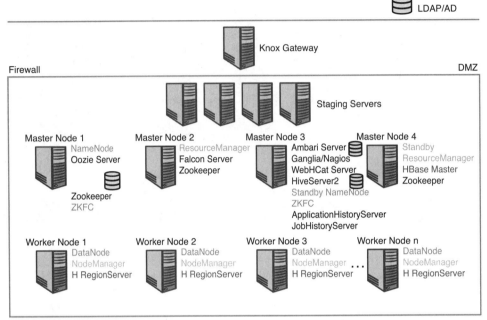

Note: There is an Ambari agent and a Ganglia agent on each node being monitored.

Figure 3.1   A Hadoop cluster (hardware and software profile).

Each server is listed with key Hadoop software processes. The master and slave server processes run as daemons in JVMs. The following is a typical list of the layers in a Hadoop cluster. Data blocks are replicated for availability. YARN and HDFS work together to make sure a job will keep running even if a worker node or disk fails. Worker nodes represent the slave servers that are running a Node Manager or DataNode daemon. A typical Hadoop cluster contains the following components:

- An LDAP or AD server for user authentication.

- HDP uses Knox to provide perimeter security through a single access point for authentication and access. Although not shown here, Kerberos is the default standard for authentication of users and services within a Hadoop cluster.

- A Hadoop cluster will use edge nodes or staging servers as access points into the Hadoop cluster network or to store data as a staging area. The edge nodes are also used to launch applications. Software for different types of data integration and data ingestion can also reside on the edge nodes.

- A number of master nodes will be configured for running the master daemons of the different frameworks that are being used in the Hadoop cluster.

- Storage and compute daemons (worker nodes) handle the I/O and compute for the data being queried or analyzed. A DataNode daemon handles the I/O and the NodeManager daemon handles the processing, and if you are running HBase, RegionServer daemons are the worker nodes that handle the local I/O. Depending on the configuration, additional frameworks might be installed on the Hadoop cluster, such as Storm, Kafka, Spark, Solr, and so on.

- Metadata repositories for the different frameworks store their information in relational databases. Ambari, Oozie, and Hive are frameworks that require a metadata repository. These relational databases must be backed up. Database failover solutions may also be implemented depending on service-level agreements.

For production environments, the software processes are distributed across the different servers. Because it is important to separate the master daemons for a framework and the slave daemon processes associated with those masters, you end up with two levels of processing. Primary master daemons and their standby daemons must reside on separate physical platforms for high availability. Examples include the NameNode and Resource-Manager daemons and their standby daemons. If you are using virtual machines, you must put in place rules to keep the primaries and standby daemons on virtual machines on separate ESXi hosts. The master and slave server workloads have different responsibilities and runtime characteristics, so the workloads should be separated from a configuration, management, and tuning perspective. Master server daemons should not be competing for resources with slave daemons in a production environment. The master server nodes should be designed for availability. The slave servers should be designed for performance. Slave servers running DataNode daemons contain all the user data. Slave servers running NodeManager daemons handle all the data processing. Traditionally, a slave server will have a DataNode and a NodeManager process; however, it is possible to separate the DataNode (storage) and NodeManager (compute) to separate worker nodes.

The HDFS and YARN frameworks address high availability and fault tolerance from a software perspective for the compute and storage nodes. Servers are added horizontally to increase the parallel processing capability, storage capacity, and throughput. Hadoop 1 scales to around 5,000 data nodes. Hadoop 2.0 is being designed to scale to 10,000+ nodes. Scalability, performance, high availability, and ease of management are improving significantly with each new release of Hadoop. Additional high availability for additional frameworks is also being added in new releases. The hardware running Hadoop is also getting faster, containing more memory, using larger network cards and larger and more disks as the price point changes with hardware.

A few years ago, slave servers would have 24GB to 48GB of memory. Now it is common to see slave servers with 96GB to 256GB of memory. Servers with 512GB of memory are starting to appear. With frameworks such as Kafka, Storm, and Spark capable of running under YARN (resource management), larger server configurations are gaining in popularity because more frameworks are running on the slave servers. Some frameworks, such as Kafka and Storm, often are designed to run on their own servers. Organizations are running Hadoop, NoSQL databases (HBase), and in-memory distributed data sets (Spark) on a single cluster. With hardware costs continuing to drop, these types of clusters might be looking at 512GB to 1TB of memory in time. In the past, slave servers would have 1GB NICs, but now, seeing a 10GB NIC in a worker node is becoming common.

A number of the frameworks, such as HDFS, YARN, and HBase, are designed with a master-slave server architecture. There are frameworks, such as zookeeper, that have their coordinated servers configured across multiple servers for availability. A Hadoop cluster is designed to be a share-nothing, distributed processing environment.

Software tools such as Ambari (Hortonworks) and Cloudera Manager (Cloudera) are used to look at the metrics collected on the system. Local operating system tools can also be used to look at the activity dependent on permissions and access. The Java Virtual Machine Process Status tool (jps) can be used to list all the Java virtual machines (JVMs) running on the current server. The jps tool displays the local VM identifier (lvmid) and JVM found running on a host. The tool reports JVMs only for those for which it has access permissions. An administrator can log in to any host running Hadoop processes and see the JVMs running. The jps command displays the JVMs using initial capital letters, but the processes are in lowercase, so use lowercase when running a Linux **ps -ef** command. The **-l** option displays a long listing. The remote.domain and port can be specified for a nonlocal host. Following are examples of running the jps tool:

```
-- The $JAVA_HOME/bin value must be defined in the PATH to run the jps
   command.
$ jps
$ jps  -l
```

Each daemon has a small application server associated with it that collects runtime metrics. Specifying the server name and correct port number enables an administrator to access these metrics. List the Fully Qualified Domain Name (FQDN) or the IP address in the URL. The listed ports might be different in your Hadoop cluster. You can look at the hdfs-site.xml, yarn-site.xml, core-site.xml, and mapred-site.xml files for defined port numbers for your cluster. Table 3.1 shows key Hadoop daemons, default port numbers, and their corresponding parameters.

Table 3.1 Hadoop Processes and Their URLs for Accessing Metrics

Daemon	ServerName:Port	Parameter
NameNode	<namenode>:50070	dfs.http.address

Daemon	ServerName:Port	Parameter
DataNode	<datanode>:50075/blockScannerReport	dfs.datanode.http.address
	<datanode>:50075/blockScannerReport?listblocks	
	<datanode>:50075/logs	
Secondary NameNode	<snamennode>:50090	dfs.secondary.http.address
ResourceManager	<rmgr_node>:8088	yarn.resourcemanager.webapp.address
NodeManager	<nodemgr>:50090	yarn.nodemanager.webapp.address
HBase Master	<hmaster>:60010	hbase.master.info.port
Region Server	<rserver>:60030	hbase.regionserver.info.port
JobHistory	<JobHistoryServer>:19888	mapreduce.jobhistory.webapp.address
Hive	<hiveserver>:9999	hive.hwi.listen.port
JMX	http://node1:50070/jmx	The "/jmx" URL exists for all Hadoop daemons.

A few notes on NameNode configuration:

- If NameNode HA is configured, the NN hostname will change to NameService ID.
- If NameNode HA is enabled, Secondary NameNode is not needed and will not exist in the cluster. A Standby NameNode will be configured with a NameNode HA configuration.

Hadoop Directory Layouts

A number of important directories exist in a Hadoop configuration. Frameworks each have their own directory to make it easy to add or remove a framework from a Hadoop configuration. These are common directories; the directory names and structures can be configured differently by an administration team. Some of the most important directories include the following default locations:

- /etc/<framework>/conf: Hadoop is made up of several frameworks. Each framework has its own configuration directory below /etc (default). Examples include the following:

/etc/ambari-agent/conf	/etc/hadoop/conf	/etc/hue/conf	/etc/pig/conf
/etc/ambari-server/conf	/etc/hbase/conf	/etc/knox/conf	/etc/sqoop/conf
/etc/falcon/conf	/etc/hcatalog/conf	/etc/nagios/conf	/etc/yarn/conf
/etc/ganglia/conf	/etc/hive/conf	/etc/oozie/conf/	/etc/zookeeper/conf

- Directory layouts (typical defaults):

  - **Configuration files:** /etc/<framework>

  - **Data:** /hadoop/data

  - **Local yum repository:** /yum/repos.d

  - **Hadoop software (binaries, libraries,...):** /usr/lib

  - **Log directory locations:** /var/log

  - **Runtime (pid files) and maintenance files:** /var/run

- Some key files in these directories include the following:

  - **Primary configuration file:** <framework>-site.xml

  - **Environmental parameters:** <framework>-env.sh

  - **Log parameters:** log4j.properties

- The following are examples of important configuration files:

  - **Environmental variables for Hadoop cluster:** hadoop-env.sh

  - **Global Hadoop configuration file:** core-site.xml

  - **HDFS configuration (I/O):** hdfs-site.xml

  - **YARN configuration file (dist. processing):** yarn-site.xml

  - **MapReduce configuration file:** mapred-site.xml

Hadoop Operating System Users

When Hadoop is installed, a number of operating system users are created in the /etc/passwd file. A number of the frameworks have super users created in the /etc/passwd file. Some of the Hadoop users include yarn, hdfs, ambari-qa, hbase, hive, oozie, hcat, mapred, zookeeper, rrdcached, apache, mysql, postgres, and sqoop.

The Hadoop Distributed File System

The Hadoop Distributed File System (HDFS) is a framework designed to store very large datasets and to process I/O at very high rates. HDFS can be configured to run on a single server or on a cluster with potentially more than 10,000 data nodes. HDFS can handle volumes now at the exabtye storage level. Over time, as the number of nodes or the number of disks or the disk sizes get bigger, this volume can increase. The number of disks and the size of the disks will determine the total storage.

10,000 nodes x 24 disks x 4TB/disk = 960,000TB or 960PB or approx. 1EB.

10,000 nodes x 72 disks x 4TB/disk = 2,880,000TB or 2,880PB or approx. 3EB.

HDFS is based on the Unix file system, but some standards were not included to emphasize performance. HDFS stores the file system metadata on master servers and the application data on the data nodes. The NameNode daemons communicate with the DataNode daemons on the worker nodes with TCP-based protocols. HDFS ensures data durability by replicating data.

HDFS stores files by separating their blocks across the disks associated with each data node. Blocks are usually broken into 64MB to 1GB sizes. This is significantly different from relational databases and data warehouses whose block sizes usually range between 8k to 16k block sizes. The HDFS default block size for HDP is set to 128MB. Other distributions often use 64MB block sizes as the default. The default block size for HDFS can be changed. Individual files and directories in HDFS can override the default block size. HDFS has a replication level, which by default is set to 3. When blocks for a file are created, they are spread across the different disks on the data node servers, and each block is replicated by default three times. The replication level can be set at the HDFS cluster level and can be overridden at the directory or the file level.

When someone runs a job to create a file, the user can add a parameter that will override the default replications level. If someone is running a development or test environment, three replicas might not be needed. Setting the replication level above three can increase data locality and reduce bottlenecks for blocks that are accessed at very high rates. The blocks are replicated so if a data node server or a disk becomes unavailable, there are still other replicas of a block that enable a job to continue. Dataset sizes, access, availability, and runtime requirements all impact the recommended block size. Larger datasets will go above the 128MB value. Over time, we can expect to see more blended (hybrid) disk solutions for Hadoop using SSD, SATA, and so on. Real-time data frameworks, such as Spark, and caching configurations might start looking at using Solid State Drives (SSDs) for performance in the future. Master daemons might consider using SAN for high availability.

HDP 2.2 added heterogeneous storage for HDFS. This is an interesting new feature that would enable an application to define the storage preference within the Hadoop cluster that could be hard disk drive (HDD), SSD, or memory. To the DataNode, this means that it is no longer one storage unit but a collection of storage types. DataNodes can now distinguish what HDD, SSD, or memory storage is. The NameNode, on the other hand, will now expect from all DataNodes in their block report to include statistics about each storage type. This is an important feature for YARN because YARN can label nodes that could have SSD drives or more memory-dense machines for time-sensitive applications. YARN might also set a group of data nodes to run a certain type of software to make sure software licensing is not violated. For example, there might be a 100 DataNode cluster, but a certain type of software is going to run on only 10 of those DataNodes (nodes running the DataNode daemon).

From a logical architecture point of view, HDFS storage architecture prior to HDP 2.2 looks something like the architecture depicted in Figure 3.2. A DataNode can be defined as a single logical unit of storage.

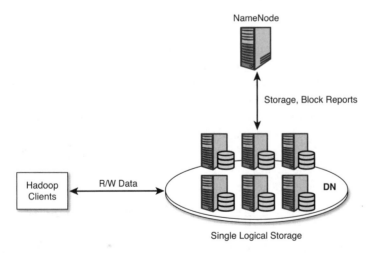

Figure 3.2   DataNode as a single logical unit.

Each heartbeat that DataNode daemons send to their NameNode daemons contains capacity and usage information. With heterogeneous storage, NameNode and DataNode daemons will now distinguish storage type and send storage and block reports based on the storage type, as shown in Figure 3.3. Hadoop clients can now choose the storage preference that matches their storage requirements—archiving, hot data placement, and replica placement. When HDFS quota is enforced, Hadoop still checks for quotas on the directory where the data is written. If it's successful, it checks for storage space. The storage preference then applies at that point whether the storage is SSD versus HDD or RAM versus HDD.

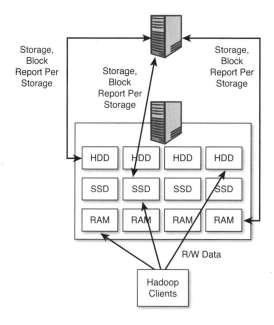

Figure 3.3   DataNode using hybrid storage.

There are future plans to add more twists to HDFS. These include the following changes:

- Enforcing expiration periods for replicas on storage types
- Providing the capability to mix and match storage types
- Support for tape drives
- Support for hot swapping failed drives

These are just some of the interesting plans for Hadoop that would make enterprises crave more.

YARN Logging

Log management is always an important part of administration. Logs are needed to debug applications, perform historical analysis, and evaluate individual tasks in an application. YARN has the capability to aggregate the logs from all the containers into a centrally configured location. When an application has finished running, there will be an application-level log directory and a per-node log that contains the logs of all the containers for an application that ran on that node. These logs can be accessed through YARN commands, a web UI, or directory from the file system where the logs are stored. Inside the MapReduce JobHistoryServer is an *AggregatedLogDeletionService* service that will periodically delete aggregated logs. The YARN **logs** command is used to display information on logs, as shown in Listing 3.1.

Listing 3.1   YARN **logs** Command

```
# yarn logs
Retrieve logs for completed YARN applications.
usage: yarn logs -applicationId <application ID> [OPTIONS]
general options are:
 -appOwner <Application Owner>    AppOwner (assumed to be current user    if
  not specified)
 -containerId <Container ID>      ContainerId (must be specified if node
  address is specified)
 -nodeAddress <Node Address>      NodeAddress in the format
  nodename:port(must be specified if container id is specified
```

The following show the syntax for the YARN command.

Print the logs for a given application:

```
$ yarn logs -applicationId <application_ID>
```

Print the logs for one container:

```
$ yarn logs -applicationId <application_ID> -containerId <Container_ID>
  -nodeAddress <Node_Address>
```

The NameNode

The NameNode is the master process (daemon) that manages all the metadata for all files stored in HDFS, which includes file hierarchy representation and block locations per file. The NameNode term can be used to refer to the hardware server on which the NameNode master daemon is running or the master daemon called NameNode.

The NameNode daemon contains a current image of all directories, files, and blocks in memory. An image also exists on the disk for persistence.

The HDFS namespace stored in memory contains directories and files in a namespace that is hierarchical. Each namespace has its own ID. The namespace ID is stored on all nodes in the cluster. This ensures that nodes with a different namespace ID might not join the cluster. No user data passes through the NameNode, nor does it store any user data. The NameNode stores only system metadata on all the files, directories, and blocks in the Hadoop cluster.

The Linux **ps** command on the NameNode server can be used to list the namenode process ID.

```
# ps -ef | grep namenode
```

Directories and file information are stored in a NameNode inode format. Inodes record information, such as the namespace, permissions, disk quotas, modification, and access times. This metadata is stored in an fsimage file. Checkpoints are maintained for the persistent image information that is stored in an fsimage file on the NameNode host's native file system. Checkpoints maintain persistent images on the disk. The NameNode contains a journal log that stores modification information in an edits.log file on the NameNode hosts native file system. The journal log is a write-ahead log file that maintains persistence. It is recommended that you store a minimum of three copies of metadata information. The NameNode automatically mirrors each copy. It is a best practice to store two local copies and one NFS mounted copy.

When a NameNode master server starts up, it restores the namespace in memory by reading the fsimage file and then replaying the edit (journal) log. There are mechanisms (configuration parameters) to keep the journal log small. A key point to understand is that the NameNode is responsible for holding the current namespace and block map data in memory. The NameNode also stores all metadata and manages the metadata and the journaling. No application data is managed or stored by the NameNode. NameNode high availability can be configured by adding a Standby NameNode.

The DataNode

The DataNode is a slave daemon process that runs on a slave server in the HDFS cluster containing application data. There is one DataNode daemon process per slave server. The term *DataNode* can refer to the server on which the DataNode slave daemon (named datanode) is running, or the daemon itself, called DataNode. Each DataNode has its own storage ID. The storage ID is generated when it first communicates with the NameNode master process. A new DataNode will also be assigned the NameNode's namespace ID during the first initialization. This storage ID will remain the same even if the server IP address or port is changed.

Each block replica on a DataNode is stored in two files. The first file contains the data and the second file contains the block metadata. The metadata contains the checksum for the block and the generation stamp. A checksum is utilized each time a data block is read or written. Block scans are performed periodically to make sure all data blocks are valid. If a data block is identified as being corrupt, it will be deleted and a replacement data block will be generated from a valid replica. The NameNode is responsible for maintaining the integrity of the data blocks. A block takes up only the space it needs up to its block size. If the final block in a file is only half filled, it will be half the size.

The Linux **ps** command can be used to list the DataNode process ID. This is a quick way to verify whether a DataNode daemon is running without having to use a GUI.

```
# ps -ef | grep datanode
```

When the DataNode daemon starts up, it looks in its configuration file to find its NameNode(s) master daemon. The DataNode sends a heartbeat communication to the NameNode(s). Information communicated includes the namespace ID, software version, and so on. If the information does not match the NameNode(s) information, the DataNode will shut itself down. The DataNode daemons also send block map reports on the status of their blocks. This is how the NameNode daemon maintains the status of all the blocks in the cluster.

The NameNode maintains the state of all the blocks in memory. The DataNodes will send a block map report to the NameNode every 3 seconds. (This limit can be configured.) Each block has a unique block ID. The block map report includes the block ID, generation stamp, and length of each block it stores. If a dataset is defined to have three replicas, the NameNode adds a replica or removes a replica if there are fewer or more than three replicas. The NameNode maintains the correct number of replicas automatically. If the NameNode does not hear from the DataNode within 10 minutes (configurable), the DataNode is considered dead and the blocks stored on it to be unavailable. Heartbeats include information such as total storage, storage in use, and the current activity. The NameNode uses this information to make decisions on block management.

DataNodes initiate heartbeats to the NameNode(s). The NameNode(s) respond to the heartbeats and send information back to the DataNodes. Information includes block management commands, such as replication and block deletes, and management commands, such as shutdown or requests for a block map report. DataNodes update the NameNode so it always contains the current state of the data in the Hadoop cluster. DataNodes are responsible for generating the replicas, taking this burden off the primary NameNode.

Figure 3.4 illustrates NameNodes and DataNodes communicating over heartbeats every 3 seconds (default). Replication of the blocks is performed by the DataNodes. Ovals represent software processes.

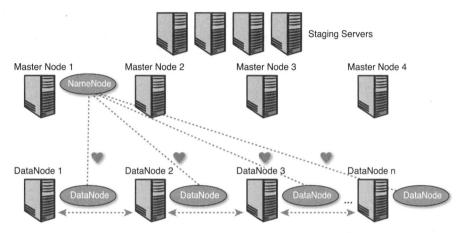

Figure 3.4   NameNodes and DataNodes communicating over heartbeats.

The Hadoop Data Directory Structure

Hadoop stores its blocks on the native OS Filesystem. For Linux, you can use ext4 or XFS. The HDFS blocks get stored in Linux directories. A Linux administrator can do a Linux **ls** command and see the individual files that make up the Hadoop blocks. The hdfs-site.xml file contains the dfs.datanode.data.dir parameter where you list all the Linux directories (separated by commas) that will store HDFS directories, files, and blocks. HDFS directories map to Linux directories defined by these parameters. HDFS creates subdirectories in Linux, which map to HDFS subdirectories to avoid putting too many HDFS blocks in individual Linux directories.

The Linux file system stores the HDFS blocks but does not manage them. As far as Linux is concerned, HDFS blocks and their metadata file are just files on the disk. When blocks are stored in HDFS, the NameNode master process receives metadata information about the blocks. HDFS has its own set of file administration commands that are completely separate from Linux. Linux sees an individual HDFS block as a local file. HDFS sees a file as being made up of multiple blocks with replicas spread across local disks in the Hadoop cluster.

HDFS file administration commands go through NameNode(s) so the NameNode(s) master process can maintain integrity of all blocks in the cluster. Do *not* use Linux file administration commands on HDFS files. The NameNode does not communicate with

Linux commands for file administration. Remember that HDFS directories and blocks span the entire cluster. HDFS file administration commands access blocks across the entire cluster. A Linux command runs only on the local server from which it is executed. HDFS stores its blocks on a Linux file system but HDFS does all file system management of those blocks. All HDFS file administration commands go through the NameNode so the metadata can be updated for storage. Because HDFS traditionally sees its storage as just a bunch of disks (JBOD), and because each disk is part of the Hadoop storage, it's often clearer to use the term Linux *partitions* instead of *directories*. A sample of storage configuration and optimization parameters is shown in Table 3.2.

Table 3.2   A Sample of Storage Configuration and Optimization Parameters

Parameter	Example	Purpose
dfs.datanode.data.dir	/hadoop/hdfs/data1, /hadoop/hdfs/data2, /hadoop/hdfs/data3, ...	Define Linux partitions to store HDFS data, files, and blocks.
dfs.datanode.data.dir.perm	750	Default permissions in HDFS.
dfs.blocksize	134217728	Default block size for cluster (128MB).
dfs.namenode.handler.count	100	Number of threads to handle RPC communication with DataNodes

Each block contains two files—the block data and its associated metadata file. There is a VERSION file in the parent directory that contains metadata information, such as the cluster_ID, storageType, layoutVersion, and so on. Linux file administration commands should not be executed on HDFS data, because all changes must go through Hadoop so the NameNode can make metadata updates. Listing 3.2 shows a sample template layout for the directories.

Listing 3.2   Sample Layout for Directories

```
${dfs.data.dir}/current/uniqueblockno_<id_1>
                       /uniqueblockno_<id_1>.meta
                       /uniqueblockno_<id_2>
                       /uniqueblockno_<id_2>.meta
                       /...
                       /subdirectory0/
                       /subdirectory1/
                       /...
                       VERSION
```

Block Placement

A Hadoop client can read or write Hadoop blocks or can launch a job (Tez, MapReduce2, and so on) to do the reading or writing. When writing a file, the Hadoop client makes a request to the NameNode for a list of DataNodes that it can use to store the blocks for the file. The NameNode will send a list of where to place the blocks back to the Hadoop client. Clients that interface with HDFS include the following:

- MapReduce2, Pig, Hive, streaming applications
- WebHDFS—REST APIs
- Sqoop and Flume
- HttpFS—REST gateway
- HDFS commands (fs, distcp, archive, balancer, fsck, dfsadmin, …)
- Hue—Contains an HDFS file browser

A write occurs to the first DataNode in the list returned from the NameNode. Replication of each block is done by the DataNodes in pipeline fashion. This takes the burden of replication off the client and the NameNode. The DataNode that receives the first block is responsible for sending instructions to another DataNode to place the second replica. This DataNode then sends instructions to a third DataNode to write the third replica. In large clusters with multiple racks, the second and third replicas are placed in the same rack, but not the rack the first replica is in. Rack awareness ensures availability in the event of a rack failure. Rack awareness must be configured. A checksum sequence for each block is created. The checksum is written to the disk along with the block. The checksum is stored in a separate file from the block. Acknowledgements of the verified checksum are sent back down the pipeline so the client gets verification that the block was written correctly. DataNodes also communicate with each other for replication.

A file is opened for writing. After the file is written to the disk, the file is closed. The blocks for the file are filled in 128MB increments (default). The last block might be only half filled, so this block will be half the size. The file cannot be updated but it can be appended to. Be aware that a different Hadoop client can read a file that is open for writing.

When a Hadoop client reads a file, it will get a list of blocks from the NameNode. The blocks are listed in order of their distance to the reader.

Figure 3.5 walks through the steps that a Hadoop client will go through to write blocks to HDFS.

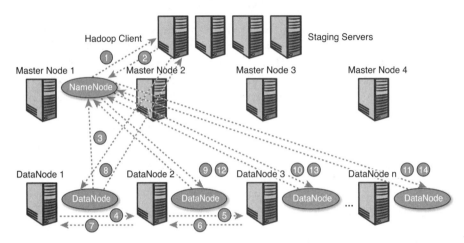

Figure 3.5   Writing blocks to HDFS with the Hadoop client.

1. The Hadoop client sends the NameNode the path and name of the file. If a path is not specified, a default path is used. For a user, the default will be the user's home directory in HDFS. The NameNode will send the client back a list of DataNodes that will hold the replicas. Each replica will have an ordered list. The client then sends the blocks to the selected DataNodes. The block replicas will be processed in an ordered pipeline. NameNode has the current state of all HDFS blocks in memory, the namespace (files and directories), and the storage utilization on each DataNode in memory.

2. The NameNode sends a list of blocks and an ordered list of replicas back to the Hadoop client. Block information is streamed to the Hadoop client, which uses a temporary directory for the block information being streamed in.

3. The Hadoop client sends the first block to a DataNode. The DataNode then writes the first block replica to disk. A pipeline with other DataNodes will be used to replicate the block.

4. The DataNode sends the instructions and block to a second DataNode. If rack awareness or virtual awareness (HVE) is set in a Hadoop cluster, the second replica is sent to a different rack and/or a different node group (if slave servers are virtualized) for HA. This second DataNode in the ordered list writes the second replica for the block. Rack awareness and HVE make sure that all the replicas are not together on the same physical server in case of some type of hardware failure.

5. The second DataNode in the ordered list sends instruction and block to a third DataNode. This third DataNode writes the third block (assuming the default is three replicas). This third DataNode will be in the same rack as the DataNode that

wrote the second replica if the Hadoop cluster is in a rack topology. Checksums are performed on all block writes. Writing the second replica to a different rack or node group meets the HA requirement. This is the default block placement policy. If there are more than three replicas, the blocks will be spread across different racks or node groups.

6. Acknowledgements are sent back through the pipeline and back to the Hadoop client.

7. Acknowledgements continue back through the pipeline.

8. Acknowledgements return to the Hadoop client.

9-11. Each DataNode will independently send heartbeats and updated block map reports back to the NameNode so the NameNode always has a current status of all blocks and DataNodes in a cluster.

12-14. These steps show the NameNode(s) responding to the initiated heartbeats from the DataNodes and sending instructions back.

Putting the placement of block replica in the context of heterogeneous storage makes it more interesting. You now have the capability to spread replicas out in different storage types (for instance, one replica in memory, another in SSD, and the third in HDD). The block replica placement must be validated with business use cases to ensure optimal configurations are still met.

NameNode Configurations and Managing Metadata

When a NameNode first comes up, it will read the current fsimage file. All the inode information gets loaded into the NameNode memory. The NameNode will then read the edits.log file; the journal information will get converted into inode information and loaded into memory. A checkpoint is performed. The current information in memory is written to a new fsimage file. The edits.log will be written to a previous edits.log file, and a new empty edits.log file will be created. Whenever the NameNode starts, the edits.log file has to be read. The length of the edits.log file impacts the startup time for the NameNode. The edits.log file is a journal log of all data changes. The NameNode cleans out the edits.log file on startup and only on startup. When a Hadoop cluster is up for a long period of time and processing data, the edits.log file can get large. Extremely high writes in a short period of time can also drive the size of the edit.log file.

There are two ways to keep the edits.log file small: the use of a Secondary NameNode or a Standby NameNode.

The Secondary NameNode has only one purpose: to periodically (every hour by default) clean out the edits.log file and build a new fsimage file. The fsimage can be replaced while the Hadoop cluster is running because the NameNode reads the fsimage only when it first starts up. The Secondary is not for failover. The purpose of configuring a Secondary NameNode is to keep the edits.log file from growing too large and increasing startup time. A Secondary NameNode is used when there is not an HA requirement for using a Standby NameNode. Here are the steps that occur to create a new fsimage file:

1. The Secondary NameNode will, at specified time intervals, copy the fsimage and edits.log file from the NameNode to the Secondary NameNode.

2. The Secondary NameNode will read the fsimage file and the edits.log file into memory and build a new fsimage file from the memory image.

3. A new empty edits.log file is created.

4. The new fsimage and edits.log file will be copied back to the NameNode. A check-point is performed marking the time when it happened.

5. The current fsimage and edits.log file will be copied to a previous file using the _N format. The new fsimage and edits.log file created by the Secondary NameNode will become the new current files for the NameNode.

The Secondary NameNode should not be used for recovery unless absolutely necessary. At a minimum, there should be three mirrored copies (configurable) of the primary NameNode metadata information. Two local copies and one NFS mounted copy should protect this metadata. In a worst-case scenario, if the primary NameNode and all copies of the metadata are unavailable, the outdated version of the fsimage and edits.log file can be used to bring up the Hadoop cluster.

Figure 3.6 shows the primary NameNode communicating with the DataNodes. The primary NameNode does *not* use the Secondary NameNode for failover. The Secondary NameNode only communicates with the primary NameNode to periodically shrink the edits.log file for short startup times for the primary NameNode. The Secondary NameNode does not provide an HA solution. A secondary NameNode is used because some customers do not need an HA solution. It is considered a best practice to configure NameNode HA by using a Standby NameNode to prevent the loss of the NameNode metadata.

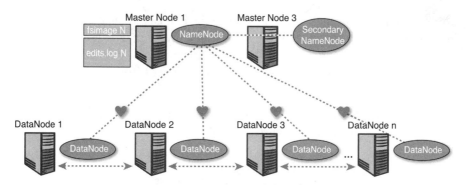

Figure 3.6   The DataNodes communicate with the Primary NameNode.

The Standby NameNode configuration is designed to be an HA solution for the NameNode. The Primary NameNode and Standby NameNode run in an active and passive mode. There is no special configuration for the Primary and Standby NameNode.

- Whichever NameNode comes up will acquire a znode lock and be the primary NameNode.

- The next NameNode will try to acquire the lock, be unable to, and will be the Standby NameNode. If someone wants one of the NameNodes to be the primary, that NameNode must be started first.

- If the primary NameNode goes down, a switch occurs and the Standby NameNode acquires the lock and will take over as the primary NameNode.

- If the original NameNode comes back, it will come up as the Standby NameNode.

The NameNode HA should have at least three zookeepers (more than one and an odd number) and at least three JournalNodes so that one of them is always arbitrating the decision on which edit log/fsimage version to use when failing over to the Standby NameNode. Both the Primary (active) and the Standby NameNode communicate with the JournalNodes to stay synchronized. During any changes to the primary node, a log entry of this change is written to the journal nodes. The standby node reads the edits from the journal nodes to stay synchronized with the primary node. DataNodes will send block information and heartbeats to the primary and Standby NameNode. Also, clients will not use the hostname of the active NameNode but the logical NameService ID that represents the NameNode HA cluster.

In an HA configuration, the metadata must be distributed to make sure there is not a single point of failure. Multiple journal nodes or an NFS configuration can be used. Using the journal nodes configuration is the recommended approach. A minimum of three journal nodes should be used. Putting the journal nodes on the master servers ensures they are on a platform configured for high availability. Only the Primary NameNode writes to the journal nodes. The Standby Namenode only reads from the journal nodes. During an HA switch, the lock is transferred to the Standby NameNode; the Standby NameNode will make sure it has read the latest entries from the journal nodes before becoming the Primary NameNode.

Figure 3.7 illustrates that only the Primary NameNode writes to the journal nodes. The Standby NameNode only reads from the journal nodes.

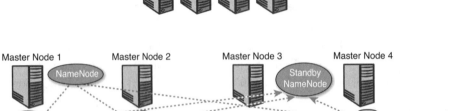

Figure 3.7   The Primary NameNode writes to the journal nodes, and the Standby NameNode reads from the journal nodes.

The HA environment is maintained by zookeeper processes. Each NameNode will have a ZooKeeper Failover Controller (ZKFC) that monitors the status of the NameNode it is monitoring. In a NameNode HA configuration, the DataNodes must send block map reports to each NameNode so the Standby NameNode can quickly become the primary NameNode. The Standby NameNode will perform checkpointing for the NameNode metadata. When running a Standby NameNode, a Secondary NameNode is not needed. The Primary NameNode manages all block operations and is the only active NameNode.

The NameNode HA can be configured to run in automatic or manual mode. Automatic mode is recommended. Manual mode requires an administrator manually perform the switch. Manual mode should be used primarily for testing.

The ZKFC processes each monitor the NameNode they are associated with and communicates with the zookeeper coordination processes (see Figure 3.8; these associations are not included in the diagram). This configuration shows the following:

- A Zookeeper Failover Controller for each NameNode.

- Three zookeeper and three journal node processes.

- The DataNodes communicate with the primary and standby NameNode.

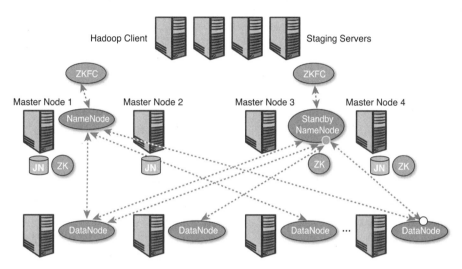

Figure 3.8 NameNode HA configuration.

Separate zookeeper processes will maintain the coordination of the HA environment. It is recommended to keep a minimum of three zookeeper coordination processes, and the number of processes should be an odd number.

Another method for protecting master processes in low-profile small- to medium-sized clusters is to put them in virtual machines and replicate the entire virtual machine with VMware Fault Tolerance. The storage for the VM needs to be on shared storage, like a SAN or a NAS. Not only the NameNode, but the ResourceManager, HBase Master, and other processes can be protected in a transparent way. VMware Fault Tolerance currently supports up to four virtual CPUs and 64GB memory (vSphere 6). Make sure the growth projections of the cluster are understood. The limit of four virtual CPUs might not change soon. This configuration must be well tested because this is a new type of configuration for Hadoop. This configuration should not be put in a high-profile Hadoop cluster until this method matures and is well tested over time. See http://www.vmware.com/resources/techresources/10301 for details.

The NameNode is multithreaded and can handle thousands of DataNodes. The NameNode configuration can be federated to support multiple active NameNodes for a single cluster. Each federated NameNode manages its own namespace and set of blocks. Business units, dev/test/production, runtime characteristics, and so on can be used to define the role of each federated NameNode. NameNodes in a federated environment work together but run individually and manage their own sets of blocks. Each NameNode can be configured with its own Standby NameNode. A federated NameNode does not need to have a Standby NameNode if HA is not a requirement. DataNodes will communicate with all the NameNodes in the cluster. This is a fairly new configuration and should be well tested and understood before going to production.

A federated Hadoop cluster can be designed in different ways. Each federated NameNode can be designed and tuned for a different purpose. Some of the different ways include the following:

- For development, testing, and production (you need to make sure production is completely protected)

- For multiple development and testing environments

- For different business units, such as marketing, sales, and auditing

- For different runtime characteristics, such as batch processing, streaming, interactive query, and/or NoSQL databases

One of the challenges is having one NameNode for different runtime characteristics that the different types of applications cannot be tuned and managed for different runtime dynamics. One NameNode can be configured for batch processing and another NameNode in the federation can be configured for interactive queries. For example, running HBase and Hadoop in the same cluster presents difficulties.

Hadoop has a balancer tool, and so does HBase. When running the Hadoop balancer, the balancer will try to distribute the blocks in HDFS so there is an even distribution of blocks across the different DataNodes. HBase has laid out the blocks for how it accesses the data. The Hadoop balancer does not recognize what is in the blocks and does not take into consideration how HBase has physically distributed the blocks. This is why the Hadoop balancer and HBase have historically not worked well in the same environment.

However, from a resource management perspective Apache Slider is going to make it easier for Hadoop and HBase to run in the same cluster. HBase and a number of other applications, such as Accumulo and Spark, can run under YARN. YARN will be able to handle resource management for applications with different runtime characteristics such as Hadoop and HBase. Slider will enable long-running applications to "slide" into YARN.

Rack Awareness

As nodes are added to a cluster, it becomes difficult to maintain a flat topology. Rack topologies are very popular with Hadoop. Hadoop makes the assumption that inner-rack

traffic is faster than out-of-rack traffic. Rack awareness can be configured for high availability on a Hadoop cluster. The first block will be placed on the local DataNode to get
the block down as quickly as possible. The second replica will be placed on a different
rack for high availability (HA). The third replica will be placed on a different node of the
second rack because HA has been addressed. Rack awareness makes sure all blocks are
not put on a single rack. Subsequent replicas will be randomly placed. The Top of Rack
(ToR) switches and aggregation switches must be configured for growth. A DataNode
will contain only one replica of a block. A sample Hadoop configuration with two racks is
shown in Figure 3.9.

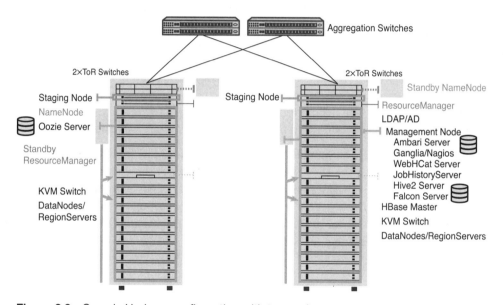

Figure 3.9   Sample Hadoop configuration with two racks.

Block Management

HDFS can be self-healing. DataNodes send the NameNode block map reports of the
blocks on their own servers. If the NameNode detects that a DataNode or the blocks on
a disk are not available within a certain time frame, the NameNode will add a new block
replica from existing replicas for the missing block. Blocks that are under replicated are
placed in a replication queue. Blocks with one replica have a higher priority, blocks with
two replicas have the next higher priority, and so on. The NameNode will ensure the
defined number of replicas for a file. If a DataNode or disk is restored, the NameNode will
detect an extra replica of a block. The NameNode will then remove a block to maintain
the defined number of blocks for the file. To address over replication, the NameNode will

remove the block from a DataNode with the least storage as long as it does not impact high availability. Block management and placement always considers high availability when rack awareness is configured. Replication can occur very fast to accommodate the number of DataNodes that exist in a cluster.

The Balancer

Over time, the blocks that are spread across a cluster can become unbalanced. When new physical hardware servers and disks are added to the Hadoop cluster, or data is deleted or moved, disk space utilization is not used when determining block placement. The balancer is a process that spreads the blocks evenly across the DataNodes to balance disk usage. The balancer must be explicitly executed; it is not an automatic process. It is recommended that you automate the process of periodically balancing the cluster. The balancer process will move blocks from DataNodes with higher disk utilization to DataNodes with lower utilization. The balancer will maintain high availability for rack awareness or HVE if configured. The balancer will maintain the correct number of replicas and the same number of racks. The balancer will try to minimize intra-rack block movement.

When running the balancer, you should provide two key inputs. The first is the defined percentage of variance across the DataNodes. You should also set the upper bandwidth of block traffic generated by the balancer to minimize the impact of currently running jobs. The higher the bandwidth the faster the balancing will occur, with increased probability of impacting current jobs. The lower the bandwidth the longer the balancing will take while minimizing the impact on existing jobs.

Maintaining Data Integrity in the Cluster

Over time, blocks can become corrupt due to memory, networking, or disk issues. It is important to ensure the integrity of the blocks in an HDFS cluster. The NameNode maintains the state. The block scanner is a process that runs over a regular interval to ensure all the blocks are valid. The block scanner runs over a three-week period by default, and an administrator might not be able to wait for the block scanner. So the administrator can run the **fsck** command manually if there is a need to manually verify that blocks are not corrupted.

Blockscanner

The block scanner is an automated process designed to run over a period of time; the default is three weeks to minimize the impact on currently running jobs. The block scanner reads block replicas and validates checksums for the blocks. Reads and writes also perform checksums. When a client reads a block, it verifies the checksum and communicates this to the DataNode. This is another verification of a block replica. The verifications for each block are stored in a log file. In a top-level directory, files are kept for the current log and the previous log. The DataNode keeps track of an in-memory list for block verification times. The verification times of a block are updated in the current log. The parameter dfs.datanode.scan.period.hours (default 504) defines the time frame for block scanning.

Example: The block scanner report can be viewed from http://datanode:50075/blockScannerReport.

Only the NameNode maintains the current state of all the blocks in the cluster. So any maintenance on blocks must go through the NameNode. If the block scanner or a client that is reading blocks sees there is an issue with the checksum, it will inform the NameNode. The block scanner and client do not repair blocks. The NameNode marks the block as corrupt. A new replica is created, and then the corrupt block is removed. The NameNode does not fix a corrupt block. The NameNode will build a new valid image of a replica and then remove the corrupt one.

HDFS Commands

HDFS commands can perform file system commands that look similar to commands performed by standard operating systems. Just remember that files in HDFS are spread across multiple blocks that contain replicas. HDFS is owned by default by the HDFS user. Table 3.3 lists the parameters in hdfs-site.xml that impact HDFS administration.

Table 3.3   HDFS-site.xml Parameters That Impact HDFS Administration

Parameter	Value	Definition
dfs.cluster.administrators	hdfs	List of hdfs admins
dfs.permissions.superusergoup	hdfs	Group for hdfs admins

HDFS operations run in HDFS based on the permission domain of the operating system user running the commands. Permissions in HDFS base use directory and file privileges similar to Linux, as shown in the Listing 3.3.

Listing 3.3   Sample Listing of the /user Directory in HDFS

```
# su - hdfs
$ hdfs dfs -ls /user
Found 6 items
drwxrwx---    - ambari-qa hdfs 0 2013-10-20 18:07 /user/ambari-qa
drwxr-xr-x    - guest     guest        0 2013-10-28 08:34 /user/guest
```

```
drwxr-xr-x     - hcat      hdfs 0 2013-10-20 15:12 /user/hcat
drwx------     - hive      hdfs 0 2013-10-20 15:12 /user/hive
drwxr-xr-x     - hue       hue 0 2013-10-28 08:34 /user/hue
drwxrwxr-x     - oozie     hdfs 0 2013-10-20 15:15 /user/oozie
```

The **hdfs dfsadmin** command has a number of options. The following **dfsadmin** command options must be run as the HDFS super user:

- -report
- -safemode enter | leave | get | wait
- -allowSnapshot <snapshotDir>
- -disallowSnapshot <snapshotDir>
- -saveNamespace
- -rollEdits
- -restoreFailedStorage true | false | check
- -refreshNodes
- -finalizeUpgrade
- -metasave filename
- -refreshServiceAcl
- -refreshUserToGroupsMappings
- -refreshSuperUserGroupsConfiguration
- -printTopology
- -refreshNamenodes datanodehost:port
- -deleteBlockPool datanode-host:port blockpoolId [force]
- -setQuota <quota> <dirname>...<dirname>
- -clrQuota <dirname>...<dirname>
- -setSpaceQuota <quota> <dirname>...<dirname>
- -clrSpaceQuota <dirname>...<dirname>
- -setBalancerBandwidth <bandwidth in bytes per second>
- -fetchImage <local directory>
- -help [cmd]

The **hdfs dfsadmin -report** command displays information on the status of the file system, such as the Configured Capacity, Present Capacity, Under Replicated Blocks, Blocks with corrupt replicas, Datanodes available, live data nodes, and so on.

```
$ hdfs dfsadmin -report
```

Entering the command **hdfs** on the shell command line returns a list of the HDFS commands, as shown in Listing 3.4.

Listing 3.4   Using **hdfs** to List the Different HDFS Commands

```
# hdfs
Usage: hdfs [--config confdir] COMMAND
where COMMAND is one of:
  dfs                  run a filesystem cmd on file systems supported in
                       Hadoop.
  namenode -format     format the DFS filesystem
  secondarynamenode    run the DFS secondary namenode
  namenode             run the DFS namenode
  journalnode          run the DFS journalnode
  zkfc                 run the ZK Failover Controller daemon
  datanode             run a DFS datanode
  dfsadmin             run a DFS admin client
  haadmin              run a DFS HA admin client
  fsck                 run a DFS filesystem checking utility
  balancer             run a cluster balancing utility
  jmxget               get JMX exported values from NameNode or DataNode.
  oiv                  apply the offline fsimage viewer to an fsimage
  oev                  apply the offline edits viewer to an edits file
  fetchdt              fetch a delegation token from the NameNode
  getconf              get config values from configuration
  groups               get the groups which users belong to
  snapshotDiff         diff two snapshots of a directory or diff the
                       current directory contents with a snapshot
  lsSnapshottableDir   list all snapshottable dirs owned by the current
                       user
  Use -help to see options
  portmap              run a portmap service
  nfs3                 run an NFS version 3 gateway
```

HDFS commands run under the permission domain of the operating system user running the command. Owner, group, and world permissions are supported similar to Linux.

Access Control Lists (ACLs) can provide additional security on files in HFS. HDFS supports absolute paths and relative paths. There is no concept of a current working directory in HDFS. A relative path will default to a user's home directory in HDFS. Table 3.4 shows some examples of running HDFS commands.

Table 3.4   Examples of Running HDFS Commands

hdfs dfs -ls -R	A recursive listing of files
hdfs dfs -mkdir /user/steve	Create a home directory for OS user
hdfs dfs -chown steve:hdfs /user/username	Change ownership for user's directory
hdfs dfs -put /tmp/mydata /user/steve	Copy file from local fs to HDFS
hdfs dfs -get /user/steve/mydata /tmp/md2	Copy file from HDFS to local fs

HDFS commands allow commands similar to Linux, such as listing files, displaying files, setting permissions, remove commands, and so on. Here is a list of HDFS commands that perform operations similar to other operating systems. The commands must begin with a prefix of **hdfs dfs**.

- -appendToFile <localsrc> ... <dst>
- -cat [-ignoreCrc] <src> ...
- -checksum <src> ...
- -chgrp [-R] GROUP PATH...
- -chmod [-R] <MODE[,MODE]... I OCTALMODE> PATH...
- -chown [-R] [OWNER][:[GROUP]] PATH...
- -copyFromLocal [-f] [-p] <localsrc> ... <dst>
- -copyToLocal [-p] [-ignoreCrc] [-crc] <src> ... <localdst>
- -count [-q] <path> ...
- -cp [-f] [-p] <src> ... <dst>
- -createSnapshot <snapshotDir> [<snapshotName>]
- -deleteSnapshot <snapshotDir> <snapshotName>
- -df [-h] [<path> ...]
- -du [-s] [-h] <path> ...
- -expunge

- -get [-p] [-ignoreCrc] [-crc] <src> ... <localdst>
- -getmerge [-nl] <src> <localdst>
- -help [cmd ...]
- -ls [-d] [-h] [-R] [<path> ...]
- -mkdir [-p] <path> ...
- -moveFromLocal <localsrc> ... <dst>
- -moveToLocal <src> <localdst>
- -mv <src> ... <dst>
- -put [-f] [-p] <localsrc> ... <dst>
- -renameSnapshot <snapshotDir> <oldName> <newName>
- -rm [-f] [-r | -R] [-skipTrash] <src> ...
- -rmdir [--ignore-fail-on-non-empty] <dir> ...
- -setrep [-R] [-w] <rep> <path> ...
- -stat [format] <path> ...
- -tail [-f] <file>
- -test -[defsz] <path>
- -text [-ignoreCrc] <src> ...
- -touchz <path> ...
- -usage [cmd ...]

Example individual commands:

```
$ hdfs dfs -cp /user/steve/myfile1 /user/steve/myfile2
$ hdfs dfs -cp /user/steve/myfile1 /user/steve/myfile2 /user/steve/dir
$ hdfs dfs -appendToFile localfile /user/steve/myfile
$ hdfs dfs -appendToFile localmyfile1 localfile2 /user/steve/myfile
$ hdfs dfs -appendToFile localfile hdfs://nn.example.com/hadoop/myfile
$ hdfs dfs -appendToFile - hdfs://nn.example.com/hadoop/myfile
```

Copy files from HDFS to the local file systems:

```
$ hdfs dfs -get /user/steve/file localfile
$ hdfs dfs -get hdfs://nn.example.com/user/steve/file localfile
```

Copy files from local file system to a destination file system (HDFS):

```
$ hdfs dfs -put localfile /user/steve/myfile
$ hdfs dfs -put localfile localfile2 /user/steve/mycooldir
$ hdfs dfs -put localfile hdfs://nn.example.com/hadoop/myfile
$ hdfs dfs -put - hdfs://nn.example.com/hadoop/myfile Reads the input from
  stdin.
```

Display contents of files:

```
$ hdfs dfs -cat hdfs://nn1.example.com/myfile1 hdfs://nn2.example.com/file2
$ hdfs dfs -cat file:///file3 /user/steve/file4
```

Count the number of directories, files, and bytes:

```
$ hdfs dfs -count hdfs://nn1.example.com/myfile1 hdfs://nn2.example.com/
  file2·
$ hdfs dfs -count -q hdfs://nn1.example.com/myfile1
```

Display information on files and directories. The fsck and du options show the effective storage space and do not display replication information.

```
$ hdfs dfs -du /user/steve/dir1 /user/steve/myfile1 hdfs://nn.example.com/
  user/steve/dir1
$ hdfs  fsck  /user/hdfs -locations
$ hdfs dfs -count -q /user/hdfs
$ hdfs dfs -du /user/hdfs
```

List files:

```
$ hdfs dfs -ls /user/steve/myfile1
```

Make directories:

```
$ hdfs dfs -mkdir /user/steve/dir1 /user/steve/dir2
$ hdfs dfs -mkdir hdfs://nn1.example.com/user/steve/dir
  hdfs://nn2.example.com/user/steve/dir
```

Move files:

```
$ hdfs dfs -mv /user/steve/myfile1 /user/steve/myfile2
$ hdfs dfs -mv hdfs://nn.example.com/myfile1 hdfs://nn.example.com/file2
  hdfs://nn.example.com/file3
```

Remove files:

```
$ hdfs dfs -rm hdfs://nn.example.com/file /user/steve/old_dir
$ hdfs dfs -rmr /user/steve/dir
$ hdfs dfs -rmr hdfs://nn.example.com/user/steve/dir
```

Set the replication level for a directory or for a file:

```
$ hdfs dfs -setrep -w 4 /user/steve/dir1
$ hdfs dfs -D dfs.replication=2  -put  /tmp/myfile3   /user/steve/myfile3
```

HDFS fsck Command

The HDFS **fsck** command will perform a file system check on HDFS blocks, but it does not repair blocks. If the **fsck** command detects a corrupt block, it will inform the NameNode, and the NameNode will then go through its procedure of replacing a corrupt block. The **fsck** command is run when an administrator is concerned there might be block corruption or needs to verify whether the blocks are okay after some situation. The **fsck** command checks for corrupt blocks, under-replicated blocks, over-replicated blocks, and the like.

The **fsck** command will not check files open for writing. The **-openforwrite** option can list these files. They are usually tagged CORRUPT or HEALTHY depending on their block allocation status.

The **fsck** command has several options:

- **<path>:** Start checking from this path
- **-move:** Move corrupted files to /lost+found
- **-delete:** Delete corrupted files
- **-files:** Print out files being checked
- **-openforwrite:** Print out files opened for write
- **-list-corruptfileblocks:** List of missing blocks and files they belong to
- **-blocks:** Print out block report
- **-locations:** Print out locations for every block
- **-racks:** Print out network topology for data-node locations

```
$ hdfs fsck /
$ hdfs fsck /user/steve/filetocheck -locations -blocks -files
```

If you run a report on the HDFS file system and save it to a file, the **-metasave** option provides additional information on the total number of blocks, number of data nodes, blocks currently being replicated, and blocks waiting for replication. You can also run the **hdfs dfsadmin -report** command and compare the differences in output. Listing 3.5 shows an example of generating a report.

Listing 3.5 Example of Running a Block Report

```
# su - hdfs
$ hdfs dfsadmin -metasave myrpt.081414
$ more /var/log/hadoop/hdfs/myrpt.081414
$ hdfs dfsadmin -report
```

The HDFS distcp Command

The HDFS **distcp** command can copy files or directories recursively within a Hadoop cluster or to a different Hadoop cluster. The **distcp** command does this by running a MapReduce job that copies the blocks. The **distcp** command can copy files and directories between Hadoop clusters that are running different versions. There is an additional parameter that you can specify with the **distcp** command if different Hadoop versions have different checksum algorithms.

Quotas and Trash

HDFS can store a lot of information, so it might be important to ensure that users do not accidently consume too much storage. HDFS provides the capability to set a space quota and/or a quota on the number of files. Quotas can be set on any directory. For space quotas, consider the replication factor. 10TB of data require 30TB of storage if the replication factor is set to 3.

Listing 3.6 sets a 30TB quota on Steve's home directory. The quota can be checked with the **-count** option and removed with **-clrSpaceQuota**.

Listing 3.6 Example of Setting and Clearing a Quota

```
$ hdfs dfsadmin -setSpaceQuota 30t /user/steve
$ hdfs dfs -count -q /user/steve
$ hdfs dfsadmin -clrSpaceQuota /user/steve
```

Listing 3.7 shows how to set and clear a quota on an HDFS directory.

Listing 3.7 Set a File Quota on a Directory, Then Clear the File Quota

```
$ hdfs dfsadmin -setQuota 2000000 /user/steve
$ hdfs dfsadmin -clrQuota /user/steve
```

Trash is designed to protect against the accidental removal of a file. Each user has a .Trash folder below the home directory. When a user removes files through an HDFS command, the file is moved to the .Trash directory. The file is kept in the .Trash directory until the trash time interval expires. HDFS commands executed through APIs do not use the trash if it is enabled.

The trash interval is the time that a file remains in the trash folder before it is deleted. The trash interval is set in the core-site.xml file with the fs.trash.interval parameter. This defines the number of minutes the file is kept in the trash folder. The default value is 360 minutes. Setting the value to 0 disables trash functionality.

The **expunge** command clears the trash.

```
$ hdfs dfs -expunge
```

Organizations that require secure deletion of sensitive data are demanding complete destruction of the data when a delete command is given. Unfortunately, there currently is no component in Hadoop that would replace the 1s and 0s in the disk for complete erasure of data. Organizations with such requirements should leverage their current tools for file deletion.

YARN and the YARN Processing Model

YARN was originally conceived and architected at Yahoo!. The project was led by Arun Murthy. Yahoo! realized that there are many deficiencies in Hadoop 1 architecture that prevented Yahoo! from scaling better and using resources more efficiently. Here are the following shortcomings of Hadoop 1:

- MapReduce was the only execution model available.

- It was limited to a maximum of 4,000 nodes.

- It was limited to around 40,000 concurrent tasks (# of tasks in the cluster).

- JobTracker became the bottleneck because it does three things at once: resource management, job scheduling, and job monitoring. Managing job life-cycle management plus resource management created a bottleneck.

- Only one HDFS namespace is possible in a cluster that potentially puts more burden on the NameNode.

- All map and reduce slots are static, which means unused memory resources weren't released when they weren't needed.

YARN is a distributed data operating system for Hadoop that is designed to manage the resource scheduling for a Hadoop cluster. YARN has completely opened up Hadoop as an enterprise data platform that can handle different types of data, execution models, and runtime characteristic with different frameworks—all under the same resource scheduling model. The previous execution model in Hadoop 1.x ran under the MapReduce execution model. Table 3.5 shows a comparison of YARN with Hadoop 2.x and the execution model that was used with MapReduce in Hadoop 1.x. YARN maintains compatibility with existing MapReduce applications.

Table 3.5 Hadoop 2 Versus Hadoop 1

	Hadoop 2.x	Hadoop 1.x
Resource Management	YARN	JobTracker/TaskTrackers
Data Processing Model	Flexible to support different types, such as batch processing, interactive queries, streaming/real-time, messaging, graph processing, and in-memory systems.	Rigid only supported MapReduce (batch processing). Iterative applications did not perform well with MapReduce, and developers were forced to make code work that required different processing models.
High Availability	Fault tolerant with resource management HA and multiple application masters.	Single points of failure. Required external HA solutions such as RedHat HA and VMware HA.
Scalability	Very scalable with 10,000+ DataNodes.	Upper limit between 4,000–4,500 DataNodes.
	100,000+ concurrent tasks.	40,000 concurrent tasks.
Efficiency	YARN containers can fully utilize DataNodes hardware.	Hard limits and Map and Reduce slots did not allow the DataNodes to fully utilize hardware resources. Often only 50% of hardware resources under MapReduce 1 were utilized.
Wire Compatibility	Protocols are wire compatible, allowing old and new servers to talk as well as supporting rolling upgrades.	Wire-compatible issues.

YARN is a distributed data operating system that can provide resource management for the entire cluster and different types of applications that are certified with YARN. Slider with YARN enables applications like HBase, Accumulo, and Storm to run under one resource management umbrella. YARN will provide predictable Service Level Agreements (SLAs) and Quality of Service (QoS) that MapReduce1 (Hadoop 1) could not provide.

As organizations put more data into Hadoop clusters, they must use a data platform that has a lot of flexibility, with high availability and scalability and that can support different types of execution models. YARN addresses all these requirements. One of the key roles of an operating system is to schedule and manage all the processing that happens on the operating system. YARN does the same thing for Hadoop. YARN schedules and manages all the processing that occurs on the Hadoop cluster. The execution model for YARN and slider has the flexibility in the future to manage processing models that have different runtime characteristics, such as batch processing (Tez, MapReduce2), interactive queries (Tez), streaming (Storm), messaging (Kafka), graph processing (Giraph), and in-memory (Spark) systems. Different runtime characteristics work with different types of data. So YARN enables Hadoop to support architectural platforms like a data lake or an enterprise data hub. Hadoop can be a single landing site that is cost effective at scale for any type of data with different processing requirements.

ResourceManager

YARN has three different types of primary processes: ResourceManagers, Node Managers, and Application Masters. The ResourceManagers and the Node Managers have system-level privileges and responsibilities. There will be a Node Manager running on each compute (worker) server that contains user data for processing. ResourceManagers and Node Managers are the system-level processes of YARN.

Node Managers are responsible for local resource monitoring (CPU, memory, storage, networking) on the slave server (worker node), reporting resource utilization and availability to the ResourceManager(s), identifying any issues and managing containers running on their local worker node. Node Managers are involved in the starting and termination of containers on the worker node. Figures 3.10 through 3.16 highlight only the YARN processes.

Figure 3.10 shows YARN before any jobs start. There will be one ResourceManager and NodeManagers on each DataNode.

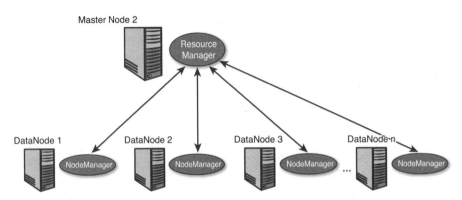

Figure 3.10   YARN before starting jobs.

Each YARN job will have its own Application Master. Each Application Master is responsible for the job life-cycle management of its specific job. As more Hadoop jobs run in the cluster, individual Application Masters will be spread across different slave servers in the cluster. This eliminates a single point of failure for all jobs as well as distributing the workload of the Application Masters. Application Masters take the workload and responsibility of job life-cycle management off of the ResourceManager. Using Application Masters this way increases the scalability of processing in Hadoop and reduces single points of failure. Different types of applications, such as MapReduce, HBase, and Spark, will all have their own Application Master.

Application Masters run user code and do not have system privileges. This prevents an Application Master from introducing malicious code into the YARN architecture. The Application Master sends a request to the ResourceManager in the form of <resource-name, priority, resource-requirement (CPU & memory), number-of-containers>.

A container is a resource lease that has the privilege of using CPU and memory on a specific worker node. Containers are allocated to the NodeManagers for running distributed processes on the DataNodes. There is flexibility where storage and networking may be added in the future. A container is a logical definition of resources (for example, 4GB of RAM, 1 CPU core) for a specific worker node. A job may run multiple containers spread across the worker nodes in the cluster.

Application Masters can work with Node Managers to launch containers that are written in C, Java, Python, Scala, and so on. A container will have information, such as the command line to start the process or JVM in the container, defined environmental variables, security tokens, jars, libraries, data files, or any additional objects required to run the code in the container.

Following is an example for determining how many containers per node can be allocated:

# of containers = min (2*CORES, 1.8*DISKS, [Total available RAM] / MIN_
CONTAINER_SIZE) where MIN_CONTAINER_SIZE is minimum container
size in GB (RAM)

The YARN launch specification API for containers is platform agnostic and does not have to be written in Java.

One of the key components of YARN is to let the ResourceManager handle the scheduling. ResourceManager has a number of modules that address security, scheduling, and the management of processing resources in the Hadoop cluster. Node Managers(s) handle the local processing on each worker node.

An Application Master will be started on a worker node to manage a job on YARN, as shown in Figure 3.11.

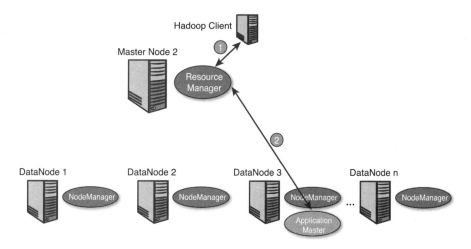

Figure 3.11 ResourceManager starts up application masters and communicates with them.

The Application Master is responsible for all the processes (containers) needed to run the job. The Application Master runs as a container. Because the Application Master is always the first container started for a job, it is referred to as container 0. The Application Master negotiates for resources from the ResourceManager. The Application Master is responsible for tracking the status and monitoring the process of the containers associated with its specific job.

When a job runs in YARN, containers are started on different worker nodes to distribute the workload across the cluster, as shown in Figure 3.12.

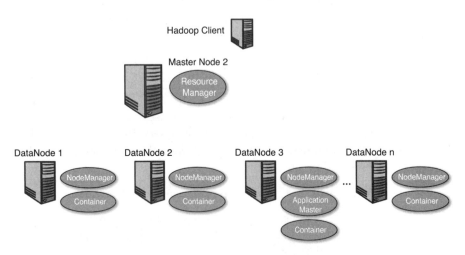

Figure 3.12   An Application Master has associated containers for each job.

The containers will be running processes that will be accessing replicated blocks on the worker nodes. Data locality, which involves trying to start processes on a worker node so the data can read locally and not across the network, will be emphasized.

The Application Master responsibility of job life-cycle management includes increasing and decreasing resources consumption, managing the flow of execution for the containers, handling issues, and performing optimizations. When the Application Master goes down, the tasks in other containers will continue to run until they are finished. The Resource-Manager will be aware that the Application Master is no longer functioning, and it will spawn a new job and tie it to the currently running jobs.

Each job will have its own Application Master, and each Application Master will manage its own containers, as shown in Figure 3.13.

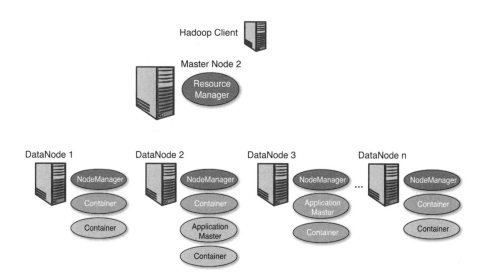

Figure 3.13 Each application will have its own Application Master and set of containers.

Steps for executing a YARN application are shown in Figure 3.14.

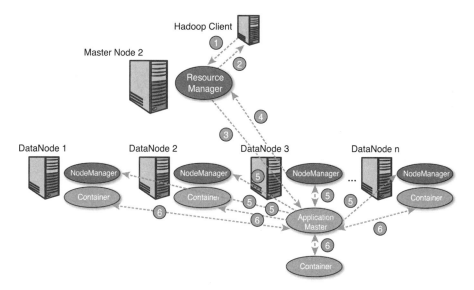

Figure 3.14 Steps for running a YARN application.

The following list details the steps of a YARN job:

1. A Hadoop client contacts the NameNode for block information for the file to be accessed or for storage to write to HDFS. Based on the number of blocks or block splits, the client will determine the amount of processing required for the job.

2. The Hadoop client submits jobs to the ResourceManager process via a public protocol.

3. The ResourceManager receives that request and validates security credentials and performs operational and administrative tasks required to run the job.

4. After the ResourceManager (scheduler) has verified that enough resources are available to run the job, the application will transition from an accepted state to a running state.

5. The ResourceManager sends a unique application ID back to the Hadoop client.

6. To start the job, the ResourceManager selects a DataNode to run an Application Master; this is also referred to as Container 0.

7. An Application Manager then coordinates the launching of additional containers across the cluster for doing the processing for the job. Container 0 can have different requirements than the other containers, so the configuration might be different.

8. The Application Master negotiates for resources with the ResourceManager and communicates with the Node Managers to execute and monitor the container activities and resource usage. The ResourceManager informs the Node Managers to let the Application Master start defined containers on a worker node.

9. The Application Master then presents the container (resource lease) to the NodeManager.

10. The NodeManager verifies the lease to make sure the Application Masters are well behaved.

Slider

The release of HDP 2.2 introduces another level of managing YARN applications—Apache Slider. Slider was created with the need to deploy long-running applications like HBase, Storm, Kafka, and many others on Hadoop. It provides easier abstractions as to how the YARN application will be developed. More importantly, this makes it easier for third-party vendors to integrate their software into Hadoop more natively via Slider. Prior to Slider, the only way to plug applications into Hadoop was by using native YARN APIs. A lot of the resource management was hand-coded, and that can be cumbersome because you must indicate in your code where to put your YARN containers, how to handle faults, and how to manipulate the application.

Now, however, Slider does most of the work for you, and the only thing you need to worry about is writing the application package. So the question is, where does a native YARN application fit now? Native applications are used when you want to create an application that is ideal for large-scale distributed algorithms with specific placement and scheduling needs.

Apache Slider is important to third-party application vendors because they can bind their applications to Slider and run their application native in YARN. For example, SAS will now be able to leverage Slider to bind their product portfolio for Hadoop. As opposed to setting up SAS servers in organizations' data centers, they can just drop their SAS servers on top of their existing Hadoop cluster. SAS can then leverage preferred HDFS storage types and YARN node labeling to improve latency requirements. Reusing the existing Hadoop cluster on top of its vendor applications makes a lot more sense. It reduces cost immensely and promotes the concept of a "multitenant" platform.

RDBMS will still be around and a critical component to enterprises. Through Slider, an RDBMS or NoSQL database can bind itself to YARN and be made available for Hadoop components to interact with. It will be an operational use case as opposed to data ingestion to Hadoop. If an organization decides to write its own YARN application that will run using a web server, this application can be registered to Slider and will interact with other Hadoop components. In short, Slider is the key to enabling any applications to integrate to any or all components in Hadoop.

Running Applications on YARN

First, you should understand how YARN works with respect to application submission and execution. Refer to Figure 3.15.

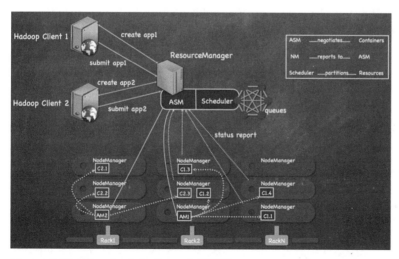

Figure 3.15 Running jobs through YARN.

What makes up YARN are the ResourceManager (RM—ApplicationsManager [ASM], Scheduler), and NodeManager(NM) components. The ApplicationsManager and Scheduler are part of ResourceManager. ResourceManager is the point of entry to all job submission requests, so all Hadoop clients will have to interface with it before a job is allocated resources. The client request must include the local files, jars, command to be executed, and environment settings. The priority of the application and number of containers are also required. All this information is necessary to ensure that an application is provided all the resources it needs to complete its job.

Figure 3.15 shows the steps to run a job through YARN:

1. Hadoop Client 1 makes an application request to ResourceManager.

2. ResourceManager parses the resource requests and communicates with ApplicationsManager so the requested number of containers is negotiated. Hadoop cluster resources are normally partitioned using Capacity Scheduler using the basic unit "queue."

3. Each queue represents the amount of memory available for use with HDP 2.2, so we can now partition CPU resources per queue.

4. After the containers are defined, it will be mapped to what queue it will be utilizing.

5. ResourceManager then returns an ApplicationId to the calling client.

6. The calling client submits the application along with the ApplicationId.

7. ResourceManager spawns an ApplicationMaster (AM) to a requested machine or rack in the cluster.

8. When the ApplicationMaster starts running, it immediately creates containers on requested nodes/racks until a minimum required number of containers is met.

9. The applications are loaded to the containers and start executing.

10. NodeManager sends a status report of the running containers and the computer resources.

11. The ApplicationMaster reports to the ResourceManager the status of the application and negotiates for more containers if required.

A couple of durability scenarios represent how faults are handled within the job execution. When one or more of the containers dies for any reason before the application completes its execution, the ApplicationMaster will renegotiate with ResourceManager, asking for more containers until its minimum number of required containers are met. ResourceManager then provides available NodeManagers where new containers will be instantiated.

Another critical path is the ApplicationMaster dying. All containers will continue to run and complete the application execution even if ApplicationMaster is no longer active. But ResourceManager will take note of this because it's not receiving any status report from the ApplicationMaster, and it will instantiate a new ApplicationMaster and register with the running containers. When containers go over their allocated memory or CPU resources, YARN kills these containers. At that point, the application will have to be given more resources and resubmit the application.

One of the powerful features of YARN is its capability to support different types of applications, such as Tez, MapReduce, HBase, Storm, Spark, Kafka, and so on. Each of these application frameworks is unique. Each will have its own ApplicationMaster that understands how to manage the execution for a specific framework. YARN can launch different ApplicationMasters each with their own specific set of code for a framework. When setting configuration parameters, the YARN parameters must be set for the containers that run on YARN; then each application framework will have its configuration parameters for its own runtime characteristics. The following is an example of key YARN parameters as well as setting parameters for running MapReduce on YARN.

There are a number of key parameters to set in the YARN environment. They include the minimum and maximum amount of memory to allocate for a container. Setting the maximum amount of memory to allocation on a slave server for all the containers determines the maximum resource utilization of the DataNode. The ratio between the virtual and physical memory also must be defined. Here is an example. Setting the values in a production environment is completely dependent on the application frameworks that are running. If the application framework code tries to exceed limits configured for YARN, the NodeManager will kill the container that tries to violate a limit. Table 3.6 shows some examples of configuring memory for containers.

Table 3.6 Key YARN Parameters in yarn-site.xml

Parameter	Value (Memory in MB)
yarn.scheduler.minimum-allocation-mb	512
yarn.scheduler.maximum-allocation-mb	4096
yarn.nodemanager.resource.memory-mb	36864
yarn.nodemanager.vmem-pmem-ratio	2.1

MapReduce2 is an execution model that runs an application in two stages with mappers and reducers. MapReduce must configure its resources for running in the YARN containers. The following parameters define how to allocate memory for a mapper and a reducer when they run in containers. Table 3.7 shows four parameters that set the Java Heap maximum value for mappers and reducers.

Table 3.7   Key MapReduce2 Parameters in mapred-site.xml

Parameter	Value (Memory in MB)
mapreduce.map.memory.mb	1536
mapreduce.reduce.memory.mb	2560
mapreduce.map.java.opts	-Xmx1024m
mapreduce.reduce.java.opts	Xmx2048m

Memory must be allocated on a worker node for the frameworks and the workloads on the frameworks. Each Hadoop cluster will have a different configuration based on their use cases and workloads. When configuring a worker node, you must make a decision as to how to allocate resources for the different types of frameworks running under YARN. The operating system, Hadoop daemons, and software agents will also take up memory and CPU. Frameworks with different execution models will have their own configuration files and sizing definitions for their containers. In Figure 3.16, compute (NodeManager) and storage (DataNode) are on the same worker node. Advanced configurations can separate compute and storage onto different worker nodes.

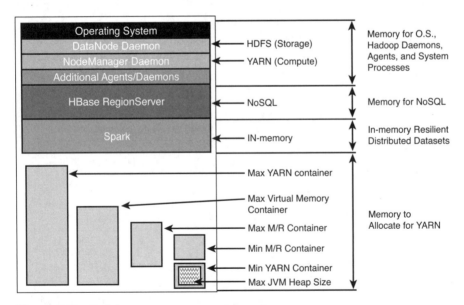

Figure 3.16   Defining memory on a worker node.

ResourceManager High Availability (HA)

ResourceManager HA is built in to the HDP distribution beginning in HDP 2.1. The ResourceManager can be scheduled to run with a high availability configuration, which will run a primary ResourceManager and a Standby ResourceManager working together in an active and passive mode. It is fault tolerant, failover is performed automatically, and it has resiliency across the entire stack. ResourceManager HA uses fencing, locking resources away from a node whose status is uncertain, to protect against a split brain. The result of a split brain is a cluster partition, where a cluster of nodes gets divided (or partitioned) into smaller clusters and then, due to data inconsistencies, proceeds to take over the resources of the other cluster as though it is the only active cluster.

ResourceManager HA has some similarities with NameNode HA and some differences. The same zookeeper (ZK) service can be used for NameNode and ResourceManager HA. ResourceManager HA does not use zookeeper failover controllers like NameNode HA. Failover functionality is built in to the ResourceManager architecture so zookeeper failover controllers are not needed.

In an HA configuration, the following information is stored in HDFS:

- The Application Master state
- The MapReduce Application Master state
- The state of the tasks that have finished
- The MapReduce job history
- YARN application history

The ResourceManager state is stored in zookeeper.

Hadoop clients and NodeManagers contact the ResourceManager. Hadoop clients and NodeManagers are configured with a comma-separated list of the ResourceManagers. Both the Hadoop clients and the NodeManagers will try to contact the ResourceManager in the order specified in the ResourceManagers list. In an HA configuration, both ResourceManager nodes are configured the same way. There is not a separate configuration for a primary and a Standby NameNode. This also simplifies the configuration for testing. Whichever ResourceManager can come up first and acquire the lock, then that ResourceManager (RMa) will be the primary. The other ResourceManager (RM) will come up and try to acquire the lock. When RM cannot acquire the lock, it will come up as the standby.

A Hadoop cluster running with a ResourceManager HA configuration will have a primary and standby ResourceManager, as shown in Figure 3.17. Only one ResourceManager will be active and will handle the scheduling for the cluster. The Standby ResourceManager maintains the current state and can become the primary ResourceManager within a few seconds after the primary has failed. Here the zookeeper processes are shown as a logical unit to simplify the drawing. Zookeeper processes will be running on separate servers.

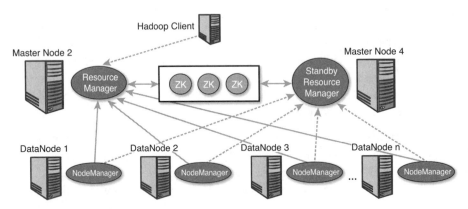

Figure 3.17   A Hadoop cluster running with an HA configuration.

What Happens During a ResourceManager Failover

Manual or automatic failover can be configured. Manual failover should be used only when it is necessary to have the administrator determine when failover can occur. Normally, a production environment will run in automatic mode.

The following steps outline what happens during a failover:

1. During a ResourceManager failover, the primary ResourceManager loses the lock with the zookeeper.

2. The Standby ResourceManager acquires the lock in the zookeeper and becomes the primary ResourceManager.

3. The active containers are killed.

4. The new primary ResourceManager reads the state from HDFS and reschedules Application Masters that will then launch their containers.

5. Completed tasks do not need to get restarted; only tasks that were in progress during the failover are restarted.

6. Clients cannot connect with the previous primary ResourceManager, so they establish a connection to the new primary ResourceManager.

7. When the failed ResourceManager comes back up, it tries to acquire the lock from the zookeeper and cannot; therefore, it comes up as the Standby ResourceManager.

8. Existing jobs continue through to completion. The architecture is designed to be resilient to failure, and no data corruption should occur during a ResourceManager failure.

- MapReduce, Tez, and Pig jobs will restart tasks that were in progress and will continue to completion.

- Hive jobs run as Tez, or MapReduce will restart the entire job.

- For Oozie workflows, the entire workflow will restart.

Be aware that Hadoop is constantly improving, so expect new features and functionality over time.

The **yarn mradmin** command has additional options for managing Resource Management HA. The following are the **yarn mradmin** HA options:

- [-transitionToActive <serviceId>]
- [-transitionToStandby <serviceId>]
- [-failover [--forcefence] [--forceactive]
- [<serviceId> <serviceId>]
- [-getServiceState <serviceId>]
- [-checkHealth <serviceId>]
- [-help <command>]

Resource Schedulers

Historically, there have been two primary schedulers in Hadoop: the Capacity Scheduler and the Fair Scheduler. There is a third scheduler, FIFO (First In, First Out); however, FIFO is not designed for multitenant clusters. The schedulers are responsible for addressing multitenancy in a single shared cluster across multiple business units, applications, and users. A scheduler also addresses data access security across shared processing and shared storage.

Historically, the Capacity Scheduler has been throughput oriented and the Fair Scheduler has been latency oriented. Both schedulers support

- Hierarchical queues
- Delayed scheduling
- Queue Access Control Lists (ACLs)

- Multi-resource scheduling

- Preemption

It is important to note that YARN controls access to cluster resources such as memory and CPU. YARN does not control access to data. Queues can be defined for YARN schedulers, and resources are allocated for the queues. Each scheduler has different priorities for allocating resources for queues. Users can be granted access to queues with ACLs, and ACLs determine which users can submit jobs to specific queues. Each scheduler has its own approach to defining ACLs.

The Capacity Scheduler is throughput oriented and runs very well in large, shared, multitenant clusters. The Fair Scheduler has worked well with environments with reduced latency for running large numbers of small jobs. Each scheduler has different priorities for allocating resources when the cluster gets busy. The Fair Sceduler tries to balance resources for all the jobs running in the cluster so every job gets a fair share of resources. HDP focuses on the Capacity Scheduler, which is emphasized here. Cloudera focuses on the Fair Scheduler.

The scheduler is a plug-in to the ResourceManager. Parameters define which scheduler is used with the ResourceManager. The Capacity Scheduler is configured with the capacity-scheduler.xml file. Capacity Scheduler is very popular in the use of enforcing SLA and QoS of jobs across different user groups. The Capacity Scheduler controls the utilization of resources in the Hadoop Cluster with queues. The following list outlines some important facts about queues:

- Users are granted access to queues.

- The queues can be hierarchical.

- Capacity management is done by setting minimum and maximum capacities for a queue and then defining user limits in the queue.

- Queues are elastic in the sense that ACLs can be applied to the queues for additional security.

- Multitenancy is controlled with limits that can be set to prevent a user, application, or queue from monopolizing resources during times of high activity.

- The Capacity Scheduler supports dynamic configurations at runtime. Queues can be added, queues can be suspended, properties changed, and ACLs modified dynamically.

- Queues can be stopped. When a queue is stopped, no new jobs can start using resources in the queue; current jobs running in the queue are allowed to finish.

The **yarn mradmin** command can be used to refresh queues after modifying the scheduler parameters.

```
$ yarn rmadmin -refreshQueues
```

Figure 3.18 shows an example of running multiple queues and their limits.

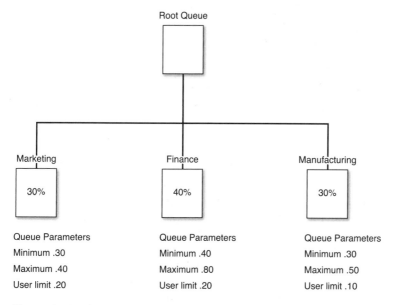

Figure 3.18 Queues determine resource allocation. Queues are hierarchical.

In Figure 3.18, the parent of all queues is the root queue. The percentage for the queues at a single level or branch must add up to exactly 100%. In the level below root, Marketing is assigned 30% of the resources, Financial is assigned 40%, and Manufacturing is assigned 30%.

The Capacity Scheduler supports elastic resource scheduling. If a queue is not using all the resources allocated and another queue is not using all its resources, then a queue can use resources up to the maximum % defined for the queue. When the system gets busy, each queue is guaranteed its minimum configuration. For example, if the other queues are not busy, the Finance queue can use up to 80% of the resources if they are available. If the system gets overloaded, the Finance group is guaranteed a minimum of 40%.

User limits can be defined on queues. Users can be assigned a minimum level of resources in a queue, or maximum limits to make sure they do not monopolize resources in a queue. An application limit can be set that defines the maximum number of applications that can be submitted to one queue. The minimum user limit tries to make sure each user has equal access to the resources in the queue, but it also makes sure that if a large number of jobs get started, they will get enough resources to complete, rather than each job getting a small percentage of the queue and all the jobs running slowly.

Table 3.8 explains the percentage of resources each user gets dependent on the number of jobs running.

Table 3.8 Queue Resource Management Makes Sure Jobs Will Finish

Number of Jobs	% of Resources Each User Gets
2	Two users will each get 50% of the queue capacity
3	Three users will each get 33.3% of the queue capacity
4	Four users will each get 25% of the queue capacity
5	Five users will each get 20% of the queue capacity
6	Six+ users will wait for the queue capacity to open up

Resource allocation is based on memory (RAM) and vcores (CPU). Resource isolation is enforced with RAM utilization limits and vcore consumption limits. Control groups (cgroups) on Linux are used to enforce vcore consumption.

Listing 3.8 shows an example of the parameters used for defining queues.

Listing 3.8 Sample Configuration of Queues

```
yarn.scheduler.capacity.root.queues = "marketing,finance,manufacturing"
yarn.scheduler.capacity.root.Marketing.capacity=30
yarn.scheduler.capacity.root.Finance.capacity=40
yarn.scheduler.capacity.root.Manufacturing.capacity=30
yarn.scheduler.capacity.root.Marketing.maximum-capacity=80
yarn.scheduler.capacity.root.Finance.maximum-capacity=100
yarn.scheduler.capacity.root.Manufacturing.maximum-capacity=80
```

Queues can have multiple levels in their hierarchy, as shown in Figure 3.19.

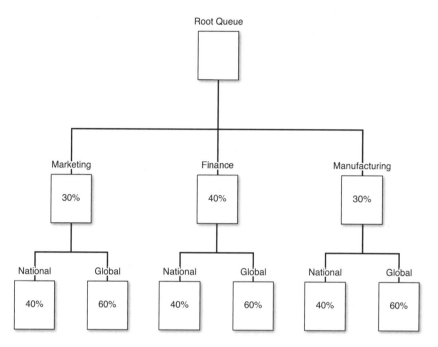

Figure 3.19   Queues can have multiple levels.

Parameters can be defined for setting up hierarchical queues to provide a lower level of granularity for business units, regions, and the like.

The following are examples of setting limits for different queues:

    yarn.scheduler.capacity.root.queues = "marketing,finance,manufacturing"
    yarn.scheduler.capacity.root.marketing.national.capacity=40
    yarn.scheduler.capacity.root.marketing.global.capacity=60
    yarn.scheduler.capacity.root.marketing.maximum-capacity=80

    yarn.scheduler.capacity.root.finance.capacity=40
    yarn.scheduler.capacity.root.finance.national.capacity=40
    yarn.scheduler.capacity.root.finance.global.capacity=60
    yarn.scheduler.capacity.root.finance.maximum-capacity=100

    yarn.scheduler.capacity.root.manufacturing.capacity=30
    yarn.scheduler.capacity.root.manufacturing.national.capacity=40

yarn.scheduler.capacity.root.manufacturing.global.capacity=60

yarn.scheduler.capacity.root.manufacturing.maximum-capacity=80

Preemption enforces SLAs based on queue priorities. Higher-priority applications do not have to wait on lower-priority applications if they have taken up all the capacity. This feature is disabled by default. The capacity scheduler will monitor priorities on regular time intervals. Monitoring will look at the current capacity, the guaranteed capacity, and then look at pending requests. Containers may be terminated during preemption. Table 3.9 lists the key preemption parameters.

Table 3.9 *Key Preemption Parameters*

xx.scheduler.monitor.enable	Turns on monitors that impact the scheduler
xx.scheduler.monitor.policy	List of classes that interact with scheduler
xx.monitor.capacity.preemption. monitoring_interval	Milliseconds (3) between invocations of policies
xx.monitor.capacity.preemption. max_wait_before_kill	Milliseconds (15) between preemption and killing container
xx.monitor.capacity.preemption. total_preemption_per_round	Max % (10) of cluster resources preempted each round

Benchmarking

Hadoop is a highly parallel and distributed platform that can scale horizontally to super computer scale. Being able to benchmark a Hadoop cluster is an important part of the overall management of Hadoop. A Hadoop distribution comes with a number of different benchmarking tools. The purpose of these tools is to put workloads on a cluster so the overall performance of CPU, processing, storage, and networking can be measured on the configuration and design of the Hadoop cluster against the hardware platform being used. The benchmarking tools are designed to put different workloads on a Hadoop cluster. A benchmark may require using more than one benchmarking tool. The tools are also used to do capacity planning on the cluster. After these tools load a data source onto a Hadoop cluster, you can use the metrics that are part of the cluster and external monitoring tools to perform the benchmark tests. The operating system, storage, and networking environments all have tools that can be used for additional metric evaluation.

Benchmarking is used on new clusters to establish baselines as well as when upgrading or modifying a cluster. Benchmarking is an excellent way to make sure the configuration of your network and storage is giving you the expected throughput. Being able to have before and after pictures can be helpful in validation or troubleshooting. Developers should consider benchmarking high-profile applications.

Hadoop is a very I/O intensive platform. Hadoop is often more memory intensive than compute intensive. It has evolved where bandwidth must be addressed for batch processing as well as latency for interactive and real-time queries. The workload the CPU and memory can generate must be balanced against the throughput of the storage and networking. Performance benchmarks must address the different types of applications and runtime characteristics of those applications (Tez, MapReduce, streaming, messaging, batch processing, interactive queries, and so on). Load-per-node, load-per-cluster, maximum number of containers per node, maximum networking bandwidth, maximum aggregate throughput, disk latency, and measuring the different types of work loads of a Hadoop cluster need to be considered.

Performance benchmarks need to look at measured simulated benchmarks, production benchmarks, and application benchmarks. Make sure you understand the workload of the benchmarking tool and what you want to measure. Benchmarking can turn into a science experiment if you are not careful. Be aware that the benchmarking tools focus on Hadoop data access patterns. In production environments, computations can be a large part of the workload in a Hadoop cluster. Concurrent Hive benchmarks might need to be run. Some benchmarks must be run with contention and others without contention.

In Hadoop 1, the only place to understand benchmark data of jobs is in the JobHistory server. It provides low-level information that system administrators can leverage to determine whether a job is using too much resources, taking too long to complete, and so on. In Hadoop 2 through YARN, these jobs are now YARN applications. So anything that is submitted to YARN for processing data is called an application. The point of entry in understanding application metrics is in ResourceManager (RM). RM knows who submitted the application, the type of the application, the queue that was used for the application, the state, progress, start time, finished time, elapsed time, allocated memory, allocated CPU cores, running containers, and much more. All these metrics provide guidance in understanding whether the application was written with optimization. MapReduce v1 is backward compatible with YARN, so all the job statistics prior to Hadoop 2 are available in ResourceManager. You can run the following command to view the job statistics prior to Hadoop 2:

```
$ hadoop job -history all <output directory>
```

Different benchmarking tools can be used. Some of the more popular ones include TestDFSIO, TeraSort, MRBench, NNBench, Gridmix, and the HiBench suite. Some of the benchmarking tools are found in the /usr/lib/hadoop-mapreduce directory in the hadoop-*test*.jar and the hadoop-*examples*.jar files. The tools in hadoop-*test*.jar include TestDFSIO, nnbench, and mrbench, and the tools in the hadoop-*examples*.jar file contain TeraSort (TeraGen and TeraValidate). The version numbers of these files will change; for example:

- hadoop-mapreduce-client-jobclient-2.2.0.2.0.6.0-76-tests.jar file

- hadoop-mapreduce-examples-2.2.0.2.0.6.0-76.jar

TestDFSIO

TestDFSIO is good way to check your OS, hardware, and Hadoop configuration and get an understanding of your I/O. TestDFSIO uses MapReduce, so it helps test the MapReduce side for a new cluster. TestDFSIO measures average throughput for read, write, and append operations. The focus is on the I/O performance for HDFS. Look at the Throughput MB/sec and Average IO rate MB/sec. Then compare that to the number of containers that can run currently on each DataNode and in aggregate. Remember that replication will also impact I/O. What matters is not just how many containers are required to run the job but how many containers can run concurrently. TestDFSIO lets you run a large number of simultaneous reads and writes. A number of mappers are run with a single reducer that generates the results. TestDFSIO is also a good way to test the environment out before looking at additional benchmarking tools.

TestDFSIO has a number of options. Listing 3.9 shows the syntax.

Listing 3.9 Syntax for Command

```
TestDFSIO [genericOptions] -read [-random | -backward | -skip [-skipSize
Size]] | -write | -append | -clean [-compression codecClassName] [-nrFiles
N] [-size Size[B|KB|MB|GB|TB]] [-resFile resultFileName] [-bufferSize
Bytes] [-rootDir] RootDirectoryName

# cd /usr/lib/hadoop-mapreduce
-- Write 20 files each 10TB in size.
# hadoop jar hadoop-mapreduce-*-tests.jar TestDFSIO -write -nrFiles 10
-size 10TB


-- Read 20 files each 10TB in size.
# hadoop jar hadoop-mapreduce-*-tests.jar TestDFSIO -read -nrFiles 10 -size
  10TB


-- Cleanup the files.
# hadoop jar hadoop-mapreduce-*-tests.jar TestDFSIO -clean -nrFiles 10
-size 10TB
```

TeraSort Benchmarking Suite

The TeraSort benchmarking suite is well known because hardware and software vendors use TeraSort as an industry comparison. It is a standard way to do benchmarks for comparisons between different companies or sources. TeraSort tests the MapReduce layers focusing on the sort phase and also testing HDFS. A TeraSort benchmark is run in three sequential steps. The first step is generating input data by running TeraGen. TeraGen might need to be used only once or a few times if you are comfortable with the input data that is created. Random data is generated with keys and values of different sizes. Values can be changed to modify the workload created. Step two is running the sort algorithms with TeraSort from the TeraGen data. The last step is validating the sorted output with TeraValidate.

For example, because a full path is not provided, the terasort-input and terasort-output directories will be created below the user's home directory in HDFS. Be aware that the number of 0s matter. Be careful with the number because it is the number of rows of 100 bytes in size. The block size set in the dbs.blocksize parameter in the hdfs-site.xml file can also impact the performance of the job. The parameters terasort-input and terasort-output are the user-given input and output directories in HDFS. Full pathnames can be used as well. Listing 3.10 shows an example of running TeraSort.

Listing 3.10   Example of Running TeraSort

```
-- Generate the input data with TeraGen and view the results.
$ hadoop jar /usr/lib/hadoop/hadoop-examples-*.jar teragen 1000000
terasort-input
$ hdfs dfs -ls terasort-input

-- Run the TeraSort using the input data created from TeraGen.
$ hadoop jar /usr/lib/hadoop/hadoop-examples-*.jar terasort terasort-input
terasort-output
$ hdfs dfs -ls terasort-input

$ hadoop jar /usr/lib/hadoop/hadoop-examples-*.jar teravalidate
terasort-output terasort-validate
Step2. CheckrecentlycreateddatainHDFS $ hadoop fs -ls terasort-validate
```

NameNode Benchmark

The NNBench tool performs load testing on the NameNode. The NameNode stores information on all files, directories, and blocks in HDFS. The NameNode processes heartbeats from all DataNodes. The NameNode configuration may include Standby

NameNodes as well as federated NameNodes. The NNBench tool runs a lot of small jobs for creating, renaming, reading, and deleting files. An example is shown in Listing 3.11.

Listing 3.11 Example of Running NameNode Benchmark

```
$ hadoop jar hadoop-*test*.jar nnbench -operation create_write \
    -maps 100 -reduces 10 -blockSize 1 -bytesToWrite 20
      -numberOfFiles 100000  -replicationFactorPerFile 3 \
      -readFileAfterOpen true
      -baseDir /benchmarks/NNBench-'hostname -s'
```

MapReduce Benchmark

The MapReduce benchmark (mrbench) tool runs a small job many times. This tests different types of runtime characteristics on the cluster. Here is an example:

```
-- Run a job 10000 times with 100 mappers and 5 reducers
$ hadoop jar hadoop-*test*.jar mrbench -maps 100 -reduces 5 -numRuns 10000
```

GridMix

GridMix is a benchmark in the Hadoop distribution that tries to model data-access patterns in Hadoop by running different Hadoop jobs (3-stage chained MapReduce job, indirect read, large data sort, reference select, and a text sort). Sort operations are emphasized. GridMix does a better job of creating different types of workloads.

The HiBench suite is increasing in popularity. HiBench is a more comprehensive suite of tools that mixes micro-benchmarks and workloads more representative of the real world. The suite contains a number of workloads (currently 8) that are broken into different categories, as shown in Table 3.10. Some of the micro-benchmarks are used in the HiBench suite. The Sort, WordCount, and TeraSort programs from the Hadoop distribution benchmark one type of MapReduce processing. The HDFS Benchmark uses Enhanced DFSIO to do an aggregated evaluation versus an average I/O value of each map task like TestDFSIO. The Web Search tools are added for large-scale indexing workloads. Machine Learning is a common workload in a Hadoop cluster, so two workloads of this type are included.

Table 3.10 Benchmark Summary

Category	Type of Workload
Micro-Benchmarks	Sort
	WordCount
	TeraSort
HDFS Benchmark	Enhanced DFSIO
Web Search	Nutch Indexing
	PageRank
Machine Learning	Bayesian Classification
	K-Means Clustering

Summary

In this chapter, we defined how YARN and HDFS work and pointed out some key considerations and tools to use. Examples of directory structure layouts and different ways to access information from the master and data node processes were covered, along with how to access the web user interfaces for each of the daemons. Both HDFS and YARN have a number of possible configurations.

For most production environments, NameNode and ResourceManager high availability are recommended. NameNode federation is also a possible configuration where multitenancy and applications with different runtime characteristics may be running on the same cluster. Configuring resource management with the scheduler is an important part of any Hadoop configuration. It is basically a critical piece in implementing multitenancy in Hadoop. Each business unit should have a guaranteed SLA or QoS. After a Hadoop cluster is configured, benchmarking is done not only for performance evaluations but also to test a newly configured Hadoop cluster. Establishing performance and throughput baselines should be part of validating a cluster configuration.

YARN provides resource management for applications with different runtime characteristics. Apache Slider will work with YARN to allow long-running applications like HBase,

Accumulo, and Storm to run under one cluster. Virtualization and Docker offer a number of configuration options for Hadoop administrators.

YARN and HDFS are the two frameworks that define how the processing and the storage work in a Hadoop cluster. YARN and HDFS are the core frameworks of Hadoop. It is important to understand how they work to better understand Hadoop. New features are constantly being added to these two frameworks with each new release. Keep up with the release nodes as new versions of Hadoop are released.

## Chapter 4

The Modern Data Platform

In the long history of humankind (and animal kind, too) those who learned to collaborate and improvise most effectively have prevailed.

—William Arthur Ward

This chapter looks at key frameworks that help define the form and functionality of the modern data platform.

Designing a Hadoop Cluster

A Hadoop cluster is a high-performance super-computer platform. The Hadoop cluster must be designed from the ground up while keeping the following key considerations in mind:

- Select a configuration from recommended hardware vendor lists. Determine what component of the hardware recommendation is not necessary, such as dual power supply on datanodes and so on. Select the right balance of CPU, memory, network, and disks to maintain throughput as the cluster grows. Bottlenecks must be avoided; at the same time, it is important to make sure resources do not go unused as the system grows.

- Determine how security will be implemented. Understand the requirements for perimeter security, authentication, and authorization inside and outside the cluster, encryption, and so on.

- Determine the configuration for edge servers. Understand how throughput will need to increase as the cluster grows.

- Design the master servers for availability. It is important to balance your HA and virtualization options, such as the following:

    - High availability options available with the Hadoop software

    - Hardware high availability (SAN)

    - Virtualization

    - Cloud high availability options

- Configure the slave servers for performance.

- Determine the data ingestion strategy and data ingestion reference architecture.

- Define the strategy for data governance. Understand metadata management, data catalog, data lifecycle management, retention time frames, and backup and recovery requirements.

- Understand the use cases the Hadoop cluster must address, and select the appropriate frameworks for the use cases.

- Define the data architecture guidelines and best practices.

- Identify which software will be used for data transformations and data analytics.

- Make it easy for users to quickly start working with the data in the cluster.

- Make sure the Hadoop cluster will meet compliance and security audits.

- Determine which execution models and frameworks will be used to satisfy interactive and real-time queries.

- Define resource management for the different business units and users.

- Always keep it simple. Complex systems fail in complex ways. The users must understand the data environment, and it must be easy to access and work with. Implementation of a data store and data catalog will make it easier for the data to be actionable.

- Understand how everyone managing and using the cluster will be trained. Projects often get into trouble due to lack of skill in managing or working with Hadoop and the data in the new environment. As the system grows and new people are brought on board, they need to be trained quickly with the right skills.

- Define resource management, groups, and so on and make sure everyone understands resource management for the cluster.

- With Hadoop 2 there are several execution models, including MapReduce2, Tez (HDP), Impala (CDH), Spark, data caching, and NoSQL. Make sure everyone understands the decision tree for which method to use for accessing the data with the Hadoop distribution and the software frameworks.

- Understand the scalability of your workforce as well as your Hadoop cluster. Overcome skill gaps. Figure out how to make Hadoop accessible and easy to use.

- Understand how Hadoop and NoSQL fit into the overall data strategy for the organization. Understand how to leverage the strengths of each data platform. Hadoop needs to integrate with the existing infrastructure.

- Test all procedures and operating guidelines until the team is comfortable managing the cluster.

While you are deciding on the previously listed areas, remember that a big data platform (Hadoop and NoSQL) is about data and being able to monetize (or gain insights into) data faster. Everything about a Hadoop cluster must work toward putting data in the hands of data scientists and analysts as quickly as possible (speed). Although Hadoop has been implemented successfully for years, relatively speaking the ecosystem is still maturing. The immaturity of the ecosystem can especially be seen in the areas of data governance and security.

Each Hadoop distribution vendor has a unique solution for data governance and security. For example, Cloudera uses Sentry and Gazzang, and Hortonworks uses Apache Ranger and works with partners for providing encryption and tokenization. For data lifecycle management, Cloudera uses Cloudera Navigator, and Hortonworks uses Falcon. Distributions such as MapR and others have their own solution for data governance and security. Understand how data governance will integrate across traditional as well as Hadoop and NoSQL. Security needs to be designed in the platform from the beginning, not bolted on later.

Data governance is not as mature in Hadoop environments and must be defined. The data catalog will have a big impact on how easily the data is consumable. One of the most difficult areas is deciding on the metadata repository. Metadata from different sources will need to go into a central metadata repository. Hadoop is adding functionality from traditional systems, and traditional systems are adding functionality found in Hadoop. MapReduce applications and R scripts can now run in some of the latest releases of relational databases and EDWs. Connectors can enable a SQL query to perform a join between data in a traditional data platform and in a Hadoop platform or a NoSQL database. Who will own the query and where will all the data reside? We are likely to see blended solutions emerging that leverage what RDBMS, EDW, Hadoop, and NoSQL platforms all do well. This blended solution is going to require the data to be consumable across different data platforms in the enterprise. This requires an organization to have a data catalog that makes the data consumable across both traditional and big data systems.

The next step is looking at the volume, growth, and retention of that data for data lifecycle management. Data arriving from different sources can and will be in different formats and layouts. Data architects need to determine the best storage format for the data. When the data lands in a Hadoop cluster, it is important the data be maintained as the original source. This original source should not be modified and should remain in its original state as a validation of the data. The types of analytics and SLAs of the data will determine the data layers and the data transformations that need to occur. Encryption in motion and encryption at rest seems like an easy solution, but it can be expensive as well. Make sure the right level of security is put in place.

Using a Hadoop cluster as a single source of data provides a lot of advantages to an organization. YARN now allows applications with different runtime characteristics to run under one resource management umbrella. HBase, Accumulo, Storm, Spark, and the like can run under YARN. Resource management can be configured to make sure applications with different run-time characteristics can all run in a single Hadoop cluster.

Data is stored in an open source environment that is relatively inexpensive compared to vertically scaled proprietary platforms. An open source environment reduces expensive data hops and copies, supports different types of data structures easily, and is linearly scalable using commodity hardware to cost effectively grow in processing, IOPS, and storage to meet organizational needs. Hadoop is a powerful data ingestion platform and can offload a lot of the ETL work of an Enterprise Data Warehouse (EDW). Hadoop can often reduce the ETL compute processes of an EDW by 30% to 40% allowing the EDW to spend its compute cycles more on analytics. Hadoop's schema-on-read supports late schema binding supporting schemas that are flexible as the data being analyzed evolves. Leverage the speed that schema-on-read provides.

Hadoop's cost effective storage allows organizations to archive data longer and even store backups in Hadoop. The capability to offload data optimization from EDWs into Hadoop is another strength of a Hadoop cluster. Data movement cost is greatly reduced because Hadoop can scale out storage for less than $100/TB using commodity hardware. Some database administration shops now joke that instead of making one backup, they make two or three copies in Hadoop. The point is for an organization to look at all the advantages that Hadoop can bring to a modern data platform and look for ways to maximize how data is transferred, stored, and analyzed to increase the monetization of enterprise data faster.

The modern data architecture is being defined by the growing needs of organizations to improve the quality and speed of analyzing data. A single source for analyzing data reduces data hops and copies of data while improving the quality of the analytics by increasing the correlation of data across different sources. Being able to store more data at lower cost also increases the accuracy of the results and significantly improves the predictive analytics capability. Requirements for a single source landing zone include the following:

- It can scale cost-effectively.

- It can handle different types of data with different run characteristics.

- It can support OLAP analytics and interactive queries.

- It can handle large volumes of data ingestion.

- It can perform analytics on large volumes of data efficiently.

Organizations have struggled for years with all the data being spread across different business units, database vendors, and technical silos. These silos are detrimental to the creation of a single data platform in a data center that can support causation, correlation, and predictive analytics of data from a variety of sources. This single data platform opens up an almost unlimited number of questions that can be asked of the data, which led to the emergence of the data lake, the latest evolution of the modern enterprise data platform. Whether the single source platform is a data lake, enterprise data hub, data reservoir, or data marshal yard, the goals are all very similar.

Bringing data together from different sources and different formats to be able to ask a richer set of questions is critical for the new level of analytics organizations are looking for. It's more of an organizational and mind-set challenge than it is a technical challenge. This type of change requires transforming how an organization thinks and works with data. This transformation requires senior management muscle to be behind the effort. Time and effort also needs to be spent in helping the business units and technical staff understand the importance and reasons behind this organizational shift around data. Large organizations are very project driven and focused. Individual projects often do not look at how its data can be of value to other business units. It's important that as different business units start loading the data into the data lake, they understand how to make data consumable for the organization. Data needs to be viewed horizontally across an entire organization. We do not want data silos being created in the data lake. The business units also need to be comfortable that the data is protected with the right level of security to trust the data in the data lake.

The data lake is a desired platform for Internet companies, banks, insurance companies, gaming companies, telecommunication firms, retail, health care, and any organization that needs to store and analyze polystructured data. A data lake needs a number of capabilities. These capabilities are provided by different frameworks in the Hadoop ecosystem. Data ingestion frameworks like Flume, Sqoop, WebHDFS, HDFS NFS, HttpFS, Storm, Spark Streaming, and Kafka support a variety of data movement capabilities. A number of different streaming solutions are also offered by different data vendors as well as third-party companies.

- Oozie provides the scheduling and workflow management for data loading, transformation, and movement. Oozie and its complex XML configuration files are not for the faint of heart. You should look for solutions and interfaces for scheduling and workflow management that are easier to work with.

- Falcon provides data lifecycle management for data archiving, backups, retention, movement, and transformation.

- Knox provides a secure authentication model and gateway for the Hadoop clusters in a data center.

- HCatalog provides the metadata repositories for schemas used to access the data.

- Hive provides the interactive SQL engine and data warehouse infrastructure for Hadoop.

- Pig is a scripting language that supports data access and transformation.

- HBase, Accumulo, MongoDB, and Cassandra offer NoSQL database capabilities. It is very common for a big data solution to contain a Hadoop and a NoSQL platform.

- MapReduce provides batch-processing capability.

- Tez (Hortonworks) provides optimized batch processing and interactive query capabilities.

- Impala (Cloudera) provides fast in-memory data access.

An organization really needs to look at how to leverage these frameworks in different ways to define solutions for use cases that are optimal as well as scalable.

As we have mentioned, understanding Hadoop is about understanding the frameworks and the features and functionality they provide, as well as how to leverage different frameworks together. Hadoop is very extensible as a platform. Additional frameworks that are not part of a Hadoop distribution can be added to provide additional features. Each new release of Hadoop introduces support for an increasing number of new frameworks. We will now take a look at these frameworks and how they help shape the data lake.

Enterprise Data Movement

Data ingestion is an extremely important part of the reference architecture for a data lake. This section looks at different frameworks for data ingestion in more detail.

Evolution of the Enterprise Data Platform

As we've discussed, relational databases and enterprise data warehouses run businesses today, and they are going to keep running the business tomorrow. At the same time we have all kinds of new data types, from different sources with large volumes of new data that organizations need to access. Vertically scalable data warehouses have difficulty storing and working with semistructured and unstructured data. Just doing simple things like having warehouses store clickstream data can be cost prohibitive for proprietary SAN storage platforms on traditional platforms. This is where Hadoop comes in. Hadoop allows these new data assets to be organized into a new a type of logically centralized enterprise data platform, with lots of possible combinations. Spark, data caching, and NoSQL are possible options for providing near real-time data access. Depending on the use cases, one or more of these options may be used.

Hadoop's framework brings a lot of flexibility to the data platform. For example, with proprietary data warehouses, most offer a proprietary bundle of BI tools, hardware, metadata, data containers, and storage. With Hadoop, each of the layers are independent yet can work together. Hadoop can leverage BI tools like Tableau, Cognos, DataMeer, MicroStrategy, Business Objects, SAS, Splunk, and Platfora, to name a few. Companies such as SAP, Oracle, IBM Teradata, and the like offer integrated solutions with Hadoop. After data lands in Hadoop, the BI tools analysts have been working with for years can be used with Hadoop. There is incredible competition to be the analytical software that runs on Hadoop.

Along with the data lake being a single landing area for very diverse types of data, the data lake can take on a lot of different roles. Some of these roles include a data ingestion engine, an initial point for exploratory BI, EDW offload optimization, backup for different data sources, a compute grid, an analytics grid, a storage grid, an archive platform, interactive and real-time processing, and as a serious data platform for analytics.

The following list specifies the various ways that data can be ingested by Hadoop:

- Hadoop can ingest data from RDBMS, flat files (XML, JSON, CSV, binary), message queue, and event data such as clickstream data.

- Data can be sent to a staging area using external tools and then loaded into Hadoop with HDFS commands or applications.

- A Hadoop distribution comes with a number of data ingestion frameworks. Oracle Data Pump, Microsoft BCP, and Teradata Fast Export are examples of external tools that can stage data into flat files for being loaded into Hadoop.

- Flume can be used to load JMS (Tibco) messages into Hadoop.

- XML, JSON, CSV, and binary files can use SCP or FTP to load data to a staging area for Hadoop.

- Flume and Storm can be used to load streaming data into Hadoop.

- The **distcp** command can be used to copy data from one Hadoop cluster to another or from within a cluster.

- Applications can be written in MapReduce, Hive, and Pig to load or copy data into a Hadoop cluster.

- Kafka, Storm, and Spark Streaming are also becoming very popular frameworks for data ingestion.

The point is that there are a lot of different use cases for loading data into Hadoop. Each has different options, depending on the volume and velocity of data that needs to be ingested into Hadoop.

Table 4.1 shows a summary of the different data sources and data transfer methods.

Table 4.1   Different Data Sources and Data Transfer Methods

Data Sources	Data Transfer Methods	Description
RDBMS and EDW	Sqoop, Informatica, Abinitio, Quest, DataStage, vendor connectors, Talend, Pentaho	SQL sources to and from Hadoop
Web Logs	Flume, Storm	Streaming into HDFS
Messages and Queues	WebHDFS, HttpFS, Flume, Storm, Kafka	Messaging data into HDFS
Files	HDFS commands, WebHDFS, HDFS NFS, HttpFS, Java, Pig, and Python	Writing files to HDFS

Table 4.2 compares EDW and Hadoop features.

Table 4.2   Comparison Between EDW and Hadoop

Layer	Enterprise Data Warehouse	Hadoop Data Platform
Architecture	Data moves to the applications	Applications move to data
Model	Relational	Nonrelational
Transactions	Transactional, ACID compliant	Nontransactional (has been non-ACID, but ACID features being added)
Structure	Schema driven	Schema-less
Schema	Schema-on-write	Schema-on-read
Storage unit	16k–32k blocks	64MB–2048MB blocks

Layer	Enterprise Data Warehouse	Hadoop Data Platform
BI Tools	Proprietary and third-party	Open source and third-party
Data structures	Hard to work with semi/unstructured data	Easily works with semi/unstructured data
Storage	Shared storage (RAID, SAN, NAS)	Nonshared storage (local disks)
Query Engine	ANSI SQL	Hive SQL (HiveQL)
Metadata	System Tables	HCatalog
Data Container	Tables	Files
Storage	Storage Area Network	Local files

Enterprise Data Movement

Hadoop is a data platform that can store data of all types and support applications with different types of runtime characteristics. The key is to bring in data from all kinds of different sources to increase the range and complexity of questions that can be asked of the data. This single source of data allows much deeper correlation questions to be considered and evaluated. With this type of capability, a goal should be to reduce the number of hops data needs to take. Each data hop is expensive to an organization. Hadoop can be a single source platform to minimize the data silos that exist in most companies.

So the movement of data from different data sources becomes a very important part of building a Hadoop data platform. Often, 30% to 60% of all the processing that occurs in an Enterprise Data Warehouse (EDW) is due to Extraction Transformation and Loading (ETL). With Hadoop being a data platform that can store data from many sources and is scalable to a super computer, we can expect the process of moving data in and out of Hadoop to be a key part of any big data solution.

ETL usually extracts the data; performs transformations to aggregate, massage, and filter the data; and then stores it. The transformation was a step normally performed before loading the data because of the high cost of SAN storage for vertically scaled systems. Hadoop storing the raw data is very important. Parts of the raw data not used today can be an important part of the decision making in the future. Massaging the data before loading it can eliminate a range of questions that you might want to ask in the future. So for a big data platform it's ELT. In analyzing data it is very important to start with the raw data that does not get updated. This raw layer becomes the source of validation for your data platform. Transformations can be performed to create additional data layers to create additional data structures and forms for more detailed analysis. Whenever transformations are performed, it is possible to corrupt the data. By keeping the raw layer untouched, the source of data validation is always maintained.

Different data architectures are available for Hadoop. One architecture that has become popular is the Lambda architecture shown in Figure 4.1, which is highlighted in the book *Big Data* by Nathan Marz. The Lambda architecture addresses data access for detailed analytics as well as a data layer for near-real-time data access. The Lambda architecture addresses the processing of arbitrary functions on arbitrary data with breaking the data into three layers.

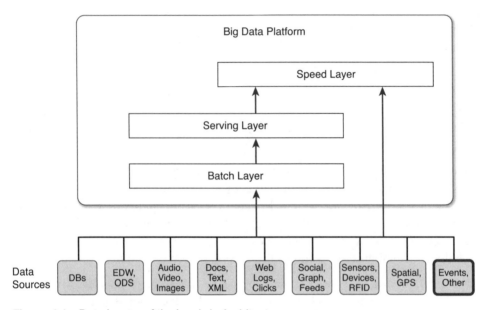

Figure 4.1   Data Layers of the Lambda Architecture

Each layer of the Lambda architecture serves different functions, which are outlined in Table 4.3.

Table 4.3   The Functions of the Layers of the Lambda Architecture

Lambda Architecture Layer	Functions of the Layer
Batch	Contains the raw original unfiltered data that is initially loaded.
	Data is transformed from this original master data layer.
	New data is created in the batch and the speed layer.
	Raw data is appended to the existing data in the batch layer.
	Batch views are generated from the batch layer.

Lambda Architecture Layer	Functions of the Layer
Serving	Can store the data from the batch views.
	Data can be transformed, massaged, aggregated, and filtered as it is loaded into the serving layer.
	Schema repositories are built to access the data in the serving layer.
	Can have indexes and can be stored in distributed databases.
Speed	New data is created in the batch and the speed layers.
	Designed to address incremental and real-time queries of the data.
	Contains the latest view of the data.
	Data is used to update the real-time views.
	Data is kept in the speed layer for a shorter defined time frame.
	Can be cached or can reside in HDFS, Spark, NoSQL, or other frameworks.

Figure 4.2 shows options for ingesting data from different types of data sources.

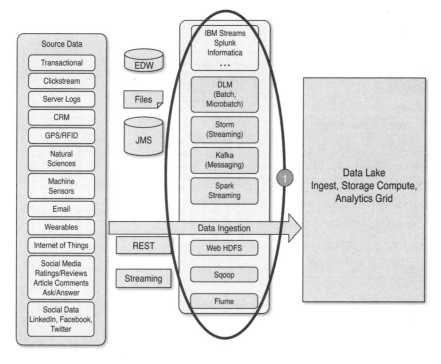

Figure 4.2   Data ingestion example.

A reference architecture must be flexible. A decoupled architecture has a lot of flexibility to handle change over time. This example layout is just one of many possible layouts. Many options exist for defining the frameworks for the different levels. The objective of Figure 4.2 is to show options for determining how to implement a reference architecture.

Hadoop is an agile platform that encourages and promotes decoupled architecture. Data outlives storage and applications and therefore implies a need to be nimble in the overall enterprise architecture. Data sources can change. Data processing gets updated. Analytical tools get swapped for business reasons. Hadoop shields organizations from this inevitable change, and Figure 4.3 is a great architecture fit for Hadoop.

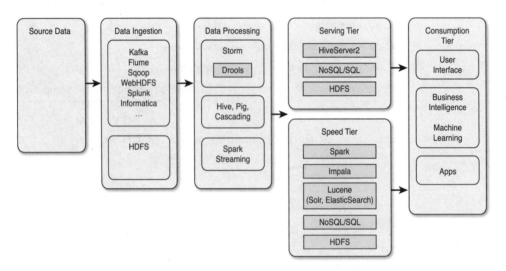

Figure 4.3   Decoupled architecture.

The Lambda architecture, shown in Figure 4.4, is also a design pattern. As we have seen, there is flexibility in how to implement the design pattern. There is also likely to be merged views across the real-time views and the batch views.

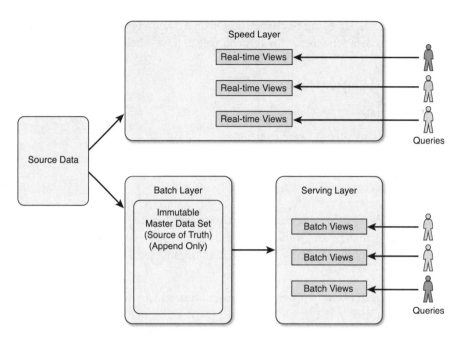

Figure 4.4   A design pattern.

As we've discussed, Hadoop and Big Data are not just about technology. They are about transforming an organization to accelerate the process of generating business value from raw data faster for competitive advantage. There has been a lot of focus on the data-driven organization. A data-driven organization uses data to make evidence-based decisions. Being data driven is important; however, the long-term goal is to be speed driven as well. A speed-driven organization focuses on improving the efficiency of going from raw data to valuable business insight. The speed driven organization must be able to build an adaptable enterprise platform that is agile enough to adjust to evolving pipelines, products, and software frameworks. Defining the correct data ingestion reference architecture for your organization is an important key to success. It's similar to designing the concepts of lean manufacturing but for data. A successful speed-driven organization is able to excel in these key areas: data ingestion, metadata management, data transformation, and data architecture.

We know that data pipelines are going to change and evolve. Data ingestion is about being able to manage change in data pipelines. Obvious changes in data pipelines include the following:

- Input sources and input types evolve.
- Output sources and data types evolve.
- Volume and velocity usually increase over time.
- Compression and encryption algorithms evolve.
- Event processing becomes more complex

Most organizations are going to have existing software investments in Oracle, IBM, SAS, Teradata, Microsoft, Informatica, and so on. Part of the data ingestion solution is deciding how to blend open source solutions with software that an organization has been using for years.

Data needs to be monetized. Hadoop provides additional flexibility with schema-on-read, so as soon as data hits the disk in the batch layer it can begin to be analyzed. NoSQL databases can load and access data without creating schemas. This enables Hadoop and NoSQL to start analyzing data quickly without a lot of upfront time to put the data in a schema for storage. Exploratory BI happens extremely fast in Hadoop. Data can then be transformed with batch views for more detailed analytics. Schemas can be defined on the data, even though the data is stored in files on HDFS. SQL statements can then begin asking more complex questions of the data using the schemas. Hadoop and NoSQL are about providing an environment of speed and agility and allowing changes to occur quickly and easily.

Blending Hadoop into the Enterprise

Relational databases and data warehouses run the business today. Prior to Hadoop, organizations utilized their data warehouse platform to store raw data and do ETL and data analytics processing. This has proven to be costly and limits the capability of an enterprise to store more or all the data desired by the business to make better business decisions. With Hadoop, organizations can quickly pick up the pace in the area of ETL and raw data offloading. This results in allowing the data warehouse to do what it's really good at—business intelligence processing. As organizations mature in their Hadoop experience, they will find new ways to leverage Hadoop to help business monetize new datasets.

A great way to get started with Hadoop is not to look at data platforms that have been hardened over years but to look for use cases with new data types and data sources. Build success with the first use cases and then look for additional data to start bringing into the

Hadoop cluster. Start to build an ETL reference architecture and gain experience ingesting data from different sources. Are there data warehouses where you can archive more of the data sooner into Hadoop? See if there are some data warehouses that you can take pressure off. Operational data stores and persistent staging areas are strong candidates for moving this data into Hadoop. Are there data warehouses where some offload optimization can be performed to allow more of the compute resources on the data warehouse to be used for analytics? Are there databases that are storing a lot of semistructured and unstructured data that Hadoop could handle more efficiently at lower cost?

If you look at any mature Hadoop environment you see data movement between Hadoop clusters, relational databases, and enterprise data warehouses, as shown in Figure 4.5. Traditional ETL occurs between the relational databases and Hadoop. The data lake can receive data from relational databases and also improve decision making with its analytics, so the Online Line Transaction Processing (OLTP) applications can make better decisions. Hadoop can perform offload optimization for the data warehouse and also handle data ingestion and transformation for the data warehouse. Hadoop has a role in the enterprise just like relational databases and data warehouses have their roles. Blending to solutions that leverage each data platform's strengths should be part of the design of a Hadoop cluster.

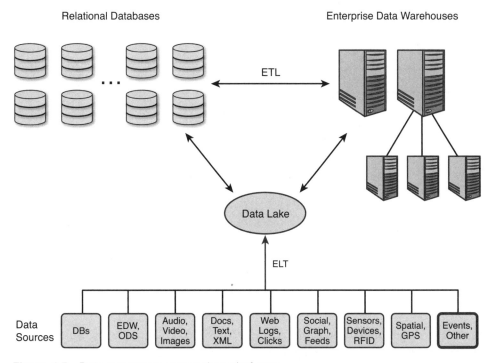

Figure 4.5 Data movement across data platforms.

Compression

Compression is an important consideration anytime large volumes of data are transferred or stored. Compression can greatly reduce storage and improve the performance of data transfers across the network. Compression also takes additional CPU processing, so the pros and cons need to be weighed. There are different compression codecs that offer different features, compression rates, and ratios. Compression codecs break into two categories: codecs with fast compression rates and codecs that can achieve high compression ratios. Fast compression rates make sense when the data is going to be used frequently. High compression codecs make sense when the data is being archived. A Hadoop cluster uses different codecs for data optimization of different datasets. Codec compression versus decompression times can vary greatly. The LZO, LZ4, and Snappy codecs are high-speed codes. The Bzip2 and Zlib emphasize higher compression rates. For compressing storage, use Bzip2 because it is splittable, which means Hadoop can parallelize the processing on any data that uses this codec. The "shuffle" phase of Hadoop can use any of the high-speed codecs such as LZO, Snappy, and others.

The Hadoop distribution comes with most of the compression codecs. LZO needs to be downloaded with a GNU license, but it is easy to download and configure. Today Hadoop comes with five compression codecs with the option to download LZO under a separate GNU license, giving us six codecs to pick from, as shown in Table 4.4.

Table 4.4 Compression Options

Codec	Splittable	Extension
LZO	NO	.lzo
Snappy	NO	.snappy
GZIP	NO	.gz
LZ4	NO	.lz4
Bzip2	YES	.bz2
Zlib	NO	.deflate

Compression codecs that support splittable files need to be considered. A codec that supports a splittable file can have multiple parallel tasks reading the blocks in a file. Non-splittable files can significantly impact performance, depending on the size of the file.

HDFS File Formats

One of the advantages of Hadoop is that data can be stored in different ways, which means someone must decide how data is going to be used and then determine the best way to store it. The following are key decisions to make when storing data:

- What file format will you use?

- Should the data be compressed?

- If you want to compress the data, in what codec storage system, such as should the data be stored in HDFS or NoSQL?

- How will the data be processed?

Remember to always view the readme files with new releases because the formats are adding more functionality with new versions of Hadoop.

The first decision is the storage system. Should the data be stored in HDFS or other options like a NoSQL database? Where is the data going to be processed? Will the data be processed from HDFS or NoSQL, or will it be loaded into an in-memory solution such as Impala, Spark, or Flink?

As for the file format, data can be stored in any of the following formats (the list is not exhaustive):

- A plain text file, as in web logs or CSV files

- A binary file

- A SequenceFile

- MapFiles

- SetFiles

- ArrayFiles

- BloomMapFiles

- XML

- JSON

- Avro

- RCFile

- Parquet

- An Optimized Row Columnar (ORC) file

The file formats all have advantages and disadvantages, depending on the processing. The best way of storing the data is determined by how the data is going to be processed and the performance of the I/O operations. Some formats are closely tied to the distribution; for example, Cloudera prefers Parquet, and Hortonworks prefers ORCFiles. However, a serializer/deserializer (SerDe) can be installed so ORCFiles can be used in Cloudera. A SerDe is basically an IO interface that either Hive or Pig can leverage to read and write files into Hadoop. It's often required for files that are not supported out-of-the-box. For example, the built-in SerDes for Hive are Avro, ORC, RegEx, Thrift, Parquet, and CSV. All these SerDes follow API implementation—initialization (for column, column names), serialization (writing to hive table), and deserialization (reading table). When an application reads the data from the serialized hive table, the SerDe implementation leverages an object inspector to properly project and interpret the rows, columns, column names, and data types through the deserializer. Additional considerations include whether the data should be splittable for higher rates of parallelization or compressed, and what the failure behavior for the format is.

It is important to keep in mind that all raw data *must* be stored in HDFS. Any processing done to the raw data produces high value data output, and the business must determine who the users of these output data are and what tools they use to make business decisions. Choosing the wrong file format can render the business tools unusable. For example, JSON is not known to be the format of choice when using BI tools for reporting or analytics purposes. In general, document-oriented formats are great for operational use cases but not for analytical tasks. Analytical tools and formats of choice might change in the future, so leaving the raw data in HDFS will enable a company to generate data in the file format that their tools can process with ease.

If a lot of columns are going to be accessed frequently, it is better to put the file in a row columnar format. If specific columns are going to be accessed frequently, it might be better to store the data in a columnar format, such as an RCFile, Parquet, or ORCFile. A columnar format can achieve significantly higher rates of compression. For example, Parquet and ORCFiles can achieve much higher compression rates and better access performance than text files, and also better than RCFiles (an older columnar format). With improvements in Hive as well as support for vectorized queries and predicate push downs (PPD), performance on columnar formats has improved significantly. Working with the different formats is pretty easy.

Here is an example of the syntax for creating an ORCFile and setting the compression codec:

```
CREATE TABLE my_cool_table (

  ...

)  STORED AS orc tbleproperties ("orc.compress"="SNAPPY");
```

If the data is going to be compressed, you must decide whether the format supports splittable compression. Being able to split files can improve processing times by increasing the level of parallelization that can be performed. File formats store the compression codec in the file header. This enables different types of compression codecs to be used easily.

SequenceFiles store the data as a binary file with key/value pairs. SequenceFiles support the data being stored in an uncompressed, record-compressed, and block-compressed format. Compressing several records in a block usually will give you better compression rates than compressing a record. Formats like SequenceFiles store metadata with the file, such as the compression codec, key and value information, a sync marker, and even user-defined data. The sync marker supports splittability for higher parallel processing.

Serialization formats such as Writables, Protocol Buffers, Thrift, and Avro all support SerDe from data structures to byte streams to data structures. Avro is becoming more popular. Avro stores the data schema in the header of each file so it is self-defining. Schema definitions can be written in JSON or in an Avro IDL. Avro is also very flexible because the read and write schemas can be different, which enables a schema to evolve over time. Avro uses sync markers similar to SequenceFiles and supports data types such as Boolean, int, float, string, enum, array, and map. Avro files can also be compressed and are splittable. Avro supports compression codecs such as Snappy, LZO, and zlib.

Compression should normally be considered when you are working with large volumes of data. There is CPU overhead with compression and decompression; however, the I/O benefits usually outweigh the CPU overhead and make it a good practice to consider compression. Compression requirements should be validated based on what the business can tolerate. For example, it is possible that ETL/ELT and analytics processing can happen at the same time within the same cluster. There will be a lot of data movement over the network due to mapreduce shuffle phase. To conserve the network bandwidth, compression can be applied for the shuffle phase. For compressing data at storage, this becomes important when the necessity to conserve disk space arises with the expense of taking a small hit on performance. So it's a trade-off that the business has to decide and be comfortable with—saving storage/network space versus performance.

Be aware that some file formats are not splittable. Some codecs provide higher rates of compression; others provide faster processing with less compression or a better balance between compression and processing speed. Sorting the data can provide higher rates of compression, depending on the similarity of the data.

The following are some of the popular codecs for processing:

- Snappy is one of the faster codecs for processing. Snappy uses container formats such as SequenceFiles and Avro for splittability.

- LZO, also one of the faster alternatives, uses files that are compressible natively so they do not need a container file, but they do require indexing. LZO is not distributed with Hadoop because of its licensing; however, LZO can be installed very easily and can be set up with just a few parameter settings.

- GZIP gives better compression rates but is not as fast. The GZIP read performance is much faster than its write performance. GZIP also must be used with container files because compression is not native.

- BZIP2 offers very strong compression ratios but is much slower. BZIP2 makes sense when storage is the primary use. BZIP2 is also splittable natively.

- MapReduce stores intermediate data on local storage. It is usually a best practice to have the intermediate data with MapReduce be compressed.

Container formats such as SequenceFiles and Avro are splittable when the compression codec does not support splittability natively.

The default formats for different tools are often not optimized for the processing of the data, so the data can be transformed when it is loaded in the destination, or it can be transformed after it has landed into HDFS. Data transformation usually puts the data in a structured format for more detailed analytics.

Knowing the classification of the file types will give some perspective on what can be done on the data. For instance, there are document-based files, flat files, and proprietary-based and binary files.

Document-oriented data spans XML, JSON, EDI, SOAP, and many more. These kinds of data are operational in nature. All can be stored in HDFS for the purpose of doing analytics, data enrichment, and archiving. But these file types are usually transformed and normalized and stored into a database table for performing typical BI processing. They can also be indexed for the purpose of tagging documents that contain errors, faults, or exceptions for investigation purposes. For example, if a SOAP message contained error codes and descriptions, an indexing tool such as SOLR can be used and made available to support operations teams for searching in real time. SOLR has a UI called Banana that can be used to customize the metrics and views on what documents can be displayed and searched.

A company in the business of providing travel booking and reservation applications worldwide captures documents across hundreds of apps and indexes them based on occurrences of application failure using SOLR. Then it exposes the indexed documents through Banana UI for near-real time trending and analysis. The time the document enters the data center to getting into the Banana UI is only 500 milliseconds or less, and the operations team can proactively identify systems having issues and resolve them in real-time fashion. This enables the company to operate its business with minimal interruption and has direct correlation to increased bookings and reservations.

Flat files like CSV, TSV, and others are some of the simplest formats that could be used directly in Hadoop for data science and business analytics without any transformation required. For example, CSV raw data can be immediately imported into Hive database table(s) without any data cleansing or manipulation. Or BI tools like SAS can directly process the raw CSV data for any computation the user wants to do.

Proprietary files like Excel and others typically require some level of data transformation and mapping tasks before it can be processed. The proprietary library is used to extract the data, and this library can be executed as a MapReduce job that will eventually put it into a format portable enough for analytics, data discovery, or machine learning purposes.

Binary files such as PDFs, JPEGs, and so on provide interesting information for business decision makers, and they store this data in Hadoop. For example, a company that's in the business of leasing business properties has transformed signed contracts into scanned PDF forms. The company ends up storing thousands of the contracts somewhere in its environment and cannot perform analytics on them on traditional systems. One example is to determine what properties the customers have and identify opportunities to extend contracts or lease more properties to its customers. Another example is to determine customers that are higher risks based on customer contracts. An Optical Character Recognition (OCR) library can be used to scan and parse the PDF images and capture texts that are relevant to what analytics the business would like to execute. The captured texts can then be stored in Hive, HBase, or HDFS. So that business users can easily pull up the contracts based on the result of the analytical processing, SOLR can be used to index the PDF images along with their captured text and apply full text searching.

Organizing Data in HDFS

Data files and Hive tables are stored in directories in HDFS. It is important to develop naming conventions and guidelines for organizing data in HDFS. Guidelines for directory and file permissions, as well as quotas, should also be defined at this time. The guidelines and best practices need to be consistent across the enterprise. There are some default directories defined with some of the frameworks, such as Hive. Consider these defaults in planning the data layouts:

- The default directories can be changed with parameter settings for the specified framework.

- Directories for files can have subdirectories for features like partitioning and buckets.

- Data layouts in HDFS tend to be denormalized and often use star-schema-type layouts.

- Because a lot of analytical queries are performed, there can be fact table and dimension table layouts.

- The following sample directory layouts are just examples, but defining standards and best practices is very important:

    - /user/<username>: Default layout for users.

    - /app: Files for running applications, files for Hive (HQL), Oozie (XML), jar files, and so on.

    - /<business-unit>: Files organized along business unit lines.

- /data or /<data-source>: Files organized by data source.

- /elt/<business-unit, source, type>: Files organized by business unit, source of data, such as logfiles or clickstream or type of file.

- /tmp: For temporal data

- /staging: Staging area, or can store in /tmp/staging.

- /backupsa

Organizations often separate data into directories for raw, staging, and final data, along with archiving and home directories for users. Consider the following example. Datalake in Hadoop can easily get toxic without some level of governance. Everybody needs sanity, and keeping the different state and type of data is essential to operationalizing the work in Hadoop.

- /datalake/raw/social_data

- /datalake/raw/financial_data

- /datalake/raw/crm_data

- /datalake/raw/sales_data

- /datalake/staging/

- /datalake/production/sales

- /datalake/production/marketing

- /datalake/archive/201504

Summary

Initially, looking at all the options in Hadoop can be overwhelming. The key is to not try to boil the ocean out of the gate. Understand your use cases. Look at how you expect your data lake to evolve over time. Look at how to make your reference architecture scalable and flexible. The flexibility is just as important as the scalability.

The Modern Data Platform for analytics is evolving quickly. Take the necessary time to understand the different options, their capabilities, their weaknesses, and their road maps. Get a solid understanding of their capabilities as well as your ability to manage the different frameworks and software solutions as a single integrated platform.

Data pipelines and data sources are evolving, so don't pick the easiest solution. Focus on where you want to take your environment in the future and prepare for that.

## Chapter 5

Data Ingestion

You can have data without information, but you cannot have information without data.

—Daniel Keys Moran

Extraction, Loading, and Transformation (ELT)

A significant percentage of the effort put into Hadoop has to do with loading and unloading data from the cluster. A number of ELT tools and third-party tools come with the Hadoop distribution (see Figure 5.1). However, the focus here is on the Hadoop tools. They include the following:

- Flume (streaming)
- Sqoop (SQL data sources)
- WebHDFS (REST APIs)
- HDFS NFS

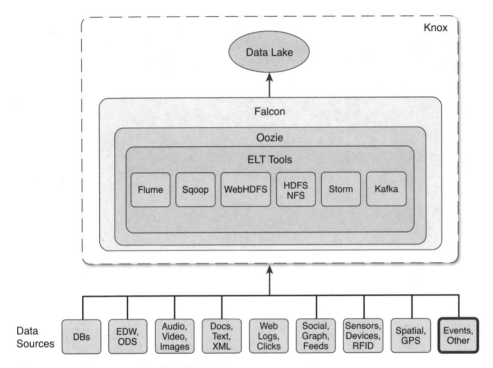

Figure 5.1   One example of ELT in Hadoop.

Storm is a popular distributed, real-time streaming and real-time computational open source framework.

Kafka is another popular open source distributed messaging system that handles very high throughput.

The building of the different data layers needs to be automated. Here are some of the tools that you can use for automation:

- Oozie is the scheduler and workflow tool for Hadoop.

- Falcon is the data and lifecycle management tool used with HDP. Falcon uses Oozie to handle scheduling of data movement operations.

- Cloudera Navigator is used with CDH.

- Knox is the authentication and security perimeter tool for Hadoop clusters.

- Kerberos handles authentication of users and services inside the Hadoop cluster.

Sqoop: Data Movement with SQL Sources

There are a number of ways to move data from relational databases, operational data stores, data warehouses, and the like to and from Hadoop. We will look at two popular methods. The first is to use a database or third-party vendors' methods for performing bulk unloads. The data is staged, and then HDFS commands or applications can be used to load the data into Hadoop. The second method is to use Sqoop, which is discussed here.

Scoop is a Hadoop client that can exchange data between SQL sources (RDBMS, data warehouses, NoSQL) and Hadoop. A JDBC driver is used to interface with the database. Sqoop can be used with any JDBC-compliant database. To use the correct JDBC driver for a database, download the .jar file and install it in the $SQOOP_HOME/lib directory (/usr/lib/sqoop/lib). The correct connect string must be specified for the database. The connect must include the server name or IP address and the database instance name; for example:

```
--connect jdbc:oracle:thin:@172.16.168.129:1521:myinst
--connect jdbc:mysql://127.0.0.1/mycooldb
```

The Sqoop job needs permission to access the database (your user ID and password) and HDFS permissions (HDFS file system name and ACL).

Database and ETL vendors have developed direct accelerated connectors for their platforms. Oracle, Teradata, Microsoft, Greenplum, SAP Hana, and Netezza have connectors. These director connectors can significantly improve the data transfer time. The following list describes some of the direct accelerated connectors:

- Teradata has an Enhanced FastLoad driver. The FastLoad driver can transfer data in parallel with multiple readers and writers. FastLoad has been around a long time to load data into Teradata. Hortonworks and Teradata developed the Enhanced FastLoad tool to support loading data directly from the source to the destination.

- The Shareplex Connector for Hadoop can be used to load data directly from Oracle into HDFS or HBase. The Shareplex Connector will replicate data in near real-time (HDFS) or real-time (HBase).

- IBM also has a very rich set of tools for ETL and streaming.

- ETL vendors such as Informatica also have solutions for Hadoop.

- Oracle built Big Data Connectors that allow for exchange of data between Hadoop and Oracle databases.

The Sqoop **import** command is used to load data from a SQL source into Hadoop or from Hadoop into a SQL target. Mappers are started to perform the data transfer operation. Each mapper establishes a connection to the SQL source and Hadoop. If the number of mappers is not specified, the default is four. The **import** command can be used to import a table, import all the tables, import a subset of data, or only the data that is returned as the result of a query.

The **export** command also supports parallel mappers running insert commands into the database. Commits happen, for example, every 10,000 transactions or 100 statements per writer. If a job fails, it will not allow a complete rollback. Verification should be performed.

Listing 5.1 shows how to load records from a relational database into Hadoop.

Listing 5.1 Create Some Simple Tables for Populating Hadoop with Sqoop

```
-- Create a MySQL database table and insert a few records.
# mysql
mysql>   CREATE  DATABASE  mycooldb;
mysql>   USE  mycooldb;
mysql>   CREATE  TABLE  mytable (id int not null auto_increment primary
  key, name varchar(20));
mysql>   INSERT  INTO  mytable  VALUES (null, 'Charles');
mysql>   INSERT  INTO  mytable  VALUES (null, 'George');
mysql>   INSERT  INTO  mytable VALUES (null, 'Steven');
mysql>   INSERT  INTO  mytable  VALUES (null, 'Cole');
mysql>   GRANT  ALL  ON  sqoopdb.* to root@localhost;
mysql>   GRANT  ALL  ON  sqoopdb.* to root@'%';
mysql>   exit;
```

Here is an example of loading data into HDFS from a MySQL table. The database password is put on the command line just for clarity. HDFS will look at the operating system user running the **sqoop** command to determine permission on the HDFS side. The table name is mytable. If a directory path is not defined on the HDFS side, by default a directory below the user's home directory will be created with the same name as the table, such as mytable. The direct parameter specifies to use the database vendor direct driver and not the default JDBC driver. Because this is a small import, a single mapper is used.

Sqoop can be a very easy way to load data into Hadoop from a relational database, as shown in Listing 5.2.

Listing 5.2 Verify the Data Loaded into Hadoop

```
-- Sqoop example. After performing the import verify data is in HDFS.
# su - hdfs
$ sqoop import --connect jdbc:mysql://127.0.0.1/mycooldb --username root
  --direct --table mytable --m 1
$ hdfs dfs -lsr mytable
$ hdfs dfs -cat mytable/part-m-00000
```

The user executing the **hdfs** commands must have permission to write in the mytable directory. Different file formats can be specified, such as the following:

- -as-textfile
- -as-sequencefile
- -as-avrodatafile

Many options can be defined, such as the following:

- List specific table columns (--columns)
- Define the field delimiter (--fields-terminated-by)
- Append to an existing dataset (--append)
- Determine how to split the data across the mappers (--split-by)
- Write a query to determine the data to import (--query)
- Define compression (--compress)

Sqoop can be used to export as well as import data between database sources and Hadoop, as shown in Listing 5.3.

Listing 5.3   Syntax for Importing Data into a Relational Database from Hadoop

```
$ sqoop import --connect jdbc:mysql://127.0.0.1/mycooldb  \
--username root --direct --table mytable -target-dir /mydatadir    \
--as-textfile --m 1
```

You can use the following help commands, along with the documentation in sqoop.apache. org, to do a lot of examples moving data between your Hadoop cluster and a relational database using Sqoop. Anyone who worked with a database loader and unloader tool will be able to work with Sqoop very easily.

It is easy to list the available options available with Sqoop, as shown in Listing 5.4.

Listing 5.4   Display Help Options with Hadoop

```
$  sqoop help
$  sqoop help import
$  sqoop help export
```

Listing 5.5 performs a SQL import and creates a Hive metadata table as part of the Sqoop operation. After the Hive metadata table is created, it can be used to access the data in HDFS. It will be completely transparent to the user running the SQL command to access the data. As far as they can tell, they are running the SQL command on a table, even though the data actually resides in an HDFS file.

Sqoop can be used to import data into Hadoop so it is immediately available to be queried using Hive, as shown in Listing 5.5.

Listing 5.5 Import Data into Hadoop Using the hive-import Option

```
-- Load data from a relational database into Hive. Then query the data
using Hive.
# mysql
mysql>   USE  mycooldb;
mysql>   CREATE  TABLE newtable (id int not null auto_increment primary
  key, name varchar(20));
mysql>   INSERT  INTO newtable VALUES (null, 'Karen');
mysql>   INSERT  INTO newtable VALUES (null, 'Cole');
mysql>  INSERT  INTO newtable VALUES (null, 'Madison');
mysql>   INSERT  INTO newtable VALUES (null, 'Gage');
mysql>   exit;


# su - hdfs
$ sqoop  import   --connect  jdbc:mysql://127.0.0.1/mycooldb   \
--username  root   --table  newtable --direct   --m 1 --hive-import
```

Hive has a command-line interface for interfacing with the data, as shown in Listing 5.6. Using the hive metadata, hive users can access the data using a SQL interface. Someone running a Hive command must have read access in HDFS.

Listing 5.6 Use Hive to Verify the Data Has Been Loaded into Hadoop

```
$ hive
hive>   show tables;
hive>   SELECT   *   FROM   newtable;
hive>   exit;
$
```

The physical files will be stored in the HDFS directory location defined by the hive. metastore.warehouse.dir property in the /etc/hive/conf/hive-site.xml file. The directory /apps/hive/warehouse is a typical default directory.

```
hive.metastore.warehouse.dir=/apps/hive/warehouse
```

HDFS commands can be used to verify the data locations in HDFS.

```
$ hdfs dfs -lsr /apps/hive/warehouse/newtable
```

The HDFS **cat** command can be used to display the contents in a data file stored in HDFS.

```
$ hdfs dfs -cat /apps/hive/warehouse/newtable/part-m-00000
```

This next command, shown in Listing 5.7, imports data into HDFS with the results of the query. The $CONDITION statement is required in the WHERE clause. This statement is replaced with LIMIT and OFFSET clauses so the data can be distributed across the mappers.

Listing 5.7 Use Sqoop to Filter Which Records Get Loaded

```
$ sqoop  import   --connect  jdbc:mysql://127.0.0.1/mycooldb   \
--username  root   --query "SELECT * FROM customers  c
WHERE s.customertype = 'commercial'
AND    \$CONDITIONS" --direct   --m 20 -as-textfile
--split-by region_id
```

The Sqoop **export** command syntax is similar to the **import** command but has some different options to support loading data from HDFS into a database. The **export** command has options like -export-dir to specify the HDFS source directory, the -update-key parameter based on the primary key for performing updates, and the -call option, which executes a stored procedure for every record using Call Mode.

Listing 5.8 exports data from HDFS into a MySQL table.

Listing 5.8 Export Data from HDFS into a MySQL Table

```
$ sqoop export
 --connect  jdbc:mysql://127.0.0.1/mycooldb
 --table mytable2
 --export-dir /mydatadir
 --input-fields-terminated-by "\t"
```

Listing 5.9 exports data from a Hive table into an Oracle database table.

Listing 5.9   Export Data from a Hive Table into an Oracle Database Table

```
$ sqoop export  --connect jdbc:oracle:thin:@172.16.168.129:1521:orcl  \
--username  sales --password sales --table SALES.Customer       \
 --export-dir /apps/hive/warehouse/customer
```

In the example in Listing 5.10, the **export** command exports and inserts data if the data does not already exist, but if the data already exists, an update is performed. This command is like an UPSERT command in relational databases.

Listing 5.10   Export Data and Insert Data if It Does Not Exist; if the Record Exists It Performs an Update

```
sqoop export --connect jdbc:oracle:thin:@192.168.166.129:1521:myorcl   \
--username sale  --password sales --table SALES.Customer     \
--export-dir /apps/hive/warehouse/newcustomers    \
-update-key  job_id -update-mode allowinsert
```

Flume: Streaming Data

Flume is a framework for streaming data into Hadoop or NoSQL. Flume can also be used to stream data into Kafka and then have Kafka stream data into Storm for processing of the data. Storm can then stream the data into HDFS for analytics and into Spark or NoSQL for real-time processing of the data.

A flume agent runs in a JVM and is configured with a stream input source (source), an event buffer (channel), and an output destination (sink). The source defines the streaming input source, the channel is the buffer, and the sink defines the destination.

A client streams events to a source. The source receives the events and sends the events to the channel buffer. Data flows from the channel to the sink, and the sink defines the destination.

There can be only one flume agent per JVM. A flume agent can have multiple sources, channels, and sinks, but there must be at least one of each, and each one must have a name associated with it. A number of predefined sources, channels, and sinks make it very easy to use an XML file to configure a flume agent and get it up and running. Events flowing from the source(s) to channel(s) to the sink(s) use a transaction model that is very reliable.

Flume must be installed on every node where a flume agent needs to run. Flume comes as part of the HDP distribution but is not installed by default.

Events

An event is made up of a header(s) and a body. An event can have multiple headers. A header is a key/value pair that can be used to make decisions with values such as time stamps, hostnames, or an event source. The body is an array of bytes.

The event flow is defined by connecting sources, channels, and sinks (see Figure 5.2). Events flow from the source through the channel to the agent.

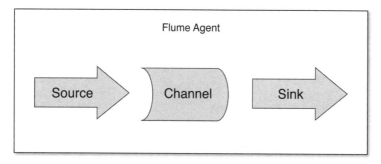

Figure 5.2   Flume agent.

Flume is not designed for very large events. Events are usually 1KB to 2KB. Video and audio events are likely not good candidates for flume.

A transaction is made up of a batch of events. The number of events in a transaction defines the transaction size. Each event has a unique sequence number. Each transaction has a unique ID.

The following are sample event headers:

```
timestamp=1379459454
hostname=mywebserver.hostname.com
```

Sources

You can configure a number of sources for a flume agent.

- A spooling directory source supports data ingestion by reading files that are put in a spooling directory. Flume will monitor the directory for new files and read them in when they appear. After the file has been read into the channel, the file is renamed.

- An Exec Source runs an application or command that generates data to standard output.

- A Log4jAppender is a Log4j plug-in that can forward logs to Flume in real time. A property logStdErr must be configured; otherwise, stderr is ignored.

- An HTTP source reads Flume events generated by HTTP POSTs and GETs. Events sent in a single post are defined as a single batch and inserted into the channel as a single transaction.

- Syslog sources generate syslog data. The syslog data can come from a syslog TCP source, a multiport syslog TCP source, or a syslog UDP source.

- TCP sources separate events with a newline.

- A UDP source handles an entire message as a single event.

- A NetCat source listens on a defined port for a server. The source looks for newlines to define the events.

- Custom sources can be defined for unique source interfaces. A Scribe can be a source and also receive data from a Scribe ingest system.

- A Scribe source can use Thrift to make sure the transfer protocol is compatible. A Sequence generator source can be used for testing.

- A JSONHandler can handle JSON formatted data and supports UTF-8, UTF-16, and UTF-32 character sets.

- An Avro source listens on an Avro port. Avro can be used to connect multiple flume agents that are input sources and collectors into multiple tiered topologies.

Channels

The *channel* is the buffer between the source and the sink. The events are held in the channel until the sink can process them. A source can write to multiple channels. The type of channel selected determines the speed and the durability of the data in the channel. Memory channels are very fast but do not guarantee against loss of data. If the memory buffer is increased significantly, the Java heap size (-Xmx and -Xms) might need to be increased.

File channels use a write-ahead log approach and are durable. The file channel will flush events to disk before acknowledging receipt of the event to the sink. If using multiple channels, make sure each file channel has a different directory path. Define directory paths on separate disks if IO contention is an issue. The data director (dataDirs) can have a comma-separated set of disks to more evenly distribute the IO if contention is high.

A spillable file channel is a combination of the memory and file channel. If memory fills up, the events spill over to disk. Any data in memory will be lost during a system or agent failure. If considering NFS, make sure you understand the IO requirements and the growth projections. A JDBC channel writes to a database and is durable. Just make sure the database writes can keep up with the data flowing through and does not become a bottleneck. Transactional guarantees are done in each channel, not across multiple flume agents. Improper sizing of the channel can lead to ChannelException or OutOfMemory-Errors issues.

Here are examples of choosing a memory channel or a file channel. The "channels" keyword is used even if there is a single channel.

```
myagent.channels.mybuffer.type=file
myagent.channels.mybuffer.type=memory
```

The following is a multiplexing selector example:

```
myagent.sources.src1.selector.type = multiplexing
myagent.sources.src1.selector.mapping.a = mychannela
myagent.sources.src1.selector.mapping.b = mychannelb
myagent.sources.src1.selector.mapping.default = mychannela
```

Flume comes with two channel selectors, or a custom selector can be written. The two prepackaged channel selectors are a replicating channel selector and a multiplexing channel selector. A replicating channel selector replicates an event to every channel it is configured with. A multiplexing channel selector can decide on which channel to put an event dependent on header information. Interceptors and a multiplexing channel selector control routing in a flume agent. Configuring the channel requires parameters as shown in Table 5.1.

Table 5.1 Configurable Parameters That Can Be Defined for a Channel

Type	Keep-alive	maxFileSize
dataDirs	transactionCapacity	minimRequireSpace
checkpointDir	checkpointInterval	
capacity	write-timeout	

Sinks

A flume agent can write to a number of sink destinations. Sink destinations include HDFS, HBase, Log, IRC, File Roll, Morphline Solr, and ElasticSearch. When writing to HDFS it is important to control how an HDFS directory fills up. Time-based escape sequences can be used to partition the data in subdirectories. You can also use format specifiers such as %Y (year), %m (month), %D (day), and %H (hour). For example:

```
myagent.sinks.mysink.hdfs.path=/flume/mypath/%Y/%m/%D/%H
```

Flume rotates files defined by the parameters hdfs.rollInterval, hdfs.rollCount, and hdfs. rollSize. Only time rotation, event count rotation, size rotation, and rotation on idle can be set for different file rollover techniques. The hdfs.batchSize sets the number of events per second. You use the codeC parameter to set the codec for compression.

Multiple flume agents can be connected to each other to form data (event) pipelines. Avro sources and sinks can be linked, and thrift sources and sinks can also be linked to form pipelines.

A sink needs to write data faster than the source can ingest data; otherwise, the channel can get stressed. Sinks are single threaded. Use load-balancing sink processors to increase the sink throughput speed. Multiple sinks for a single channel can improve performance for high-activity time frames. A sink processes events from only a single channel. You need to spend some time to understand what type of compression codec to use. After you have thoroughly tested your Flume data flow, it is important to understand growth projections and the throughput capability of the Flume topology.

Event serializers can be used to convert a Flume event to another format for output. The text serializer is the default. The HDFS file time can also be defined to specify the output format.

Events can be sent to different sinks for load balancing or failover. The routing behavior is defined by the sink processor. The sinkgroups property is used to define how to work with multiple sinks. A sinkgroup is defined, and then the sinks are assigned to the sinkgroup. The processor type is then set to load_balance or failover. Failover will switch to another sink within a group if the current sink fails.

Following are sink configuration examples:

- myagent.sinkgroups=mygrp
- myagent.sinkgroups.mygrp.sinks=mysink1,mysink2
- myagent.sinkgroups.mygrp.processor.type=failover
- myagent.sinkgroups.mygrp.processor.priority.mysink1=5
- myagent.sinkgroups.mygrp.processor.priority.mysink2=10

Table 5.2 shows the parameters as part of the sink configuration.

Table 5.2 Example of Configurable Parameters That Can Be Defined for a Sink

Type	hdfs.inUseSuffix	serializer.syncIntervalBytes
Channel	hdfs.round	hdfs.fileType
hdfs.path	hdfs.roundValue	hdfs.writeType
hdfs.filePrefix	hdfs.roundUnit	hdfs.threadsPoolSize
hdfs.fileSuffix	hdfs.rollInterval	hdfs.roolTimerPoolSize
hdfs.maxOpenFiles	hdfs.rollSize	processor.type
hdfs.timeZone	hdfs.rollCount	processor.selector
hdfs.batchSize	serializer	processor.backoff
hdfs.codeC	serializer.appendNewLine	processor.priority.Name
hdfs.inUsePrefix	serializer.compressionCodec	processor.maxpenalty

Configuring a Flume Agent

Flume agent sources can include another flume agent communicating over RPC using Avro, or network streams such as Syslog or Netcat, Log4J, or commands writing to standard output. Flume channels can be no-durable memory, files, or databases using JDBC. Flume destinations are defined with sinks. Sinks can include HDFS, HBase, JMS, and Avro.

A flume agent uses a Java property file with key/value pairs to configure the flume agent. Multiple flume agents can be configured in a single property file. When starting up a flume agent, an argument can be passed to identify which agent should be started. Each property for an agent needs to be associated with an agent name. Here the agent is named myagent. Each agent must have its sources, channels, and sinks named. Each source, channel, and sink must also be named. Arguments for any source, channel, or sink must use the name as a prefix in the definition.

```
myagent.sources=<definition of sources>
myagent.channels=<definition of channels>
myagent.sinks=<definition of sinks>
```

You must provide the agent with the name of the sources, channels, and sinks. These names will then be used to define the sources, channels, and sinks. The agent (myagent) uses the source (mysource), the channel (mybuffer), and the sink (mysink) for configuring the agent. The names are then used to connect the source to the channel and subsequently to the sink to define the event flow in the agent.

Next, you must define Flume for a Netcat source. Listing 5.11 shows a simple example for showing how to set an event flow through a flume agent. A Netcat source opens a socket and listens on a port for incoming events. Logger is a sink that is popular for testing and debugging event flows. The example uses Logger to log events using log4j. You can save this configuration in a file called my.conf.

Listing 5.11   How to Set an Event Flow Through a Flume Agent

```
# Define the source, channel and sink names
myagent.sources=mysource
myagent.channels=mybuffer
myagent.sinks=mysink

# Configure the source and channel. Connect the source and the channel.
myagent.sources.mysource.type = netcat
myagent.sources. mysource.bind = 0.0.0.0
myagent.sources. mysource.port = 12345
myagent.sources. mysource.channels = mybuffer
myagent.channels.mybuffer.type = memory
myagent.channels.mybuffer.capacity=100

# Configure the sink and connect the channel and the sink.
myagent.sinks.mysink.type = logger
agent.sinks.mysink.channel = mybuffer
```

The agent needs to be started using the configuration file called my.conf. In this configuration the agent name is myagent. This example overrides the log4j default of writing to a flume.log file and instead appends to the console. The log level is specified with INFO. This command starts the JVM for the flume agent using the my.conf file. Make sure paths for all listed files are correct. This example uses relative paths.

```
$ flume-ng agent -n myagent -c conf -f my.conf -Dflume.root.logger=INFO,
  console
```

You can test the flume agent using a telnet or nc command. The agent log file will show the string in a hexadecimal and String form.

```
$ telnet 12345
Hello, this is a test of my first Flume agent <return>
```

Defining a Flume Topology

Flume monitoring can be done using Ganglia, JSON over HTTP, and JMS.

Flume topologies are very flexible. Flume topologies support multiple data streams in a single flume agent, fan-in and fan-out topologies, and multitiered Flume topologies.

Listing 5.12 shows an example of configuring Flume to collect syslog information and then forward the data stream to a collector flume agent on an edge node for a Hadoop cluster. The syslog server will be writing to TCP port 514, and the flume agent collecting the information will write to Avro port 4545. The collector flume agent on the Hadoop edge server will be listening on port 445 and then will write to HDFS.

Listing 5.12 Sample of a Syslog Server Configuration File

```
...
# Provides UDP syslog reception
#$ModLoad imudp
#$UDPServerRun 514

# Provides TCP syslog reception
#$ModLoad imtcp
#$InputTCPServerRun 514
...


--Flume configuration file.
myagent1.sources = mysource
myagent1.channels = mychannel
myagent1.sinks = mysink

# Define the source
myagent1.sources.mysource.type = syslogtcp
myagent1.sources.mysource.port = 514
ambari.sources.mysource.host = localhost

# Define a memory channel
myagent1.channels.mychannel.type = memory
myagent1.channels.mychannel.capacity = 2000
myagent1.channels.mychannel.transactionCapacity = 200

# Describe the sink
myagent1.sinks.mysink.type = avro
myagent1.sinks.mysink.hostname = 172.16.168.129
myagent1.sinks.mysink.port = 4545

# Define the event flow with the source, channel and sink
myagent1.sources.syslog_source.channels = mychannel
myagent1.sinks.mysink.channel = mychannel
```

Start the flume agent. This flume agent sends its output to an Avro port. A collector flume agent will be configured next to receive the input from myagent1 flume agent.

```
$ flume-ng agent -n myagent1 -f  myconf.properties
```

This second flume agent needs to read the events being sent to it from the first agent. This flume agent will read the Avro stream and will write to HDFS. You can check the configuration for this flow in Listing 5.13.

Listing 5.13   Flume Agent Reading the Avro Stream and Writing to HDFS

```
myagent2.sources = logagent
myagent2.channels = mychannel
myagent2.sinks = myhdfs

# Connect the source to the Avro event stream.
myagent2.sources. logagent.type = avro
myagent2.sources. logagent.bind = 0.0.0.0
myagent2.sources. logagent.port = 4545

# Connect the sink to HDFS and set a file format.
myagent2.sinks.myhdfs.type = hdfs
myagent2.sinks.myhdfs.hdfs.path = hdfs:/flume/logevents/%y-%m-%d/%H%M/%S
myagent2.sinks.myhdfs.filePrefix = logevents-
myagent2.sinks.myhdfs.round = true
myagent2.sinks.myhdfs.roundValue = 10
myagent2.sinks.myhdfs.roundUnit = minute

# Set the memory channel buffer
myagent2.channels.mem_channel.type = memory
myagent2.channels.mem_channel.capacity = 2000
myagent2.channels.mem_channel.transactionCapacity = 200

# Connect the source, channel and sink
myagent2.sources.logagent.channels = mychannel
hue.sinks.sink_to_hdfs.channel = mychannel

Start the collector Flume agent. Logger can be
$ flume-ng agent  -n myagent2 -f myconf2.properties
```

Flume can be used to load date into different sources very easily, as shown in Figure 5.3.

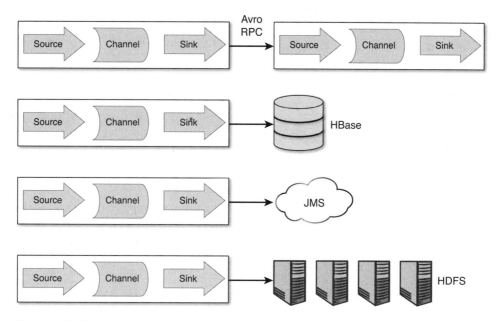

Figure 5.3   Flume agents can be configured to write to different sinks (destinations).

A popular flume configuration is to have one flume agent generate the data stream for another flume agent. You may have a flume agent running on a web server communicating with a flume agent on a gateway server in the Hadoop cluster that then streams the data into HDFS (see Figure 5.4). If there are multiple web servers, there may be a fan-in configuration aggregating the data in a collector flume agent that then loads the data into HDFS (see Figure 5.5).

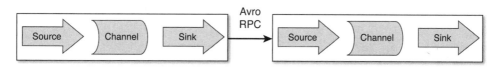

Figure 5.4   Flume agent on web server streaming data to flume agent on gateway server.

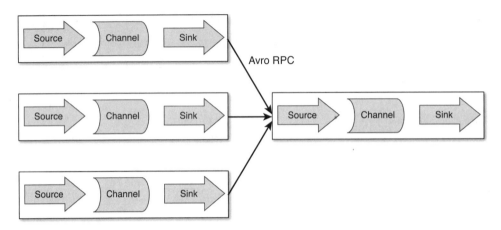

Figure 5.5   Multiple flume agents running on separate web servers may be aggregating their data streams to a collector flume agent.

Flume can be installed from a defined HDP repository, as shown in Figure 5.4.

```
$ yum install -y flume
```

Interceptors

The event or message body can get modified with interceptors that can be part of the event stream in a flume agent. Interceptors can modify, filter, and remove events. Multiple events can be changed together, depending on the complexity of the data processing. For example, multiple interceptors can process the events as they flow between the source and the channel (see Figure 5.6). The order of processing the interceptors is set in the property definitions shown here:

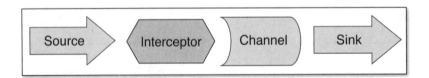

Figure 5.6   An interceptor can be written to process and manage the data as events flow between the source and the channel.

```
myagent.sources.mychannel.interceptors = myint1 myint2 myint3
```

The interceptor type can be set in a separate parameter for each interceptor. Table 5.3 defines the different interceptor types.

Table 5.3 Interceptor Types and Their Definitions

Interceptor Type	Definition
Host	Add the server name or IP address in the event header. Static headers can be added to events to also define the source, such as a specific web server.
Static	Add a static value.
Timestamp	Adds or updates a timestamp for event headers.
UUID	Defines a unique value to all events.
Regex Filtering	Searches for a regular expression and filters values.
Regex Extractor	Searches for a regular expression and gets selected values and places them in header to create an identifier or tag.
Morphline	A morphline configuration file defines a chain of filtering that pipes events from one command to another.

Channel selectors use a fan-out strategy. A replicating channel selector will replicate an event to all the configured channels, as shown in Figure 5.7. The interceptor can process the data so the channel selector can make decisions as to what channel to send an event to. A multiplex channel selector writes events to a subset of channels. Replication and multiplexing enable an event to be replicated to different channels or sent down the stream of a specific channel. Load balancing distributes events with a group in a round-robin or random fashion. Custom channel selectors can also be written.

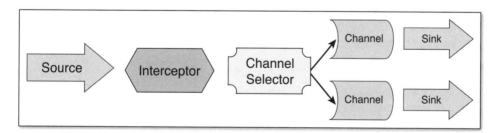

Figure 5.7 A replicating channel selector will replicate an event to all the configured channels.

A medical device can record information on a patient as well as the components in the medical device. The patient information may be monitoring the blood pressure, heart rate, and other vital signs. The medical device can also collect information from sensors on the status of the different components in the device. The interceptor can process the data and make appropriate changes and filters, and after that, the channel selector can determine where to send the event.

Flume Sink Processor provides load-balancing capabilities when multiple sinks are grouped together. If one or more of the sinks fail, the Sink Processor automatically fails over to the other active sink, as shown in Figure 5.8.

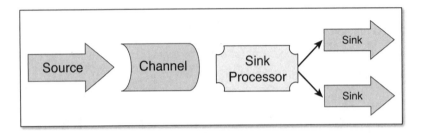

Figure 5.8   Sink processes are designed for failover or load balancing.

There could be multiple agent sources where all of them feed into one channel. The use case could mash up data sources into one single entity. A high-level diagram is shown in Figure 5.9.

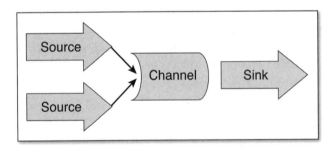

Figure 5.9   Fan in configuration.

Flume has a fan out strategy where, based on an occurrence of a specific value from a source field, the data is routed to the target channel. For example, if the customerType attribute has a value of "consumer" it goes to the first channel; if the value is "business", it goes to the second channel. Figure 5.10 shows the fan out strategy.

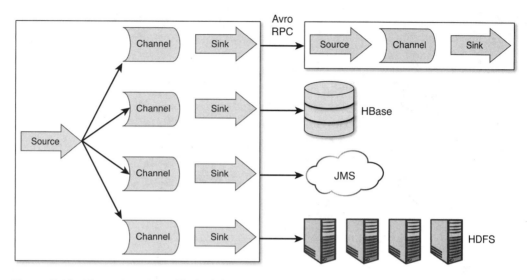

Figure 5.10   Fan out strategy. Each sink can have its own destination.

Flume can be set up to have topologies for failover purposes, as shown in Figure 5.11. It can also be multitiered, as shown in Figure 5.12.

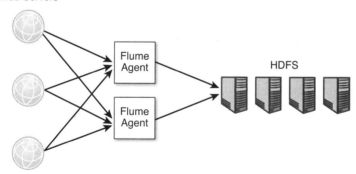

Figure 5.11   Topologies can be configured for failover.

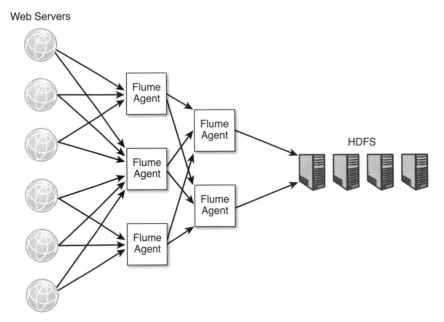

Web Servers

Flume Agent

Flume Agent

Flume Agent

Flume Agent

Flume Agent

HDFS

Figure 5.12   Flume topologies can be multitiered.

Flume Configuration Considerations

Configuring a flume agent requires allocating enough memory for all the flume agents that are in the flume topology. Flume agents need permission to write to all directories defined in the configuration. Make sure there is enough disk storage during high activity times. If using a file channel time the file system must have enough storage allocated. Directory permissions must be defined when required. The JVM and heap sizes need to be configured for the flume agent JVM.

Each flume agent needs to use the flume environmental variables and have its property and log4j properties files properly defined. Primary flume configuration files include the following:

- /etc/flume/conf/flume-env.sh

- /etc/flume/conf/flume-conf.properties

- /etc/flume/conf/log4j.properties

To protect from data loss, use file channels and not memory channels. Depending on the version of Ambari, it might be necessary to write a monitoring script for the flume agents. But as of Ambari 1.7, flume agent monitoring is now available. JMX metrics can also be set up to monitor Flume activity. It is important to use some mechanism to monitor the flume agents and, if they fail, to restart them quickly. It can also help to make sure the Flume collectors (aggregators) are behind a network load balancer. This can help during periods of high activity. Using a virtual IP address (VIP) can also help.

Before implementing a Flume topology, make sure the growth and velocity projections are well understood. Multitiered topologies can help with load balancing and failover and can handle increases in activity during different time frames. Event routing can also be performed at the different tiers.

Start with the log files to help identify any issues. Validate the configuration in the flume_env.sh script and the configuration properties file. Verify the pipeline is correct. Get everything working with default values, and then tune parameters. Try to isolate the problem at the source, channel, or sink layer. If using multitiered topologies, verify each tier. If using several flume agents, understand the ratio of sinks to cores on the system. Tuning the batch sizes can improve performance, especially as the number of sinks increases. Additional sinks may help the throughput to the destination. Make sure the sinks are at least as fast as the sources so that the channel does not become a bottleneck. Setting the sink to Null can eliminate the sink as the issue. Set the source to an Exec or Sequence generator source to test the source. Use a memory sink to verify the channel is not the issue.

WebHDFS: Data over HTTP

WebHDFS is a framework that enables HDFS commands to be executed from a server that does not have Hadoop software installed. WebHDFS uses HTTP Representational State Transfer (REST) APIs to execute HDFS commands. WebHDFS is built in to HDFS so it can execute all HDFS commands. HDFS can read and write files, make directories, modify permissions, and rename files. WebHDFS can copy data between different versions of HDFS.

REST can be used with firewalls and is independent of any language. Read and write calls will get redirected to the DataNodes. Kerberos (SPNEGO) and Hadoop delegation tokens can be used for authentication. A WebHDFS process called HttpFS can be used for additional security.

WebHDFS must be enabled in the Hadoop cluster to be used. WebHDFS can be enabled during installation if using Ambari or can be enabled by setting the dfs.webhdfs.enabled parameter equal to true. If you are setting up a secure cluster, you need to set the dfs.web.authentication.kerberos.principal and the dfs.web.authentication.kerberos.keytab parameters.

Common Linux tools like curl and wget can be used to access HDFS from scripts and the command line. The Linux **curl** command is well known and is very protocol friendly. Following are some sample WebHDFS commands.

Create a directory called /webdata/sep2014:

```
$ curl -i -L "http://<server>:50070/webhdfs/v1/webdata/sep2014/
webdata?op=MKDIRS
```

Read a file called mytest in the directory /webdata/sep:

```
$ curl -i -L "http://<server>:50070/webhdfs/v1/webdata/sep2014/
mytest?op=OPEN
```

List the entries in the home directory for the HDFS user:

```
$ curl -i -L "http://<server>:50070/webhdfs/v1/user/hdfs/
webdata?op=LISTSTATUS
```

Create a new file. This is a two-step process. Create the path and then load the file. The servername must be provided for your environment.

```
$ curl -i -X PUT "http://<servername>:50070/webhdfs/v1/webdata/oct2014/
$ curl -i -PUT -T testdata.txt "http://<servername>:50075/webhdfs/v1/
webdata/oct2014/testdata.txt?op=CREATE&namenoderpcaddress=<servername>:8020
&blocksize=1048576&overwrite=false&user.name=hdfs
```

HttpFS: Proxy Server

HttpFS (Hadoop HDFS over HTTP) is a way to access a proxy server to use REST APIs through an HTTP gateway. HttpFS can be used to copy data between clusters running different versions of Hadoop. HttpFS can access data in HDFS using commands like **curl** and **wget**. The webhdfs client can also access HttpFS using HDFS commands. The default port for HttpFS is 14000.

HttpFS is a separate service from HDFS. HttpFS runs in a Tomcat application server. HttpFS can work with firewalls and can use Kerberos and SPNEGO as well as pluggable authentication methods. HttpFS commands are similar to running WebHDFS commands, as shown in the following examples:

Create a directory in HDFS. Use the servername where HttpFS is running:

```
$ curl -X POST http://<servername>:14000/webhdfs/v1/user/hdfs/
newdata?op=mkdirs
```

Read a file:

```
$ curl  http://<servername>:14000/webhdfs/v1/user/hdfs/mynewfile.txt
```

List the contents of the new directory:

```
$ curl http://<HTTPFS-HOST>:14000/webhdfs/v1/user/hdfs/newdata?op=list
```

The Linux proxy user for HttpFS is set in the Hadoop core-site.xml. Replace <proxy-user> with the appropriate Linux username. Also list the appropriate servername; an IP address is used in Listing 5.14.

Listing 5.14   Update HDFS core-site.xml

```
<property>
  <name>hadoop.proxyuser.<proxy-user>.hosts</name>
  <value>172.168.168.129</value>
</property>
<property>
  <name>hadoop.proxyuser.<proxy-user>.groups</name>
  <value>*</value>
</property>
...
```

Run the httpfs.sh script to start and stop HttpFS.

```
$ bin/httpfs.sh start
```

WebHCat

WebHCat can execute HCatalog commands and run applications on the Hadoop cluster through REST APIs. MapReduce, Pig, Hive, and Streaming applications can be executed on a server without Hadoop software through WebHCat. WebHCat has its own server that needs to be managed separately.

WebHCat was previously named Templeton. The Templeton reference is still used for backward compatibility.

```
$ /usr/lib/hcatalog/sbin/webhcat_server.sh start
$ /usr/lib/hcatalog/sbin/webhcat_server.sh stop
```

The key WebHCat administration files include webhcat_server.sh, webhcat-site.xml, and webhcat-log4j.properties. The administration files must reside on the same server where the WebHCat server is running. The four main files for WebHCat administration include the webhcat_server.sh, webhcat-site.xml, and webhcat-log4j.property files. The default HTTP port for the WebHCat server is 50111.

Kerberos and SPNEGO credentials can be used for authentication. WebHCat commands can use a Knox gateway for authentication. The WebHCat URL is http://hostname.port/templeton/v1.

HTTP requests are sent to access Java, Pig, and Hive applications and HCatalog DDL commands. Application requests are processed by the WebHCat servers and will include a destination where the results should be stored in HDFS, as shown in Figure 5.13.

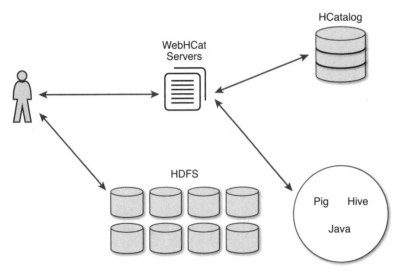

Figure 5.13 HTTP commands can be sent to different sources.

Verify WebHCat is installed and up and running:

```
$ curl -i http://localhost:50111/templeton/v1/status
```

Sample command of running a Java MapReduce application:

```
$ curl -v -i -k -u <userid>:<passwd> -X POST \
    -d jar=/dev/my-coolapps.jar -d class=coolapp1 \
    -d arg=/apps/input -d arg=/apps/output \
    'http://172.16.168.129:50111/templeton/v1/mapreduce/jar'
```

Defining the user in a GET and POST table command:

```
$ curl -s
'http://172.16.168.129:50111/templeton/v1/ddl/database/default/table/
  mytable?user.name=karent'
$ curl -s user.name=karent  -d rename=mytable2
'http://172.16.168.129:50111/templeton/v1/ddl/database/default/table/
  mytable'
```

Log file locations can be defined in the templeton-log4j.properties file. The main WebHCat server files include templeton.log (log4j), templeton-console.log (stdout), and templeton-console-error.log (stderr).

Oozie: Scheduling and Workflow

Oozie is a workflow and scheduling service framework for Hadoop. The Oozie server runs as a servlet in an embedded Tomcat server. The Oozie client runs the Oozie commands. Oozie stores the scheduling and workflow information in a metadata repository. The metadata repository for Oozie can be Derby, HSQL, MySQL, Oracle, and PostgreSQL. Derby is the Oozie default for Apache; however, HDP uses MySQL as the default metadata repository.

The Oozie console is a simple web interface to get the status of Oozie jobs. Organizations do not want to run multiple schedulers. Enterprise schedulers can be used to execute Oozie workflows. REST APIs can also be used to execute Oozie workflows.

Data ingestion, transformation, backups, and archiving can all be automated by Oozie. Data often gets transformed into multiple layers requiring multiple programs processing the data. Oozie can run data processing from the following sources as job streams:

- Tez
- MapReduce
- Streaming
- Pig
- Hive
- Distcp
- Java applications
- ssh
- Email
- Shell scripts

A *workflow* is a set of tasks to be executed in a defined order. Oozie manages the workflow. An Oozie bundle is a method for packaging coordinator and workflow jobs.

The Oozie scheduler can be triggered by data or time conditions. An application that is part of the workflow stream can define parameters like queues and input and output directories. The default port for Oozie is 11000, and the default administration port is 11001.

Oozie can be configured to run with HTTPS. Oozie can use Kerberos and SPNEGO for authentication.

Key configuration files for the Oozie framework include the following:

- oozie-env.sh: Environmental file
- oozie-site.xml: Server configuration file
- oozie-log4j.properties: Logging file
- adminusers.txt: Administrative users

Log files for the Oozie framework include the following:

- oozie.log: Web services log file
- oozie-ops.log: Messages for administration monitoring
- oozie-instrumentation.log: Instrumentation data
- oozie-audit.log: Auditing data

Oozie uses the Hadoop Process Definition Language, which is an XML-based language. The workflow defined in the Oozie XML file is a set of actions that are organized in a Direct Acyclic Graph (DAG). A DAG contains vertices (nodes and actions) and has directed edges that connect the vertices to define the order of actions. A DAG has a beginning node and an ending node and does not circle back to the beginning. An Oozie job defines its parameters in a Java properties file (job.properties) or an XML configuration file. Workflows can contain fork and join nodes. Decision nodes have control statements that determine the work flow.

An Oozie DAG has a beginning and an ending node, as shown in Figure 5.14. After an action is performed, decisions about the next step can be made.

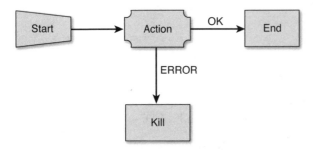

Figure 5.14   An Oozie DAG has a beginning and an ending node.

Oozie can support a variety of workflows with join, fork, and decision nodes, as shown in Figure 5.15.

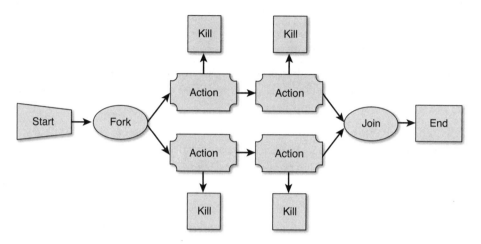

Figure 5.15 Oozie supports multiple workflows using join, fork, and decision nodes.

Oozie uses callbacks and polling to know the status of different tasks and actions.

The oozied.sh script that is used to start, run, and stop the Oozie server runs as the OS user that owns the Oozie installation directory. The logs/oozie.log file can be checked to make sure Oozie started properly.

Use the following to start the Oozie server as a daemon and check the status:

```
$ bin/oozied.sh start
$ bin/oozie admin -oozie http://localhost:11000/oozie -status
```

You can access the Oozie web console to look at the status of a job by going to http://<oozie-server>:11000/oozie/.

Oozie contains a command-line tool, oozie, for performing administration tasks and managing jobs. The oozie tool contains a number of command options for job operations, jobs status admin operations, validation of a workflow, running pig or hive jobs, and getting syntax and version information:

```
oozie job <OPTIONS>
oozie jobs <OPTIONS>
oozie admin <OPTIONS>
oozie validate <ARGS>
oozie pig <OPTIONS> -X <ARGS>
oozie hive <OPTIONS> -X <ARGS>
```

```
oozie mapreduce <OPTIONS>
oozie info <OPTIONS>
oozie help
oozie version
```

Oozie jobs normally contain three components:

- The job.properties file contains the parameters that are passed to Oozie at runtime. This file resides where the Oozie job is submitted. The job.properties file also points in HDFS where the workflow.xml file resides.

- The workflow.xml file contains the instructions for running the Oozie job. The workflow.xml file must reside in HDFS so the application running the job can find the file. An Oozie job can contain parallel processes that are spread across multiple data nodes.

- An Oozie library directory must also reside in HDFS. The library directory contains the jar files and any additional files needed to run the applications that are part of the Oozie job flow.

The Oozie Job Command

The Oozie **job** command can be used to start, kill, run, suspend, resume, submit, rerun, and get information on jobs, as shown in Table 5.4.

Table 5.4   Oozie Job Options

Command	Description
- dryrun	Test the coordinator or workflow without running
-info <arg>	Get information on a job
-kill <arg>	Terminate a job
-log <arg>	Specify the job log
-rerun <arg>	Rerun a job
-resume <arg>	Resume a job
-run	Run a job
-start <arg>	Start a job
-submit	Submit a job
-suspend <arg>	Suspend a job

The following is an example of checking the status of an Oozie system:

```
$ oozie admin -oozie http://localhost:11000/oozie -systemmode normal
```

The following is an example of validating the workflow for an Oozie job:

```
$ oozie validate newworkflow.xml
```

The following is an example of testing the workflow for a job without executing it:

```
$ oozie job -oozie http://localhost:11000/oozie -dryrun -config
  newjob.properties
```

The following is an example of submitting an Oozie job:

```
$ oozie job -oozie http://localhost:11000/oozie -config newjob.properties
  -submit
job: 25-34958494454848-oozie-newjob
```

The following is an example of submitting a MapReduce job:

```
$ oozie mapreduce -oozie http://localhost:11000/oozie -config
  newjob.properties
```

The following is an example of submitting a Pig script:

```
$ oozie pig -oozie http://host:11000/oozie -file my.pig -config
  job.properties
-PINPUT=/user/gage/input -POUTPUT=/user/gage/output
-X -Dmapred.job.queue.name=reports
```

The following is an example of submitting a Hive script:

```
$ oozie hive -oozie http://host:11000/oozie -file myhive.sql -config
  job.properties\
-Dfs.ddfault.name=hdfs://localhost:8020 -PINPUT=/user/gage/input \
-POUTPUT=/user/gage/output -X -Dmapred.job.queue.name=reports
```

The following is an example of starting Oozie jobs and checking the status:

```
$ oozie job -oozie http://localhost:11000/oozie -start
  25-34958494454848-oozie-newjob
$ oozie job -oozie http://localhost:11000/oozie -info
  25-34958494454848-oozie-newjob
```

The following is an example of suspending and resuming Oozie jobs:

```
$ oozie job -oozie http://localhost:11000/oozie -suspend
  25-34958494454848-oozie-newjob
$ oozie job -oozie http://localhost:11000/oozie -resume
  25-34958494454848-oozie-newjob
```

The following is an example of how Oozie jobs can be terminated:

```
$ oozie job -oozie http://localhost:11000/oozie -kill
  25-34958494454848-oozie-newjob
```

Access in Oozie

Be careful about disabling Oozie security—this makes everyone an admin user.

Oozie has a set of authorization rules for users, ACLs, and administrators:

- Users have read access to all jobs and write access to their jobs.

- Users can have additional write access to jobs dependent on ACL privileges.

- Users have read access to admin operations.

- Administration users have write access to all jobs and write access to all administration operations.

Falcon: Data Lifecycle Management

Falcon is Hadoop's framework for data management, data pipeline processing, lifecycle management, and data discovery. Falcon uses declarative definitions to perform data orchestration and management operations. Typical data in Hadoop is loaded in a raw format and is often transformed and massaged into different data layers by running Tez, Pig, and Hive scripts. The data is often transformed to allow BI tools to perform detailed analytics.

The data pipeline to transform the data can get very complex quickly when you start looking at data governance, late data, failure handling, impact analysis, archiving, replication, auditing, replication across clusters, retry policies, lineage, tagging, retention levels, eviction, and validation of data quality. Relationships need to be documented and tracked. Trying to manage this with Oozie workflows can quickly become unmanageable.

Manual coding of Oozie XML files will become error prone and difficult to manage. Large organizations might need to run tens of thousands of Oozie workflows a day. Trying to hand-code XML documents for complex Oozie workflows is not realistic. Falcon enables you to define the data pipeline for governance.

Falcon runs as a standalone server in the Hadoop cluster, as shown in Figure 5.16. Falcon focuses on maintaining the dependencies and the relationships between the entities.

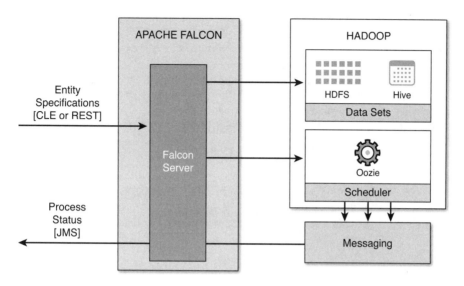

Figure 5.16 Falcon runs as a standalone server.

Oozie is the default scheduler for Falcon, although Falcon is designed to be able to integrate with other schedulers. A user defines specifications that get sent to the Falcon server using the CLI or REST APIs. Falcon gets the specifications and converts them into actions for the workflow scheduler. The Falcon server uses Oozie as the workflow engine. Falcon autogenerates and orchestrates the Oozie workflows.

Falcon uses JMS for messaging. Falcon's metadata is stored on HDFS. The default port for Falcon is 15000.

Falcon can replicate data to another Hadoop cluster. Falcon will manage the entire process workflow from staging, cleansing, conforming, and then storing the resultant processed data. Ambari can be used to manage Falcon. Falcon will use a number of .xml files.

Each cluster has a cluster specification file. This file defines endpoints for writing to HDFS, submitting jobs, executing Oozie, accessing the Hive metastore, and issuing alerts, as shown in Listing 5.15.

Listing 5.15 Sample XML File for Falcon

```
<?xml version="1.0"?>
<cluster colo="myCluster" description="mycoolCluster" name="myCluster"
xmlns="uri:falcon:cluster:0.1">
 <interfaces>
        <interface type="readonly" endpoint="hftp:
          //sandbox.hortonworks.com:50070" version="2.2.0" />
```

```
    <interface type="write" endpoint=
     "hdfs://sandbox.hortonworks.com:8020" version="2.2.0" />
    <interface type="execute" endpoint="sandbox.hortonworks.com:8050"
     version="2.2.0" />
    <interface type="workflow" endpoint=
     "http://sandbox.hortonworks.com:11000/oozie/" version="4.0.0" />
    <interface type="messaging" endpoint=
     "tcp://sandbox.hortonworks.com:61616?daemon=true"
     version="5.1.6" />
 </interfaces>
  <locations>
      <location name="staging" path="/myapps/falcon/myCluster/staging"/>
      <location name="temp" path="/tmp"/>
      <location name="working" path="/myapps/falcon/myCluster/working"/>
   </locations>
</cluster>
```

The specification file defines the cluster to Falcon:

```
$ falcon entity -type cluster -submit -file oregonCluster.xml
```

A dataset specification file defines how often the data is processed, late arrival time frames, and sources, permissions, and destination paths, such as HDFS or Hive tables, as shown in Listing 5.16.

Listing 5.16   *Falcon Example*

```
<?xml version="1.0" encoding="UTF-8"?>
<!-- A data feed generated twice a day. -->
<feed description="Raw data feed" name="myDataFeed"
    xmlns="uri:falcon:feed:0.1">
    <tags>externalSystem=2014data,classification=secure</tags>
    <groups>myEvalDataPipeline</groups>
    <frequency>hours(12)</frequency>
    <late-arrival cut-off="hours(5)"/>
    <clusters>
        <cluster name="myCluster" type="source">
            <validity start="2014-04-01T00:00Z" end="2014-12-31T00:00Z"/>
            <retention limit="days(60)" action="delete"/>
        </cluster>
    </clusters>
    <locations>
        <location type="data"
```

```
        path="/user/mydata/falcon/data/${YEAR}-${MONTH}-${DAY}-${HOUR}"/>
        <location type="stats" path="/none"/>
        <location type="meta" path="/none"/>
    </locations>
    <ACL owner="mydata" group="users" permission="0755"/>
    <schema location="/none" provider="none"/>
</feed>
```

Use the following to submit the dataset specification to Falcon:

```
$ falcon entity -type cluster -submit -file myDataFeed.xml
```

Listing 5.17 shows how to define a process specification.

Listing 5.17 Defining a Process Specification

```
<?xml version="1.0" encoding="UTF-8"?>
<process name="myIngestProcess" xmlns="uri:falcon:process:0.1">
    <tags>pipeline=myDataPipeline,owner=mydata,externalSystem=2014Data
    </tags>
<clusters>
        <cluster name="myCluster">
            <validity start="2014-04-01T00:00Z" end="2014-04-01T00:00Z"/>
        </cluster>
    </clusters>
    <parallel>2</parallel>
    <order>FIFO</order>
    <frequency>hours(12)</frequency>
    <outputs>
        <output name="output" feed="myDataFeed" instance="now(0,0)" />
    </outputs>
    <workflow name="myWorkflow" version="2.0.0"
    engine="oozie" path="/user/mydata/falcon/ingest" />
    <retry policy="periodic" delay="minutes(15)" attempts="3" />
</process>
```

Use the following to submit a process flow to Falcon and schedule the processing:

```
$ falcon entity -type process -submit -file myIngestProcess.xml
$ falcon entity -type feed -schedule -name myDataFeed
$ falcon entity -type process -schedule -name myIngestProcess
```

Kafka: Real-time Data Streaming

You might wonder whether Kafka is the same as Flume. It's not. Both were created to perform data streaming ingestion to Hadoop, but the underlying architecture is very different. Kafka was developed at LinkedIn with the need to have a unified platform for handling all the real-time data processing. They wanted to switch from using batch-oriented file aggregation of their user activity data to a real-time publish-subscribe system. At LinkedIn, Kafka supports multiple subscribing systems and delivers more than 55 billion messages to consumer applications. It is possible to have 1 million writes per second per machine in Kafka, provided all the optimization configuration has taken place.

Why is ingesting activity data in real time so critical at LinkedIn? LinkedIn's earnings come from three key revenue streams: Hiring Solutions, Marketing Solutions, and Premium Subscriptions. The common denominator for all these revenue streams is the knowledge and monetization of user identity. The more precise the ad placement is to a specific audience based on who they are and what their interests are, the more customers are acquired for the advertiser or marketer. The ad placement happens in real time based on current user activity. Kafka doesn't place the ads in real time, but it provides real-time intelligence on what the consumer is doing where a real-time data processing framework like Storm can pick it up and then decide where to load the ad.

With the booming Internet of Things (IoT) business, Kafka would be the perfect fit for ingesting all sensor data that continuously generate data, which can represent both user activity and system activity. For example, Synapse Wireless, a Huntsville, Alabama, company, is trying to solve the critical problem of patient infections at hospitals. It has deployed sensors on all hospital rooms from door entries to soap dispensers and other areas. So when a nurse goes into a room, a sensor fires off and detects the nurse's badge. Once detected, a server from the back end starts monitoring the nurse. The sensors continuously monitor the nurse. If the nurse doesn't wash his or her hands within 30 seconds, the sensors sends a reminder alert to the nurse's badge. This brings two wonderful things for the hospital: avoiding any legal suits due to inappropriate care that led to serious infections and understanding how their nurses or resources are interacting with their patients. The sensor data are all captured by Kafka, and Storm is used in coordination with Kafka to do real-time business logic processing.

Let's take a high-level look at the architecture of Kafka as shown in Figure 5.17. Producers send messages over to the Kafka cluster where, in turn, these messages are delivered to the consumers. The communication between these clients and Kafka servers is done with high performing, language agnostic TCP protocol. You can use a variety of programming languages for the Kafka clients. Topic, on the other hand, is where messages get published. A Kafka cluster is composed of however many brokers are present. Each broker could be its own server. All messages are written to page cache (OS) and are eventually saved to disk. This is why writing to Kafka is very fast.

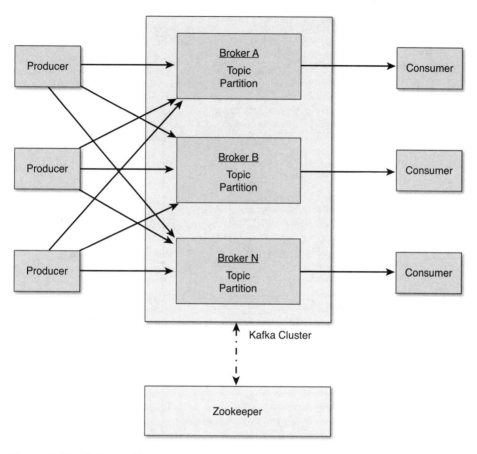

Figure 5.17   Kafka architecture.

Topic

A *topic* is a feed name where messages are published. A topic consists of partitions—ordered and immutable sequences of messages that are continuously appended to. Partitions provide scale and parallelism. Topic is also distributed across Kafka servers. One can configure the number of replicas per partition for fault tolerance purposes. The replica is not intended for parallel processing. Partitions also follow the leader-follower principle. The leader partition handles all the read-write requests, and the followers just replicate. When the leader fails, one of the followers is automatically made the leader. A topic can have one or more partitions (P0, P1, P2, and so on). When messages are written to the topic, the consumers retrieve the oldest data first, and then go through the sequence of writes until they get to the freshest message, which is shown in Figure 5.18.

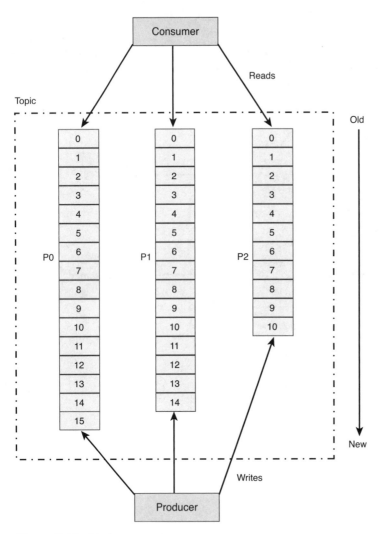

Figure 5.18　Topic concept.

There are two ways to create a topic: via the CLI or autocreate it via broker configs. Take, for example, the CLI approach. The following command specifies replica, partition size, and the topic name. We want to make sure that the creation of topic gets registered with zookeeper so its state can be tracked. The kafka-topics.sh is located under the bin folder of your Kafka install.

```
kafka-topics.sh --create --zookeeper localhost:2181 --replication-factor 1
--partitions 1 --topic mordor
```

To check whether the topic was created, use the --list option:

```
kafka-topics.sh --list --zookeeper localhost:2181
```

The response should show the name of the topic that was previously generated, which was "mordor."

Producer

Producer is responsible for generating the messages and identifying which message needs to go to what partition in a topic. The publication of the message to partitions can be done via a round-robin or by using a message key. Producer has CLI or API that can be used to send messages. CLI is really meant for troubleshooting issues, and API is preferred. As an example, check the CLI command that follows. Using the same topic name and after running the command, you are now able to send messages via the command line. You can start typing the messages and separate them out using newlines.

```
kafka-console-producer.sh --broker-list localhost:9092 --topic mordor
```

When implementing Producer clients using the API, the following classes are used:

- **kafka.javaapi.producer.Producer<K,V>:** This is a generic Java object that requires two parameters. The first parameter is the partition key and the second is the type of message, such as String.

- **kafka.producer.KeyedMessage<K,V>:** This is a wrapper for the message that will be sent to Kafka. It requires at least the topic name and the message. For organizing the messages, it is recommended that you use the topic key and partition key. The topic key is synonymous with a message category. The partition key acts like a bucket to group messages with the same key attribute value.

- **kafka.producer.ProducerConfig:** This object dictates to the Producer the following information:

  - The location of the Kafka brokers where messages will be sent

  - The serializer requirements

  - The partitioning object

  - Requirements for message acknowledgement

- **kafka.producer.Partitioner:** This is an interface that is implemented to define the logic on how the partition key is calculated. If the messages have large cardinalities, it is recommended to use this. The function partition() is used to define the business logic for the partition key.

Consumer

This is the Kafka client that consumes the message from the topic. It uses the concept of consumer group, where a consumer object behaves both as a queue and publish-subscribe clients. For instance, a consumer behaves like a queuing client if all the consumer instances belong to the same consumer group. A publish-subscribe messaging behavior occurs when all the consumer instances belong to different consumer groups. The Kafka consumer group name is global to the Kafka cluster (see Figure 5.19).

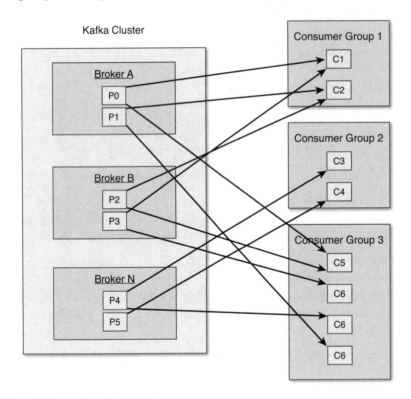

Figure 5.19   Consumer groups.

This shows a Kafka cluster with three servers/brokers. One partition can support multiple consumers or consumer groups. Subscribers of the messages are actually a cluster of consumers, and the order of the messages is guaranteed, in contrast to traditional asynchronous messaging. Suppose, for example, that a given topic mordor has two partitions, P0 and P1. You can do a quick check on whether the topic is receiving messages by running the following command:

```
kafka-console-consumer.sh --zookeeper localhost:2181 --topic mordor
  --from-beginning
```

This dumps the messages from topic mordor into the standard output.

So the question is, what if the broker that wrote the message to topic mordor went down; are the consumers still able to read from the topic? Yes. This is the fault-tolerance feature of Kafka where the brokers are decoupled from the topics.

There are two consumer APIs, but the one that covers most use cases is the High Level Consumer API. The other is called Simple Consumer API, which requires more configuration and implementation. Let's dig deeper into the high level API.

If the consumer doesn't care about the message offset in a partition, and all it wants to do is pull the data, the High Level Consumer API is more than sufficient. There are some design considerations on how a high level consumer is implemented. You want to make sure that your consumer is multithreaded and that all threads are utilized as much as possible. As a general rule, the number of threads should not be more than the number of partitions. Also, if guaranteeing the order of the message is critical, do not allocate multiple partitions per thread. The following are the Java classes that are utilized (at minimum) to implement a simple consumer:

- **kafka.consumer.ConsumerIterator:** This is an iterator object that holds all the message streams for consumption. It can be designed to run all the time until it is interrupted.

- **kafka.consumer.KafkaStream:** A map of the streams that listen on each topic for incoming messages.

- **kafka.consumer.ConsumerConfig:** A lot of the error handling is done for you automatically, but you must indicate where to store state information—that is, message offsets for a particular topic and partition. The following are the minimum properties that can be used to pass along to Kafka:

  - **zookeeper.connect:** One Zookeeper instance that stores message offsets.

  - **zookeeper.sync.time.ms:** The amount of time in milliseconds that is allowed between a Zookeeper follower and its master before a failure occurs.

  - **auto.commit.interval.ms:** The frequency of updating offsets written to Zookeeper.

  - **zookeeper.sync.timeout.ms:** The amount of time in milliseconds that Kafka waits for Zookeeper to respond to a request before stopping and continuing to consume messages.

  - **group.id:** Consumer Group identification.

- **java.util.[HashMap, List, Map, Properties, concurrent.ExecutorService, concurrent. Executors]:** These are utility interfaces used to create thread pools essential to configuring how many threads are provided per topic. Because Kafka waits for a brief amount of time before sending a message offset update to Zookeeper, it is possible that a message can be consumed that is not synced to Zookeeper. So when a consumer client crashes and restarts, that same message will be replayed. To handle this type of scenario, always implement a clean shutdown. The following methods must be called after waiting for about 10 seconds:

  - **ConsumerConnector.shutdown():** Kills the connection to Kafka.

  - **ExecutorService.shutdown():** Kills all threads invoked by Consumer.

As you've seen, Kafka is an extremely fast and scalable messaging bus. Consumers can be written to send the data to different sources. Kafka also has interfaces to Storm, and Storm has predefined connectors (bolts) to different destinations. Over time we can expect to see more producers and consumers predefined and available for Kafka. At the same time, Kafka and Storm can be combined, which enables Kafka to be the messaging bus to define the data pipeline and enables Storm to do the data processing and store the data in the defined destination.

Just as Kafka has components such as producers and consumers, Storm has its set of components. Tuples are data structures in the stream. Spouts generate streams of data. Bolts handle data processing (aggregations, functions, joins, alert logic, reads/writes to data stores) and persistence and can send data to new bolts.

Figure 5.20 shows a sample workflow generated by Storm spouts and bolts.

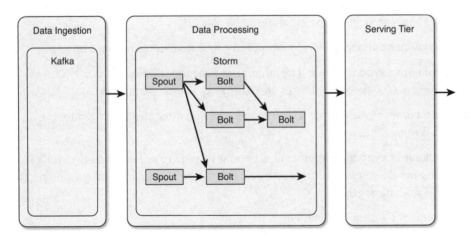

Figure 5.20   Example workflow generated by Storm spouts and bolts.

Installing and Configuring Hadoop

Throughout this book we are constantly emphasizing that Hadoop is all about the data. Before installing Hadoop, the focus must be on the data. Determine the different use cases for Hadoop. Get an understanding of the initial data sources, the data types, the volumes of data, and growth projections. Define the goals of the Hadoop cluster and measurements for success around data analytics. What questions and answers are you looking for from the data?

Data projections will help define the initial hardware profile for the cluster. There are a lot of options for the hardware and software profile of a Hadoop cluster. Step through the advantages and benefits of the following considerations:

- Using a physical versus virtual configuration
- Using a private or a public cloud
- Using a hardware appliance
- Defining a rack topology
- Which frameworks to use
- Using a local repository, or not
- Selecting which NoSQL databases to work with
- Selecting the type of analytics software to use

The hardware profile can vary significantly for different Hadoop clusters. Designing the master nodes for availability presents a number of options. DataNode configurations can vary from 64GB to 256GB of memory. A DataNode may use two 1GB bonded cards or a 10GB network card. The most important part of a DataNode configuration is that the hardware profile must be balanced. Can the throughput of the storage and network balance the processing capability of the memory and CPUs? The security requirements for the data need to be well understood. What will the configuration of the gateway servers be?

The configuration of the Hadoop platform can vary from site to site. What frameworks will be used from the distribution? Will frameworks be added that are not part of a default distribution? There are a lot of NoSQL databases, each with different features and benefits. The data architecture and schema designs and the data ingestion methods for ELT need to be understood.

Manual Versus Ambari

Hadoop installations vary between different releases of the software. However, Hadoop distribution vendors do a good job of providing step-by-step instructions for how to do GUI installs or manual installs on their websites.

At doc.hortonworks.com, you'll find links for hardware recommendations and manual RPM installs. There is a separate link to the Ambari documentation and the steps for doing an Ambari install. For installation and management there are two approaches: a manual install using RPMs or an Ambari install using a GUI interface. The long-term direction of the HDP distribution is to use Ambari as the tool for installation, provisioning, management, and monitoring of a Hadoop cluster.

Almost all proof of concept (POC) projects are done using Ambari. Ambari's GUI interface makes it very easy to provision and set up a Hadoop cluster. It requires a lot more up-front skill and knowledge to install and manage a Hadoop cluster manually. There have been historical reasons for managing Hadoop manually, but as time goes on more and more new clusters are managing Hadoop with Ambari. Earlier releases of Ambari did not scale to thousands of nodes, but Ambari is maturing as an enterprise product.

Ambari is recommended for a number of reasons:

- Management of a Hadoop cluster needs to be automated; otherwise, as the Hadoop cluster scales, it will become unmanageable.

- The creation of scripts to automate a Hadoop cluster not only requires a lot more skill at the beginning, but the maintenance of the scripts can become a monster that must be constantly fed as the cluster grows in size and complexity.

- It's going to be harder and harder not to use Ambari. Ambari supports HA features, Kerberos, Storm, Tez, Falcon, and the like. If you don't use Ambari you have to manage all the different frameworks individually and manually.

- One nice feature of Ambari is the REST APIs are open, so organizations that want to maintain consistency with their enterprise management products and execute Ambari commands through the REST APIs can maintain management consistency across the organization.

Figure 5.21 shows that tools from Microsoft, Teradata, Openstack, HP, and the like can be used to execute Ambari commands.

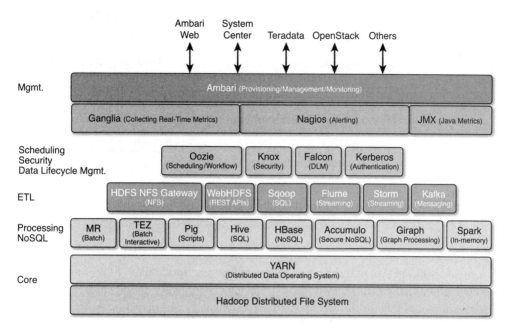

Figure 5.21 Enterprise Management tools can be used to manage a Hadoop cluster with REST APIs.

Be aware that you must use Ambari to manage HDP, or you must do it manually; you cannot do both. HDP stores its configurations in XML files. If you update the HDP configuration files manually, some automation tools, such as Puppet or Chef, must be used to propagate the changed files across the cluster. Ambari does this automatically by storing the configurations in a metadata repository and making changes to the configuration files from the metadata repository.

So if an administrator makes a manual change to a configuration file, those changes are not updated in Ambari's metadata repository. Then, if later an administrator uses Ambari, Ambari updates the changes from the metadata repository and overwrites the changes made manually.

The HDP distribution separates the HDP software stack and Ambari into separate releases. This enables each to be upgraded independently of each other. The documentation has also been separated.

Summary

As you can see, a lot of data ingestion tools exist for Hadoop. Because each has its own purpose, which one to use for what use case can easily become confusing. We discussed tools that can ingest data in real time, streaming, and batch. You should start with a base configuration of the ingestion tools and start using them. As the experience grows, advance data ingestion optimization will become relatively easy. Also, note that if you are already using a data transfer tool that is certified with Hadoop, that will be the easiest route to take to quickly onboard data to HDFS. The important thing is to get as familiar as you can with all the ingestion tools so that you can make an educated decision about which tools would be right for your enterprise.

## Chapter 6

Hadoop SQL Engines

> *Data is the new oil. No: Data is the new soil.*
>
> —David McCandless

One of the biggest decisions in the design of a Hadoop ecosystem is selecting the SQL engines for the use cases. You have to ask yourself, for different types of applications and projects, should we use Hive on Tez, Impala, Spark SQL, Phoenix for HBase, and so on? The decision gets harder as each new release adds functionality that overlaps other SQL engines. In this chapter we discuss Hadoop SQL engines and two of the primary tools that use these engines, Hive and Pig.

Where SQL Was Born

In the early days of computing, everything was file based and only geeks could parse and process such data. With RDBMSs, SQL became the universal language of data processing for developers, analysts, and business executives. The language was so easy to use, it became critical to the enterprise as the basic foundation of business decisions. Organizations started piling so much data onto their RDBMS systems that it quickly exhausted their capacity and introduced new problems, such as cost, scale, and performance, into the equation. Massive Parallel Processing architecture was then developed, and it brought about the Enterprise Data Warehouse (EDW) environment that we know today. EDW carried over the SQL language, and adoption was relatively easy and rapid. However, new datasets kept coming up, and 85% of this new data was unstructured, which cannot easily be stored in EDW systems.

The velocity of data keeps getting faster, and volume is exponentially increasing. Mark Zuckerberg of Facebook, Steve Jobs of Apple, Jack Dorsey of Twitter, and internet giants in Palo Alto created innovations that would generate so much data that EDW systems could no longer manage the workload nor scale economically. Yahoo! quickly realized this in 2005 and built its own platform to accommodate this massive amount of data and named it Hadoop. At that time, it was back to square one—no SQL engine was provided. Rather, heavy computer programming was involved to analyze data. Everybody understood SQL, and to maximize the potential of Hadoop, Hive was created to provide SQL compliance.

SQL in Hadoop

In the early days of Hadoop, only people with Java skills were able to create jobs and process data. Writing MapReduce jobs was not something business analysts would do. Hadoop was born to run as an intelligence platform, and yet developers were the only ones who could interact with it. But to decrease the time required to achieve value from the data, the business side needs to be involved. It was an ironic situation. Internet giants like Yahoo!, eBay, Facebook, and others that have a large pool of developer talent were the only ones taking advantage of the power of Hadoop, which drives traffic to their web properties and converts it to revenue. A shortage of talent in Hadoop impeded commercial enterprises in adopting it. It's still true today but the environment has improved significantly. So what was the first step that drove the widespread adoption of Hadoop? Let's start with Facebook.

Back in 2007, Facebook was using commercial RDBMS as its data warehouse. It had 15TB of data at that time. It was running some analytics for it on Ad Platform, which was taking days, and scaling its data warehouse quickly became an issue. Facebook was growing rapidly, and so was the quantity of its data. Storing petabytes of data became a requirement, and its RDBMS data warehouse became very limiting. So it ventured into Hadoop and realized its power from storing petabytes of data to processing jobs in minutes to hours, in contrast to days in RDBMS.

Facebook's daily data ingestion back in 2007 was 15TB, and now it's ingesting at least 600TB per day. But it still had the challenge of improving its analysis of data, and Hadoop had to reach broader audiences where analysts and business managers could interact with Hadoop as they wanted. MapReduce took them to a phenomenal level, but Facebook's growth wasn't stopping, and it was time to let decision makers get their hands on Hadoop. So it built Hive, which is the SQL engine for Hadoop. It was a great success, and business users loved it.

As of today, Facebook is running at least 300PB of data in Hive to do data analytics. Hive is so powerful that people who came from RDBMS backgrounds are now able to do the same work in Hadoop. Facebook later donated Hive to the Apache Software Foundation (ASF). That was the start of the growth in the adoption of Hadoop. SQL language was a universal way of interacting with data that almost everybody understands. However, the innovation of Hive did not stop there.

Hive became well known as a batch-oriented SQL tool, creating the perception that it is too slow to be used for interactive and real-time queries. Hortonworks and the ASF community rallied together to improve Hive and created an initiative called Stinger. Stinger was basically divided into three innovation areas—increase SQL compliance, improve SQL query speed, and enable Hive to scale to hundreds of PBs. All these were completed in early 2013. This resulted in creating Tez as an in-memory execution engine for Hive, ORCFile as the Hive storage format for querying with speed, and Cost Base Optimizer to generate query statistics. The same group of organizations are pushing Hive again and initiated another project called Stinger.next.

Phase I of Stinger.next, which completed December 2014 (part of HDP 2.2), included features such as ACID capabilities, allowing insert, update, and delete. Temporary tables were also added. There's a difference in what RDBMS ACID typically does because it can process row by row. With Hive ACID, it still takes blocks of rows and processes them. In the next release(s), ACID will allow for multistatement transactions with BEGIN, COMMIT, and ROLLBACK features. There are also improvements to Cost Based Optimizer for function pushdown and added support to star and bushy joins. Storm can now stream events directly into Hive as well. So any dashboard, applications, and tools that are pulling data from Hive will now get data in milliseconds.

Phase II of Stinger.next, which is slated for the second half of 2015, is even more interesting. The community is pushing Hive to reach latencies in milliseconds. Tez will play a part in Hive's new architecture, but a new component is being built called Live Long and Process (LLAP) that will utilize heavy in-memory processing. LLAP will be running on DataNodes that will use extensive caching, reuse compressed columnar data in memory, and off-heap. Hive on Spark is in the works, and this will introduce Spark to a wider group of people with SQL skills. Hive is used to pull data and resultsets that are automatically converted to RDD, ready for Spark function(s) processing. Machine learning can then be invoked via Hive.

The last phase of Stinger.next is geared toward making Hive SQL 2011 analytics compliant. Richer data types, functions, and other data warehouse capabilities will be made available. Materialized views will be included. Organizations have multiple Hadoop clusters geographically dispersed and want the capability to run one query across all of them.

Hadoop SQL Engines

The query execution engine for Hive was based on MapReduce, and that was a good start. After Hive penetrated a broader audience, users eventually realized that they needed to run the queries faster. As mentioned earlier, Stinger was completed and Stinger.next was initiated to reach the goal of responding to a query in milliseconds, with the help of Tez, which is to be completed in the second half of 2015. During this journey, Hadoop distributors built something new to address the query speed issue. Impala was born out of Cloudera, Spark SQL was innovated by Databricks, Phoenix was developed by SalesForce. com, HAWQ was born out of Pivotal, BigSQL from IBM, Flink from ASF, and Apache Drill mainly influenced by MapR. It might seem like a long list, but it continues to grow and it becomes very challenging for organizations to decide which one to use. Each tool claims to have unique feature sets compared to others. It could be SQL compliance, speed, scalability, interoperability, portability, security, ease of use, and so on. What adds to the difficulty in deciding which SQL engine to use is that all these are evolving rapidly with aggressive road maps, and the SQL engines are starting to overlap in multiple areas.

Let's talk about what decision process must be considered and focus on some use cases that lay out strengths and weaknesses of each SQL tool for Hadoop.

Selecting the SQL Tool For Hadoop

Remember that the decision you make today might change tomorrow. Hadoop is moving very fast, and the entire ecosystem of tools has to catch up. Choose what you need now, but continue to watch out for other tools for the future. Be ready to adjust when the need arises. Let the decision making begin.

SQL Multi-execution Support

Across the enterprise, it is common to see the need for batch, interactive, and real-time data processing. A nightly job needs to run and crunch large amounts of data. When business users hit their offices at 9 a.m., they start running queries to generate interactive business reports. Executives start looking at real-time dashboards powered by SQL queries. A lot of SQL tools are out there, but they are all part of the same toolbox as Hadoop. This echoes the thought, "Use the right tool for the right job." Table 6.1 explains the SQL tools and what type of execution they support—memory or IO, or both. Executing SQL in memory provides the fastest response, where queries take subseconds. But this has limitation on how much data can be processed, and it's all dependent on how much memory the Hadoop cluster has overall.

Table 6.1 Hadoop SQL Execution Support

SQL Tool	Execution	Characteristics
Hive	Memory (Tez)	Runs on Tez for in-memory processing that can scale from tens and thousands of TBs. Tez enables interactive queries for Hive. Tez determines how much memory is available and runs the job in waves if there isn't enough memory for all data. It enforces data pipelining in memory.
Hive	IO MapReduce(2)	Proven at hundreds of TBs to PBs of batch data processing. All processing is disk based.
Impala	Memory	Has its own daemon for processing queries. Limitation is on how much data it can store in memory for processing. Great at simple queries on one large table.
Spark SQL	Memory	All data processing is done in memory.
HAWQ	IO	Has one query processing module per node for query execution that utilizes IO to complete a job.
HAWQ	Memory (Gemfire XD)	In-memory transactional support through Gemfire XD.
BigSQL	IO	Disk-based processing.
Apache Drill	IO	Leverages HDFS, Hive, and HBase for storage but doesn't use YARN. Has its own daemon called DrillBit that exists on all DataNodes for query execution.
Presto	Memory	Its goal is the same as Tez—utilize memory for data pipelining to reach "interactive querying" capabilities.
Phoenix	IO	Utilizes HBase as its storage mechanism and capitalizes on HBase's low latency IO performance for interactive query.

Closeness to Hadoop Core

Any tool, including SQL, should leverage the power that Hadoop brings. It means that a SQL engine shouldn't run beside or on Hadoop, but in it. A tool that takes advantage of YARN definitely inherits the speed and scale of processing essential for crunching terabytes to petabytes of data. If it leverages HDFS as its primary storage, any data dropped into HDFS can be exposed to SQL querying, and there's no limitation on what data can be queried. A tight integration with YARN and HDFS means that resources are being utilized more effectively, and managing and operating the SQL engine becomes second nature to the Hadoop admin.

Table 6.2 describes the different SQL tools in terms of their native integration with Hadoop.

Table 6.2 Native Hadoop SQL Engine Support

SQL Tool	Hadoop Native	Characteristics
Hive	Yes	Driven by the Apache open source community with the backing of Hortonworks and other big vendors. There were 144 developers across at least 30 companies that compose the hive community. Leverages YARN for computing and HDFS as primary storage.
Impala	No	Primarily driven by Cloudera. Doesn't run on YARN. It has its own daemon for processing queries. Leverages HDFS to store raw data and records in HBase.
Spark SQL	Yes	Leverages YARN for resource management. Spark SQL is still maturing, and there isn't a lot of support yet from analytics vendors.
HAWQ	No	Doesn't run on YARN but has direct access to HDFS. It has query processing unit per node for query execution.
BigSQL	No	Not YARN native and uses General Parallel File Systems (GPFS) as primary storage, in contrast to HDFS.
Apache Drill	Yes (HDFS)	Leverages HDFS, Hive, and HBase for storage but doesn't use YARN. Has its own daemon called DrillBit that exists on all DataNodes for query execution.
Presto	Yes (HDFS)	Designed for interactive ad-hoc query. Primary storage is HDFS but supports Hive as storage backend and others.
Phoenix	No	Brings relational database to Hadoop and uses HBase as primary storage. One trillion row table can be queried in fewer than 10 seconds.

Ecosystem Endorsement

What good is a SQL engine, even if it's close to perfect, if there's very little endorsement from third-party vendors that specialize in data analytics? Organizations want to preserve their existing investments, and any tool that they bring in to their infrastructure should introduce little to no changes. Moving an RDBMS user to a Hadoop SQL engine should be transparent. Users of BI tools shouldn't notice when their application utilizes Hadoop's SQL engine. It is a natural choice to pick a SQL engine that's mostly supported by existing, commonly used data analytics systems. The cost of maintaining an existing data analytics system should remain flat.

There are two levels of endorsements—certification and joint engineering. Certification basically means that a third-party data analytics tool can work with specific version(s) of the Hadoop SQL engine. The goal is to make the integration work. There may be some gaps in functionality because of some integration limitations. With joint engineering, it's a deeper partnership between third-party data analytics like SAS, Tableau, and others with SQL engine vendors. Both sides have dedicated engineers working together not only to make it work but define the roadmap on how both products work in the future. This kind of partnership benefits organizations in three ways. First, they will have strong support and voice to influence how both products should evolve. Second, they can keep the tools they love and continue using them. Third, the product releases of the vendor and Hadoop SQL engine will be so close to each other that organizations can use the latest and greatest technology that supports critical business decisions.

Table 6.3 outlines what third-party vendors are currently supporting which Hadoop SQL tool.

Table 6.3   Hadoop SQL Engine Ecosystem Endorsement

SQL Tool	Endorsement Level	Characteristics
Hive	High	All major players in the data analytics space have invested and adopted Hive to support data analysts on Hadoop through the Hive SQL interface. SAS, Tableau, Microstrategy, SAP, HP Vertica, Teradata, Pentaho, and many more support Hive. The adoption is so high because of the Stinger initiative. It brought Hive closer to ANSI SQL 92 Standard and made it possible to do interactive queries.
Impala	Medium	Not many data analytics vendors have adopted Impala, but there are at least six of them as listed on Cloudera's website.
Spark SQL	Low	Spark SQL is very new, but it is gaining attention across the big data space. There's a very active open source community behind it. We have yet to see adoption from analytics vendors.
HAWQ	Low	HAWQ was innovated by Pivotal and is a proprietary tool, but Pivotal decided to slowly open source components of HAWQ. As of today, HAWQ is closely tied to Pivotal's product portfolios.
BigSQL	Low	Mainly run by IBM and fairly a new product. It runs on its BigInsight Hadoop distribution.
Apache Drill	Low	Conceptualized by MapR and donated to Apache. Specifically designed for semistructured, nested data processing. There's not a lot of traction happening yet, but the concept is very interesting.
Presto	Low	Relatively new and mainly governed by Facebook.
Phoenix	Medium	Gaining traction in the open source community. Hortonworks is backing Phoenix, and it's part of their distribution.

Portability

Writing SQL queries and executing them on different frameworks is a data analyst's nirvana. It goes with the saying, "Use the right tool for the right job." A query execution framework could be designed in such a way that it can process TBs to PBs of data. But then it can switch to interactive mode and possibly to the millisecond response time. Another query execution framework would be useful for doing interactive queries. Perhaps a different workload is required to run in-memory query processing specifically targeted for machine learning. This kind of flexibility provides businesses the capability to make the right decision at the right time with the right tool.

Another thing to consider is when the time comes that you have to move from one big data platform flavor to another, make sure that all the work previously done can be migrated fairly easily.

Table 6.4 highlights the portability of each SQL engine for Hadoop.

Table 6.4 Hadoop SQL Engine Portability

SQL Tool	Portable	Characteristics
Hive	Yes	Considering its very close compliance with ANSI SQL 92, there will be less work porting SQL DML and DDL statements to other SQL engines. Hive can also switch its execution engine from MR to Tez and soon on Spark as well.
Impala	Yes	It's a little behind on ANSI SQL 92 compliance, and it would take a lot of query adjustments to make it work. The only Hadoop distributor that's adopting it is MapR. There are no other execution engines that it can run on.
Spark SQL	No	Relatively new, and we have yet to see it maturing. The idea of running queries in memory is very attractive.
HAWQ	Yes	HAWQ was just donated to Apache as an open source project. This could get interesting because a lot of the full SQL syntax support is available. It runs only on Pivotal HD today, but due to its full SQL compliance support, queries will be easily migrated to other Hadoop platforms.
BigSQL	No	Proprietary to IBM and still maturing.
Apache Drill	No	It supports Hadoop and NoSQL platform as its backend storage. We have yet to see SQL compliance improving.
Presto	Yes	Besides supporting its own execution engine, it has connectors to Hive and Cassandra.
Phoenix	No	Only tied to HBase as its backend storage and doesn't support other execution engines.

Support

Few organizations will adopt a product—even if it's great—if it has subpar support. With Hadoop becoming mainstream, it is critical to choose a SQL engine that is backed by not only the vendor's deep engineering expertise but also a big community of commercial and noncommercial entities. Everybody claims to have the best support in the big data industry, but due diligence must be done by reaching out to customers who are vendor references and getting third-party assessments from the likes of Forrester Research and Gartner.

Table 6.5 outlines the level of commercial and community support for each SQL tool.

Table 6.5 Hadoop SQL Engine Support

SQL Tool	Enterprise Support	Characteristics
Hive	Yes	Hortonworks and its partners support it. All major data analytics tools support it—not only from a commercial support point of view, but how much support the Apache community is providing to Hive to push its innovation. At least 17 organizations are creating innovations in Hive.
Impala	Yes	Cloudera provides support. There's no Apache community involved, and only Cloudera is pushing the innovation.
Spark SQL	Yes	Databricks provides support, but at least 14 other organizations are heavily involved in pushing the innovation and will provide support to the community and also commercially.
HAWQ	Yes	Pivotal provides support today, but since it was donated to Apache Software Foundation, other Hadoop distributors can take advantage of it. A growing support base will eventually expand.
BigSQL	Yes	IBM provides support, and it's proprietary.
Apache Drill	Yes	MapR provides support, but a growing number of committers is an indication that community support is coming.
Presto	No	Early stages and, as of this writing, community is mainly Facebook.
Phoenix	Yes	Hortonworks provides support for it. Seven organizations are part of the community that is driving the innovation.

Adoption Rate

The ones who truly prove and push the limits of any technology are the Internet giants. That's why BigTable was born at Google, Hadoop was innovated by Yahoo!, Cassandra was created at Facebook, Kafka was developed by LinkedIn, and there are many others. Most of them provided their innovations via open source. It is this trend that drives the commercial space to listen intently and carefully to what these big tech firms can offer to the community. For organizations that have the software engineering power plants, it's easier for them to try out these open source technologies and push them to production. But others who are more concerned with running the business tend to get something that works out-of-the-box—in short, enterprise ready. This is where mainstream adoption of technology takes place. This level of simplicity, ease of use, and enterprise readiness propels a SQL engine to mass adoption. This is what separates hype from reality.

Table 6.6 illustrates adoption maturity for each SQL tool.

Table 6.6   Hadoop SQL Engine Adoption

SQL Tool	Adoption Rate Level	Characteristics
Hive	High	This was the first SQL tool in Hadoop and has rapidly been adopted since.
Impala	Low	Only Cloudera customers are the adopters.
Spark SQL	Low	A lot of talk and interest exist for this tool, but it's yet to be tested in the enterprise.
HAWQ	Low	Only Pivotal HD customers adopted it.
BigSQL	Low	Relatively new, and there isn't any information on what commercial industry is using it in production.
Apache Drill	Low	MapR has been driving this, and we have yet to see adoption speed up.
Presto	Low	Very slow adoption exists because there isn't a community that is involved yet.
Phoenix	Medium	This is getting attention due to its capability to process a trillion rows in seconds.

SQL Compliance

The more SQL compliant the tool, the more work the business can do. If limitations exist, they shouldn't stop an organization from running some level of complex queries. The sheer amount of data Hadoop has brings a wealth of information that fuels the success of a company. Multiple data sources need to be transformed, joined, aggregated, and computed. These capabilities must be the minimum requirement. A proof of concept between SQL engines is pretty common, and it's done to validate which SQL engines support the organizations' business requirements. It doesn't stop there, but it also warrants the need to understand what features are going to be supported in the future.

Table 6.7 describes each SQL tool's compliance with the ANSI SQL 92 standard.

Table 6.7   Hadoop SQL Engine SQL Compliance

SQL Tool	ANSI SQL Compliance	Characteristics
Hive	High	Very close to ANSI SQL 92. Apache community currently working on making it SQL 2011 Analytics compliant and will be completed in 2015.
Impala	Medium	Has some catching up to do with ANSI SQL 92 compliance.
Spark SQL	Low	Relatively new and has some work to do to get close to ANSI SQL 92.
HAWQ	High	Ahead of the game in terms of full SQL compliance.
BigSQL	Low	Relatively new.
Apache Drill	Low	Relatively new.
Presto	Low	Relatively new.
Phoenix	Medium	Has some catching up to do to get close to ANSI SQL 92 compliance.

Security

As of today, there are verticals using Hadoop to store sensitive data. Security compliance to mandated regulations is a minimum requirement to keep data safe. A SQL engine that provides this support and even goes further is an ideal candidate. The more granular the security controls, the better. HIPAA and PCI for example, require data to be encrypted. Voltage, Protegrity, DataGuise, Gazzang, and Vormetric provides this capability in Hadoop. The Apache open source community is also busy working on making Transparent Data Encryption (TDE) in Hadoop production ready in Q3 2015. So a native encryption support is coming. The SQL engine must seamlessly work with security tools that Hadoop provides and its ecosystem.

Table 6.8 defines the security support for each SQL tool.

Table 6.8   Hadoop SQL Engine Security

SQL Tool	Security Strength	Characteristics
Hive	High	Along with Apache Ranger support, Hive provides RBAC-style security controls. Knox validates and filters Hive requests to prevent unauthorized access to Hive service. Support for Kerberos is available for strong authentication. Voltage, Vormetric, Protegrity, and DataGuise provide data at rest encryption in Hive. HDFS Transparent Data Encryption is in technical preview that could potentially provide native encryption in Hadoop. Data in transit encryption is also supported.
Impala	High	Utilizes Sentry and Kerberos as its security controls for data access. Support for Gazzang is available to encrypt data at rest. Data in transit encryption is also supported.
Spark SQL	Low	Supports only shared secret authentication scheme.
HAWQ	High	Utilizes Kerberos for authentication. Uses Protegrity for data encryption. Data in transit encryption is also supported.
BigSQL	Medium	Utilizes LDAP for authentication.
Apache Drill	Low	No mention of security model in the documentation.
Presto	Low	No mention of security model in the documentation.
Phoenix	High	Leverages Ranger to protect HBase tables and Kerberos for strong authentication. It will take advantage of HDFS TDE for data at rest encryption. Has full support for data in transit encryption.

Now Getting Groovy with Hive and Pig

Hive enables analysts, managers, and programmers to use SQL to access and process data stored in HDFS and NoSQL databases. Pig is a scripting language that can be used to access, process, and transform data in Hadoop. HCatalog is a table and storage manage layer that enables schemas to be created that can be accessed from different languages and tools.

In previous chapters we covered how HDFS commands can be used to put data in HDFS. Some examples follow:

Load data from STDIN using the - operator:

```
$ hdfs  dfs  -put  -  /user/hdfs/mydata/mynewfile.txt
```

Load data from a local file to HDFS:

```
$ hdfs dfs -put  mylocalfile.txt  /user/hdfs/mydata/newhdfsfile.txt
$ hdfs dfs -copyFromLocal  /tmp/mytmpfile.txt    \ /user/hdfs/mydata/
  mytmpfile.txt
```

We will now take a look at the data frameworks.

Hive

Hadoop applications can be written in Java, Python, Pig, and so on. All these languages are excellent tools for different types of solutions. Despite the power of all the languages to do low-level processing, SQL is still the best way to access data when possible. Pig is a scripting language that provides a lower level of granularity for manipulating data. Pig can be helpful when the data transformations in HDFS get too complex for SQL. Various GUI interface tools will create the SQL and Pig application code. Writing a MapReduce2 or Tez program in Java can take hours or days. Being able to write high-level queries in SQL or by using query tools is the fastest way to access data when SQL is the right tool. The primary way you use SQL in Hadoop is to use the Apache Hive framework. Hive and Pig also support Tez in the latest releases.

The Hive framework defines an ETL/data warehouse infrastructure on top of Hadoop. The underlying data can be stored in files in HDFS or other data storage systems like HBase or Accumulo. Data can be stored in HDFS with different pluggable data format handlers (SerDes) and be spread across disks on multiple servers. When a Hive table is defined on a file in HDFS, it is transparent to the user accessing the table how the data is organized or what format the data is in. Hive provides a data warehouse layer on top of Hadoop by supporting concepts such as databases, tables, columns, partitions, and buckets to underlying data that can be stored in different formats. Databases allow tables to have separate namespaces to avoid naming conflicts.

Users, managers, and analysts can then run SQL queries on the Hive tables. Query tools that support JDBC or ODBC can be used to query Hive tables. Leading business intelligence and visualization tools can be used to query data in HDFS using Hive tables. Hive currently allows queries, inserts, updates, and deletes. It's important to understand that Hive and HDFS are not a relational database. Hive tables can map to structured and unstructured tables. This provides the flexibility of running joins between data from different sources and data storage formats. The driver processes the SQL statement by performing the parsing, compilation, optimization, and execution of the code. Hive uses modules that act as interpreters to execute the MapReduce2 or Tez code.

HiveQL

Hive supports a query language called HiveQL. HiveQL is not ANSI SQL compliant, but in every release of Hive more ANSI SQL functionality is added. Hive was initially designed for Petabyte scale data. With the Stinger initiative and Tez, Hive can also be used to run interactive queries in Hadoop. Hive lets users write highly parallel applications or interactive queries without having to understand the architecture or the underlying data formats. SQL statements running HiveQL will get transformed into a MapReduce or Tez job (based on the parameter setting), and a cost-based optimizer can optimize the execution plan and the join.

A Hive query will go through an execution process similar to an RDBMS with a few differences. When a Hive query is executed, it will be parsed and a lexical scan will be performed on it; an execution plan will be defined for the query, and then the command will be executed. These steps are similar to how an RDBMS processes a SQL statement. The difference with Hive is that based on parameter settings, a Hive statement will be transformed into a MapReduce2 or a Tez execution model. This transformation is transparent to the user. Similar to RDBMS, query and join optimization can be performed with hints if the cost-based optimizer does not create an ideal execution plan for the dataset. Star schemas, cubes, and dimensions are supported in Hive similar to RDBMS. However, the join optimization plans are different in Hive compared to an RDBMS. Hive uses log4j for its logging. The default log level is INFO. Audit logs can also be generated by Hive.

Hive and Beeline Command-Line Interface (CLI)

The **hive** command can be executed to work with Hive with interactive command-line mode. The hive set option will display environmental variables.

The HiveServer is a service that enables clients to submit SQL requests to Hive using different programming languages. HiveServer2 became available beginning in Hive 0.11. Both HiveServer and HiveServer2 provide a container for the Hive execution engine. HiveServer2 has a number of advantages, but the two primary ones are better concurrency and authentication of users. Beeline is the interface to use with HiveServer2. The hive command line is used with HiveServer(1). Beeline is a replacement for the Hive CLI client with HiveServer2. HiveServer2 also has a new RCP interface that has more options for JDBC and ODBC clients. HiveServer2 is designed to replace the HiveServer, but the HiveServer2 is still maturing, so a number of companies are still using the HiveServer.

Hive and Beeline can run queries for the HiveServer or HiveServer2 in interactive command-line mode or can run queries from the command line or from a file.

Help is available for the **hive** and **beeline** command-line arguments:

```
$ hive -H    or   hive -h
$ beeline -h
$ beeline --help
```

The following commands show how to start Hive with interactive mode, to run a query on the command line, or to run a script from a file:

```
$ hive
$ hive - e  'SELECT …'
$ hive -f    filename
$ beeline
$ beeline -e  'SELECT …'
$ beeline -f    filename
```

Variables can be set at the command-line argument or by using the **set** command within the command-line interface.

Following is the syntax for setting Hive variables with the Hive CLI:

```
$ hive -d key=value
$ hive --define key=value
$ hive --hivevar key=value
```

Following is the syntax for setting Hive variables with the Beeline CLI:

```
$ beeline --hivevar key=value
```

Defining Hive configuration variables in command line in Hive CLI:

```
hive --hiveconf key=value
```

The HiveServer2 can be started and stopped manually.

```
$ $HIVE_HOME/bin/hiveserver2
$ $HIVE_HOME/bin/hive --service hiveserver2
```

Hive can execute SQL code from a script.

```
$ hive -f /myscripts/mreport.hql
```

Hive can run shell commands in the Hive shell.

```
hive>  ! ps -ef | grep hive
```

Hive can execute SQL code from a script, as shown in Listing 6.1.

Listing 6.1   Run a Hive Script

```
$ hive -f /myscripts/mreport.hql


$ hive
hive> set;
hive> CREATE TABLE   mynewtab (myid INT, name STRING);
```

Partition tables are defined differently than a lot of RDBMS platforms. The partition column is a virtual column. The partition is derived from a specific dataset that the data is loaded into. The LOAD DATA LOCAL option will load data from an operating system directory. If the LOCAL keyword is not used, data will be loaded from an HDFS directory.

Listing 6.2 shows a sample command to create a table.

Listing 6.2   Sample CREATE TABLE and LOAD Commands

```
hive> CREATE TABLE  myparttab (id INT, name STRING)
      >    PARTITIONED BY (ds STRING);


hive> LOAD DATA LOCAL INPATH '/sampledata//myparttab.txt'
      > OVERWRITE INTO TABLE myparttab;
hive> LOAD DATA LOCAL INPATH '/sampledata//mynewtab.txt'
      > OVERWRITE INTO TABLE invites PARTITION (ds='2014-07-01');


hive> CREATE TABLE  newdata (
      >      id INT,
      >      name INT,
      >      status INT,
      >      createtime STRING)
      >   FIELDS TERMINATED BY '\t'
      >   STORED AS TEXTFILE;
hive> ALTER TABLE newdata ADD COLUMNS (cold_data INT);
hive> DESCRIBE  mynewtab;
hive> SHOW TABLES;
hive>  SELECT m.myid, m.name   FROM mynewtab m
   >   WHERE m.ds='2014-07-01';
hive>  SELECT t.id FROM mypartab;
hive> SHOW TABLES '.*tab';
hive> ALTER TABLE newdata RENAME TO olddata;
hive>  exit;
hive> DROP TABLE olddata;
```

Run a query from the command line in silent mode:

```
$ hive -S -e  "SELECT * FROM myparttab"  > /tmp/parttab.out
```

After starting up beeline with interactive mode, you need to connect to the HiveServer2. The default transaction isolation level is TRANSACTION_REPEATABLE_READ. The default user ID and password for hive is hive/hive.

Listing 6.3 shows how to use beeline, the recommended tool for any CLI administration because it's more secure than the legacy hive CLI.

Listing 6.3   Example Working with the Beeline CLI

```
#  beeline
Beeline version 0.13.0.2.1.1.0-237 by Apache Hive
beeline> !connect jdbc:hive2://127.0.0.1:10000 hive
  hive org.apache.hive.jdbc.HiveDriver
0: jdbc:hive2://127.0.0.1:10000> show databases;
+-------------------+
| database_name  |
+-------------------+
| default          |
| mydb             |
| yourdb           |
+-------------------+
3 rows selected (1.802 seconds)
0: jdbc:hive2://127.0.0.1:10000> dfs -ls /user;
+----------------------------------------------------------------------+
|                                                     DFS Output        |
|                                                                      |
+----------------------------------------------------------------------+
| Found 6 items                                                        |
|                                                                      |
| drwxrwx---    - ambari-qa hdfs         0 2014-03-25 06:57 /user/ambari-qa  |
| drwxr-xr-x    - guest     guest  0 2014-04-01 07:02 /user/guest      |
| drwxr-xr-x    - hcat      hdfs   0 2014-03-25 06:48 /user/hcat       |
| drwx------    - hive      hdfs   0 2014-03-25 06:19 /user/hive       |
| drwxr-xr-x    - hue       hue    0 2014-04-01 07:02 /user/hue        |
| drwxrwxr-x    - oozie     hdfs   0 2014-03-25 06:24 /user/oozie      |
+----------------------------------------------------------------------+
7 rows selected (0.127 seconds)
0: jdbc:hive2://127.0.0.1:10000> !quit
```

Tables by default are stored in the directory defined by the hive.metastore.warehouse.dir parameter in the hive-site.xml file. The default location can be overridden by defining a path in HDFS. The table will be created as a subdirectory in the defined path. The user must have permission to write in the path directory.

The hive.metastore.warehouse.dir parameter is shown in Listing 6.4 on where it's configured.

Listing 6.4   Setting the Default Directory for Hive Tables

```
<property>
    <name>hive.metastore.warehouse.dir</name>
    <value>/apps/hive/warehouse</value>
  </property>
```

Listing 6.5 shows the creation of a table and defines the storage location in HDFS.

Listing 6.5   Create Table Overriding the Default Directory Path

```
CREATE TABLE subscriber (
  ID INT,
  fName STRING,
  lName STRING,
  initdate TIMESTAMP,
 regionid INT
 ) ROW FORMAT DELIMITED
   FIELDS TERMINATED BY ','
 LOCATION  '/user/gage/subscribers/;
```

HiveServers

Hive uses the HiveServer service that contains an execution engine for processing JDBC or ODBC drivers from a Hive client or SQL tools. The HiveServer2 supports concurrent Thrift clients and has improved authentication (Kerberos) and authorization over the previous HiveServer. HiveServer2 can allow all connections to connect or can authenticate connections using Kerberos or LDAP. The hive.server2.authentication parameter can be set in the hive-site.xml file. Secure Socket Layer (SSL) can also be defined between

HiveServer2 and clients. HiveServer2 is recommended, but it is possible to run HiveServer concurrently if there are reasons to run older applications on HiveServer, such as some applications using native HiveServer1 Thrift bindings. The ports for HiveServer2 and HiveServer can be set with parameters in the hive-site.xml file or with the HIVE_SERVER2_THRIFT_PORT and HIVE_PORT environmental variables.

The HiveServer2 service is shown in Figure 6.1.

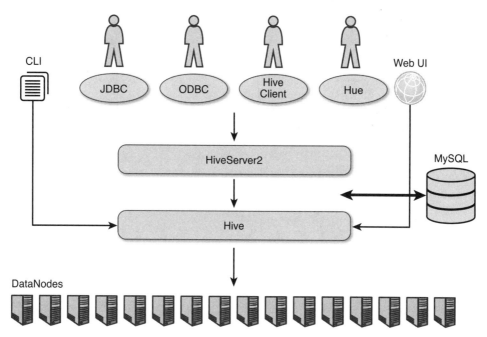

Figure 6.1   HiveServer2

Beeline can connect to the secure HiveServer2 and uses HiveServer2 Thrift APIs. The hive shell will connect to the nonsecure HiveServer instance.

If running HiveServer2 and HiveServer1, make sure they are configured on different ports, as defined in Listing 6.6.

Listing 6.6   Setting Default Port Values

```
<property>
  <name>hive.server2.thrift.port</name>
  <value>10001</value>
</property>
<property>
  <name>hive.port</name>
  <value>10000</value>
</property>
```

Authentication is defined with the hive.server2.authentication parameter. The default is NONE. See the Listing 6.7 configuration example.

Listing 6.7   Setting Authentication Level

```
<property>
  <name>hive.server2.authentication</name>
  <value>NONE</value>
  <description>
    Client authentication types.
        NONE: no authentication check
        LDAP: LDAP/AD based authentication
        KERBEROS: Kerberos/GSSAPI authentication
        CUSTOM: Custom authentication provider
                (Use with property hive.server2.custom.authentication.class)
  </description>
</property>
```

Hive uses a metadata repository to store all its table definitions and system information. MySQL, PostgreSQL, Oracle, and Derby can be used. JDBC and ODBC connections will go through the HiveServer2. The metadata repository can reside on the same server as the HiveServer2 or on a remote server.

Apache Thrift

Apache Thrift is an Interface Definition Language (IDL) that supports cross-language services with languages like Java, Python, PHP, Perl, C++, JavaScript, Node.js, CSharp, Delphi, and Cocoa. Thrift is used to define data types and service interfaces using an IDL file. The compiler will then generate the code to use RCP clients to access data. The Thrift code generation engine gets the IDL file and creates client and server RPC libraries. This allows a Java programmer to transparently interface with a Python application without having to write interface code. Thrift supports Boolean, byte, 16-bit signed integer, 32-bit signed integer, 64-bit signed integer, double, string, structs, as well as list, set, and map containers. The goal of Thrift is to provide reliable communication across different programming languages.

A Hive client can be used with Java, Python, PHP, C++, and so on to access Hive tables. Additionally, functionality can be added to Hive queries with User Defined Functions (UDFs). Hive also supports unions, arrays, maps, and structs.

Data Types, Operators, and Functions

Following is a list of the primitive data types:

- Integers
- TINYINT—1-byte integer
- SMALLINT—2-byte integer
- INT—4-byte integer
- BIGINT—8-byte integer
- Boolean type
- BOOLEAN—TRUE/FALSE
- Floating point numbers
- FLOAT—Single precision
- DOUBLE—Double precision
- String type
- STRING—Sequence of characters in a specified character set

Complex types are made up of primitive and other composite data types. Complex types include Structs, Maps (key/value tuples), and Arrays (indexable lists). Hive supports relational, logical, and arithmetic operators, and built-in single row and aggregate functions. Hive keywords, operators, and functions are not case sensitive.

SHOW Commands

Show commands make it easy to get information on database objects and details on tables. The show commands have additional options not shown here. With Hive, a Schema and a Database are interchangeable.

- **SHOW DATABASES:** Display list of all databases.

- **DESCRIBE DATABASE** *dbname*: List details of a database.

- **SHOW SCHEMAS:** Display list of all databases.

- **SHOW TABLES:** Display information on tables in a database.

- **SHOW PARTITIONS page_view:** List partitions for a table.

- **DESCRIBE page_view:** List the columns and their data types.

- **DESCRIBE EXTENDED page_view:** Display detailed information on a table.

- **SHOW ROLES:** Display role information.

- **SHOW FUNCTIONS:** Display information on functions.

- **DESCRIBE FUNCTION <function_name>:** Display information for a specified function.

- **DESCRIBE FUNCTION EXTENDED <function_name>:** Detailed function info.

More on Hive Tables

Partitioned tables can add partitions when new data is loaded. Make sure that if a location is defined, it is the directory where the files are loaded. Partitions can be added, renamed, and dropped. Data can be preloaded into a separate table and then converted to a partition with the EXCHANGE option. Partitions are stored as metadata definitions. However, data can be loaded before a partition is created. An administrator can execute the ALTER TABLE with the ADD PARTITION option to create new partitions. The **MSCK REPAIR TABLE** command can be run to add metadata about partitions that do not have metadata. This command is used when the partition data exists in HDFS but not in the metastore definitions. Views can be created on tables. Indexes can be created, altered, and dropped. Indexes can be used to improve queries on specific columns to avoid full table or partition scans. Index partitioning will match the partitioning of the table. Indexes cannot be defined on views. Functions can be permanent or temporary. Temporary functions are temporal and last only for the life of the session.

Table and column names are not case sensitive. SerDe and property names are case sensitive. Comments for tables and column comments need to be in single quotes. Use the EXTERNAL keyword when you do not want to tie the table metadata definition to the data. A table defined with the EXTERNAL keyword will not delete the data with the **DROP table** command. EXTERNAL is used when the data is created before the TABLE is defined. Often the data can be used by multiple sources. An internal table (Hive managed) does not include the EXTERNAL keyword. The data will be deleted along with the table definition with an internal table definition. Hive tables can access data stored in delimited text, Sequence file (compressed), Avro (converts Avro into Hive schema and data types), RCFILE (record columnar file), ORCFile (optimized row columnar format), JSON, XML, and other formats.

- The STORED AS TEXTFILE format should be used if data is stored in plain text.

- The STORED AS SEQUENCEFILE format should be used if data needs to be compressed.

- The INPUT and OUTPUTFORMAT allow the format name to be defined as a literal.

- The STORED AS PARQUET is used for Parquet columnar storage.

- The STORED BY format is used when working with nonnative tables (HBase, Accumulo).

Hive Syntax

We're now going to take a look at Hive syntax and some sample commands to show that Hive is a very easy environment to transition to for those experienced with SQL. At the same time, the SQL tools around Hadoop are maturing significantly, and SQL is becoming a point-and-click environment similar to RDBMS environments.

A number of data types are available. The data types are getting close to being consistent with the ANSI SQL standard.

Data Types

Table column data types:

- TINYINT, SMALLINT, INT, BIGINT

- BOOLEAN

- FLOAT, DOUBLE

- STRING

- BINARY

- TIMESTAMP

- DECIMAL

- DECIMAL(precision, scale)

- CHAR, VARCHAR
- ARRAY < data_type >
- MAP < primitive_type, data_type >
- STRUCT < col_name : data_type [COMMENT col_comment], ...>
- UNIONTYPE < data_type, data_type, ... >

The following are sample row formats:

- DELIMITED [FIELDS TERMINATED BY char [ESCAPED BY char]]
    - [COLLECTION ITEMS TERMINATED BY char]
    - [MAP KEYS TERMINATED BY char] [LINES TERMINATED BY char]
    - [NULL DEFINED AS char] (Note: Only available starting with Hive 0.13)

- SERDE serde_name
    - [WITH SERDEPROPERTIES
    - (property_name=property_val, property_name=property_val, ...)]

File formats:

- SEQUENCEFILE
- TEXTFILE
- ORC, RCFILE
- INPUTFORMAT input_format_class OUTPUTFORMAT output_format_class

DDL Commands

Here is a list of HiveQL DDL statements:

- CREATE, ALTER, DROP DATABASE
- CREATE, TRUNCATE, DROP TABLE
- SCHEMA, VIEW, FUNCTION, INDEX
- DROP DATABASE/SCHEMA, TABLE, VIEW, INDEX
- TRUNCATE TABLE
- ALTER DATABASE/SCHEMA, TABLE, VIEW

- MSCK REPAIR TABLE (or ALTER TABLE RECOVER PARTITIONS)

- SHOW DATABASES/SCHEMAS, TABLES, TBLPROPERTIES, PARTITIONS, FUNCTIONS, INDEX[ES], COLUMNS, CREATE TABLE

- DESCRIBE DATABASE, table_name, view_name

Command Syntax:

Listing 6.8 provides all commands and the options to create a Hive database, table, partition, view, and index.

Listing 6.8 Syntax for the CREATE DATABASE | Schema Command

```
CREATE (DATABASE|SCHEMA) [IF NOT EXISTS] database_name
  [COMMENT database_comment]
  [LOCATION hdfs_path]
  [WITH DBPROPERTIES (property_name=property_value, ...)];
DROP (DATABASE|SCHEMA) [IF EXISTS] database_name [RESTRICT|CASCADE];
ALTER (DATABASE|SCHEMA) database_name
    SET DBPROPERTIES (property_name=property_value, ...);
CREATE [EXTERNAL] TABLE [IF NOT EXISTS] [db_name.]table_name
  [(col_name data_type [COMMENT col_comment], ...)]
  [COMMENT table_comment]
  [PARTITIONED BY (col_name data_type [COMMENT col_comment], ...)]
  [CLUSTERED BY (col_name, col_name, ...) [SORTED BY (col_name [ASC|DESC],
    ...)] INTO num_buckets BUCKETS]
  [SKEWED BY (col_name, col_name, ...) ON ([(col_value, col_value, ...),
    ...|col_value, col_value, ...])
  [
   [ROW FORMAT row_format] [STORED AS file_format]
   | STORED BY 'storage.handler.class.name' [WITH SERDEPROPERTIES (...)]
  ]
  [LOCATION hdfs_path]
  [TBLPROPERTIES (property_name=property_value, ...)]
  [AS select_statement]

CREATE [EXTERNAL] TABLE [IF NOT EXISTS] [db_name.]table_name
  LIKE existing_table_or_view_name
  [LOCATION hdfs_path]
ALTER TABLE table_name ADD [IF NOT EXISTS] PARTITION partition_spec
[LOCATION 'location1'] partition_spec [LOCATION 'location2'] ...
partition_spec:
```

```
: (partition_col = partition_col_value, partition_col = partiton_col_
  value, ...)

ALTER TABLE table_name PARTITION partition_spec RENAME TO PARTITION
  partition_spec;

ALTER TABLE table_name_1 EXCHANGE PARTITION (partition_spec) WITH TABLE
  table_name_2;

ALTER TABLE table_name PARTITION partition_spec RENAME TO PARTITION
  partition_spec;

MSCK REPAIR TABLE table_name;

ALTER TABLE table_name DROP [IF EXISTS] PARTITION partition_spec, PARTITION
  partition_spec,...

ALTER TABLE table_name DROP [IF EXISTS] PARTITION partition_spec IGNORE
  PROTECTION;

ALTER TABLE table_name ARCHIVE PARTITION partition_spec;
ALTER TABLE table_name UNARCHIVE PARTITION partition_spec;

ALTER TABLE table_name [PARTITION partitionSpec] SET FILEFORMAT file_format

ALTER TABLE table_name TOUCH [PARTITION partitionSpec];

ALTER TABLE table_name [PARTITION partition_spec] ENABLE|DISABLE NO_DROP;
ALTER TABLE table_name [PARTITION partition_spec] ENABLE|DISABLE OFFLINE;

ALTER TABLE table_name CHANGE [COLUMN] col_old_name col_new_name column_
  type [COMMENT col_comment] [FIRST|AFTER column_name]

ALTER TABLE table_name ADD|REPLACE COLUMNS (col_name data_type [COMMENT
  col_comment], ...)
```

Syntax for the CREATE VIEW command.

```
CREATE VIEW [IF NOT EXISTS] view_name [(column_name [COMMENT column_
  comment], ...) ]
[COMMENT view_comment]
[TBLPROPERTIES (property_name = property_value, ...)]
AS SELECT ...
```

```
DROP VIEW [IF EXISTS] view_name

ALTER VIEW view_name SET TBLPROPERTIES table_properties

CREATE INDEX index_name
ON TABLE base_table_name (col_name, ...)
AS index_type
[WITH DEFERRED REBUILD]
[IDXPROPERTIES (property_name=property_value, ...)]
[IN TABLE index_table_name]
[
   [ ROW FORMAT ...] STORED AS ...
   | STORED BY ...
]
[LOCATION hdfs_path]
[TBLPROPERTIES (...)]
[COMMENT "index comment"]

DROP INDEX [IF EXISTS] index_name ON table_name

ALTER INDEX index_name ON table_name [PARTITION partitionSpec] REBUILD

CREATE TEMPORARY FUNCTION function_name AS class_name

DROP TEMPORARY FUNCTION [IF EXISTS] function_name

CREATE FUNCTION [db_name.]function_name AS class_name [USING
  JAR|FILE|ARCHIVE 'file_uri' [, JAR|FILE|ARCHIVE 'file_uri'] ]

DROP FUNCTION [IF EXISTS] function_name
```

HCatalog

HCatalog is a table interface and storage management layer that is built on top of the Hive metastore. HCatalog is a component of Hive. HCatalog projects table definitions to provide a relational view of the data. HCatalog uses Hive's DDL for table management. HCatalog allows the schema definition to be extracted from Pig, Hive, Tez, MapReduce, and streaming applications. This allows an abstract table definition to be created that can be shared across different types of applications. If a table definition needs to change, it can be changed in one place versus in every application. Applications can access these table definitions and access data transparent of the underlying data storage formats. Applications can use the abstract table definition and not be concerned about the data storage format—text files, SequenceFiles, ORC files, or RCFile. HCatalog can support any format that a serializer-deserializer (SerDe) can be written in. HCatalog uses Hive's SerDe class for serialization and deserialization. Data can be stored in these tables, and these tables can reside in databases in a Hive data warehouse. Partitions and buckets can be defined on these tables. HDFS will use directories to organize the data for these table definitions. A custom format requires the serializer and deserializer to be defined with an InputFormat, OutputFormat, and SerDe definition.

An example of different types of applications that can access data in HDFS is shown in Figure 6.2.

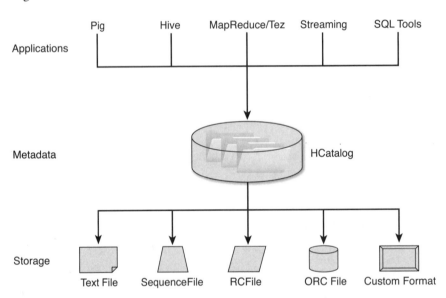

Figure 6.2   HCatalog definitions abstract schema definition from applications.

HCatalog interfaces include the Pig HCatLoader and HCatStorer interface and the MapReduce HCatInputFormat and HCatOutputFormat interface. Hive has direct access to the metadata. The Pig interfaces are used in Pig scripts to access and write data to HCatalog managed tables. Hive/HCatalog allows schema definitions to be shared across data management tools such as Teradata. Teradata's SQL-H, which runs on top of HCatalog, can use HCatalog definitions to access data in Hadoop. HCatalog also provides a notification when new data arrives. Workflow tools like Oozie can subscribe to notifications from HCatalog and will receive notifications, for example, when new partitions are added to a table.

Pig

Apache Pig is a software framework that provides the Pig Latin scripting language for analyzing data, performing ETL operations as well as iterative processing. Pig came out of Yahoo and became an Apache project. Pig can work with all kinds of data formats, therefore the name Pig, because a Pig will eat anything. Pig Latin allows programmers to be able to write programs that can read and write data from Hadoop without having to write low-level detailed Java programs. Pig and Hive can overlap in terms of the capability to process data. However, with Pig being a scripting language, Pig can perform more detailed processing of data than Hive. Pig scripts can run using the Tez or the MapReduce execution model. As of HDP 2.1, the ORC format is not supported, but that will be addressed in a future release.

Pig can be started in cluster or local mode. The default is cluster mode, which accesses data in HDFS. If started in local mode, Pig will access the local file system and run from the local host. Pig scripts can be executed with the Pig executable from the command line, interactively in the grunt shell, or embedded in Java. The PigServer class can be used to execute Pig scripts from Java applications.

Pig Latin is the language used to write Pig scripts. Pig Latin statements end in a semicolon and can span multiple lines. Statements in a Pig script are processed by an interpreter and then get added to a logical plan if they are valid. Statements in the logical plan do not execute until a **DUMP** or **STORE** command is performed. Except for LOAD and STORE, which perform I/O, Pig operators receive a relation as input and deliver another relation as output. Pig Latin scripts usually have the following layout:

1. Read data from the file system (LOAD statement).

2. Process the data.

3. Generate output (STORE writes to Filesystem and DUMP writes to STDOUT).

The Pig grunt shell can be started in cluster and local mode—a number of command options are available in the shell. Pig statements executed in the grunt shell need a semicolon at the end of the statement.

The grunt shell supports a number of file system commands on HDFS with options such as **mkdir, ls, put, mv, cat, rm, rmf**, and so on. Grunt shell commands do not need a terminating semicolon.

It is important to note that remove commands are not confirmed and are not recoverable, so be careful. There is no oops option.

Table 6.9 summarizes some of the commands available in the shell.

Table 6.9   Grunt Shell Commands

Shell Command	Description
help	Display help options.
fs	Introduce Hadoop file system shell commands.
sh	Execute OS shell command.
exec	Execute Pig script.
run	Execute Pig Scripts with access to grunt environment.
kill	Terminate Hadoop job using unique job id.
describe	Display the schema for an alias.
explain	Display the execution plan.
dump	Execute the alias and display results to STDOUT. Initiate a logical plan to be executed as a physical plan and running as a Tez or MapReduce job.
set	Set execution parameters for Pig (case sensitive). Pig shell variables can be defined and reviewed.
rmf	Removes files and directories without confirmation.
quit	Exit from the grunt shell.
store	Send results of a query to a directory in HDFS. Initiate a logical plan to be executed as a physical plan and running as a Tez or MapReduce job.
illustrate	Initiate a logical plan to be executed as a physical plan and running at Tez or MapReduce job.

Single line comments can be defined with a double dash (--). Multiline comments are defined with /* ... */.

Pig jobs running as MapReduce can be monitored using the job history web UI. The grunt shell keeps a command-line history that can be reviewed and accessed using the up and down arrows on the keyboard. The grunt shell, unlike HDFS, has the concept of a present working directory. The **cd** command can be used to change directories.

To review some samples of the Pig CLI commands, see Listing 6.9.

Listing 6.9   Sample Commands with the Pig CLI

```
$ pig
grunt> help
grunt> /* Comments in the shell
grunt> can be multi-lined */
grunt> fs -mkdir /user/hdfs
```

```
grunt> fs -ls /user
grunt> fs -put /etc/passwd   /user/hdfs/newpasswd
grunt> fs -mv  /user/hdfs/newpasswd /user/hdfs/newfile1
grunt> fs -cat /user/hdfs/newfile1
grunt> fs -rmf /user/hdfs/newfile1              -- remove is not confirmed
grunt> sh date
grunt> kill  job_0004
grunt> set debug 'on'
grunt> aliases;
grunt> set DEFAULT_PARALLEL 10
grunt> exec  mycoolscript.pig
grunt> exec -param v1=E  -param v2=SW  mycoolscript2.pig
grunt> set java.io.tmpdir /tmp2
grunt> set
grunt> a = LOAD 'provider' AS (name, status, rating, region);
grunt> run mycoolscript3.pig
grunt> quit

$ pig -x local
```

Running Pig Scripts

For a sample command of running Pic scripts in local or cluster mode, see Listing 6.10.

Listing 6.10   Running Pig Script in Cluster and Local Mode

```
$ java -cp $PIGDIR/pig.jar:$HADOOP_CONF_DIR  org.apache.pig.Main my_first_
  script.pig
$ java -Xmx256m -cp pig.jar org.apache.pig.Main -x local my_local_
  script.pig
```

Pig Latin Operators and Statements

Pig Latin contains a number of operators to use to access data, troubleshoot applications, and process data. These operators are not case sensitive. Field names, aliases, and User Defined Functions (UDF) are case sensitive. A relation is a way of storing a dataset that is the result of a Pig processing statement. An alias is the name associated with a relation and is not a variable. This is one of the reasons aliases are not predefined, nor do they have a data type associated with them. Field names and aliases must start with a letter and contain only alphanumeric or underscore characters that are part of the ASCII character set.

A number of Pig operators can be used for loading, processing, and filtering data, as shown in Table 6.10.

Table 6.10   List of Pig Operators

Operator	Description
DUMP	Display results onscreen.
LOAD	Read data.
STORE	Writes result to a file in a file system.
FILTER	To process tuples or rows of data.
DISTINCT	Eliminates duplicate tuples.
FOREACH	To process column data.
GROUP	Organizes data into a single relation.
COGROUP	To group data.
JOIN	Join data from two or more relations.
LIMIT	Limits the number of tuples in output.
DESCRIBE	Display the schema of a relation.
EXPLAIN	Display the logical or physical execution plans to compute a relation.
ILLUSTRATE	Display the step-by-step execution of statements.
ORDER	Sorts a relation.
JOIN	Performs an inner or outer join.
UNION	Merge the contents of two or more relations.
SPLIT	To separate the contents of a relation into multiple relations.
SAMPLE	Generate a random sample of data of a stated size.
STREAM	Directs dataset to a program.
FLATTEN	Unnests bags and tuples.
CROSS	Calculates the cross product of relations.

Aliases and Field Names

The alias called myalias stores the results of the dataset (relation) generated by the **LOAD** command. The fieldnames are name, status, rating, and region. Fieldnames can be used as shown in Listing 6.11. Each fieldname holds the current value of each column value that is part of the relation resultset.

Listing 6.11   Example Working with Aliases

```
$ pig
grunt> myalias = LOAD 'provider' AS (name, status, rating, region);
grunt> describe provider;
grunt>  NE_region  = FILTER myalias BY (region='NW');
grunt> rating_group = GROUP NE_region BY rating;
grunt> DUMP  rating_group;

TextLoader can be used to load text data into an alias.
$ pig
grunt> mynewalias = LOAD 'provider.txt' using TextLoader();
```

Pig Data Types

Pig supports a number of different data types. The tuple, bag, and map complex types can be nested.

Pig supports a number of data types, as shown in Table 6.11.

Table 6.11   Pig Data Types

Data Type	Description
int	32-bit signed integer
long	64-bit signed integer
float	32-bit floating point number
double	64-bit floating point number
chararray	String of Unicode characters
bytearray	Array of bytes
boolean	True or false
datetime	Date-Time value (1970-01-01T00:00:00.000+00:00)
bigdecimal	A precision integer for large whole numbers
biginteger	A precision real number for large values
tuple	An ordered set of values (Cole Trujillo,C,1,NW)

bag	An unordered set of tuples
	{
	(Cole Trujillo,C,1,SW),
	(Karen Schmitt,O,1,NE),
	(Sudhir Gupta,C,2,SE)
	}

map	Key-value pairs [name#Cole Trujillo, status#C,rating#1,region#SW]

Schemas

A schema is a list of fields that define a dataset for a relation. Names and data types can be assigned to the fields. Schemas are defined with the AS keyword or the LOAD, STREAM, and FOREACH operators. When a schema is defined, error checking is performed during the parse phase. If a schema is not defined, Pig will make its best interpretation of how to work with the data. Schemas are not required but are recommended. Schemas can be defined with the fieldname and field data type. The format is to provide the fieldname (alias), colon, and then a data type (myfield:int). If the field data type is not provided, the field data type will default to a bytearray. If a schema is not defined, the field will be unnamed, and field data type will default to a bytearray.

The following are examples of simple and complex types:

```
myalias1 = LOAD 'person1'  AS (name:chararray, active:boolean,
  mdate:datetime);
myalias2 = LOAD 'person2'  AS (name:chararray,
              T: tuple (active:boolean, status:int, rating:int),
              mdate:datetime);
myalias3 = LOAD 'person3' AS (name:chararray, ,C: bag {CC: tuple(t1:int,
  t2:int, t3:int)});
myalias4 = A = LOAD 'person4' AS (P:map []);
```

Error Handling

A Pig script will by default try to run all jobs that are part of the script. The return code can be evaluated to understand the success of the job run. The Pig log files can be reviewed to verify the success of store commands. Each store command will have an output directory path. The return codes shown in Table 6.12 will provide the result of the job run.

Table 6.12 List of Return Codes

Return Code	Description
0	All Pig statements succeeded.
1	Retrievable errors.
2	All Pig statements failed.
3	Some Pig statements may have failed.

The **-F** or **-stop_on_failure** commands can be used to have a Pig script terminate when the first job fails.

```
$ pig -F  mycoolscript.pig
$ pig -stop_on_failure  mycoolscript.pig
```

Table 6.13 shows a summary of operators, commands, and functions.

Table 6.13   Operators and Functions for Pig

Arithmetic	+, -, *, /, %, ?
Comparison	== !=, >, <, >=. <=
Null	is null, is not null
Boolean	AND, OR, NOT
File Commands	**cat, cd, copyFromLocal, copyToLocal, cp, ls, mkdir, mv, pwd, rm, rmf**
Functions	avg, min, max, sum, count, count_star, concat, size, diff, IsEmpty, tokenize

Summary

The Hadoop ecosystem supports a number of different SQL engines. SQL engines like MapReduce2 are designed for processing large batch jobs efficiently. SQL engines like Tez support batch, interactive, and real-time queries. SQL engines like Spark and Impala are designed to support interactive and real-time queries. A Hadoop cluster is likely to run multiple SQL engines to support different types of applications.

Hive is the de facto standard for running SQL workloads in Hadoop. The community is continually pushing innovation in Hive to accommodate the big data needs of organizations. We have seen what Hive does and its semantics for performing DDL and DML statements. As of today, Hive is heavily used in the analytics space. We learned that HCatalog is extremely useful in terms of managing metadata for hive database tables that can be exposed to pig, hive, applications, and BI tools. As you can see, Hive supports data analytics.

Pig, on the other hand, can get handy for ETL processing. We learned that it provides functions packed with transformation capabilities that allow for writing very short, efficient lines of codes.

## Chapter 7

Multitenancy in Hadoop

In the long history of humankind (and animal kind, too) those
who learned to collaborate and improvise most effectively have
prevailed.

—William Arthur Ward

Successful communities and organizations must be able to collaborate and share common sources in a way that protects the individuals (tenants) and the shared sources. A data lake has the same requirements. A data lake must provide a level of multitenancy that can logically isolate the tenants to protect the physical shared sources (data). This chapter introduces you to the concepts of isolating data, resources, and processes in a Hadoop cluster that is meant to enforce desired, acceptable service-level requirements across different types of applications and jobs.

There are regulations—legal and business requirements—that drive the need to separate data and processing from other organizations or groups. A shared data lake can easily become a "data maintenance" nightmare without disciplined data governance. The users in a data lake must have the isolation defined in such a way that there is confidence that the shared sources are properly protected.

Hadoop 1 had no capability to support a multitenant cluster. The open source community quickly realized that for the adoption to continue, multitenancy around Hadoop had to be solved. Hadoop 2 with YARN and HDFS 2 was designed to address the areas around multitenancy in the data lake. It's important to understand that Hadoop 2 does not just solve technical challenges. Hadoop 2 capabilities are driving all the new business application developments and innovation around the concept of a shared Hadoop cluster.

Although vendors can choose to use YARN or not, it is critical for organizations to consider the benefits of YARN because it truly makes a Hadoop cluster multitenant. It enforces Service Level Agreements (SLAs) and Quality of Service (QoS) across functional business units. Any applications with different programming paradigms and runtime characteristics can now be run in Hadoop as well. The picture for the multitenant Hadoop environment is complete with Apache Ranger facilitating the protection of the shared data by providing the centralized security management for Hadoop. Multitenancy can be implemented with either physical or logical separation of access to data. Organizations that provide services to customers who require dedicated environments can request physical segmentation of the infrastructure. On the other hand, the logical separation of infrastructure and data is a pretty common technique used to realize cost savings, but it is more challenging to implement. We focus on the logical separation of data in this chapter.

There are three key aspects to multitenancy: security, storage, and processing isolation. Multitenancy is not only specific to data storage and data processing isolation in Hadoop but to individual frameworks or services that directly impact how data is handled in general. This includes HBase, Storm, Kafka, Spark, Knox, Solr, YARN, and many more. Collaborating in a shared Hadoop environment requires careful configuration that delivers satisfactory usage of these Hadoop services and/or components as well as data. If no controls are in place to balance the Hadoop needs across different users, a lot of them will be stepping on their toes. A multitenant Hadoop environment has three levels of SLAs that are supported: batch, interactive, and real-time. A marketing group might need real-time job processing, whereas EDW would require batch and interactive processing. This kind of setup must be enforced and maintained at all times. Different business units and users must be able to have confidence that their SLAs will be met.

Securing the Access

The choices made to apply security controls to data must not limit the capability of an organization, business unit, or group to access their data easily. Security controls should not introduce any unnecessary restrictions and limitations that would render the Hadoop cluster useless. In other words, provide enough data access on a "need to know" basis.

Lowering or eliminating the risks of compromising data involves applying typical security at all levels in the enterprise—data center, network, OS, application servers, databases, and so on. Standard security best practices still apply to Hadoop, but there are several security controls specific to Hadoop to ensure users and groups are provided correct permissions to access the data intended for them to view or process.

There are a lot of things to consider for securing the services and data in a Hadoop cluster. This includes authentication, authorization, audit, and data protection. Centralized administration of security across the cluster lowers the risks of inconsistent security configurations that could potentially break security protocols.

Authentication

Authorization without authentication is not secure. It is the first step to securing access to any kind of resources. There are two levels of authentication: user-level and service-level authentication. Hadoop commonly utilizes Active Directory (AD) or an LDAP server for user authentication and Kerberos for service authentication. Both AD and LDAP are mature and heavily used by organizations to provision user accounts that need access to systems. Hadoop takes advantage of this to simplify user provisioning as Hadoop clusters grow. The security environment gets more complicated to manage as users change roles and move to different business units. The question is, how do we use this in Hadoop?

The Apache Software Foundation (ASF) community created Apache Knox for the purpose of intercepting requests to Hadoop clusters and performing checks to ensure no unauthorized users can get inside Hadoop. Knox provides perimeter security and leverages AD/LDAP to authenticate users and determine what Hadoop services they have access to. A good example is users from the BI team who need access to Hive, and that's the only service they need. Others, like Hadoop job submitters, need to have access only to either Falcon or Oozie services. Data scientists might need access to more than one service, such as HDFS, Pig, Hive, Spark, and others. All these rules can be plugged into Knox. Besides mapping what user role has access to what services, Knox also has the capability to filter based on the combination of IP address, user ID, user group, and Hadoop services.

It is even more challenging when organizations choose to deploy their Hadoop clusters in the cloud. Security architects don't typically expose their internal authentication framework to the cloud. If they do, it forces security teams to think differently. Either they must put another instance of AD/LDAP in the cloud, or they must use the cloud vendor's authentication product to authenticate users. Others are pushing Hadoop to go in the direction of OAuth and Security Assertion Markup Language (SAML). OAuth is an authorization framework that separates the authorization requests into three areas: resource owner, authorization server, and resource server. When clients want to access a protected resource, they ask for an authorization grant from the resource owner. Then that authorization grant is sent to the authorization server, where it returns an access token. The client then takes that token and sends it to the resource server and in turn sends the protected resource or data. If you're familiar with single sign-on and what it does, you've learned SAML. SAML is essentially single sign-on where a user requests access to a service from a service provider. The service provider in turn sends a request to an identity provider that eventually provides the response with its corresponding access assertions. All of this exchange of request and response happens within the web browser. There's currently no support for OAuth and SAML, but the open source community is considering adding it.

Figure 7.1 shows the best practice for securing Hadoop along with other components necessary for analytical processing. Figure 7.1 presents a step-by-step authentication process from different entry points.

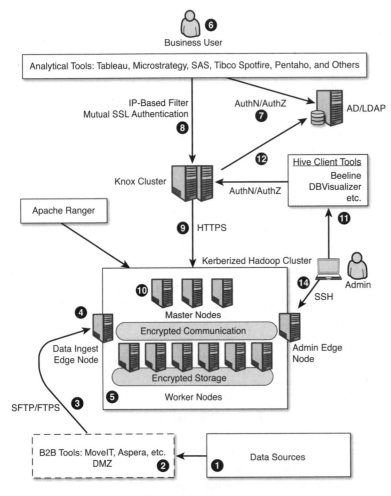

Figure 7.1   Hadoop security architecture.

Step 1.   The data source in this case comes from a different network, private or public. The data could be sensitive or nonsensitive. It could represent data that requires compliance in any of the following: HIPAA, PCI, PII, PHI, and so on. When this data gets transferred it requires secure authentication and a secure channel for the data delivery. The organization that hosts the data has the option of either pushing the data through typical B2B secure connections or allowing an external entity to pull it via an approved protocol. The process that takes place here involves exchanging firewall rules, certificates, and location of data.

Step 2.   The receiving organization has the B2B infrastructure normally within a demilitarized zone (DMZ) environment that is used to accept incoming files from an external provider. Based on firewall rules and certificates, the authentication happens between data source and DMZ. The authentication can happen in either direction. After data is received, the B2B tool either securely stores it into a NAS/SAN/NFS file system or pushes it to a different secure location. This is where security architects will spend more time determining whether it makes sense to encrypt at the file system server because storage array vendors already have some built-in encryption at the disk level. But what makes this more interesting is that data still has to travel into Hadoop. If the encryption solution is tied only to the hardware level and can't function when data leaves the storage array, this limits the capability of Hadoop to encrypt/decrypt data seamlessly. Storage appliances typically don't have an operating system (OS) installed, and it is the underlying dependency that a lot of the encryption vendors are able to work with. To resolve this limitation, the same data should be moved to a location where an encryption tool can immediately encrypt data as it lands and transparently decrypt it for Hadoop when data is needed for processing. This is where a data ingest edge node comes into play. This edge node has the necessary Hadoop client tools to perform data movement from itself to HDFS.

Step 3.   If the B2B tools have secure access to the data ingest edge node—that is, FTPS, SFTP, SCP, where it can be authenticated—then it can move the data from the DMZ to an edge node. A security conscious organization will not like this approach because a DMZ-bound tool is now going into a segmented network that is intended only for internal use. So the immediate thought will be to instead have the data ingest edge node use certificate-based authentication with DMZ B2B tools and then move the data to itself. After data lands in the edge node, it is encrypted immediately. How does this happen?

Let's take, for example, Vormetric. Vormetric has an agent that can be installed on the edge node and all nodes in the cluster. These agents have the policy for encrypting data that is running all the time. All Hadoop components above the OS work with the encryption agent transparently. The agent waits for data to come and immediately encrypts it when it gets stored on the disk. So before any data lands anywhere in the Hadoop cluster, all nodes have the encryption agents. At this point, data ingest edge node is now ready for Hadoop clients to push the files from edge node to HDFS.

Step 4.   A Flume Hadoop client can be used to pull all the files from an edge node and store the data in HDFS. But before that happens, Flume must be authenticated with Kerberos. Why Kerberos? It is better to authenticate with Kerberos for all machine service accounts; it performs better and provides stronger authentication because passwords are not sent over the wire at all. User accounts are typically provisioned through AD or LDAP. Flume must use wire encryption from the edge node to the NameNode/DataNode(s) to protect data in transit. The highest threat of compromising sensitive data happens internally to organizations. So all links between the source of the data to Hadoop and to integrated tools must be encrypted to provide an added layer of protection on top of encrypted data at rest.

Step 5.   After data lands in HDFS, it is encrypted. All access to HDFS requires authentication via Kerberos or AD/LDAP. If the cluster was deployed in the cloud and is utilizing cloud vendor-specific storage such as S3, Binary Large Object (BLOB) storage, and the like, there's more work to do because a lot of the encryption vendor's software does not normally work with these kinds of cloud storage. Cloud vendors do provide their own encryption of data at rest, and it's up to the organization to decide how to integrate that with their Hadoop deployment to ensure their data is protected.

Step 6.   Users at this stage are typically business users who want to access data from Hadoop, more specifically Hive, and run their analytical reports. They typically use tools that are ODBC or JDBC compliant, such as Tableau, Datameer, Microstrategy, and SAS. These tools must integrate with AD/LDAP and Knox for authentication purposes.

Step 7.   Business users are first authenticated via AD/LDAP before they can do anything with their analytical tools. If the authentication scheme is based on SSO, like SAML, OAuth2, or SiteMinder, it poses some challenges to Knox because Knox doesn't fully support these protocols yet. The only SSO support Knox has is working with user identity in the request header provided by SiteMinder.

Step 8.   When users start sending queries to Hive, all the requests are intercepted by Knox. The integration between Knox and BI Tools is protected via SSL. The question at this point is, will the user be authenticated via AD/LDAP the next time the user sends query requests? It is definitely possible because Knox supports AD/LDAP for authentication, but the downside is that AD/LDAP will be overloaded with authentication requests for every single query to Hadoop. So to alleviate this high volume of authentication, Knox can be turned on to provide a user session through cookies. This enables users to keep their JSESSIONID, and they don't have to reauthenticate with Knox until the session ends. This makes Knox stateful and could have implications on performance. To get the balance of the two authentication approaches, a mutual SSL authentication can be enforced between the BI Tool and Knox so that users will never have to authenticate again. User identity can be passed down to Knox instead and cascaded to Hive for authorization and auditing purposes. It makes the authentication process a lot simpler. This authentication with Knox is happening at the application level because the user is already authenticated and a trust is already established between the BI Tool and the user. Knox supports authentication via username and password, but it is an inconvenience to users to provide these credentials every time they submit a request to Hadoop.

Step 9.   Suppose a Hive query request is sent over to Hadoop and is received by Knox; Knox knows that the request is for Hive query processing. Before the requests go to Hive, Knox is required to authenticate them with Kerberos. After the Hive query requests are authenticated, they are handed off to the HiveServer2 for processing.

Step 10.   At this point, the user identity from the request is available for checking permission levels on the requested database, tables, and columns based on the username. Apache Ranger maps the username to the Hive database policy to determine the access that the user has. When the query runs, proper permissions are applied for the requesting user and all events tied to the user and query are recorded for auditing purposes. You might ask, why kerberize the Hadoop cluster? We don't want any impersonation happening within the cluster. All services or components within Hadoop must be authenticated, and Kerberos is very lightweight and does not impact the job performance. Kerberos has also been around a long time and is trusted by infrastructure teams. Kerberos tickets used for authentication are stored in cache and have a lifetime that is long enough to prevent the need to reauthenticate every time a service request is received. It is common for a Kerberos ticket to have a lifetime of eight hours, which normally maps to the user's working hours.

Step 11.   This is a different point of access to Hadoop and has a different purpose. Administrators typically use tools that are meant for investigation or troubleshooting in the cluster. Tools like Beeline, DBVisualizer, and the like still need to be authenticated via Knox. This throws a different light on authentication versus business users because the admins have low frequency access to the cluster, and it is fine to tie the Hadoop administrator authentication to AD/LDAP.

Step 12.   When the admin opens up a connection from Beeline, the JDBC/ODBC driver connects to Knox over HTTP and must be authenticated. Knox captures the user account information, such as username and password. Then it sends it off to AD/LDAP for authentication. After the user is authenticated, the request is granted access to Hive, and it follows the same process at this point as in steps 9 and 10.

Step 13.   Administrators can also access the Hadoop cluster nodes via SSH, and their authentication will be at the POSIX level. It is assumed at this point that the trust between the users and their machines has been established via AD/LDAP authentication before an SSH request can be issued.

This description provides an overview of how all the pieces work when it comes to authentication. You'll notice that there are two edge nodes, for data ingestion and for administration. This is an important best practice to avoid combining the access of the administrator with the business data.

Auditing

Knowing that organizations will be storing massive amounts of data of varying formats and types in Hadoop, it makes sense to have some level of governance. It is typically required to have audit logging for three reasons: compliance, security, and diagnostics. Auditors want to have full traceability on what's happening with business data in and out of Hadoop. Logging events that Hadoop services generate is the first step, but integrating and correlating events across the entire Hadoop software stack is the ultimate goal. Hadoop already logs all events and the Apache Software Foundation (ASF) community had made big progress in trying to consolidate these events into one place. At this point, Apache Falcon logs all events that relate to data pipelining and data processing in Hadoop. Falcon has the capability to enrich data pipelines with metadata that describes the location of data, the job that read the data, the user or group that owns the data, the permission levels, and much more. The open source community is also actively developing graphical representations of the data lineage within Falcon. Apache Ranger is another place where authentication attempts, security policy names, user/groups, timestamps of data access, and resources used are recorded in granularity.

Organizations that have implemented Security Information and Event Management (SIEM) systems like Splunk SIEM can be integrated with Hadoop to capture audit information in one place and also derive security analytics information for auditors and security experts to consume.

Authorization

ACLs provide the basic foundation of a multitenant environment. ACLs define who has access to what data, files, objects, or resources and what operation they can perform. ACLs protect against any unauthorized access to resources and services in Hadoop and help enforce users' access to data on a "need to know" basis. The ACL is essential to all the following components of your environment: the operating system, the web and system applications, databases, networks, and Hadoop. When a request is made to a resource, Hadoop checks the ACL definitions and decides whether the requester is permitted to access the data and if the requested operation is authorized. Apache Ranger enforces this ACL-based security in Hadoop where an administrator can easily manage access to both nonsensitive and sensitive data across different Hadoop components. Ranger simplifies the ACL policy life cycle by providing a centralized administration of authorizing access to HDFS, Hive, and HBase data. Ranger provides consistent fine-grained controls and integrates with Active Directory and LDAP.

The expectation is that the next release of Ranger will include Knox and Storm ACL policy definitions and that the open source community will not stop there but will continually move all ACL-security related configurations of Hadoop services into Ranger. It is possible in the future that Ranger agents, responsible for enforcing ACL rules in Hadoop components, will be made extensible where custom applications that require interaction with Hadoop services in the enterprise can leverage Ranger through an agent registration interface. In short, Ranger will eventually be the overarching piece in the Hadoop ecosystem that will enforce authorization on all services and data in Hadoop.

Next we'll discuss the architecture of Ranger, which is shown in Figure 7.2, and how it enforces these fine-grained controls to Hadoop.

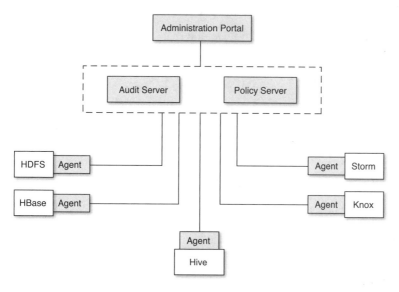

Figure 7.2 Apache Ranger architecture.

In Figure 7.2, Ranger has four components: Admin Portal, Audit, Policy, and Agent. All these components are key to managing the access to all the data stored or being processed in HDFS, HBase, Hive, Storm, and Knox. One instance of Ranger can manage the security policy definition and enforcement across multiple clusters onsite or offsite.

The Admin Portal is a web-based UI that enables a security admin to easily and efficiently manage users and groups and their permissions for resources they are allowed to read, write, or execute.

A policy enables an admin to identify a resource path (in HDFS /datalake/customer/financial) that needs to be secured. One or more groups and one or more users are assigned to have access to this resource and permissions could be one or more of the following: Read, Write, Execute. These permissions can be configured to be recursive relative to the resource. With Hive, the resource is the database, its tables, and columns where similar assignment of users and groups are made using one or more of the following permissions: Select, Update, Create, Drop, Alter, Index, and Lock. The resources that can be protected in HBase are tables, its column families, and columns where users and groups are mapped to one or more of the Read, Write, and Create permissions.

Auditing enables an admin to verify whether access controls and permissions are being enforced. Auditing provides information around what resources are being accessed by users at what time and whether they were successful in processing the resource. A user or group who's been denied access to resources multiple times could be an indication that they have a need to access the data, and further examination of their current permissions can be made. It could also indicate an anomaly that needs to be investigated.

The agent shown in Figure 7.2 is a lightweight Java daemon that is embedded into a Hadoop component like HDFS, Hive, HBase, Storm, and the like that acts as an authorization provider to enforce security policies as defined from the policy server. These policies stay in memory, but further plans to store policies in HDFS or locally are under way. These agents are decoupled from the audit and policy servers, so if either or both audit and policy servers go down, the agents are still running and enforcing Hadoop security rules.

Data Protection

Data protection comes in two flavors: data in transit encryption and data at rest encryption. Sensitive data that flows in and out of Hadoop needs to be encrypted. Organizations that demand encryption are typically in the health care and financial space. For decades, encryption has been a proven practice that prevents sensitive data from getting exposed. Man-in-the-middle attacks, where an intruder is sniffing data from a network, are prevented when sensitive data that flows in and out of Hadoop is going through an encrypted network channel. Insider attack damage can be minimized by ensuring that sensitive data in Hadoop is encrypted as it is stored.

Data in Transit Encryption, a.k.a. Wire Encryption

Intermediary Hadoop components receive data before it lands into HDFS. These are typically the data ingestion tools. Data access tools need to use an encrypted channel when presenting processed data to business users. In the previous chapter, we discussed different ingestion tools like Sqoop, Flume, WebHDFS, WebHcat, and Kafka. Each has its own configurations for wire encryption, and we discuss those separately. The data access tools that present processed data to users have better, consistent protection because Apache Knox supports SSL over HTTP, and most, if not all, of the services in Hadoop have REST APIs that can be protected over this encryption protocol.

Wire Encryption for Flume

Flume has sources, channels, and sinks, which all support wire encryption. This section identifies the properties that would enable wire encryption for each.

Avro Source has a property called ssl for encryption purposes. When this property is set to true, it also requires the keystore and keystore-password properties. An option to set the Java keystore is also available by specifying the property keystore-type and possible values could be JKS or PKCS12. Avro Sink also has an ssl property that can be set. The following properties can be set along with ssl: truststore, truststore-password, truststore-type, and trust-all-certs. Do not use the latter in production because SSL server certificates of Avro Sources are not validated. There are other sources and sinks, but only Avro supports wire encryption at this time.

Flume supports multiple channels, but only File Channel has the option for wire encryption. The following properties should be used:

- **encryption.activeKey:** Key used to encrypt data

- **encryption.cipherProvider:** Cipher provider type

- **encryption.keyProvider:** Key provider type

- **encryption.keyProvider.keyStoreFile:** Keystore file path

- **encrpytion.keyProvider.keyStorePasswordFile:** Path to keystore password file

- **encryption.keyProvider.keys:** List of all keys

- **encyption.keyProvider.keys.*.passwordFile:** Path to optional key to password file

Wire Encryption for WebHDFS

HDFS has a wrapper for HTTP access called WebHDFS. It can be set up to use HTTP over SLL for either one-way or two-way encryption. For one-way encryption, only the SSL client validates to the server, whereas two-way encryption requires that both the client and the server identify each other. This can be challenging to set up and incurs more performance overhead. The focus of this section will be on one-way SSL encryption setup.

The following properties must be set to enable one-way SSL encryption:

- hadoop.ssl.require.client.cert=false
- hadoop.ssl.hostname.verifier=DEFAULT
- hadoop.ssl.keystores.factory.class=org.apache.hadoop.security.ssl.FileBasedKeyStoresFactor
- hadoop.ssl.server.conf=ssl-server.xml
- hadoop.ssl.client.conf=ssl-client.xml

For WebHDFS to pick up this SSL configuration, you must make the following changes in hdfs-site.xml file. If you are using Ambari, you should go to the **HDFS service**, **Config** tab and make the following changes:

- dfs.http.policy=HTTPS_ONLY
- dfs.client.https.need-auth=true (optional for mutual client/server certificate validation)
- dfs.datanode.https.address=$hostname:50475
- dfs.namenode.https-address=$hostname:50470

The Hadoop SSL Keystore Factory must have an ssl-server.xml file configuration. Hadoop SSL Keystore Factory manages the SSL keys and certificates that the Hadoop core services use to communicate with other services in the Hadoop cluster over the HTTP protocol. With HDP, there's an ssl-server.xml configuration example that you can copy and paste. It can be found in /usr/hdp/2.2.0.0-1084/etc/hadoop/conf.empty/ ssl-server.xml.example. The path mentioned will change when new HDP releases are out. Copy it and rename it ssl-server.xml; then make the changes shown in Listing 7.1.

Listing 7.1 Hadoop SSL Parameter Settings

```
<property>
<name>ssl.server.truststore.location</name>
<value>/etc/security/serverKeys/truststore.jks</value>
<description>Truststore to be used by NN and DN. Must be specified.
</description>
</property>
```

```
<property>
<name>ssl.server.truststore.password</name>
<value>your_password_here</value>
<description>Optional. Default value is "".
</description>
</property>

<property>
<name>ssl.server.truststore.type</name>
<value>jks</value>
<description>Optional. The keystore file format, default value is "jks".
</description>
</property>

<property>
<name>ssl.server.truststore.reload.interval</name>
<value>10000</value>
<description>Truststore reload check interval, in milliseconds.
Default value is 10000 (10 seconds).
</description>
</property>

<property>
<name>ssl.server.keystore.location</name>
<value>/etc/security/serverKeys/keystore.jks</value>
<description>Keystore to be used by NN and DN. Must be specified.
</description>
</property>

<property>
<name>ssl.server.keystore.password</name>
<value>your_password_here</value>
<description>Must be specified.
</description>
</property>

<property>
<name>ssl.server.keystore.keypassword</name>
<value>your_password_here</value>
```

```
<description>Must be specified.
</description>
</property>

<property>
<name>ssl.server.keystore.type</name>
<value>jks</value>
<description>Optional. The keystore file format, default value is "jks".
</description>
</property>
```

Now you'll make some changes to the client properties. Copy the /usr/hdp/2.2.0.0-1084/ etc/hadoop/conf.empty/ssl-client.xml.example and rename it to ssl-client.xml; then make the following property changes:

```
ssl.client.truststore.location=/etc/security/clientKeys/all.jks
ssl.client.truststore.password=clientTrustStorePassword
ssl.client.truststore.type=jks
```

After making all the file changes, copy them to all the nodes in the cluster. You must restart all the Hadoop services afterward so the changes take effect. You can do this in Ambari or via the command line.

Wire Encryption for Knox

Knox is the perimeter security for Hadoop. There is some confusion about the differences between Knox and a firewall. A firewall can apply rules based on what ports and IPs are allowed to communicate with Hadoop, whereas Knox exposes only one endpoint and authenticates all requests via AD/LDAP and based on the user's permissions. The user's permissions can allow access to one or more Hadoop service. For example, for BI users, the Hadoop services they have access to might be only Hive. Others might have access to Oozie to submit a job. A sample integration is shown in Figure 7.3. Knox is meant to secure business user access to the Hadoop cluster. Knox is geared toward users who are going to use an analytics tool to query data from Hive, for example. The protocol used by this tool will be JDBC/ODBC over SSL to ensure that the link between business users and Hadoop is encrypted. Queries from Knox to Hadoop also use the SSL protocol to maintain the same security. A typical question that comes up with Knox is, does it scale? It's good to have a holistic security model for Hadoop, but you need to make your decisions carefully so that Hadoop performance doesn't take a big hit. Knox doesn't ingest data but rather receives query requests and pushes them down to Hadoop, then streams the query resultsets back to the analytics tool. It's a CPU-bound process. It is recommended that you have at least two Knox instances in a production environment for high availability and a load balancer to front them in a round-robin fashion. Knox, like other areas of Hadoop, can be virtualized.

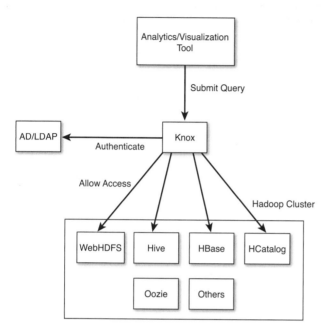

Figure 7.3   Knox integration architecture.

There are concerns about the business user being authenticated twice or more. The analytics tool authenticates the business user once, and when the request goes to Knox, the same authentication is applied again for the same user. If users submit a lot of requests to Hadoop, their requests always get routed to AD/LDAP. To alleviate the load on AD/LDAP, Knox and the analytics tool can be set up to have mutual SSL authentication. At this point, the username or the group name is passed straight to Hadoop. Based on their permissions, Knox grants access to the services, and Apache Ranger uses the user identity to provide access to the requested data.

Knox supports SiteMinder and IBM Tivoli Access Manager for Federation/SSO authentication. The out-of-box support for Federation/SSO authentication is a simple process that inspects HTTP headers to extract the username and/or group name for the authenticated user. That information then gets passed down to Knox and then down to Hadoop services for the purposes of keeping track of the user activity. This is useful when auditing requirements are needed.

There is also wire encryption support for Remote Procedure Call (RPC) and Data Transfer Protocol (DTP) that are being used by the master and worker nodes. This is to ensure that data traveling back and forth within the cluster is running across an encrypted channel. Hortonworks has detailed documentation that discusses how to set this up; go to docs.hortonworks.com and choose the latest release documentation and look for information on wire encryption. Table 7.1 shows at high level the different Hadoop protocols that are supported for encryption.

Table 7.1   Data in Motion Encryption Matrix

Communication Protocol	Communication Point	Supported Encryption
TCP/IP	Data transfer that happens between client to Hadoop cluster and intracluster communication	Encrypted Data Transfer Protocol and SASL
REST	WebHDFS and Knox	REST over SSL Knox over SSL SPNEGO—framework that extends Kerberos to support web applications
JDBC/ODBC	HiveServer2	SSL
RPC	Hadoop Client to cluster or intracluster	SASL
HTTP	NameNode and RM	HTTPS
	MapReduce Shuffle	Encrypted MapReduce Shuffle

Data at Rest Encryption

Government agencies and industries such as finance and health care are pushing the requirements for securing sensitive data in Hadoop. When organizations adopt the data lake implementation model of Hadoop, it is likely that sensitive data will be stored. Sensitive data could mean data deemed sensitive by compliance standards such as PCI, HIPAA, PII, or data that is outside the scope of compliance standards but treated as sensitive by business. Depending on how organizations interpret the approach to encrypting data, solutions could range from using hardware, volume, OS, and application encryption levels. Business must understand and accept trade-offs. For example, is performance a critical requirement while encrypting data? Performance degrades as the encryption goes from cell to field to table/file, database/folder, to volume to hardware. If performance is not an issue, then it makes things a lot simpler but at a cost. Why? Because HDFS doesn't have a notion of node labeling, and even if it has storage preferences, it doesn't guarantee that sensitive data will be stored on the preferred storage type all the time. Node labeling is essentially a way to tag one or more machines in the cluster and make Hadoop clients aware that the labeled machines are for a specific purpose that these clients can use. This means that the entire cluster must be encrypted, rather than just sections of it. This could get expensive, even if the amount of sensitive data stored in a cluster is 1% of the total data. To balance the cost and performance, a lot of organizations are preferring to use something flexible where files and or attributes can be encrypted.

Multiple vendors provide data encryption at rest in Hadoop, such as Voltage, Protegrity, DataGuise, and Vormetric. What we see in the field is that organizations want to reuse their existing encryption tools with Hadoop. This becomes easy when one of the tools they use is among the four mentioned. Otherwise, either they buy from one of these vendors or work with Hadoop vendors to certify their existing encryption tool and make sure that encryption/decryption of data is seamless. Depending on the demand for that current tool and how quickly the Hadoop vendor certifies, the certification process can take from 60 to 120 days.

There are no production-ready native Hadoop encryption capabilities at this time, but the open source community has released a technical preview of HDFS Transparent Data Encryption (TDE). Hortonworks has released a blog that you can find at www.hortonworks.com/kb/hdfs-transparent-data-encryption. The technical preview shows how to use TDE along with Key Management System (KMS). Organizations that started with Hadoop prior to TDE have also used an open source encryption tool called LUKS that encrypts at the volume level.

Next, we'll map different encryption levels across the entire stack, as shown in Figure 7.4.

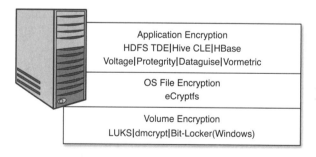

Figure 7.4 Encryption levels for Hadoop.

The question is, when does it make sense to use volume encryption over the others? Typically, when all data is considered to be sensitive, a volume encryption makes more sense. OS file encryption becomes relevant when there's a mix of sensitive and nonsensitive files that are being stored. As mentioned earlier, the cost becomes more significant as the encryption solution becomes more of a blanket approach versus "pick and encrypt."

Application encryption follows the latter option, where organizations have more granular policies for encrypting sensitive data. For example, for HDFS, identify the zone, which is a directory; then when data gets dropped there, it is automatically encrypted. For Hive, the database, tables, or column can be selectively encrypted. The benefit is a balance of cost and performance.

Next, we discuss the components that make up TDE. Figure 7.5 shows the different parts of HDFS TDE along with some keywords that are critical to remember. Table 7.2 shows the acronym definitions used in the diagram.

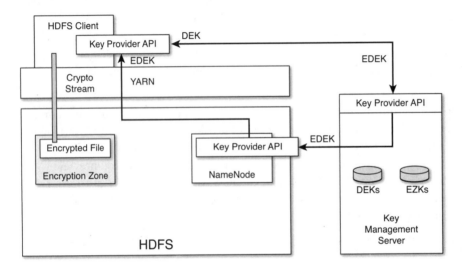

Figure 7.5   HDFS TDE architecture.

Table 7.2   HDFS TDE Acronyms

Acronym	Description
EZ	Encryption Zone, which is one (or more) HDFS directory.
EZK	Encryption Zone Key: The master key for a specific zone.
DEK	Data Encryption Key: A unique key associated with each file. EZ key used to generate DEK. Data Encryption Key (DEK) is a key that is specific to a file. All files within an EZ get their own DEK. The DEK key is basically generated from the EZ key.
EDEK	Encrypted Data Encryption Key (EDEK): A necessity so that the keys are not exposed. This minimizes the risk of security breaches if the keys are compromised.

Encryption Zone (EZ) is where all files and directories are encrypted. A Hadoop or security administrator normally defines the policies on EZ and how that maps to ownership and permissions of the encrypted data. Either a legal or a specific compliance business unit that is familiar with local and federal regulations requirements should be working with the security administrator so that the correct policies are properly enforced. An encryption key is assigned to an EZ that serves as the master key. So there will be one master key per EZ and one EZ per HDFS directory.

The KMS sole purpose is to store all encryption keys and expose a REST interface when these keys need to be used. You might ask, what if I already have an existing KMS? HDFS TDE is designed to leverage any enterprise KMS, but HDFS TDE KMS is not mature enough yet and organizations should probably use their own enterprise-ready KMS that has gone through a rigorous security review, validation, and approval process. This existing KMS system is something that is embedded into their enterprise, and their security operation team does not have access to multiple KMS systems. The open source community built an open source KMS system for the purpose of providing something that can be immediately used but with some rough edges. As it matures, it may become an option for others.

The Key Provider API allows HDFS NameNode and HDFS Client to communicate with the KMS so that data can be encrypted and decrypted seamlessly.

For more information about HDFS TDE configuration, you can go to hadoop.apache.org; go to the latest documentation release and search for "Transparent Encryption" under HDFS.

Isolating the Data

Acquisitions, business rules, or weak data governance normally brings about the existence of siloed database systems. If nobody wants to take ownership of the siloed system, it makes it even harder to analyze data. A data lake in Hadoop breaks down these siloes and enables an organization to pool all its data into one single place for data analysis, regardless of format and size. If careful governance is not implemented in the data lake, data can quickly become messy, especially with hundreds or thousands of TBs or PBs of data. Defining the storage quota, access controls, and archiving policy are key ingredients for ensuring that data is isolated from others.

Enforce HDFS Space and Name Quota

In HDFS, name and space quotas are available to control the amount of data stored for each directory or file. A name quota is a hard limit on the number of files and directories allowed for its parent directory. If a quota is exceeded, the file or directory creation process will fail. A newly created directory that doesn't belong to a quota-constrained directory does not have the associated quota. If this new directory was assigned a quota of one, it will remain empty. The largest quota for a directory or file is Long.Max_Value.

Space quota, on the other hand, is the hard limit on the number of bytes used by files defined at its parent directory. When a directory that is under its quota is renamed, the quota is still enforced. Any operation that would result in a quota violation will fail. This could either be block allocations, increasing the replica count, or renaming a directory where it would exceed the quota. If the quota is set to zero, file or directory creation succeeds, but no blocks are added to the new file or directory. The size of the quota set always includes the block replication.

Both name and space quotas are persistent with fsimage. When quotas are set or removed, it creates journal entry.

In the example in Figure 7.6, four directories are allocated in HDFS. Each directory will be configured to have its own quota. You must identify how much storage each directory can accommodate. Storage space is normally influenced by historical data capture and projected annual data growth for existing datasets and/or new sources of data. Typically, a space quota makes more sense because keeping track of the number of files and directories is cumbersome. It is easier to make projections on storage allocation requirements in Hadoop if you're using space quota. But we will show how both types of quota are set in HDFS.

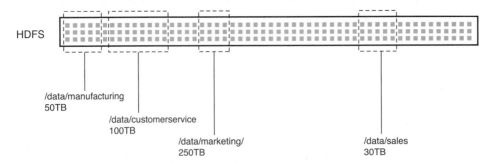

Figure 7.6   HDFS space quota.

In Figure 7.6, there are four directories, and each has its own space quota requirements in TB. Let's start with space quota first. Setting the quota requires the hdfs super user account. The following commands show how to set quotas for all directories:

```
$ hdfs dfsadmin -setSpaceQuota 50t /data/manufacturing
$ hdfs dfsadmin -setSpaceQuota 100t /data/customerservice
$ hdfs dfsadmin -setSpaceQuota 250t /data/marketing
$ hdfs dfsadmin -setSpaceQuota 30t /data/sales
```

The suffix t on the quota limit is terabyte. You can use g for gigabytes. If there's no prefix, it defaults to bytes. When checking to see whether the quota was enforced, you can run the following command, which displays the quota information all at once for all the directories:

```
$ hadoop fs -count -q /data/manufacturing /data/customerservice
  /data/marketing /data/sales
```

There are a total of eight columns as a result of executing this command. Here are the descriptions of each column:

> Column 1—Name quota size allocated
>
> Column 2—Remaining name quota size
>
> Column 3—Space quota size allocated
>
> Column 4—Remaining space quota size
>
> Column 5—Directory count
>
> Column 6—File count
>
> Column 7—Content size in bytes
>
> Column 8—File/directory name

The following tabular data is the output from running the **hdfs quota** command with the -count option that shows whether the storage quota was enforced. For example, the first line shows that the current quota limit for the directory /data/manufacturing is 50TB.

```
none   inf   54975581388800   54975581388800   2 0 0 /data/manufacturing
none   inf 109951162777600  109951162777600   1 0 0 /data/customerservice
none   inf 274877906944000  274877906944000   1 0 0 /data/marketing
none   inf  32985348833280   32985348833280   1 0 0 /data/sales
```

Notice that the output of the quota query includes both space and name quota details. It is also possible that a mixture of name and space quotas exist. The following command creates a subdirectory under /data/manufacturing:

```
$ hadoop fs -mkdir /data/manufacturing/sensor
```

We know that /data/manufacturing is using a space quota. Now let's make the sensor folder use a name quota and set it to 1000:

```
$ hdfs dfsadmin -setQuota 1000 /data/manufacturing/sensor
```

Let's check and see the quota count for each of the specified directories:

```
$ hadoop fs -count -q /data/manufacturing /data/customerservice /data/
  marketing /data/sales /data/manufacturing/sensor
```

```
none   inf   54975581388800   54975581388800   2 0 0 /data/manufacturing
none   inf  109951162777600  109951162777600   1 0 0 /data/customerservice
none   inf  274877906944000  274877906944000   1 0 0 /data/marketing
none   inf   32985348833280   32985348833280   1 0 0 /data/sales
1000   999      none                      inf   1 0 0 /data/manufacturing/sensor
```

The result shows the name quota size allocated and remaining name quota size for /data/manufacturing/sensor, which is 1,000 and 999 directories/files, respectively.

Quota can change and even be removed. Running the same command for name and space quota to set the quota with a new number of files/directories or bytes respectively will work. Clearing or removing the quota is very straightforward. To clear or remove the name quota, run the following command:

```
$ hdfs dfsadmin -clrQuota /data/manufacturing/sensor
```

That will remove the quota for the sensor directory only. When running the report quota, the following will result:

```
$ hadoop fs -count -q /data/manufacturing/sensor
none   inf   none   inf   1   0    0 /data/manufacturing/sensor
```

Here's the command for clearing space quota:

```
$ hdfs dfsadmin -clrSpaceQuota /data/manufacturing
none   inf   none   inf   2   0    0 /data/manufacturing
```

It will remove the quota set for the manufacturing directory. A single command can be performed to remove multiple quotas all at once just by appending the target directories at the end of the command.

NameNode Federation

NameNode Federation is available in Hadoop 2, and it enables a single Hadoop cluster to have several HDFS "block pools," where each pool belongs to its own unique namespace. This has no implication on security, but the main goal is to give each group, business unit, organization, or entity the capability to have a dedicated HDFS namespace. The namespace then becomes dedicated for a specific business unit or group. Instead of enforcing quotas where the namespace is shared across all users and processes, NameNode Federation enforces namespace isolation. A Hadoop cluster that doesn't use NameNode Federation has only one namespace, as shown in Figure 7.7.

Figure 7.7   Hadoop without NameNode Federation.

With NameNode Federation, you can have more than one namespace, as shown in Figure 7.8. You can have as many NameNode servers as you want, as long as it provides value to the business. You'll notice there are many block pools in the cluster where each of them belongs to its own respective namespace. This block pool will then be used by a business unit dedicated to them to store any data. It is still recommended to enforce name and space quotas for each namespace. This kind of setup can also be used to separate development, test, and production environments if the cluster is large enough to warrant it.

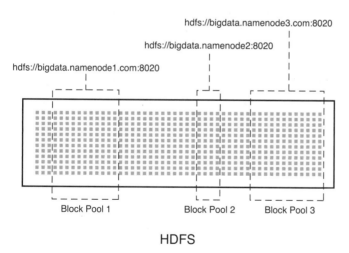

Figure 7.8   Hadoop with NameNode Federation.

On the contrary, most of the organizations prefer having different clusters for different environments. It follows the typical software environment legacy setup, which is particularly important for regulated industries where a validated environment setup is mandatory.

When NameNode Federation is configured and set up in the cluster, a new ClusterID is autogenerated that will be used to identify all the nodes in the cluster. This is the ID that will be used to format the other NameNodes in the cluster. A Cluster Web Console is available to monitor the federated NameNodes.

Access Controls

Hadoop data components such as HDFS, Hive, and HBase have their own native security controls, but these native security controls are not sufficient for an enterprise operating in an environment where their data is governed by federal mandates and regulations. Apache Ranger will fill in the gaps and make a strong, centralized way to manage data security across all components of Hadoop. Ranger has a user-friendly UI that will allow for Create, Update, Delete (CRUD) operations on security policies. Ranger in HDP 2.2 now exposes a REST API to define and manage security policies that can be integrated with other applications or run on a command-line interface like curl.

HDFS, Hive, and HBase have their own metadata repository for configuring policies. Each metadata repository maps to one cluster. If an enterprise has four clusters, such as Dev, Test, Prod, and DR, there will be four repositories for each Hadoop component. For instance, HDFS will have hadoopdev, hadooptest, hadoopprod, and hadoopdr policy repositories. Figure 7.9 shows a policy repository for HDFS, HBase, and Hive, which indicates that only one cluster is available for configuration. Remember that Ranger can configure policies for as many clusters as are available across the data centers.

Figure 7.9   Ranger policy repository.

Figure 7.10 shows a sample repository of policies for HDFS. The resource path represents the hdfs directory or data that needs to be controlled. For instance, the path /datalake/customer1/sales is made available only for the analytics group. Any user belonging to this group will have access to this path. Because it's recursive, any subdirectories created will be visible to the same group.

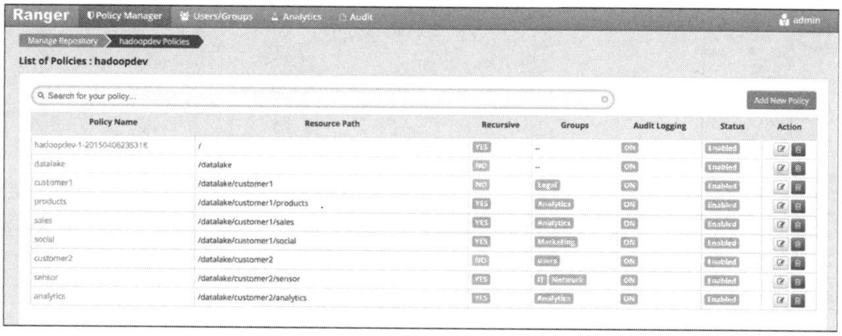

Figure 7.10   HDFS defined policies.

If you click on the row where /datalake/customer1/sales is located, you will see the permissions provided for the analytics group on this resource, as shown in Figure 7.11. This provides information about the following factors:

- Who created the policy

- At what time the policy was created

- What group has access to which resources

- What permissions are configured for the group

The Ranger administrator can create policies where one resource can be accessed by multiple groups and/or users with varying permissions. Delegated administration for each policy repository is also possible. This makes sense for an organization with large groups of users who will be utilizing a shared service Hadoop cluster.

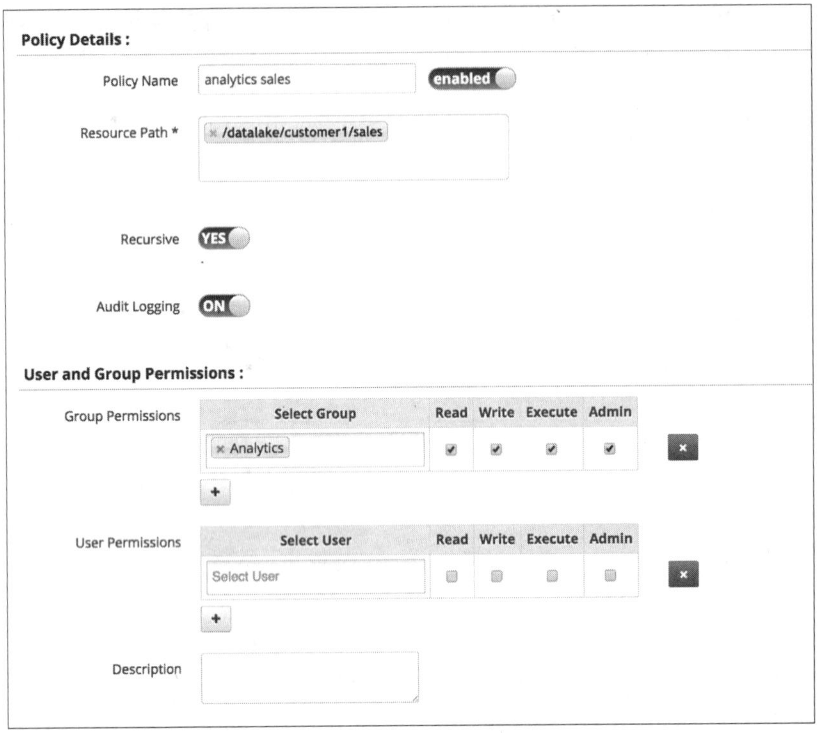

Figure 7.11   HDFS data policy details.

For Hive, the policies look like the one in Figure 7.12. The very first policy where the Database Name is * means that logging is on for all tables and columns. There's no negative policy in Ranger. Negative policy basically means one cannot configure to not allow access to a specific resource in HDFS. Only users and groups that are called out in the policy will have access and permissions to databases, tables, and columns. You'll notice that you can also apply access controls to UDFs.

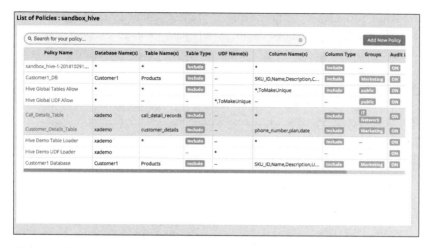

Figure 7.12   Hive defined policies.

Clicking the second row that has the Customer1 database and Product table shows the policy information in Figure 7.13. There's one table with five columns for the Marketing group to perform operations on, such as selecting, updating, alerting, indexing data, and many more. You have the option of configuring inclusion or exclusion of the columns. The configuration in Figure 7.13 is an inclusion configuration.

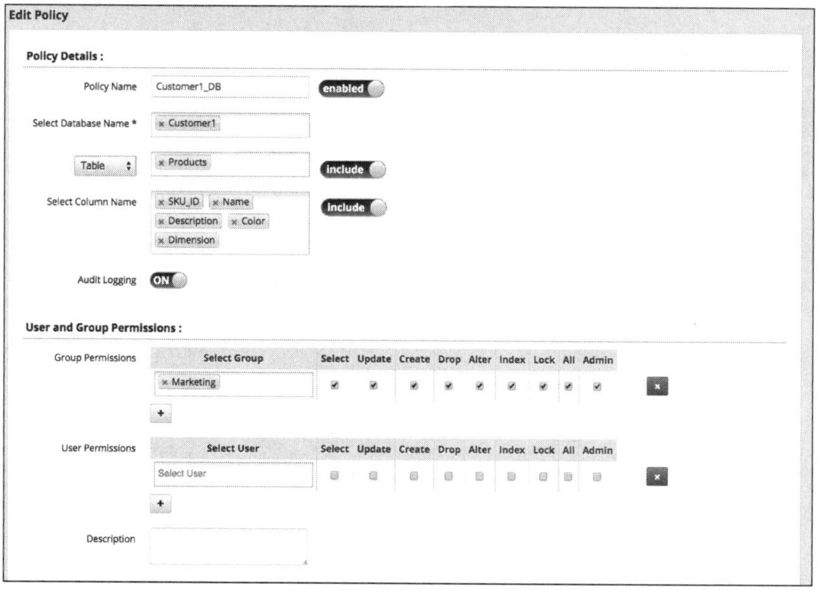

Figure 7.13   Hive policy details.

HBase, on the other hand, provides security controls for tables, column families, and columns, as shown in Figure 7.14. The Hive database policy provides access only to what is needed by specific users or groups.

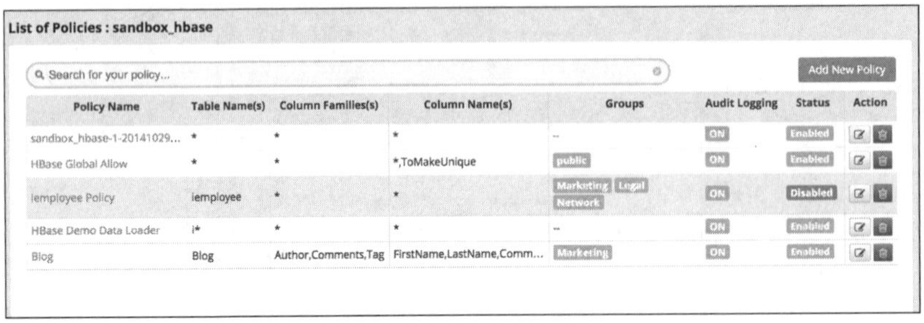

Figure 7.14   HBase defined policies.

You'll also notice an Edit button on the action column, which enables you to edit the policy. Figure 7.15 shows the policy in edit mode as well. You'll see that the Blog HBase table has one group and one user permitted to read and read/write/create/admin, respectively.

Figure 7.15   HBase policy edit mode.

Archive Carefully

When a multitenant cluster is supported and managed by IT, they have to know not to mix data when the archive process is initiated. Segregation of the data still needs to be enforced when it gets archived. It is a good practice to archive separately those datasets that cannot coexist with others. Archive destination could be in different places depending on what is good for the business. It could be in the same Hadoop cluster, in a remote Hadoop cluster, in NFS, or in the cloud. Business must establish rules and policies around usage of the archived data. If archived data needs to be pulled and made available in the Hadoop cluster within an hour for further processing, this affects the destination of the archive data. It is best to store archive data in the same Hadoop cluster or in a remote Hadoop cluster for this kind of setup. When the archive set is rarely accessed, then it is best to store that data either in the cloud or in an existing local NFS system in the data center.

The following command is used to perform archiving in Hadoop:

```
hadoop archive -archiveName name <source> <destination>
```

The -archiveName is the name of the archive you want to use—basically, the filename for the archive; for example, customer1.har. The source could be multiple hdfs paths separated by whitespace.

After archiving, if you want to validate your data, you can list the files by running the following command:

```
hadoop fs -lsr har:///user/Hadoop/customer1.har
```

To inspect the contents in the archived file, you can run the following sample command:

```
hadoop fs -cat har:///user/Hadoop/customer1.har/product/headphones.txt
```

Isolating the Process

A lot of organizations these days are implementing a data lake where different business units share the same Hadoop cluster. This is often referred to as a *shared services cluster*, which provides the benefit of maximizing the infrastructure and provides richer data integration. The common question asked with a data lake is, how can I ensure that my job runs according to my SLA? Can I be guaranteed that my job will finish when expected? Will Hadoop maintain data isolation as it is running jobs? In YARN, all jobs or applications are isolated from others. YARN's Capacity Scheduler provides all the elements in Hadoop that will partition the computing resources based on RAM. HDP 2.2 provides another feature that allows for isolating cpus via cgroups. With the combination of memory and CPU resources, SLAs are better enhanced for each application across the cluster. Network partitioning is not yet available in the Capacity Scheduler. All these resources are defined in the Capacity Scheduler's queue. A queue represents a certain percentage of the overall available computing resources in the cluster. A queue has the following attributes:

- Short queue name

- Full queue path name

- List of associated child queues and applications

- Guaranteed capacity of the queue

- Maximum capacity of the queue

- List of active users and their corresponding resource allocation limits

- State of the queue

- Access control lists governing access to the queue

Let's draw an example of how this works, using Figure 7.16 as a reference. Assuming you have 100 DataNodes in the cluster and each node has 128GB of memory, the total aggregated memory is 12,800GB, or roughly 12.8TB. Hadoop won't be able to consume all this memory because a certain portion of it is reserved for system memory and HBase memory. The general rule is that reserved system memory is normally 24GB, with another 24GB of memory reserved for HBase. The total available memory now for Hadoop is 12,752GB, or 12.7TB. Considering that all the business units in Figure 7.16 will be utilizing the cluster, each of the units has an allocated memory that will be used for running jobs. This basically represents the queue where the total available memory was sliced into different pieces and spread across different child queues.

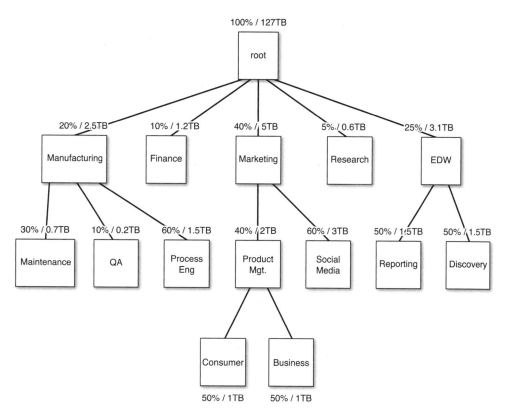

Figure 7.16 Capacity scheduler queue setup.

All queues start at the root queue, which represents the total pool of memory available (12.8TB) in the cluster. The sole purpose of establishing queues is to prevent any group or any user from hogging all the resources in the cluster, preventing others from submitting any jobs. For SLAs and QoS to be met, queues must be enforced. Consider Figure 7.16 and look at the Manufacturing group. They were allocated 20% of the total resource; that is 20% of 12.7TB, which equates to 2.5TB of memory. This amount of memory is split into three queues: Maintenance, QA, and Process Engineering, where each has 30%, 10%, and 60% of the 2.5TB of available memory.

Consider this scenario. Maintenance and Process Engineering queues are not being used, but Susie from QA just started a job that consumed 2TB of memory. YARN will acknowledge that this is valid because the total available memory for Manufacturing is 2.5TB. Fred from Process Engineering afterward started submitting an application that would require 1TB of RAM. Fred's application will have to wait until Susie's job finishes so resources can be reclaimed. If Fred's application has higher priority over Susie's and preemption is turned on in YARN, Susie's jobs will be killed almost instantly so that Fred's application can run first.

Preemption will be very useful in maintaining order and queue policies across the cluster. Preemption is particularly useful for an organization that has varying degrees of urgency to complete its applications/jobs.

To enable the Capacity Scheduler, go to /etc/hadoop/conf/yarn-site.xml file and look for the property yarn.resourcemanager.scheduler.class; enter the value org.apache.hadoop.yarn.server.resourcemanager.scheduler.capacity.CapacityScheduler. This turns on the Capacity Scheduler, but to adjust its settings, the file /etc/hadoop/conf/capacity-scheduler.xml file must be modified to suit organizational needs. Any changes to this file will be reloaded when Capacity Scheduler restarts. When a Hadoop Admin wants to reload the changes immediately, the command **yarn rmadmin -refreshQueues** can be run.

Setting Up Capacity Scheduler Queues

Using Figure 7.16, our capacity-scheduler.xml queue would look something like that shown in Listing 7.2.

Listing 7.2   Parameters for Configuring Capacity Scheduler Queues

```
<property>
<name>yarn.scheduler.capacity.root.queues</name>
<value>manufacturing,finance,marketing,research,edw</value>
<description>The top-level queues below root.</description>
</property>

<property>
<name>yarn.scheduler.capacity.manufacturing.queues</name>
<value>maintenance,qa,processeng</value>
<description>child queues under manufacturing</description>
</property>

<property>
<name>yarn.scheduler.capacity.marketing.queues</name>
```

```
<value>productmgt,socialmedia,processeng</value>
<description>child queues under marketing</description>
</property>

<property>
<name>yarn.scheduler.capacity.productmgt.queues</name>
<value>consumer,business </value>
<description>child queues under productmgt</description>
</property>

<property>
<name>yarn.scheduler.capacity.edw.queues</name>
<value>reporting,discovery </value>
<description>child queues under edw</description>
</property>
```

Summary

Creating a data lake around a shared service Hadoop cluster requires the users to be able to trust that security is properly implemented and to have confidence the data is properly protected. Defining the right strategy around multitenancy is critical to success. This chapter addressed key areas of multitenancy as well as how important it is to have an integrated strategy. It touched upon the concept and implementation of multitenancy in Hadoop that requires strong security controls and data and process isolation. Determining the right queue configuration per entity, business unit, or organization requires careful coordination and SLA/QoS benchmark validation. When moving data from one cluster to another or any location for backup and disaster recovery purposes, ensure that data integrity and isolation are preserved.

## Chapter 8

Virtualization Fundamentals

"Nature teaches beasts to know their friends."

—Coriolanus

The quote "Nature teaches beasts to know their friends" is about understanding the importance of coexisting peacefully with other groups. As Hadoop evolves and increases its role around enterprise data, it is going to require that IT groups, traditional data platforms, Hadoop, virtualization, and cloud services all work together to deliver data platforms that provide organizations with a competitive edge.

Throughout this book we constantly emphasize the importance of using big data to increase the speed so that your organization can use data to make business decisions. We've also discussed that big data is evolving extremely fast. Open source is helping accelerate the innovation around big data. Hadoop frameworks are adding new processes and new capabilities, and new frameworks are maturing and being added to production environments. The platforms running big data need agility, flexibility, and adaptability to handle the rate of change around big data.

The entire concept of Hadoop is based on software frameworks that are extensible. Hadoop platforms need to be just as extensible. As Hadoop clusters become more popular, customers are starting to look at how they can leverage virtualization, cloud services, and containers to handle the fast evolving Hadoop ecosystem. Before we look at virtualizing Hadoop we need to build some basic knowledge around virtualization.

The next two chapters focus on virtualization basics and best practices. It is best to understand virtualization terminology and concepts before looking at how to virtualize Hadoop.

Hadoop. We will then bring everything together in the following chapters by looking at how virtualization, the cloud, and containers can provide increased agility and speed to Hadoop platforms. VMware big data extensions, such as the Hadoop Virtual Extensions (HVE), containers, and cloud services are like a disruptive "tidal wave of change" sweeping through data centers. This wave of change needs to be understood. Virtualizing Hadoop is the focus of the last chapters in the book.

Why Virtualize Hadoop?

Infrastructure teams need platforms that are highly reliable and available and meet performance requirements. Historically, these platforms have been physical servers. However, the computer industry has reached a tipping point where now every year more new systems are chosen to run on virtual servers versus physical servers. The reason is that virtual servers offer significant infrastructure and management advantages over physical servers. Virtualization is not required to leverage cloud services, but virtualization is heavily used in cloud services and hosting companies.

Organizations are moving more and more to software platforms (virtual servers) and away from hardware platforms (physical servers) for the availability, stability, flexibility, and performance needed for business and mission-critical systems. Virtual servers can usually run with single-digit performance overhead and in some situations can even run faster than physical servers (yes, it's true). So if Hadoop can run on virtual servers that meet performance requirements and can leverage the advantages of virtual servers, then infrastructure teams and data teams need to do their due diligence on understanding the benefits of virtualizing Hadoop.

One of the hot focus areas around Hadoop is Hadoop as a Service (HaaS). There are multiple ways of deploying HaaS. The following are some of the more popular ways:

- Hadoop running the Hortonworks Data Platform (HDP) on Microsoft Hyper-V and Windows Azure. Some highlights include the capability to run Linux on Windows Azure.

- Deploying Hadoop using a hosting company like Rackspace on an OpenStack platform.

- Using Amazon Web Services (AWS) as a compute service for Hadoop.

- Deploying HaaS using hosting companies like HP Cloud Services and telecommunication companies.

- Using VMware software to deploy Hadoop in cloud infrastructures and VMware's Software-Defined Data Center (SDDC) architecture.

Let's start by talking about hypervisors. Many hypervisors exist in the industry, ranging from vSphere (VMware), Hyper-V (Microsoft), OVM (Oracle), and KVM (Red Hat), as well as containers such as Docker. This book focuses on VMware virtualization for deploying HaaS. There are a number of reasons we chose VMware:

- VMware's dominance of the virtualization market. As of 2013, VMware still has almost 60% of the virtualization market according to the IDC. A number of large corporations are more than 70% virtualized with VMware, and CIO studies (IDC) indicate CIOs are resistant to move away from VMware.

- VMware's product maturity. VMware VMs have been running on public, private, and hybrid clouds, as well as Macs and PCs for years.

- VMware has strong management solutions around virtualization, cloud infrastructures, and the Software Defined Data Center (SDDC).

- VMware is very involved with the Apache Software Foundation and OpenStack. VMware has contributed the Hadoop Virtualization Extensions (HVE) and code for project Serengeti. Serengeti is designed to automate the deployment and management of Apache Hadoop on virtual environments such as vSphere. This supports a multitenant architecture that enables multitenant Hadoop jobs to expand and contract within the same Hadoop data platform.

- VMware's SDDC is very comprehensive and supports the management of different types of virtual machines (VMs).

- With VMware's market dominance and product maturity, there are a tremendous amount of books, blogs, whitepapers, and videos on VMware products. There are companies that have been running tens of thousands of VMware VMs for years. The largest percentage of virtualization/cloud expertise and experience is in the VMware ecosystem.

Virtualization is all over Hadoop today. Following are examples of using virtualization with Hadoop:

- Hadoop distribution vendors offer downloadable VMs, making it easy to learn Hadoop as well as develop and test algorithms without stressing a development or test Hadoop cluster.

- Hosting companies such as AWS, Rackspace, HP, and telecommunication companies offer Hadoop clusters running in VMs that are available at the click of a button. These are great environments for development, testing, and proof of concept projects. As companies have great success with these environments, they look at taking the next step and running the Hadoop clusters in production in the cloud.

- Organizations wanting to deploy Hadoop in a private cloud with the option of moving to a hybrid or public cloud.

- Projects looking at virtualizing the Hadoop master servers and running the Hadoop worker nodes on physical servers.

- Running virtualized Hadoop master servers and using HVE to make the Hadoop cluster virtual aware and running the Hadoop worker servers on virtual servers.

- Using the VMware Hadoop Virtual Manager to automate deployment, to enable elasticity, and to enable multitenancy.

Today's virtualization software is significantly faster than a few years ago and runs with extremely low overhead. Remember the days when experts would say you can't run enterprise systems on Java because Java is too slow? Now the most critical systems in the world run on Java. In fact, all the Hadoop daemons and processes run in Java Virtual Machines (JVMs). Virtualization has gotten extremely lightweight and fast over the past few years. Depending on the environment, in the field we have seen that virtual servers can usually run with less than 10% overhead. Table 8.1 shows that Hadoop processes can easily run in a highly configured VM and stay within maximum limits.

With vSphere 5.5, each VM in an ESXi host can have up to 64 vCPUs, 1TB of RAM, a network of 36GB/s, and up to 1,000,000 IOPS. The latest CPUs are significantly faster than the previous generation, and virtualization can leverage hyperthreading. The latest processors have numerous features built in to them to optimize virtualization, as shown in Table 8.1.

Table 8.1 Upper Limits of a VM

Performance Capacity	ESXi 5.5
Benchmark: 1M IOPS with 1 microsecond of latency (5.1)	1 μs
vCPUs per VM	64
RAM per VM	1TB
RAM per ESXi Host	4TB
Network	36GB/s
IOPS/VM	1,000,000
Virtual disk size	62TB

VMware's virtualized servers leverage x86 hardware, which can scale linearly at relatively low cost to build high-performance super-computer systems. The average Hadoop server profile easily fits with VM maximum limits.

So if Hadoop can run in virtual infrastructures with minimal overhead and can run with higher availability than physical servers and with increased operation flexibility, technical infrastructure teams and architects need to understand the benefits of virtual platforms. Before we look at the benefits of running a virtual infrastructure, let's get started with some virtualization basics and terminology.

Introduction to Virtualization

A few concepts are fundamental about virtualization. First, running software in VMs abstracts the physical hardware, including memory, CPU, networking, and storage. This abstraction enables VMs (virtual servers) to be able to provide feature/functionality that is not available with physical servers. Second, virtualization is usually a precursor to using cloud services. Virtualization is not required to provide cloud services; however, almost all cloud services are delivered through virtualization. Management is a key factor in day-to-day operations that have significant advantages with virtualization. The management feature will be elaborated as we discuss virtualization.

There are different types of clouds, such as private, public, hybrid, and community. In this book we focus on private (on-premise) clouds. Most production Hadoop cloud deployments start out as a private cloud that is managed by an organization's internal IT department and is normally run inside the corporate firewall. However, hosting companies can manage the private cloud from their sites. Also, the cloud is increasing in popularity for doing Hadoop or NoSQL Proof of Concept (POC) projects. After you virtualize, a VM can easily be moved to a different site. This capability can also be used to move an environment from a private to a public cloud or from a public cloud to a private cloud. Because a VM abstracts the underlying physical hardware, when Hadoop is virtualized, hardware migration issues go away.

VMware Terminology

VMware vSphere is a suite of products and features that provides VMware's Infrastructure as a Service (IaaS) and cloud services for organizations and service providers. One product within the vSphere suite is the VMware virtualization software ESXi. ESXi is VMware's type one hypervisor. The hypervisor is the scheduler that provides CPU, memory, storage, and networking resources to VMs.

An administrator installs ESXi software on a clean physical server (ESXi host). The ESXi software contains the hypervisor (resource scheduler), which is also referred to as the VMkernel. A hypervisor is a thin software layer that schedules the physical resources of CPU, memory, storage, and networking that a VM needs. The hypervisor has a very small and lightweight footprint (approximately 150MB disk storage) that makes it extremely fast and provides a small security profile. Hadoop daemons and the operating system do not know they are running in a VM. It's actually the CPU, memory, storage, and networking that are being virtualized. Management is done through remote tools.

There are two types of hypervisors, a type one (native or bare-metal) and a type two (hosted) hypervisor.

- A type one hypervisor runs directly on a physical server with no software layer between the hypervisor and the physical hardware. This is why a type one hypervisor is called a bare-metal hypervisor. This hypervisor is designed to be extremely fast for production environments. VMware ESXi, Oracle VM, Linux KVM, Hyper-V, and Citrix XenServer are all examples of type one hypervisors. Hypervisors are different in their functionality and features. Hypervisors such as VMware, Hyper-V, OVM, and KVM have many similarities, but they are also different. Just like Oracle, SQL Server and MySQL are relational databases for which there are significant differences in how they do things as well as in the environments and ecosystems where they run. So it is with hypervisors.

- A type two hypervisor runs on top of an operating system such as Windows (VMware Workstation) or Mac OS (VMware Fusion). Type one hypervisors are designed for running server workloads with high performance. Type two hypervisors are designed for running VMs on existing operating systems that require using general-purpose schedulers in the operating systems. Each VM has its own operating system and software environment. A type two hypervisor is great for running multiple VMs on laptops and PCs. VMware Workstation, Parallels, and VirtualBox are additional examples of type two hypervisors.

The x86 architecture has different levels of authorization. Operating system instructions have traditionally run in level 0 (to get access to hardware) and the applications usually run in level 3. The x86 architecture has different levels of privilege from an authorization of rights. These levels of privilege are related to concentric rings of privilege on the CPU registers. These concentric rings of protection allow only certain types of operations to be run within their borders. For example, application code runs within an outer ring at the level of the CPU, but operating system code that is responsible for controlling the hardware, scheduling, and managing control operations typically runs at the level 0 ring of privileges. When virtualization began taking over the hardware management jobs, it took over the OS jobs and ran instead at ring 0 privilege. This is partially what is meant when we say full virtualization uses binary translation and directs executing techniques for performance.

Occasionally, a feature of level 0 privilege was associated with another feature of the OS that the hypervisor wouldn't normally perform. This caused applications not to perform as well. CPU chip makers detected these issues from customers and redesigned the chip with a new ring of protection called -1. It allowed a new level of privilege for the hypervisor;

the OS would run code at level 0 and applications run at level 3. This enabled the code job to be run with the proper permissions and each component to execute codes with the proper level of privilege. Full virtualization uses binary translation and direct execution techniques for performance. The VM also supports direct execution of the processors for performance. This fully abstracts the operating system from the hardware. Allowing the guest operating system to be decoupled from the hardware provides tremendous portability and flexibility.

When an operating system runs on a traditional physical server, the operating system must go through software interfaces to get access to the physical resources. Virtual memory maps, adapters and drivers from hardware vendors have provided the interface. Now instead of going through the hardware vendor interfaces, the operating system goes through the VMware interfaces. The advantage of this is the operating system sees a consistent virtual interface (software stack) no matter what the underlying hardware is. This consistent presentation or view across an organization provides two very important components for success: a controlled consistent software stack and the capability to achieve a very high level of standardization. A consistent software stack gets rid of all the nickel-and-dime errors that occur with working with different hardware vendor drivers, adapters, and patch sets. A high level of software standardization creates high availability derived from fewer mistakes and fewer variables in computing. This consistency and standardization is one of the many reasons enterprise environments insist on virtualization for serious business-critical applications.

Terminology and Concepts

We look at virtualization in more detail in the next section; however, we need to introduce a few terms and concepts before explaining the benefits of virtualization.

- A host machine (physical server) contains the physical cores, physical memory, physical network cards, and physical storage adapters. Physical servers running VMware software must be x86 platforms. Companies such as Dell, Cisco (UCS), HP, and IBM offer supported platforms. Read the VMware Hardware Compatibility Lists (HCL) to purchase platforms optimized for running virtualization software.

- An ESXi host is a physical server running VMware software (hypervisor) that manages the scheduling of resources (CPU, memory, storage, networking). Individual VMs then run on the ESXi host.

- Multiple VMs can run on an ESXi host.

- Each VM is completely independent and runs its own OS software.

- Each VM can also be referred to as a guest.

- The OS and software running in each VM requests resources through the Virtual Memory Manager (VMM). The VMM communicates with the hypervisor (VMkernel).

- VMware tools provide paravirtualization software and drivers that communicate with the underlying hardware. For example, these VMware tools allow for optimized performance using paravirtualized network drivers. These drivers support advanced networking configurations and are significantly faster than the default drivers.

- A set of ESXi hosts can run as a VMware DRS/HA cluster. This enables VMs to transparently move from one ESXi host to another ESXi host in the same DRS cluster.

As shown in Figure 8.1, the VMkernel (hypervisor) runs on top of a physical server. The hypervisor contains components like a scheduler, memory allocator, and vSwitches (networking). Each guest VM has its own completely independent OS and software environment.

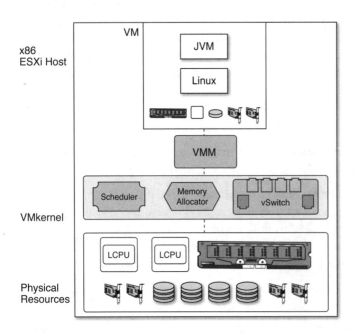

Figure 8.1 An ESXi host.

This diagram displays several key points about an ESXi host running multiple individual VMs:

- It is completely transparent to the software (OS and Hadoop daemons [JVM]) that they are running in a VM. The CPU, memory, storage, and networking resources that a VM needs are virtualized. So a Hadoop administrator can manage Hadoop the same way in a VM as in a physical server.

- The hypervisor (VMkernel) is a very thin, lightweight scheduler that transparently allocates the resources that the VMs request.

- Each VM is referred to as a guest machine. The OS running in the VM is referred to as the guest OS. Each VM is a machine; it is a software machine and not a physical machine.

- The VM's guest operating system goes through virtual memory maps, a virtual software adapter, and a virtual NIC to get access to physical resources. As far as the operating system is concerned, the virtual interfaces are interfaces to physical resources.

- VMs have their own CPUs, memory, hard disks, NICs, parallel/serial ports, SCSI controllers, USB controllers, video cards, and keyboards. Their resources are virtual instead of physical.

- The Virtual Machine Monitor (VMM) is a lightweight interface between the VM and the VM kernel. The VMM manages each VM's memory allocation.

- Hadoop processes are not aware that they are running in a VM, with one exception. Hadoop Virtual Extensions (HVE) make sure the Hadoop cluster is aware it is running in a virtual infrastructure. The reason for HVE is to make sure two replicated blocks do not end up on two VMs on the same host for high availability of the blocks. This is discussed later.

Figure 8.2 highlights VMs on an ESXi host that are completely independent. The VMkernel (hypervisor) with the Virtual Memory Manager abstract out the physical resources from the VMs.

Figure 8.3 shows two ESXi hosts running four VMs using shared storage. The VMM provides the hardware abstraction for each VM. The VMMs then go through the VMkernel to get access to the physical resources. Each VM has its own virtual NIC. Each VM's virtual NIC is configured to access a specific ESXi host's physical NIC through an internal or an external switch. A best practice is to have Hadoop worker nodes running with local storage. vCenter Server is a single point of management for the virtual infrastructure.

The OS, databases, and apps are not aware of being in VM.

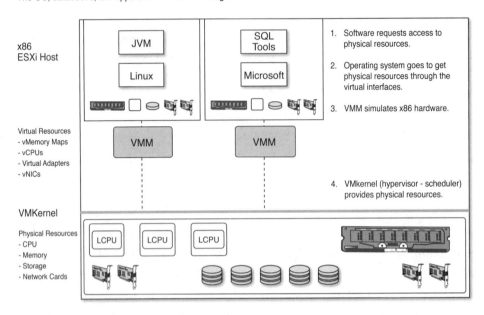

Figure 8.2 Operating systems and software processes do not know they are running in a VM.

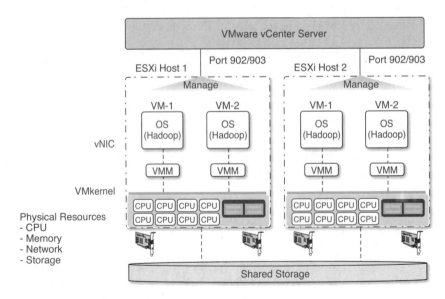

Figure 8.3 Two ESXi hosts running multiple VMs.

When Hadoop processes come up, they look in their configuration files for qualified server names for other Hadoop processes they communicate with. As far as the Hadoop processes are concerned, they are communicating with processes running on other servers. The Hadoop processes are not aware whether the processes are running on virtual or physical servers. We get into more detail about virtualizing different types of servers running Hadoop in the virtualizing Hadoop chapters.

It is important that overhead be minimal to virtualize tier one platforms with performance SLAs. VMware accomplishes this with a combination of binary translation, paravirtualization, and hardware assist.

- **Hardware-assisted virtualization:** Processors from Intel and AMD continue adding more features to enhance the performance of virtualization at the processor level. Hardware-assisted virtualization is also transparent to the guest operating system and the software it is running.

- **Paravirtualization:** Paravirtualization is used in special areas where performance is very sensitive, such as in drivers, and can significantly improve operating system performance. Paravirtualization uses a call interface to allow the guest operating system kernel to communicate to the hypervisor that it needs to perform special privileged CPU and memory operations. This takes the pressure off the hypervisor to perform binary translation and reduces performance overhead around memory management operations. Paravirtualization is not transparent to the guest OS because it uses special drivers that work only on virtual platforms.

Virtualization Infrastructure Advantages

A Hadoop cluster has different layers and different types of servers. There are master servers and worker nodes. A Hadoop cluster usually has servers running client software, staging data as edge servers, and using LDAP or Microsoft Active Directory servers. Servers can be virtualized, as well as networks and the storage. At this point we are focusing only on virtualization concepts and terminology. Virtualizing Hadoop is discussed in later chapters.

Management of the nonvirtualized data center comes with a number of serious problems from a management point of view. The cost of capital expenses ties up assets that could be better spent on your business or enterprise core competencies, not to mention the additional cost of operational staff, greater floor space, and excessive cooling costs for an ever expanding data center. Having Hadoop physical deployments as the only option places the enterprise at risk of being a financial money pit. Management would have limited options when it comes to the cost of equipment, staffing, physical plant size, and operational demands. Abstracting the hardware enables Hadoop administrators to leverage the following virtualization features to improve availability, scalability, optimization, and manageability:

- **vMotion:** Enables you to move a running VM transparently to a different ESXi host with zero down time and no loss of transactions. Hadoop and the operating system do not know a vMotion move occurred. vMotion can be used when a physical server has planned maintenance. vMotion can also provide zero-downtime migration without a shared disk solution.

- **DRS/HA cluster:** Enables you to spread VMs across multiple ESXi host servers. A VM can be independent of the specific ESXi host (physical server) it is running on. This is excellent if you are running a Hadoop master server that is using a shared disk solution. Hadoop worker server processes are usually tied to local disks running on a specific ESXi host. If an ESXi host fails, the DRS/HA cluster can start up the VMs that were on the failed ESXi host and can restart the VMs on other hosts in the DRS/HA cluster if there are no local dependencies.

  ESXi hosts maintain heartbeats and are aware of the VMs running on other ESXi hosts in the cluster.

- **HA:** If there are no local dependencies, high availability automatically starts up a VM on a different physical server if the original ESXi host fails. It takes five mouse clicks to configure HA. Other HA solutions often have a lot of complexity that increases an administrator's workload, and the complexity can itself create downtime. HA increases the availability of the VMs and reduces the administrator's workload around this area.

  - Rules can be defined to set the order and priority of VMs starting on the cluster if an ESXi host fails.

  - Affinity and anti-affinity rules can be configured to make sure VMs stay together or to make sure VMs reside on separate hosts. For example, you would not want a primary and its standby system both running on the same ESXi host.

- **vSphere App HA:** Provides protection from application failures. vSphere App HA policies support the restarting of application services.

- **Resource pools:** Can guarantee that VMs with strict SLAs always have the compute resources they need.

- **Distributed Resource Scheduler (DRS):** Enables you to load balance VMs across a DRS/HA cluster. Administrators can set rules and make decisions about when a VM is allowed to move from one host to another with no downtime. This feature makes sure the hardware utilization is properly distributed across a DRS/HA cluster. This increases the robustness of the environment Hadoop is running in. A VM must not have any local dependencies (local disk) before you can move it.

- **Distributed Power Management (DPM):** Enables you to move VMs from one host to another, power down host servers that are not being utilized, and then power the host servers back up when there is sufficient utilization. This can help reduce environmental costs. Customers can save a lot of money on electricity, air conditioning, and so on when there is very little activity (holidays, weekends). A VM must not have any local dependencies (local disk) before you can use this feature.

- **Fault Tolerance (FT):** Enables you to mirror a VM on a separate host, so if the original environment goes down, the mirrored environment becomes the primary, and a new secondary environment is created. Previous to vSphere 6.x, fault tolerance currently supported one vCPU. vSphere 6.x supports four vCPUs.

- **Templates:** You can tune the OS, drivers, patches, and agents for a VM and save the image as a golden template. A new VM can be created in minutes with a single click.

- **Cloning:** You can right-click on a running VM and create a new VM by providing new IP address, hostname, and so on to make sure the new VM environment matches the original one exactly in terms of latest patches, kernel settings, and the like.

- **vCenter Converter:** Enables you to move the operating system and environment from a physical machine to a virtual machine running on a different host. When hardware reaches an end of life, the environment can move into a VM running on the latest hardware. Legacy systems will run faster than ever before on the latest hardware and be under the protection umbrella of the virtual infrastructure.

- **vAppliance:** A tuned and customized VM can be created as a vAppliance and then deployed to different environments. A virtual appliance is deployed using an Open Virtualization Format (OVF) file. OVF is also used by XenServer, VirtualBox, IBM, OpenStack, and Microsoft.

- **vApp:** A set of VMs can be deployed together as a vApp. When a Hadoop environment needs other machines running a DNS server, LDAP server, application server, or third-party software, a vApp might be the best option.

- **vCenter Server:** A single management platform for managing VMs and ESXi hosts. vCenter Server has additional plug-ins for vSphere Update Manager and the vCenter Site Recovery Manager (automation of disaster recovery).

- **vCenter Operations Management Suite (vCOPs):** You can collect statistics from a Hadoop cluster and use advanced analytics to increase the monitoring of Hadoop. vCOPs will learn the Hadoop environment over a period of time (two weeks) and understand what is normal and not normal. For example, a VM might run at 90% utilization, but that might be normal for Wednesday and Thursday afternoons. vCOPs will learn that this is normal and not require alerts to be customized for different types of run levels. This not only reduces administration but can also detect when things might not be normal. This enables you to become aware of something that is running in a nonnormal environment and often allows you to fix a future problem before it impacts performance or availability.

- **Resource Management:** If a Hadoop cluster is running multiple VMs across a DRS/HA cluster, CPU capacity prioritization, Storage I/O Control, Network Control, and resource pools can be used to guarantee VMs with critical SLAs can be met, and busy neighbors do not impact high-profile VMs.

- **Storage vMotion:** Enables the transparent movement of VM disk files containing Hadoop data from one server to another over the network.

- **Virtual networks:** Virtual networking abstracts the physical networking layer. Virtualized networks provide the same advantages to networks that virtual servers provide for hardware. Simplified management, elasticity, scalability, reduced administration, and provisioning are all benefits of software-defined networking.

  - Two VMs running on the same host and connected to the same vSwitch can communicate without going to the physical network. This greatly increases bandwidth and lowers latency.

  - Distributed network switches enable each network switch to be configured from a central management point (vCenter). If a change is made in vCenter, the change is then reflected in all the virtual NICs that use the distributed switch. Each distributed switch has a local definition in the individual ESXi hypervisor. So if vCenter goes down, it does not impact all the VMs using the distributed switch. vCenter would need to be restarted before new configuration changes could be made to the distributed switch.

  - There is support for 40GB cards.

- The following are additional networking features:

  - **Enhanced SR-IOV:** Communicates Port Group-specific properties.

  - **Traffic filtering:** Controls allowing or dropping selected traffic.

  - **QoS tagging:** Can mark network packets for high profile traffic types to support SLAs.

  - **Packet capture:** Captures packets for troubleshooting.

- **Virtual security:** Security can also be a software-defined service by abstracting out physical storage devices. Integrated firewalls, virtual private networks, and gateway options have a lot more options in a virtual infrastructure.

- **vSphere Data Protection:** VMware's backup and recovery tool. Data Protection is available for free and is deployed as a virtual appliance. It is fully integrated with the vSphere environment, is agentless, and does image-level backups to disk. There is direct host recovery, so there is no dependency on the vCenter Server. This is for the backup of an individual VM. Data stored in HDFS that is distributed across different servers requires different backup solutions.

  - vSphere Data Protection Advanced is available at an additional cost.

  - vCenter Single Sign On is available for multidomain environments.

VMware Tools

VMware tools software is a set of VMware utilities that improves the performance of the VM guest operating system. VMware tools is installed in the VM's guest operating system. It is strongly recommended that you install VMware tools and get the version up to date. For Hadoop Data Platform, consider it a requirement. Some of the key utilities include the following:

- Optimized network device drivers

- Perfmon monitoring features

- Synchronizes the VM guest OS time with the host operating system

Virtual Networks

Because networking is such a significant feature to a well-designed Hadoop cluster, this section provides more clarity to basic network virtualization details that can easily be employed for a virtualized Hadoop cluster.

Virtual networks enable VMs to communicate with other VMs and physical machines. Virtual switches define how virtual networks work. A virtual switch is a software definition in the hypervisor. We discuss two types of switches: a standard switch (vSwitch) and a distributed switch (dvSwitch).

There are two connection types for virtual switches:

- **VM port groups:** Connect VMs to the network.

- **VMkernel ports:** Support management and hypervisor services.

  - Hypervisor services include IP storage, vMotion activity, and fault tolerance.

  - Management communication supports administration activity.

Networking characteristics can be defined at the virtual switch level, the port group level, and the port level.

Virtual Switch Diagram

There are three key components of a virtual switch:

- **VM port group:** Enables several ports to share network characteristics. Certain types of Hadoop daemons and processes might have a different network profile than production servers of a different type. LDAP servers and web servers have different network profiles.

    - Security characteristics can be defined at the port group level, such as security, traffic shaping, and NIC teaming policies.

    - NIC teaming policies can be defined at the port group level, such as load balancing, failover, and failback.

- **VMkernel port:** Supports iSCSI, vMotion, FT, and management network activity.

- **Uplink port:** Uplink ports connect to a physical NIC.

There are different strategies for designing virtual switches. For example:

- There can be one virtual switch supporting different port groups and different VMkernel ports (see Figure 8.4).

- There can be individual virtual switches for different types of port groups, as well as for iSCSI, vMotion, FT, or Management.

Figure 8.4 shows a single virtual switch configuration and a multiple virtual switch configuration for different network streams.

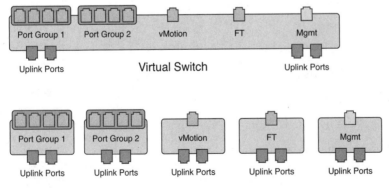

Figure 8.4 Configuration displaying one virtual switch and multiple virtual switches.

Following are key fundamentals about virtual switches:

- Virtual switches can enable VMs on the same ESXi host to communicate. Virtual switches can also enable the VMs to communicate with other VMs on other ESXi hosts and physical servers.

- Virtual switches are Layer 2 switches (OSI model).

- Two virtual switches cannot connect to the same physical NIC.

- A single virtual switch can communicate with two physical NICs for load balancing and failover, for example.

- A VM must go through the following steps to get network connectivity to a physical NIC:

  1. VMs are configured with a virtual NIC (vNic).

  2. The vNICs are mapped to a port in a virtual switch.

  3. The port is mapped to an uplink in the virtual switch.

  4. The uplink maps to a physical NIC (pNIC).

  5. The uplinks use vmnics (virtual network adapters) to interface with the virtual switch.

- An internal virtual switch is not connected to a physical NIC.

- An internal switch enables two VMs on the same host to communicate using the internal switch.

- Two VMs on the same ESXi host can communicate over the same internal switch in an ESXi host to achieve speeds close to bus communication speed because they do not have to go through the physical NICs.

Virtual Distributed Switch

If you are running a cluster, using standard switches, and a set of Hadoop daemons needs its network profile modified, each standard switch must be modified on each ESXi host. Over time, network characteristics and settings need to be modified. This process is not only high maintenance, it is also prone to errors.

If you are using a distributed switch and the network characteristics for a set of VMs change, the distributed switch can be updated, and that change is then reflected across the entire cluster. With a distributed virtual switch, a change is made in the following locations:

- **The management plane:** The management plane has the centralized network definitions.

- **The data plane:** The data plane has the local distributed definitions within the ESXi host. If the vCenter server goes down, all the VMs associated with the distributed switch use the local definitions until vCenter is up again. All networking works normally, no distributed configuration changes can occur until vCenter is up again.

Figure 8.5 shows the data plane is stored locally, eliminating vCenter as a point of failure.

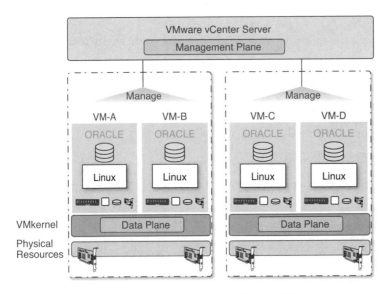

Figure 8.5   Data plane information is found in the VMkernel.

VLANs

A VLAN creates a logical grouping of virtual switch ports. This logical grouping enables the virtual ports to work as if they were on their own physical segment. VLANs can be defined at the port level group.

Virtualization Is the Path to Cloud Technology

Deploying development, test, and proof-of-concept Hadoop clusters in the cloud is increasing significantly. Rackspace, HP Cloud Services, and the telecommunication companies are increasing their services for Hadoop. Hosting companies are always trying to maximize the use of their hardware, so the nodes in a Hadoop cluster are usually virtualized. Virtualization offers many features that allow the maximum utilization of cloud services for Hadoop.

Here are two independent vendor definitions of the cloud and one from VMware.

- **The NIST Definition of Cloud Computing:** Cloud computing is a model for enabling ubiquitous, convenient, on-demand network access to a shared pool of configurable computing resources (for example, networks, servers, storage, applications, and services) that can be rapidly provisioned and released with minimal management effort or service provider interaction.[1]

- **Cloud Computing:** A computing capability that provides an abstraction between the computing resource and its underlying technical architecture (for example, servers, storage, networks), enabling convenient, on-demand network access to a shared pool of configurable computing resources that can be rapidly provisioned and released with minimal management effort or service provider interaction. This definition states that clouds have five essential characteristics: on-demand self-service, broad network access, resource pooling, rapid elasticity, and measured service. Narrowly speaking, cloud computing is client-server computing that abstract the details of the server away; one requests a service (resource), not a specific server (machine). Cloud computing enables Infrastructure as a Service (IaaS), Platform as a Service (PaaS), and Software as a Service (SaaS). Cloud computing means that infrastructure, applications, and business processes can be delivered to you *as a service*, over the Internet (or your own network).[2]

- **VMware:** Cloud computing is an approach to computing that leverages the efficient pooling of an on-demand, self-managed virtual infrastructure that is consumed as a service. Sometimes known as utility computing, clouds provide a set of typically virtualized computers that can provide users with the capability to start and stop servers or use compute cycles only when needed, often paying only upon usage. See more at www.vmware.com/cloud-computing/public-cloud/faqs.html#sthash.J7t6k3d1.dpuf.

As mentioned earlier, there are different types of clouds, such as private, public, hybrid, and community. In this book we focus on Hadoop technology that fits all types of clouds. Most Hadoop cloud deployments start out in public clouds (as a test or proof of concept). After your deployment is virtualized, a VM can easily be moved to a different site. If supported, this capability can also be used to move an environment from a public cloud to a private cloud or from a private cloud to a public cloud. Because a VM abstracts the underlying physical hardware, after Hadoop is virtualized it no longer has to deal with difficult, slow, and restrictive hardware migrations. A straight path to the cloud enables Hadoop to offer a mainstream enterprise the power of big data without undoing all the effort of companies to make IT agile and powerful.

IT exists to serve the needs of its organization, and cloud offers elasticity, efficiency, availability, and ease of management. Elasticity allows nondisruptive adjustment up or down of computing resources to meet the needs of big data. Efficiency is achieved in the cloud by paying only for actual usage. Availability in the cloud could be as simple as rolling back a change created during testing or recovery of a Hadoop project to a disaster site. Another benefit of the cloud is management that handles multiple departments in isolated, secure networks, and with simplified monitoring that is responsive and predictive. To maintain the best of both private and public cloud features, one possible path is a hybrid cloud for Hadoop deployments. The basic idea is having a private cloud sized to normal workloads, allowing companies full control over compliance and security obligations. But with a hybrid cloud, the enterprise could adopt to seasonal changes or growing usage with a public cloud provider. A hybrid cloud is ideal for big data organizations because it is difficult to predict accurately the workloads from one month to the next or test and development requirements. The point is to give Hadoop administrators a path or direction to build a steady and long-lasting career using an IT department as a service broker. Other books give clarity to options regarding the cloud, and we want to be sure Hadoop is in alignment with those options.

Summary

The advantages of virtualization, including management, availability, scalability, and optimization, would be compelling reasons to virtualize Hadoop if they were the only reasons. The trend for virtualization is so entrenched with the enterprise, the better question is, "How do I virtualize Hadoop?"

Let's face it, virtualization is constantly used in Hadoop development, Hadoop proof of concepts, small Hadoop projects, and large one-off Hadoop projects. But with time it will become increasingly clear that Hadoop and big data projects are a core enterprise competency. If big data is vital to the enterprise, we must maximize our stewardship of IT assets from hardware, people, and processes to deliver IT faster, easier, and cheaper. In addition, learning to virtualize Hadoop opens a path for Hadoop administrators to fully participate in the cloud. Why should you care about all this? Simply because today's businesses ask IT to fulfill its mission to serve the businesses' objectives. Adapt to your customers or be abandoned by that same customer is the new atmosphere within which all businesses must survive. We are not suggesting there is only one way to do Hadoop. We are saying that without a wide range of practical offerings or options, your company's value is limited. If you can't meet all the customers' needs, they will find the company that can. That is why we say "virtualize" and do it in such a way that you have a straight path to the cloud.

References

1. NIST Special Publication 800-145: http://csrc.nist.gov/publications/nistpubs/800-145/SP800-145.pdf

2. http://cloudtimes.org/glossary/

## Chapter 9

Best Practices for Virtualizing Hadoop

"The fool doth think he is wise, but the wise man knows himself to be a fool."

—William Shakespeare, *Measure for Measure*

The goal of this chapter is to establish a general knowledge of virtualization best practices used with any business-critical application. Best practices depend on context and the current configuration and platform. This chapter contains areas to consider for tuning and configuration for any high throughput platform. There is always more to learn in configuring virtual infrastructures for production environments. Later, these practices will be expressed in the context of vSphere 5.5 Big Data Extensions.

Running Virtualized Hadoop with Purpose and Discipline

Excellence in production platforms, virtualized or not, needs to be enterprise configured at every level. Think like an architect creating a perfectly fitted and balanced design. If you are going to run Hadoop on Linux, you need to properly define BIOS settings, Linux kernel parameter settings, network driver and storage adapter settings, and the Hadoop cluster that is tuned for heavy workloads. A virtual infrastructure also needs the right hardware, BIOS settings, driver and adapter settings, and so on, just like a physical environment needs to be optimized. A highly optimized enterprise platform is like a relay race. Each runner individually contributes and all handoffs need to be flawless, but the total team effort is what wins the race. Like a relay race, weaknesses in any aspect will be revealed at the point you need results the most. Virtualization tends to unify and coordinate the whole rather than silo the contributing pieces.

Consider best practices as the wisdom of experience. Generally, these practices have yielded good results. Best practices are recommended guidelines dependent on the requirements, environment, and skill set of the people involved. But best practices are not always absolutes; they depend on context. However, settings and best practices can have trade-offs. Every situation must be evaluated to determine whether the trade-offs are justified. Just as administrators build their corporate best practices and standards for business-critical applications, there needs to be a set of best practices and standards for virtual infrastructures running Hadoop. The point is to have a mindset toward excellence, purpose, and the discipline of standard practices.

The good thing is that there are many virtualization whitepapers, blogs, knowledge base articles, and best practices. The problem is that they go out of date, are infrequently updated, and often come from vendors who have a lot of knowledge but want everyone to drink their Kool-Aid. Therefore, we will use field knowledge and lessons learned to discuss best practices from the perspective of achieving operational excellence of the Hadoop infrastructure that happens to be running in a virtual infrastructure.

The best Hadoop administrators have always been infrastructure aware. The nice thing about Hadoop running on x86 commodity hardware is that a single individual can understand the entire technology stack that Hadoop runs on—from the operating system (Linux or Windows), to the local disks, CPU cores, memory, and network cards. The more people understand the infrastructure around Hadoop, the better job they can do in designing, performance tuning, and troubleshooting Hadoop in a virtual infrastructure. Context is everything when considering best practices. For example, Hadoop might be running in a virtual infrastructure; therefore, someone must have an excellent understanding of virtualized platforms. The VMs running on ESXi hosts might be using resource pools, running in a DRS/HA cluster, using VMware Big Data Extensions, using virtual switches, and running in virtual networks. Hadoop has different run-time characteristics than relational databases and application servers. The platform running Hadoop must be tuned for Hadoop's runtime characteristics.

Hadoop is different from a lot of other enterprise applications that can be virtualized. A Hadoop cluster has master nodes and worker nodes. It is a best practice to separate Hadoop's master server nodes from the worker nodes. In a virtual infrastructure, it is even more important. The reason is if the worker nodes are virtualized, the Hadoop cluster must be configured to be virtualization aware. The master nodes are virtualized with one strategy while the worker nodes are virtualized with a different strategy. Master nodes are configured for availability, and the Hadoop master nodes need to leverage the benefits of virtualization for availability. When virtualizing the worker nodes, the worker node VMs must be finely tuned for the OS used, storage technology, and network characteristics. For now the key is to understand that a configured VM makes a significant difference in the VM running similar to a physical server.

If something is running poorly, someone must be able to quickly determine whether it is a Hadoop/application problem, a virtual infrastructure problem, or a hardware problem. This is where knowledge of the infrastructure comes into play. The better Hadoop administrators are at understanding the virtualization infrastructure, the better they are at troubleshooting Hadoop in that environment.

A poorly performing virtualized Hadoop environment can be an experiment in disaster if there is not strong virtualization expertise. Systems bound to sluggishness and characterized by improperly configured BIOS, storage, networking, and VMware tool settings, or not following virtualization best practices, will induce pain and anguish. Hadoop administrators must be able to talk to VMware administrators the same way they talk to the different infrastructure teams. Hadoop administrators who know how to use esxtop or look at performance metrics or look at a customized read-only interface in vCOPs will be happy virtual team members. Teaching a few Hadoop administrators what they need to understand to diagnose problems in a virtual infrastructure will go a long way toward supporting the virtualization of Hadoop. Making a few Hadoop administrators become vHadoop administrators will create harmony and peace in the enterprise.

The Discipline of Purpose Starts with a Clear Target

It is important to define goals for the virtualization of your Hadoop servers. To achieve the benefits of virtual servers, Hadoop administrators must learn how to use and trust the virtualization features. Virtual servers have advantages over physical servers. These advantages need to be leveraged. Hadoop administrators should have the following goals with virtualization:

- Higher levels of standardization by abstracting the hardware and having a single image of the software stack for the virtual machine. This requires building golden images according to best practices and corporate standards. This should reduce trouble tickets by a noticeable amount. There needs to be separate images for master servers, worker nodes, and clients. If you are running NoSQL, or frameworks on individual clusters, they will require separate golden images.

- Faster server provisioning and deployments with cloning and templates. Be able to create new VMs on demand in a few minutes. Work on reducing corporate overhead so paperwork and red tape do not slow down the process.

- Avoid VM creep (sprawl). It is so easy to create new VMs, and when people learn they can create them in minutes, everybody wants one. Then the number of VMs increases like rabbits. VMs take resources. The more VMs you create, the more the resources they consume that have to be shared. Just because it's easy to create a VM does not mean someone should automatically get one. Also, it is important to remove VMs when they are no longer being used. You must decommission a virtualized Hadoop slave server; you cannot just remove the VM.

Virtualizing Different Tiers of Hadoop

Master nodes need to leverage virtualization to maximize availability and management. The following best practices can help you get the most out of your master nodes:

- Use RAID and shared storage.

- Hadoop features, such as YARN, NameNode High Availability, and NameNode Federation, can use virtualization to enhance their capabilities.

- Consider leveraging vMotion and DRS for the master nodes. You can use vMotion to move targeted VMs on to new hardware with zero downtime.

It is a best practice to have a Hadoop cluster run in its own network and not share any network traffic.

A Hadoop cluster is made up primarily of two tiers of servers—master servers and worker nodes. Master server access needs to be limited. It is common to have a firewall for a Hadoop cluster and a firewall around the master servers. Take advantage of network virtualization using VLANs and network fencing to provide an additional level of software security. There are master servers that do not have HA capability, so virtualization can add additional HA features to minimize down time.

Hadoop 2.6 has HA features for the NameNode(s), Resource Manager, HBase, and the Ozzie Server built in to the Hadoop distribution. The Hadoop roadmap lists future frameworks having HA built in. Leverage the built-in HA that is part of Hadoop and coordinate that with VMware HA or Fault Tolerance. Fault Tolerance can provide server failover with servers (currently up to four vCPUs).

VMware HA can support a number of the Hadoop master servers, such as Ambari Server, HiveServer2, and Zookeeper processes that do not currently have a built-in Hadoop HA solution. RDBMS metadata repositories for Ambari, HiveServer2, and Ozzie can also be virtualized. Improve high availability by leveraging virtualization features as defined corporate standards for vMotion, Storage vMotion, Resource pools, port groups (vDS), Network and Storage I/O control, DRS, HA, FT, and HA App-Aware. Hadoop clusters can have additional frameworks, such as Storm, Kafka, Hue, Spark, Shark, Accumulo, Cassandra, and Giraph. The processes that run these frameworks should be considered for virtualization as well.

Set up anti-affinity rules for the following:

- Primary NameNode(s) and Standby NameNode.

- Primary Resource Manager and Standby Resource Manager.

- Primary Ozzie Server and Standby Oozie Server.

- RDBMS metadata repositories often use replication. For example, if using MySQL for the metadata repositories, it is a best practice to make sure the primary MySQL server and the replicated MySQL server reside on separate ESXi hosts.

- Zookeeper processes.

Affinity rules should be considered for the following:

- Primary master servers and their corresponding Zookeeper Failover controller

- Metadata repositories and their backup servers

- WebHCat Server, JobHistory Server, Oozie Server, and Falcon Server

At virtualized Hadoop cluster creation time, the node group (virtual) topology and the physical topology is made known to the system by means of configuration files and by turning on the HVE features. This is applicable when the virtual machines containing the NameNode and DataNode processes are using local, direct-attached disks, which is one viable choice for them. This is covered in more detail in Chapter 12, "Virtualizing the Hadoop Worker Nodes." The use of local disks eliminates some of the features of virtualization, such as vMotion and DRS. This is okay because the worker nodes use Hadoop and HDFS features to maximize availability. The worker nodes must leverage the virtualization features for management and administration.

The HA features of virtualization can provide additional protection for Hadoop frameworks. Virtualization can reduce the total cost of ownership (TCO) around Hadoop. Higher utilization of CPUs requires fewer physical machines to run Hadoop. Focus on reducing CapEx, OpEx, and Energy costs. Be aware that Hadoop has different runtime characteristics than other applications that are virtualized. Also be aware that Hadoop master nodes and worker nodes have different runtime characteristics as well. Look at the typical operations performed on Hadoop clusters and how virtualization features can reduce downtime and increase flexibility in administration.

Batch processing applications on Hadoop run until they are finished. Be extremely careful about overconfiguring VMs on ESXi hosts running Hadoop. Consider resource pools to protect Hadoop SLAs. Hadoop clusters are very I/O intensive. Tune to minimize virtualization overhead at the storage layer.

Site Recovery Manager (SRM) gives you an additional way to automate movement of a Hadoop cluster from a primary to a secondary site. The advantage of using SRM is the automation of disaster recovery to another site. By default, it also provides great documentation for this process with its internal scripts. These features all express a series of practices that embrace a vast array of disciplines to enable availability, scalability, management, and optimization. These disciplines are the general targets that must be considered in virtualizing any critical business system.

Tier 1 Is Not Tier 2 or Tier 3

One of the biggest issues we see in the field is that customers have been running tier 2 and tier 3 virtualized platforms for years. The problem is these platforms often have not been enterprise optimized for running tier one applications. We then see customers not achieving the performance expectations when virtualizing business-critical applications, and it's because they have not followed the best practices. When we show them best practices, they start getting the performance numbers they were expecting. The point here is to go through all the Hadoop best practices for virtual infrastructures with the necessary due diligence and properly test them. At customer sites, we consistently see that most problems and support tickets were generated from not following best practices and from inadequate monitoring. A breakdown is shown in Table 9.1.

Table 9.1 Causes of Support Tickets

Area	Percentage of Support Tickets
Storage Network	75%
Network	10%
Lack of best practices and inadequate monitoring	10%
Other	5%

Industry Best Practices

Hadoop services are network and storage latency sensitive. With the heavy workloads of Hadoop clusters, it is very important to maintain balance across a Hadoop cluster and avoid bottlenecks in memory, processing storage, and networking, especially with the latest versions of Hadoop supporting interactive query capability. Virtualization gives administrators the capability to respond to changes in the environment quickly. One of the key benefits of virtualization is the capability to achieve consolidation and get higher utilization of your hardware, especially because network communication on the same hosts occurs at the speed of the communication bus. When the system is heavily used, the environment must be configured to make sure VMs with SLAs have the resources they need to meet their SLAs.

When we talk about best practices, remember that best practices are dependent on their context. It's not unusual to look at two sources and find best practices that conflict with each other. The reason for the conflict could be the context. Here is a perfect example of two highly recommended solutions that contradict each other.

One best practice is to never overcommit VMs running applications with performance SLAs. Then, protect the VMs with features like resource pools, allocation management such as storage I/O control and network I/O control (NetIOC), and so on. This approach is strongly recommended when someone starts virtualizing high-profile Hadoop platforms, especially because the virtual environment is always guilty until proven innocent when it comes to performance. It is critical that your customers be very confident that the virtual infrastructure teams can guarantee the right levels of performance when they start virtualizing.

Another best practice is to allow some level of overcommitment of VMs. This is a great way to leverage all the features of virtualization and get every ounce of utilization out of your hardware that you can. However, this approach requires the virtual infrastructure team to have a lot of expertise and experience around latency-sensitive environments and understand how to protect VMs to make sure their SLAs are met. If you overcommit when you start virtualizing, and your expertise cannot match what you are trying to accomplish, it's like putting a 16-year-old in a brand new high-performance Corvette. The results are pretty similar. The biggest problem with using this approach is that customers often do not have adequate guidelines to protect the resources of the sensitive VMs when the environment grows or encounters increased utilization. Make sure that VMs are sized correctly, or make sure you can control overcommitment.

vSphere can control resource sharing with its algorithms for fair share CPU scheduling, memory entitlement, network I/O control, storage I/O control, and resource pools. The key point in this example is that latency-sensitive environments need to perform operations at the millisecond level. You can't have your users lose confidence in using VMs simply because you didn't do your due diligence. This concern applies even more to a new big data project because doubts exist about the performance overhead of virtualization. Concerns loom that infrastructure is a money pit and burdens the business. All this can be avoided by having a focus on building out the Hadoop platform from the context of what is tried and true.

A goal of best practices is to reduce the possibility of errors and minimize variables when troubleshooting. Therefore, you should consider doing the following:

- Develop best practices and make sure they are consistently followed.

- Build analytical skills and metric knowledge around the four areas you are virtualizing: memory, CPU, storage, and networking.

- Teach Hadoop administrators the key metrics they need to understand about the virtual infrastructure so they can determine whether an issue is a virtualization issue or a Hadoop issue.

- Your benchmarking should enable you to create consistent and reproducible results that you can compare against. Metrics should always be quantitative.

- Understand dependencies and interdependencies.

- With VMware, develop best practices around vCenter vSphere Operations Manager and additional adapters like Hyperic or the management and monitoring software you are using. Understand this is going to take time and the development of skill and expertise.

- It is important that Hadoop administrators know all about the virtual infrastructure. Hadoop admins and vAdmins need to work together. When there is a Hadoop (application) issue, the whole team must be able to quickly determine whether it is a VM problem or a Hadoop problem. The following tips can help you determine the problem and troubleshoot it:

  - What are the key metrics for virtualization? Learning to understand the key metrics with tools such as vCenter Operations manager will be helpful. Getting very good at esxtop is a requirement.

  - Your systems should have custom vCenter Operations Dashboards for Hadoop administrators to be able to look at the virtual infrastructure the same way they would look at storage and networking in physical server environments.

With any infrastructure, it comes down to people, processes, and technology. Also, keep it simple because complex systems fail in complex ways. Hadoop clusters grow horizontally. Automation must be emphasized from the very beginning, and good design is critical. The practices and guidelines put in place must be scalable. It's important to develop internal best practices, management processes, and guidelines for managing and monitoring a virtualization environment. Make sure your infrastructure management is ready to handle tier 1 workloads and the dynamics they can create.

Remember, in many enterprise environments these practices already exist; it's a matter of bringing the Hadoop administrators, data architects, and system and platform architects into the team.

VMware Best Practices—Where Do I Start?

The more solid and robust the virtualization infrastructure is and the better this infrastructure has been configured, the better Hadoop will run. There are five vital virtualization keys for Hadoop:

- Make sure virtualization maximizes the availability of the master nodes.

- Virtualization needs to be configured for performance for the worker nodes.

- Virtualization adds to the advantages of features such as NameNode HA, Resource Manager HA, Ozzie HA, NameNode Federation, and YARN by producing a data center that is more available, less expensive, and has greater flexibility. All are discussed later in the book.

- For Hadoop to be managed virtually, worker nodes must be rack aware (if rack topology is used) and virtual aware. Hadoop Virtual Extensions (HVE) enable this awareness to become a reality; providing worker nodes with the capability to maximize performance and reduce the management and administration of the worker nodes. HVE accounts for efficient uses of hardware without breaking Hadoop's capability to recover from failures and be a robust product.

- Virtualization increases the flexibility of the Hadoop cluster and assists with Data Lifecycle Management, such as backups and other processes that run in the Hadoop cluster. Understand the runtime characteristics of different frameworks (such as Storm, Kafka, and NoSQL databases) and how their VMs need to be optimized.

- A virtualization strategy must be aware of the entire infrastructure (such as staging servers, edge servers, HDFS NFS Gateways, HTTP Gateways, Hadoop clients, and management servers) that makes up the Hadoop cluster.

Build your virtualization best practices the same way you would build a house—from the ground up.

- **Hardware:** Purchase the right hardware from the vendor hardware compatibility lists (HCL).

- **BIOS:** Set the right BIOS settings. The latest hardware and CPUs are adding numerous features to leverage virtualization. Leverage BIOS settings focused on availability for master nodes and performance for worker nodes.

- **Storage:** Use storage best practices that are a combination of your virtualization provider and your storage teams. Hadoop platforms are very I/O intensive, so minimizing virtualization overhead around I/O is a very high priority.

- **Network:** Use networking best practices. The right settings and drivers make all the difference. Virtual networks and NSX offer a lot of advantages to Hadoop clusters.

- **Virtualization:** Try to stay on the latest version of VMware tools to get the most recent paravirtualized network and storage drivers. It is important to use the right drivers and settings.

- **Internal standards:** Define corporate standards and follow them. Define resource pools, DRS rules, resource pool management, guidelines for vMotion, and so on. Companies often get in trouble by not defining these standards properly and then not following them. Then Hadoop has problems and virtualization is blamed when the problem was due to not following the best practices.

- **Skills:** Develop performance tuning and troubleshooting skills. Most important, communicate, communicate, communicate to make sure Hadoop administrators are working well with all infrastructure teams supporting virtualization.

- **VM Management:** Make sure best practices and corporate standards are being followed as the virtual infrastructure grows. As infrastructures grow, SLAs will continue to be met if guidelines are being followed.

Guidelines Around Overcommitment and Disk Latency

Overcommitting allows somewhat higher utilization of your hardware, but overcommitment must be done with caution and awareness. Here are a few general guidelines:

- Overcommit your development and test environments as much as you can, staying within common sense and meeting defined requirements. Overcommit allows cost savings related to the amount of hardware used, the energy to run the hardware, and less staff to run the development environment.

- Try not to overcommit production high-profile environments unless your expertise is ready for it. Initially, be conservative and do not overcommit production environments with SLAs. Build success and confidence in your users so that they can trust virtualized Hadoop platforms.

- After you develop the right level of expertise, you can overcommit some production environments if you have guidelines that make sure SLAs are always met. Understand where bottlenecks occur. Worker nodes are constantly adding and removing YARN containers for different jobs. Make sure overcommitment does not impact application YARN containers.

- Do not overcommit virtual resources until the runtime characteristics of a production Hadoop cluster are well understood. Your team must be good with resource pools, setting DRS priorities and rules, I/O controls (Storage and Network), SR-IOV, and so on. Saying you absolutely do not overcommit production environments is a simple answer, but it is not always a correct answer.

VMware has benchmarked the throughput and disk latency for virtual infrastructures. Storage latency is dependent on the storage hardware topology. VMware announced at recent VMWorlds that it has achieved these numbers:

- vSphere 4.1—5 microseconds
- vSphere 5.0—2 microseconds
- vSphere 5.1—1 microsecond with 1 million IOPS in a VM

Most companies run benchmarks in a controlled environment to maximize the results. You might not be able to achieve these same results; however, be aware that these numbers have been reached.

There will be a slight increase in CPU usage due to the hypervisor allocating resources. There is minimal overhead of going through the hypervisor, but it does require some CPU cycles. However, this should be minimal.

Disk latency is minimal if best practices are followed. The point is to benchmark your throughput and disk latency following best practices and understand your storage hardware's capability.

Hardware

All hardware should meet the requirements in the hardware compatibility lists (HCL).

- When you choose hardware, be aware that CPU compatibility is important for vMotion. vMotion impacts DRS and DPM.

- Hardware-assisted virtualization has a significant positive impact on performance. This happens by making use of areas or rings of privilege available to critical processing like VMkernel code. This privilege enables the VMkernel to manage the VM more efficiently. Go to the Edit virtual machine settings for a VM and choose the Options tab to get access to the virtualization settings.

- The following discussion is technical in nature but I want to make sure the big idea is clear. X86 processors place code in special areas within the CPU before processing the code or executing on the data. These special areas contain priority of when they get time in the CPU, and the privilege at which the code operates is related to where the code is placed. Before hardware virtualization assist, two types of code OS and Hypervisor code, such as virtual memory monitoring, would compete for priority or privilege. With the existence of hardware virtualization there now exists two noncompeting places of privilege and priority for OS and Hypervisor code to run. Here are the details: hardware-assisted CPU virtualization assistance, VT-x (Intel), and AMD-V (AMD) trap system-sensitive operations and reduce the overhead of supervisory-level code. This gives the virtual machine monitor (VMM) the capability to decide whether it should use hardware-assisted virtualization (HV) or binary translation (BT). Although HV is usually faster, BT is faster in a few situations. The complexity of both the performance and security of code is a problem not effectively managed by administrators. Enabling the VMkernel to use hardware assist to intelligently place code scheduled to run on the CPU ensures that applications will perform their best.

- Hardware-assisted Memory Management Unit (MMU) virtualization, also called rapid virtualization indexing (RVI) or nested page tables (NPT: AMD) and extended page tables (EPT: Intel) can reduce memory management overhead.

- With software MMU the guest OS has to map guest virtual memory to guest physical memory in guest page tables. This requires ESXi to use "shadow page tables" that directly map guest virtual memory to host physical memory addresses.

- Hardware-assisted MMU eliminates shadow page tables by managing both guest virtual to guest physical translations and guest physical to host physical translations in hardware. This eliminates overhead from managing page tables in software but the two-level scheme in the translation lookaside buffer (TLB) introduces a new source of overhead. However, the net result is nearly always a benefit.

- To make sure the TLB does not encounter additional overhead in caching direct guest virtual memory to host physical memory address translations, use large memory pages for the hypervisor and the guest OS. The essence of this configuration is for data to be near the CPU for processing by holding it in this TLB cache. Obviously, the chance is greater for a TLB to have the needed data if the pages of memory are larger. Large pages (2MB memory pages) can reduce TLB misses. Be aware that using large pages can impact transparent page sharing. For this reason, when configuring hardware-assisted MMU, virtualization also configures large pages. Large pages are the default in vSphere and in recent versions of Linux (through transparent huge pages).

Always disable physical hardware devices that will not be used in the VM. This is good not only from a security and management perspective but also for performance. The operating system must be optimized for running Hadoop. Disabling unused devices can free interrupt resources, eliminate polling on unused devices, and eliminate blocks of memory that they can take up. These devices include the following:

- USB controllers
- Floppy drives
- COM ports
- Optical drives
- LPT ports
- Network interfaces
- Storage controllers

VMware Tools

Virtual hardware version 10 is part of vSphere 5.5. This version is not backward compatible. Always try to be up to date on the latest hardware version. This is always a balance between the latest versus the most tested. The latest versions of OS, network drivers, virtual tools, CPUs, and memory all improve performance and reduce overhead in virtualization.

PVSCSI drivers provide up to 30% CPU savings and 12% I/O improvement.

BIOS

Always make sure you are running the latest version of your BIOS, and double-check your settings after performing an update.

- Enable Turbo Boost in the BIOS if your processors support it. Consider disabling C-states from an ESXi perspective and not the BIOS, if possible, but for high latency environments it might be best to disable C-states in the BIOS.

- Make sure all processor sockets are enabled and all cores for each socket are enabled.

- You normally want to keep NUMA enabled by disabling node interweaving. Try to keep all memory accesses within one socket by configuring VMs that fit on one NUMA node. This will allow NUMA optimizations.

- Turn on hyperthreading.

- Turn on all hardware-assisted virtualization features. Leverage Hardware Assist with VT and memory management.

- Hardware assisted CPU virtualization.

- Hardware assisted memory virtualization.

  Hardware assist enables both memory and the CPU to function.

- Set Static High Performance or OS control for power.

- Try to avoid CPU affinity.

- Avoid Direct Path I/O unless you absolutely need the small amount of additional performance it gives you. Direct Path I/O can improve performance by bypassing the vNIC and giving a VM direct access to a physical NIC. You gain performance but lose some virtualization features, such as vMotion. It is important to understand the trade-offs and the performance gain.

- Leave the memory scrubbing rate at the manufacturer's default unless otherwise recommended.

- Consider interrupt coalescing. Adaptive coalescing is usually something to avoid in latency sensitive environments.

- Consider turning off power management schemes for maximizing performance. The best way of controlling this is at the ESXi level and not the BIOS level. Set power management in the BIOS to OS Controlled Mode or the equivalent. Then set power management with ESXi.

- Adaptive coalescing may introduce latency. Consider disabling coalescing.

vSphere

The vSphere Flash Read Cache enables flash resources to be used by the hypervisor. The read caching is completely transparent and is managed like CPU and memory. The Flash Read Cache can improve performance for latency sensitive environments.

vSphere Replication supports VM-level replication to different sites. There is support for multiple point-in-time copies and Storage vMotion. Integration with SRM can be used to automate the disaster recovery process.

VM

A Latency Sensitivity level can be set for VMs. Go to the VM Options tab and set the level to High. The options are Low, Normal, Medium, and High.

Memory and CPU

Memory and CPU allocations are managed differently in a virtual infrastructure. For memory, you must carve out specific chunks. For CPU, you share time slices.

CPU ready time is the amount of time a vCPU is waiting for time slices from a physical CPU.

Hypervisor NUMA scheduling and related optimizations are broken into two categories.

VMs that have cores that fit in a single NUMA node are allocated memory local to a NUMA node. The goal is to keep the memory local to the NUMA node on the socket. Depending on memory availability, memory accesses will be local, reducing memory access latencies. NUMA works by a one-step access to the data and code needed. You can think of it like efficiency of motion: if you can do something with fewer steps, this efficiency opens the door to higher performance and more reliable results, solving the problem it was designed to resolve.

VMs with more cores than what fit into a physical NUMA node are referred to as *wide-NUMA virtual machines*. Optimizations try to keep memory access local but might need to periodically access memory in a different NUMA node.

Memory

Virtualization supports a number of features to manage memory. They include ballooning, transparent page sharing (TPS), allocation management (shares, reservations, limits), memory compression, and hypervisor swapping.

- **Transparent page sharing:** Multiple copies of memory are automatically mapped to one location in physical memory.

- **Ballooning:** During the tug-of-war for memory resources, the oldest memory areas are swapped out to disk.

- **Compression:** Take memory pages with greater than 50% compression ratio and compresses them. Compression is better than swapping.

- **Allocation management:** Provides resource management if not enough resources are available.

- **Hypervisor swapping:** Should be avoided if possible.

All the listed memory management techniques are based on small host memory pages. The transition from large to small (and back) host memory pages is transparent to the user. Although the techniques themselves often incur little overhead, there can be a significant indirect performance penalty because of the use of small memory pages. Defining full memory reservations for a Hadoop instance prevents memory management techniques from being used. Overconfiguring vCPUs that you are not using creates overhead. Idle vCPUs take a certain amount of overhead to maintain.

The following are considerations for production Hadoop environments:

- Minimizing the contention over memory by sizing VMs correctly is preferable to using memory management (ballooning, TPS, memory compression, swapping) features unless you can make sure SLAs are always met.

- Do not disable page sharing or the balloon driver. Although you might not plan to use these features, they are useful safeguards.

- If you use ballooning, configure it to let you know there is memory pressure. If you have swapping issues over a period of time, it is likely to be reflected in performance issues.

- If you have swapping or paging at the guest level, the guest memory is underprovisioned. In the field we have seen Hadoop clusters get better I/O throughput performance when swapping is turned off on all worker nodes.

- The standard conservative approach has been to turn off transparent page sharing (VM level setting). If you are working with vSphere 5.1 or later, it is recommended to keep transparent page sharing on. However, for Hadoop servers it is still best to not overcommit memory unless your team has a lot of experience and expertise managing it.

- Make sure the VM is a little larger than the guest memory usage.
- Enable hyperthreading.
- Keep full memory reservation (DRS or resource sharing setting at VM level).
- Non-Uniform Memory Access (NUMA) nodes—on every motherboard an amount of physical memory belongs to a physical socket. There can also be multiple NUMA nodes on one socket. For example, a 12-core socket can be broken into two NUMA nodes. A software process running in a VM can request memory, and the physical CPU can cross another physical socket to get the memory. Virtual NUMA passes NUMA topology to the guest operating system.
- The hypervisor tries to keep the vCPU for a VM local to a socket's memory. Be aware that NUMA migrations can occur for load balancing, which can create some performance latency.

CPU

The goal is to minimize the number of sockets (or NUMA nodes) a VM has to use. Set the VMware parameter `numa.vcpu.preferHT=True` to keep the vCPUs to the minimum number of physical sockets. Hadoop often needs more threads than cores, so this setting can see increased performance.

- Memory must be managed in a VM the same way it is managed on a physical server running Hadoop. Understand how much memory is being used in the VM and how much memory is idle.
- Try to avoid CPU affinity; it creates two types of problems:
  - The VM tied to a CPU with CPU affinity cannot use another vCPU, but other VMs can use the CPUs the VM is using.
  - With CPU affinity, a VM loses that capability to use vMotion. Hadoop worker nodes should not be moved with vMotion in most situations.
- DRS anti-affinity rules can be used to keep VMs with high CPU activity separated.
- Not all systems can leverage CPU and memory virtualization features. Application servers, LDAP servers, and so on may be more I/O driven. Be aware of which resource is stressed.
- If the network cards are at 100% activity, this will impact the CPU load.

Storage

Storage is always about understanding throughput, IOPS, and disk latency. Understand your I/O usage patterns and thresholds and times of high activity. Benchmark and confirm that you are achieving the true throughput of your hardware. Bad settings and configurations can keep the true throughput of the system from being achieved. It is important to understand the total IOPS your disk system can handle. The following equations can help you to figure the IOPS of your system:

Total Raw IOPS = disk IOPS x number of disks

Functional IOPS = (disk IOPS x write%)/ (RAID overhead) + (Raw IOPS x Read%)

You must find a balance between performance and capacity. Larger drives usually provide poorer performance. The more spindles you have, the more IOPS you can generate. Set the right multipathing strategy and use path balancing when possible. Round-robin should be considered with Asymmetric Logical Unit Access (ALUA). Plug-ins can also be used.

Improper storage configuration is often the culprit with performance issues. A major percentage of disk performance issues are media related, so it is crucial to understand your payload (throughput) and your IOPS. The following are areas to validate:

- Minimize high activity systems sharing physical resources if possible.

- Understand your network bottlenecks. Transitioning to a smaller number of links can impact performance during high activity.

- Try to avoid putting high-performance cards in slower PCIe slots.

Additional considerations:

- Jumbo frames (maybe < 10% more important for 10GbE).

- For Tier 1, 10GbE is a better choice than 1Gb.

- For latency-sensitive environments such as Hadoop, the interrupt rate on the network adapter should be increased on the ESXi server.

- Look at VAAI (xcopy/write_same). The value of VAAI (VMware API Array Integration is to offload the effort of storage from being the job of the VMkernel on an individual ESXi host that would consume CPU, memory, storage, and networking resources and allow the storage array to take over these operations. These metrics would enable you to know whether the array is doing the work rather than the ESXi host.

- File Block Alignment – impact 10% – 40% improvement.

- I/O concurrency (Async I/O) 9% performance improvement.

- Vmxnet TX coalescing, 2% improvement in performance.

Using flash drives for the vSphere infrastructure has crossed the tipping point. A vSphere flash infrastructure can be built using PCIe flash cards or SSD drives. Many companies are starting to use hybrid storage solutions with certain frameworks where disk performance is critical to meet SLAs.

Setting the maximum queue depth for Fibre Channel HBA cards can help SAN contention when the command queues are being stressed.

If there is just one VM on a LUN, set the maximum queue depth.

If there are multiple VMs on a LUN, also look at the Disk.SchedNumReqOutstanding.

VMware vStorage APIs for Array Integration (VAAI) can offload some operations to the storage hardware, as opposed to performing the operations in the hypervisor.

Considerations for SANs:

- Look at block zeroing for improving performance of eager-zeroed thick disk creation as well as first-time write performance on lazy-zeroed thick disks and thin disks. This is true for all disks, including local storage.

- When using SANs, look at hardware-accelerated cloning (fully copy or copy offload).

- Make sure the SAN and local storage are properly configured according to your storage vendor's recommended settings. End-to-end speeds must be consistent for SANs. The SAN must connect to the SAN switch at the same speed the SAN switch is connected to the ESXi HBA.

Considerations for NAS:

- Hardware-accelerated cloning can also be beneficial on NAS. Storage vMotion does not leverage this feature on NAS.

- Using NAS native snapshots for creating VM linked clones and VM snapshots offloads the overhead from ESXi to NAS. This feature requires hardware version 9 or later.

- For local storage, make sure the write-back cache is configured according to your storage vendor.

All the recent performance benchmarks performed by VMware comparing VMFS (VMDK) or RDMs show negligible performance differences between the two. So you should choose VMFS or RDMs independent of your objectives and the feature or functionality you want to leverage. VMFS enables you to leverage all the virtualization features.

RDMs is a good choice when you want to leverage features of your storage vendor or if you want to make a cautious transition to virtualization.

Hadoop high -profile environments need to focus on performance. Following are general rules for Hadoop storage:

- LUNs for Hadoop node files must be created as EAGERZEROTHICK.

- Storage multitiering strategies are increasing in popularity.

- Snapshots are stored with the VMX file. Make sure there is sufficient space.

- Customers are using SSDs more often, and storage vendors are including them in multitiered storage solutions.

Networking

CPUs keep getting faster, so VMs can process more, often putting pressure on network I/O. Each release of vSphere takes this into consideration. vSphere 5.5 supports up to eight 10GbE NICS on an ESXi host. The following are some network considerations:

- Separate VM traffic from the vMotion, iSCSI, and management traffic. This provides better security and scalability as the environment grows.

- Activity for vMotion should occur on its own separate network. Ideally, use a separate physical network and, if necessary, use a VLAN to segment the vMotion traffic.

- Try to stay away from MSI and MSI-X modes if you are using passthrough devices in a Linux kernel. This might work better in future Linux releases.

- Try to organize physical NICs for a specific network service. Network services can also be separated by using port groups with different VLAN IDs.

- PVLANs and their designs can be used to control traffic between virtual networks with uplinks to pNICs and virtual networks without uplinks.

- VMkernel network adapters should be configured to the maximum transmission unit (MTU).

- Load balancing determines which NIC a VM will use for its uplink. You should not have VMs with high I/O activity on the same uplink (physical NIC).

- Use the latest recommended virtual adapters. It is currently vmxnet3, but follow the latest best practices. Do not use the default virtual network drivers for enterprise level workloads.

- VMs stay on the uplink they are using until an event occurs. Understand settings for the NIC link state change, beacon probes, timeouts, and so on.

- Jumbo frames are recommended. If you use jumbo frames, make sure they are enabled end-to-end.

- If you use IP hash, make sure the physical switch supports IP hash (EtherChannel).

- Make sure to design your network with system failure in mind. Minimize all points of failure.

Additional settings to look at

- Checksum offload

- Large receive offload (LRO)

- TCP segmentation offload (TSO)

- Ability to handle multiple Scatter Gather elements per Tx frame

- With VXLANs, look at NIC support for offloading encapsulated packets.

Esxtop

Esxtop is an easy tool for Linux-oriented Hadoop administrators to get comfortable using, especially if they are used to tools such as top, iostat, vmstat, and the like. An administrator needs to understand these metrics and how to look at them. For example, different workloads can have the same utilization (%UTIL) but have different overhead costs (%SYS).

Esxtop can be used to quickly see whether your environment is overloaded.

Look at the first line of the esxtop CPU panel. If the load average is 1 or above, the system is overloaded.

View the usage percentage for the physical CPUs on the PCPU line. If the usage is between 90%–95%, the system is close to being overloaded.

A lot of metrics can be viewed with esxtop, including the following:

- **MEMSZ:** Memory size; how much memory is configured for the VM (memory size).

- **GRANT:** Amount of physical memory the VM currently has.

- **SZTGT:** Size target; memory the hypervisor wants to allocate to a resource pool or a VM.

- **TCHD:** Touched; the estimated amount of memory that's been used for a VM.

- **TCH_W:** Working set writes.

- **SW*:** Swap metrics (current, target, reads, writes).

- **NUMA statistics:** The %local memory value ideally should be 100.

CPU metrics:

- **%SYS:** Percentage of CPU usage consumed by the system or VMkernel

- **%RUN:** Percentage of total scheduled time to run.

- **%WAIT:** Percentage of time in blocked or busy wait states.

- **%UTIL:** Physical CPU utilization.

- **%IDLE:** Percentage of time that the CPU is idle.

- **%WAIT:** %IDLE is used to understand I/O wait time.

Storage metrics:

Esxtop can be used to look at the storage adapter (d), the VM (v), and the disk device (u). Key values include the following:

- **QUED/USD:** Command queue depth.

- **CMDS/s:** Commands per second.

- **MBREADS/s:** Count of megabyte read operations per second.

- **MBWRTN/s:** Count of megabyte write operations per second.

- **DAVG:** High numbers indicate the ESXi host storage adapter should be looked at. The problem could be because the storage processor is overloaded, bad overloaded zoning, or the RAID set does not have enough spindles to handle the IOPS needed.

- **KAVG:** High numbers mean there might be an issue with the ESXi storage. Look at queue issues (queue being full) or driver issues.

- **DAVG + KAVG = GAVG:** DAVG is the average disk latency, accounting for speed of operations along the path or at the end of the operation in a storage array; thus, disk latency and KAVG is the average latency or time accounted for by VMkernel to place a storage workload on the storage path (to begin a storage operation). GAVG is the global average accounted for from the sum of both VMkernel and disk latencies.

- **Aborts:** The DAVG or KAVG are likely exceeding thresholds (5000ms). The aborted command will be repeated, but this will create performance delays for the VM.

Summary

Virtualizing Hadoop requires an understanding not only of virtualization but also of the strategies for virtualizing master nodes and virtualizing worker nodes. Master nodes need to leverage the virtualization features to maximize availability. Worker nodes must be configured for virtual awareness and also for using the virtualization features to maximize performance and reducing the overall management of worker nodes in a Hadoop cluster.

One of the big challenges in virtualizing Hadoop is that Hadoop experts often do not understand virtualization, or they fear adding additional complexity into a Hadoop cluster. However, virtualization can offer high availability in areas that Hadoop does not address at this time. Virtualization can also offer improvements in flexibility, agility, and time to deliver; therefore, we have provided a pathway to explore the more significant details you might need to address to get maximum results from your virtualized big data projects.

## Chapter 10

Virtualizing Hadoop

> *Throughout history, people with new ideas—who think differently and try to change things—have always been called troublemakers.*
>
> —Richelle Mead, *Shadow Kiss*

In this book, we've discussed the variety of technology options available with Hadoop and the industry direction toward converged data, cloud deployments, data-driven applications, and open source. Open source has changed how organizations look at solving problems, and it is an area where platforms and ecosystems are being created. Open source can now mitigate risk. These technology options are continuing to evolve with the high-profile activity around predictive analytics and the innovation of open source.

We have constantly emphasized that one area of focus should be on building the culture and sense of urgency of a speed-driven data organization. A speed-driven data organization focuses on getting the data in the hands of the analysts and data scientists as quickly as possible to accelerate the speed of generating business value from the data. Hadoop and big data are platforms for accomplishing this objective.

We've also seen that big data is context driven. When people talk about big data, they can be talking about Hadoop, with NoSQL solutions like HBase, Cassandra, Aerospike, MongoDB, and so on; in-memory solutions such as Spark and Flink; massively parallel processing (MPP) query engines like Cloudera Impala and Apache Drill; and distributed search tools such as Apache Solr or Elasticsearch. Hadoop is not required for a big data solution; however, Hadoop is often the central data hub around different big data components. Most organizations also have data warehouse platforms in place from companies such as HP, Oracle, IBM, Teradata, Netezza, and Greenplum. There are often integration solutions such as Informatica, Splunk, Ab Initio, Pentaho, and Quest, to name a few. There are high-performance analytics tool decisions to be made from companies such as SAS, SAP, IBM, HP, Oracle, Revolution Analytics, Datameer, Tableau, Alpine Data Labs, HP Vertica, Microstrategy, Platfora, and Actian. Weeding through the Hadoop distributions, NoSQL platforms, in-memory solutions, and large vendor and niche solution providers to determine the best combination for areas such as architecture, platform, data governance, integration, security, SQL engines, analytics, and visualization tools takes time. With all the different software components and tools involved in a Hadoop ecosystem, organizations must determine how to manage Hadoop and create the enterprise operational efficiencies necessary to manage a Hadoop ecosystem.

It is important to not get lost in the technologies or products we went through in the preceding paragraph. Determine which solutions can best help you accomplish your goals. Be able to answer the following questions:

- What is the best way to leverage our existing data platforms with emerging platforms to generate business insight faster?

- Where is the best data platform for persisting data?

- What query engines and compute platforms do we need to work with for our use cases?

- What are the existing skill sets of our teams, and how do we get the expertise to run production applications in the evolving enterprise data platform?

- How do we win the war on talent?

- How do we leverage our existing data platforms while reducing the data silos and improving the analytics and decision making for the organization?

- What is the best way to deal with the dynamics of existing data silos and data territories and the politics of existing and emerging technologies?

- How do we maintain or evolve our culture and management of data platforms?

How Are Hadoop Ecosystems Going to Be Managed?

Hadoop is a set of open source extensible software frameworks designed to be put together like LEGO blocks. However, these Hadoop frameworks and the software they touch are getting more complex, as discussed in the previous sections. The difficulty of managing a Hadoop ecosystem is increasing significantly each year. Defining an enterprise solution around security, compliance, governance, backups, disaster recovery, and so on for all these components is a challenge. Organizations such as Pivotal, EMC, IBM, HP, and Hitachi are bringing powerful solutions to the Hadoop ecosystem, which bring additional choice considerations. How do we find the right mixture of open source versus proprietary software? It will be different for every company. At the same time, an incredible amount of bureaucracy surrounds existing infrastructure teams. Asking existing infrastructure teams to manage different components of a Hadoop ecosystem on physical servers and to provide the platform supporting rapid change as well as all the networking, disaster recovery, governance, and security around the data is not trivial. Solving organizational data fragmentation and dealing with the complexity involved in building an enterprise Hadoop ecosystem can significantly slow the progress in achieving the benefits of a big data platform.

A Hadoop ecosystem cannot be just a blending of the best-of-breed software frameworks and applications. There must be some integration of all the components. There also must be a way to control cost structures and reduce the risk that is inherent in transformation projects. Organizations realize they are moving into a data-driven world, and the capability to analyze data and turn it into business value quickly is critical for success. We come back to the challenge of tying everything together.

Building an Enterprise Hadoop Platform That Is Agile and Flexible

So, the 50-million-dollar question is, how do we put together a solution that helps achieve the goal of being data-driven with an enterprise platform that is agile and flexible? Rapid change at low cost is a key ingredient for innovation. Therefore, successful strategies for deploying big data solutions can't look at hardware solutions for deploying physical servers using data center models that worked 10 or 20 years ago. Big data platforms must support the data-driven organization by providing an environment that supports fast deployments, rapid change, new proof of concept projects, and the flexibility to support an environment that is constantly evolving. Hadoop workloads are not constant. The modern data architecture associated with a Hadoop cluster is designed to run applications with different types of workloads in the same cluster. A Hadoop environment needs a level of automation so the administration complexity does not increase linearly as the environment evolves. Creating big data platforms should be like playing a game of LEGOs. Someone must be able to easily add, remove, and change pieces with a platform that is stable through rapid changes.

The platforms that provide the best solutions for speed, agility, flexibility, and adaptability while delivering the lowest-cost solution today are virtualization and cloud platforms. Containers look like a key future solution as well, but containers are still maturing. However, the evolution of containers with Hadoop is something to keep an eye on.

Clarification of Terms

In discussions where we refer to virtualization, we are focusing on the scheduling of CPU, memory, networking, and storage resources through a type one hypervisor. A type one hypervisor runs directly on the physical hardware without an operating system. This is why type one hypervisors are referred to as *bare-metal hypervisors* or as a hardware virtualization engine.

Using hypervisors and containers are two ways of achieving operational efficiencies. Hypervisors virtualize the CPU, memory, networking, and storage around the software stack of operating system, drivers, applications, and the like in a virtual machine. Containers support the sharing of an operating system creating very lightweight software modules that can share software binaries. Figure 10.1 diagrams this. When we talk about containers, we are referring to containers similar to Docker. A Docker engine enables several isolated containers to execute their own runtime instance of an operating system. Each container uses its binaries and libraries from the host operating system while a virtual machine runs in its own guest operating system with its own binaries and libraries contained within the virtual machine. Virtual machines and containers are two ways of abstracting the physical resources. With virtualization, there is an entire infrastructure for management, monitoring, and provisioning, as well as networking and storage virtualization. Virtualization is a very mature proven technology, whereas Docker containers are a new, emerging technology.

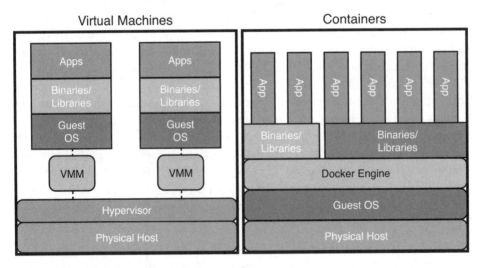

Figure 10.1   Virtual machines versus containers.

The Journey from Bare-Metal to Virtualization

At one time, all data centers were physical. When VMware started in 1998, the thought that the physical components of a computer could be represented through software was considered crazy. Administrators and developers were also so exhausted they were considered crazy. Why were they so exhausted? Because of long days of tedious and repetitive work with constant calls at night to resolve fragile issues around contention, availability, and scale. Ironically, their very expensive hardware was frequently underused.

The perception was that even if virtualization could work, it would overutilize the physical resources to the point that it wouldn't provide any value. Thankfully, developers knew that it would help them with rapid deployments, quick changes, and building and tearing down test developments and test environments. Deadlines were more reachable and things just worked.

This technology was originally a hosted solution, where the virtual machine was built on x86 hardware with Windows, Linux, and, later, the Mac OS. Many companies ran VMware Workstation, VMware Fusion, or VMware Player to get various jobs done. The value of being able to run practically any program from any operating system became very compelling to the IT community.

Fast forward about three or four years, and VMware introduced virtualization software that worked directly on bare-metal x86 hardware. All of a sudden, you were seeing all the benefits of virtualization on the servers rather than on desktops and laptops. What benefits? The first clear winner was time savings. The rapid speed of deployment made tedious work a breeze. Soon the people paying for the infrastructure realized that hardware utilization could be better optimized, so boxes went from 14% utilization across an organization to 70%–80% utilization without a reduction in quality of service. Granted, at first it was used only on servers with a light workload. However, the cost savings piled up because of the more efficient use of hardware, fewer servers to handle the same workload, and a reduction in the cost of electricity and cooling. Suddenly, IT could save time and money while getting work done.

The new functionality enables each virtual machine to be isolated and running its own software stack from the operating system down to the applications. Each virtual machine can be completely independent within its own functionality and capable of running the same from ESXi host to ESXi host. This led to simplifying the methods for redistributing individual virtual machines to maintain high performance on each virtual machine. This also led to elegant availability solutions that often restarted themselves on failure. The IT department started to look good and gain greater confidence in virtual infrastructures. Over time, VMware improved the software's features to handle many of the toughest workloads. This never would have happened without hardware following virtualization in one innovation after another.

Why this history tour? Because by the year 2011 the world of servers had changed so much that there were more virtualized servers than bare-metal servers. This has set up an unnatural tension with big data and Hadoop. By not seriously considering virtualization as a viable option, you are asking data center operators to return to the days of wasting money, wasting time, and looking bad to business units with outdated deployments. Virtualization software is extremely stable and runs business-critical applications today. In the next year, the industry will see more virtualization of different Hadoop components and more examples of Hadoop moving into the cloud.

Why Consider Virtualizing Hadoop?

Hadoop was originally developed to run on commodity physical servers. This greatly reduced costs and enabled organizations to run batch-oriented analytics at a fraction of the cost of traditional databases and data warehouses. Hadoop has also always been about virtualization and abstraction of resources. Today, Hadoop virtualizes the compute, storage, and network resources across a distributed cluster and makes it transparent to the developer how the cluster is composed. YARN took the next step and virtualized how OS resources are utilized across all the nodes in a Hadoop cluster. The Hadoop schedulers can now guarantee resources across a cluster for all kinds of applications with different runtime characteristics. Containers are going to provide the next level of isolation for Hadoop clusters. So the concept of virtualization and abstraction is not new to Hadoop. Virtualization hypervisors can take Hadoop to the next level of abstraction.

Hadoop ecosystems now have a lot more frameworks, in-memory solutions, distributed search engines, NoSQL databases, integration layers, analytics, and visualization software that can be part of a big data platform. Significant new features are constantly being added at an amazing rate. These are all components that need to work together as the systems evolve and grow. Working with all these as separate components is a management nightmare. Using standards and implementing best practices through each individual framework and component of a big data platform is not how to create speed, agility, and flexibility. There must be some consistent management infrastructure that is the glue and facilitates a speed-driven environment.

The problem with using physical servers is that they are too rigid and cannot adjust to the speed, agility, and flexibility requirements of a big data environment. Also, a number of the big data components do not have high availability solutions built in. Virtualization high availability features are easy to implement and can strengthen the overall big data platform. All the big data systems were designed to be like LEGO blocks that can be easily added and removed. However, networking, security, resource management, and monitoring need to be managed as a single environment.

Virtualization can be that key. Virtual machines enable infrastructure teams to work with virtual machines as software containers that can abstract out all the hardware issues of different drivers, interfaces, and dependencies from hardware vendors. Hardware becomes outdated. Hadoop DataNodes a few years ago were 48GB to 64GB of memory, but over the past few years they have grown to 96GB, 128GB, 256GB, and bigger. A physical server is fixed in size, so the administrator must configure the software for that size. By putting virtual machines on an ESXi host, there are now options for sizing the ESXi hosts and virtual machines for the appropriate workloads. Moving a virtual machine from one hardware platform, or even one data center, to another is very easy compared to moving physical hardware or changing to a new physical hardware platform. Virtual machines will greatly reduce the amount of testing that needs to be done when moving to new environments because the software stack is abstracted out from the physical layer and the proprietary drivers and software stack. As the physical infrastructure evolves over time, virtual machines abstract out the hardware, enabling infrastructure updates to be performed at a fraction of the time and cost of manipulating physical hardware.

Benefits of Virtualizing Hadoop

The benefits of virtualization can significantly improve the operational efficiencies of the Hadoop cluster. Additional benefits include the following:

- Provide a consistent management infrastructure that facilitates a speed-driven data environment. A virtual infrastructure can significantly improve areas of weakness in Hadoop, such as security, governance, disaster recovery, monitoring, and enterprise infrastructure management.

- Flexibility to separate the compute and storage layer. You will likely want to grow/ flex your compute layer more often than your data layer. Having the compute layer reside on separate (virtual) machines enables this to happen more quickly.

- With virtualization, you can share hardware with other groups or business units if spare cycles are available. Many physical clusters run at 60% or less of their CPU and memory capacity. That spare power can be utilized through virtualization.

- Reducing the Total Cost of Ownership (TCO). As a Hadoop cluster grows with more frameworks, NoSQL databases and BI/Visualization tools and more tenants are added; having software workloads tied to fixed size physical servers is inefficient.

- Reduce time and administration for provisioning. Provision in minutes instead of days, weeks, and months, which leads to faster data center management.

- Quickly grow and shrink a cluster based on workload demand. Sizing the Hadoop cluster to service any particular application can be quite difficult. Virtualization helps by enabling the user to scale up or scale down and then run the application quickly under different configurations.

- Accelerate innovation by reducing the cost of implementing change.

- Secure multitenancy; efficiently share resources with strong VM isolation.

- Virtualization makes it easier to set up a self-service environment to increase developer productivity and improve the quality of testing. It can also make it easy for different business units to explore types of workloads, frameworks, configurations, and so on.

- Improve security and networking with all the big data frameworks and environments.

- Keep the cost of entry into big data low for business units. For business units the difficulty in trying out new environments (POCs) can make it extremely difficult to try to adopt big data solutions. Virtualization can significantly reduce the application development lifecycle.

Virtualized Hadoop Can Run as Fast or Faster Than Native

A virtual infrastructure can have performance advantages over physical servers. Multiple virtual machines in the same ESXi host can reduce network overhead for the right workloads. Virtualization facilitating the separation of resources for compute and storage can allow better utilization of hardware resources, leading to better performance. A virtualized Hadoop cluster should be expected to run with single-digit overhead, and in some cases run as fast as or faster than native performance.

VMware has a recent performance study on virtualizing Hadoop using vSphere 6 in which tests conducted with TeraSort showed that virtualized Hadoop can perform at up to 12% better than native performance. This test made use of stacking several virtual machines onto one host server. So in certain cases, virtual Hadoop can outperform the native setup. The size of the ESXi host, size of virtual machines, and workload activity determine the optimum number of virtual machines to run on an ESXi host. In this performance study configuring for TeraSort

- One VM per ESXi host was slower than native performance.

- Two VMs per ESXi host were as fast as native performance.

- Four VMs per ESXi host were 12% faster than native performance.

- Ten and 20 VMs per ESXi host were still faster than native performance.

Figure 10.2 shows a performance comparison with multiple VMs per host.

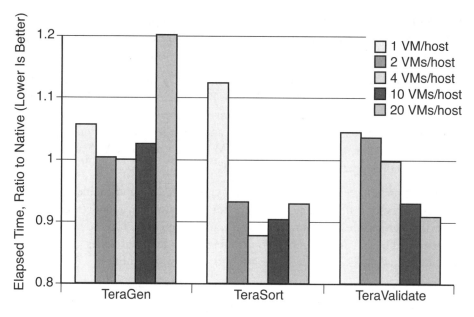

Figure 10.2   Virtualization can perform nearly as fast or as fast as native.

It is strongly recommended to read the whitepaper DOC-28678, "Virtualized Hadoop Performance with VMware vSphere6 on High-Performance."[1] The paper helps illustrate the importance of right sizing your hardware environment, Hadoop tuning, and performance tuning the virtual infrastructure, and how these tasks have a big impact on reducing latency and improving throughput.

Depending on workloads, if you are able to create smaller virtual machines, you can perform more total tasks per host. Virtualization makes it easier to right size each of the servers in a Hadoop environment, which allows more resources for more demanding servers (virtual machines). This is one feature area that can contribute to faster performance. For low-latency requirements, some production and performance test environments might still require physical servers. That does not mean that corresponding development and test clusters can't be virtualized. Also, there will be a number of servers that are part of the Hadoop ecosystem that would be good candidates for being virtualized.

As we discussed in Chapter 9, "Best Practices for Virtualizing Hadoop," memory configuration is especially crucial. A large part of Hadoop is made up of Java Virtual Machines (JVMs) running across a distributed cluster. Hadoop daemons run in JVMs. YARN mappers and reducers running in containers are also JVMs. Being able to start up JVMs is one of the first steps in determining the capacity of a Hadoop cluster. One area of tuning a Hadoop cluster is tuning the JVMs in the cluster. Java metrics, such as JVM Free/Total memory, Guest OS memory usage, Garbage Collection (GC) rate, and duration of GC, all need to be well understood. Hyperic can also be used to monitor JVMs.

It is important to clearly understand how to performance tune a virtualized infrastructure for Hadoop and to follow the best practices. NUMA, Buffer cache, Memory DIMMs, and Translation Lookaside Buffer (TLB) are all important considerations. We talked about the importance of following virtualization best practices and guidelines for Hadoop in Chapter 9. Having two virtual machines each on its own NUMA node versus one VM on two NUMA nodes can improve performance by up to 10%.

VM-based isolation makes it easier to provide security, protect data, and enable efficient utilization of resources for different types of workloads. Virtualization supports different configurations that can enable an organization to maximize a configuration to better utilize hardware resources. This keeps an organization from adding additional nodes just to solve bottlenecks. The following list describes three ways to set up worker nodes:

- **Combining compute and storage:** This is the historical and default configuration for Hadoop. The ResourceManager and DataNode daemons run on the same worker node.

- **Separating compute and storage:** If workloads utilize more compute or storage resources, then by separating compute and storage more resources can be allocated with better efficiency. You should consider two things. First, you will likely want to grow or flex your compute layer more often than your data layer. Ensuring that the layers reside on separate (virtual) machines enables that to happen more quickly. Second, many customers want to carefully protect the access to their business data in HDFS form. This means they want to centrally control it, not spread it out across many servers in the data center. Having the HDFS storage layers separate from the compute layers facilitates this. There is not a lot of expertise currently with this configuration. Time will be needed to build the expertise of the team supporting this configuration.

- **Having multiple tenants share the same storage:** There can be different Hadoop clusters that need to share the same data. Instead of trying to maintain separate Hadoop clusters, there can be one shared storage solution. Then there can be separate tenants or Hadoop resources that share the same storage. Time is needed to understand the dynamics around solving multitenancy this way.

Part of considering a virtual infrastructure for Hadoop is looking at the long-term benefits that an enterprise virtual infrastructure and the software-defined data center (SDDC) can bring to the entire Hadoop ecosystem. It's also important that the right people are making the decisions. A lot of the best short-term decisions often end up in bad long-term decisions. It's a common mistake to put more emphasis on building a Hadoop cluster than on maintaining it.

As a Hadoop cluster gets bigger, has more tenants, and increases its profile in an organization, the more administration tasks need to be automated or simplified. The cluster administration cannot increase in workload or complexity as the Hadoop cluster grows. Administrators often think of using automation tools such as Chef or Puppet, which have traditionally been used by Linux system administrators for configuring and maintaining multiple servers. Although these are great tools, all the scripts created by administration teams end up becoming monsters that have to be fed due to their high maintenance. They require a great deal of work dealing with day-to-day administration tasks, failures, backups, updates and upgrades, and disaster recovery. It's important to think one to two years into the future about how you want your organization to manage your Hadoop ecosystem.

Coordination and Cross-Purpose Specialization Is the Future

Some virtualization administrators have been virtualizing for years. There are lots of books and whitepapers on how to virtualize. Surprisingly, the current issue is that most of the experienced virtualization administrators do not understand the complexity of big data. There are big silos in IT, and administrators are so focused on their own areas they can't see into other technical areas. Merging Hadoop and virtualization requires strong technical expertise on both sides but also requires a blending of knowledge. Virtualization administrators must understand the technical challenges of big data to build the right enterprise platform. While Hadoop administrators need to know enough about virtualization to understand how to leverage its features, they also must have confidence that they can troubleshoot and tune their environment in a virtual infrastructure. Time needs to be best making sure the Hadoop experts understand the infrastructural benefits of virtualization.

One of the key things to create alignment is to define a path toward integration. Organizations need the operational capabilities of virtualization, cloud services, and Hadoop to maximize the vision of a speed-driven organization built around data. This can almost be compared to a DevOps theme. Hadoop has traditionally been run like a developer environment, and now it needs to fit into a day-to-day operations mode.

There are a number of ways to do this. If your team is strong in Hadoop, start gradually building up skills in virtualization and go through the path of starting to virtualize low-profile environments and gradually move to higher-profile environments. Move from virtualizing development, Proof of Concept (POC) environments, testing, and then production. This is something that takes time, but it is a safe path and it enables your team to build confidence and skill around virtualizing Hadoop. If you are new to Hadoop, you can start off with Big Data Extensions (BDE) and build your skills as you grow your Hadoop environment. This requires the team to have time to build skills around virtualizing Hadoop before the Hadoop cluster goes to production.

Cloud services, virtualization, and containers are going to play a role in Hadoop clusters. The point is, we are saying you have choices about how to manage Hadoop and its infrastructure. It's about getting different areas of technology that do not know each other's strengths and weaknesses and building awareness of capabilities. Both sides are technical and need to be shown the advantages of working together. Technical expertise is about voice as well as details. In this environment, success requires thinking like both a virtualization administrator and a Hadoop administrator. Developers and anyone working with Hadoop development, POC, and test clusters will love the operational benefits of virtualization. Then as skills, expertise, and confidence increase, leveraging those benefits in a production Hadoop environment can be realized.

Barriers Can Be Organizational

Virtualization experts can bring a lot of operational advantages to Hadoop. Virtualization experts have been focused on operational efficiencies, automation, security, and so on for years. Hadoop administrators are still trying to define and build an operational platform, with large areas such as security and operational management areas that still need to mature. Most Hadoop administrators aren't even thinking about site recovery. Coordination and cross-purpose specialization of technical teams is the future. This coordination across different teams is required for a sustainable solution. The integration of all these moving parts is an ever-evolving story.

Virtualization offers a lot of advantages that directly address the requirements for speed, agility, flexibility, and adaptability that are needed on big data platforms. However, virtualization has many nontechnical challenges to overcome. Many of these challenges have to do with the lack of detailed technical knowledge around virtualization, a willingness to recognize the limitations around using physical servers, and leaders willing to step up and invoke change. Another challenge is that software vendors are concerned about their software and the implementation of their solutions. These are all significant barriers but ones that can be overcome through knowledge, awareness, and educating teams on the benefits of virtualization. This also emphasizes that part of the big data journey is organizational transformation.

Virtualization Is Not an All or Nothing Option

Virtualization works extremely well as a blended solution. Everything does not need to be virtualized at once. Using virtualization for Proof of Concept (POC) projects, development and test environments are a natural progression for using virtualization with the production components of big data. Developing the skill and expertise to virtualize a production Hadoop environment takes time. It also takes time for the team to develop the confidence it takes to work with a virtualized environment. Virtualizing Hadoop one step at a time is a great way to build confidence in infrastructure teams as well as business units.

Rapid Provisioning and Improving Quality of Development and Test Environments

As more projects move into a big data solution, there are going to be POC projects, different development scenarios, quality assurance tests, and so on. This is where the advantages of virtual machines create a massive positive impact. Mixed-use cases and mixed workloads can live well together on a suitably prioritized virtual environment. Resource pools can separate these workloads from each other and prioritize a subset of them over others.

Virtual appliances provide flexibility for testing different scenarios. A virtual appliance is an image of a virtual machine that is preconfigured for a specific environment. A virtual appliance can be open or closed. An open virtual appliance environment can be modified. A closed virtual appliance is delivered as a complete system and is not intended to have its environment modified. Virtual appliances provide developers, business analysts, and quality assurance testers with download environments that they can work with. Each person can have an individual environment to work with. This reduces the amount of administration work for the infrastructure teams and enables developers to get working environments on demand. A virtual appliance is easy to work with and can create economies of scale.

A vApp takes the concept of a virtual appliance to a new level. A vApp is a set of virtual machines preconfigured to work together. When a vApp is implemented, unique IP addresses, server names, and so on can be created for the deployment. With almost a push of a button, an entire pretested environment can be delivered to a technical team. Following is a very small set of examples of vApps:

- A multitiered Hadoop cluster with clients, metadata repositories, master servers, and worker nodes.

- Configurations using different distributed search engines such as Solr or ElasticSearch.

- A multitiered Hadoop cluster with NoSQL and in-memory solutions such as Spark or Impala.

- Completely configured NoSQL environments such as HBase, Accumulo, Cassandra, Mongo, Riak, Aerospike, and so on.

- Data ingestion environments including the following:

  - Flume and Kafka

  - Kafka and Storm

  - Kafka and Spark Streaming

- Development environments with Eclipse, Maven, Ant, Snappy, Spring, Java, Python, Scala, and so on. These environments can be complex environments that are deployed easily to development teams on Windows, Macs, and existing clusters.

- Deployments of different Hadoop distributions such as Cloudera, Hortonworks, and MapR.

- Hadoop clusters with different security or network configurations.

- Deployments of different versions of a Hadoop distribution with different frameworks.

In a large organization, business units use Cassandra, Spark, or Solr. Over time, other business units will try to determine what is the best configuration for their use cases. When a vApp can be deployed in a short time, it enables organizations to try different deployments easily to confirm what is best for their use cases. Virtualization used this way can greatly accelerate business units moving to big data and leveraging the benefits sooner. We've talked about how innovation can occur more easily when there is a low cost to rapid change. Virtualization provides that lower cost of ownership and facilitates rapid change to support an environment for innovation.

In some Hadoop environments, it can take months to get the hardware for some type of deployment and then weeks before the environment is set up. In a virtualization environment with vApps and virtual appliances, pretested environments can be deployed to a team in a matter of minutes. The improvement in testing, reduced errors, and fewer mistakes—as well as greatly accelerating a team's time frames for delivery—is immeasurable. Technical infrastructure teams can build environments as vApps and then deploy them easily in the future. Be aware that virtual appliances and vApps are new to Hadoop environments due to lack of expertise and awareness. There is not a lot of experience out there with them. Start slowly with them. They have been proven over the long term in Hadoop; however, they have some advantages that should be considered. Just be aware that this is a bleeding-edge solution as far as Hadoop is concerned.

Being able to run the Hadoop components on virtual machines provides a lot of features and functionality to those components. There are also a number of options available through virtualization that are not available with physical servers. Leveraging cloud services that usually leverage virtualization in addition to containers will add even more options to a big data solution.

Improve High Availability with Virtualization

A Hadoop cluster is made up of a number of components that need to be highly available:

- Master Server processes, such as NameNode, ResourceManager, Zookeeper, Falcon Server, Ambari or Cloudera Manager, Application History Server, WebHCat Server, HBase Master, metadata repositories, and so on

- Worker node processes such as DataNode, NodeManager, HBase RegionServer, and the like

- Client nodes

- Edge or staging servers

- LDAP or Active Directory servers

- Software nodes that support BI, visualization, governance, data integration, and so on

Some of the Hadoop master daemons have high availability features, like NameNode, ResourceManager, Oozie, Zookeeper, and HBase Master. Other Hadoop master daemons, along with their metadata repositories, do not have built-in high availability. Client nodes, Edge servers, and software vendor nodes often do not have high availability built in. The worker nodes address high availability with the Hadoop software. YARN and HDFS provide high availability for the worker nodes.

Features such as VMware high availability, Distributed Resource Scheduler, and vMotion can have a very positive impact on availability due to hardware failure, software failure, and even maintenance for the master servers, software servers, and client nodes that do not have high availability built in. A number of these features require a shared disk solution, but virtualization and a shared disk solution for these nodes are often a lower-cost solution and provide an easier software environment to maintain.

Use Virtualization to Leverage Hadoop Workloads

Hadoop workloads can vary significantly. Some Hadoop clusters have extremely heavy workloads, whereas others can have spikes of activity. Traditionally, compute and storage have resided together. However, fixed compute and storage coupled together can lead to low utilization and a lack of flexibility. The problem with this is that not all Hadoop jobs will use the same level of compute and storage resources. If there isn't enough compute power or there is a lack of storage resources, the solution is often to add more nodes. Separating compute and storage resources can lead to better utilization of hardware, decreasing the tendency to add more nodes when there are bottlenecks in just one place. Creating multiple virtual machines that are right sized on the same ESXi server can also provide performance advantages.

Hadoop in the Cloud

More and more companies are looking at how to leverage Hadoop with cloud services. Companies such as Rackspace and Altiscale and hardware vendors and telecommunications companies provide on-premise solutions to take the pressure off of internal organizations. Companies such as Amazon, Google, IBM, Microsoft, and HP provide hosting services for big data platforms. IBM Bluemix offers an open cloud architecture for deploying applications in the cloud. Virtualization is not a requirement for cloud services but virtualization is usually a key component to leverage all the benefits of cloud services.

Organizations providing Hadoop-as-a-Service are delivering solid solutions that are reliable and perform well out of the box. Cloud organizations are going to be viable options for organizations to get an environment up in minutes versus internal organizations waiting months to get hardware in and set up. Virtualized environments can help internal infrastructure teams deliver solutions with the speed and agility of cloud hosting organizations. Cloud organizations are going to put pressure on internal infrastructure teams to improve their quality of service as well as their time to delivery.

Big Data Extensions

VMware's Big Data Extension (BDE) is a set of management tools designed to facilitate running Hadoop on a virtualization platform. Serengeti is an open-source project initiated by VMware to support the deployment of Hadoop in a virtual environment. BDE

- Is a commercially supported version of Project Serengeti.

- Is a part of VMware vSphere and is not a standalone product.

- Integrates with vSphere vCenter to help manage Hadoop in a vSphere environment. BDE supports Apache Hadoop, Hortonworks, Cloudera, and MapR distributions.

- Is managed and controlled through the vCenter server.

- Facilitates the rapid provisioning of Hadoop in a virtual infrastructure as well as supporting leading Hadoop management tools such as Cloudera Manager and Ambari.

- Can provide the management interface for Hadoop, or through APIs, leverage existing Hadoop management tools.

BDE can create the virtual machines but, in BDE 2.1, the Hadoop management tools will install the software transparently to the administrator. BDE can call the appropriate APIs to perform the installation. This enables BDE to focus on what it does best and to leverage what the Hadoop distribution management tools can do, instead of BDE trying to do everything. BDE can work with a user self service using tools such as vRealize Automation.

This self service can deliver infrastructure and application services through an IT catalog. Some virtualization features like vSphere Storage DRS are not available with BDE. Additional features of BDE include the following:

- Enables self-service provisioning of Hadoop clusters in a private cloud with vCloud Automation Center. This allows Hadoop-as-a-Service for end users.

- Supports deployments of Hadoop and HBase.

- Provides elastic scalability by separate compute and data layers. Enhances multitenancy.

- Allows flexible solutions for local storage, shared storage, and hybrid storage solutions.

BDE is a virtual appliance integrated as a plug-in to the vCenter server. The virtual appliance contains two virtual machines: a Serengeti Management Server and a Hadoop Template Server. The Serengeti Management Server focuses on building the cluster, configuring the virtual machines, and defining the master server and worker nodes. The Serengeti Management Server also clones the Hadoop template to support scaling out the cluster.

It's important to work with VMware and not only get the best practices and guidelines for Hadoop but also get their latest checklist for BDE. There is a list of items to check off to make sure the environment has been properly set up for running Hadoop with the BDE software.

The Path to Virtualization

There are a lot of different ways to virtualize a Hadoop environment. Multiple options exist between private, public, and hybrid clouds, as well as virtualizing different areas of Hadoop. The following describes one successful path.

Before virtualizing servers that require low latency, make sure virtualization can meet the low latency service level agreements (SLA). VMware has performed a number of performance studies and reference architectures that can help with this. Remember that the CPU, memory, storage, and networking configuration is a mathematical model that defines the resource and throughput capability of the cluster. Performance test numbers must tie back to the CPU, memory, storage, and networking capabilities of the hardware. Along with identifying imbalances that create bottlenecks, the scalability and throughput for the physical hardware must be identified. Latencies, especially around storage and networking, need to be identified. If virtualization cannot meet the SLAs, do not virtualize those servers. Make sure to build the appropriate level of expertise and confidence before moving to the next level of virtualization.

- Look at using cloud hosting companies that specialize in virtualizing Hadoop. This is a great way to get development started or get a POC project going sooner.

- Start with POC projects where the goal is the testing of use cases. This can be an easy, low-cost entry into virtualizing Hadoop.

- Build virtualized development environments.

- Build virtualized quality assurance and test environments.

- Virtualize servers that are not part of the Hadoop master or worker nodes.

- Virtualize NoSQL databases.

- Virtualize the Hadoop master servers.

- Virtualize the Hadoop slave servers.

We are going to see Hadoop being deployed more and more in private clouds. It will begin with test and development clusters. Even production servers will find traction in the private clouds. Solutions provided by Amazon Web Services (AWS), Amazon Elastic Compute Cloud (Amazon EC2), Microsoft Azure, Rackspace Cloud, IBM Bluemix, Altiscale, and the telecommunications and hardware firms are going to make it easier and easier to set up Hadoop-as-a-Service. Internal infrastructure teams providing physical servers for running Hadoop may be the easy and safe short-term solution but will have a very hard time competing on cost and delivery results without looking at virtualization.

We can also expect organizations to want to see how they can leverage external storage solutions such as S3. The more an organization looks at the importance of being a speed-driven organization, the more important virtualization and the cloud are going to become. The added isolation of Linux containers and image management should also be considered, especially because many companies are being delayed in the big data journey by the slow pace at which their internal infrastructure teams can implement Hadoop ecosystems today.

The Software-Defined Data Center

The software-defined data center at its essence is understood by simply imagining all the components in any data center. What is required to support a company's computing needs? VMware has compiled a series of interlocking products that allow all the control of the data center to be done through software. This means it is possible to automate, integrate, and reconfigure the data center as needed by the demands of the business. For instance, there is an inherent competition between configuring for latency versus throughput that has yet to be resolved within performance turning. Administration teams need to set up metrics around throughput and latency.

This is a tremendous advantage in our ever-changing industry. Are you building a big data environment for the moment or for the future? Are you stuck in the technology of the 1990s or are you building for service that might be onsite private or might be public depending on the project or need? Somewhere down the road, organizations will need to make sure their cloud and big data strategies are aligned. If you get too far down the road without aligning these two important areas, it will be a lot more difficult and less seamless. Organizations might want the flexibility to run big data workloads in-house on virtual platforms and then, if so desired, move them to a public cloud environment seamlessly, without changing the application or infrastructure.

Some of our readers are Hadoop specialists and went to training to learn how all this complexity for a big data platform fits together. Did you consider that educational groups or departments have been under constant demand to set up and tear down environments? So what did they do? Most training organizations are using some form of virtualization—either cloud provisioned Hadoop or a virtual machine to provide you a training environment. This is another very good reason to virtualize—experimenting in rapid setup and tear-down of different clusters and cluster sizes. This is the same pattern that we saw between 2000 and 2013 when developers used virtualization for less critical workloads in the data center, and then this evolved into virtualizing business-critical applications. This trend is so pervasive that today more new servers are being virtualized versus being configured for bare metal. This isn't a fad or a hype cycle; this is a trend that will not reverse. Organizations have no plans to go back to bare-metal servers, especially as organizations deploy more cloud services. To borrow the title from Marc Andreessen's article from the *Wall Street Journal*, "Software Is Eating the World," including your data center.[2] At best, it is just a matter of time as more mature and solid products like VMware Software Defined Datacenter (SDDC) consume more components in the Hadoop ecosystem.

The key is to have the courage to adapt. The levels of complexity in Hadoop and in the Software Defined Datacenter are significant. However, we are at a place in IT environments where we need to take our hands off the hardware and allow software to manage all this complexity. That means the critical value we need from big data is going to require a new focus on providing service to the businesses we serve. In other words, change means making sure people, processes, technology, and business costs are in alignment. This is where organizational transformation is so important. Hadoop and the goals of big data cannot be achieved by just installing software. Creating a speed-driven organization and an environment for innovation requires a clear vision of the goal to be accomplished for an organization. The reason the authors choose to work with VMware Press is because VMware has had a solid track record of supporting the enterprise for many years. So briefly, by illustration of interlocking products, let's look at some of the advantages virtualization might afford a big data deployment.

First, consider how Hadoop has gained traction because it assumes that hardware fails and so it builds in data redundancy, and the software provides high availability on the worker nodes. The vCenter and vSphere software has native capability to restart failed virtual machines on other physical nodes with high availability. It also has the capability to pick critical nodes that are four vCPUs or fewer and run them with zero downtime by fault tolerant (FT) protection. So a key component of the virtualization advantage is to have virtualization high availabilities support critical nodes in the Hadoop ecosystem, which does not have high availability functionality. Consider addressing high availability from a virtualization enterprise perspective versus doing it for each individual component of a Hadoop ecosystem one by one.

Second, the vSphere system can adapt to processing and memory demands by use of distributed resource control moving workloads from one server or storage array to another to prevent bottlenecks. These are critical day-to-day operational features that make today's enterprise more robust and reliable. All these features have been available in one form or another within the software for years. Virtualization enables the administrators of a data lake to have a higher degree of protection and performance in the day-to-day operations.

Virtualization has been evolving similar to Hadoop. A significant change that has occurred with VMware vSphere virtualization is how networking and storage has now been abstracted to complete the software-defined data center. Consider how much effort is required to be efficient, agile, and in control without software-defined features. For years, companies would deploy a VM in minutes, but it then took days for networks to be configured and storage to be provisioned. A software-defined data center now simplifies network and storage management.

Virtualizing the Network

Recently, NSX has given networks the capability to separate the control plane (how the network is to behave or be configured) versus the data plane (the transportation of the network data from one location to another). The implication of this separation is revolutionary, enabling networks to be provisioned rapidly. VMware is also committed to building security into its products from the ground up. This is a remarkable advantage gained by using vSphere in a Hadoop deployment. Why? For example, currently security is still evolving within a number of Apache projects. Bound by physical node management, the solutions for network security are usually perimeter based. Many organizations have had unfortunate incidents where attackers breached the perimeter and then moved freely within the enterprise data center. Network micro segmentation, which has been operationally unattainable in manual networks but is built in to NSX, enables security controls over a group of virtual machines, down to even a single VM. These software-defined automation capabilities and inherent security in NSX can deliver a very efficient foundation to any Hadoop deployment. The one thing that is clear in the Hadoop ecosystem is constant innovation. To handle constant change, forward-thinking leaders can use software-defined networking to implement Hadoop.

Networking is not the only innovation in software-defined computing. Storage has recently gone through an explosion of changes with converged products and flash technology. Yet the software-defined refinements might in the end produce the most valued benefits. VMware introduced vSAN in the vSphere 5.5 vRealize Suite, and now it has introduced Virtual Volumes. At the heart of these improvements is the concept of object storage. The critical issue is policy-based management where you define rules for minimum and maximum requirements, such as ReadOps, WriteOPs, ReadLatency, or WriteLatency. In essence, the policy determines the required capacity, performance, and availability requirements of the VM. Object-based storage assures the VM's storage always adheres to the rules of its construction. This is wildly powerful because now no matter where the VM lives, if it is in compliance with its policies, the VM storage will deliver the same level of performance. Few realize that the ultimate power of storage objects lies in the ease to reconfigure storage to the changing demands a VM might face. This capability to reconfigure storage allows very fine control over a virtual machine's critical storage needs.

In other words, think about all the applications that are part of a Hadoop ecosystem. Some data platforms, such as NoSQL, might need a defined number of failures to tolerate, or a number of disk stripes per object, or flash cache and read cache reservations, or object space reservations (thin or thick provisioning). These properties are examples of components commonly associated with CAP theorem. Roughly, CAP theory states that in the event of a network partition (P) the system can be designed for consistency (C) or availability (A). This theorem has led to two out of three generalizations. The only problem is that with object storage, the granularity is refined. With objects, you can individually define characteristics such as availability, coherence, consistency, durability, latency, throughput, scaling, or locality, to name just a few properties. No longer is customizing applications a one-time hardened decision regarding trade-offs; instead, it's a policy-based dynamic decision determined on a per-application basis. This means that a policy can be set, it will be maintained, and if it's inadequate, you can reset the policy and check the results. Virtualized storage is emerging as a powerful ally to all the various demands of a broad Hadoop project. Software-defined storage continues the story of control, agility, and efficiency. In addition, security policies can be maintained within the policies. These are features every Hadoop administrator needs to address or at least understand.

To summarize, vSphere is a complete foundation for a software-defined data center, and it makes the road to cloud management a much more reasonable path. Hadoop can move from concept to production through many phases and never miss a requirement.

Virtualization has incredible architectural and operational flexibility, which the fast evolving Hadoop environment can leverage.

vRealize Suite

Consider that VMware has added a powerful set of management tools under the umbrella of the vRealize Suite into the data center mix. Four of these tools in particular give distinctive advantages to the big data process. vRealize Automation enables regular users and developers to provision entire systems from a self-service portal, manage the governance of these systems by role-based access control, and manage the entire lifecycle of the provision, including removing the virtual machines when the job is completed. This means a blueprint could be created for all the operating systems, applications, and application configurations of each component of Hadoop and be applied to a physical box, a VM, or a cloud deployment and run with the same settings from place to place. This would rapidly improve the development cycle of create, test, and place in production. By deploying Hadoop clusters or components through software automation rather than manual methods or scripts, it will make it easier to troubleshoot problems that arise. To aid in the monitoring and management of the data center, vRealize Operation can monitor both the emerging trends that affect performance and forecast capacity requirements for CPU cycles, memory, network, and storage.

vRealize Operations use a robust set of analytics to determine the trends for each metric in a system or for remote dynamic thresholds in such a way that it's possible to receive early warnings about performance problems. You might ask, what is all this going to cost my organization? vRealize Business is a tool that tracks all the significant cost for IT and displays it in dashboards so that every business unit knows what they are consuming. Together, these products interlock to give a new level of control, agility, and efficiency that is impossible for manual-only management. Organizations want more choice and custom capabilities in their day-to-day operations. So the company can choose the best of breed in each area of the data center.

The final management tool to highlight could easily be considered the "glue" behind the software-defined data center. This tool is vRealize Orchestrator. This product has a track record of more than 7 years within VMware and is standard with the base vCenter installation. vRealize Orchestrator allows for the extreme flexibility of automation. If any product has a REST API or SOAP API or a plug-in, vRealize Orchestrator can automate the operations between the two products. Using either prebuilt workflows or JavaScript, Orchestrator can take any manual task that can be performed between VMware products and third-party software and automate the operation.

As these tools get tested in the Hadoop world and people develop experience with them in Hadoop they can open new possibilities for how to manage and deliver Hadoop platforms.

It would be a huge task to accomplish all this work from scratch, but the truth is most Fortune 1000 companies already have some or all of the virtualization infrastructure in place. It is a matter of making use of it with Hadoop distributions. That is why it is so critical to see that the issue of virtualized Hadoop is more of a mental roadblock than a technical hurdle. If you want to build a Hadoop ecosystem that supports data science for today and tomorrow, virtualization is the foundation for a solid future. A virtualized data center can make all your day-to-day operations from agility to efficiency to control more manageable.

The authors don't want to force anyone in any direction but want to enable you to make good choices. The key point is to do your due diligence around your cloud and your big data strategies. A lot of virtualization already exists in every Hadoop ecosystem, so it is a matter of time before it consumes this world as it has every other. Why—because it's true that software is eating the world!

Summary

Virtualizing a Hadoop or big data environment has the potential to have a very positive impact on the speed of deployments, operational flexibility, platform adaptability, reduced downtime, and simplified management, as well as reducing the total cost of ownership. The best cost reduction is often hard to quantify, especially around areas such as the speed of deployments, flexibility, adapting to change, and reduced downtime. These are critical factors for success but are often not easily measured.

A lot of organizations might not be ready to put a production cluster in a virtualized environment. Not all the reasons are technical. Others might not have the right use cases and workloads for running elastic data and compute nodes. Working through the costs of virtualizing Hadoop as well as virtualizing the worker nodes is something that has to mature. Organizations are struggling with all the vendors who want to add expensive proprietary software costs to an inexpensive commodity hardware environment that is open source. However, virtualization is not an all-or-nothing solution. The point is that you have a choice. What's hard is that often the choice is not just about technology. It's also about people, staffing, costs, individual's comfort level, and so on. As we've been saying all along, Hadoop is about giving your organization a competitive advantage by being able to bring business value from data sooner. As you continue to achieve the goal of being a speed-driven organization, there are ways virtualization can help you realize those goals sooner and easier.

Virtualizing Hadoop is still on the bleeding edge of the Hadoop world. Be aware that vSAN, NSX, virtual appliances, and vApps are new to the Hadoop world as well. A number of these virtualization features have not been sufficiently tested in Hadoop environments, and they need time to mature and for people to develop expertise with them in Hadoop. We introduced them here because it is important to understand all the tools in the toolbox. We are trying to point out possible future options but also point out they must be better understood with Hadoop platforms. Also, virtual appliances and vApps offer enough advantages that they should be considered at least for development and POC environments as the industry knowledge around them with Hadoop increases. An understanding of vSAN and NSX capabilities may also be helpful in looking at how networking and storage is going to be managed as the Hadoop cluster evolves. However, the benefits that virtualization brings to Hadoop can be significant. Also, Hadoop requires highly flexible yet cohesive environments, and a virtual infrastructure can be the glue to a Hadoop ecosystem.

The general movement is toward hybrid cloud solutions where the local private cloud addresses compliance, security, and data protection, with some areas moving into the public cloud while retaining the same look and feel. Hadoop's evolving central role in data analytics is going to be primarily in the private cloud with some areas using the public cloud. We are trying to show that there are multiple paths, with different degrees of speed and difficulty, that involve everything from a very gradual adoption to jumping in all at once. We also expect the use of containers to increase in Hadoop clusters, especially in the development and test areas.

References

1. DOC-28678, "Virtualized Hadoop Performance with VMware vSphere6 on High-Performance" whitepaper: http://www.vmware.com/files/pdf/techpaper/Virtualized-Hadoop-Performance-with-VMware-vSphere6.pdf

2. Marc Andreessen's article from the *Wall Street Journal*, "Software Is Eating The World": http://www.wsj.com/articles/SB10001424053111903480904576512250915629460

## Chapter 11

Virtualizing Hadoop Master Servers

Our experience over seven or eight years has been that when customers start using virtualization, they have a preliminary notion of what virtualization is. But once they get in and start using it, they see it's like a Swiss Army knife, and they can use it in many different ways.

—Raghu Raghuram

Virtualization is like a Swiss army knife; it has many ways that it can help you. However, this presents a number of challenges. The first is that today most people still do not understand how virtualization works or how to leverage a lot of its features and functionality. The second is that building an enterprise virtual infrastructure is not a trivial endeavor. However, if you build it right, virtualization and the concepts around the software-defined data center will forever change how your organization manages servers for the Hadoop ecosystem. Virtualizing Hadoop is a journey. Technical skills and experience have to be developed one step at a time. Infrastructure teams must learn how to design the infrastructure, how to implement best practices, and how to troubleshoot and tune a Hadoop environment running on a virtual infrastructure. Even if a company is experienced with virtualization, it is still new to virtualizing Hadoop. Software vendors want to minimize the possibility of anything impacting the perception of performance around their software. The top priority of most software vendors is not lowering the total cost of ownership (TCO) for your environment or improving the operational efficiency, agility, and flexibility of your Hadoop ecosystem. However, virtualization will give you all of those benefits. Make sure your organization is driving how you want to operationalize Hadoop.

Virtualizing Servers in a Hadoop Cluster

Infrastructure teams and Hadoop teams must have confidence in the virtualization infra-structure. This comes from working with systems that have been virtualized and gaining confidence in being able to troubleshoot and tune them. When issues come up, teams gather confidence that they can identify whether it is a virtual infrastructure issue or an operating system, software, or Hadoop issue. Confidence also comes from seeing that, if tuned and configured properly, software running in VMs can run with minimal overhead. An infrastructure team must develop the skills in virtualizing different parts of a Hadoop cluster, such as setting measurements, tracking tickets of various types, and resolving those tickets. Determine the maturity of the skill set that is required for each layer of virtual-ization before you virtualize the next level.

Customers who express reluctance to virtualize the worker daemons (compute and storage) often have no trouble at all virtualizing the master daemons. The master daemons are often some of the first servers to be virtualized. Master daemons are not put under the same type of performance stress as the worker daemons. For development, test, or proof of concept (POC), Hadoop clusters' master daemons may be put on the same ESXi hosts as the Hadoop worker daemons, but it is not recommended unless there is limited hardware. When provisioning clusters, you should always follow a repeatable pattern that follows best practices. Numerous reasons exist to keep the master daemons and the worker daemons separate in a Hadoop environment.

There are several ways to start virtualizing the Hadoop environment, including the following:

- Virtualize different layers one at a time:
    - Virtualize servers that touch the Hadoop cluster.
    - Virtualize security and third-party software servers.
    - Virtualize frameworks, NoSQL databases, and SQL engines that for different reasons will run in the Hadoop network but as separate clusters.
    - Virtualize edge/gateway/staging servers.
    - Virtualize Master servers.
    - Virtualize workers.
    - Virtualize DR sites.

- Virtualize different Hadoop clusters one at a time:
    - Virtualize the development environment.
    - Virtualize test and quality assurance environments.

- Virtualize production environments.

- Virtualize DR sites.

Virtualizing the Environment Around Hadoop

Virtualization of the servers that touch the Hadoop cluster is a good first step. LDAP or AD servers are easy to virtualize. They have high availability solutions within their own software that are enhanced with the high availability features of virtualization. Most medium and large organizations have been virtualizing these authentication servers for years. After the user authentication servers, it is good to take a look at other software servers that touch the Hadoop cluster. Additional security servers make good candidates for virtualizing.

The next set of servers to virtualize are the edge or staging servers. These servers are the starting point for data that is being loaded into HDFS. Applications will also be launched to run on the Hadoop cluster from the edge or staging servers. Any additional servers running third-party software that touches the Hadoop cluster should be virtualized next.

Virtualizing the Master Hadoop Servers

Virtualizing the master servers is one of the key steps in building a virtual platform for Hadoop. One of the primary goals for the design and configuration of the master servers is high availability. This makes them an ideal candidate for virtualization. Virtualizing the master servers significantly increases the enterprise robustness of these servers.

A list of the master Hadoop servers to virtualize depends on which distribution is used and which frameworks are installed with the distribution. Other frameworks that may be installed can be independent open source frameworks but are considered part of the core frameworks for a specific installation. One of the goals of the Open Data Platform (ODP) is to create a standard distribution of core Hadoop frameworks that enables software vendors to test their software against and validate with.

Here is a sample list of the frameworks that can be virtualized. Additional processes, such as the LDAP, Distributed PRC (DRPC), port mapping processes (portmap), Network file system processes (nfs3), Storm processes (nimbus, supervisor...), and so on, might need to be virtualized depending on the Hadoop configuration. The master servers should be put on different hosts based on the high availability (HA) requirements for each of the Hadoop daemons. If features like the vSphere distributed resource scheduling (DRS) or VMware high availability are used, there are different rules about where virtual machines can move. For example, you would not want the virtual machine running the standby ResourceManager to end up on the host where the primary ResourceManager is running. VMs for the Hadoop daemons can have different priorities and different affinity and anti-affinity rules.

Organize the Hadoop daemons in virtual machines and ESXi hosts based on HA and management requirements. If the Hadoop ecosystem includes NoSQL and products such as Spark, Impala, Flink, Storm, and Kafka, they will need to be organized around virtual machines and hosts for their individual software resource requirements as well. Make sure that the rules around these virtual machines are clearly defined. An example is not to put a primary daemon and its standby daemon on the same ESXi host.

Another nice thing about virtual machines is they are easy to create and work with. Most physical Hadoop clusters have three to four hosts for the master Hadoop daemons. With virtual machines it might be better to have four to six virtual machines for managing the master Hadoop daemons. Make sure that you understand the ramifications for how the Hadoop master servers are spread across the ESXi hosts. More flexibility exists in defining the rules for the management of the daemons with virtual machines than with physical servers. However, if someone wants a lower level of granularity for controlling the HA requirements, affinity and anti-affinity rules, and VMware DRS/HA rules, having a few extra virtual machines to spread the daemons across provides a lot more flexibility to be able to create the right management infrastructure. It is important to have a specific reason for each Hadoop daemon and where it is placed in the virtual infrastructure. Hadoop cluster performance requires low-latency communication between the worker nodes and the master servers. To maintain low latency, it might be best to have the NameNode and ResourceManager Hadoop daemons run in their own dedicated virtual machine. Each cluster configuration is unique; the point is that with virtual machines there is more choice. Do not lose sight of this when creating the plans for the virtual machines. Remember that the rules must be periodically evaluated as the ecosystem grows and changes. Evaluation of support tickets should be monitored over regular time frames to confirm that the Hadoop daemons are properly organized in the vSphere DRS/HA cluster. The following is a list of key master server daemons in a Hadoop ecosystem. This list will change depending on a specific configuration or software release.

- Oozie Server
- NameNode
- Standby NameNode
- ResourceManager
- Standby ResourceManager
- Falcon Server
- Ambari Server
- Ganglia/Nagios
- Zookeeper

- Knox Gateway

- HBase Master

- JobHistoryServer

- ApplicationHistoryServer

- HiveServer

- HiveServer2

- WebHCat Server

Figure 11.1 shows examples of master Hadoop dameons to virtualize.

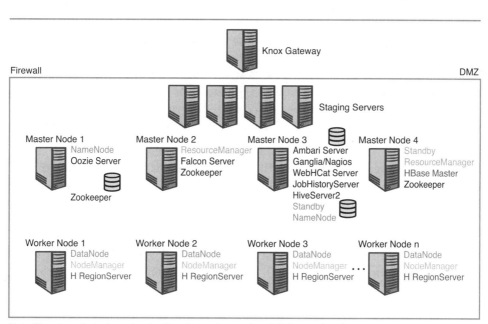

Figure 11.1   Examples of master Hadoop dameons to virtualize.

After the Hadoop master daemons have been spread across different virtual machines, the virtual machines can be right-sized for the workload they need to support. This enables the extra resources remaining after the master servers are placed to be spread across the rest of the virtual infrastructure, or for the resources not already allocated to be dynamically allocated to different areas during high activity periods. This flexibility does not exist with physical servers.

Although high availability is the priority around the master Hadoop daemons, the performance is also important. Follow all the best practices outlined around making sure that the Hadoop daemons have the resources they need to meet SLAs. Do not overcommit resources for the environment around the master Hadoop daemons, and make sure resource pools are protecting their resources.

One of the decisions around virtualizing the master servers is whether to use shared storage. There are advantages and disadvantages for both sides. Shared storage protects the Hadoop master daemons from disk failure and at the same time adds additional cost, complexity, and required expertise to the Hadoop environment. Shared disk also allows all features of virtualization to be available for the Hadoop master daemons. However, if this Hadoop cluster is being deployed into an existing virtualized data center, it is likely that shared storage of some form is already available there for the master virtual machines to use. The features available for vSphere HA, Application HA, Distributed Resource Scheduler (DRS), and fault tolerance may be considered for the Hadoop master daemons. DRS can also have a positive impact on performance by making sure the resources are evenly distributed across the vSphere hosts. It is important to work with vendors and confirm whether these features have been tested with Hadoop platforms. More advanced features need confirmation that they have been tested and have been confirmed to run with Hadoop.

Earlier chapters discussed SAN, iSCSI, and NFS. There are pros and cons for each of the different storage solutions. Make sure the storage that you select can meet the performance requirements. The performance of the disks is important. VSAN writes go to solid-state disks (SSD) and the read cache hits come from the SSDs. The ratio between SSD and HHD will have an impact on performance, but it's the universal debate of speed versus cost. It is also recommended that you use 10Gb links between hosts in the ESXi VSAN cluster. The 1Gb links will work, but the 10Gb links are recommended. Make sure the SATA or SAS disk speeds can meet the performance requirements. The RAID controller and the write-back cache size will impact performance here. Make sure the write-back cache is nonvolatile so there aren't any issues with data loss or corruption.

Another important decision is whether to use physical (raw device mappings) or virtual file formats (VMFS). There really isn't a performance difference between the two file formats, so the decision should be based on which format provides the most advantages for a specific configuration. Use the virtual file formats if the goal is to leverage as many of the virtualization features as possible. It is recommended to use the VMFS format in all cases, except where rapid switching to a physical system is required.

Make sure that all the standard best practices are followed. Provision the storage to be thick provisioned eager-zeroed for all disks containing data for the master Hadoop daemons. Monitor the storage performance by looking at the physical SCSI adapter that will give you information on the primary and replica activity, the data store performance, and the virtual machine level performance. Administrators need to get very good at understanding the metrics around these areas. Too often when a performance problem occurs, the immediate reaction is that there is too much performance overhead with virtualization. In fact, the problem is usually due to not following best practices for design and configuration, especially in the areas of storage and networking.

Another choice in high availability is whether to use VMware fault tolerance (FT). Fault tolerance protects a virtual machine so there is continuous availability in case of a server failure. Failover to the secondary virtual machine makes sure there is no disruption in service. Some of the master Hadoop daemons, such as the NameNode, ResourceManager, and Oozie server, have high availability built in to their framework, but others do not. FT may be an option to consider for the frameworks that do not have HA built in. FT may also be a consideration for the relational databases that are serving as the metadata repositories for areas such as the Ambari Server, Hive Server, and the Oozie Server.

Administrators must decide whether they want to use database options such as setting up a MySQL server with replication. Setting up a MySQL cluster is not necessary for the workload the metadata repositories get. A MySQL database server set up with replication and something like Distributed Replicated Block Device (DRBD) may be another option. With fault tolerance, there is some overhead, but the high availability it brings to master Hadoop daemons that do not have high availability built in provides an easy way to add this important capability. The point is there are multiple choices as to whether to use VMware HA options, database HA options, and so on. The cost, the complexity of administration, the skill sets of the teams, and the Hadoop SLAs will direct you to the right solution.

If you use a SAN or virtual SAN, vMotion can be used when you need to perform maintenance. An administrator can use vMotion to move a virtual machine from one host to another with no down time. With the vSphere DRS/HA and Application HA, this might be all that is necessary to meet availability requirements for the Hadoop components that do not have HA built in. The nice thing about vSphere DRS/HA is that it's easy to maintain and does not add to the complexity of administration after it is running. Hadoop is open source, and if you are not careful, a lot of unnecessary third-party products can add complexity and cost to a Hadoop cluster.

Virtualizing Without the SAN

The decision not to use SAN or virtual SAN means some of the features, such as VMware DRS/HA, will not be available. There is still tremendous value in keeping the master Hadoop daemons virtualized. All the agility and flexibility as well as on-demand resource management can still be leveraged by the virtual machines. Virtualized networking will also secure the Hadoop cluster to a large degree. This is important because Hadoop security is still maturing. Networking can be virtualized just like compute resources are abstracted. This enables network capacity to be optionally segmented into logical area networks that are attached to specific environments and applications. These logical networks can span physical boundaries. This provides the capability to change and scale the logical networks without needing to reconfigure physical network hardware. As the Hadoop cluster evolves and workloads change, firewalls, VPNs, load balancers, and network settings can be easily modified.

Logical networks eliminate the issues of IP addressing when moving workloads. As more business units access data in the data lake, virtual networking enables multitenancy at scale. Logical networks also allow network segments to be isolated. This means two POC Hadoop clusters can have the same server names and IP addresses because they are running in their own isolated environment. This makes it not only easier to provision new Hadoop clusters but also eliminates a significant amount of errors and administration costs.

An important area that most Hadoop environments do not pay proper attention to is having a high-quality development and testing environment. The quality of the development and testing of Hadoop clusters impacts the quality of the Hadoop production cluster(s). As Hadoop evolves, there will be requests for different types of Proof of Concept (POC) projects. The capability to stand up Hadoop clusters quickly is important. A vApp (that is, a collection of virtual machines that are always deployed as a unit) can be an excellent way to stand up new Hadoop clusters that have proven configurations. With the vApp being a container of multiple virtual machines, a vApp of the master servers can be created to deploy an exact duplicate in development, test, and POC environments. Now these environments are leveraging the configurations that are used in production environments. The vApps contain all the resource controls and network configurations to ensure they are exact copies of a production environment. Test the vApp in multiple scenarios before deploying.

Summary

The primary design goal for the platforms running the Hadoop master daemons is availability. Second, the Hadoop master servers will need the flexibility to support change and evolution of Hadoop software itself, physical server hardware, software, and networking and storage hardware and requirements. Virtualization adds a lot of important functionality and features to a Hadoop cluster for achieving both goals.

In this chapter we have shown how virtualization brings a lot of benefits and features to the Hadoop master servers that can be leveraged by infrastructure teams. An organization has more choices for configuring a Hadoop cluster with virtualization, and more choices are good. Virtualization experts will want to solve problems with virtualization; Hadoop experts will want to solve problems using Hadoop and open source frameworks, and so on. There is a difference between configuring a Hadoop cluster for a performance proof of concept (POC) and configuring a Hadoop cluster for a production environment with all the management that production implies. Virtualization, infrastructure, and Hadoop experts need to get in a room with a whiteboard and lay out how the Hadoop cluster should be maintained and managed to meet current SLAs as well as the constant evolution of the Hadoop ecosystem. Everyone needs to leave their egos at the door and listen to all the teams' reasons for one approach over another. In the same way a data lake eliminates data silos, a Hadoop cluster running in a virtual infrastructure reduces the technical silos around the different technical teams. Agility, flexibility, maintainability, and elasticity can all be improved through running Hadoop on a virtual infrastructure.

## Chapter 12

Virtualizing the Hadoop Worker Nodes

Two roads diverged in a yellow wood. I took the one less traveled by, and that has made all the difference.

—Robert Frost

In this chapter we look at different ways of virtualizing the worker nodes in a Hadoop cluster—those nodes that contain the NodeManager, Application Master, Containers, and DataNode processes as their Hadoop roles. The standard native configuration that you might have seen up to now has been to combine compute processing (NodeManager, Application Master, Container) and storage (DataNode) on each Hadoop worker node. We will initially use that approach here when we virtualize the worker nodes and then show how you can go beyond it for flexibility reasons.

The design approaches in this chapter make the assumption that there are separate considerations for the Hadoop master servers from the Hadoop workers—and that these may be hosted on separate virtual and physical machines. There have been successful Hadoop clusters where these two main types of nodes have been mixed[1] on one host server, but for larger Hadoop clusters we consider the separation of the two to be important.

A Brief Introduction to the Worker Nodes in Hadoop

In this discussion, we treat a "worker node" as the Hadoop-specific set of processes or daemons that have in the past been run on a physical machine. As we develop the virtualization approach, we will see that these processes run just as well on a set of virtual machines. In fact, a portion of the performance testing done at VMware's and its partners' labs in the past few years focused on comparing the two approaches, native and virtualized. Virtualizing the Hadoop workers, however, enables us to choose new design patterns, and there are advantages to be gained from other designs.

Our concept of a Hadoop node is the virtual machine equivalent of a physical machine to begin with, to take the most straightforward approach to virtualizing.

The NodeManager process, running on a worker node, manages the compute processing for that node. The DataNode process on a worker node takes care of the storage and retrieval of the data blocks on that node.

Each job running in the YARN environment will also have an Application Master process running on one of the worker nodes. The Application Master manages the acquisition of resources (CPU power and memory) for containers that perform their part of the compute work for a specific job. You may think of containers as Java processes here, although the path is open to use of other forms of containers, such as Linux containers (LXC). Containers are spread out across the worker nodes under the direction of the Application Master.

Starting and stopping containers is the responsibility of the NodeManager on each node. The NodeManager starts a container after it is given an assignment of certain compute resources for containers to use by the Application Master. The NodeManager may stop a container prematurely if instructed to do so by the ResourceManager master process.

Combining all the preceding processes on to one physical node has been the regular way of doing things in the native form of Hadoop up to now. The first important design point is that given the decision to virtualize the Hadoop workers, you do not have to construct your worker nodes differently. Your virtualized Hadoop worker (with the Hadoop processes running in a virtual machine) may be a replica of a native, physical worker in terms of processes.

As we shall see however, separating the compute and data storage functionality can provide added flexibility in allocating and using the various resources.

From a worker design perspective there are a number of considerations:

- To combine the compute processing (NodeManager) and the data (DataNode) processing in the same virtual machine or to separate them out into separate virtual machines.

- Whether to have one virtual machine per ESXi host (physical server) or multiple virtual machines on an ESXi host. This includes determining the size of each virtual machine and how many YARN containers can run in each virtual machine for the compute processing.

- What storage design to choose for the two main roles (NodeManager and DataNode). This is a very important choice for any Hadoop cluster. Considerations include the choice of local direct-attached storage (DAS), SAN-based storage, Flash storage, Network Attached Storage (NAS), and hybrid models that use more than one storage mechanism.

- Whether to have completely separate clusters or to combine data storage and have different Hadoop clusters sharing the same storage. This helps with the issue of managing separate Hadoop clusters that have significant amounts of common data in them.

Deployment Models for Hadoop Clusters

This section discusses different design layouts for deployment of the workers that make up a Hadoop cluster. Figure 12.1 shows the topology choices. Here, the term *compute* refers to the NodeManager daemon and its associated containers in the Hadoop architecture; the term *data* refers to the DataNode daemon.

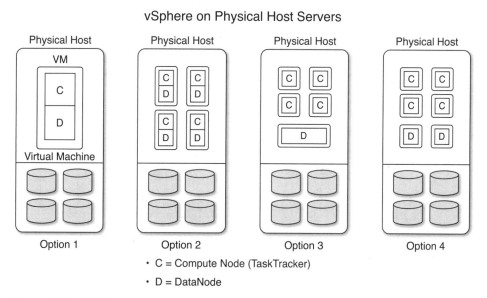

Figure 12.1   Choices for deployment of the Hadoop roles on virtual machines.

Virtualizing the worker nodes has a number of general approaches from a storage perspective. They involve using direct-attached or shared storage for HDFS data and other data, though of course you can combine the two types of storage in one design. We discuss these storage options along with the concepts of unifying or separating the compute and data Hadoop components.

In options 1 and 2 in Figure 12.1, the compute and data daemons are combined into one virtual machine. In options 3 and 4, they are separated into individual virtual machines. These general models of combined and separated roles have different benefits, which are discussed in the following sections along with the architectural variants of each one. The term *NodeManager* from this point on also refers to the containers and Application Master that it controls, particularly when referring to the I/O access that is done.

The Combined Model

In the combined model, the NodeManager and DataNode processes are executing together within the same virtual machine. This is the approach that would have been used in a native environment. It is not the only deployment model to consider, however, but it can be the basis for comparing a virtualized Hadoop cluster with a native one. Figure 12.2 shows an example of the combined model, option 1, in simplified form. For illustration purposes, we show one worker virtual machine (shown as a Hadoop Virtual Node) on one host ESXi server, the virtualization host. Several such virtual machines can run together on a vSphere host server, and that is the more common case. Many vSphere servers can be present in a cluster. We have seen examples of hundreds of vSphere servers being deployed in this way in larger Hadoop clusters, with multiple worker virtual machines on each server.

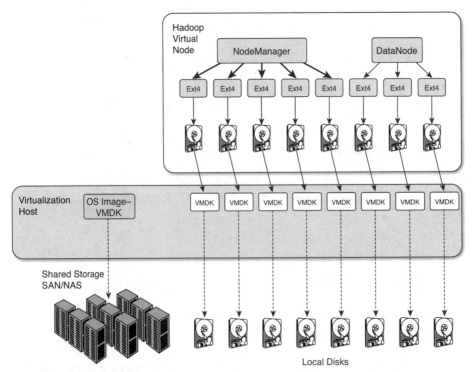

Figure 12.2   A virtualized deployment of the combined compute-data model.

This example shows a vSphere host server that has eight local direct-attached disks as well as a connection to a SAN or NAS shared-storage device. If no local disk storage is available, alternatives exist for deploying the design, which are discussed later in this section. In our example, eight virtual machine disk (VMDK) files are present, stored on individual datastores that are mapped to the eight locally attached disks; that is, one VMDK file per disk.

For those who are new to virtualization, a *datastore* is a term in vSphere for storage that abstracts away from the particular nature of the physical disk or disks it represents. A datastore is a container for a virtual machine's VMDK files, and it is created by the vSphere administrator in the vCenter tool as part of the normal vSphere setup phase. That datastore is then associated with a particular disk device in the hypervisor after it is attached to the server. VMDKs (and their associated files) are files that are managed by the hypervisor. They are the virtual disks that store the operating system and application data for a virtual machine. The VMDK files are placed into a datastore when you first create the virtual machine.

These VMDK files contain operating system data, HDFS data, or other data needed by the virtual machine. For the more important scalable Hadoop clusters, we would recommend separating the "system" data or operating system data from the "application" data onto separate VMDK files and separate datastores. For small development and testing clusters this is not so important.

A vSphere server can have many local direct-attached storage disks, if they are available. Some vSphere host servers have 24 or more DAS disks in current Hadoop deployments. The Hadoop distribution vendors recommend having as many direct-attached disks as possible for performance reasons. Having more direct-attached disks provides more aggregate I/O bandwidth, and that is very important for optimizing performance with Hadoop. The NodeManager and DataNode processes may be configured to share the physical disks through the use of a common datastore, but in this example, each process has its own exclusive access to its own set of physical disks, through the use of separate datastores. That is achieved through mapping one datastore to one physical disk and then assigning the individual datastores/VMDKs to a particular directory or partition used by the different processes in the virtual machine's operating system.

Figure 12.3 shows a set of virtual machines on the same server. You can choose to use two or more virtual machines per server, depending on the need. These virtual machines contain the same Hadoop processes and data that a physical worker would contain (that is, the combined model). The traditional layout for the guest operating system is on a local partitioned disk. The guest operating system disk for a virtual machine can also be placed on the SAN-based shared storage. This protects the guest OS disk against failures and can provide more safety than storing the guest OS on local disk. If no shared storage is available, the guest OS system and swap disks can be placed on a vSphere datastore that is mapped to a pair of dedicated local disks that are configured with RAID0, giving added protection. This is described in http://www.vmware.com/files/pdf/VMW-Hadoop-Performance-vSphere5.pdf and http://www.vmware.com/resources/techresources/10452 and is another mechanism to ensure that the OS is protected against disk failure.

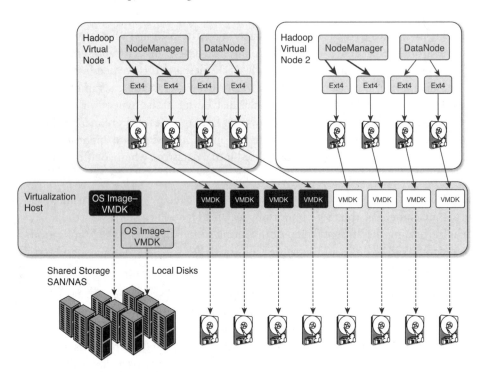

Figure 12.3   Multiple virtualized Hadoop nodes per host server.

Deploying multiple virtual machines concurrently on a vSphere server host enables better resource utilization when their workloads are suitably matched to the hardware. Multiple Hadoop nodes per host server, where each node is contained in a virtual machine of its own, have been shown to improve the overall system performance in comparison with a native or physical implementation.[1, 2] Those studies show that the overall completion time for a job can be reduced by adding more virtual machines to a host server. Beyond a certain number of virtual machines, however, the capacity of the physical server might be fully occupied, and the gains diminish. Guidelines for determining the optimal number of virtual machines are mentioned in the preceding references and in Chapter 9, "Best Practices for Virtualizing Hadoop."

The deployment of the combined model in Figure 12.3 with more than one worker virtual machine per ESXi server host has eight DAS disks divided across the various workloads— that is, across the virtual machines.

In Figure 12.3, four VMDK files are allocated to four datastores for each of the two virtual machines shown. Each datastore is mapped to one local physical disk. This means that all traffic to one VMDK uses one dedicated physical disk. This separation of disk access prevents contention for the same disk between the two virtual machines. The NodeManager and DataNode processes in each virtual machine do not share the VMDK files and the physical disks. The two processes are separated from each other as far as access to disks is concerned. If the particular performance requirements of the deployed applications require it, a set number of disks can be allocated in this way exclusively to the virtual machine or to one process within it. The disadvantage of this approach is that there are fewer disk spindles handling the I/O from any one virtual machine or process within it at any time. You can choose to share or separate the disks among the virtual machines through the use of vSphere VMDKs and datastores in this way, depending on your performance needs.

The Separated Model

As an alternative to the combined model, the DataNode and NodeManager processes can be separated onto different virtual machines. This separation brings the benefit of disconnecting the lifetime of the NodeManager process from that of the DataNode at the virtual machine level.

As a result, the DataNode virtual machines can live independently of the NodeManager virtual machines, and vice versa. The number of NodeManager virtual machines can be varied independently of the DataNode virtual machines present at any given time. This separation of the compute processing from the storage is referred to as the Data/Compute separation model.

This model has the benefit of allowing scale-out at the compute layer (through adding more virtual machines) while the storage/data layer in general tends to remain stable. Compute nodes can be added for different types of workloads. For example, NodeManagers can be added or removed from the system without affecting the DataNode (the storage component) that in the previous combined model shared a virtual machine with it.

The same principle applies to increasing the number of DataNodes, although that is likely to happen less frequently. If a new DataNode were to be added to a Hadoop cluster, a data rebalancing procedure would then be needed to spread parts of the HDFS dataset out to the new DataNode. This data rebalancing work can be network-bandwidth intensive and time consuming, especially if a job is executing at the time. The more likely scenario is that the user chooses expansion or contraction of the number of NodeManager virtual machines over time to match the current compute layer capability to the needs of the jobs being executed.

Administrators can choose either to start a new NodeManager in a new worker virtual machine and join it to an existing cluster or decommission a NodeManager from a Hadoop cluster and remove the virtual machine in which that process ran from the working set. This type of flexibility allows the resource distribution to match the workload utilization. The approach shown in Figure 12.4 shows two virtual machines running on the same host server, with compute and data separated.

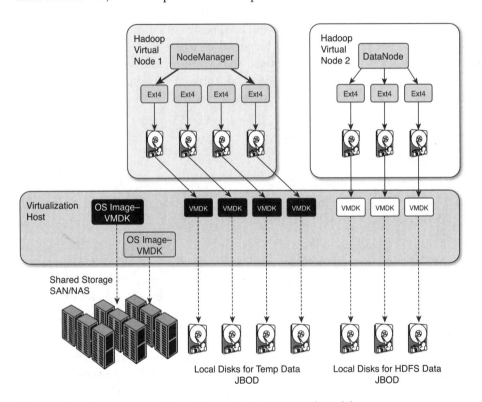

Figure 12.4   Deployment of the data compute separated model.

One virtual machine is dedicated to running the NodeManager while the other holds the DataNode process. These two virtual machines communicate closely to achieve the same effect as the combined model does. However, now we can add new NodeManager virtual machines at will, increasing the power of the compute layer of the Hadoop cluster.

As shown in earlier designs, the placement of the guest operating system disks and the swap disks on shared storage may be done in the same way as the combined-model deployment. In this architecture, it is possible that some of the local disks might be shared between a DataNode and a NodeManager (or compute) node through the use of common datastores. However, we show a design in Figure 12.4 that depicts the optimal separation of the consumers of I/O bandwidth—in other words, one that does not share physical disks across the two virtual machines. Separate local storage spindles, mapped through datastores, are used here for the VMDK needs of the NodeManager (the shuffle and temporary data) and the DataNode (the HDFS data). Shuffle data and temporary data in Hadoop is that data used in the middle of MapReduce processing for spills from memory and for data that is in transit between Mapper and Reducer processes. Temporary and shuffle data are written to local directories on the worker nodes and are not stored in HDFS.

An advantage of this approach is that all available disk spindles can participate in the I/O traffic. A disadvantage of sharing disks across the virtual machines is that the two important processes (the NodeManager and DataNode) can compete for access at the same time. This can occur if temporary data is being written by the NodeManager at the same time as HDFS data is being read or written to by the DataNode, for example. That scenario is avoided by isolating the virtual machines to disks or datastores of their own.

The local, or direct-attached storage approach can require extra effort in managing the individual disks independently because of the sheer number of disks spread out across the servers. However, local storage can be cost effective and provide optimal performance in many situations. The trade-off here is between the added burden of managing all the local DAS disks (compared to managing a central storage model) against the scalability gains to be achieved from it. The DAS approach spreads the data out across the servers in your datacenter, making it more challenging to control access to data and back up and restore data as opposed to a more centralized storage system.

Network Effects of the Data-Compute Separation

The data-compute separated deployment design model causes a change in the networking data flow between the Hadoop components, as shown in Figure 12.5.

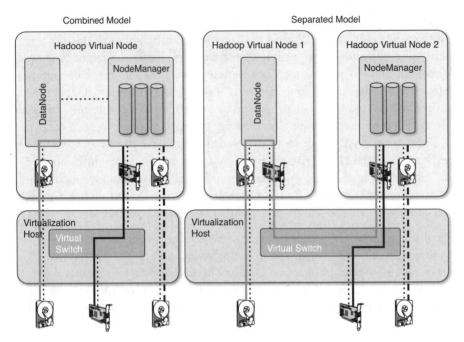

Figure 12.5 Network data flow in the combined model versus the data compute separated model.

The light gray path on the left side of Figure 12.5 shows the data flow between the NodeManager and DataNode processes when they are executing within the same virtual machine. The light gray data path also shows the disk access by the DataNode. The black line represents communication between this virtual machine and others on the network.

The right side of Figure 12.5 shows the network traffic between the NodeManager and DataNode when they are separated into individual virtual machines. When these two processes are separated, the network traffic between them goes over the network stack in the guest OS of each virtual machine as normal, then on to the virtual switch implementation in vSphere, as shown by the gray line on the right side.

A virtual switch is a software component in the vSphere virtualization platform that, among other functions, logically connects two virtual machines. A virtual switch can be associated with a physical switch, although the virtual switch can also exist independently of any physical switch.

When two virtual machines are located on the same vSphere host server and are connected to the same virtual switch, the network traffic between them traverses the virtual switch in memory. This traffic does not need to be carried on a physical switch or handled by the physical network adapter on the host. This enhances the performance of network traffic between the virtual machines, although there is a small impact.

The differences between the two deployment models (the combined and separated models) have been measured and are described in technical detail in http://labs.vmware.com/vmtj/toward-an-elastic-elephant-enabling-hadoop-for-the-cloud.[3] The trade-off is the extra cluster-sizing flexibility gained by having these Hadoop roles separated from one another, while their virtual machines are on the same vSphere host.

Separating the two Hadoop roles into different virtual machines can also provide data-security benefits. Visibility of the HDFS data can be restricted through careful attention to access control on the DataNode virtual machine and by placing the HDFS data into a vSphere datastore that is separated from the NodeManager data.

We also must consider the storage needs of the temporary data used in the MapReduce processing. This data is by default stored in locations on the local file system of the guest OS in the virtual machine where the NodeManager is executing. It is therefore outside of HDFS control. The dashed vertical lines to the right side of each section in Figure 12.5 represent the NodeManager process accessing the local temporary or shuffle data, which is often called *temp data*.

Each compute virtual machine has its own temporary data space, the size of which is closely related to the design of the specific Hadoop applications using it. For example, the TeraSort Hadoop benchmark application requires a temp data space size that is at least twice its input dataset size. On the other hand, the related TeraGen and TeraValidate applications do not require significant temporary data space. This part of the design requires careful measurement by looking at the application behavior with its data before the Hadoop cluster is constructed.

The Shared-Storage Approach to the Data-Compute Separated Model

This section discusses another model for data storage that uses a shared storage mechanism for certain parts of the design and retains the separation discussed earlier between the compute nodes (the NodeManagers) and the data/storage nodes (the DataNodes).

Figure 12.6 shows a SAN- or NAS-based hybrid topology for the data-compute separated deployment model.

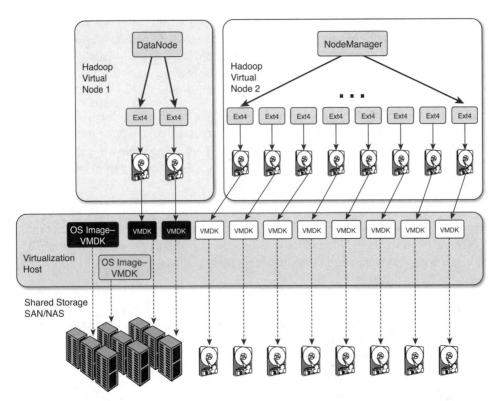

Figure 12.6   Using SAN storage with the data-compute separated deployment model.

The advantage to using shared storage is that it provides reliability, through VMware HA and other features, for the virtual machines hosted on it. Using shared storage for parts of the Hadoop configuration also increases the storage utilization alongside existing vSphere deployments. This model could be used to reverse the storage mechanisms shown earlier, placing the VMDK files of the NodeManager on the shared storage and those of the DataNode on the local storage. This last approach is less commonly used because the bandwidth required for the temporary data can potentially outweigh that required for the HDFS data. Measure the achievable disk bandwidth to the shared storage device carefully in either case, and compare it with the aggregate bandwidth needed by the virtual machines and the servers hosting them.

With the deployment model shown in Figure 12.6, the data disks of the DataNode virtual machine can be increased to cater to the application's HDFS dataset. The temporary data is required for the mapper-phase output, the shuffle phase of the MapReduce algorithms, and possibly also for spills in both the map and reduce phases. These parts of the data are handled by the NodeManager and its associated containers.

The temporary data size, as mentioned earlier, is highly application dependent. Assessing the size and growth rate of this data at an earlier phase of design is recommended. Providing adequate space on the SAN, or on local storage, to cater for both types of data is a necessary step in this design.

The following are alternative options to this model if no SAN or NAS access is available in the user's data center but scalability is required:

- Use direct attached disks for the temporary data storage.

- Use NFS-based storage.

- Use local solid-state disks (SSDs) for storing the temporary data.

The second and third options can be used in situations where deployments of virtualized Hadoop are being made on blade servers, where the physical slots on the servers are insufficient for direct-attached disks.

Local Disks for the Application's Temporary Data

For some applications, a significant portion (up to 75% in some cases) of the disk I/O bandwidth is consumed in writing to and reading the temporary data that is used while the MapReduce sort and shuffle phases are executing. The temporary data, as mentioned, is written to and read from the local node's file system directories and is not stored in HDFS. Work is in progress on storage of temporary data within HDFS for future Hadoop releases, but that work is not commonly used at the time of writing.

Speed of access to both the HDFS data and the temporary data is important for the efficiency of the application's algorithms. This means that higher-bandwidth disk access is ideal for the HDFS and the temporary data. Those higher levels of bandwidth might necessitate alternative strategies to using SAN or similar storage technology for these types of data. This is a calculation that uses the total I/O bandwidth available to the storage divided by the number of consuming servers, and it applies to all the models discussed here.

Each shared storage or SAN device's I/O bandwidth characteristics are vendor and model specific, and because they change as new models appear on the market they are not discussed in detail here. When there is a higher-specification read/write bandwidth supported by the local direct-attached disk approach, that design can be more suitable for storing the HDFS and/or the temporary data. This trade-off requires careful calculation of capacity, bandwidth, and costs.

The Shared Storage Architecture Model Using Network-Attached Storage (NAS)

The most prominent example of the shared storage model uses a network attached storage (NAS) device for all the HDFS data. The EMC Isilon storage mechanism provides an elegant way of deploying HDFS that is popular among many adopters of Hadoop on vSphere. The Isilon storage device is made up of an expandable set of file servers that are networked together using high-speed Infiniband networking. The operating system that manages this infrastructure, OneFS, provides a layer of software that exports the HDFS interfaces and provides the standard Hadoop RPC communication protocols. The file servers within the Isilon machine contain a set of NameNodes and DataNodes that behave, from a data requestor perspective, exactly like the Hadoop processes discussed earlier. One of the benefits of this approach is that in managing the HDFS data, the OneFS operating system uses a data storage algorithm that reduces the need for multiple replicas of data blocks.

In the model shown in Figure 12.7, all the application's HDFS-based data is stored on the Isilon NAS device. Other data, such as the system disks for the virtual machine operating systems, are held in VMDK files that are mapped to the separate shared-storage mechanisms on the left side of the diagram. These guest operating system VMDK files could also be stored on local attached disks, if they were available.

When implementing Hadoop clusters, users frequently want to leverage their existing virtual infrastructure, which is commonly supported by shared storage or SANs. Their main interest is to minimize change, so keeping their existing servers and making use of an Isilon storage system is an option.

The Isilon approach simplifies the design for the HDFS data where the host systems have a limited amount of or lack local storage. Having decided on this approach, the focus for virtualization now shifts to the storage for the ResourceManager and NodeManager processes, or the "compute" roles. The temporary data that is used by the NodeManager is shown here on direct attached disks, as shown in previous models. This temporary data is not required to be backed up and secured in the same way as the HDFS data is. As discussed earlier, when performance is a primary concern and bandwidth demands are significant, ideally the temporary data is placed on local storage. But if the local storage option is limited or not available, the following alternative approaches can be used:

- Use SSD storage, if available, for the temporary data.

- If only SAN shared storage is available, the temporary data must be placed on the shared storage. This may, however, limit the scalability of the system.

- Temporary data can also be placed on the Isilon device, but care should be taken that this traffic does not interfere with the HDFS traffic.

All other application data that would be handled by the NameNode and DataNodes is securely stored on the Isilon device. Traffic to and from the Isilon storage is carried over dedicated high-speed network interfaces for speed of access.

In situations where several host servers exist with many locally attached disks, managing them can prove to be a significant systems management task. A distinct advantage of this NAS-based design is that it centrally stores and secures access to the HDFS data while still providing access to the data through the normal Hadoop interfaces. Another is that any data that is loaded onto the storage through other protocols, such as NFS, SMB, and HTTP, are now visible through HDFS without an ingestion step.

This Isilon design reduces the amount of administrative time spent on the management of locally attached disks on the host servers, thus saving costs. Figure 12.7 shows a virtualized Hadoop compute layer communicating over the network with an Isilon storage system that presents the HDFS protocols to the compute virtual machines. In Figure 12.7, the temporary or shuffle data is shown as being stored on direct attached disks, thereby relieving the Isilon storage of that task. That temporary/shuffle data can itself also be stored in a separate area on the Isilon, if needed.

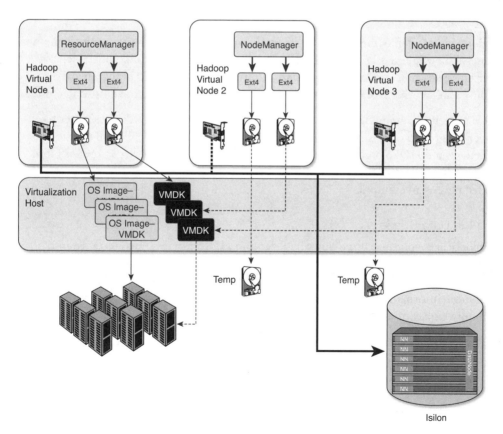

Figure 12.7   A deployment model based on NAS storage.

Deployment Model Summary

In the earlier sections, you learned that there are several models for deployment of the Hadoop workers on virtual infrastructure. We provide some guidelines for choosing between them and for integrating ideas from several models into your own design. There is no one right model, particularly when the applications being deployed have different storage and performance requirements. Considerations other than performance can take precedence here, such as security or backup/recoverability of the data or cost of the overall solution.

Refer to the *VMware vSphere Big Data Extensions Administrator's and User's Guide*[4] for detailed deployment steps and parameters to use for these models. After you choose a design that is capable of meeting application needs, you can then create a detailed plan for the other computing resources that the server hosts will use, including storage sizing, CPU, memory, availability, networking, and hardware layout configurations.

Storage Sizing

A Hadoop cluster deployment often starts small, with a cluster that grows as the load on it increases. The vSphere Big Data Extensions tool provides support for scaling a deployed cluster up or down in size, using the design patterns discussed earlier in this chapter, such as adding a full worker node or adding a compute-only worker node to an existing cluster.

Storage capacity is an important initial determination to make. This requires a user to predict data growth over time and to consider temporary data and replicated data for the MapReduce and HDFS algorithms. The required data space can be three times or more the size of the input data that is first loaded into the cluster. A storage-sizing exercise is provided next as an example.

Sizing the Data Space

Data blocks are replicated three times by default in HDFS, so this must be taken into account when sizing the data space for the DataNode virtual machines in particular. This is calculated differently if the HDFS storage mechanism is an EMC Isilon storage device; more information on that can be found in the "EMC Hadoop Starter Kit" https://community.emc.com/docs/DOC-26892.

The HDFS data block replication factor can also be configured differently for different Hadoop applications, at the user's request.

The following is a disk-sizing exercise example:

- We make the assumption that the data volume grows by approximately 3TB per week.
- By default, HDFS is set up to contain three replicas of each data block.
- Therefore, 9TB of extra storage space is required per week.

- We add a value of 100 percent of the input data size for the temporary space, resulting in 12 TB per week.

- Assuming that we have server machines with 12 x 3 TB disk drives, the calculation of the number of machines needed to support one year's worth of data would be (52 x 12)/36 = 17 machines. This figure does not, however, include the data storage needs of the vSphere hypervisor itself, which should also be taken into account. More guidance on that storage can be found in the vSphere Administrator documents.

Availability

The design of Hadoop ensures that a Hadoop cluster is resilient to many common failures, such as server or storage failure. The majority of servers in a Hadoop cluster are worker nodes. Hadoop has built-in failure-recovery algorithms to detect and repair a job when a worker node fails. The Hadoop scheduler detects that a task has failed on a worker node and restarts that task either on the same node or on another node that contains the correct data. Data blocks are replicated in HDFS so that if a virtual machine containing one copy of any data block becomes unavailable, the replica for that block can be found on another host in that replica group. VMware has put code in place in the Apache Hadoop code itself to handle situations where virtual machines are replicating each others' data blocks. For safety, those code contributions to the Apache source ensure that these virtual machines are on separate servers. This is described later in this chapter.

Best Practices for Virtualizing Hadoop Workers

This book has an entire chapter on virtualization best practices; however, after talking about virtualizing the Hadoop workers, we felt it worthwhile to take a second pass over some of these considerations. This section introduces best practices for setting up each of the main compute resources—disk I/O, CPUs, memory, and so on—when preparing them to run Hadoop-based workloads. Many of these best practices apply equally to other types of workloads on vSphere.

As a general recommendation, a virtualized Hadoop cluster should reside on the most up-to-date hardware available. This will enable optimal specifications for clock speed, core count, hyperthreading, and caching.

Disk I/O

The following best practices apply to the disk I/O mechanisms employed in virtualizing Hadoop:

- For optimal performance, the more direct-attached disks available on the servers that support the Hadoop worker nodes, the better. Because the NodeManagers and DataNodes depend heavily on disk I/O bandwidth, having more available disks decreases the likelihood that requests will execute together on a single disk device and thereby cause an I/O bottleneck. There are examples earlier in this chapter of host servers with eight local disks, but it is not uncommon with Hadoop workloads to have servers with 24 direct-attached disks today. One Hadoop distributor recently recommended using 32 local direct-attached disks for larger servers. Such an environment qualifies as a "power user" and has some disadvantages. The performance work done at VMware shows that three to four disks per DataNode process give better results, so that is a general guideline to follow.

- Use 1 to 1.5 disks per core or virtual CPU when possible. This recommendation is consistent with that of the Hadoop distribution vendors. Having more independent disks increases the management attention required compared with a centralized, shared-disk system. For the architect, this is a trade-off between the stated performance benefits and the cost of managing the independent disks.

- Provide at least 120Mb per second of disk bandwidth per core or per virtual CPU. For SATA disks, that equates to roughly one disk per virtual CPU.

- For power-user applications, disks operating at 7200RPM or higher have performed well. This type of disk setup requires more management oversight than does a centralized SAN arrangement.

- RAID is not required on disks that contain HDFS data, because the HDFS system replicates its data blocks regardless. If RAID controllers are present in the storage subsystem being used, the disks should be configured to use pass-through mode if available. If pass-through functionality is not available for the RAID controller, a single LUN or virtual disk should be created in RAID0 format on each physical disk.

Note   The term *virtual disk* here is a vendor-specific concept and does not refer to a VMDK.

- In keeping with the recommendations of Hadoop distributors for native systems, provided there is flexibility of choice, the LVM, RAID, and IDE technologies should not be used in the I/O-intensive areas of virtualized Hadoop systems.

- Ensure that the local disk controller has enough bandwidth to support all the local disks.

- Ensure that write caching is enabled for DAS devices in particular when using them for virtual machine data storage.

Refer to the Isilon documentation for best practices when choosing that platform as the HDFS storage mechanism.

Ensure Partitions Are Aligned on Disk Devices

To store virtual disks, vSphere uses datastores, which are logical containers that hide the specifics of physical storage from the virtual machines and provide a uniform model for storing virtual machine files. Datastores deployed on block storage devices use the VMFS format, a special high-performance file system format that is optimized for storing virtual machines.

Disk-datastore alignment is very important in achieving I/O operational efficiency in the virtualization environment, as it is in the physical one. Alignment is required at two levels: at the vSphere host server level and within the guest OS of each virtual machine.

Alignment at the vSphere Server Host Level

Utilize the vSphere Web Client user interface to achieve alignment when creating a datastore on a disk. vSphere automatically aligns partitions on the disks that it controls.

There might be situations where alignment must be done over many disks and where using the vSphere Web Client user interface would involve much repetitive and error-prone work. For these situations, custom scripts are developed and used by operations personnel to execute the alignment on a larger scale.

Guest OS Disk Alignment

The vSphere Big Data Extensions tool automatically handles disk alignment at the guest OS level in a virtual machine during the provisioning of a Hadoop cluster. On a Linux guest OS, use the **fdisk -lu** command to verify that partitions are aligned.

Virtual CPUs

The following set of best practices apply to the arrangement of virtual CPUs in the virtual machines supporting the worker nodes in Hadoop.

- At least two virtual CPUs are recommended for any virtual machine that is executing a significant Java process, such as the main Hadoop worker processes. See "Enterprise Java Applications on VMware - Best Practices"[5] for more details.

- For optimal performance, it is recommended that you not overcommit the physical CPUs on the vSphere host. Ideally, the total number of virtual CPUs across all virtual machines on a host server should be equal to the physical core count on that server. This ensures that a virtual CPU doesn't have to wait for a physical CPU to be available before it can execute. When this occurs, we normally see an increase in %Ready time as measured by vSphere performance tools. When hyperthreading is enabled in the BIOS, the total number of vCPUs can be configured to twice the number of physical cores, if the objective is to achieve the maximum performance outcome from the system.

- You should enable hyperthreading for host servers that are managed by vSphere when the host servers are handling Hadoop workloads.

- Virtual machines that fit within the number of cores in a socket, and that use the associated memory for that socket, often perform more efficiently than virtual machines that span multiple sockets. Therefore, it is recommended that you limit the number of virtual CPUs in any virtual machine to a number that is less than or equal to the number of cores in a socket on the target hardware. See the related discussion of NUMA in the "Memory" section that follows.

In the virtualized Hadoop performance work described in "Virtualized Hadoop Performance with VMware vSphere 5.1,"[6] the particular hardware used had two sockets per server, with four cores per socket. Hyperthreading was enabled so that 16 logical processors were present in total. In those tests where four virtual machines, each with four vCPUs, were executed on the system, the performance results were close to that of the native equivalent (within 5%). In those cases described in "Virtualized Hadoop Performance with VMware vSphere 6 on High-Performance Servers - Performance Study,"[7] the results were up to 12% better than the native results, such as in the TeraSort case. With a higher number of sockets or cores per socket on different hardware, a greater number of virtual machines could be executed in similar fashion while obeying the guidelines on fitting the virtual machines within a socket size.

Memory

The following best practices apply to the organization of memory for the virtual machines supporting the Hadoop worker nodes:

- The sum of all the memory configured in the virtual machines on a server should not exceed the size of physical memory on the host server.

- Avoid exhausting the memory of the guest OS within the virtual machine itself. Each virtual machine has a configured memory size that limits its addressable memory space. When a set of memory-hungry processes, such as the Hadoop roles, is executing in the guest OS, ensure that there is enough guest OS memory space configured to enable those processes to execute without incurring memory page swapping at the guest OS level.

- To increase speed and efficiency, nonuniform memory access (NUMA) segments the server's main memory into parts that are closely associated with individual processors. Each of these parts is a NUMA node and has a particular size on any one server architecture. By designing a virtual machine's memory size to fit within the boundary of a NUMA node, the resident Hadoop workload's performance should not be affected by cross-NUMA node migrations or accesses. A group of virtual machines can be designed to fit well within a NUMA node also, giving similar benefits. Virtual machines with memory space that spans more than one NUMA node can incur performance impacts through use of cross-node memory accesses.

- The physical memory of a vSphere host server should allow for the memory requirements of the vSphere hypervisor and for the overhead incurred by each virtual machine. A general guideline is to set aside 6 percent of physical memory for the hypervisor's own use.

- Use a memory-to-core ratio of at least 4GB of memory to one core or virtual CPU.

Virtualized Networking

This section lists the best practices for virtual networking in the context of the Hadoop worker nodes.

- Use dedicated network switches for the Hadoop cluster and ensure that all physical servers are connected to a Top-of-Rack (TOR) switch.

- Use a bandwidth of at least 1Gb per second to connect servers running virtualized Hadoop workloads. If available, a 10GBps switch for connecting servers will give significant benefits.

- Provide between 200mb per second and 600mb per second of aggregate network bandwidth per core, depending on the network requirements of the system.

    Example: 100-node Hadoop cluster

    - 100x16 cores = 1,600 cores

    - 1,600x50MB per second = 80GB per second

    - 1,600x200Mb = 320Gb of network traffic

    - 1,600x600Mb per second = 960Gb per second of network traffic

Typical servers have dual network ports. In many cases, two ports are not enough for ESXi hosts. In configuring ESXi host networking, consider the traffic and loading requirements of the following:

- Management network

- Virtual machine port groups

- IP storage (NFS/iSCSI, Fiber Channel over Ethernet)

- vSphere vMotion

- Fault tolerance

The virtual machines within the Hadoop cluster might also require network connectivity to the corporate network. When designing this portion of the infrastructure, there should be no dependencies on a single network adapter or on a connection to a single physical switch. Redundant pathways for virtual machine–to–virtual machine traffic should be planned into the design.

Scalability is another consideration. The larger the environment grows, the more dynamic it becomes and the harder it becomes to manage the network configuration and keep it consistent across all the hosts in a cluster.

The Hadoop Virtualization Extensions (HVE)

Knowledge of the topology or physical layout of the data center, racks, and hosts that it is operating in is a central part of the original Hadoop design. Making the Hadoop software aware of the virtualization topology on which it is now hosted brings significant benefits to it in the areas of performance and robustness. This section describes a set of technology contributions that VMware has made to the open source Apache Hadoop project. The Hadoop Virtualization Extensions on VMware vSphere 5[8] have been adopted into the core functionality of the Apache project and have been implemented by the main Hadoop distributions. Several areas of innovation within the Hadoop Virtualization Extensions make Hadoop aware of the virtualization topology for better data placement, data lookup, and component placement. In this section we concentrate mainly on the data placement part of HVE. More information on the other parts of HVE can be found in the full technical description.

When implemented on native or physical systems, the Hadoop infrastructure is made aware of the physical topology on which it is operating through user-supplied entries in standard configuration files. This information tells Hadoop about the data centers, racks, and nodes (or physical machines in the original case) on which it is deployed. This is shown in Figure 12.8.

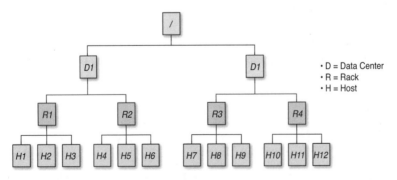

Figure 12.8 The native Hadoop topology components.

In Figure 12.8 we see that the Hadoop system is aware of hosts, racks, and data centers in a containment relationship. Rack awareness can be configured for a Hadoop cluster. Rack awareness makes sure that a single rack will not contain all the replicas for a data block.

However, when virtualization is introduced into the Hadoop layout, another layer is needed in the topology to enable the system to understand that components are deployed on virtual machines that live on one or more servers. This new concept is given the name *NodeGroup*. A NodeGroup represents a set of virtual machines that are running on the same host server (all virtual machines within one NodeGroup share the same host server). This enables users to express within the Hadoop topology the fact that two DataNode processes, executing in their individual virtual machines and potentially containing replicas of the same blocks of data, should not be run on the same physical host. This is referred to as virtual awareness. Rack awareness and virtual awareness can be defined for the same cluster. This makes sure that all the replicas for a given data block do not end up in the same rack and that the placement of block replicas conforms to the concept of a node group. All virtual machines in a node group are executing on the same ESXi host. This additional layer in the topology that allows for more understanding of virtualization concepts in Hadoop is shown at the NodeGroup or NG level in Figure 12.9.

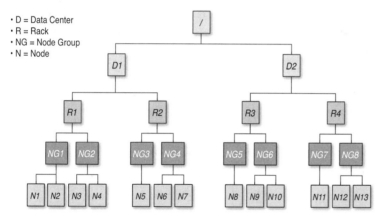

Figure 12.9 The new NodeGroup layer added to the Hadoop topology.

With the HVE-based addition to the Hadoop system topology, it is now possible to separate out the virtual machines that contain DataNodes in such a way that no two DataNodes that maintain replicas of the same data block will run on the same host server. If the latter were allowed, an opportunity would exist for one host server failure to stop two or more virtual machines from executing. Those virtual machines may be replicating each other's data blocks. This would put those data blocks at risk. An example of the two forms of data block placement is shown in Figure 12.10.

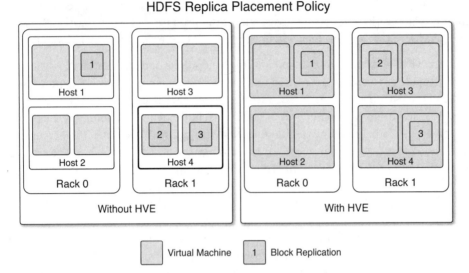

Figure 12.10   Replica data block placement with HVE and without HVE enabled.

In Figure 12.10, the left side of the diagram represents a system without HVE enabled. Because this environment does not have virtualization awareness in its data placement algorithms, it would be possible to have two replicas of a data block contained in two virtual machines that occupy the same host server. HVE is enabled on a Hadoop cluster, through three steps:

1. Upload to the BDE Management Server a topology file that contains the details of the racks and servers.

2. Connect to the BDE Management server (as described in the User and Administrator Guide for BDE).

3. Enter the following command to the BDE command line interface as in the following example:

```
cluster create --name myCluster --topology HVE
```

After HVE has been enabled for the cluster, the approach to data block replication is seen on the right side of Figure 12.10. In that case, no two virtual machines containing DataNodes that are replicating each other's HDFS data blocks are allowed to live on the same server host, leading to higher availability in the event of a host failure.

HVE also enables other functionality, such as replica choosing policies, so that whenever the HDFS client seeks a data block, the nearest replica is found. This is an optimization of the path to get to a data block and is described in more detail in "Hadoop Virtualization Extensions on VMware vSphere 5."

Figure 12.11 summarizes the contributions of the HVE work to the subprojects within Hadoop. As can be seen in Figure 12.11, all the major components of Hadoop are influenced by HVE.

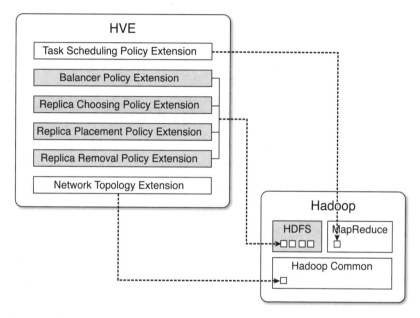

Figure 12.11   Summary of the modules with Hadoop that HVE touches.

The HVE technology for HDFS is implemented at the time of writing in all the major distributions of Hadoop, including Cloudera CDH 5.3 and Hortonworks HDP 2.2.

Summary

As Hadoop ecosystems grow and become more complex, the platform running the Hadoop environment needs the capability to handle the change that will occur within the workloads and the different versions and use cases for that platform. Virtualizing the Hadoop worker layer provides that level of flexibility, and virtualizing also enhances the level of performance monitoring to allow an infrastructure team to be proactive in the management of the Hadoop ecosystem. The different design scenarios discussed in this chapter provide a number of solutions for the worker virtual machines in a Hadoop cluster. The virtualization environment contains management and monitoring capabilities required to support a Hadoop production environment. The HVE extensions enable a Hadoop cluster to be aware of the virtualization parts as well as being rack and host aware for the placement and retrieval of data. Virtualization provides new design approaches to the architect, and it simplifies the operational functions for a Hadoop cluster.

References

1. A Benchmarking Case Study of Virtualized Hadoop Performance on VMware vSphere 5: http://www.vmware.com/files/pdf/VMW-Hadoop-Performance-vSphere5.pdf

2. Virtualized Hadoop Performance with VMware vSphere 6 on High-Performance Servers: http://www.vmware.com/resources/techresources/10452

3. Toward an Elastic Elephant—Enabling Hadoop for the Cloud: http://labs.vmware.com/vmtj/toward-an-elastic-elephant-enabling-hadoop-for-the-cloud

4. VMware vSphere Big Data Extensions Administrator's and User's Guide: https://www.vmware.com/support/pubs/vsphere-big-data-extensions-pubs.html

5. Enterprise Java on VMware vSphere—Best Practices: http://www.vmware.com/resources/techresources/10876.

6. Virtualized Hadoop Performance with VMware vSphere 5.1: http://www.vmware.com/resources/techresources/10360.

7. Virtualized Hadoop Performance with VMware vSphere 6 on High-Performance Servers - Performance Study: http://www.vmware.com/resources/techresources/10452

8. Hadoop Virtualization Extensions on VMware vSphere 5: http://www.vmware.com/files/pdf/Hadoop-Virtualization-Extensions-on-VMware-vSphere-5.pdf

Resources

vSphere Big Data Extensions: http://www.vmware.com/hadoop

Apache Hadoop 1.0 High Availability Solution on VMware vSphere: http://www.vmware.com/files/pdf/Apache-Hadoop-VMware-HA-solution.pdf

Project Serengeti: http://www.projectserengeti.org/

Scaling the Deployment of Multiple Hadoop Workloads on a Virtualized Infrastructure: http://www.intel.com/content/www/us/en/software/intel-dell-vmware-scaling-the-deployment-of-multiple-hadoop-workloads.html?wapkw=hadoop+virtualization

Deploying Latency-Sensitive Applications on VMware vSphere: http://www.vmware.com/resources/techresources/10220

Protecting Hadoop with VMware vSphere 5 Fault Tolerance: http://www.vmware.com/files/pdf/VMware-vSphere-Hadoop-FT.pdf

Apache Hadoop Storage Provisioning Using the VMware vSphere Big Data Extensions: https://www.vmware.com/files/pdf/products/vsphere/VMware-vSphere-BDE-Storage-Provisioning-Whitepaper.pdf

VMware vSphere VMFS: Technical Overview and Best Practices: http://www.vmware.com/files/pdf/vmfs-best-practices-wp.pdf

VMware vSphere Resource Management Guide: http://pubs.vmware.com/vsphere-55/topic/PDF/vsphere-esxi-vcenter-server-55-resource-management-guide.pdf

Deploying Virtualized Hadoop Systems with VMware Big Data Extensions: A Deployment Guide: http://www.vmware.com/files/pdf/products/vsphere/Hadoop-Deployment-Guide-USLET.pdf

EMC Isilon Hadoop Starter Kit: https://community.emc.com/docs/DOC-26892

## Chapter 13

Deploying Hadoop as a Service in the Private Cloud

"There was a time when every household, town, farm or village had its own water well. Today, shared public utilities give us access to clean water by simply turning on the tap; cloud computing works in a similar fashion. Just like water from the tap in your kitchen, cloud computing services can be turned on or off quickly as needed. Like at the water company, there is a team of dedicated professionals making sure the service provided is safe, secure and available on a 24/7 basis. When the tap isn't on, not only are you saving water, but you aren't paying for resources you don't currently need."

—Vivek Kundra

The Cloud Context

Organizations today are working to develop their cloud strategies. At the same time, other sections of the organizations are developing their big data strategies. Somewhere down the road, these strategies must be aligned. It is likely that the world of Hadoop will be a mixture of native/physical and virtualized implementations for some time. Tremendous advantages are achieved in building development and test environments using virtualization. Over time, we can expect some big data projects to use the cloud and some production servers to be virtualized. Virtualizing Hadoop should start while Hadoop is getting started in an organization. Some organizations choose to wait until Hadoop has become a very high-profile application platform and then look to see how to tie in their cloud and virtualization strategies. However, several case studies have shown that getting Hadoop workloads onto the virtualization base early in the adoption phase helps them learn more quickly and achieve more flexibility.

Stakeholders for Hadoop

This chapter describes a solution for use of Hadoop within a private cloud; that is, a cloud implementation that is contained within the organization or enterprise boundary. Security, privacy, and data safety are often the motivations for organizations to keep their cloud private rather than publicly visible. The rapid provisioning and hardware independence traits that are found in the public cloud are also desirable in the private cloud; the two forms of cloud deployment share many of the same mechanisms. It is also feasible to have a blend of the two forms, called a hybrid cloud, where the applications can be moved back and forth between the private and public clouds. Let's take a look at describing the private cloud for Hadoop as a service.

Different stakeholders within an organization want separate Hadoop clusters for their own purposes, though they might share common data in some cases. Some of these stakeholders include the big data application developers, the quality assurance testing personnel, the production staging test teams, and the production application support teams. Additionally, those teams that are responsible for providing central IT services to their business units within an organization need the capability to provide to their internal customers a provisioning function for the varieties of Hadoop platforms. The developers need to experiment with their application designs in a safe sandbox area that does not affect other communities. The testing community must execute suites of tests that can run at length in an automated fashion. Central architecture and service provider groups seek economies of scale by having a common infrastructure and design approach to service these users.

All these parties want the capability to rapidly provision Hadoop clusters as the need arises, without having to deal with lower-level infrastructure concerns such as storage and networking details and without requiring a manual permission process that is driven by a central authority. These users' Hadoop clusters are expected to appear at unpredicted intervals of time; they live for some time and then are possibly decommissioned after they have served their business purpose. This rapid provisioning and deprovisioning functionality is ideally achieved using a cloud management platform and using virtual machines as the unit of deployment for the various parts of the system. Underlying that cloud management platform is a common set of compute and storage resources that is virtualized and allocated to different user communities in isolated resource pools.

Within organizations, because hardware resources are limited, some controls over the Hadoop cluster provisioning process are needed. These controls often consist of a workflow process containing steps to be taken before the provisioning process completes. An example of a workflow step is an automatic approval to provision clusters of a certain size, for example. Another step could be a manual checking process to determine whether the size of the cluster is larger than predefined sizes.

To claim that a private cloud implementation exists for achieving all of the preceding goals, certain factors are required to be fulfilled by a system. Those factors are as follows:

- End users are able to provision instances of Hadoop clusters from a customizable web portal without being concerned about the infrastructure deployment details.

- A catalog of sample Hadoop clusters of various sizes is available for the end users to choose from and customize to their specific needs.

- The deployment of a cluster is automated so that very little, if any, user intervention is required.

- The workflow for deploying a cluster might require some management intervention.

- The deployment process does not require the user to have knowledge of individual physical machines, storage mechanisms, or networks. It is expected that the Hadoop components can be deployed on portable virtual machines.

- There are time and space constraints on how long any particular Hadoop cluster can live before it becomes a candidate for decommissioning.

The following discussion gives the private cloud viewpoint on this landscape, where the full deployment of a Hadoop cluster is done within the enterprise walls.

VMware created a custom integrated solution to achieve the preceding set of goals. The solution is built using two products from the VMware vCloud Suite portfolio: the vRealize Automation (vRA) platform (known previously as the vCloud Automation Center) and the vSphere Big Data Extensions (BDE) feature set that is part of vSphere 5.5 and later.

vRA is a cloud management platform and toolkit that allows for multitenancy, application catalogs, application blueprints, entitlements, and end-user application provisioning using a web portal as the interface. vRA uses the BDE and vCenter management features to handle the infrastructure components (such as deploying a virtual machine on to a server) under the covers, and it exposes the appropriate level of abstraction to the user, depending on the user's role. A full description of the features of vRA is given in VMware vRealize Automation—Documentation Site at https://www.vmware.com/support/pubs/vRA-pubs.html.

Integration Features

The solution described here deals with different classes of users of Hadoop-as-a-service. Two important user roles that are present here, among others, are those of the Tenant Administrator (TenantAdmin) and the Tenant User. The vRA and BDE products, when integrated together, provide a solution that enables the provisioning of Hadoop as a service for the tenant users. In the solution, the following operations are exposed through a web browser interface; that interface is implemented using the web portal functionality provided by the vRA cloud management platform.

Creating a Basic Hadoop Cluster

This operation enables the user to create a basic Hadoop cluster from an existing catalog entry. The catalog entry is placed there by a service architect who wants to supply this particular functionality to the end user. The Hadoop cluster is composed of three types of nodes: the master, worker, and client nodes. Each node is deployed in a virtual machine when the full cluster is deployed by the user. The master node contains the NameNode and ResourceManager daemon processes, and the worker node contains the DataNode and NodeManager processes. The client node contains the client, Pig, Hive, and Hive-server, among other roles. For more information on the roles of the various Hadoop nodes, see Chapter 7, "Multitenancy in Hadoop."

Creating a Compute-Only Cluster

This operation creates a Hadoop cluster without HDFS functionality in it. The idea is that the HDFS components are supplied by a separate file system or a storage device. This type of cluster has three parts: master, worker, and client. The tenant-user supplies the address of an external HDFS mechanism that fulfills the DataNode and NameNode roles, at cluster creation time. The master node virtual machine in this deployment scenario contains only the ResourceManager Hadoop role, and the worker node contains just the NodeManager role. The client node contains the same roles as it does in the basic Hadoop cluster.

Creating a Data-Compute Separated Cluster

For this deployment type, the data and compute resources will be separated onto different virtual machines. There are four types of nodes here: master, data node, compute node, and client. The master node contains the NameNode and the ResourceManager roles. The data node contains the Hadoop DataNode role; the compute node contains the NodeManager role, and the client contains the same roles as mentioned in the "Creating a Basic Hadoop Cluster" section earlier in the chapter.

The service architect in vRA creates a blueprint service for the three operations given earlier. When creating the blueprint service, the service architect configures the infrastructure resources that are defined in the Big Data Extensions domain (the resource pool, networks, and datastores) to isolate the infrastructure-level resources between the tenants.

After a Hadoop cluster of one of the above types has been created by an end user using the vRA portal, the tenant user can carry out a set of operations on that cluster, such as starting, stopping, and resizing the cluster. These operations are described in the next section.

The User Experience

After a set of catalog services has been published in vRA, the tenant-user can view those items in the catalog and then request the deployment of a Hadoop cluster using one of the entries in the catalog as a pattern.

Create a Hadoop Cluster

A tenant-user who has the entitlement Hadoop as a Service enabled can use Hadoop cluster creation items within the vRA tool, such as Create a Cluster, Create a Compute-Only Cluster, and Create a Data-Compute Separated Cluster.

When users have chosen the type of deployment they want to use, the vRA tool gives them the option to supply a description and reasons for approval of the proposed new cluster, if needed.

Then users are asked to provide a name for the new Hadoop cluster. After this is done, the tenant-user customizes the configuration of each type of node in the normal BDE style. Examples of the types of customization allowed here are the number of virtual CPUs or the amount of memory that the virtual machine has for a particular role. BDE provides small, medium, and large profiles as examples to make the users' choice easier in this area. The customization of one type of virtual machine size is shown in Figure 13.1. This customization can also be done for the worker nodes. In the screen shown in Figure 13.1, users are allowed to choose the number of virtual CPUs, memory size, and storage size for the master virtual machines that will be created subsequently.

Figure 13.1   Configuring the size of the master nodes.

After the appropriate data has been submitted, a new request will be shown on the vRA Requests screen, and the user observes the provisioning process by using the vCenter screens or by using the command-line features of the BDE Management Server. The BDE command used here is the **cluster list** command, whose output is shown in Figure 13.2. The Hadoop distribution used in this example is Apache, although it could be configured for any of the well-known distributions. The different Hadoop roles are shown within a Group Name, which represents a virtual machine type. There may be several instances of that virtual machine type in the eventual deployment.

```
CLUSTER NAME              :  basic
AGENT VERSION             :  2.2.0
APP MANAGER               :  Default
DISTRO                    :  apache
AUTO ELASTIC              :  N/A
MIN COMPUTE NODES NUM     :  N/A
MAX COMPUTE NODES NUM     :  N/A
IO SHARES                 :  NORMAL
STATUS                    :  RUNNING
AD/LDAP ENABLED           :  false

GROUP NAME  ROLES                                          INSTANCE  CPU  MEM(MB)  TYPE    SIZE(GB)
-------------------------------------------------------------------------------------------------
master      [hadoop_namenode, hadoop_resourcemanager]      1         1    5000     SHARED  8
client      [hadoop_client, pig, hive, hive_server]        1         1    3748     SHARED  10
worker      [hadoop_datanode, hadoop_nodemanager]          2         1    3748     LOCAL   10
```

Figure 13.2   Output of the **cluster list** command from the BDE CLI tool showing the new cluster.

Run the **cluster list** command and, after a short period of time, the new Hadoop cluster is shown as created, and it appears as an item on the vRA Items page.

Resizing a Hadoop Cluster

After tenant-users create a Hadoop cluster using vRA, they can execute resource actions. Looking at the Actions available on the new cluster in vRA in Figure 13.3, users can click Resize Cluster in the Actions box.

Figure 13.3   Actions available on a cluster in the vRA solution—right side of screen.

In the Resize Cluster dialog box, the user provides a description for the resize operation and the reason for performing the action. The user then chooses the node type that will be resized. The BDE Server supports scaling the worker nodes of a cluster in and out by increasing or decreasing the number of virtual machines serving that cluster. The user chooses the new number of worker nodes. After submitting the request, the status of this cluster is UPDATING.

Figure 13.4 shows the parameters for resizing the Hadoop cluster. Here, the cluster is being resized to contain two worker virtual machines. This can be any number up to the capacity of the system to support it.

Figure 13.4   Screen from vRA showing a request to resize a Hadoop cluster.

After a short period of time, the resizing job completes. To verify that the resize operation completed successfully, check the Worker IPs field, which gives the set of IP addresses that are now being used by virtual machines.

Overview of the Solution Architecture

As part of the integration of the vSphere Big Data Extensions with VMware vRealize Automation, the VMware engineering team developed a custom vCenter Orchestrator (vCO) plug-in. vCenter Orchestrator is a standard component within the VMware vCenter Server. The vCenter Server tool is used to manage virtual machines and the hardware that underlies them. vCenter Server is present in the vast majority of data centers that have VMware technology implemented today. It is a foundational component of the VMware vCloud Suite of products.

vCenter Orchestrator (delivered as part of vCenter) enables a set of actions on virtual machines and associated resources to be sequenced in a workflow so that the operator's task is made easier. It has a workflow composer design tool built in to it. Within the vCO plug-in that was built for this particular integration, some workflows will invoke the workflows of other vCO plug-ins also. This is done to configure the Big Data Extensions host and REST operations. All other workflows are designed to call the REST API of the Big Data Extensions Server to carry out many kinds of Hadoop deployment operations. The workflows built in the vCenter Orchestrator server are exposed to vRealize Automation for the purpose of configuring blueprint services in the vRA catalog or resource actions that will become visible to the end users. An example of one screen from the creation of a blueprint in vRA is shown in Figure 13.5.

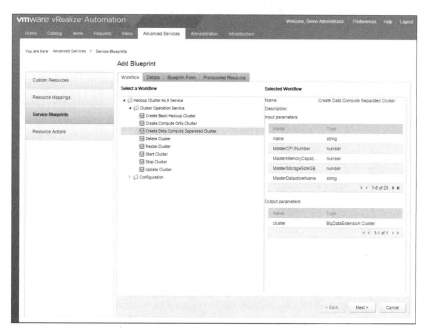

Figure 13.5   Adding a new blueprint in the vRA environment.

After the suitable access entitlements are completed and the blueprints are published into the vRA catalog of available applications, the tenant users can begin to execute deployments in a Hadoop-as-a-service fashion. Figure 13.6 shows the architecture for the integration of vRA (formerly called vCloud Automation Center or vCAC) with the BDE tool through the VCO workflows.

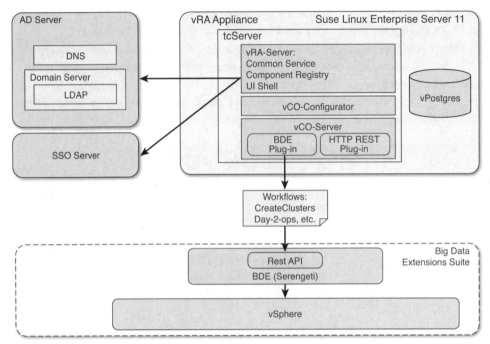

Figure 13.6   The solution architecture for the integration of BDE with vRA.

Summary

Providing a facility for Hadoop-as-a-Service is an important goal of many organizations. What they want to achieve, simply put, is the capability to provide a variety of different Hadoop infrastructures for hosting applications to their user communities while abstracting the low-level technical implementation details away from those end users. The integration solution described in this chapter enables that Hadoop-as-a-Service end goal for cloud tenant users. The solution described here brings together a cloud management technology, vRealize Automation, and a Hadoop cluster provisioning technology, VMware Big Data Extensions, to implement this functionality. That same solution has been customized to meet the needs of the enterprise by several Hadoop consumer organizations today.

In a Hadoop-as-a-Service environment, the tenant users can easily perform common Hadoop cluster provisioning and management administrative tasks. Tenants are separated by virtue of having separate resource pools and clusters in which their Hadoop clusters live. These separate environments can be given different priorities for execution by the administrator, according to the business need. This fulfills one of the main goals of virtualizing Hadoop in the sense that the pool of available hardware is safely shared across different Hadoop user communities in the enterprise. More technical details on this architecture can be found in https://community.emc.com/docs/DOC-39529 and http://www.vmware.com/files/pdf/products/vsphere/VMware-vSphere-Adobe-Deploys-HAAS-CS.pdf for those who are interested in pursuing this virtualization-based approach.

References

VMware vRealize Automation—Documentation Site: https://www.vmware.com/support/pubs/vRA-pubs.html

VMware vSphere Big Data Extensions User's and Administrator's Guide: https://www.vmware.com/support/pubs/vsphere-big-data-extensions-pubs.html

VMware vSphere Big Data Extensions website: http://www.vmware.com/bde

Virtualizing Hadoop in Large Scale Infrastructures: https://community.emc.com/docs/DOC-39529

Adobe Deploys Hadoop-as-a-Service on VMware vSphere: http://www.vmware.com/files/pdf/products/vsphere/VMware-vSphere-Adobe-Deploys-HAAS-CS.pdf

## Chapter 14

Understanding the Installation of Hadoop

Technology presumes there's just one right way to do things and there never is.

—Robert M. Pirsig

Technology is nothing. What's important is that you have a faith in people, that they're basically good and smart, and if you give them tools, they'll do wonderful things with them.

—Steve Jobs

Map the Right Solutions to the Right Use Case

Let's clarify why we presented the quotes of these two famous men. First, these statements are not true for all technologies, but they are for most of them. Second, Steve Jobs is absolutely right. Even the best technology cannot be effective if it is used incorrectly and by the wrong people.

What can we say about Hadoop in light of the quotes?

First, never trust anyone who says that Hadoop will save your life or that Hadoop is the only technology that can provide the right answers and is the "most advanced" in the world. This is not true, unless you know what exact business challenge or use cases need to be solved. This is especially important with how fast technology is evolving around Hadoop. People go to the latest conferences or read the newest whitepapers, and they hear or read that NoSQL, Spark, Hadoop, or other third-party tools are the best way to go. Slow down and make sure the solutions being considered map to the use cases.

Second, NO technology in the world can be used by itself without the right people involved in the design and implementation of the idea behind the technology.

I worked with Hadoop in general and HDP in particular as an architect and administrator for several years. After installing, tuning, and troubleshooting some of the largest Hadoop installations in the world, I can tell you the following:

- Always do your homework and try things before implementing them on a big scale.

- Never trust "automated procedures" unless you clearly understand what is happening under the hood.

- Always try to clearly define your objectives and needs for yourself. This is especially important when presenting for customers or management. Until you understand what you are trying to accomplish, you will not be able to present things correctly.

- There is always more than one way to solve a problem. Do not be bound to only one solution.

- Most important, believe in yourself!

Thoughts About Installing Hadoop

The installation of Hadoop has gotten significantly easier with each new release. Tools such as Ambari and Cloudera Manager provide tools for installing and provisioning Hadoop. VMware BDE enables you to create blueprints and deploy not only Hadoop clusters but all the other servers that are required to support the Hadoop ecosystem with the push of a button.

There is one thing you must be very careful about with all the nice automated tools and easy point-and-click buttons. When something breaks or a button is pushed, someone must understand how Hadoop works. Also, sometimes a company needs to have a custom installation and configuration done and then have a "blueprint" created for automatic deployment. This chapter takes you through the manual installation of Hadoop so you can understand all the pieces that need to be in place to make Hadoop work.

It is critical for the Hadoop administrator to understand the manual installation and configuration procedure and have a deep understanding of the Hadoop infrastructure layout and configuration. It is also important for the person installing the Hadoop cluster to have the right mindset. For example, paying attention to detail is critical. Cleaning up a partly functional cluster is harder than starting clean. Doing things correctly the first time is critical. The required skill sets are also important. Understand the typical issues that people come across when installing Hadoop for a particular release or ecosystem. Sometimes, when they install Hadoop, customers see warnings but ignore them. Warnings were related to hostnames, network configurations, and other issues in the cluster environment. You should have a list of all parameter and configuration settings when you begin the installation. A cluster that is not properly installed can get up and running but have a lot of issues later. Then you will need to reinstall the Hadoop cluster. So taking care with every installation step is critical to a successful installation.

A Few Words on Best Practices

Try to keep the Hadoop cluster within a single network segment if the cluster size allows it. Spreading Hadoop across multiple network segments will not break it but will significantly increase the amount of maintenance for the production grade system.

Always surround a Hadoop cluster with firewalls. Users should not be able to connect to cluster nodes directly (unless the user is an administrator). Hadoop servers contain logging and other sensitive information; access to them needs to be protected.

Some Thoughts on Installing Hadoop

Always consider these two important rules: RTFM ("Read the favorite manual," or words to that effect) and KISS ("Keep it simple, stupid"). In other words, be prepared before asking questions, and do not overcomplicate things. Complex systems fail in complex ways. After Hadoop is installed, consider the maintenance of the cluster. Focus on the long-term maintenance of the cluster, not just the installation of a specific configuration.

Now we'll look at an example of an actual implementation of a Hadoop cluster on a small scale, but having a fully working distributed system after completing the exercise.

The Hortonworks Data Platform (HDP) distribution is selected for this manual installation because of its commitment of being 100% open source and 100% free. We will use HDP 2.2 for the installation example, and we will perform a manual installation using Hortonworks hosted repositories. Our lab environment contains three nodes, installed with the minimal CentOS 6.6 setup. All the required prerequisites are installed on all nodes (ntp, wget, unzip, JDK, and so on). The Java Development Toolkit (JDK) installed by Oracle provides an RPM Package Manager (rpm) to the default location (/usr/java). Using the default JDK installation, we have static JAVA_HOME: /usr/java/default, which is not changing if the JDK upgraded or modified. This provides a stable environment for upgrades.

Compliance with all prerequisites is crucial because the cluster will not function during or after install if one is missed. Please visit the following URL to review all the HDP prerequisites: http://docs.hortonworks.com/HDPDocuments/HDP2/HDP-2.2.4/ HDP_Man_Install_v224/index.html#ref-09cc282d-3bdc-4513-8dcb-990f06845697.

Finally, all the installation instructions seem to assume that installations must be performed as root but there are no options to install HDP using a "nonroot" account. Enterprises today do not want to use the root account to install software components.

Configuring Repositories

Yum repositories must be configured on each server to complete HDP installation, so we will download the HDP repository file to each of the cluster nodes. To download the HDP repository, run the following command:

```
[root@hdp22-1 ~]# wget -nv http://public-repo-1.hortonworks.com/HDP/
  centos6/2.x/GA/2.2.0.0/hdp.repo -O /etc/yum.repos.d/hdp.repo
2015-02-17 21:43:39 URL:http://public-repo-1.hortonworks.com/HDP/
  centos6/2.x/GA/2.2.0.0/hdp.repo [605/605] -> "/etc/yum.repos.d/
  hdp.repo" [1]
```

After you download the repo file, you must perform repositories synchronization:

```
[root@hdp22-1 ~]# yum repolist
```

To verify the configuration of the repositories, execute the following command:

```
[root@hdp22-1 ~]# yum list "hadoop*"
```

The JDK also must be installed on all nodes. All JDK installations must be identical across the cluster.

Listing 14.1 shows how to install the JDK on all nodes. Look at the documentation for the Hadoop release being installed, and then work with the latest JDK that is stable. Verify what JDK versions are supported.

Listing 14.1 Install the Java JDK

```
  [root@hdp22-1 ~]# yum install jdk-7u75-linux-x64.rpm
Loaded plugins: fastestmirror
Setting up Install Process
Examining jdk-7u75-linux-x64.rpm: 2000:jdk-1.7.0_75-fcs.x86_64
Marking jdk-7u75-linux-x64.rpm to be installed
Loading mirror speeds from cached hostfile
 * base: mirrors.kernel.org
 * extras: centos.mirrors.tds.net
 * updates: mirror.spro.net
Resolving Dependencies
--> Running transaction check
```

```
---> Package jdk.x86_64 2000:1.7.0_75-fcs will be installed
--> Finished Dependency Resolution
Dependencies Resolved
======================================================================
 Package
 Arch Version   Repository Size
======================================================================
Installing:
 jdk x86_64 2000:1.7.0_75-fcs   /jdk-7u75-linux-x64 197 M
Transaction Summary
======================================================================
Install 1 Package(s)

Total size: 197 M
Installed size: 197 M
Is this ok [y/N]: y
Downloading Packages:
Runningrpm_check_debug
Running Transaction Test
Transaction Test Succeeded
Running Transaction
   Installing : 2000:jdk-1.7.0_75-fcs.x86_64             1/1
Unpacking JAR files...
     rt.jar...
     jsse.jar...
     charsets.jar...
     tools.jar...
     localedata.jar...
     jfxrt.jar...
   Verifying  : 2000:jdk-1.7.0_75-fcs.x86_64             1/1

Installed:
  jdk.x86_64 2000:1.7.0_75-fcs

Complete!
[root@hdp22-1 ~]#
```

When the repositories are configured and accessible and the JDK is installed on all nodes, you can start the HDP installation.

Installing HDP 2.2

For the purpose of this book, we will install and configure a basic three-node cluster containing the following core components: HDFS, YARN, MapReduce2, and Hive. The rest of the ecosystem components are installed similarly, so we will not concentrate on a "full" cluster setup here.

Environment Preparation

Before starting installation, a number of tasks should be completed. Make sure you have the information for each node, such as server names, IP addresses, and the like. Also verify whether you have identified what processes and software are going to go on each node. First, you should create the user accounts and groups.

Table 14.1 shows a list of key Hadoop services and the user IDs and groups that run them.

Table 14.1   Typical System Users and Groups

Hadoop Service	User	Group
HDFS	hdfs	Hadoop
YARN	yarn	Hadoop
MapReduce	mapred	hadoop, mapred
Hive	hive	Hadoop
Zookeeper	zookeeper	Hadoop

Listing 14.2 sets up the primary users used by Hadoop.

Listing 14.2   Set Up Users and Groups for Hadoop

```
# Adding HDP internal users and groups
groupadd -f -g 1024 hadoop

# HDFS user
useradd -c "Hadoop HDFS" -d /var/lib/hadoop-hdfs -s /bin/bash --groups
  hadoop -u 1001 -U hdfs
echo "export JAVA_HOME=/usr/java/default" >> /var/lib/hadoop-hdfs/.bash_
  profile
echo "export PATH=\$PATH:\$JAVA_HOME/bin" >> /var/lib/hadoop-hdfs/.bash_
  profile
```

```
# YARN user
useradd -c "Hadoop Yarn" -d /var/lib/hadoop-yarn -s /bin/bash --groups hadoop
   -u 1002 -U yarn
echo "export JAVA_HOME=/usr/java/default" >> /var/lib/hadoop-yarn/
   .bash_profile
echo "export PATH=\$PATH:\$JAVA_HOME/bin" >> /var/lib/hadoop-yarn/
   .bash_profile


# MapReduce user
useradd -c "Hadoop MapReduce" -d /var/lib/hadoop-mapreduce -s /bin/bash
   --groups hadoop -u 1003 -U mapred
echo "export JAVA_HOME=/usr/java/default" >> /var/lib/hadoop-mapreduce/
   .bash_profile
echo "export PATH=\$PATH:\$JAVA_HOME/bin" >> /var/lib/hadoop-mapreduce/
   .bash_profile


# ZooKeeper user
useradd -c "ZooKeeper" -d /var/run/zookeeper -s /bin/bash --groups hadoop -u
   1004 -U zookeeper
echo "export JAVA_HOME=/usr/java/default" >> /var/run/zookeeper/.bash_profile
echo "export PATH=\$PATH:\$JAVA_HOME/bin" >> /var/run/zookeeper/.bash_profile


# Hive user
useradd -c "Hive" -d /var/lib/hive -s /bin/bash --groups hadoop -u 1006 -U
   hive
echo "export JAVA_HOME=/usr/java/default" >> /var/lib/hive/.bash_profile
echo "export PATH=\$PATH:\$JAVA_HOME/bin" >> /var/lib/hive/.bash_profile
```

Hortonworks provides a set of companion files that include components' configuration templates as well as several useful scripts.

Download the companion files from the repository server:

```
[root@hdp22-1 ~]# wget http://public-repo-1.hortonworks.com/HDP/
   tools/2.2.0.0/hdp_manual_install_rpm_helper_files-2.2.0.0.2041.tar.gz
```

Use the scripts shown in Listing 14.3 to set the environment variables and to create the required directories. It is recommended that you include those scripts in the .bashrc file. You must edit the script directories.sh file to provide the directory information.

Listing 14.3 This Script Sets Up the Hadoop Environment Before Starting the Install

```
    [root@hdp22-1 scripts]# cat usersAndGroups.sh
#!/bin/sh

#
# Users and Groups
#

# User which will own the HDFS services.
export HDFS_USER=hdfs

# User which will own the YARN services.
export YARN_USER=yarn

# User which will own the MapReduce services.
export MAPRED_USER=mapred

# User which will own the Pig services.
export PIG_USER=pig

# User which will own the Hive services.
export HIVE_USER=hive

# User which will own the Templeton services.
export WEBHCAT_USER=hcat

# User which will own the HBase services.
export HBASE_USER=hbase

# User which will own the ZooKeeper services.
export ZOOKEEPER_USER=zookeeper

# User which will own the Oozie services.
export OOZIE_USER=oozie

# User which will own the Accumulo services.
export ACCUMULO_USER=accumulo

# A common group shared by services.
export HADOOP_GROUP=hadoop
```

```
[root@hdp22-1 scripts]#


[root@hdp22-1 scripts]# cat directories.sh
#!/bin/sh


#
# Directories Script
#
# 1. To use this script, you must edit the TODO variables below for your
  environment.
#
# 2. Warning: Leave the other parameters as the default values. Changing
  these default values will require you to
#  change values in other configuration files.
#


#
# Hadoop Service - HDFS
#


# Space separated list of directories where NameNode will store file system
  image. For example, /grid/hadoop/hdfs/nn /grid1/hadoop/hdfs/nn
export DFS_NAME_DIR="/data1/hdfs/nn";


# Space separated list of directories where DataNodes will store the
  blocks. For example, /grid/hadoop/hdfs/dn /grid1/hadoop/hdfs/dn /grid2/
  hadoop/hdfs/dn
export DFS_DATA_DIR="/data1/hdfs/dn /data2/hdfs/dn";


# Space separated list of directories where SecondaryNameNode will store
  checkpoint image. For example, /grid/hadoop/hdfs/snn /grid1/hadoop/hdfs/
  snn /grid2/hadoop/hdfs/snn
export FS_CHECKPOINT_DIR="/data2/hdfs/snn";


# Directory to store the HDFS logs.
export HDFS_LOG_DIR="/var/log/hadoop/hdfs";


# Directory to store the HDFS process ID.
export HDFS_PID_DIR="/var/run/hadoop/hdfs";


# Directory to store the Hadoop configuration files.
```

```
export HADOOP_CONF_DIR="/etc/hadoop/conf";


#
# Hadoop Service - YARN
#


# Space separated list of directories where YARN will store temporary data.
  For example, /grid/hadoop/yarn/local /grid1/hadoop/yarn/local /grid2/
  hadoop/yarn/local
export YARN_LOCAL_DIR="/data1/yarn/local /data2/yarn/local";


# Directory to store the YARN logs.
export YARN_LOG_DIR="/var/log/hadoop/yarn";


# Space separated list of directories where YARN will store container log
  data. For example, /grid/hadoop/yarn/logs /grid1/hadoop/yarn/logs /grid2/
  hadoop/yarn/logs
export YARN_LOCAL_LOG_DIR="/data1/yarn/logs /data2/yarn/logs";


# Directory to store the YARN process ID.
export YARN_PID_DIR="/var/run/hadoop/yarn";


#
# Hadoop Service - MAPREDUCE
#


# Directory to store the MapReduce daemon logs.
export MAPRED_LOG_DIR="/var/log/hadoop/mapred";


# Directory to store the mapreduce jobhistory process ID.
export MAPRED_PID_DIR="/var/run/hadoop/mapred";


#
# Hadoop Service - Hive
#


# Directory to store the Hive configuration files.
export HIVE_CONF_DIR="/etc/hive/conf";


# Directory to store the Hive logs.
export HIVE_LOG_DIR="/var/log/hive";
```

```
# Directory to store the Hive process ID.
export HIVE_PID_DIR="/var/run/hive";


#
# Hadoop Service - WebHCat (Templeton)
#

# Directory to store the WebHCat (Templeton) configuration files.
export WEBHCAT_CONF_DIR="/etc/hcatalog/conf/webhcat";

# Directory to store the WebHCat (Templeton) logs.
export WEBHCAT_LOG_DIR="var/log/webhcat";

# Directory to store the WebHCat (Templeton) process ID.
export WEBHCAT_PID_DIR="/var/run/webhcat";


#
# Hadoop Service - HBase
#

# Directory to store the HBase configuration files.
export HBASE_CONF_DIR="/etc/hbase/conf";

# Directory to store the HBase logs.
export HBASE_LOG_DIR="/var/log/hbase";

# Directory to store the HBase logs.
export HBASE_PID_DIR="/var/run/hbase";


#
# Hadoop Service - ZooKeeper
#

# Directory where ZooKeeper will store data. For example, /grid1/hadoop/
  zookeeper/data
export ZOOKEEPER_DATA_DIR="/data1/zookeeper/data";

# Directory to store the ZooKeeper configuration files.
export ZOOKEEPER_CONF_DIR="/etc/zookeeper/conf";

# Directory to store the ZooKeeper logs.
```

```
export ZOOKEEPER_LOG_DIR="/var/log/zookeeper";

# Directory to store the ZooKeeper process ID.
export ZOOKEEPER_PID_DIR="/var/run/zookeeper";


#
# Hadoop Service - Pig
#

# Directory to store the Pig configuration files.
export PIG_CONF_DIR="/etc/pig/conf";

# Directory to store the Pig logs.
export PIG_LOG_DIR="/var/log/pig";

# Directory to store the Pig process ID.
export PIG_PID_DIR="/var/run/pig";


#
# Hadoop Service - Oozie
#

# Directory to store the Oozie configuration files.
export OOZIE_CONF_DIR="/etc/oozie/conf"

# Directory to store the Oozie data.
export OOZIE_DATA="/var/db/oozie"

# Directory to store the Oozie logs.
export OOZIE_LOG_DIR="/var/log/oozie"

# Directory to store the Oozie process ID.
export OOZIE_PID_DIR="/var/run/oozie"

# Directory to store the Oozie temporary files.
export OOZIE_TMP_DIR="/var/tmp/oozie"

#
# Hadoop Service - Sqoop
```

```
#
export SQOOP_CONF_DIR="/etc/sqoop/conf"

#
# Hadoop Service - Accumulo
#
export ACCUMULO_CONF_DIR="/etc/accumulo/conf";

export ACCUMULO_LOG_DIR="/var/log/accumulo"
[root@hdp22-1 scripts]#
```

The script shown in Listing 14.3 sets up the working environment for the Hadoop cluster and creates required folders. This enables you to see under the covers how the Hadoop directories and the like are set up. You must have a working knowledge of shell scripts to go through this.

On execution, the script shown in Listing 14.4 provides feedback with the environment set.

Listing 14.4   Display the Environment Being Set Up

```
[root@hdp22-1 scripts]# cat helper.sh
#!/bin/bash
. ./usersAndGroups.sh
. ./directories.sh

env

echo "Create namenode local dir"
mkdir -p $DFS_NAME_DIR
chown -R $HDFS_USER:$HADOOP_GROUP $DFS_NAME_DIR
chmod -R 750 $DFS_NAME_DIR

echo "Create secondary namenode local dir"
mkdir -p $FS_CHECKPOINT_DIR
chown -R $HDFS_USER:$HADOOP_GROUP $FS_CHECKPOINT_DIR
chmod -R 750 $FS_CHECKPOINT_DIR

echo "Create datanode local dir"
mkdir -p $DFS_DATA_DIR
chown -R $HDFS_USER:$HADOOP_GROUP $DFS_DATA_DIR
```

```
chmod -R 750 $DFS_DATA_DIR

echo "Create yarn local dir"
mkdir -p $YARN_LOCAL_DIR
chown -R $YARN_USER:$HADOOP_GROUP $YARN_LOCAL_DIR
chmod -R 755 $YARN_LOCAL_DIR

echo "Create yarn local log dir"
mkdir -p $YARN_LOCAL_LOG_DIR
chown -R $YARN_USER:$HADOOP_GROUP $YARN_LOCAL_LOG_DIR
chmod -R 755 $YARN_LOCAL_LOG_DIR

echo "Create zookeeper data dir"
mkdir -p $ZOOKEEPER_DATA_DIR
chown -R $ZOOKEEPER_USER:$HADOOP_GROUP $ZOOKEEPER_DATA_DIR
chmod -R 755 $ZOOKEEPER_DATA_DIR
```

Listing 14.5 sets up the core directories for the Hadoop installation.

Listing 14.5   Core Directories for the Hadoop Installation

```
[root@hdp22-3 scripts]# ./helper.sh
YARN_USER=yarn
OOZIE_PID_DIR=/var/run/oozie
FS_CHECKPOINT_DIR=/data2/hdfs/snn
HOSTNAME=hdp22-3.1fedotov.com
MAPRED_USER=mapred
HBASE_USER=hbase.
OOZIE_TMP_DIR=/var/tmp/oozie
SHELL=/bin/bash
TERM=xterm-256color
PIG_PID_DIR=/var/run/pig
HISTSIZE=1000
SSH_CLIENT=192.168.56.1 55971 22
ZOOKEEPER_USER=zookeeper
YARN_PID_DIR=/var/run/hadoop/yarn
MAPRED_LOG_DIR=/var/log/hadoop/mapred
HBASE_LOG_DIR=/var/log/hbase
ACCUMULO_USER=accumulo
WEBHCAT_LOG_DIR=var/log/webhcat
```

```
ZOOKEEPER_DATA_DIR=/data1/zookeeper/data
ACCUMULO_LOG_DIR=/var/log/accumulo
SQOOP_CONF_DIR=/etc/sqoop/conf
SSH_TTY=/dev/pts/0
WEBHCAT_CONF_DIR=/etc/hcatalog/conf/webhcat
USER=root
HDFS_USER=hdfs
OOZIE_LOG_DIR=/var/log/oozie
DFS_DATA_DIR=/data1/hdfs/dn /data2/hdfs/dn
YARN_LOCAL_LOG_DIR=/data1/yarn/logs /data2/yarn/logs
ACCUMULO_CONF_DIR=/etc/accumulo/conf
ZOOKEEPER_CONF_DIR=/etc/zookeeper/conf
HIVE_PID_DIR=/var/run/hive
HIVE_LOG_DIR=/var/log/hive
PATH=/usr/local/sbin:/usr/local/bin:/sbin:/bin:/usr/sbin:/usr/bin:/root/bin
MAIL=/var/spool/mail/root
HADOOP_GROUP=hadoop
PIG_LOG_DIR=/var/log/pig
WEBHCAT_USER=hcat
HBASE_CONF_DIR=/etc/hbase/conf
PWD=/root/hdp_manual_install_rpm_helper_files-2.2.0.0.2041/scripts
ZOOKEEPER_LOG_DIR=/var/log/zookeeper
PIG_CONF_DIR=/etc/pig/conf
OOZIE_DATA=/var/db/oozie
HDFS_LOG_DIR=/var/log/hadoop/hdfs
LANG=en_US.UTF-8
HADOOP_CONF_DIR=/etc/hadoop/conf
OOZIE_CONF_DIR=/etc/oozie/conf
WEBHCAT_PID_DIR=/var/run/webhcat
YARN_LOG_DIR=/var/log/hadoop/yarn
PIG_USER=pig
HISTCONTROL=ignoredups
HOME=/root
SHLVL=2
HIVE_USER=hive
ZOOKEEPER_PID_DIR=/var/run/zookeeper
DFS_NAME_DIR=/data1/hdfs/nn
YARN_LOCAL_DIR=/data1/yarn/local /data2/yarn/local
LOGNAME=root
SSH_CONNECTION=192.168.56.1 55971 192.168.56.17 22
```

```
LESSOPEN=||/usr/bin/lesspipe.sh %s
OOZIE_USER=oozie
MAPRED_PID_DIR=/var/run/hadoop/mapred
HBASE_PID_DIR=/var/run/hbase
G_BROKEN_FILENAMES=1
HDFS_PID_DIR=/var/run/hadoop/hdfs
HIVE_CONF_DIR=/etc/hive/conf
_=/bin/env
Create namenode local dir
Create secondary namenode local dir
Create datanode local dir
Create yarn local dir
Create yarn local log dir
Create zookeeper data dir
```

The following command will verify whether the data directories are set up properly after executing the scripts in Listing 14.5:

```
[root@hdp22-1 scripts]# ls -l /data*
```

After setting all the required environment variables and creating all the required directories, you can proceed to the installation.

Installing HDFS and YARN

HDFS and YARN are core HDP services, and usually both are installed on all existing clusters. It is a very rare case when only HDFS is used as redundant storage without running any processing on the cluster. So, we will install both HDFS and YARN on our cluster.

First, we must install the HDP binaries. All the dependencies that are required by the product are pulled automatically by YUM.

```
[root@hdp22-1 scripts]# yum install hadoop hadoop-hdfs hadoop-libhdfs
  hadoop-yarn hadoop-mapreduce hadoop-client openssl -y
```

To increase the usable cluster capacity, HDFS uses data compression. Compression libraries must be installed to use data compression, so the next step is to install the LZO and Snappy compression libraries:

```
[root@hdp22-1 scripts]# yum install snappy snappy-devel -y
```

After you complete installing the packages, you need to configure core services.

Setting Up the Hadoop Configuration

Sample configuration files are provided with companion files. Copy configuration files to the HDP configuration directory, and then modify it to reflect the names and locations that correspond to your environment. These sample configuration files are templates for setting up your environment.

1. To set the correct YARN and MapReduce memory settings, we will use the helper script along with the rest of the helper files, as shown in Listing 14.6.

Listing 14.6 Set Up the Parameters for YARN Containers, MapReduce, and Tez

```
[root@hdp22-3 scripts]# ./hdp-configuration-utils.py -c 1 -m 4 -d 2 -k
  False
Using cores=1 memory=4GB disks=2 hbase=False accumulo=False
 Profile: cores=1 memory=3072MB reserved=1GB usableMem=3GB disks=2
 Num Container=3
 Container Ram=1024MB
 Used Ram=3GB
 Unused Ram=1GB
 yarn.scheduler.minimum-allocation-mb=1024
 yarn.scheduler.maximum-allocation-mb=3072
 yarn.nodemanager.resource.memory-mb=3072
 mapreduce.map.memory.mb=1024
 mapreduce.map.java.opts=-Xmx768m
 mapreduce.reduce.memory.mb=2048
 mapreduce.reduce.java.opts=-Xmx1536m
 yarn.app.mapreduce.am.resource.mb=1024
 yarn.app.mapreduce.am.command-opts=-Xmx768m
 mapreduce.task.io.sort.mb=384
 tez.am.resource.memory.mb=2048
 tez.am.java.opts=-Xmx1536m
 hive.tez.container.size=1024
 hive.tez.java.opts=-Xmx768m
 hive.auto.convert.join.noconditionaltask.size=134217000
[root@hdp22-3 scripts]#
```

2. Edit the core-site.xml file and modify the properties.

```
<property>
  <name>fs.defaultFS</name>
  <value>hdfs://hdp22-1.lfedotov.com:8020</value>
</property>
```

3. Edit the hdfs-site.xml file and modify the properties shown in Listing 14.7.

Listing 14.7   Define Primary Data Locations for HDFS

```
<property>
  <name>dfs.datanode.data.dir</name>
  <value>/data1/hdfs/dn,/data2/hdfs/dn</value>
</property>
<property>
  <name>dfs.namenode.checkpoint.dir</name>
  <value>/data2/hdfs/snn</value>
</property>
  <property>
    <name>dfs.namenode.checkpoint.edits.dir</name>
    <value>/data2/hdfs/snn</value>
  </property>
  <property>
  <name>dfs.namenode.name.dir</name>
  <value>/data1/hdfs/nn</value>
</property>
  <property>
  <name>dfs.namenode.http-address</name>
  <value>hdp22-1.1fedotov.com:50070</value>
</property>
  <property>
  <name>dfs.namenode.secondary.http-address</name>
  <value>hdp22-2.1fedotov.com:50090</value>
</property>
```

4. Edit the yarn-site.xml file and modify the properties shown in Listing 14.8.

Listing 14.8   Set Up YARN Primary Directories as Well as Ports and Memory Parameters

```
<property>
  <name>yarn.log.server.url</name>
  <value>https://hdp22-3.1fedotov.com:19888/jobhistory/logs</value>
</property>
<property>
  <name>yarn.nodemanager.local-dirs</name>
  <value>/data1/yarn/local,/data2/yarn/local</value>
</property>
```

```
<property>
  <name>yarn.nodemanager.log-dirs</name>
  <value>/data1/yarn/logs,/data2/yarn/logs</value>
</property>
<property>
  <name>yarn.resourcemanager.address</name>
  <value>hdp22-3.1fedotov.com:8050</value>
</property>
<property>
  <name>yarn.resourcemanager.admin.address</name>
  <value>hdp22-3.1fedotov.com:8141</value>
</property>
<property>
  <name>yarn.resourcemanager.hostname</name>
  <value>hdp22-3.1fedotov.com</value>
</property>
<property>
  <name>yarn.resourcemanager.resource-tracker.address</name>
  <value>hdp22-3.1fedotov.com:8025</value>
</property>
<property>
  <name>yarn.resourcemanager.scheduler.address</name>
  <value>hdp22-3.1fedotov.com:8030</value>
</property>
<property>
  <name>yarn.resourcemanager.webapp.address</name>
  <value>hdp22-3.1fedotov.com:8088</value>
</property>
<property>
  <name>yarn.scheduler.maximum-allocation-mb</name>
  <value>3072</value> <!-- Example: "2048" -->
</property>
<property>
  <name>yarn.scheduler.minimum-allocation-mb</name>
  <value>1024</value> <!-- Example: "682" -->
</property>
<property>
  <name>yarn.nodemanager.resource.cpu-vcores</name>
  <value>2</value> <!-- Example: "2" -->
</property>
```

```
<property>
  <name>yarn.nodemanager.resource.memory-mb</name>
  <value>3072</value> <!-- Example: "2048" -->
</property>
  <property>
  <name>yarn.nodemanager.resource.percentage-physical-cpu-limit</name>
  <value>100</value> <!-- Example: "100" -->
</property>
<property>
  <name>yarn.timeline-service.address</name>
  <value>hdp22-3.1fedotov.com:10200</value>
</property>
<property>
  <name>yarn.timeline-service.webapp.address</name>
  <value>hdp22-3.1fedotov.com:8188</value>
</property>
<property>
  <name>yarn.timeline-service.webapp.https.address</name>
  <value>hdp22-3.1fedotov.com:8190</value>
</property>
```

5. Edit the mapred-site.xml file and modify the properties shown in Listing 14.9.

Listing 14.9   Set Up Primary Parameters for MapReduce

```
<property>
  <name>mapreduce.jobhistory.address</name>
  <value>hdp22-3.1fedotov.com:10020</value>
</property>
 <property>
  <name>mapreduce.jobhistory.webapp.address</name>
  <value>hdp22-3.1fedotov.com:19888</value>
</property>
<property>
  <name>mapreduce.map.java.opts</name>
  <value>-Xmx768m</value> <!-- Example: "-Xmx546m" -->
</property>
<property>
  <name>mapreduce.map.memory.mb</name>
  <value>1024</value> <!-- Example: "682" -->
```

```
</property>
<property>
  <name>mapreduce.reduce.java.opts</name>
  <value>-Xmx1536m</value> <!-- Example: "-Xmx546m" -->
</property>
<property>
  <name>mapreduce.reduce.memory.mb</name>
  <value>2048</value> <!-- Example: "682" -->
</property>
<property>
  <name>mapreduce.task.io.sort.factor</name>
  <value>100</value> <!-- Example: "100" -->
</property>
<property>
  <name>mapreduce.task.io.sort.mb</name>
  <value>384</value> <!-- Example: "273" -->
</property>
<property>
  <name>yarn.app.mapreduce.am.resource.mb</name>
  <value>1024</value> <!-- Example: "682" -->
</property>
<property>
  <name>yarn.app.mapreduce.am.command-opts</name>
  <value>-Xmx768m</value> <!-- Example: "682" -->
</property>
```

6. Edit the container-executor.cfg file:

```
yarn.nodemanager.local-dirs=/data1/yarn/local,/data2/yarn/local
yarn.nodemanager.linux-container-executor.group=hadoop
yarn.nodemanager.log-dirs=/data1/yarn/logs,/data2/yarn/logs
banned.users=hfds,bin,0
```

You have now completed the installation and configuration of the core HDP services. You can proceed to starting the core services.

Starting HDFS and YARN

In this section, let's start by formatting and starting HDFS. We are executing all commands on the same machine because we have a single node installation for HDFS and YARN.

1. Start by formatting HDFS.

```
[root@hdp22-1 ~]# su - hdfs
[hdfs@hdp22-1 ~]$ hadoop namenode -format
DEPRECATED: Use of this script to execute hdfs command is deprecated.
Instead use the hdfs command for it.
```

2. The command for setting up the secondary NameNode daemon is as follows:

```
[root@hdp22-2 ~]# su - hdfs
[hdfs@hdp22-2 ~]$ /usr/hdp/2.2.0.0-2041/hadoop/sbin/hadoop-daemon.sh
   --config /etc/hadoop/conf start secondarynamenode
starting secondarynamenode, logging to /var/log/hadoop/hdfs/hadoop-
   hdfs-secondarynamenode-hdp22-2.lfedotov.com.out
```

3. Verify that the secondary name node is running:

```
[hdfs@hdp22-2 ~]$ /usr/java/default/bin/jps
16186 SecondaryNameNode
16247 Jps
[hdfs@hdp22-2 ~]$
```

4. Use the following command to start the DataNode daemon on the worker nodes:

```
[hdfs@hdp22-1 ~]$ /usr/hdp/2.2.0.0-2041/hadoop/sbin/hadoop-daemon.sh
   --config /etc/hadoop/conf start datanode


[hdfs@hdp22-2 ~]$ /usr/hdp/2.2.0.0-2041/hadoop/sbin/hadoop-daemon.sh
   --config /etc/hadoop/conf start datanode


[hdfs@hdp22-3 ~]$ /usr/hdp/2.2.0.0-2041/hadoop/sbin/hadoop-daemon.sh
   --config /etc/hadoop/conf start datanode
```

5. Next you need to verify the HDFS functionality. Check the NameNode UI by connecting your browser to the NameNode URL: http://hdp22-1.lfedotov.com:50070/dfshealth.html. The NameNode page displays, as shown in Figure 14.1.

Figure 14.1   NameNode UI.

6. Create the hdfs user directory in HDFS:

```
[root@hdp22-1 ~]# su - hdfs
[hdfs@hdp22-1 ~]$ hadoop fs -mkdir -p /user/hdfs
[hdfs@hdp22-1 ~]$ hadoop fs -ls /
```

7. Copy a file into HDFS and list the file:

```
[hdfs@hdp22-1 ~]$ hadoop fs -copyFromLocal /etc/passwd passwd
[hdfs@hdp22-1 ~]$ hadoop fs -ls /user/hdfs
```

Congratulations, you now have a fully functional HDFS (see Figure 14.2).

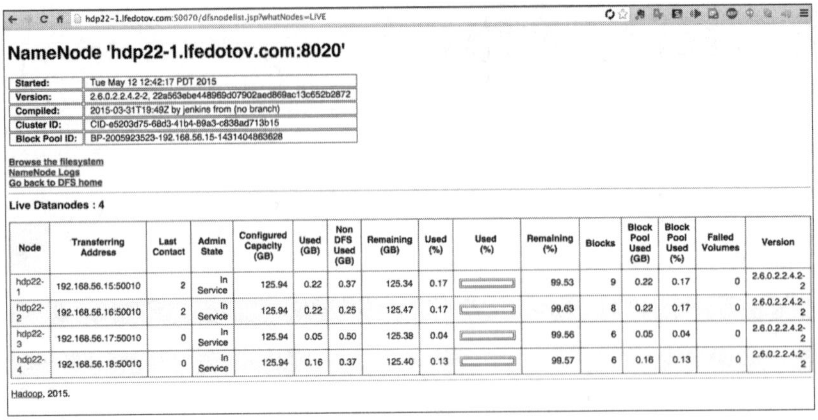

Figure 14.2   DataNodes view in NameNode UI.

Start YARN

The ResourceManager is the master daemon that handles resource management for the Hadoop cluster. This master daemon should be started before starting the worker daemons.

1. Execute the commands shown in Listing 14.10 from the ResourceManager server to start ResourceManager and verify whether it is running.

Listing 14.10   Start Up the YARN ResourceManager Daemon and Verify It Is Running with the **jps** Command

```
[root@hdp22-3 ~]# su - yarn
[yarn@hdp22-3 ~]$ export HADOOP_LIBEXEC_DIR=/usr/hdp/2.2.0.0-2041/hadoop/
   libexec
[yarn@hdp22-3 ~]$ /usr/hdp/2.2.0.0-2041/hadoop-yarn/sbin/yarn-daemon.sh
   --config /etc/hadoop/conf start resourcemanager
starting resourcemanager, logging to /var/log/hadoop-yarn/yarn/yarn-yarn-
   resourcemanager-hdp22-3.lfedotov.com.out
[yarn@hdp22-3 ~]$ /usr/java/default/bin/jps
16752 Jps
16592 ResourceManager
[yarn@hdp22-3 ~]$
```

2. Execute the commands shown in Listing 14.11 from all NodeManager nodes to start all Node Managers.

We will use each system as a worker node because it is a small configuration.

Listing 14.11 Start Up the NodeManager Daemons

```
[root@hdp22-1 ~]# su - yarn
[yarn@hdp22-1 ~]$ export HADOOP_LIBEXEC_DIR=/usr/hdp/2.2.0.0-2041/hadoop/
  libexec
[yarn@hdp22-1 ~]$ /usr/hdp/2.2.0.0-2041/hadoop-yarn/sbin/yarn-daemon.sh
  --config /etc/hadoop/conf start nodemanager

[root@hdp22-2 ~]# su - yarn
[yarn@hdp22-2 ~]$ export HADOOP_LIBEXEC_DIR=/usr/hdp/2.2.0.0-2041/hadoop/
  libexec
[yarn@hdp22-2 ~]$ /usr/hdp/2.2.0.0-2041/hadoop-yarn/sbin/yarn-daemon.sh
  --config /etc/hadoop/conf

[root@hdp22-3 ~]# su - yarn
[yarn@hdp22-3 ~]$ export HADOOP_LIBEXEC_DIR=/usr/hdp/2.2.0.0-2041/hadoop/
  libexec
[yarn@hdp22-3 ~]$ /usr/hdp/2.2.0.0-2041/hadoop-yarn/sbin/yarn-daemon.sh
  --config /etc/hadoop/conf
```

3. Start the MapReduce JobHistory Server. The container-executor program runs the containers as the user that executes the application. The NodeManager uses this program to start and kill containers. A setuid is defined for this program so the containers can switch to the user that executes the containers. The container-executor script sets up permissions for all local files used by the containers, such as jars, shared files, intermediate files, log files, and so on. Change the permissions on the container-executor file on all NodeManager nodes, as shown in Listing 14.12.

Listing 14.12 Set Up the Permissions for the Container-Executor File and Verify They Are Correct

```
[root@hdp22-1 ~]# ls -l /usr/hdp/2.2.0.0-2041/hadoop-yarn/bin/container-
  executor
---Sr-s--- 1 root yarn 36504 Nov 19 11:56 /usr/hdp/2.2.0.0-2041/hadoop-
  yarn/bin/container-executor
[root@hdp22-1 ~]# chown -R root:hadoop /usr/hdp/2.2.0.0-2041/hadoop-yarn/
  bin/container-executor
[root@hdp22-1 ~]# chmod -R 6050 /usr/hdp/2.2.0.0-2041/hadoop-yarn/bin/
  container-executor
[root@hdp22-1 ~]# ls -l /usr/hdp/2.2.0.0-2041/hadoop-yarn/bin/container-
  executor
---Sr-s--- 1 root hadoop 36504 Nov 19 11:56 /usr/hdp/2.2.0.0-2041/hadoop-
  yarn/bin/container-executor
[root@hdp22-1 ~]#
```

4. Execute the commands shown in Listing 14.13 from the JobHistory server to set up your directories on HDFS.

Listing 14.13   Set Up Permissions for the JobHistory Server and Verify They Are Correct

```
[root@hdp22-3 ~]# su - hdfs
[hdfs@hdp22-3 ~]$ hadoop fs -mkdir -p /mr-history/tmp
[hdfs@hdp22-3 ~]$ hadoop fs -chmod -R 1777 /mr-history/tmp
[hdfs@hdp22-3 ~]$ hadoop fs -mkdir -p /mr-history/done
[hdfs@hdp22-3 ~]$ hadoop fs -chmod -R 1777 /mr-history/done
[hdfs@hdp22-3 ~]$ hadoop fs -chown -R mapred:hdfs /mr-history
[hdfs@hdp22-3 ~]$ hadoop fs -mkdir -p /app-logs
[hdfs@hdp22-3 ~]$ hadoop fs -chmod -R 1777 /app-logs
[hdfs@hdp22-3 ~]$ hadoop fs -chown yarn /app-logs
 [hdfs@hdp22-3 ~]$
[hdfs@hdp22-3 ~]$ hadoop fs -ls /
Found 3 items
drwxrwxrwt   - yarn   hdfs        0 2015-02-19 14:40 /app-logs
drwxr-xr-x   - mapred hdfs        0 2015-02-19 14:40 /mr-history
drwxr-xr-x   - hdfs   hdfs        0 2015-02-19 14:20 /user
[hdfs@hdp22-3 ~]$
```

5. Execute these commands from the JobHistory server to start History Server:

```
[root@hdp22-3 ~]# su - mapred
[mapred@hdp22-3 ~]$ export HADOOP_LIBEXEC_DIR=/usr/hdp/2.2.0.0-2041/
   hadoop/libexec
[mapred@hdp22-3 ~]$ /usr/hdp/2.2.0.0-2041/hadoop-mapreduce/sbin/
   mr-jobhistory-daemon.sh --config /etc/hadoop/conf start
   historyserver
```

Verifying MapReduce Functionality

Try browsing to the ResourceManager, which looks like that shown in Figure 14.3 (http://hdp22-3.lfedotov.com:8088/).

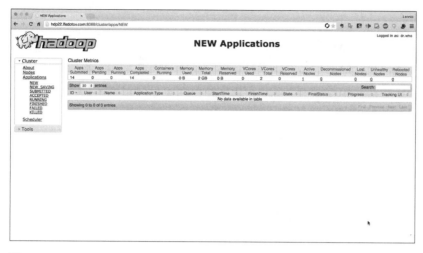

Figure 14.3   ResourceManager UI.

To verify MapReduce functionality, follow these steps:

1. Create a $CLIENT_USER and add it in the users group (this user should exist on all cluster nodes).

```
[root@hdp22-3 ~]# useradd client
[root@hdp22-3 ~]# usermod -a -G users client
```

2. As the HDFS user, create a /user/client.

```
[root@hdp22-3 ~]# su - hdfs
[hdfs@hdp22-3 ~]$ hdfs dfs -mkdir /user/client
[hdfs@hdp22-3 ~]$ hdfs dfs -chown client:client /user/client
[hdfs@hdp22-3 ~]$ hdfs dfs -chmod -R 755 /user/client
[hdfs@hdp22-3 ~]$ hadoop fs -mkdir /tmp
[hdfs@hdp22-3 ~]$ hadoop fs -chmod 777 /tmp
```

3. Additional preparation for running map/reduce jobs is also needed in HDP 2.2:

```
[root@hdp22-3 ~]# su - hdfs
[hdfs@hdp22-3 ~]$ hadoop fs -mkdir -p /hdp/apps/2.2.0.0-2041/mapreduce
[hdfs@hdp22-3 ~]$ hadoop fs -chown mapred /hdp/apps/2.2.0.0-2041/
    mapreduce
[hdfs@hdp22-3 ~]$ logout
[root@hdp22-3 ~]# su - mapred
[mapred@hdp22-3 ~]$ hadoop fs -put /usr/hdp/2.2.0.0-2041/hadoop/
    mapreduce.tar.gz /hdp/apps/2.2.0.0-2041/mapreduce
[mapred@hdp22-3 ~]$ hadoop fs -ls /hdp/apps/2.2.0.0-2041/mapreduce
```

```
Found 1 items
-rw-r--r--      3 mapred hdfs     191314810  2015-02-19  14:56  /hdp/
   apps/2.2.0.0-2041/mapreduce/mapreduce.tar.gz
[mapred@hdp22-3 ~]$
```

4. Run the smoke test as the $CLIENT_USER using Terasort and sort 10GB of data.

```
[root@hdp22-3 ~]# su - client
[client@hdp22-3 ~]$ hadoop jar /usr/hdp/2.2.0.0-2041/hadoop-mapreduce/
   hadoop-mapreduce-examples.jar teragen 10000 /tmp/teragen
```

At this point we have fully functional YARN and MapReduce components. The core HDP cluster is installed, configured, and functional (see Figure 14.4).

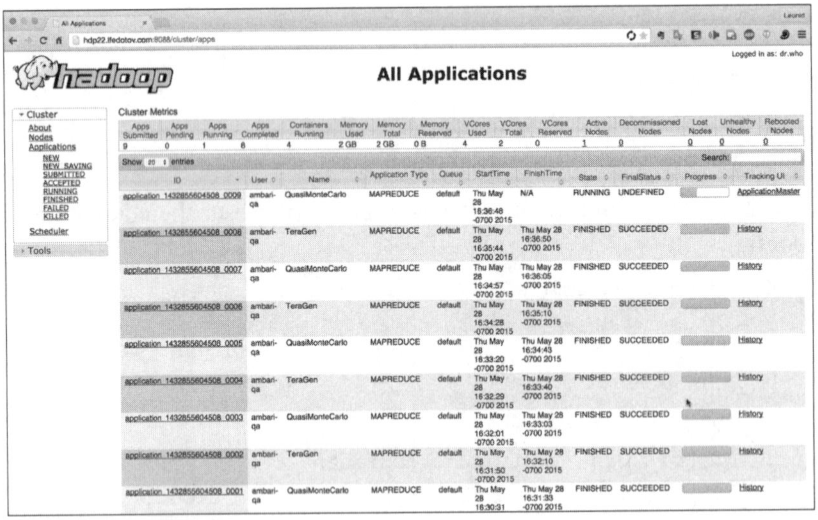

Figure 14.4   Completed Jobs in Resource Manager UI.

Installing and Configuring Hive

Now that we have installed, configured, and are running the cluster, we can add Hive and HCatalog to it. Apache Hive is a tool for creating higher-level SQL queries using HiveQL; the tool's native language can be compiled into sequences of MapReduce programs. HCatalog is a table and storage management layer for Hadoop that enables users with different data processing tools to more easily read and write data on the grid.

Installing and Configuring MySQL Database

For Hive to run, you must install and configure the database for Hive Metastore first. The default Metastore database is MySQL, so you need to set it up on our cluster node.

First, install MySQL:

```
[root@hdp22-2 ~]# yum install mysql-server
```

After the installation completes, you should start MySQL and set the password for user root. We will use the word hadoop as a password for the root user.

```
[root@hdp22-2 ~]# /etc/init.d/mysqld start
```

Now you should create and grant the required privileges to the user who will own the Hive Metastore database. We will use the username hive with the password hive.

```
[root@hdp22-2 ~]# mysql -u root -phadoop
```

Installing and Configuring Hive and HCatalog

After you have run and configured the MySQL database for the Hive Metastore, you can continue to install and configure Hive and HCatalog.

```
[root@hdp22-2 ~]# yum install hive hive-hcatalog
```

Copy the Mysql Java connector to the /usr/hdp/2.2.0.0.-2041/hive/lib folder:

```
[root@hdp22-2 ~]# cp /usr/share/java/mysql-connector-java-5.1.17.jar /usr/
  hdp/2.2.0.0-2041/hive/lib
```

All required local directories were already created earlier when you ran the directories.sh helper script.

Now you need to set the Hive configuration. To do this, edit the /etc/hive/conf/hive-site. xml file and set the following properties in it, as shown in Listing 14.14.

Listing 14.14   Set Up the Parameters for Hive in the hive-site.xml File

```
<property>
  <name>javax.jdo.option.ConnectionURL</name>
  <value>jdbc:mysql://hdp22-2.lfedotov.com:3306/
   hive?createDatabaseIfNotExist=true</value>
  <description>Enter your JDBC connection string. </description>
</property>
```

```
<property>
  <name>javax.jdo.option.ConnectionUserName</name>
  <value>hive</value>
  <description>Enter your MySQL credentials. </description>
</property>

<property>
  <name>javax.jdo.option.ConnectionPassword</name>
  <value>hive</value>
  <description>Enter your MySQL credentials. </description>
</property>

<property>
  <name>hive.metastore.uris</name>
  <value>thrift:// hdp-book.1fedotov.com:9083</value>
</property>
```

For Hive to function correctly, you need to create the required directories in HDFS.

- The Hive home directory:

```
[root@hdp22-2 conf]# su - hdfs
[hdfs@hdp22-2 ~]$ hadoop fs -mkdir -p /user/hive
[hdfs@hdp22-2 ~]$ hadoop fs -chown hive:hdfs /user/hive
```

- The Hive warehouse directory:

```
[hdfs@hdp22-2 ~]$ hadoop fs -mkdir -p /apps/hive/warehouse
[hdfs@hdp22-2 ~]$ hadoop fs -chown -R hive:hdfs /apps/hive
[hdfs@hdp22-2 ~]$ hadoop fs -chmod -R 775 /apps/hive
```

- The Hive scratch directory:

```
[hdfs@hdp22-2 ~]$ hadoop fs -mkdir -p /tmp/scratch
[hdfs@hdp22-2 ~]$ hadoop fs -chown -R hive:hdfs /tmp/scratch
[hdfs@hdp22-2 ~]$ hadoop fs -chmod -R 777 /tmp/scratch
```

You have completed the Hive setup and configuration at this point. You are ready to start the services and validate the Hive functionality:

```
[root@hdp22-2 ~]# su - hive
[hive@hdp22-2 ~]$ nohup /usr/hdp/2.2.0.0-2041/hive/bin/hive --service
  metastore>/var/log/hive/hive.out 2>/var/log/hive/hive.log &
[1] 27413
```

Run the following command to start the HiveServer2:

```
[hive@hdp22-2 ~]$ nohup /usr/hdp/2.2.0.0-2041/hive/bin/hiveserver2 > /var/
  log/hive/hiveserver2.out 2 > /var/log/hive/hiveserver2.log &
[2] 27999
```

Beeline is a command-line utility to communicate to HiveServer2 and submit queries.

Now you can use Hive to load and query data.

Example: Using the HCatalog functionality, load the /etc/passwd file as a table to Hive, then run multiple select queries on it. Each query will initiate a MapReduce job. The result and status of the MapReduce job can be monitored through the YARN UI (Listing 14.15).

Listing 14.15   Use These Simple Commands to Verify Hive Is Set Up Properly

```
[hive@hdp22-2 ~]$ hcat -e "drop table passwd"
OK
Time taken: 1.024 seconds
[hive@hdp22-2 ~]$ hcat -e "create table passwd (name string, passwd string,
uid int, gid int, commentary string, home string, shell string) ROW FORMAT
  DELIMITED FIELDS TERMINATED BY ':' location 'hdfs:///user/hive/passwd'"
OK
Time taken: 1.546 seconds
[hive@hdp22-2 ~]$ hcat -e "describe passwd"
[hive@hdp22-2 ~]$

[hive@hdp22-2 ~]$ hadoop fs -ls .
[hive@hdp22-2 ~]$

[hive@hdp22-2 ~]$ hive
hive> describe passwd;
hive> select * from passwd;
hive> select count(*) from passwd;
hive> select name, home, shell from passwd where uid > 1000;
hive> exit;
[hive@hdp22-2 ~]$ hadoop fs -ls .
 [hive@hdp22-2 ~]$ hadoop fs -ls passwd
 [hive@hdp22-2 ~]$
```

Figure 14.5 shows the completed MapReduce jobs initiated by Hive.

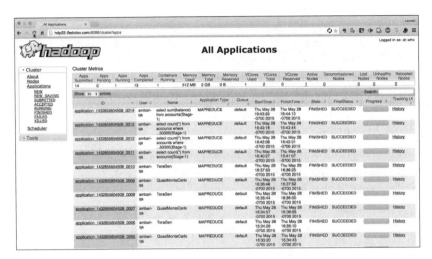

Figure 14.5   ResourceManager UI shows completed MapReduce jobs initiated by Hive.

Summary

This chapter takes you through the basic installation and verification of a Hadoop cluster. At the end of this installation, Hadoop is up and running with HDFS, YARN, MapReduce, and Hive/HCatalog functionality. However, today not many people perform a manual installation. HDP provides installation and management functionality through a product called Ambari. Big Data Extensions also support automated installs. Using the GUI tools for installs offer a number of advantages; however, we recommend that Hadoop administrators learn what the GUI tools are doing so the configuration is well understood.

TIPS:

- Always preinstall all required HDP packages during the system provisioning time. This will save a lot of time on setting up and configuring the cluster.

- If you are expanding an existing cluster by adding new nodes to it, you must not only install the HDP packages at the same time as you perform system provisioning, you also must load all needed configuration files (taken from one of the existing slave nodes). This way, the new nodes will be available immediately after provisioning. They will be added to the running cluster automatically on the first reboot after installation.

- Always consider setting up HA for HDP components and for MySQL database, which is used as a metadata storage.

- There is no need to back up the cluster data located in HDFS. HDFS provides built-in data redundancy. However, it is a good practice to back up the NameNode data periodically. You should also back up the cluster configuration files and the Hive Metastore database.

## Chapter 15

Configuring Linux for Hadoop

"What you get by achieving your goals is not as important as what you become by achieving your goals."

—Henry David Thoreau

The installation and management of a Hadoop ecosystem is a journey, not a destination. The Hadoop ecosystem is constantly evolving; customers are looking at using Hadoop-as-a-Service and aligning their big data strategies with their cloud strategies. Customers are going to leverage automated installs with different management tools, but someone still needs to make sure all the individual components, such as the Linux operating system, are installed and optimized for running Hadoop and its components. Hadoop now runs under one set of code that can run on Windows or Linux. In this chapter we focus on Linux.

Laying out a well-designed Linux architecture for a Hadoop cluster is a critical factor for success. In this chapter, we lay out the optimal foundation for Linux reference architecture for a Hadoop cluster.

Platform architecture lays a successful foundation for Hadoop. Right sizing for Hadoop is another important component that includes the correct CPU architecture, RAM capacity, storage capacity, NIC setup, switch configuration of workload patterns, and so on. A solid Linux configuration is one important component of that foundation. We focus on creating a lean and secure Linux infrastructure for Hadoop that will perform consistently with each build. Best practices and lessons learned in the field on how to build an enterprise Linux platform for a Hadoop cluster are shared. The goal of a Hadoop Linux configuration is to minimize administration and maintenance while achieving maximum availability for

Hadoop master servers and maximum performance for worker nodes. Key topics include optimizing kernel parameters, disk layout, file system considerations, proper partition alignment, setting up the network interfaces, and reviewing storage considerations.

Supported Linux Platforms

To start, let's discuss the supported platforms for Linux deployments for HDP2. HDP2 is supported on the following Linux distributions:

- Red Hat Enterprise Linux 5.x or 6.x

- CentOS (Community Enterprise Operating System) 5.x or 6.x

- Oracle Linux 5.x or 6.x

- SLES 11 SP1+

- Ubuntu 12

Only 64-bit architectures on x86 platforms are supported. The discussions of Linux in this chapter predominately cover Red Hat. RHEL, Centos, Oracle Linux, SLES, and Ubuntu are all valid and popular versions of Linux. For a proof of concept or testing out Hadoop, you might need only the Hadoop cluster to be up and running for 30 to 45 days. If that is the case, an unsupported version of Linux might be the best cost-effective option. If you need the cluster for more than a 30-day proof of concept, you can leverage CentOS, a Linux distribution that is a free, enterprise-class, community-supported computing platform.

Different Deployment Models

There are three deployment models for Hadoop. A production environment should be using the fully distributed model. The following list outlines the benefits of each model:

- **Standalone:** Hadoop is deployed in a single JVM running on a local file system. This model is designed for developers to develop and test code. This enables a developer to walk through application code one step at a time as the code is executing.

- **Pseudo distributed:** This Hadoop cluster is deployed with all the processes defined by configuration files; however, the entire cluster is deployed on a single system. This is also an excellent platform for developers or for someone who wants to learn Hadoop administration. You can start working with Hadoop even if you don't have the resources to run several VMs or physical servers. Vendors provide downloadable VMs with this configuration.

- **Fully distributed:** This is a Hadoop cluster with master servers and worker nodes spread across multiple servers (either virtual or physical).

Linux Golden Templates

You must spend some time and energy to understand what a Linux golden image template should encompass in your virtualized infrastructure. You might opt to create and maintain golden image VMs for master node and data node servers. Master node servers must have disks/LUNs allocated from the storage array and need high availability considerations. For example, a single disk drive can be used for the operating system; however, using two drives for the operating system with RAID 1 mirroring would be better. You might opt to create a single template for both the master node and the data node and flip the configurations with a shell script, or you might opt to maintain two separate templates because the design and architecture between the two might be significantly different in your organization. A PXE boot may also be considered. PXE will work on physical or virtual servers. This also adds agility when updating a distribution.

The concept of creating a golden image applies at all levels of the stack. We do not stop at the virtual machine layer. You need to create golden images for the OS layer, the cluster software layer, and the networking component layer. After all these components are properly vetted, you can create a golden image VM template that encompasses all the layers of the stack.

Before you can create a golden image VM template, you must create a golden image OS. This does not occur overnight but can be accomplished easily. The template needs to start from a minimal installation option of the Linux operating system with all unnecessary daemons disabled. The template must have the basic components, such as VMware Tools. You should not have installed components such as X Windows (X.org, KDE, GNOME, and so on), RPMs, or executables. The golden image should be optimized for Hadoop; therefore, it should not have any packages installed that will not be used by a Hadoop node. The Linux image for Hadoop nodes should be stripped of all unnecessary services. Run only required services for all Hadoop nodes. When installing Hadoop, usually only services such as SSH and NTP are required. Also be careful about using IPTables. Hadoop workloads can vary greatly in network usage. IPTables can add to the difficulty in identifying network issues.

A lot of collaboration should occur between the system administrators as to standards and policies. Furthermore, someone must be the "owner" of the templates to make sure the entire standard build is applied to the golden image template. As you mature within the organization, you can develop automation to simplify the build process and those parts of the builds that require manual intervention. The level of automation will dictate how long it takes to provision the Linux VM. From the beginning, automation is very important. A Hadoop cluster is a high-performance parallel-processing environment that is designed to scale linearly. Hadoop clusters can grow to hundreds and thousands of nodes.

One of the best benefits of virtualization is that you can clone a new VM with just a few clicks. Cloning VMs exponentially increases the time to provision over bare metal servers. The cloning process with VMware provides extreme value to a virtualized environment to rapidly provision Hadoop nodes.

Building a Linux Enterprise Hadoop Platform

The Hadoop cluster is only as solid as the foundation on which it runs. A well-designed Hadoop cluster contains the following:

- Hardware designed and selected from reference architectures and recommended hardware compatibility lists.

- The hardware configuration should take into account any additional frameworks or software, such as Spark, Impala, HBase, Hawq, and the like. There needs to be enough memory and CPU for running MapReduce as well as the extra packages. If more memory and CPU is added, make sure the disk I/O and network speed is sufficient. This may require going to 10GB network cards. Larger data nodes might require considering larger network cards.

- 10GB network cards have gone down significantly in price. Over time, if you switch to hardware configurations that are bigger, the 10GB cards will have a longer life. When using a 10GB card, set an active/passive configuration. With 1GB cards, a bonded configuration is recommended and setting to active/active. With 1GB, using bond-mode 4 (lcap) has worked well. Fiber is still expensive. With copper, both Twinax and Cat6 RJ-45 work well, but remember there is a distance range of about 7 meters.

- NIC tuning is somewhat dependent on the hardware and drivers used. Be aware of TCP Offload Engine (TOE); this moves a lot of the TCP stack onto the NIC. TOE also requires custom drivers. Watch out for TCP Segment Offloading (TSO), which reconstitutes Ethernet frames into packets before handing them to the kernel. If issues are encountered, consider turning this off.

- The operating system and file systems must be optimized for running under the workloads Hadoop clusters can generate.

- A current version of Java for running Hadoop daemons and processes in Java Virtual Machines (JVMs).

Figure 15.1 shows a Hadoop ecosystem, which can contain a number of frameworks.

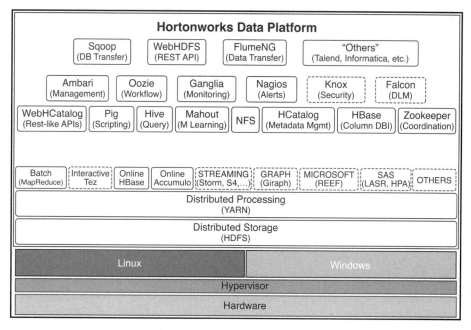

Figure 15.1 Hadoop-Hortonworks data platform.

As Hadoop administrators, we want to focus on creating golden images for the different types of nodes that make up the Hadoop ecosystem. We need to create a golden image for master nodes, worker nodes, Hadoop clients, management servers, edge nodes, LDAP nodes, and any other type of node that will be used in the Hadoop cluster. We can automate all the preceding components to simplify and reduce the amount of time to provision a Hadoop cluster.

The reference architecture for a Hadoop cluster can vary widely depending on the types of data ingestion, workload, and integration with other data platforms in an enterprise. Following are a few best practices for most Hadoop platforms:

- A Hadoop platform should be self-contained and not share any network traffic with any external systems.

- A Hadoop cluster usually has gateway systems used as edge servers for staging data, contain Hadoop clients, NFS gateway servers, and so on.

- Rack and virtual awareness must be configured for rack and virtual topologies.

- Servers running the master daemons in a Hadoop cluster should be optimized for availability.

- Master server daemons that have high availability features such as NameNode and ResourceManager should have HA configured.

- Hadoop uses a lot of logs, local temporary files, and so on. Hadoop jobs that run out of HDFS or local space will eventually fail. These dynamic directory locations need to be properly monitored.

- Slave server configurations are getting bigger as the price of hardware goes down. 10GB NIC cards have reached a price point where they will become common as well.

- Hadoop can use RAID for master servers. Hybrid storage solutions will also become more commonplace. Tiered storage, such as NL-SAS/SAS, SATA, SSD, and RAM enables Hadoop to select the right storage device for the right data access pattern. Hot data can reside in SSD, whereas RAM can be used for real-time compute and lookup, and SATA can be used for archiving cold data. Local disks should be used for the slave servers.

- Store backup copies of master daemon data on shared storage.

- Master servers have dual power supplies, network cards, and so on to eliminate single points of failure.

- Slave nodes in a Hadoop cluster should be optimized for performance.

- Use local disks for performance and throughput scalability.

- YARN and HDFS manage the availability and robustness of the worker nodes in a Hadoop cluster; therefore, RAID and redundant hardware are not necessary.

Let's start with one of the foundational components of the Hadoop cluster, the operating system (OS). Hadoop workloads can create a high number of parallel processes, lots of network traffic, and a large number of files. These workloads require a different type of Linux configuration than what one would expect to see on a database server or web server. Creating an optimized OS does not happen overnight but can be established with some architectural review and careful planning. There must be a lot of collaboration among the system administrators as to standards and policies for the corporation. Furthermore, someone in the group must be the "owner" and champion the evolution of the golden image template. Many companies make the mistake of not doing the work necessary to maintain the golden image template after it is established.

After we create templates for our OS, we must deploy them. As we mature within the organization, we can build automation to simplify the provisioning process and slowly remove parts of the builds that require manual intervention. The level of automation dictates how long it takes to provision the Linux VM—the more you automate, the less time it will take.

Selecting the Linux Distribution

It is up to the administrator as to which supported operating system distribution is used. Depending on OS licensing agreements, a customer can use an enterprise license to deploy Red Hat, Oracle Linux, Suse, and so on across all nodes in the cluster. A hybrid solution of different guest operating systems can also be used. For example, you can install the Red Hat Enterprise Linux (RHEL) on all master nodes and use CentOS for all worker nodes. Free distributions of CentOS can reduce the licensing costs. However, if you are using a hybrid solution, it is recommended that you use the same release for all nodes. For example, you can leverage RHEL 6.6 for all master nodes and Centos 6.6 for all worker nodes.

Optimal Linux Kernel Parameters and System Settings

Taking a Linux environment from the default installation to the optimal configuration for Hadoop processing in a virtualized infrastructure involves changes and enhancements. Enterprise Linux administration techniques are required to operate a high-performance Hadoop cluster. Critical industry best practices are revealed in the upcoming sections.

epoll

We do not want to be in a predicament where we encounter out-of-file descriptor errors in a Hadoop cluster. We need to increase the per-process limits on the number of files that a single user or process can have open.

If you are on Linux kernel 2.6.28, the default epoll file descriptor limit of 128 is not adequate. This setting happens to be too low for Hadoop and should be increased to 4,096. You can modify this parameter by adding or modifying the /etc/sysctl.conf file:

```
fs.epoll.max_user_instances = 4096
```

or modifying the dynamic /proc file system:

```
echo 4096> /proc/sys/fs/epoll/max_user_instances
```

After you make the appropriate changes to the /etc/sysctl.conf file, you can execute the **sysctl -p** command to dynamically reload the kernel parameters. You can verify the settings by executing the **sysctl -a** command. Alternatively, you might want to make the entries dynamically by modifying the entries to the /proc file system. Modifying the /proc file system setting is lost on the next reboot, but it can be handy for trying out different values.

Disable Swap Space

The idea of disabling swap space usage on the Linux server can be perceived as an unthinkable thought for some enterprise Linux system administrators because they have set it for years. You should aggressively monitor swap usage utilizing tools such as Ganglia and native commands such as top, mem, and vmstat.

For the data nodes, for optimal performance and best practice adherence, you should disable swap. There are two ways you can disable swap. The first and most extreme method is to disable swap by executing the **swapoff** command with the **-a** option:

```
#swapoff -a
```

To ensure that swap does not become reenabled after a server reboot, you need to comment out the swap entry in the /etc/fstab file as shown here:

```
LABEL=SWAP-sda2        swap              swap    defaults        0 0
```

Another way to minimize or disable swapping is by setting the vm.swappiness Linux kernel parameter. By default, this parameter on Red Hat Linux 6 is set to 60. The valid range for the vm.swappiness parameter is 0 to 100. A value of 100 indicates that the Linux kernel should aggressively swap Hadoop application data to disk as much as possible. Aggressive swapping on a heavily utilized Hadoop cluster can cause Hadoop operations to time out or even fail as I/O operations to the disk become overly excessive. To completely disable swap activity, set this parameter to a value of 0.

Disable Security During Install

Security-Enhanced Linux (SELinux), originally developed by the United States National Security Agency (NSA), is a Linux security kernel module that provides access control security policies. We highly recommend that you disable security on all nodes in the cluster during the installation phase. Both SELinux and IPTables (firewall) should be disabled. Security can then be turned on after the installation is complete.

Disable SELinux

By default, SELinux is enabled with Red Hat 6. You can execute the **sestatus** or **getenforce** command to obtain the SELinux status and the SELinux policy being used.

```
# getenforce
```

To enforce SELinux:

```
# sestatus
SELinux status:                 enabled
SELinuxfs mount:                /selinux
```

```
Current mode:                    enforcing
Mode from config file:           enforcing
Policy version:                  24
Policy from config file:         targeted
```

You can dynamically change the SELinux current status from "enforcing" to "permissive" by executing the following command:

```
# setenforce 0
```

To completely disable SELinux set the SELINUX=disabled option in the /etc/selinux/ config file:

```
# This file controls the state of SELinux on the system.
# SELINUX= can take one of these three values:
#        enforcing - SELinux security policy is enforced.
#        permissive - SELinux prints warnings instead of enforcing.
#        disabled - No SELinux policy is loaded.
SELINUX=disabled
```

If you modify the /etc/selinux/config file, you will need to reboot the server for SELinux to be completely disabled.

Disable IPTables

IPTables is a powerful firewall built in to most Linux kernel distributions. During the installation phase, we recommend that you disable IPTables. You can also issue the command **service iptables status** to confirm whether the IPTables services are running. To disable IPTables from future autostartup, execute the **chkconfig** command. To instantly stop IPTables, issue the **service iptables stop** command. Passing the status option to the **service** command will provide the current status of IPTables.

```
# service iptables stop
iptables: Setting chains to policy ACCEPT: filter          [ OK ]
iptables: Flushing firewall rules:                         [ OK ]
iptables: Unloading modules:                               [ OK ]
# chkconfig iptables off
# service iptables status
iptables: Firewall is not running.
```

You also need to stop ip6tables with the **service ip6tables stop** command. You will want to disable IPTables until the cluster is functional:

```
chkconfig -level 345 iptables off
chkconfig -level 345 ip6tables off
```

IO Scheduler Tuning

The Completely Fair Queuing (CFQ) works well for common Linux workloads. For Hadoop on bare-metal implementations, the deadline scheduler is the preferred option. However, for virtualized Hadoop clusters, the noop scheduler is the best practice recommendation. The scheduler is configured in the Linux kernel parameters file. For example, in the /boot/grub.conf file, set the elevator parameter to noop.

Check Transparent Huge Pages Configuration

Linux 6 has a new feature called Transparent Huge Pages (THP), which is enabled by default. THP was intended to shield the complexity of configuring huge pages to the system administrators and developers. Manual configuration of huge pages can be inconvenient and difficult to get right. Huge pages are assigned at boot and are usually used for highly static memory allocation, such as with Oracle databases, while Hadoop is moving toward more elastic models. THP is an abstraction layer that automates the creation, management, and use of huge pages.

THP is important for Hadoop performance but has a subfeature called Compaction, which has been known to cause performance issues with Hadoop workloads. You must disable compaction with the following command:

```
echo never > /sys/kernel/mm/redhat_transparent_hugepage/defrag
```

Limits.conf

Because our Hadoop cluster is a multiuser system, we will need to set some resource constraints for users on the system. Limiting the number of processes per user for the service accounts is important for running a stable system. To limit user process, you can set the shell limit, at the user, group, or system level, by adding entries to the /etc/security/limits.conf file.

The /etc/security/limits.conf file defines process resource limits for users. Linux administrators can specify hard and soft limits for users in the pam_limits module. A soft limit is like a warning, and a hard limit is a ceiling limit. A hard limit cannot be changed by the user. Hard limits can be changed only by the root user. A soft limit, however, can be changed by the user but cannot exceed the hard limit. You must set two parameters in the limits.conf file:

- **nproc:** Sets the maximum number of processes as address space limit
- **nofiles:** Sets the soft limit for the number of file descriptors a user process can have open at one time

Starting in Oracle/Red Hat Linux 6, we recommend creating a file for setting the nproc/ nofile values in the /etc/security/limits.d directory: /etc/security/limits.d/90-hadoop.conf. To validate the changes, execute the **ulimit -a** command for the max user processes setting.

Be careful not to set your limits too low for both soft and hard limits, because these are mere limits and do not actually consume system resources.

```
*    soft    nofile    32768
*    hard    nofile    32768
*    soft    nproc     65536
*    hard    nproc     65536
```

Partition Alignment for RDMs

Misaligned file systems can cause poor performance for Hadoop workloads. On Linux, the first 63 blocks are reserved for the master boot record (MBR). The first data partition starts with offset at 31.5KB. This offset often produces misalignment situations on the memory cache or RAID configurations of a lot of storage arrays, leading to performance degradation due to overlapping I/Os.

For Raw Device Mappings (RDMs), there are some programs and utilities to properly configure partition alignment, such as GNU Parted, fdisk, or sfdisk. We recommend using the parted native OS executable to manually configure the correct alignment against any device name. GNU Parted is the partition editor leveraged to manipulate partitions. With the Parted command, you can add, remove, resize, clone, or modify partitions on the disk. Here's a sample code to create a partition alignment of 1M with the GNU Parted executable:

```
# /sbin/parted -s /dev/sdb mklabel gpt mkpart /dev/sdb1 xfs 2048s 32.0GB
```

The following list includes other tasks that you can perform with GNU Parted:

- With the -s option, you can script out the command-line options so that user intervention is not prompted.

- The mklabel option creates a new disk label for the partition table. You must pass in the gpt (GUID partition table) value for the label type.

- You can use the mkpart option to create a partition; specify the device name, file system type, and the start and end points for the partition, where the start and end points can be either in sectors, MB, or GB. (Each sector is 512 bytes, so you should have 2048 for 1MB.)

Most importantly, we use GNU Parted rather than fdisk because with GNU Parted, you can create partitions over the 2TB limit. To check for partition alignment on an existing device, run the following command:

```
# /sbin/parted -s /dev/sdb print
Model: VMware, VMware Virtual S (scsi)
Disk /dev/sdb: 34.4GB
Sector size (logical/physical): 512B/512B
Partition Table: gpt


Number  Start   End     Size    File system  Name       Flags
 1      1049kB  32.0GB  32.0GB               /dev/sdb1
```

File System Considerations

The Hadoop Distributed File System is platform independent and can function on top of any underlying file system on Linux. Linux offers a variety of file system choices, each with caveats to keep in mind regarding HDFS. Linux offers three popular options for file systems for Hadoop:

- ext3
- ext4
- XFS

Yahoo! has publicly stated the adoption of ext3 file system for its Hadoop deployments. For those who are risk averse, HDFS on ext3 is a good option because it has been publicly tested on Yahoo!'s cluster and is a safe choice for the underlying file system.

Starting in Red Hat 6, ext4 is the default file system; ext4 is the successor to ext3. ext4 has numerous new features, such as the following:

- Better performance with large files
- Delayed allocation of data, which adds a bit more risk with unplanned server outages
- Decreased fragmentation and improved performance

Ext4 was introduced in 2008 and provides support for huge file sizes and file systems. A single huge file can be up to 16TB, and the ext4 file system can be up to 1 exabyte (1EB). Directories in ext4 can contain up to 64,000 subdirectories; directories in ext3 can have up to 32,000 subdirectories. ext4 introduces extent-based allocation, which stores contiguous blocks together in a larger unit of storage. This is particularly important for Hadoop as reads and writes of data happen in larger blocks. Many experienced administrators prefer ext3 or ext4 to XFS because ext3 and ext4 are more widely supported and appear to have fewer reliability problems. We recommend the ext4 file systems for the master nodes.

XFS, created in 1993 by Silicon Graphics Inc. and ported to Linux in 2001, is a 64-bit high-performance journaling file system. XFS offers numerous features and performance capabilities that make it the preferred file system type for all DataNode disks for performance reasons. XFS file systems are equally partitioned across *allocation groups*. You can think of each allocation group as a separate file system that manages its own inodes and free space. Having multiple allocation groups for a file system allows for parallelism without degraded performance. Each allocation group can be up to 1TB in size.

We cannot discuss all the desirable features of XFS, but the following list covers the most relevant features:

- XFS offers massive scalability with features such as variable block sizes and extent-based allocation.

- The 64-bit file system is conceptually capable of handling file systems as large as 8 exabytes.

- XFS provides the delayed space allocation support for buffered writes to file systems. This feature leverages the lazy evaluation technique for allocation of extents based on the configuration of the underlying storage device, effectively reducing fragmentation problems and increasing performance.

- XFS can offer near raw I/O performance.

- XFS can provide direct I/O high throughput by allocating direct memory access between an application and a storage device.

- XFS has the built-in internal mechanisms to freeze the file system for simplified hardware-based snapshots.

- Oracle Linux 6.4 offers support for XFS as part of its distribution.

- Red Hat offers XFS support with additional licensing cost and calls it the Scalable File System Add-On. Even though the XFS file system can scale up to exabytes, Red Hat supports only files systems of less than 100TB.

- CentOS by default provides XFS support with no additional cost.

- mkfs.xfs is part of the xfsprogs RPM package, but it does not come with the basic server installation of either Red Hat or Oracle Linux. If mkfs.xfs does not exist on your data nodes, you should install the executable with yum.

The following example shows the command to run to establish the recommended mount options and file system settings when you use XFS:

```
# /sbin/mkfs.xfs -f -L DISK1 -l size=128m,lazy-count=1 -d su=512k,sw=6 -r
  extsize=256k /dev/sdb1
mkdir -p /data1
mount /dev/sdb1 /data1
```

For the I/O controller configuration, Just a Bunch of Disks (JBOD) and RAID0-per-spindle are common configurations. With RAID0 on each spindle, the controller can provide an additional layer of caching. This can provide a performance boost. If the drive is used as a straight pass-through, the RAID card will not be used.

Lazy Count Parameter for XFS

Performance gains can be achieved by formatting the file system using large log buffers and enabling lazy-count. The lazy-count parameter changes the method of logging various persistent counters in the superblock. Leaving the default value for the lazy-count to 1, the superblock is not modified or logged on every change of the persistent counters. Information is stored in other parts of the file system to be able to maintain the persistent counter values without the need to maintain them in the superblock. This can provide improvements in performance on some configurations.

Mount Options

Linux has two mount options for file systems that we are interested in: noatime and nodiratime. As a general best practice for Hadoop file systems, you should always enable noatime for ext3, ext4, and XFS file systems in /etc/fstab. Important tips include the following:

- Turning on noatime implicitly means that nodiratime is enabled as well.

- Read accesses do not cause the atime information to be updated.

- Do not confuse last access time with last modified time. With last modified time when a file is changed, the modification date is updated.

- If you do not set noatime, each read access for files and directories results in a write operation.

- This mount option can lead to significant performance gains because access to files and directories is not logged.

Entries in your /etc/fstab should look similar to the following entry:

```
LABEL=DATA1 /data1 xfs     allocsize=128m,noatime nodiratime,logbufs=8,
  logbsize=256k nobarrier   0    0
```

Write barrier support is enabled by default in XFS. Write barriers ensure file system integrity using write caches, even during a power loss. Barriers should be disabled for RAID configurations with battery-backed controller cache. The allocsize parameter on the XFS file system preallocates disk space before writing to a file and enables you to optimize streaming performance. This prevents fragmentation on the XFS file system. By increasing the number of log buffers and their size (controlled by logbufs and logbsize mount options), you can enable XFS to handle enqueue pending file and directory operations more efficiently.

A couple more mount options for XFS that are worthy of mentioning to further optimize streaming performance are largeio and inode64. The largeio parameter enables the file systems to expose the file system stripe width rather than the page cache size. This allows for the Hadoop cluster to leverage the high bandwidth to easily determine the optimum I/O size for the underlying file system. For file systems greater than 1TB in size, you must also specify the inode64 parameter in your mount option. By default, with the 32-bit inodes, XFS places all the inode information on the first 1TB of a disk. For example, if you happen to have a 32TB disk, all the inodes reside on the first 1TB. This can result in strange behavior where the file system will report a disk full status when you have plenty of available free space, and performance on the file system will deteriorate. By specifying the inode64 option for file systems greater than 1TB, the inodes are placed in the location where the data resides, thus minimizing disk seeks.

I/O Scheduler

Four I/O schedulers available on Linux are suited to perform better under different workload conditions:

- The default is the fair queuing scheduler, which provides a good compromise between latency and throughput.

- Noop is the simplest of the I/O schedulers and leverages the FIFO queueing model and request merging. Noop assumes that the I/O performance optimizations are taken care of somewhere else in the I/O stack. Noop is ideal for solid-state disks or flash-based systems where the read/write head has been proven to not impact application performance. Noop scheduler is the best practice of virtualized environments. In a nutshell, the Linux OS has a scheduler, and so does the hypervisor. We want to leverage the hypervisor scheduler over the VM OS scheduler because leveraging both schedulers has proven to provide suboptimal results.

- Anticipatory scheduling is similar to the deadline scheduler but is heuristic. The anticipatory scheduler "anticipates" subsequent block requests and caches them for use. Anticipatory scheduler has been documented to improve performance in workloads like Apache web servers but has been documented to decrease performance in database workloads.

- Deadline scheduler is lightweight and tries to put a hard limit on latency by guaranteeing a start service time for a request.

Starting from Red Hat 5, the I/O scheduler on any particular block device can be changed dynamically without a reboot at runtime. Virtualization changes how the I/O scheduler should be set up on the guest VM because the hypervisor also performs I/O optimizations and disk scheduling. You do not want to schedule I/O at the hypervisor layer or at the guest layer because it impacts I/O performance to VMDKs and RDMs. The guest VM should allow the hypervisor to sort out I/O requests instead of trying to do it at the guest VM level by setting the scheduler to Noop.

You can dynamically set the I/O scheduler to Noop by executing the following command:

```
echo noop > /sys/block/DEV1/queue/scheduler
echo noop > /sys/block/DEV2/queue/scheduler
```

You can execute the following script to validate whether your disks are set up for Noop:

```
# find /sys/block/*/queue -name scheduler -exec sh -c 'echo -n "$0 : " ;
  cat $0' {} \;
...
/sys/block/sdaaa/queue/scheduler : [noop] anticipatory deadline cfq
/sys/block/sdaab/queue/scheduler : [noop] anticipatory deadline cfq
/sys/block/sdaac/queue/scheduler : [noop] anticipatory deadline cfq
/sys/block/sdaad/queue/scheduler : [noop] anticipatory deadline cfq
/sys/block/sdaae/queue/scheduler : [noop] anticipatory deadline cfq
/sys/block/sdaaf/queue/scheduler : [noop] anticipatory deadline cfq
...
```

Be aware that the preceding approach for setting the I/O scheduler is not persistent across reboots. You can edit the /etc/grub/grub.conf file to set the boot parameter elevator=noop on the active kernel to make changes permanent. Following is a sample grub.conf file that demonstrates how this is done:

```
default=0
timeout=5
splashimage=(hd0,0)/grub/splash.xpm.gz
hiddenmenu
title Red Hat Enterprise Linux Server (2.6.18-238.el5)
        root (hd0,0)
        kernel /vmlinuz-2.6.18-238.el5 ro root=/dev/VolGroup00/LogVol00
          rhgb quiet elevator= noop
        initrd /initrd-2.6.18-238.el5.img
```

Disk Read and Write Options

The read performance of a disk can be significantly improved by adjusting the read-ahead option to a higher value using the **blockdev** command. The default value is 256 sectors. By default, the Linux OS will read 128KB (256 x 512 bytes) of data in advance so that data is already in memory cache before the program needs it. We recommend that you set this value to a much higher number to achieve the read performance of sequential file reads on large files. We recommend starting with a value of 2048 and increasing the value as you validate performance improvements. You can set the read-ahead size with the **blockdev** command. The actual read-ahead intelligent algorithm is adaptive, so setting a high value will not impact performance for small random reads.

To check the current **blockdev** status of all block devices, issue the command **blockdev --report**. To check for a specific disk, you can narrow your search by specifying **blockdev --getra** [*device name*] (that is, **blockdev --getra /dev/sda**). Another option is to look at **/sys/block/**[*device name*]**/queue/read_ahead_kb** (that is, **cat /sys/block/sda/queue/ read_ahead_kb**).

To adjust the read-ahead value to 1 MB, use the --setra parameter:

```
# blockdev --setra 2048 /dev/sda
```

To make the changes permanent upon system reboot, add the **blockdev** command entries in the /etc/rc.local file.

If you are experiencing many I/O requests to your Hadoop cluster, you can increase the queue length by increasing the value in /sys/block/<device_name>/queue/nr_requests.

```
# echo 512 > /sys/block/sda/queue/nr_requests
```

Each request queue has a limit on the amount of I/O request descriptors for each read and write I/O. By default, the value for the number of reads and writes that can be queued is 128. We recommend changing the number of schedulable requests to a value of 512. Similar to the **blockdev** command, you must add these commands to the /etc/rc.local file to make the changes permanent upon system reboot.

Storage Benchmarking

Storage I/O calibration and benchmarking is a critical component for heavy Hadoop workloads. Most companies do not do any kind of I/O benchmarking before or after the implementation. We suggest that you perform benchmarking before installing any software. The objective of the benchmarking is to identify I/Os per second (IOP) capabilities, latency, and throughput for the storage that is presented to the cluster nodes while identifying latency. Through the benchmarking, you can proactively identify storage,

HBA, disk layout, or multipathing issues before laying down any software. The goal of the benchmarking is to produce a report that displays the read and write capabilities of the storage, identify maximum throughput for the specified workload, and determine potential latency issues within the storage subsystem.

I/O benchmarking is a relatively simple process. Your benchmark criteria must include read/write ratios, latency requirements, and throughput for the simulated workload. You need to estimate the percentage of write activity relative to the percentage of read activity for the presumed workload. Based on the percentage of writes to read and the RAID implementation, you will be able to decipher the output from the following various tools:

- I/O Analyzer from VMware
- Bonnie ++
- IOzone
- Linux/Unix dd
- Oracle Orion

Of all the tools in the preceding list, we prefer VMware's I/O Analyzer for Hadoop I/O benchmarking. I/O Analyzer is the recommended tool for a virtualized infrastructure because it integrates host performance data from ESXi. VMware supplies I/O Analyzer as a virtual appliance that can be downloaded from the I/O Analyzer page at https://labs.vmware.com/flings/io-analyzer. I/O Analyzer can be leveraged to collect storage performance tests and automate storage performance analysis for graphical output. I/O Analyzer can leverage IOmeter to generate a synthetic workload or a trace replay tool to mimic an application workload.

Java Version

The following Java runtimes are supported for Hadoop:

- Oracle JDK 1.6.0_31 64-bit
- Oracle JDK 1.7 64-bit
- Open JDK 7 64-bit

Java 7 is supported on HDP 1.3.2 and HDP2. Java 6 is end of life and should be avoided. You can download the latest Oracle 64-bit JDK (jdk-7u76-linux-x64.tar.gz) from Oracle's download site. At the time of writing this book, HDP 2.2 is the latest stable release and Java 7 is the preferred version.

You should download only the 64-bit version of Java, either the RPM version or the tar.gz version. We recommend that you uninstall the previous version of Java before you install the new version.

Red Hat 6 Update 5 comes shipped with Java 1.7u45 natively.

```
# java -version
java version "1.7.0_45"
OpenJDK Runtime Environment (rhel-2.4.3.3.el6-x86_64 u45-b15)
OpenJDK 64-Bit Server VM (build 24.45-b08, mixed mode)
```

Set Up NTP

You should synchronize your system time between your master servers and data nodes by enabling the NTP daemon. You should always configure NTP to use internal clock servers from your data center rather than clock servers from the public domains (*.ntp.org).

For the Hadoop cluster, we recommend that you enable NTP with the -x option to allow for gradual time changes, which is also referred to as *slewing*.

To set up NTP with the -x option, you need to modify the /etc/sysconfig/ntpd file, add the desired flag to the OPTIONS variable, and restart the service with the **service ntpd restart** command.

```
# Drop root to id 'ntp:ntp' by default.
#OPTIONS="-u ntp:ntp -p /var/run/ntpd.pid -g"
OPTIONS="-x -u ntp:ntp -p /var/run/ntpd.pid"
```

After you modify the ntpd file for the -x option, you must synchronize the files across all the master servers and data nodes. Here's a simple scp one-liner script to synchronize the ntpd file across all the nodes in the cluster:

```
# for i in rhel02 rhel03 rhel04; do scp ntpd ${i}:$PWD; done

ntpd                                100%  255     0.3KB/s   00:00
ntpd                                100%  255     0.3KB/s   00:00
ntpd                                100%  255     0.3KB/s   00:00
```

You can check your current NTP configuration by checking the process status and grepping the results for the NTP daemon. In the example that follows, we start the ntpd service and check to confirm that the settings are correct with the **ps** command:

```
# service ntpd start
Starting ntpd:                                    [  OK  ]
```

```
# ps -ef |grep -i ntp
ntp        3496     1  0 10:38 ?          00:00:00 ntpd -x -u ntp:ntp -p /var/
   run/ntpd.pid
root       3500  2420  0 10:39 pts/1      00:00:00 grep -i ntp
```

As the final step, NTP must be configured for automatic restarts. Execute the **chkconfig ntpd on** command on all the cluster nodes.

Enable Jumbo Frames

Jumbo frames are Ethernet frames with more than 1500 bytes of payload maximum transmission units (MTU). Enabling jumbo frames provides the capability for an Ethernet frame to exceed the IEEE 802 specification for an MTU of 1500 bytes up to a maximum of 9000 bytes. When an application sends a message greater than 1500 bytes, it is fragmented into 1500 bytes, or smaller frames from one end-point to another. Setting the message size to 9000 bytes can improve network throughput performance. Setting jumbo frames can also reduce server overhead in CPU usage when transferring larger files. Because the packets are bigger, fewer packets are needed to send the same data. This can result in faster transfers and less CPU overhead on both the transmitting and receiving servers.

Jumbo frames should be enabled as part of your standard golden image. With jumbo frames, you need to configure the network interfaces on the OS, the distributed switch, and the physical switch itself. Enabling jumbo frames is especially important if you are working with 10gigE network interfaces.

To enable jumbo frames, type the following command as root to set the new MTU to 9000:

```
# ifconfig eth0 mtu 9000
```

To make the changes permanent, modify the network interface configuration file specific for the network interface. In our example, we are modifying the eth0 file by adding the MTU=9000 parameter at the end of the file.

```
# cat /etc/sysconfig/network-scripts/ifcfg-eth0 |grep MTU
MTU=9000
```

After jumbo frames are enabled for the OS, you can leverage the **ping** command with the -M, do, and -s options for end-to-end jumbo frames connectivity testing including switch support. We also leverage the -c option to send two iterations of the **ping** command.

```
ping -M do -s 8972 -c 2 dn01a

PING dn01a (10.17.33.31) 8972(9000) bytes of data.
8980 bytes from dn01a (10.17.33.31): icmp_seq=1 ttl=64 time=0.017 ms
8980 bytes from dn01a (10.17.33.31): icmp_seq=2 ttl=64 time=0.018 ms
```

The important parameter is the -s option where you can specify the packet size. Any value larger than 8972 bytes will result in an error for the **ping** command. With the **ping** command, the packet header has reserved 20 bytes of IP header and 8 bytes of ICMP header data. The default packet size for the **ping** command is 56 bytes if you do not include the ICMP header data or the IP header bytes.

In addition to enabling jumbo frames, you should also disable IPV6. Review the section at the end of this chapter for why you need to disable IPV6.

Additional Network Considerations

The following two network-related settings can affect Hadoop performance. The default setting for the net.core.somaxconn Linux kernel parameter is 128. This parameter defines the maximum number of pending connection requests for any listening queue or the number of connections that the server can set up at a given time. We recommend changing this setting to 1024 to help bursty requests from the NameNode and Resource-Manager. If the listen queue is saturated because of too many simultaneous connection requests, additional connections will be refused.

In addition to this kernel parameter, we recommend setting the txqueuelen network interface parameter. A higher value is recommended for servers connected over high-speed Internet connections that perform large data transfers. The default value for the txqueuelen is 1000. We recommend setting this to 4096 or higher to better accommodate the bursty traffic seen in the network traffic of Hadoop clusters.

The following command will dynamically modify the network settings:

```
# sysctl -w net.core.somaxconn=1024
```

You can append the net.core.somaxconn=1024 entry to the /etc/sysctl.conf file to make this change permanent after reboots.

You can modify the txqueuelen for a network interface with the following command:

```
# ifconfig eth0 txqueuelen 4096
```

To make the changes permanent, you can add the line /sbin/ifconfig eth1 txqueuelen 4096 to the /etc/rc.local file.

Enable NSCD

Name Service Cache Daemon, or nscd, is a daemon that provides caching facilities for the most common name service requests. Enabling nscd also helps when you have network hiccups. Nscd is a small footprint daemon, and almost no configuration is needed. Hadoop nodes are network-based applications and issue a lot of name lookups, especially for HBase and distcp. By enabling nscd, you can reduce the latency of service requests and impact on shared infrastructure. By enabling the nscd, you can see performance improvements when using naming services like DNS, NIS, NIS+, and LDAP.

Before you start using nscd, you should first modify the configuration file /etc/nscd.conf and disable the nscd options for passwd, group, and netgroup by modifying the enable-cache lines to "no" as shown here:

```
# cat /etc/nscd.conf |grep enable-cache |grep -v \^# |sort -k3
    enable-cache    netgroup    no
    enable-cache    group       no
    enable-cache    passwd      no
    enable-cache    services    yes
    enable-cache    hosts       yes
```

Next, start the nscd services with the **service start nscd** command. You enable nscd to start on server reboot by issuing the **chkconfig** command:

```
# chkconfig -level 345 nscd on
```

To confirm that nscd is enabled, issue the **nscd** command with the -g parameter, which prints the current configuration statistics. To list all the valid options for nscd, pass the -? parameter.

Disable IPv6

Apache Hadoop is currently not supported on IPv6 networks. It has been developed and tested on the IPv4 network stack. At the time of writing this book, Apache Hadoop requires IPv4 to work, and only IPv4 clients can communicate with the cluster. Set the following options in the respective files to disable IPV6:

```
/etc/sysctl.conf   :  net.ipv6.conf.all.disable_ipv6 = 1
/etc/sysconfig/network   : NETWORKING_IPV6=no
/etc/sysconfig/network-scripts/ifcfg-eth0 : IPV6INIT="no"
```

After you complete the preceding steps, restart the network and execute the **ifconfig -a** command to validate that there is no ipv6 address.

Summary

When a Hadoop cluster is designed and configured, it is important to determine that the Hadoop master servers are optimized for availability and the Hadoop worker nodes are optimized for performance. Ideally, the worker nodes should be designed to be replaceable because they are likely to be added on a periodic basis and taken offline occasionally.

In this chapter, we reviewed the Linux optimizations needed to configure a Hadoop cluster. The chapter started by determining the right Linux distribution for your master and DataNodes. It looked into optimizing the kernel parameters and choosing the right file system and file system options. It then discussed performance considerations for disabling swapping and memory optimizations. Next, it reviewed disk performance considerations and storage benchmarking. The chapter concluded with network considerations pertinent for optimizing the Hadoop cluster.

Hadoop Cluster Creation: A Prerequisite Checklist

The following table is an essential checklist of data items to have ready before you set up your first Hadoop cluster. You should use a tool such as vSphere Big Data Extensions to assist with the provisioning, monitoring, and maintenance of the clusters. Many of the terms used here are taken from the vSphere Big Data Extensions User and Administrator Guide.

Category	Check to Perform or List of Details	Explanation
1. Networking		
DHCP	An IP address and FQDN can be assigned for all VMs to be provisioned.	
Static IP range	An IP address and FQDN can be assigned for all VMs to be provisioned.	
DNS	Supplies a hostname for all VMs.	
	Supports forward and reverse lookups.	A and PTR records present for all provisioned VMs.
Management network	Is the management network separated from the data network?	Might be ideal for performance reasons.
2. Storage		
Storage mechanism for VMDK files		For example, SAN/local DAS/NAS/other.
Storage mechanism for HDFS data		For example, Isilon/DAS.
Storage mechanism for shuffle/temp data		For example, DAS, Flash.
Storage capacity for VMDK files		
Storage capacity for HDFS data		Take the replication factor (default = 3) into account here.
Storage capacity for shuffle/temp data		
All datastores added have unique names		Both vSphere and BDE require the datastore name to be set up.
2a. Direct Attached Storage (DAS)		
Configured as JBOD or RAIDxx disks	<enter your data here>	Can set aside 1 or 2 spindles per machine for VM images.
Number of disk drives per host		The more disk drives per host the better.

Category	Check to Perform or List of Details	Explanation
Number of disk drives per processor core		1 to 1.5 disk drives per processor core is considered ideal for performance reasons.
Rotation speed, bandwidth (Mb/sec), and type of drive (SAS, SATA)		For example, 7200 RPM, 180 Mb/sec, Serial ATA Disk Drives
2b. Network Attached Storage		
Usernames, group names, zones required for access		Pay particular attention to the mapping of groups and user IDs on Isilon to those on each compute node.
Notes on Datastores		Datastore free space must be greater than the Hadoop cluster data size. Take the Hadoop replication factor into account. It is normally set to 3, though it can be adjusted.
3. Resource Pool(s) for Hadoop Clusters		
CPU capacity		
Memory capacity		
4. Creating a New Hadoop Cluster		
New cluster name		Supply a unique cluster name.
Application Manager		Choose one from the list of application managers that were added into BDE previously. For example, Cloudera Manager, Ambari.
Hadoop distribution and version		Choose from the list that Application Manager supports.
Local Repository URL		For use by Cloudera Manager or Ambari to download packages from

Category	Check to Perform or List of Details			Explanation
Cluster Deployment Type	Types are Basic, HBase, Data-Compute Separation, Compute-Only Cluster (Isilon). Compute-Workers-Only, HBase-Only or Customized Cluster.			See the section "About Hadoop and Hbase Cluster Types" in the BDE Admin and User Guide.
Cluster configuration specification file				If you choose to customize the cluster, you may supply a cluster specification filename.
Virtual Machine Sizes (Node Groups in BDE)				**Please insert your values in the following table.**
DataMaster Node Group (NameNode)	vCPUs:	Memory Size:	Disk Size:	
ComputeMaster Node Group (ResourceManager)	vCPUs:	Memory Size:	Disk Size:	
Worker Node Group (NodeManager, DataNode)	vCPUs:	Memory Size:	Disk Size:	
Client Node Group (Hive, Pig clients)	vCPUs:	Memory Size:	Disk Size:	
HBase Master Node Group (HBase Master Server)	vCPUs:	Memory Size:	Disk Size:	
New Cluster Topology				
Topology Type				Examples: HOST_AS_RACK, RACK_AS_RACK, HVE, NONE
Network or set of networks to be used	HDFS network: MapReduce network: Management network:			These are the network names from the list created in BDE. You can separate the HDFS, MapReduce, and Management networks.
Resource pool or pools				Select one or more resource pools that the new cluster will use.
Administrative password (can be set here or generated)				This is to allow access to the VMs in the new cluster.

Big Data/Hadoop on VMware vSphere Reference Materials

Deployment Guides

- Virtualizing Hadoop—a Deployment Guide:

  http://www.vmware.com/bde under Resources -> Getting Started

  or more directly: http://www.vmware.com/files/pdf/products/vsphere/Hadoop-Deployment-Guide-USLET.pdf

- Deploying Virtualized Cloudera CDH on vSphere using Isilon Storage—Technical Guide from EMC/Isilon:

  http://hsk-cdh.readthedocs.org/en/latest/hsk.html#deploy-a-cloudera-hadoop-cluster

  or find the latest version at https://community.emc.com/docs/DOC-26892

- Deploying Virtualized Hortonworks HDP on vSphere using Isilon Storage—Technical Guide from EMC/Isilon:

  http://hsk-hwx.readthedocs.org/en/latest/hsk.html#deploy-a-hortonworks-hadoop-cluster-with-isilon-for-hdfs

  or as above, https://community.emc.com/docs/DOC-26892

Reference Architectures

- Cloudera Reference Architecture—Isilon version:

  http://www.cloudera.com/content/cloudera/en/documentation/
  reference-architecture/latest/PDF/cloudera_ref_arch_vmware_isilon.pdf

- Cloudera Reference Architecture—Direct Attached Storage version:

  http://www.cloudera.com/content/cloudera/en/documentation/
  reference-architecture/latest/PDF/cloudera_ref_arch_vmware_local_storage.pdf

- Big Data with Cisco UCS and EMC Isilon: Building a 60 Node Hadoop Cluster
  (using Cloudera):

  http://www.cisco.com/c/dam/en/us/td/docs/unified_computing/ucs/UCS_CVDs/
  Cisco_UCS_and_EMC_Isilon-with-Cloudera_CDH5.pdf

- Scaling the Deployment of Multiple Hadoop Workloads on a Virtualized Infrastructure (Intel, Dell, and VMware):

  http://www.intel.com/content/www/us/en/software/intel-dell-vmware-scaling-the-
  deployment-of-multiple-hadoop-workloads.html?wapkw=hadoop+virtualization

Customer Case Studies

- Adobe Deploys Hadoop-as-a-Service on VMware vSphere:

  http://www.vmware.com/files/pdf/products/vsphere/VMware-vSphere-Adobe-
  Deploys-HAAS-CS.pdf

- Virtualizing Hadoop in Large-Scale Infrastructures—technical white paper by EMC:

  https://community.emc.com/docs/DOC-41473

Performance

- Virtualized Hadoop Performance with VMware vSphere 6 on High-Performance
  Servers:

  http://www.vmware.com/resources/techresources/10452

- Virtualized Hadoop Performance with VMware vSphere 5.1:

  http://www.vmware.com/resources/techresources/10360

There are some very useful best practices in the preceding two technical papers.

- A Benchmarking Case Study of Virtualized Hadoop Performance on vSphere 5:

  http://www.vmware.com/resources/techresources/10222

- Transaction Processing Council—TPCx-HS Benchmark Results (Cloudera on VMware performance, submitted by Dell):

  http://www.tpc.org/tpcx-hs/results/tpcxhs_results.asp

- ESG Lab Review: VCE vBlock /systems with EMC Isilon for Enterprise Hadoop:

  http://www.esg-global.com/lab-reports/esg-lab-review-vce-vblock-systems-with-emc-isilon-for-enterprise-hadoop/

vSphere Big Data Extensions (BDE)

- VMware BDE Documentation site:

  https://www.vmware.com/support/pubs/vsphere-big-data-extensions-pubs.html

- VMware vSphere Big Data Extensions—Administrator's and User's Guide and Command Line Interface User's Guide:

  https://www.vmware.com/support/pubs/vsphere-big-data-extensions-pubs.html

- Blog articles on BDE Version 2.1:

  http://blogs.vmware.com/vsphere/2014/10/whats-new-vsphere-big-data-extensions-version-2-1.html

  See the embedded blogs from the Hadoop distro vendors also.

- VMware Big Data Extensions (BDE) community discussion:

  https://communities.vmware.com/message/2308400

- Apache Hadoop Storage Provisioning Using VMware vSphere Big Data Extensions:

  https://www.vmware.com/files/pdf/VMware-vSphere-BDE-Storage-Provisioning.pdf

- Hadoop Virtualization Extensions (HVE):

  http://www.vmware.com/files/pdf/Hadoop-Virtualization-Extensions-on-VMware-vSphere-5.pdf

- Container Orchestration on vSphere with Big Data Extensions:

  https://labs.vmware.com/flings/big-data-extensions-for-vsphere-standard-edition

Other vSphere Features and Big Data

- Protecting Hadoop with VMware vSphere 5 Fault Tolerance:

  http://www.vmware.com/files/pdf/techpaper/VMware-vSphere-Hadoop-FT.pdf

- Toward an Elastic Elephant—Enabling Hadoop for the Cloud:

  http://labs.vmware.com/vmtj/toward-an-elastic-elephant-enabling-hadoop-for-the-cloud

- Apache Flume and Apache Scoop Data Ingestion to Apache Hadoop Clusters on VMware vSphere:

  https://www.vmware.com/files/pdf/products/vsphere/VMware-vSphere-Data-Ingestion-Solution-Guide.pdf

- Demos of Big Data Extensions:

  https://www.youtube.com/watch?v=doOCAQNSgeU&list=PL9MeVsU0uG662xAjTB8XSD83GXSDuDzuk

Index

vmware®

Increase Your Value—Get VMware Certified

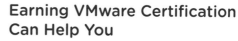

Earning VMware Certification Can Help You

- Develop practical skills as you gain technical expertise

- Advance your career and obtain new responsibilities

- Increase your job satisfaction

- Improve career recognition and financial compensation

- Gain a hiring advantage when applying for a job

Learn more about VMware certification at
www.vmware.com/certification

informIT.com THE TRUSTED TECHNOLOGY LEARNING SOURCE

PEARSON

InformIT is a brand of Pearson and the online presence for the world's leading technology publishers. It's your source for reliable and qualified content and knowledge, providing access to the top brands, authors, and contributors from the tech community.

✦Addison-Wesley   **Cisco Press**   EXAM✓**CRAM**   **IBM** Press.   **que**   **PRENTICE HALL**   **SAMS** | Safari

LearnIT at InformIT

Looking for a book, eBook, or training video on a new technology? Seeking timely and relevant information and tutorials? Looking for expert opinions, advice, and tips? **InformIT has the solution.**

- Learn about new releases and special promotions by subscribing to a wide variety of newsletters. Visit **informit.com/newsletters**.

- Access FREE podcasts from experts at **informit.com/podcasts**.

- Read the latest author articles and sample chapters at **informit.com/articles**.

- Access thousands of books and videos in the Safari Books Online digital library at **safari.informit.com**.

- Get tips from expert blogs at **informit.com/blogs**.

Visit **informit.com/learn** to discover all the ways you can access the hottest technology content.

Are You Part of the IT Crowd?

Connect with Pearson authors and editors via RSS feeds, Facebook, Twitter, YouTube, and more! Visit **informit.com/socialconnect**.

informIT.com THE TRUSTED TECHNOLOGY LEARNING SOURCE   **PEARSON**

✦Addison-Wesley   **Cisco Press**   EXAM✓**CRAM**   **IBM** Press.   **que**   **PRENTICE HALL**   **SAMS** | Safari

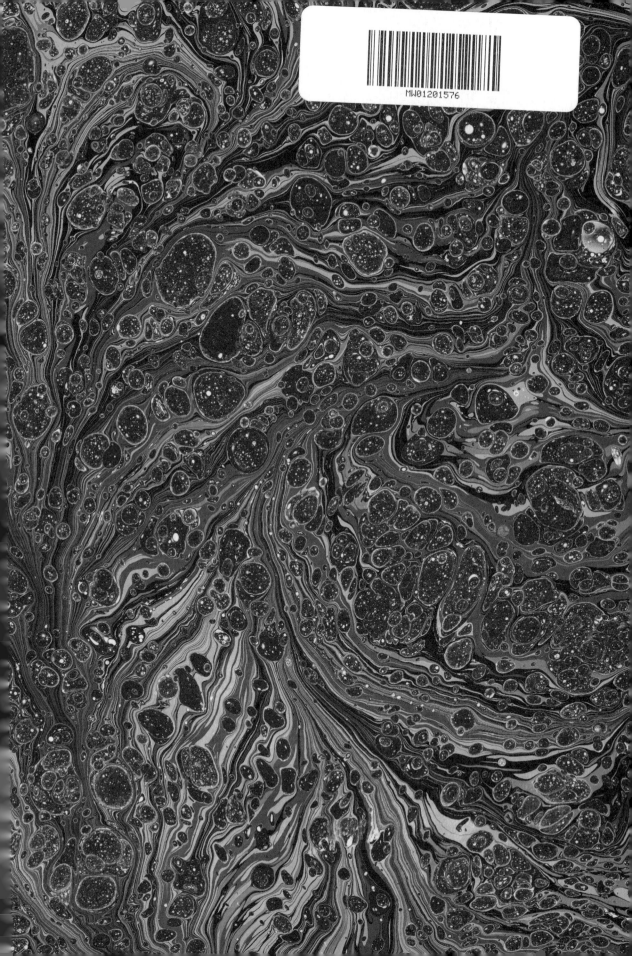
MW01201576

The Spanish in the SS and Wehrmacht

The Spanish in the SS and Wehrmacht

1944 – 1945

The Ezquerra Unit in the Battle of Berlin

Eduardo Manuel Gil Martínez

Schiffer Military History
Atglen, PA

ACKNOWLEDGMENTS

Erik Norling, Luis E. Togores, Augusto Ferrer, Fernando Sánchez, Antonio Carrasco and Francisco Martínez, for their invaluable help.

Translation from the Spanish by Linda Robins da Silva.

Book Design by Francisco A. Martínez Canales and Stephanie Daugherty.
Additional photographs and military resources: Almena

Copyright © 2012 by Schiffer Publishing.
Library of Congress Control Number: 2012944437

All rights reserved. No part of this work may be reproduced or used in any forms or by any means – graphic, electronic or mechanical, including photocopying or information storage and retrieval systems – without written permission from the copyright holder.

The scanning, uploading and distribution of this book or any part thereof via the Internet or via any other means without the permission of the publisher is illegal and punishable by law. Please purchase only authorized editions and do not participate in or encourage the electronic piracy of copyrighted materials.

"Schiffer," "Schiffer Publishing, Ltd. & Design," and the "Design of pen and inkwell" are registered trademarks of Schiffer Publishing, Ltd.

Printed in China.
ISBN: 978-0-7643-4271-4

This book was originally published in Spanish under the title,
Españoles en Las SS y la Wehrmacht, 1944-45,
by Almeda Ediciones, Madrid, Spain.

We are interested in hearing from authors with book ideas on related topics.

Published by Schiffer Publishing Ltd.
4880 Lower Valley Road
Atglen, PA 19310
Phone: (610) 593-1777
FAX: (610) 593-2002
E-mail: Info@schifferbooks.com.
Visit our web site at: www.schifferbooks.com
Please write for a free catalog.
This book may be purchased from the publisher.
Try your bookstore first.

In Europe, Schiffer books are distributed by:
Bushwood Books
6 Marksbury Avenue
Kew Gardens
Surrey TW9 4JF, England
Phone: 44 (0) 20 8392-8585
FAX: 44 (0) 20 8392-9876
E-mail: Info@bushwoodbooks.co.uk.
Visit our website at: www.bushwoodbooks.co.uk

FOREWORD

Luis E. Togores

Without a doubt the 250th Infantry Division of the Wehrmacht, known as the Spanish Volunteer Division, the famous "Blue Division", is, of all the military units that participated in the Second World War, one of the most written about. The list of titles numbers more than several thousand, which suggests that the subject has already been exhausted. However, nothing could be further from the truth.

In Spanish universities doctoral theses continue to be written about the "soldiers", such as that recently defended by Pablo Sagarra dealing with the Division chaplains, or the completed thesis awaiting examination by chemist Ángel Carralero on its health services. However, perhaps, that which is most notable is the interest which the subject stirs in publishers and, above all, for the public which show rare loyalty and buy, with military discipline, all the titles dealing with this subject which appear in bookshops. This has been shown by the recent success of books such as Las fotografías de una Historia, la División Azul (Photographs of a History, the Blue Division), with more than 10,000 copies sold, or Atlas of the División Azul (Atlas of the Blue Division) by Carlos Caballero, which sold a similar number of copies.

Currently, the greatest challenge lies in ensuring that a significant number of this enormous list of books published in Spanish is translated, at least into English, German and Russian. It is true that some works have appeared in English – such as those by Kleinfeld and Tambs or Wayne Bowen – but in general these are works of a general nature which rarely include the new and significant contributions which are constantly being provided by Spanish researchers and publishers on these subjects.

Among the books which have come out, the continued publication of the memoires of members of the division deserve to be mentioned, although they are made up of accounts which are basically very similar, they continue to provide a fundamental contribution to the reconstruction of this, very important, part of Spain's participation in the Second World War. Unfortunately, these testimonies are coming to an end, since the passing of time is causing the continual and unstoppable disappearance of the members of the Division; even so, it is worth mentioning the emergence of some books of memoires such as that by José María Blanch, recently published with the title Memorias de un soldier of the División Azul (Memoirs of a Soldier from the Blue Division).

All of this shows that the Blue Division continues to be a source of interest for many generation of Spaniards interested in the history of Spain. There are many young people who, attracted by the heroic deeds of the Division, get involved in reading about history and engage with specialist Internet forums, which is very positive from a nation who is generally reluctant to find out about its own history. A "well done!" to the members of the division, who continue, like El Cid, to notch up victories after their deaths. Together with these readers, new and old, a succession of authors is emerging who continue to deal with the studies and research into the participation of the Spanish in the Second World War. In regards to the presence of the Spanish in the last months of the war, there are limited bibliographic resources and testimonies. It is curious how in this section there is only the autobiographical testimony of Miguel Ezquerra to go on, which is very difficult to prove, as none of the Spaniards fighting for the Third Reich in the final stages have left written accounts of their experiences apart from the aforementioned exception. In addition, there is neither a good bibliography of and about the Spanish workers who worked for the German Nazis nor information about these events by the diplomats and Spanish workers who stayed in Germany during the last months of the war. There is a lack of information on the Soviet side and, to a lesser extent, from the western allies on the presence of Spanish volunteers at the end of the Second World War in the German ranks. It seems there is still a lot of research to be undertaken.

Among the new authors currently emerging either from the ranks of professional historians or from affection and dedication to Spanish military history is Eduardo Manuel Gil Martínez, who, with curiosity and scholarship, adds to the history of the division with the pages following this introduction with the title The Spanish in the SS and in the Wehrmacht, 1944-1945: The Ezquerra Unit in the Battle of Berlin.

As said previously, much has been written about the period between the moment when Serrano Suñer let forth the cry, "Russia is guilty!" until the return of the volunteers of the Blue Division to Spain. Little is known about the Blue Legion, and especially about the small groups of volunteers who, contravening orders from Spain, decided to continue fighting for Nazi Germany. There are the works of Fernando Vadillo, the aforementioned memoires of Miguel Ezquerra and publications on the Waffen-SS by Marbella author Erik Norling. There is also the rigorous research currently being carried out by Xavier Moreno Juliá on the Blue Legion but little more. The book which follows this prologue can be added to this small group of publications on the last stage of Spanish exploits in the Second World War.

Editorial Almena, in its line of specialist texts on Military History, has brought out a work that, without a doubt, will awaken interest in those curious about the last stage of the Spanish presence in the fight alongside Germany against the Soviet Union, allowing them to easily and enjoyably get close to the least known stage of the Spanish effort in the fight against Soviet Communism. These pages give an account of the Spanish participation in the Battle of Berlin, described day by day, from Friday April 20 to Thursday May 3, 1945, by the author, and also include maps, uniforms, weapons and the combatants' tactics as well as a biography of Miguel Ezquerra together with the other protagonists of these events, which will help readers to understand the events narrated and explained by Eduardo Gil in his book.

Almost seven decades have gone by since the departure of the first Spanish volunteers for Germany, but for many readers and writers it seems like it only happened yesterday.

CONTENTS

PROLOGUE

This book aims to remember the history of some of the Spanish who fought in the Second World War on the German side. It is completely without any political purpose, it aims only to reconstruct some events in the closest possible manner to the texts which I have looked at.

Fortunately, the intervention of Spanish troops posted in the German Armed Forces is better known in Spain thanks to the increasingly numerous works which have appeared in recent years. The majority of these books deals with the Spanish incorporated into the Wehrmacht, the widely known Blue Division and its successor the Blue Legion. Worth singling out is the immense work, in all senses, by Fernando Vadillo "Gran crónica of the División Azul" (*Grand Chronicle of the Blue Division*); *Morir en Rusia* (*Dying in Russia*), by Carlos Caballero; the mainly photographic *Las fotografías de una historia. La División Azul* (*Photographs of a History. The Blue Division*), by Luis E. Togores and Gustavo Morales, and the work by Kleinfeld and Tambs, *La Division española de Hitler* (*Hitler's Spanish Division*). Books describing the adventures of the Spanish posted to the Luftwaffe and Kriegsmarine, have also come out recently, such as *Escuadrillas azules en Rusia* (*The Blue Squadrons in Russia*), by Santiago Guillén and Carlos Caballero or *Bajo las banderas de la Kriegsmarine* (*Under the Flags of the Kriegsmarine*), by Alfonso Escuadra.

After the end of the more or less "official" intervention of the Spanish in the war which came about as a consequence of allied pressure on the Spanish government, there were hundreds of Spaniards who stayed in the service of the Reich. These "irreducibles" have been dealt with very seldom in books, although again in a very apt manner by Fernando Vadillo. Among these last Spaniards there is a small group that took part in the final defense of Berlin. Information on them is basically provided by the aforementioned book by Vadillo and the biography of Miguel Ezquerra, who was head of the Spanish unit under discussion at that time.

The decision to write this work was born of the need to have a work that discusses the role of the Ezquerra Unit in the last days of the Reich, putting it in the framework of the events which happened during the Soviet attack on the German capital.

The fact that there is an increasing number of more detailed and better documented publications on the last days of the III Reich, such as *La última batalla* (*The Last Battle*), by Cornelius Ryan; the wonderful, *Berlín. La caída: 1945*, (*Berlin, The Fall: 1945*) by Anthony Beevor; *Hitler's Last Bastion*, by Franz Kurowski; *Berlin 1945*, by Peter Antill, or the series of French magazines *Hors Serie Historica* "Berlin 1945", which allow us to know with more certainty how the events unfolded in those difficult days of the definitive Soviet assault on Berlin, and about the confrontations between them and the garrison of the capital.

It is hoped that this book will allow us to know these men better, men who in many cases gave their lives defending a land where they were not even born. They decided to continue in the armed fight against Communism as it was the last bastion of the cause. This was also the case for many of the troops which defended the capital of the Reich, amongst which, apart from the Germans and Spaniards, were French, Estonians, Latvians, Swedes, Belgians, Romanians, Italians, etc. Although these non-German contingents did not have many men, they did demonstrate what would be the first Pan-European attack on Communism.

It is true that the scant sources available dealing with the concrete case of the participation of Spanish troops under Spanish command in the defense of Berlin are regarded with a degree of caution, above all Ezquerra's autobiographical book. Despite this, and taking into account the inaccuracies that can appear in any work of this type, they should be considered as a reference tool which will serve as a structure for more details about the events which took place during those difficult days at the end of April and the beginning of May in 1945.

At the same time as aiming to give information about the violent last days of the Reich in the German capital, I am also carrying out a brief investigation without wanting to undertake an exhaustive study of the presence of other Spaniards posted in the Waffen-SS as well as in the actual German Army from 1944 to May 1945. A veil of darkness has fallen over these men and little is known about their activities during the last year and a half of the Second World War. Fortunately, there are publications and books that tell "a little of this and a little of that" about these men. I am referring to authors who are renowned in this little known "closed world" of the Second World War such as Jean Pierre Sourd, with his works *True believers* and *Croisés d'un idéal*; Spanish writer, Carlos Caballero Jurado, with *Los últimos de*

los últimos. El batallón fantasma (*The Last of the Last: The Ghost Battalion*) and *El batallón fantasma. Españoles en la Wehrmacht y Waffen-SS, 1944-45* (*The Ghost Battalion, The Spanish in the Wehrmacht and Waffen-SS, 1944-45*). Others include Antonio Muñoz, with various books dealing with minority subjects of the world conflict; or Fernando Vadillo, with his work *Los Irreductibles* (*The Irreducibles*) in the "Gran Crónica of the División Azul" (*Grand Chronicle of the Blue Division*); or Erik Norling, with his work on the *Wallonien*, in which he puts emphasis on the Spanish who served in it; as well as smaller, but no less interesting works, such as the article by Gregorio Torres on "Españoles en las Waffen-SS en Italia", (*The Spanish in the Waffen-SS in Italy*), or Wayne Bowen, with "The Ghost Battalion: Spaniards in the Waffen-SS, 1944-1945."

The events that related here are another glorious chapter in the book of Spanish history, showing men who are true to their ideals, defending them until the end. Men who decided to choose the difficult path of honor at any cost and who did not know the meaning of the word surrender. This book then is a small but deserving homage to those Spanish who, in memory of their Spanish ancestors in the defense of Numantia, joined the Carthaginian army in Zama, the glorious tercios in Rocroi, the heroic men of Spanish fleet at Trafalgar or the last of the Philippines, even knowing the end that was about to befall them, were able to keep fighting until the end, without giving rise to weakness, keeping the spirit of combat alive, keeping their dignity and staying loyal to their ideals. This is a homage to them.

Eduardo Manuel Gil Martínez
Seville, 2010

INTRODUCTION

The existence of Spanish troops posted in the ranks of the Waffen-SS during the defense of the city of Berlin in the last days of the Third Reich, has been something which has been silenced within the actions of the Spanish in the Second World War.

What is known, although not in any detail by most Spaniards, is the existence of the popularly known Blue Division, which came about as a response to the people' s clamor after the German Army' s attack on the USSR in June 1941. This was shown by a large demonstration in Madrid orchestrated mainly by the Falange which evidenced the desire to fight the Soviets in their own country in order to retaliate for their support of the Republican side during the Spanish Civil War, and at the same time partly settle the debt accrued with Germany for its support of the national side. It was during this demonstration that Serrano Súñer, Secretary of State and president of the Political Junta of the Falange, from one of the balconies of the headquarters of the General Secretariat of the Movement gave his well known address: "Comrades, this is no time for speeches; but time for the Falange to now declare its conviction: Russia is guilty!, guilty of our Civil War. Guilty of the death of José Antonio, our founder. And of the deaths of so many comrades and so many soldiers who fell in this war due to the aggression of Communist Russia. The extermination of Russia is demanded by history and the future of Europe […]."

Due to the great popular enthusiasm generated by this, he managed to recruit thousands of volunteers from the soldiers and civilians who then lined up to enlist at the recruitment offices which were created for this purpose. It is said that some young recently graduated officers, who had not fought in the Spanish Civil War, faced with the scene of a world war in front of them, could not miss the chance offered to them of going to the front. In addition, young university students with a thirst for adventure, or with the romantic ideal of defending their belief in God and their homeland, seized the idea of enlisting in the Spanish Volunteer Division.

The official Spanish position at the beginning of the world conflict was neutral despite a large percentage of the population being pro-German; expressed thus in a decree: […] officially affirming the state of war which unfortunately exists between England, France and Poland on one side, and Germany, on the other, the present decree orders, the strictest neutrality of Spanish subjects […].

On June 12, 1940 a position of "no belligerence" was adopted, similar to that of Italy before it became involved in the armed conflict. Despite this first step taken by Spain towards Germany, the negotiations for its entrance in the war by the Secretary of State, von Ribbentrop, did not end in Spain joining the Axis due to lack of understanding on both sides. Therefore, the situation in which Spain found itself with regards to Germany was somewhat complex.

The invasion of the Soviet Union allowed for the pressure put upon Francisco Franco by Adolf Hitler to be alleviated, by means of the dispatch of a Spanish expeditionary force to

Russia. This was considered by the Germans, in principle, as a first step towards Spain's gradual entrance into the war.

This dispatch of troops to be included in the German Army would also allow for part of the debt accumulated by Spain to be indirectly paid to Germany for its help in the Spanish Civil War.

In July 1941, an initial contingent of some 18,000 men under the command of General Agustín Muñoz Grandes (who would be relieved by General Emilio Esteban-Infantes in December 1942), left for Germany in order to, after suitable training received at the Grafenwöhr camp, become part of the German Army under the name of the Infanterie *Division 250* (250th Infantry Division).

From September 29 of the same year the unit would fight as part of the 16th German Army in the Army Group North. From then on the Spanish would take part in a number of actions against the Soviets in such resonant and memorable places as Novgorod, the River Volkhov, Lake Ilmen and Krasny Bor.

On December 12, 1942, General Muñoz Grandes received the order to return to Spain in spite of the German opposition to their departure. Two days later Adolf Hitler conferred the Oak Leaves on the General for the Knight's Cross of the Order of the Iron Cross which he already had. The command of the Division fell to the general who had, until then, been the second commander, General Emilio Esteban-Infantes Martín, who would later also be awarded the Knight's Cross of the Iron Cross.

Due to pressure from the allies, the Spanish government was obliged, on September 24, 1943, to withdraw the Blue Division (its last war action was to repel a Soviet attack on October 5, 1943). Nevertheless, it kept a contingent of 2,269 men involved in the unit known as the Blue Legion, with the added aim of avoiding possible setbacks by the Germans when repatriating the majority of the Division.

The Blue Legion began to form on October 20, 1943, being officially created the following November 17 with the level of regiment and under the command of Colonel Antonio García Navarro. The repatriation of the members of the Blue Division was carried out in a series of steps, being completed before the end of December 1943.

Obviously, allied pressure forced Spain to permanently cut the help it was supplying to Germany. On February 20, 1944, the *Führer* and Francisco Franco agreed on the repatriation of the Blue Legion. The repatriation order arrived at the Legion's command post on March 3. And on March 6, at 11:34, in Lechts, Coronel García Navarro delivered his last address to the legionnaires: "[…] There is sad and important news: Spain, in agreement with the German Government, will take part in the difficult, even tragic, step of agreeing to our repatriation.

[…] Return proud of having fulfilled your obligations! […] Proud because Spain demanded this of us and because it did this without hesitation.

[…] Now an order. The hardest that I have given to the Legion. Nobody will show they are happy! I already know that you are not, as I see tears in the eyes of many and emotion from everyone. We cannot feel happy, however great the desire to return to Spain, to be reunited with our loved ones or because family difficulties or other abandoned affairs, require our presence.

Nobody will be happy: Spain is in mourning and the Legion is in black. Black with seriousness, with feeling, with the bitterness of returning.

[…] You will carry, today on this day of mourning, empty rifles, like those at a burial or during Holy Week, because, and I say this again to you, this is a day of mourning for our Country."

The Blue Legion (or Spanish Legion of Volunteers-SLV) received the official farewell of the 18th Army in Pruna on the 14th; General Lindemann directed a last address to the Spanish and decorated a number of officers and soldiers.

On the 16th the legionnaires handed in the weapons they were carrying apart from knives for self defense. On the same day the first contingent of Spanish left by train for Könisberg (nowadays known as Kaliningrad, part of the Russian Federation), where they arrived three days later. There they assembled at the Stablack Süd military installations.

On the 21st they handed in the last weapons and part of the uniform, and with this the Legion was considered to be dissolved the following day, although it took two weeks to hand in their German uniforms in Wilmehoff, and wear Spanish uniforms. The stipulated withdrawal of the Blue Legion, was carried out therefore between March (on the 31st the first repatriated members arrived at Irun) and April 1944 (during the 11th or the 17th, depending on sources, the last men arrived, amongst whom were their colonel and the Staff Officers of the SLV), having taken four days to complete the journey from Könisberg to Irun. The repatriation started with the Third Flag, followed by the First and Second flags, finishing with the Staff Officers.

For different reasons, some Spaniards decided not to return to Spain despite the risk run by those who had collaborated with the German Armed Forces of losing their Spanish nationality.

These men, mostly ex-members of the Division and the Legion, together with others who had crossed the Spanish border to join the German Armed Forces and many Spanish citizens working in the Reich, who had lost their jobs due to the incessant allied bombing on German industry, decided to fight as part of German troops.

After the withdrawal and dissolution of the Blue Legion (March 1944), the interven-tion of the Spanish into the Axis was illegal, which did not stop some volunteers from refusing to return to Spain and other Spaniards from crossing the border into France. Many of them ended up, after various ups and downs, joining units belonging to the *Waffen-SS* (such as the *Wallonien* or Norland divisions), others were assigned to the 3rd Mountain Division or to the 357th Infantry Division.

There were also Spaniards fighting against the partisan guerrilla in Yugoslavia (August 1944) forming part of the 8th Company of the 2nd Battalion of the 3rd Regiment of the Brandenburg Division, which also fought against the partisan guerrilla in Italy. And, as an epic climax, in this group of Spaniards that according to various sources, numbered up to approximately 1,000 men, in the last year of the war a combat unit called *Einheit* or *Einsatzgruppe Ezquerra* (after the name of its leader) would be formed, a unit integrated into the 11th SS Grenadiers SS Nordland (original name 11.SS-Panzergrenadier-Freiwilligen-Nordland Division), which would become involved in the defensive combat of the capital of the Reich.

Although there are reports from the Spanish diplomatic corps on its existence, the only direct source which deals with it is the book entitled *Berlin, a vida o muerte*, (Berlin, life or death) written by the leader of the unit, Miguel Ezquerra.

These memoires, as they are do not match other accounts, have given rise to incredulousness on the part of many regarding the events they recount.

It is true that regarding the battle in Berlin, Ezquerra tells of a number of events where he and his men risked their lives in the violent combat which they carried out under intense continuous artillery fire and Soviet gunfire, with some surviving due to nothing short of a miracle. Considered equally miraculous is the fact that Ezquerra, despite eventually being captured by the Russians, managed to escape and return to Spain by covering hundreds of kilometers through difficult paths in a Europe where war had recently finished, along paths where many of the men that were returning to their homes were held by allied or Russian forces, or betrayed by informers ending up being captured.

Anyone who has lived through these events, simply by having survived them, deserves at least to be listened to and for there to be a certain decree of willingness to believe in the possibility that the unexpected events being recounted may be true. Events can be more or less precise, which is why they can be considered fictitious. He can be given the same vote of confidence which any man who risks his life for his ideals deserves. This, together with the fact that he is a Spanish soldier with many years of service and combat and, that he voluntarily joined the German side in spite of its imminent defeat, are proof of his spirit and ability to fight, as well as that of the men who joined his unit.

Another event that has also been questioned regarding the account given in Ezquerra' s book, is the decoration that he was awarded by Adolf Hitler. Whether this is true or not, it certainly was the case that in those last days plenty of medals were awarded to the defenders of the capital, which is why, whilst knowing that there will never be any hard proof of this, it can be accepted as true that this really happened as recounted in the book.

The existence of this unit is therefore quite unknown, and not often talked about in books. This text aims to elaborate on these facts, as well as the particular characteristics of the combat in Berlin and the suffering undergone by these Spaniards to defend an ideal and their military pride, despite the particularly adverse situation they found themselves in.

Capitalizing on the ever more numerous texts dealing with the combat in Berlin, this book aims to fit into the information already available and as far as possible, into the dates of the various action of the men under the command of Ezquerra in the streets of Berlin.

It will also look at the uniforms, emblems and weaponry used by these men during the days when they were battling on the streets of the German capital. Lastly it will look at the characteristics of the fighting in the city.

The lack of winter camouflage uniforms turned the Spanish into easy targets during the SDV combats on the Eastern front.

PREVIOUS PAGE: Inspection of the troops.

Various members of the Division pose for the camera in a snowy Russian forest.

A trip in a horse drawn carriage to relax for a few minutes away from the tension on the Russian front.

General Muñoz Grandes with various German High Commanders visiting the SDV.

The Spanish good sense of humor was essential when dealing with the severity of the Russian winter.

The immense size of the USSR meant supplies by rail were of vital importance for the troops of the Reich.

Members of the Division wrapped up against the freezing Soviet climate.

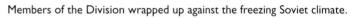

Campaign mass for the members of the division.

The motorization of the Spanish Division forces was minimal, as the SDV was categorized as self-transporting.

Soldier from the Division resting on the Russian front. The metallic emblem of the yoke and arrows can be seen on the side of his cap.

The uniform of the Spanish in the SDV was the same as that of the Germans, with the addition of the Spanish shield on the right arm. When some of them joined the *Wehrmacht* in the last year of the war, there was practically no difference from their German comrades.

Visit from General Esteban-Infantes
to the offices of the newspaper of the
SDV. *La Hoja de Campaña* in Reval.

Esteban-Infantes during his visit
to Reval (present day Tallin).

Visit from General Esteban-Infantes to the rearguard service of the *Wehrmacht*.

On both pages (above).
Images of an academy for training
Wehrmacht sub officers which
General Esteban-Infantes visited
during his command of the SDV.

On both pages (below)
Commemorative meal for
General Esteban-Infantes in the
Narva Transmissions School.

Below: Esteban-Infantes together with
Colonel Göring, head of the Narva
Transmissions School.

General Esteban-Infantes leaving with various officers in a visit to some installations of the Kriegsmarine in the Baltic.

General Esteban-Infantes giving the Great Cross of Military Merit to Field marshal von Klücher, head of the Army Group North, in June 1942.

Sub officer of the SDV with his MP-40 around his neck and two stick grenades at his waist.

SDV anti-tank post. The increase in the armament of the Soviet combat tanks rendered the Spanish anti-tank weapons obsolete. In the last year of the war the *panzerfaust* became the "star" weapon against the all powerful Soviet armored vehicles.

Gunner and assistant from a MG-34 machine gun team of the SDV with camouflage smocks on the Russian front.

A soldier carrying a sign of the 263rd Infantry Regiment under the command of Colonel Vierna Trápaga.

Two Spanish soldiers waiting crouched down by the protection of their barricade.

MG-34 machine gun team with the gunner at the front followed by his helper transporting two boxes of ammunition.

Commander Osés, of the 250th Mobile Reserve Battalion of the SDV. Its unit, mostly made up of professional soldiers, showed evidence of Spanish soldiers' combat ability on Soviet terrain.

A guard of honor accompanying the coffin of a fallen member of the division being transported by a cart in Russian territory.

The sad farewell to a comrade on Russian soil.

General Moscardó visited the SDV between November and December 1941 under the command of Muñoz Grandes. Whilst there, he attended the burial of one of the fallen Spanish soldiers.

Photographs courtesy of Luis E. Togores.

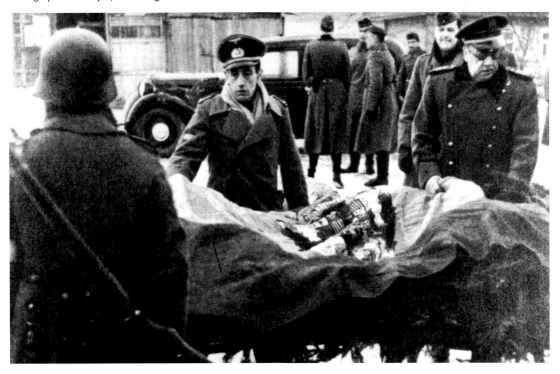

German and Spanish flags cover the coffins of two bodies of division members who fell in the fight against the Soviets. Photograph courtesy of Luis E. Togores.

General Esteban-Infantes at the burial of a division member. *Photograph courtesy of Luis E. Togores.*

"I had a comrade ...
one of the best of all."

Photographs courtesy of Luis E. Togores.

Riga Cemetery, the resting place of men of various nationalities who made up the German Armed Forces. *Photograph courtesy of Luis E. Togores.*

Prayer for the dead in the Königsberg hospital cemetery. *Photograph courtesy of Luis E. Togores.*

Not all the members of the division were able to be buried properly, as the picture shows, due to the pressure put on the Spanish-German lines by the Soviets.

BELOW. Russian women attend the burial of SDV soldiers. The civilians' good treatment of the Spanish allowed for certain links of affection to be created between some of them. *Photographs courtesy of Luis E. Togores.*

Memorial to the fallen at the cemetery of the campaign hospital of the SDV, otherwise known as the 250th Infantry Division of the *Wehrmacht*. *Photograph courtesy of Luis E. Togores.*

General Muñoz Grandes inspecting the troops that are going to be repatriated after their difficult time on the Russian front. *Photograph courtesy of Luis E. Togores.*

The time to leave is approaching and the men, piled into their wagons, are surprised to see General Muñoz Grandes, their current leader. Below. Many division members cannot hide their joy as the time to go home approaches despite being crowded together in the railroad cars taking them to the rear guard. Photographs courtesy of Luis E. Togores.

General Muñoz Grandes smokes a cigarette whilst he addresses a farewell to the first group from the SDV being repatriated. The cold Soviet climate can be seen in the uniforms used by the Spanish. Below: Another moment from the first repatriation of members of the Division in March 1942, which was personally attended by General Muñoz Grandes with the SDV staff officers. *Photographs courtesy of Luis E. Togores.*

Farewell between comrades before leaving for Spain after being on the Eastern front. On the right sleeve of the soldier with a moustache is the Silver Palm of the Falange, one of the most important decorations of the Party. General Muñoz Grandes was always well liked by his men, in the lower photograph he is seeing off the first group of volunteers returning to Spain after serving on the Russian Front for seven months. *Photographs courtesy of Luis E. Togores.*

Division members return to Spain being looked after by German women personnel. *Photograph courtesy of Luis E. Togores.*

Javier Sánchez Carrilero with comrades on the repatriation train. The good humor of the Spanish was maintained on many occasions despite the circumstances of their time spent on the Russian Front. *Photograph courtesy of Luis E. Togores.*

Opposite page.
Spanish military
ex-combatants in Russia

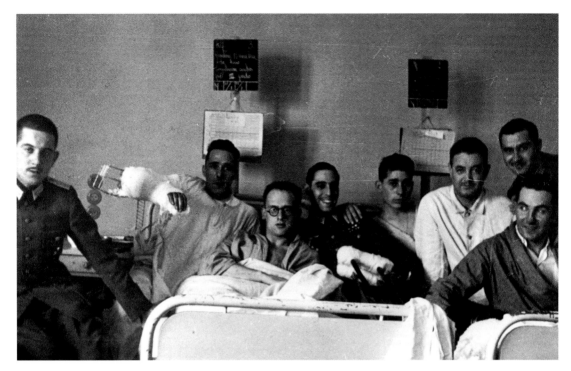

Various wounded from the SDV pose for the photograph in the rearguard hospital.
Photograph courtesy of Luis E. Togores.

Parade of a group of ex-division members after their return to Spain from the Eastern Front.
Photograph courtesy of Luis E. Togores.

Return of Colonel Pimentel to Spain after his time in the SDV.
Photograph courtesy of Luis E. Togores.

Return of Colonel Pimentel, head of the 262 Infantry Regiment
of 250th Infantry Division of the *Wehrmacht*, with his men.
Photograph courtesy of Luis E. Togores.

Mass reception for General Muñoz Grandes at the North Station in Madrid December 18, 1942.
Photograph courtesy of Luis E. Togores.

Wounded members of the SDV in the Maudes hospital in Madrid.
Photograph courtesy of Luis E. Togores.

This proud
veteran of the
Russian Front
shows a mixture
of German and
Spanish insignias.
*Photograph courtesy
of Luis E. Togores.*

Three SDV veteran
attend classes
at Complutense
University
wearing their blue
shirts bearing
the *Wehrmacht*
eagle, the Iron
Cross Second
Class and other
Spanish emblems.
*Photograph courtesy
of Luis E. Togores.*

General Esteban-Infantes presides over the act of formation of the SDV in the presence of General German Kleffel. Underneath. Speech by General Esteban-Infantes at another instance of the act of formation of the SLV and the departure of the last members of the division. *Photographs courtesy of Luis E. Togores*.

The Spanish soldiers, despite initial negative impressions on the German High Command, won their respect and affection with their countless SDV and SLV actions. *Photograph courtesy of Luis E. Togores.*

Colonel García Navarro in the act of saluting one of his decorated men. *Photograph courtesy of Luis E. Togores.*

This photograph presided over by Colonel García Navarro shows the heterogeneous uniform of boots, pants, belts, jackets and caps used by the German Armed Forces in the last years of the conflict. Below: Spanish soldiers, dressed for combat, it was not for nothing that many of the members of the SDV and the SLV, veterans of the Spanish Civil War, were always a desired comrades for German soldiers. *Photographs courtesy of Luis E. Togores.*

Colonel García Navarro, head of the SLV, with General Amado Loriga to his left. The latter played a significant role in the recruitment of members to the SLV. *Photograph courtesy of Luis E. Togores.*

Three legion members sharing some cigarettes. *Photograph courtesy of Luis E. Togores.*

Colonel García Navarro talks
to his staff officers in Pruna.
Photographs courtesy of Luis E. Togores.

Formation of the SLV with the national flag in Stablack-Süd.
Photograph courtesy of Luis E. Togores.

Spanish soldiers pose next to three comrades belonging to the Flemish
Legion on some artillery. *Photograph courtesy of Luis E. Togores.*

Award of a decoration to Colonel García Navarro shortly before his return to Spain.
Photograph courtesy of Luis E. Togores.

Visit from a German delegation to the SLV installations accompanied by its leader.
Photograph courtesy of Luis E. Togores.

Four SLV members pose with their Spanish uniforms with German insignias in the Stablack-Süd barracks. Below: Inspection of the three SLV flags, already with their Spanish uniforms, by the head of the Königsberg Army Corps, General Wodrig. After the official dismissal of the SLV from the German Armed Forces, the story began for hundreds of Spanish who, even with the risk of losing their nationality, continued the war on the German side. *Photographs courtesy of Luis E. Togores*..

For many of the members of the Legion, amongst whom was Ricardo Botet, the war was still not over, which is why they decided not to return to Spain and to enlist again in the German Armed Forces. Left: Colonel García Navarro at a moving farewell of the SLV.

Below: Despite its short existence the SLV knew how to maintain the legacy of courage, pride and devotion left by the SDV in its fight against the Soviets.

Photographs courtesy of Luis E. Togores.

The SLV, after this ceremony, no longer belonged to the *Wehrmacht*.

Below: Various Spanish and German leaders pose for the photographer, amongst whom can be seen Colonel García Navarro (first on the left) and General Walter Model (third on the left).

Photographs courtesy of Luis E. Togores.

Shot of the moment when Colonel García Navarro informed the SLV of the repatriation of its men, "… The news is sad and significant. Spain, in accordance with the German Government, is taking the painful, even tragic, step of agreeing to our repatriation." *Photograph courtesy of Luis E. Togores.*

Arrival of General Lindemann and Colonel García Navarro at the general barracks of the 121st German Infantry Division in December 1943.

Below. Image of the farewell ceremony.

Photographs courtesy of Luis E. Togores.

THE FORMATION OF UNITS
ON VARIOUS FRONTS

Spain did not take part in the Second World War however many Spaniards did on one side or another.

After the Civil War, Francisco Franco's regime found itself in debt, in moral and material terms, to Adolf Hitler's Germany and Benito Mussolini's Italy, which, together with the affinity with their government, led to activities to align Spain inside the Axis.

As the situation in Spanish after three years of war was far from suitable for taking on new clashes and as Francisco Franco was aware of this, this alliance was never able to fruition.

The invasion of the Soviet Union by the Axis troops led to the Spanish government, as mentioned previously, meeting the demands of many ex-combatants, as well as that of the young men who had not had the opportunity to fight in the Spanish Civil War, posted in the Spanish Division of Volunteers (SDV), commonly known as the Blue Division to continue the fight against communism which had already started in the Spanish confrontation. The volunteers were mainly people with strong ideological convictions, enabling them to act with immense drive and courage when the time came to fight despite the complicated situation they had to face on the Northern Soviet Front.

The onset of the Second World War and strong pressure by the allies to withdraw Spanish troops under German command, led the Spanish government to consider the possibility of repatriating the Blue Division (integrated into the German Land Army) and the Blue Squadron (integrated into the German Armed Forces).

Among the threats which led to the withdrawal of the Blue Division in November 1943 was the allied plan to invade the Canary Islands. Politically, the circumstances were rather too complex for the Spanish government to manage to keep a balance between the Axis and the allies, but on the other hand there was the strong desire of thousands of members of the division not to leave their comrades fighting against the Soviets in the lurch. All of this led to the withdrawal being carried out in two parts. Firstly, the Blue Division was repatriated, with its last war action taking place on October 5, the same day on which the order to abandon the Front was received. It was officially dissolved on November 17 and its last members left the Front on December 24, 1943. When the SDV left some 2,200 men stayed in Russia still integrated into the German Army, in a unit called the Spanish Legion of Volunteers (SLV) also known as the Blue Legion, at the orders of Colonel Navarro. On November 17, General Esteban-Infantes signed the order to create the SLV. This Legion was incorporated into the heart of the 121st German Infantry Division.

However the government of the allies were not prepared to allow this clever "double play" by the Spanish government, and increased their communication with the Spanish authorities putting even more pressure on them, until they achieved the Legion's withdrawal from the Front, and the repatriation of its men to Spain. The return began on March 17; the transmissions unit started off the departure, followed by other small units. The first train with soldiers arrived at the Spanish border on March 28, and the last on April 11, 1944. Therefore, by April 12, 1944 all the members of the Blue Legion were on Spanish land, with only small groups left in Germany who were in charge of completing all the documentation, selling off left over materials and repatriating the Spanish patients from the hospitals in Königsberg and Riga; at least this was their function in theory, but, as will be seen, this was not exactly the case.

Among many of the men who had been ordered to withdraw the idea of leaving their comrades was taking root when the situation began to become very tense on the Eastern Front. The fight for them was not over. This situation encouraged some of them to stay on in Germany and continue with their fight against Bolshevism; but again, strong pressure from the allies forced the Spanish government to consider any Spanish military personnel who did not return with their expeditionary contingent as deserters. When reading texts on this matter it should be remembered that in that period the Royal Decree, promulgated on June 24, 1889, was in force, stating that any citizen who served in a foreign army in war would lose their nationality unless the citizen in question was in possession of special permission from the Head of State. Specifically, Article 25 of the First Title of the First Book of the Spanish Civil Code states this in the following manner (published by Royal Decree July 24, 1889):

1. Spaniards who are not native will lose their nationality:
    a) When, for a period of three years, they exclusively use the nationality that they have renounced when taking Spanish nationality.
    b) When they voluntarily enter into armed service or assume political office in a foreign country against the express prohibition of the Government.

2. The final ruling that the interested party has taken by falsehood, deception or fraud, the acquisition of Spanish nationality results in such an acquisition being nullified, if there will be no adverse effects for third parties in good faith. The act of nullifying will be carried out by the Public Prosecutor's office or by virtue of denunciation, within fifteen years.

Based on this the Spanish government was able to convert a large number of men who opted to continue fighting into stateless people, however the in the title of this article it clearly states: "The Spanish who are not native will lose their nationality…", by this it can be understood that it is not directed at Spaniards who are native, in other words, the majority of Spaniards.

In any case, the Spanish government, possibly without being able to admit that all those who were doing military service in warring nations would lose their Spanish nationality, thought that each day the support given to the powers of the Axis was less productive and that it would be more politically correct to avoid the presence of Spanish military units in the conflict as much as possible. This situation was reflected in the official declaration from the Spanish government in January 1944 with which it showed its opposition to those with Spanish nationality being incorporated in the various military organizations in Germany (the text of this official declaration is missing, but its existence is recorded in various texts dealing with the subject).

This official declaration aimed to put an end to the clandestine crossing of the Spanish-French border by Spaniards who had been encouraged by the German secret service in Spain and by Falangist leaders to join the German Armed Forces.

However, Clyde Clark (taken from the Gutenberg webpage) comments that the Spanish legislation in force between December 21, 1943 and January 1, 1945 guaranteed amnesty to those recruited by other countries or deserters who stayed abroad. (Clark, *Evolution of the Franco Regime* (n.p., 1951), 442, 555-56). Although reference should be made to the existing law, which was published by Royal Decree on July 24, 1889, as previously mentioned, and that was possibly used incorrectly to achieve the government's intended aim.

The government's aim was to put the Spanish "volunteers" between a rock and a hard place: this tough decision had to be made by all those whose intention it was to stay at their posts facing the unrelenting Soviet advance. This led to many of them eventually abandoning their idealism and "romanticism" and coming back down to earth. The war was beginning to seem lost for the countries of the Axis and Spain could not maintain the policy that three years earlier brought it closer to them.

But these vicissitudes would not stop a significant handful of solders from persevering with their idealism and staying with German troops. These men would not be alone, as from Spain, in the most pro-German circles, a rather high number of men (mostly ex-combatants from the Blue Division), given the circumstances, thought about returning to Germany to join independently.

From before the Blue Legion's repatriation, in some circles close to the Falange, the training of a new unit of Spanish troops to be in the service of the Germans was planned. The recruitment had to be carried out in secret to avoid being found out by Francisco Franco's government, and it was undertaken mainly in Spain itself using the meetings of the Falange and groups of veterans from the Blue Division.

Other volunteers stayed in Germany openly, as since the departure of the Legion to Spain, some men were "invited" by German officials to stay in the conflict by enlisting in Wehrmacht units. Yet other Spanish combatants were Spanish workers who had worked in the Reich for a long time and considered enlisting in the German army to be economically and socially beneficial.

In addition some of the exiled Spaniards (former Republicans) who were recruited after having served in Reich work battalions, had in some cases been obliged to wear the German uniform. Exceptional cases of men who preferred to serve together with other Spaniards than stay in the conditions in which they found themselves.

Spanish authorities gave the order to "armor" the Pyrenees border passes, in direct contact with occupied France. The Civil Guard received strict orders to block the pass, with the order to shoot if necessary. And even though these orders were carried out to the letter, it is true that in some cases these members of the Civil Guard could not help but feel great respect towards these men who risked their lives and even their own nationality to cross a border which would take them to the chaos of war once again. Some of these men, former members of the Division, did not forget the oath to fight against Bolshevism that they had taken together with their German comrades in arms: "I swear to God, that in the fight against Bolshevism I will unconditionally obey the Captain General of the armed forces, Adolf Hitler, and as a loyal soldier I am ready, whenever called upon, to give up my life for this oath."

Although many of them were shot at or even shot down when they tried to cross the border, others managed to get to France, where the Germans who knew the situation in Spain, received them with practically open arms. To organize them, the Germans established recruitment stations where they

	E 44	F 44	M 44	A 44	M 44	J 44	JU 44	A 44	S 44	O 44	N 44	D 44	E 45	F 45	M 45	A 45	M 45
SONDERSTAB F																	
STABLACK SÜD				15		PRIMEROS											
VIENA (B. FANTASMA)						PRIMEROS											
HALL TIROL (101 Y 102)																	
BRANDENBURG (102) y FRANCIA																	
BRANDENBURG (YUG)																	
SKORZENY (ANT BRAN DE FRANCIA)																	
EZQUERRA (OP.ESP CON BRAN Y JAGDVERBANDE SKORZENY)						SEGUNDA QUINCENA	ENTRE BR Y SS	ENTRE BR Y SS	SS								
SD																	
3 GJD (101)																	
STOCKERAU (B. GERMANOCROATA) (101 y 102)													HASTA 25				
24 GJD (102)																	
357 DI (101 Y 102)															FINALES		
WALLONIE																	
29 SS													PRIMEROS				
U.EZQUERRA (NORDLAND)																	
BOZEN																	
DIRLEWANGER																	
17 LUFTWAFFE FELDDIVISION ¿?																	

Approximate indication of the period and length of time spent by Spanish soldiers in the various military units they served in from January 1944. In the first column the *Waffen-SS* and SS units are shown with a shaded background. The other units belong to the *Wehrmacht*, apart from the last one which belongs to the *Luftwaffe*. In the other columns, the dark shade shows the length of time the Spanish spent in these units in a documented manner, whilst the light gray shows stays not documented by the author, even though they may be true according to the indirect dates above them. The 17.*Luftwaffe Felddivision* appears with a question mark, as there is no data at all of Spanish soldiers being in its ranks, although there are some who speak of the possible existence of some Spaniards in it. Obviously, if this is true, it would only be a handful of individuals who had joined up completely independently.

One of the few images of Spanish soldiers in SS uniform. This is the *SS-Oscha* Camargo (to the left of the picture) during the spring of 1945 near to Rodengo-Saiano, in Brescia, in some maneuvers with his unit, the I/WGRdSS81, posted in the 29.*Waffen Grenadier Division der SS italiana (courtesy of Erik Norling).*

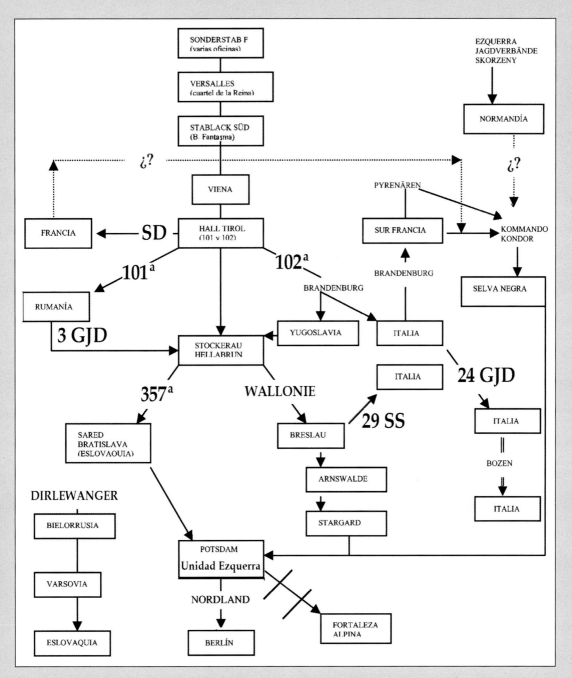

Distribution of the units in which Spanish soldiers were posted from 1944. The solid lines show the transfer of Spaniards between units. The dotted lines show the transfers which were not officially documented. The continuous double line shows the transfer of men which was possible, but not sufficiently demonstrated. The two diagonal lines which show the transfer of a unit to the supposed Alpine fortress, show that the unit did not arrive at its destination. The question marks show that there is doubt as to whether the transfer of men happened as shown and which unit is actually affected.

were given documents and signed up to the German Armed Forces.

The existence of Spaniards posted in the *Waffen-SS* did not go unnoticed by the Spanish authorities, proof of which are two letters sent to the State Department from the Spanish Embassy in Berlin regarding this subject.

The letter dated May 11, 1944 states: Information has been received that currently many ex-combatants from the Blue Division are clandestinely crossing the Pyrenees border, they are doing this safe in the knowledge that they will be well received by the German authorities […] a number of these ex-combatants have been encouraged to enlist in the Flemish Legion of the SS to return to fight on the Russian Front. (A.M.A.E File R-1079).

In another letter sent on July 6, 1944, the Spanish ambassador in Berlin informed the Spanish Secretary of State about the clandestine presence of Spaniards in the German Armed Forces; the following documents this: […] Many of these Spaniards are flaunting national emblems (meaning Spanish emblems) on their uniforms apart from those belonging to the SS […]. (A.M.A.E., File R-1079).

The units of Spanish volunteers, both of the *Heer* and the *Waffen-SS* were set up during 1944 and the first half of 1945 thanks to men from different backgrounds enlisting. The Spaniards who were enrolled were those who were working in Germany in the summer of 1944 and came mainly from two well defined groups; some came from the total of 50,000 workers who left the Reich after the signing of the agreement between the Spanish and German governments in August 1941; others were Spanish emigrants in France, amongst them were those who were there before the Civil War and those who arrived afterwards (meaning the Republicans who fled to France and after the German invasion of the country were recruited by the German authorities, especially for the Todt Organization, a German construction and engineering group which used a significant amount of forced labor).

Although there were obviously all types of ideas, it is clear that many of the workers joined the volunteers' unit more for ideology than for the possibility of leaving the increasingly dangerous factories of the Reich, also targets of the Allied Forces' bombing raids, without forgetting what might occur by deserting should a suitable opportunity arise.

The other group that supplied men to these units of volunteers was that of the aforementioned veterans of the SDV and the SLV who opted to stay in Germany when they were discharged.

The recruitment units (belonging to the *Sonderstab F*) were under the leadership of Dr. Edwin Maxel, who had been part of the staff of the German liaison unit in the Blue Division and was head of this unit and the Blue Legion. He returned to Spain with the Legion, acting from the German Embassy as coordinator of recruitment in direct contact with the *SS-Brigadeführer* Hansen (*El Batallón Fantasma*, Carlos Caballero). The origins of the *Sonderstab F* go back to 1941, when it was created under the command of D. Helmuth Felmy (the initial from his surname was what gave the unit its name), although the relationship of the *Sonderstab F* with the Spanish goes back to the beginning of 1944. The *Sonderstab F* which was in action from January 1944 until August of the same year in the south of France had "offices" in the border areas near to Andorra, Port Bou, Hendaya, and Puigcerdá, with its main headquarters in the city of Lourdes.

Once registered at the headquarters of the *Sonderstab F*, the new recruits were sent to a induction camp in the Quartier of the Reine (Reina barracks) in Versailles. There they were met by Luís García Valdajos, veteran of the Division and the Blue Legion, who was in Versailles, stationed at the Stablack Süd (Eastern Prussia) training centre with the mission of coordinating and escorting the Spanish contingent to Stablack, after they had completed the admissions process and had a medical examination. A small number of men was recruited by the SD (Security Service) to be posted to a new unit created in February 1944: the *Einsatzgruppe Pyrenären* of the *Sonderstab F*, sent to do anti-partisan work by infiltrating the resistance. This mission was favored by the plentiful presence of Spanish anti-fascistas in the maquis of the region. Among the Spanish recruited by the SD there were also exiled Republicans in France who would eventually end up serving as spies.

From June 1944, a group of Spaniards was put into action by the *Sicherheitsdienst* (SD). Its missions were carried out mainly in the Southeast of France, although there are also reports of its participation in actions against the French resistance and against the allies in Normandy. The Spanish embassy in Berlin estimated that toward the summer of 1944 there was approximately 1,500 Spaniards working for the German security services in France, although this figure was possibly exaggerated. This led to official protests by the Spanish government but the German diplomatic corps claimed not to know the facts, justifying them as isolated cases and admitting their inability to do anything about the situation.

The first group of Spaniards under the command of García Valdajos were due to arrive at Stablack around April 15, 1944. Once there, the men were given training, despite the fact that many of them had been combatants previously. That, those men, who were in many cases were more experienced than the average member of the German Army, had to be trained again, struck many as absurd, but, for better or worse, the German organization worked in this fashion. The number of Spanish received at Versailles reached 300 in May 1944 and a number close to 400 in June. After the relevant men were selected they were sent to Eastern Prussia, and were posted in the *Freiwilligen Einheit Stablack* (Stablack Volunteers Unit) under the command of Artillery Captain Wolfram Gräfe and lieutenants Loinant and Panther. Various non-commissioned officers, some information and propaganda officers and a few female assistants (around five or six) also served in the unit. All of them were German and mainly came from the Liaison Staff Officers with the Blue Division and the SLV. The aim was that the complete staffing of this unit would firstly be made up of staff officers and three companies of three grenadier sections each (nine men): it was also considered necessary to create two back-up companies (reserve and training).

In Stablack Süd, García Valdajos' previous title of lieutenant was recognized after the first contingent of men arrived. Once the Spanish were settled in García Valdajos took on an administrative control role in the training of new recruits until June (6th), leaving the purely military tasks to the charge of Miguel Ezquerra. On June 7 García Valdajos moved to Paris to undertake a combat course against the maquis aimed at SS-SD officers, after which he did not return to the training center.

An important fact to bear in mind is that in Stablack Süd they would not accept volunteers who had work, or what amounts to the same thing, they would not recognize the jobs or decoration of those who had served in the SLV or in the SDV. All of them had to serve as soldiers. It was also decided that the Spanish soldiers would wear the uniform of the *Wehrmacht*, receiving the salary of the German soldiers.

The Spanish received the uniform of the *Heer* without any specific emblem denoting nationality and swore an oath to follow Hitler. They later received all equipment with a great variety of weaponry, as well as complete training that included German classes.

At the end of April or beginning of May 1944 the *Spanisches Freiwilligen-Einheit* (Spanish Unit of Volunteers) was created in Stablack, with an initial contingent of close to 250 men, distributed, as had been planned previously into staff officers and three grenadier companies, as well as two back-up companies.

The Unit, which the Spanish posted there began to call the "Ghost Battalion" after its "theoretical" inexistence. The training of the unit did not become more than a rumor amongst the Spanish in Germany, it was never made public there because of the opposition from Franco's government to Spanish citizens continued fighting for the *Wehrmacht*.

All the men that had been "picked" by the Reich, were sent to Stablack Süd, leaving the Versailles barracks practically empty of Spanish troops, after their immediate transfer to Eastern Prussia. In regards to this, a telegram from the Foreign Command Unit of the OKW (*Wehrmacht* High Command) dated May 16, 1944 reports the presence of a single Spaniard in the Versailles barracks, whilst one officer and ten more men had left for Königsberg five days earlier. NARA T77/885/5634629.

At the beginning of June 1944, the unit moved from Stablack to Stockerau and Hollabrun, near to Vienna (the first some fifteen kilometers from the capital and the second twenty-five kilometers away), where the complete unit received the name of *Freiwilligen Einheit Stockerau*. On the outskirts of Vienna, the reserve units (*Freiwilligen Ersatzbataillon*, located in Hollabrun) and training units (*Freiwilligen Ausbildungbataillon*, located in Stockerau) were installed and its third company was still in the process of being set up with the volunteers who continued to arrive (between June 8 and July 20 there were around one hundred and fifty). Its

first companies, already complete, left Solbad Hall im Tirol (this place went by this name between 1938 and 1974, currently it is called Hall im Tirol), near to Innsbruck, to undergo eight weeks of training as mountain troops. The complete unit would receive the name of *Freiwilligen Einheit Solbad Hall*. This training was always led and overseen by officers who had liaised between the Blue Division and the *Heer*. As it was growing, the unit had a mix of young German officers and Spanish officers who were the ex-officers of the Blue Division who joined the unit as has been previously detailed, as simple soldiers, having to rise up through it on their own merits.

In Stockerau, Spanish troops were commanded by German SS Artillery Captain Wolfram Gräfe, who was already known to them as he had led the unit in Stablack Süd.

Lastly the wishes of many Spaniards did not come true, that of serving together in an entirely Spanish unit. In reality it was not the right moment to do this as a Spanish unit could have caused protests from the Spanish government, an increase in allied pressure on Spain, or the subsequent risk of opening up a new front after an allied landing on the Iberian Peninsula. Despite this, there were those who did not wish to form part of any unit that was led by the Spanish, as can be seen in a note from the Command of Foreign Units of the OKW dated May 10, 1944, which reports the dispatch to Königsberg of sixty Spaniards recruited in France who had shown a desire to serve in the German Armed Forces under German command, preferring it to Spanish command (T77/885/5634630). Despite being a unit of volunteers, some complaints quickly arose, mainly resulting from the culture clash and different disciplinary styles between the Spanish and the Germans. As a consequence, around fifty men requested a transfer to a *Schutzkommando* (armed guard and escort units) of the Todt Organization in the south of France.

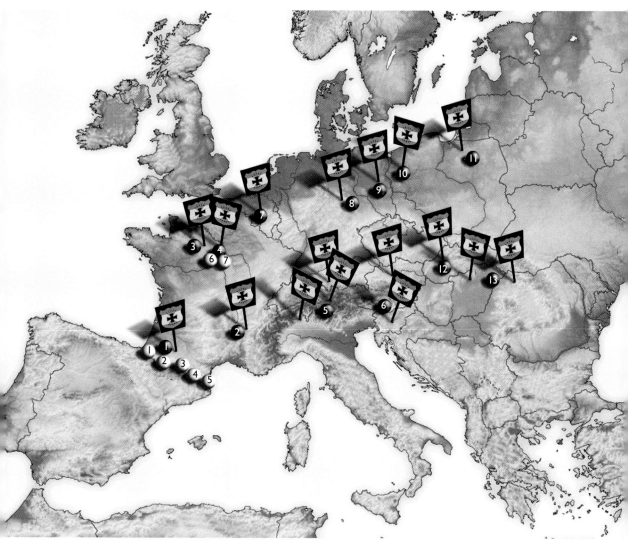

On this map of Europe the white circles in the foreground show the places in France connected with the "recruitment" of the Spanish who wanted to enlist in the German Army after crossing the Pyrenees border.

1. Hendaya
2. Lourdes
3. Andorra
4. Puigcerdá Border

5. Port Bou
6. Versailles
7. Paris

In the background, and shown with black circles, are the various places throughout Europe where Spanish solders were in barracks or fought after the repatriation of the SLV posted in the units of both the *Wehrmacht* and the *Waffen-SS*.

1. Area of the French Pyrenees. Anti-partisan fight.
2. Area of the lower French Alps. Anti-partisan fight.
3. Normandy landings.
4. La Reina barracks. Versailles
5. Northern Italy. Anti-partisan fight.
6. Northern Yugoslavia. Anti-partisan fight.
7. Belgium. Battle of Ardennes.

8. Battle of Berlin.
9. Defense of the River Oder area.
10. Various confrontations. Eastern Front.
11. Various confrontations. Eastern Front.
12. Training in various Austrian locations.
13. Combat in Romania and Slovakia

Note: The symbol used on this map, used by members of the SDV and SLV, is used throughout the book to show the presence of Spanish volunteer units, but it is not necessarily used by other volunteers.

As regards the Spanish volunteers who fought with the *Waffen-SS* and their security forces, it is completely impossible to establish a total number, but there is some agreement that during the summer of 1944 there must have been around 1,000 Spanish (Berlin Document Center microfilm, T354, A3343, U.S. National Archives).

In June 1944, when two Spanish companies arrived at Solbad Hall im Tirol they acquired the official name of *101.Spanische-Freiwilligen Kompanie* and *102. Spanische-Freiwilligen Kompanie*, the former was under the command of lieutenant Panther and the latter under the command of second lieutenant Leiffen.

The *101.Spanische-Freiwilligen Kompanie* had four rifle and one command squad, there is no concrete data on the 102nd, which may have been similar, taking into account that a third company was being formed. The name of the complete unit was *Freiwillige Einheit Solbad Hall.*

At this barracks, as previously stated, the Spanish were trained mainly in exercises specifically for mountain troops (this would determine in the future the areas to which they would be sent to fight) as well as learning how to handle all types of weapons. The camp, near to the city, was located on a tree covered hillside. An old building which had long before functioned as a convent was the command headquarters of the companies training there.

During this training period the by now "typical" clashes between the Spanish and the Germans returned, culminated in the killing of a German soldier by a Spaniard called Echevarría. Obviously, the fact that Spanish soldiers who had been in command served as privates did not help when it came to being treated appropriately by the Germans.

The probable number of men who managed to "meet" in Solbad Hall im Tirol was at least 200 in each of the two compa-

nies formed, with more men arriving at the barracks little by little. Some men who had no training at all were transferred in some cases to the Todt Organization.

After the training was finished in August 1944, the soldiers were posted to German units as diverse as the 357th Infantry Division, the 3rd Mountain Division or anti-partisan units of the 3rd Regiment of the *Brandenburg* Division. Another Spanish contingent served in the SD, and around fifty men carried out anti-partisan tasks in the area of the Pyrenees until they were transferred to the *Jagdverband* of Otto Skorzeny.

The 101st Company, together with the *3.Gebirgs-Division* (belonging to the *XVII Armee Korps* of the Ukrainian Army Group South of the *Wehrmacht*), left from Solbad Hall im Tirol by train for Vienna, from where it left for the outskirts of Budapest. Before leaving Austrian territory, in Vienna, it suffered an Allied aerial attack which it responded to with anti-aerial machine guns carried for that purpose on the railroad convoy. It was the section under the command of Corporal Pérez Eizaguirre which, in turn, had to fight against the attacking planes, resulting in the Corporal being wounded.

After the bombing, the train continued on its way to the Hungarian capital, Budapest. From there it left for the Hungarian city of Debrecen, but not without waiting for a group of sappers to put the parts of the railroad track back in working order as they had been broken after the aerial attacks which occurred in Hungary. From there, in the middle of August 1944 and under the command of second lieutenant Panther, it eventually continued toward what would be its final destination: Bukovina (a region in the north of Romania and Moldavia, to the southeast of Ukraine and the south of the Galitzia region).

The train stopped at the Romanian station of Vatra-Dornei, part of the district of

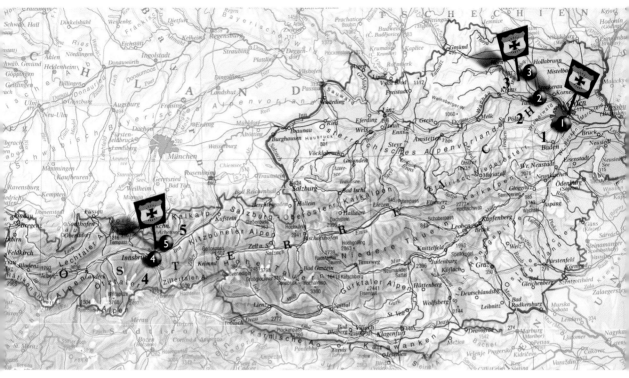

Various locations in Austria where Spanish units were stationed during their reorganization and training after the dissolution of the SLV.

1. Vienna.
2 Stockerau.
3 Hollabrunn.

4 Innsbruck.
5 Solbad Hall im Tirol.

Cámpulong. There the men of the 101st left the train to camp for two days on the outskirts of the town. On the third day Panther ordered the men to ready themselves, and after passing inspection they were sent to the positions of the *3.Gebirgs-Division*, seventy kilometers away, a distance that the Spanish covered on foot. When they arrived their main order was to collaborate with the *3.Gebirgs-Division* to keep the mountain passes open at the places where the German troops would withdraw towards the west in the face of continued pressure from the Red Army.

The Spanish covered villages such as Iacobeni, Valea Putnei and Pajorita, in their new operations front. They eventually arrived at their destination forty-eight hours after their departure from Vatra Dornei, to join the 1st Battalion of the *3.Gebirgs-Division* in Cámpulong (nowadays Cîmpulung Moldovenesc), on the banks of the River Moldova. In just eleven days the Spanish had

Route followed by rail by the 101st Company from Solbad Hall im Tirol to Cámpulong, (Romania) to join the 3.*Gebirgs* Division. The last stretch was completed by foot (see next page).

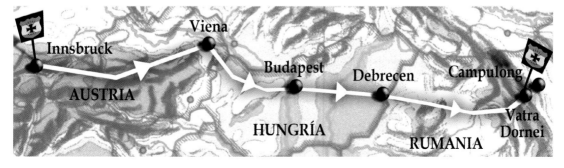

gone from the secure Tyrol to the front lines of a front that was threatened with collapse and being run over by the unstoppable Soviet "red wave."

When the Ukrainian Army Group South of the Wehrmacht collapsed in the face of the Soviet offensive, the *3.Gebirgs-Division* fought for the control of the mountain passes of the Eastern Carpathian Mountains, suffering significant losses (according to different sources there were between fifty-seven and seventy dead, prisoners and disappeared). The tasks that the Spanish undertook would serve to halt the Soviet advance as much as possible, allowing the withdrawal of the German army to be protected: blowing up bridges, sabotage of railroads and roads, establishing defensive posts at strategic points, etc. The Spanish acted in small groups that allowed for precise and silent face to face attacks.

On August 27 Romania changed sides after the coup d' état that deposed Marshal Antonescu, leaving the troops of the Axis in the Carpathian Mountains in an even more complicated situation. The Spanish withdraw from their position to about three kilometers from Cámpulong from August 31 due to the imminent danger of being trapped behind enemy lines.

The 101st Company was then pursued by regular Soviet troops as well as, for some days, Romanian Allies. Many Spanish were killed in this fighting. The survivors of this company were those who covered the withdrawal of the last German forces over the Cámpulong Bridge over the Moldova, blowing up the bridge when the last of the troops had crossed over; next they turned to the southeast in search of Vatra Dornei.

A group of Germans in vehicles finished off the procession of German troops that were fleeing to safer territories in the west, blocking the roads with the aim of halting the rapid Soviet advance.

The Spanish fell back leaving behind villages which became part of the battle front;

Route followed on foot by the Spanish 101st Company from Vatra Dornei to Cámpulong (Cîmpulung Moldovenesc) to join the *3.Gebirgs* Division. To the right a modern map of the east of the Romanian province of Suceava. The places where there are records of the Spanish having passed through on the way to the front are marked.

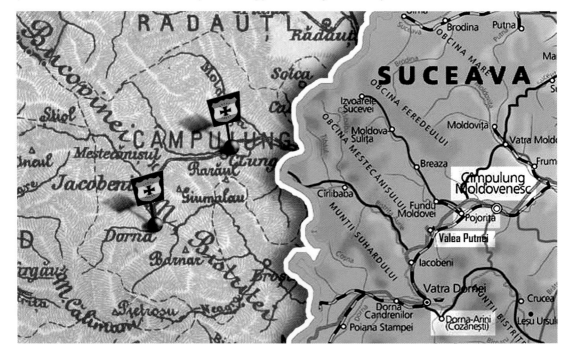

On this page are two pictures of comrades in arms of the Spanish volunteers in the German mountain troops. Above. Soldiers of the 3. *Gebirgsdivision* protecting the withdrawal of their comrades opening fire with a 7.5cm piece of artillery of the type called *leichtes Infanteriegeschütz* 18.

To the right, an expert sniper belonging to the 3. *Gebirgsdivision*. The picture is of *Gefreiter* Matthäus Hetzenauer (1924-2004). This young Austrian served in the *Gebirgsjäger* Regiment-144. He is considered the best "ace" of the Wehrmacht snipers with 345 confirmed deaths. He was awarded the Knight of the Iron Cross on April 17, 1945, a few days before the end of the war.

eventually fortifying themselves on a hill called Muntii Sureanuluni, thirty kilometers from Cámpulong. The remainder of the battered company were left isolated in enemy territory, due as much to the speedy withdrawal of the German troops as the unstoppable Soviet advance towards Hungary, supported by the help given by armed groups mainly belonging to the Romanian Communist Party which did not stop pursuing them.

A complete feeling of abandonment and dejection set in among the eighteen Spanish who remained under the command of a German second lieutenant whose name has not been recorded. The skirmishes continued day after day, although the rugged landscape covered in enormous pine trees and full of craggy terrain favored the Spanish. In spite of this, they suffered losses such as that of Ramón Pérez Eizaguirre, who was captured when leaving his position in one of the barricades defending the Spanish to seek out food in nearby shepherds' huts. This volunteer had carried out the same task on other occasions to procure milk, corn and other food, and had been hit on one occasion by Soviet marksmen but, as luck would have it, on September 20 another encounter with the ever increasing Russian patrols this time resulted in his capture.

The men of the 101st were finally able to leave behind the dangerous Romanian mountains to enter into no less dangerous Hungarian territory. The aim of the meager group of Spanish was to reach the relatively safety of Austria, leaving behind the unoccupied lands of Hungary. Possible they managed to "hook up to" a goods train that took them to their destination, as Vadillo suggests in his book *Los Irreductibles*. Worn out and tattered by nearly two months of continued combat and significant physical and emotional wear and tear, there were possibly only a dozen or so Spanish survivors who were able to join up with their compatriots in Stockerau and Hollabrunn at the end of October. The

Spanish troops together with the *3.Gebirgs-Division* received various commendations, decorations and promotions due to their performance in the Carpathians.

It is possible that a number of the men that made up a Company (102nd) were given the task of carrying out tasks in the fight against the partisans in Yugoslavia toward the middle of August (possibly the 16th), establishing their general barracks in Celje, in German Sachsenfeld, (part of the municipality of Zalec), in present day Slovenia.

It seems that the Spanish, commanded by Lieutenant Ortiz, were integrated into the 8th Company of the 2nd Battalion of the 3rd Regiment of the *Brandenburg* Division, although there are some doubts as to which unit they were assigned to. This unit became a Franco-Spanish company and was led by either Captain Stregner (according to Gerard LeMarec in *Les français sous le casque allemand*) or Captain Traege, (according to Antonio Muñoz in *Forgotten Legions*).

It would appear that, this unit was formed of a total of 250 men, amongst whom the Spanish were a minority, as at least 180 came from France. Some of these men stayed in the north of Yugoslavia with the order to fight against Tito's partisans, although it is not recorded that there were actually many encounters with them. Another group extended its anti-partisan tasks across Italy headed by lieutenants Ortiz and Demetrio to follow the 7th Company, which was mainly Italian in origin.

They fought against the Italian partisans in places such as Bevagna, Perugia, Arsoli,Carsoli, Avezzano and Terni. After that they were in the Arezzo and Cittá di Castello areas, later joining up with other "brandemburgers" to the north of Turin in September 1944 (in Ivrea specifically), from which they withdrew to the south of France.

At the end of October, as a result of the advance of the Soviet Army and Tito's

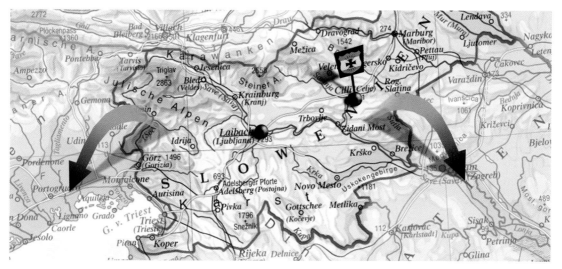

Map of Slovenia showing Celje and the capital Ljubiana. The Spanish of the 102nd Company posted in the 8th Company of the 2nd Battalion of the 3rd Regiment of the *Brandenburg* Division carried out action in the area of Celje in August 1944. Various units of these troops were active in the north of Italy (left) and of Yugoslavia (right).

Yugoslavian forces, the Spanish troops located in the north of Yugoslavia withdrew first to Hollabrunn and in December to Stockerau.

Regarding the troops stationed in the north of Italy, during this withdrawal some of the Spanish posted in them stayed behind, being absorbed into the *59.SS-Gebirgsjäger-Regiment* of the *24. Waffen-Gebirgs-(Karstjäger)-Division der SS del Sturmbannführer Werner Hahn*. Here they assembled in a Spanish company under the name *5.Kmp./II.Btl. (Spanish-Kmp.)*, belonging to the *SS-Gebirgs-Regiment 59*, under the command of *W-Ustuf.* José Ortiz Fernández. Other names of the Spanish members of this company are: *W-Ustuf* Trápaga, who, according to Sourd in his book *Croisés d´un idéal*, held the rank of *Oberscharführer*, Antonio Pardo and Federico Martínez (information taken from the *Axis History Forum AHF*). According to Ortiz's testimony, he undertook a training course in Solbad Hall im Tirol to become an officer of the *Waffen-SS*, after which he recruited Spaniards for factories and prison camps on the outskirts of Vienna. With these men he increased the potential of his 5th Company of the 2nd Battalion, which he would command with the rank of *Untersturmführer*. The section heads were Trápaga and *Unterscharführer* Meleiro, Ozores, Millán and Solís, all veteran sergeants of the Spanish Division of Volunteers except Trápaga, who due to passing the medical examination, (also according to Sourd), could not join them.

The *Karstjäger* fought from November 1944 mainly in the Friuli-Venezia Giulia region, in northeast Italy, and also in the west of Slovenia, as well as in Croatia, with considerable success. The Spanish company was fully operative with an approximate number of 100 men (according to Sourd) between November and December, taking part in anti-partisan missions in Villach and Pontebba and later in Tolmezzo. According to Sourd, in March 1945 it was in action in the Trieste area in the battle for the city of Gorizia (on the present day border between Italy and Slovenia) against Tito's partisans. According to the testimony of a German veteran of the Karstjäger, the Spanish company proved itself to be very aggressive in the fights which mainly took place in the Chiaporano sector, where the fight ended up in face to face combat. Many of

69

the wounded in these fights were transferred to campaign hospitals in Udine and Gorizia. The final stage ended in tragedy, after Gorizia was taken by the partisans, the wounded were massacred. Among them were at least fourteen Spanish of the *Karstjäger*.

On April 8 (although according to Sourd there are other sources which put these events in March) the section commanded by *Oberscharführer* Trápaga was surrounded on the Ponte di Canale, suffering significant losses.

The men of the *Karstjäger* in the last days of the war also fought in the regions attacked by the English troops, coming up against the famous "Desert Rats" of the 8th Army.

Particularly in the last stages of the conflict the task of the German Division was to locate the groups of the Italian resistance and Yugoslavian partisan communists, becoming more and more involved in the missions of brutal excesses and atrocities. Especially fierce was the behavior of the Italian members of the Division, as well as that of the Slovenians and Croatians, in the operations carried out in their countries, to the east of the Italian area of operations.

After the surrender of the German Army, in the first few days of May 1945, the Spanish volunteers received authorization to flee and try to get back to Spain; despite this, the fighting against Tito' s Yugoslavian partisans in Trieste lasted until May 5 1945, after British troops (8th Army) had already occupied all of this area as well as the city (May 2).

The men who stayed in Yugoslavia withdrew in October to Austria. The fighting continued during the withdrawal to the River Drava, as well as the area of Slovenia, under German control until the last day of the war, or Carinthia (Kärnten en German) in Austria until May 10, where they finally surrendered to American troops two days after the surrender of the Reich (according to Sourd, the date of the final surrender of these men was May 9).

Men from this 102nd Company in Italy and Yugoslavia abandoned the rape and pillage, among the many atrocities committed in the confrontations they had mainly with Yugoslavian partisans and to a lesser extent the Italian partisans.

Among the luckiest of those who did not flee and who stayed behind, were those who handed themselves in to American troops, ending up imprisoned in concentration camps; but many of them were captured and killed by partisans. Some of them tried to escape to the Spanish Consulate in Venice, but were unsuccessful due to the impressive pressure put on them by the new pro-communist Italian authorities. Others tried via Milan, but were discovered by communist partisans who dashed their hopes to return to the country. Eventually, some of them, such as Sergeant José María Ozores, did manage to escape and return to Spain after surviving many difficulties and dangers in the north of Italy.

The arrival of the escaped Spanish was so significant, that in November 1945, months after the conflict had ended in Europe, a couple of hundred Spaniards stayed in Italy in the hope of being repatriated by the Spanish Embassy. Of them, the majority were veterans of the *Karstjäger* and, to a lesser degree, other units, Sourd states that this included the Ezquerra Unit, and some ex-workers in the Reich.

As regards the Spanish of the Brandenburg withdrawn to France, the staff officers of the E Army Group, situated in the south of France, tried to form a company of Spanish legionnaires. According to Antonio Muñoz (Forgotten Legions, page 198), men of the *8.Kompanie II.Bataillon 3.Regiment "BR"*, sub unit where the Spanish were stationed, made up the so-called *Streifkorps Biscaya* as part of the *Streifkorps Süd-Frankreich*. Joining with these men, led by lieutenant Demetrio from July 1944, were some Spanish from the Todt Organization, constituting the so-called

SS *Karstjäger* in action. Below, handling a piece of mountain artillery.

Below: Conveniently covered and camouflaged, the men of the *Karstjäger* Division during combat training in the open.

Einsatzgruppe Pyrenären, which fought the maquis in the south and southeast of France. The unit was made up of around fifty men.

According to Sourd, this *Einsatzgruppe Pyrenären* was made up directly from the *Sonderstab F* way back in January 1944, although this point is debatable as there is no other source confirming it, more credible is the "*Brandenburg*" origin of the unit.

During its period of activity the *Einsatzgruppe Pyrenären* distinguished itself in the anti-partisan fight against the maquis (very plentiful in south east France). As many of these maquis had previous fought for the Republic during the Spanish Civil War, in the course of the aggressive clashes there were many examples of extreme cruelty from both sides.

During the existence of the *Einsatzgruppe Pyrenären* it happened that a couple of men stationed in the SD were temporarily posted to this unit with the task of "hunting" an important member of the OSS (U.S. Office of Strategic Services) which used the Pyrenees as an operations camp in strict collaboration with the French Resistance. One of these men was Rufino Luís García Valdajos, who had been posted to the *Sonderstab F* and was "captured" by the SD, which he would join with the rank of SD *Obersturmführer*. The other man, also Spanish, a friend and comrade of García Valdajos was Ricardo Botet Moro, also "captured" in Stablack Süd by a SD officer, called either Ellis or Ehlers (according to Sourd).

Returning to the location of the OSS agent in the Pyrenees, it seems that this was not possible as, according to the Spanish agents in the SD, they were "abandoned" somewhere in the southeast of France with civilian clothes and a sum of money to live on for a while but they did not have exact information as to where, how and when to capture the American agent. The result was that which Botet relates: "We did not try to find anyone. We did not completely unders-

tand the orders and neither did we have any idea where to start the search" (in Sourd).

Miguel Ezquerra, who had also been "captured" by the SD, incorporated with the rank of *SD Hauptsturmführer*, took part in various anti-guerrilla missions in the spring and summer of 1944 in the south of France.

The Spanish *Einsatzgruppe Pyrenären* unit should have been formed in Pamiers (in the French district of the department of Ariége), although as it was the summer of 1944 after the Normandy landing, it was difficult to organize, as there were not a few who were waiting for the allied occupation in order to "disappear." Eventually the *Einsatzgruppe Pyrenären* withdrew from France together with the Streifkorps Süd-Frankreich during the summer of 1944 when faced with the advance of the allied forces.

In September, when the *Abwehr* (German intelligence service) was in the process of being absorbed by the *Sicherheitsdienst* (SD) (security service), the *Streifkorps Süd-Frankreich* was transferred to the *SS-Jagdverband Südwest*, a formation under the command of *Obersturmbannführer* Otto Skorzeny. (Sourd states that these facts occurred in June, although after consulting different sources it seems more credible that it happened in September, taking into account that in July there was an assassination attempt on Hitler which accelerated the process).

The *SS-Jagdverband Südwest* of Skorzeny had the force of a small regiment, with the following organization (according to facts from Sourd):

- *Stab und Kampfschule.*
- *SS Jadgeinsatz Italien* (made up of Italian volunteers).
- *SS Jadgeinsatz Nordfrankreich* (made up of French volunteers).
- *SS Jadgeinsatz Südfrankreich* (made up of French and Spanish volunteers).

The fading armored German forces were still feared rivals for their opponents until the end of the conflict. In the photograph, a Panther tank meets with SS *Panzergrenadier* troops.

The changeover to the Skorzeny unit by men belonging to the *Brandenburg* unit was motivated by the change of task which was assigned to the latter. After the plot on July 20, 1944 to kill Hitler, Canaris and other high commands of the *Abwehr*, that controlled the Division, were connected with the events. Immediately the control of the Division passed over to the SD, to later be turned into a conventional combat unit (although considered élite), and as the *Infanterie-Division Brandenburg* was sent to the eastern front. Around 1,800 men from the *Brandenburg* managed to be transferred to the *SS-Jagdverband* from *Obersturmbannführer* Skorzeny, "attaching"

themselves to their special operations on the western front.

Possibly, Demetrio's men were attached to the *Einsatzgruppe Pyrenären*, perhaps some men of "special operations" under the command of Miguel Ezquerra belonging to Skorzeny's unit, (they had already taken part in the Normandy sector, around 20-30 men according to Sourd), together with the so-called *Kommando Kondor* attached to the *SS-Jagdeinsatz Süd-Frankreich*. This unit was posted to a base near to the Alsatian area of Molsheim to fight the infiltrations of French collaborators in the liberated regions.

These Spanish, according to Sourd, like their comrades of other nationalities, participated in various training courses in sabotage tactics and special operations. These courses took place in Tiefenthal and Wiesbaden between October and November 1944 (lasting three weeks) and also an advanced course between the months of January and March 1945 (lasting a total of three or four days). From January 1945, the Spanish of the *Kommando Kondor* became part of the reconnaissance and sabotage in the rearguard of the 7th US Army.

In April 1945, the *SS-Jagdverband Südwest* joined with the *SS-Jagdverband Mitte*; at that time the latter was personally led by Skorzeny.

The remainder of these troops fought on the western front in April 1945, after passing through the centre of the concentration of Spanish troops in Potsdam in the charge of Ezquerra. As their mission these men had to make up part of the defensive system of the Alpine fortress (Alpenfestung in German, a large area of German resistance in the Bavarian and Austrian mountains which was never created), the imminent German collapse and the multiple difficulties involved in moving about stopped their arrival in the area, leading to them being dissolved in the last days of the war fleeing toward the Austrian mountains, dressed in civilian clothes and with the aim of taking any opportunity to return to their native country.

Going back to October 1944 will show how the remainder of these Spanish units that fought in Yugoslavia (102nd Company) were grouped together, in Stockerau and Hollabrunn, with those that fought in the Carpathians (101st Company), and with the third company that was formed of the volunteers that had continued to arrive (the "leftovers" of the *Sonderstab F* were transferred to Stockerau in Autumn of 1944, where they stayed until the end of the war carrying out recruitment work and organization of the recently arrived Spanish).

Although the project of creating a unit of Spanish volunteers was still in force during this period, the *SpanischesFreiwilligen-Einheit* was incorporated into the Croatian reserve brigade (*Kroatisches-Ersatz-Brigade*) which provided replacements for the German-Croatian divisions of the 369th, 373rd and 392nd *Wehrmacht*.

Then, the *Freiwillige Ausbildungbataillon (Spanische)* was formed, stationed in Stockerau. This unit served under the control of the *Ersatz Ausbildungsbrigade* of Croatian volunteer infantry divisions of the *Heer* commanded by Colonel Klein, with the Reserve Battalion, *Freiwillige Ersatzbataillon (Spanische)* being stationed in Hollabrunn.

According to Georg Tessin, it was January 30 1945 when the Spanish volunteer companies 101st and 102nd *Freiwilligen-infanterie-kompanien (spanischen)* were created in Stockerau, with the members of these reserve and training companies of the *SpanischesFreiwilligen-Einheit*, with its dissolution.

These companies were assigned to the 357. Infanterie-Division. However this theory does not seem to have any foundation, because, as previously stated, in Hall im Tirol there were reports of the existence of the Spanish 101st and 102nd Companies.

A note in the file of the Command of Foreign Units of the OKW, dated December 16, 1944 gives information about the dismantling of the Spanish company in Army Group South, as well as the Spanish Training Battalion, including the liaison personnel which had already been in service in the Spanish Legion, as well as the Replacement Battalion of Spanish volunteers in the XVII Military District centralized in Vienna. All the personnel were absorbed by the SS. NARA T77/885/5634561 (*U.S. National Archives and Records Administration*).

The "waiting" situation of these Spanish troops stationed in Stockerau allowed for the "abandonment" of the Austrian barracks by 33 men for the *28.SS-Freiwilligen Panzergrenadier-Division Wallonien* to be recorded from these early dates of December 11-17, 1944; later there will be details of the transfer of these men. Faced with this situation, the commander of the Croatian unit demonstrated, to the command of his Military District in Vienna December 19, 1944, his most energetic protest against this "recruitment" carried out on the men under his jurisdiction by this unit of the *Waffen-SS*. Likewise he managed to confiscate the travel permit obtained by the *Waffen-SS* from a man called Rafael Barrio Toquero who seemed to be one of the men who was trying to join the Walloons. (He had served in the anti-tank unit of the 269th Regiment of the SDV and later in the Legion), (Guttenberg).

As can be seen in the note from the Command of Foreign Units OKW dated December 16, 1944, in principle the exit of Spanish to the SS units had official backing, although very possibly this was not the transfer process to SS units that must have been planned in the Command of Foreign Units OKW In spite of this, and as will be seen later, this "official" transfer of the Spanish to the *Waffen-SS* would stop, with the unit that the Spanish were sent to becoming the 357th Infantry Division, which did not belong to the *Waffen-SS*.

On January 25 1945 the Military District XVII (Vienna) posted 101st and 102nd Spanish Volunteer Companies as reinforcements for the 357th Infantry Division after dissolving the training and replacement battalions of the volunteers in Stockerau and Hollabrunn. The companies were assigned suitable German liaison personnel (two officers, forty-four men and six translators for each company), and were sent to Sared (a city near to Bratislava, known in German as Pressburg), where this unit was located. The untrained personnel were assigned as work-force for the work units. (NARA T79/94/672-3). These men served in the 357th until the end of March 1945.

However at the beginning of February 1945 some of these men were sent to the *28.SS-Freiwilligen-Panzergrenadier-Division Wallonien,* following their comrades who had "escaped" midway through the previous month. Continuing with the events which took place in Stockerau from November 1944, the men who did not "desert" the *Wallonien* and stayed with the German-Croatian Brigade from September 1944 became attached to the 357th Infantry Division and were deployed to Slovakia, toward the east of Bratislava, to be precise between the cities of Levice and Neutra (Nitra in German). The members of the 101st were the first to leave to join the new unit, arriving by train to the outskirts of a place which could have been called Vajka (or perhaps, as F. Vadillo suggests, another name), on the banks of the River Hron, tributary of the Danube. The members of the 102nd Spanish Company left later, on February 6, from Stockerau, although after a U.S. air attack it was not until the 10th that the train finally managed to leave, passing through Bratislava on the 11th, after having left Vienna, and stopping in Leoben on the 12th, and on the 13th in Nitra. Following this route, on the 14th they reached Vrable, on the outskirts of the River Zitava.

Eventually, the men of the 102nd arrived at their destination on the 16th, alighting at the small settlement of Kisgyekduyer, a few kilometers from their post on the second German defensive line. They stayed there for just two days, after these forty-eight hours had passed they set off for the first line of fire.

Men from the 101st Spanish Company and the 102nd continued to be attached to the various units of the 357th Division, which, toward the middle of January had been withdrawn from the front to get more supplies, choosing Neutra, in the face of the heavy attack of these troops from the 2nd Ukrainian Front under the command of Field Marshal Malinovski. The Spanish stayed in front of the 6th Soviet Armored Army belonging to the 2nd Ukrainian Front.

That same January they met the Soviets in Nagy Kalna, around fifty kilometers to the north of the River Hron (Gran, in German). In February they took part in the counterrattack against the head bridge of the Hron under the command of the *I.SS-Panzerkorps*. At the end of March there are reports that the Spanish took part in the battle of the River Hron, where they also suffered several losses. During this period the men formed part of the 8th Army, taking part in the German defensive line that ran exactly along the aforementioned river in the south of Czechoslovakia, between January 31 and March 2.

Fernando Vadillo gives an account of the vicissitudes of thirty or so men from the 102nd Spanish Company, they found themselves on March 8 on the outskirts of Kisgyekduyer, near to Vráble. From these positions they watched the waters of the River Hron, and until the 23rd they managed to keep their positions, as Kurt Jentsch (the head, and also interpreter, of the small Spanish group) received the order to withdraw to the second line. After two days, the group was in Uibarch, where, together with their German comrades posted there, they had to face a powerful Soviet attack. After resisting heroically, they received a new order entrusting them with the mission of clearing a road of enemies and later defending it so that mountain batteries could replace withdrawn German forces. From this moment, permanent withdrawal began, open to an attack at any moment from the Soviets or increasingly daring partisans.

The new withdrawal in formation was carried out with the group of Spanish in villages such as Topol´cany, Bánkovce, Traincín and later Nove Mesto na Váhom (Neustadt, in German,) where they arrived on the last day of March. Later they continued to Myjava (on the present day border between the Czech Republic and Slovakia), where they arrived on April 2, then they reached Stráznice on the 4th of the same month and on the following day the railroad station of Belusa. There, they were accepted on a train which took them to Hollabrun, where they arrived on April 6.

However they did not stay long in the Austrian barracks, as they received the order to leave the following day in a train to Pilsen which enabled them to arrive at the German town of Hof on the 11th. In the barracks where they were gather they spent a week resting from all their previous exploits, after seven days they were provided with civilian clothes and given compulsory discharge from the German Armed Forces; at the same time they were handed documents proving their status as workers contracted by the Government of the Reich, which would later avoid accusations about these men who had voluntarily supported the German war effort until the very end.

Returning to the situation in which the 357th Infantry Division found itself in March 1945, a month during which it took part in bloody conflicts, the reduced Division had no choice but to withdraw from fighting in the direction of Bratislava and Vienna. Around forty kilometers on from Neutra, the 357th again occupied new defensive positions under the operational control of the *Panzerkorps Feldherrnhalle* commanded by *General der Panzertruppen* Kleemann. They were again steamrollered by the Soviets, heading toward the northeast, specifically toward the area of Brno (Moravia).

In the first days of May the remainder of the destroyed 357th Division withdrew again pushed by the Soviet machine in the direction of Iglau (Jihlava, in Czech) and Deutsch-Brod (Havlikcuv-Brod, in Czech), where they eventually surrendered to their pursuers. Only

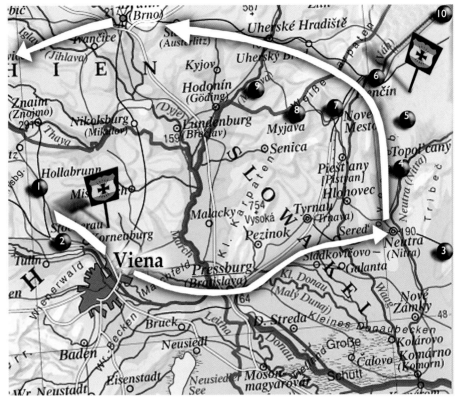

Path followed by the 357th Infantry Division of the *Wehrmacht* from leaving its barracks in Austria until Slovakian territory (hypothetically until Nitra) and its subsequent withdrawal in combat when faced with the advances of the Soviet Army, from Nitra to Ceska Budejovice (to the east) passing by Brno. (February-May 1945).

Places in the Austrian-Slovakian area to the north east and northeast of Vienna which men from the 102nd Spanish Company passed through while they were part of the 357th Infantry Division:

1. Hollabrun;
2. Stockerau;
3. Vráble;
4. Topol´cany;
5. Bánkovce;
6. Traincín;
7. Nove Mesto na Váhom;
8. Myjava;
9. Stráznice;
10. Belusa.

some men who were separated from the main part of the unit managed to break the seize by heading to Büdweis (Ceské Budejovice, in Czech) to join the Americans. Although they managed this, they fell into the hands of the Soviets again when they were handed over by the Americans and transferred together with the rest of those captured from their unit to the Soviet camps of Schachty, Charkov, Stalino and even Moscow.

It is practically impossible to know for sure what happened to the men who fought in the 357th Division, although it is very possible that most of the Spanish volunteers fell in combat and very few were made prisoners by the Soviets. This group includes the case of Corporal Jorge Mayral Mora (born in Don Benito), veteran of the SDV and of

the SLV, part of the 102nd Spanish Company and finally attached to the 357th, that was captured by the Soviets on March 20 1945 in the combat next to the River Hron when he commanded a squad of Spanish volunteers. Others who fell into the hands of the Soviets that same day were, Manuel Báez Gil (from Cadiz), Miguel Climent Sebastián (from Alicante), Manuel Rodríguez Martín (from the Canary Islands), Jesús Corral Martín (from Santander), Benjamín Vázquez García (from Galicia) and Juan Martínez García de Vadillo (from Murcia).

Returning now to the story of the whereabouts of the dispersed groups of Spanish, there were some transfers to the SS Walloon Division. It seems this event took place due to the intervention of Antonio Alfonso Van

Horembeke, a Belgian nationalized Spaniard who participated in the Civil War and who was at that time stationed in the state department of FET-JONS in Vizcaya. Van Horembeke left for Germany at the end of March 1944 with the aim of gathering together some Spanish to enlist them in the Flemish Legion of the *Waffen-SS*. In the first group of Spanish recruited for the Wallonien there were various noncommissioned officers with a good deal of experience in combat, with the Division as well as the Spanish Legion, on the eastern front. Amongst them were Zabala, Ocañas, Cabrera, Vadillo and Pinar, who immediately took up their old posts, lost until that moment. Later another group of Spanish arrived due to the intervention of Beltrán de Guevara (an old friend of Horembeke who had joined the Wallonien in the first contingent that came out of the Croatian Reserve Brigade) from Stockerau and Hellabrun that was heading for Hemmendorf, where it was found by the then Reserve of the Wallonien.

At the end of September in Poland, Van Horembeke met with a Walloon noncommissioned officer called Paul Kehren, also a veteran of the Tercio, and together they established contact with Leon Degrelle (Leader of the Belgian SS volunteers) to suggest to him the integration of Spaniards into the ranks of the *28.SS-Freiwilligen-Panzergrenadier-Division "Wallonien."* Degrelle, always in need of new reinforcements for his diminished troops, considered it to be a unique opportunity so he accepted the idea and entrusted this mission to Van Horembeke. The latter entered into contact with the *SS-Ostuf* (first lieutenant) Luís García Valdajos, due to his knowledge of the state of the Spanish in the German Armed Forces. In September or the beginning of October 1944 there was an meeting in the Hotel Adlon in Berlin between García Valdajos, Botet Moro (acting as interpreter) and Leon Degrelle, who once and for all managed to convince the Spaniard of his incorporation in to the *Wallonien*, which happened on November 1st.

García Valdajos, Kehren and Van Horembeke began to carry out their recruitment tasks in all the places where they could find Spaniards from November to December. Evidently, important areas were the camps of Stockerau and Hollabrunn, where, as previously stated, there were many Spaniards who "deserted" to join the Walloon Division. Another significant "source" was the Spaniards who worked in factories or even served in other *Wehrmacht* units.

It is difficult to know exactly how many men joined the Belgians from both camps, but from these volunteers and those recruited in other areas a semi-independent unit was formed commanded exclusively by Spaniards and under the command of García Valdajos.

At the end of November 1944 the first contingent of Spanish volunteers found themselves concentrated in the camp that the Walloon Division had in Breslau. The final number of Spanish who swelled the Wallonien could have reached over a hundred according to some, although more possibly it reached 240-350 men in January of 1945 (this is an approximate number as, understandably, there are various opinions. Sourd confirms that it was around 350, Caballero Jurado raises the figure to 350-400, and the testimony of Albert Steiver, reduces it to about 240). Whilst he was completing the Spanish formation, Botet Moro was sent to the *SS Panzergrenadierschule Kienschlag*, in Prosetschnitz (Czech Republic), from where he would return, according to Sourd, with the rank of *Standarten Oberjunker*.

In the *"Wallonien"*, the fight against the common Soviet enemy allowed for the links between the Spanish and the Walloons to be strongly established. The Belgian *SS-Sturmbannführer* Franz Hellebaut said that they were joined to the only battalion of the 70th SS Infantry Regiment of the

Three German soldiers at an observation post waiting for the arrival of the Soviet advance. The Spanish had to face the Soviet troops in most of the various units of the *Wehrmacht* and of the *Waffen-SS* that they were attached to.

Soldiers from a SS unit resting after destroying a Soviet armored vehicle. In the battle for Stargard, the Spanish in the *Wallonien* had to face, with a degree of success thanks to the use of the *panzerfaust,* the Soviet combat tanks.

1. A young sixteen year-old Botet Moro during the Spanish Civil War.
2. Botet Moro in the *Wehrmacht* uniform, which he wore in the SDV as well as the SLV, later using the *Waffen-SS* uniform in the *Wallonien* and in the Ezquerra Unit which was posted in Nordland.
3. Impeccable studio photograph of Botet Moro as *SS-Oberscharführer* of the *Wallonien*.
4. A worn out Botet poses for the identity card picture taken in 1946 in an English prisoner of war camp for his repatriation to Spain.

Photographs courtesy of Augusto Ferrer-Dalmau

Division, under the command of *SS-Hstuf* (Captain) Robert Denie, allowing for the formation of a third company within this (3rd Company of the first and only battalion of the *70.Grenadiere-Regiment*, the 3/I/70). Chosen as liaison officer for the rest of the Division to the *SS-Ustuf* (second lieutenant) Rudi Bal, who spoke Spanish as he had lived in Argentina some years before. The Walloons and the Spanish troops left Breslau and were stationed first in Olderhof (on the outskirts of Hannover) and later were sent to the area of Renania, where they were prepared for a possible intervention in the battle of Ardennes. In the end they did not intervene, although on December 24, 1944 a group of Spanish under the command of *SS-Oscha* (second lieutenant) Ricardo Botet were in the area of Marmagen (Nettersheim) joined with a group of men from the *SS-Ostuf* Derriks.

Once they had left the western front they moved on in February to Stettin (present day Szczecin) and the sector of Stargard (present day Stargard Szczeciski), on what today constitutes the German-Polish border.

Although the head of the Spanish was García Valdajos, Bal effectively became the head of the company when his comrade, at the end of January 1945, stayed in the area of Remagen, with Berlin being the next place where there is news of him, during the beginning of the formation of the Ezquerra unit, when the troops of the Wallonien were sent to the front. This decision was motivated mainly by, as mentioned previously, García Valdajos' excellent capabilities in organizational and administrative tasks, better than those of command of the troops in combat.

In the final phases of the training there was another transfer of men between units, meaning a group of around thirty Italian volunteers (the figure suggested by Sourd is fifty, the highest of the sources consulted), made up of Italian workers in Germany and Italian emigrants residents in Belgium, were granted permission to join the *29.Waffen Grenadier Division der SS (Italienische Nr.1)*, mainly made up of Italians.

Together with the Italians should be added around ten or twenty Spanish who perhaps preferred to transfer to another area of conflict closer to Spain. This small group of Spanish, under the command of the *SS-Oscha* Camargo and of the *SS-Uscha* Martínez Alberich, joined the Italian Division, in a section of the *SS-Regiment 81* of the *29.Waffen Grenadier Division der SS (Italienische Nr.1)*. Its missions consisted in fighting against activities of the partisans, only facing regular American troops at the end of the conflict in the last days of war in Europe with acceptable results, given the circumstances. They may have taken part in free combat on the outskirts of Trieste and Brennero, although there are no confirmed facts. In January 1945 they reached the area of Rodengo-Saiano, where the training base of the Italian Division was. As a postscript, it should be added that most of the men who surrendered from this unit to the partisans were immediately executed.

From the middle of January 1945, the previously relatively inactive Soviets unleashed a strong offensive that broke the Vístula front, reaching the River Oder in a few weeks, leading to the German forces having to withdraw and renew their defenses. To achieve the establishment of a secure defensive front, new troops were claimed on the first line of the eastern front; amongst them was the Walloon unit (magnificently studied by Norling).

On January 27, the Wallonien and another unit, also of Belgian origin, the *27.SS-FreiwilligenGrenadier-Division "Lange-marck"* received the order to head to the front, without knowing exactly what their destination was. On January 28 they boarded various trains that after leaving behind the western region of the Reich, that took them to Stargard, where most of the men of the *Wallonien* arrived on February 6. Not all of them arrived, as the Company of the Staff officers and the 1st Battalion of the *SS-Freiwilligen-Grenadier-Regiment 69* due to a mistake by the *Deutsche Reichsbahn* (German railroad service), alighted in Stettin.

Returning to the Spanish of the *28.SS-Freiwilligen-Panzergrenadier-Division*, on the first day of February 1945, when the *Wallonien* was already deployed in the area of Stargard, near to Stettin (Szczecin), it received various expeditions of Spanish arriving from Vienna and Berlin. With these volunteers the three sections of the 3rd Company were complete and a fourth section was created in the 1st Company of the same battalion (an independent section that would be attached to the 5th Company of the Walloon *SS-Ustuf* Albert Steiver.) These last reinforcements very probably came from 101st and 102nd companies, as well as a few workers recruited at the last minute. As some of these workers were lacking suitable military preparation it was preferable to send them back to their place of origin. Steiver in his memoires entitled *Krussow-1945 Wallons et espagnols* bears witness to the actions of the Spanish posted there.

With *SS-Hstuf* Denie being absent, Steiver took on the command of the battalion as well as the task of making the incorporation of new Spanish as useful as possible, these men had to immediately face a long march of around thirty-five kilometers before reaching their position on the front. Steiver, calculated that around 260 of the men arrived, although the number was possibly less.

The heads of each of the three sections that made up the company were the *SS-Oscha* La Fuente (according to Sourd, his job was that of *Waffen-Hauptscharführer der SS*) and Lorenzo Ocañas (according to Sourd, his job was that of *Waffen-Oberscharführer der SS*), acting as commander in his duties with the company *SS-Oscha* Ricardo Botet (according to Sourd, his job was that of *Standarten Oberjunker*), who combined this task with that of head of the 1st Section. Other volunteers who made up the officers and noncommissioned officers in the company were Pedro Zabala, Juan Pinar, Cabrejas and the aforementioned Van Hoorembeke, who had returned to service after his activity as recruiter for the *Wallonien*.

The fourth section formed from the recently arrived Spanish, stayed attached as a support unit to Steiver's 1st Company, which participated in the battle of Stargard. This section stayed under the command of sergeant Abel Ardoos (perhaps in reality this was under Ardoz, as his rank, according to Sourd, was *Waffen-Hauptscharführer der SS*). They were prepared for combat as they were well equipped with heavy machine guns and anti-tank weapons, as well as a camp kitchen. With the leadership of this section falling under Ardoos his knowledge of French and German were key.

Near to Stargard, according to Sourd, some Spanish had a misunderstanding with a German officers and his soldiers. The incident was caused by the immediate judgment passed on three Polish women who had been accused of stealing potatoes from German stores, with the result that after being arrested they were sentenced to death. By chance the Belgian *Hauptsführer* Denie and the Spaniard

Botet Moro, together with another group of unknown Spanish, arrived at the farm where the sentence was to be carried out. Eventually, after a great deal of discussion with threats on both sides, the Spanish and Denie managed to free the women, although not without being issued with a final threat by a German officer: to have to appear before a war council. Shortly afterwards, during the departure to new positions, Sourd states that five of those involved became separated from the column and were able to kill the German officer and some of his men to avoid them avenging themselves for the previous events, but this is not confirmed.

Returning to the general position of the men of the Wallonien, they were deployed in a part of the front where they coincided with many men of different nationalities who were part of the German defensive framework assembled in the area of the River Óder. There, Norwegians, Swedes, Danes, Flemish, Walloons, Dutch, French, Estonians, Latvian and Spanish fought to halt the powerful Soviet steamroller.

The vanguard of the Red Army drew near to the southeast of Stargard and the advance of these two Belgian units, both the Flemish and the Walloons was urgently required. The area given to the Walloons for defense was in the south of the city of Stargard, with only the battalion of the 2nd Regiment in which the Spanish forming the 3rd Company were integrated remaining as a reserve force.

Officers of the SS *Wallonien* Division pose for a photographer in the *Kienschlag* officers school, (Botet also spent time at this school), among them (6) are the Spaniard Lorenzo Ocañas, who was part of the Ezquerra Unit in the battle of Berlin, where he was captured. These are some of the names of some of the members of the SS next to Ocañas in the photo, such as Serlet (1), Suain (2), Foulon (3), De Goy (4) y Hancisse (5). Photograph courtesy of Augusto Ferrer-Dalmau.

It was the 2nd Armored Army and the 61st Soviet Army Corps who faced the Walloon unit. On February 7, the battle for Arnswalde, thirty kilometers to the south of Stargard, reached its decisive point, on February 10 the Soviet forces revived their attack against the city of Stargard, whilst the Spanish carried out various incursions in territory occupied by the Red Army, demonstrating great bravery and ferocity in all of them.

On the 11th, the 1st Company of the I Battalion of the *SS-Freiwilligen-Grenadier-Regiment 69*, temporarily attached to the *10.SS-Panzer-Division Frundsberg*, tried to conquer the village of Klutzow supported by some of the increasingly scant aerial and armored units, as well as a good handful of men, amongst which there were some Spanish. The attack came to a halt after the aerial and land support ended, with the Walloons and Spanish given the task of defending the sector of Krüssow-Stargard (present day Kluczewo-Stargard Szczeciski, Poland). Inevitably, Krüssow fell into Soviet hands, which meant that on February 13 the Walloons withdrew to Wittichow (today called Witkowo) and Schneidersfelde (today Radziszewo). The 3rd Company, the Spanish company, together with the 6th Company of Rooryck and the 1st Company of Lecoq, took up position to the south of Streesen (present day Strzyno in Poland).

On February 16, 1945 *Operation Sonnenwende* (Solstice) began, which had the participation of, amongst others, the *SS Frundsberg, Nordland, Langemarck, SS-Polizei, Nederland* and *Wallonien* Divisions, all under the group command of the *SS-Obergruppenführer* Felix Steiner. The aim of this operation was to take advantage of the fact that the Soviets, after the significant advances achieved during its offensive in January 1945, had left their flanks uncovered. With a view to taking advantage of this situation, the Germans had to carry out a two-pronged offensive movement to corner the troops and crush them. One of these "prongs" left from Pomerania and the other from Hungary, but the cruel reality of the state of the German Armed Forces would stop them gaining the means necessary to carry out the maneuver, and therefore the main aim of the German offensive was to manage to contact the troops situated in Arnswalde (present day Choszczno), which is something they managed on February 18 with a cost of great and irreplaceable losses and without managing to permanently stabilize the front line.

The main direction of the attack ran in charge of the *Nordland*, using the *11.Panzerabteilung Hermann von Salza* as battering ram and on both sides the two regiments of the Division: the *Norge*, to the east, and the *Denmark*, to the west. The men of the *Langemarck* and of the *Wallonien* covered the western flank, meeting with the *Frundsberg* and the *SS-Polizei* in the direction toward the River Oder; whilst the eastern flank remained covered by the Dutch of the *Nederland* and by the *Führer Grenadierdivision*. Days 19 and 20 were witness to intense fighting in the surrounding areas of Arnswalde, beginning the final withdrawal of all the forces to the south of the River Inha on the 21st.

The later reorganization of the forces who were still standing in this sector led to the *Wallonien* staying under the control of the more powerful Nordland.

On February 27 the Soviets advanced with the aim of surrounding the troops situated in Stargard, starting the battle for the city. There, the Walloon troops were ready on the outskirts of Kollin (present day Kolin), around fifteen kilometers from Stargard. The number of losses was again high, so that the only battalion of the *SS-Freiwilligen-Grenadier-Regiment 70* (also called 3/I/70), where the Spanish

Leon Degrelle, in both pictures, in front of his Walloon unit in Estonia. The close contact he had with his men even on the first line made him a well liked commander.

Many Spanish finished up being integrated in the *Wallonien* Division, taking part in the fighting in Krüssow-Stargard in Pomerania.

were posted was disbanded, and its troops were divided between the two battalions of the *SS-Freiwilligen-Grenadier-Regiment 69*. Here, the Spanish, matched up with the Walloons, destroyed the Armored Soviets, mainly the well known T-34, with its new anti-tank weapons (the feared panzerfaust), halting their advance as much as possible. There are reports of a fight in which the Spanish, armed with panzerfaust, took on a group of T-34, destroying one, catching up with another and forcing the withdrawal of the rest.

The patrols that the Spanish had to carry out wore down more and more their already tattered ranks, after being surprised at times by the deadly response of their opponents, always lying in wait for the movements of the Spanish.

During this period the 1st Company of Steiver and therefore the section of Ardoos were temporarily assigned to the Frundsberg Division.

On March 3, the remains of the disappeared I Battalion of the 70th SS Regiment of Infantry Division covered the withdrawal of the *Wallonien* along the Baltic coast.

On March 4 Stargard was permanently abandoned, with the Walloons and the Spanish of Ardoos being the last to withdraw, covering the civilians who were trying to flee to the west and the military units that, when scattered, sought the rearguard lines.

There were twenty-eight days of almost continuous combat which permanently debilitated the section of the Spanish that served in the 1st Company of Steiver. The losses in this section reached 90% of its members; although there are no exact figures available to confirm the veracity of this information, it provides an approximate idea of the significant debilitation of the section. The Spanish who were part of the 3rd Company also suffered significant losses, up to the point that, as pre-

viously mentioned, they were posted in the *SS-Freiwilligen-Grenadier-Regiment 69*.

Only around sixty Spanish managed to escape the surrounding of Stargard in Pomerania at the beginning of March 1945; Rudi Bal, the head of the Spanish company at that time, fell in combat on March 6 in front of his men, leaving them under the command of Pedro Zabala and Ricardo Botet.

The survivors of Stargard were regrouped in Scheune, south of Stettin, where they of all formed part of a defensive line north of Berlin.

They were there for a short time, as immediately afterwards the Spanish posted in the Walloon Division received orders to converge on the outskirts of Potsdam, something that took place at the beginning of March taking advantage of the fact that the units of the III German Corps of the SS withdrew toward the capital of the Reich.

It is possible that some of the Spanish did not withdraw to Potsdam and that they continued on until the end of the conflict with the Walloon unit scattered among their companies. Leon Degrelle, in an interview given in 1969 to the Madrid newspaper Arriba, stated that he had Spanish volunteers under his orders until the end of the war, which is possibly true, although there are no other documents or concrete information of the time confirming this.

Among the men who left for Potsdam after leaving the Wallonien was Ricardo Botet. When they arrived at their destination they were integrated into a new unit under the command of Ezquerra who was directing the Spanish who had arrived from one place or another. Ricardo Botet confirmed this with this statement: "We received the order to go to Potsdam where all the Spanish were being regrouped in a single unit, captained by Miguel Ezquerra Sánchez, we knew it was bad to abandon our comrades of the *SS-Wallonie* with whom we had fought and shed blood for a shared ideal. When we arrived in Potsdam we stayed in a school for military orphans and there we found a huge circus spectacle, there were more sergeants than soldiers, quarrelsome legionnaires, down and outs, disoriented people who did not know where to go and old veterans of the D.A and other units of the *Wehrmacht*, approximately between 100 and 150 all in all. Of all of them, I remember a legionnaire who was Ezquerra's escort, he had his face completely covered in tattoos and had an enormous belt of the Tercio with two pistols, one each side. Years later, I was told that he died buried among the ruins of Berlin."

It was in Potsdam where the Ezquerra Unit was born, a unit that would defend the centre of the capital of the Reich together with a range of defenders of many nationalities against the Russian steamroller that was already advancing to the gates of the city.

Ezquerra, after recovering from wounds suffered at the battle of the Ardennes, and García Valdajos were given the task of gathering together all the Spanish as far as possible, taking them out of their various military units where they were posted, also recruiting the Spanish workers in the industries of the Reich, or in general any Spaniard living in Germany who showed suitable physical aptitude and was the right age for service. In this case, facilitating the creation of this new Spanish unit, he played an important part in helping General Faupel.

The resulting unit was totally heterogeneous, in its ranks there was a mixture of old legionnaires (veterans of the wars in Africa), veterans of the Spanish Civil War, of the Blue Division and of the Blue Legion, ex-members of the *Wallonien* Division, as well as the aforementioned workers who having been working in the Reich now found themselves in many cases unemployed after the destruction of German industry; as well as Spanish members of the Todt Organization,

Falangists recruited from Madrid and Spanish who for different reasons found themselves imprisoned in German jails.

Miguel Ezquerra then received orders from the German High Command to track down the Spanish who were likely to enlist in his combat unit in different German cities and towns and in this sense, started to have some tensions in his relationship with the Spanish embassy, as it was, as much as it could, trying to repatriate the Spanish who were still following the Reich, and therefore the founding the creation of a unit Spanish combatants in the SS contradicted the intentions of Rodríguez del Castillo, the last representative of the Spanish embassy in the Berlin of the III Reich.

In fact (as Vadillo recounts), in the middle of the month of April, between the 12th and the 16th, Gonzalo Rodríguez del Castillo managed to evacuate around 200 Spanish workers by railroad. From the 14th, the Spanish embassy in Berlin had no electricity supply (like many other buildings in the affected city) and Rodríguez del Castillo transferred its functions to the building that the Falange had in the Berlinstrasse. It was there where he made his last calls to manage to evacuate all the Spanish who were in Berlin, using radio announcements as well as embassy notices in the newspapers to do so.

However the situation became extreme in the capital of the Reich and shortly afterwards on the 19th, it was the Spanish diplomatic corps with Rodríguez del Castillo who abandoned the city immediately. A small caravan composed of six cars and a motorbike with the flag and number plate of the Diplomatic Corps left the capital by one of the magnificent freeways of the road network of the Reich heading east, and then going north east, in the direction of Hamburg. During the trip they mixed with thousands of military and civilians on their way to one place or another (both fleeing

from the Soviets and on their way to meet them) and they had to undergo numerous road checks by the Police, the Army, the SS and other security forces.

Their legal diplomatic papers allowed them to continue on their way and try to escape the hell which enveloped most of Germany. The difficult nature of the trip was reflected by two of the vehicles of the Spanish caravan having to be abandoned.

On April 24th when the Spanish passed by Wusterhausen, they were informed by German security forces of the presence of Russian troops only twenty kilometers from the freeway they were travelling on, in fact they had taken the nearby town of Neuruppin. They speeded up their journey as much as possible, as being captured by the Soviets, despite their belonging to the Diplomatic Corps, could have had an unpredictable result. In two days, on April 26, they were in the city of Lübeck; from there they "jumped" to Hamburg, and two days later they left for their final destination: Copenhagen.

After the German surrender and entering occupied Denmark on May 5, there were days of uncertainty among the Spanish led by Rodríguez del Castillo, uncertainty that ended when, in the middle of the summer (July 24), due the intervention of troops from the United Kingdom, they were transferred in an RAF plane to London, where their dangerous escape from a German Reich that was falling apart minute by minute ended.

Going back in time again to March 1945, the story returns to Potsdam, a place near the capital of Germany, where the Spanish combat group that would go down in history as the Ezquerra Unit was formed, although its first leader was the *Obersturmführer* Luís García Valdajos, who, as has been noted previously, was always chosen for organizational tasks due to his wide experience in this area, as well as his capabilities for combat.

It was he who suggested the command go to Miguel Ezquerra Sánchez, an officer with a great deal of experience as officer in the first line of fire.

At the beginning of April 1945, the unit, called *Einheit Ezquerra* in German (some authors call it the *Einsatzgruppe Ezquerra*) was made up of two companies stationed in Potsdam where the last volunteers were collected.

Vadillo, in his book *Los irreductibles*, tells how the *Unterscharführer* Ramón Baillo Fernández was sent by Miguel Ezquerra from Berlin for the recruitment of Spanish volunteers for the unit commanded by José Ortiz (mentioned previously) to Tolmazzo, near to Udine. Evidently, no efforts were spared to activate this last Spanish unit, which would shortly afterwards enter into combat. Ezquerra recounts in his book how some survivors of these Belgian and French SS divisions were integrated in his unit, unfortunately there is no information in the documentation available of either of these French or Walloon units that corroborates this fact. It was possible that at some point during the fights for Berlin some men from these units ended up temporarily fighting together with his comrades from the Spanish unit.

To locate the recruitment and training center of these Spanish troops in Potsdam, the German High Command offered an old school for military orphans that had also been an officers school. It was there where they were given, mainly light, weapons, and later, in Berlin, they were permanently re-equipped.

The days passed with light training being given to the volunteers, in theory designed more for those who had not been in recent active military service, as was the case with the ex-workers of these industries of the Reich. The prevailing atmosphere, despite the complexity of the situation, was one of expectancy and a desire to begin combat. There were not volunteers for nothing, although it should be borne in mind that some men were more motivated than others, and in spite of this volunteer spirit, it is possible that some men did desert during the days of training, as well as during the actual battle of Berlin. There are no reliable details, but it is possible that the total number of deserters reached around fifty.

The new company, from the Ezquerra unit, directly descended from the 101st,, was known by this name in some studies and in others simply as the Ezquerra Unit. These remaining members of the original 101st remained permanently integrated into the *11.SS-Freiwillingen PanzergrenadierNordland Division* when the war front was close to Berlin.

As well as the Spanish already mentioned in SS formations, there was news of the existence of a reduced number posted in other units under the SS. In the *SS-Polizei Freiwilligen Bataillon Bozen*, it is reported that between twenty and thirty-one Spanish were in its ranks, and in the 1st Company of the *Dirlewanger* Brigade, it is reported that there were approximately six.

According to Sourd, in an internal document belonging to the *SS Sonder Bataillon Dirlewanger* dated April 14, 1944 the names of six Spanish appear. At least one of them, with the surname Rodríguez, had been transferred to this unit from the SS command in Prague. Another document, this time dated April 15, 1944, gives information about the *Dirlewanger* incorporated in the *SS Kampfgruppe Anhalt* (Anhalt combat group of the *Waffen-SS*), to take part in the *Frühlingfest* Operation in Belarus under the command of the *SS Obersturmbannführer* Günther Anhalt. In this combat group, in which, according to Sourd six Spaniards took part, as well as the *Dirlewanger* there were also the *SS-Polizei Regiment* 2 and 24, as well as other smaller units.

Little more is known of the Spanish posted to this unit (penitentiary in origin, as among its troops there were dangerous criminals and delinquents), although it can

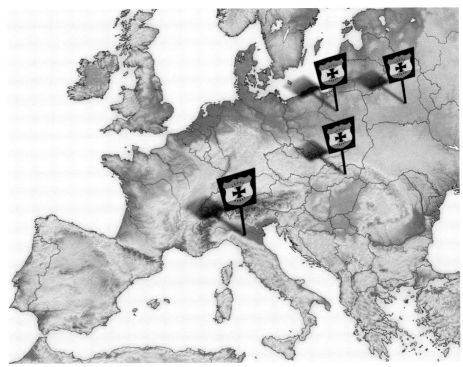

Area in which Spanish troops posted in the *Dirlewanger* Brigade (northeast Europe) and in the *SS Polizei Freiwilligen Bataillon Bozen* (north Italy) were located.

be assumed that they remained in it until the end of the conflict (those who survived, obviously, although there are no details regarding this subject), being able to take part in suppressing the uprising which took place in Warsaw, where the members of this unit were the perpetrators of many atrocities against the Polish people and even against their own German comrades in other units who tried to avoid their outrages.

Supporting this is the information provided by Sourd in his book *Croisés d´un idéal*, in which he refers to the testimony of a veteran of the Spanish Division of Volunteers called Jorge Oriente who had known a Spanish veteran of the *Dirlewanger*. This veteran, whose name he did not recall, had told him about his journey around Germany (after having served in the Spanish Division of Volunteers), which had taken place after he had crossed over the Franco-Spanish border clandestinely to finish up in Stablack, where together with another dozen Spanish sent there, their previous jobs were not recognized. The dissatisfaction of this group led to them going under court martial and being sentenced to serve in a disciplinary unit, which was none other than the *Dirlewanger*. In this unit individuals from different backgrounds such as *Waffen-SS*, *Heer* or even civilians convicted of various crimes mixed together.

All the Spanish stayed in the same section and took part in the anti-partisan action in Belarus (it is almost certain that this was the previously mentioned Operation *Frühlingfest*), that took place between May and June 1944. Also, the anonymous veteran told Jorge Oriente that they took part in the fighting to crush the popular uprising in Warsaw in August 1944. Following this, and already in full withdrawal from the Soviet steamroller, they reached Slovakia; there he contacted the Spanish consulate and managed to finally obtain false documents as a Spanish worker which enabled him to get to Spain.

Regarding the men integrated in the *SS-Polizei Freiwilligen Bataillon Bozen*, the little challenged theory surrounding the Spanish who served in this Police unit is based on the diverse origin of the background of these men, dealing with stragglers from the Spanish unit (the Blue Legion is mentioned), or men from the *24. Waffen Gebirgs Division Karstjäger*, as the *1. Btl./ SS-Pol.Rgt. Bozen* coincided at the end of April 1945 in the same area of deployment as the *Karstjäger*, the area of Tarvisio (Tarvis in German, situated in the province of Udine, in the region of Friuli-Venezia Giulia). Of the approximately 100 men who served in this mountain unit, twenty or thirty could have been authorized to join the *Polizei*, remaining in Italy until the end of the war fighting against the partisans. There is documentary evidence in the form of a list which shows six Spanish volunteers as having fallen in the north of Italy whilst serving in the *SS-Polizei Regiment Bozen* possibly during March and April 1945. According to the German archives of the WASt (German War Records Office), at least three of them are still in the cemetery at Costermano. According to Sourd in his book *Croisés d´un idéal*, there is a document dated May 11, 1945 which mentions the existence of twenty-five Spanish belonging to the *SS-Polizei Freiwilligen Bataillon Bozen*.

If it is true that in the previous units most of the Spanish are found under the flags of the Third Reich, there are also references (Sourd) to Spanish in the Kriegsmarine (Naval Reserve 28, in Sennheim), in coastal artillery units in Estonia, in the Todt Organization, in the NSKK (National Socialist Motorists Corps), in the Speer Legion or even in an artillery regiment of the *17. Luftwaffenfelddivision* during the summer of 1944 on the Normandy coast

The members of the *Dirlewanger* Brigade appear covered by camouflage masks in many pictures taken at the end of 1944 and the beginning of 1945, as in the examples shown here.

The photo below was taken during the free combat on the streets of Warsaw in the days of the rebellion (August 1944).

Men from a *SS-Polizei* (police) regiment, like the Bozen, where some Spanish served. Some of the weapons they were carrying were second level in general and were much more suitable for anti-partisan clashes than for fighting regular armies on the front.

Men from the *SS-Polizei Bozen* Volunteers Regiment, in which some Spanish served, pose for the camera somewhere in the north of Italy. It can be seen that they are carrying a significant supply of grenades together with various automatic weapons from Italy, the Breda M-1930 light machine gun that the second soldier to the left is carrying on his shoulder can be clearly made out.

(it is true that there are no known documents regarding this and that, in Antonio Muñoz's book, *Göring´s Grenadiers* there is no reference to the existence of these Spaniards; although there could be other Spanish who individually were incorporated into this unit).

There must have also been some men with dual nationality (Spanish and German), who having been considered as *volksdeutschen* could have been in any other German formation. There are reports of a Federico Lux who served in the *Nordland* Division, and was killed on the Narva front (Narwa in German).

The *Wehrmacht* passing over to the SS was not automatic, nor specifically organized beforehand, but it was events which made the Spanish who were in Stablack Süd in the *Wehrmacht* finish up in many cases in *Waffen-SS* units. As previously mentioned among the vicissitudes suffered by the 102nd, some of the Spanish who made up its ranks were transferred to the *24.Waffen-SS Gebirgs Division Karstjäger* in October 1944;

but the definitive step took place when many of the Spanish who were at the camps in Stockerau and Hollabrunn "self transferred" to the *28.SS Freiwilligen Panzer-Grenadier Division Wallonien*.

There is no evidence that they kept the numbers 101 or 102 when they joined the Walloon unit. For this reason there is not proof of the existence of these sometime mentioned *101.Spanische-Freiwilligen Kompanie der SS* or of the *102.Spanische-Freiwilligen Kompanie der SS*. Only when the Ezquerra Unit was formed were at least two companies attached nominally to the *Nordland* created, and these two companies were able to recover the name that they had in Hall im Tirol (101st and 102nd) however in this case belonging to the SS, in any case, there is no hard evidence to confirm this fact.

As a final assessment on the presence of the Spanish from 1944 in various German units, it must be taken into consideration that neither the number of men in service, nor their distribution, made this human contribution especially significant for the progress of the war. It must be remembered that it is very complicated to establish a true figure for the Spanish volunteers that after the repatriation of the Blue Division and later of the Spanish Legion Volunteers joined the *Waffen-SS* security forces, *Wehrmacht* and other formations, although the figure can be rounded up to 1,000 men, as stated in the microfilm T354, A3343 from the *Berlin Document Center, U. S. National Archives*.

Without taking into account their low number and independently of political connotations, their participation in the war can, in general, be viewed as a worthy, and in some cases heroic, contribution, to the annals of the Spanish military history of the XX century, as they knew how to believe, fight and die doing their country proud. It is also necessary to mention the presence of Spanish on the side of the western allies and in the Red Army who also fought for their ideals and it is only fair to recognize that all those men deserve a place which is underlined in Spanish military history.

Photograph of Ricardo Botet (to the right) when he was posted to the SDV in 1941. *Photograph courtesy of Augusto Ferrer-Dalmau*

SS soldiers sheltering, waiting for the enemy. The Spanish troops of the Wallonien meet their old Soviet enemies again, but now inside the Reich.

1

2

3

4

1. M-43 army tunic

There were four basic types of SS army tunic: the 1937 model, the 1941 model, the 1942-43 model and the 1944 model. The 1942-43 model, shown in the picture, was made from dyed-field gray wool with a five-button front and non-pleated pockets; this model, like the 1941 tunic, no longer had the bottle green collar of the 1937 model.

2. M-44 army tunic

This model was similar to the U.S. army tunic known as "Ike" as it was also a short tunic of a type which is now known as a flight or "bomber" jacket. The two lower pockets and the lower part of the M-43 tunic were removed in order to save material, which was essential during wartime. It is almost certain that this model of army tunic and that shown before were those issued to the German soldiers at the last minute, meaning that it is highly likely that these were also those used by the Spanish included in their ranks.

3. M-44 camouflage army tunic

On March 1st 1944 the camouflage drill uniform became regulation wear, either used over the standard cloth uniform or worn alone. It was a dot style camouflage (*Erbsenmuster*) of five colors. The tunic shown here has shoulder boards like those used by the Panzer Grenadiers (with green piping), and would have been the type mainly used by the Spanish involved in the defense of Berlin.

4. SD sleeve patch

At the end of 1938 the SS started using a new range of diamond-shaped insignias to be worn on the lower part of the sleeve. Between 1939 and 1940 the SS expanded their range of ribbons and sleeve patches to more than thirty ribbons and over a dozen different diamond-shaped patches. The patch shown here is the type used by the *Sicherheitsdienst* (Reich Security Service) for its troops. As stated in the main text, some Spanish soldiers were recruited by this service.

1. M-1942 helmet
The 1942 model was the last produced by Germany during the Second World War and only differed from previous models in a few minor details, such as a thinner edge and different-shaped air vents. This type was made from a manganese-silicate steel alloy. The helmet shown here has a second pattern decal.

2. M-1940 helmet with type B oak leaf camouflage cloth cover
This type of camouflage (*Eichenlaubmuster*) was used throughout the war, and like all the camouflage patterns designed up to 1944 has a predominantly brown color scheme for fall/winter and, as shown here, a mainly green one for spring/summer.

3. M-43 officer's cap
The M-43 field cap (*Einheitsfeldmütze*), shown here is a model from the end of the war made in wool of medium quality, probably made in a concentration camp. Although it has the piping in silver thread which was typical of the officers' clothing, the emblem on the front is a version for soldiers in a model which came into use from 1944 onwards.

4. M-43 soldier's cap
Comparing this photograph with the previous one, differences can be seen between the officer's caps and the soldier's caps. In this case, in terms of the materials used to make them, the difference which is most obvious is the edging in silver thread on the officer's cap; however, the front emblems on both, of which there were many types made, are those used by the troops. All the headgear on this page was part of the kit used by the Waffen-SS in the last few months of the war, meaning that they were undoubtedly also used by the Spanish included in their ranks.

5. Collar tab for noncommissioned officers and soldiers
The soldiers wore tabs with the runes on both sides of the collar, whilst the officers wore the runes on the right side and the emblem denoting their rank on the left side. In the fall of 1940 it was stipulated that the collar tabs must be worn on the army tunic and on the field uniform. Like the previous pieces, the tabs for officers were made in silver thread, which was also used to edge the 60x40 mm piece.

6. Metal eagle and SS skull
These metal pieces were made to be worn on the officers' peaked caps, the eagle (*Hoheitsadler*), belonging to the SS, above and the skull (*Totenkopf*) below. Although rules dictated that these insignias should only be used on peaked caps (*schirmmütze*), over time they were also used unofficially on other headgear, such as the M-43 leather winter caps.

1. Eagle arm patch for officers
In contrast to the other branches of the German Armed Forces, who wore the national eagle (*Hoheitsadler*) on the right breast of the tunic, the SS wore it on the left arm, above the elbow. The patch shown here is made from metallic silver thread and was designed to be worn on an officer's uniform. There are many variations of this patch.

2. Eagle arm patch for noncommissioned officers and soldiers
The other photograph shows the differences between the eagle arm patch (*Hoeitsadler*) for officers and the patch for soldiers, as the latter is made in white thread. The eagle arm patches were brought into use in 1935 and derive from the eagle cap patch which was developed that same year.

3. Knight's Cross of the Iron Cross with Oak Leaves
The *Ritterkreuz des Eisernen Kreuzes mit Eichenlaub* was established in 1940 as a grade immediately superior to the Knight's Cross of the Iron Cross. Of the 7,313 Knight Crosses awarded during the Second World War, only 882 were with Oak Leaves; one of these was awarded to General Muñoz Grandes, first commander of the Blue Division.

4. Knight's Cross of the Iron
The *Ritterkreuz des Eisernen Kreuzes* was a grade of the 1939 version of the Iron Cross established in 1813. It was the highest decoration in Germany, awarded in recognition of extreme bravery on the battlefield or for outstanding military leadership. Included in this group were the only two Spaniards to be awarded this decoration: General Muñoz Grandes and General Esteban-Infantes (although, as described in main text of the book, Miguel Ezquerra claims to have also been a recipient). Based on the September 1st 1939 renewal of the Iron Cross, this decoration was worn on a ribbon around the neck and could be awarded to soldiers of any rank and to allies of the Third Reich.

5. Iron Cross 1st Class
The Iron Cross (*Eisernen Kreuzes*) was restored as a German decoration, rather than Prussian, as it had been previously, in 1939. The Iron Cross was awarded for bravery in combat and for other military contributions on the battlefield. The 1st Class Cross was a metal badge worn in the center of the left-hand breast pocket of either the dress or everyday uniform. It was a progressive award; in other words, it was only awarded to those who had already earned the right to wear the 2nd Class Cross. During the Second World War around 300,000 1st Class Crosses were awarded, of which 135 went to Spanish soldiers.

6. Iron Cross 2nd Class
The 2nd Class Cross was worn on a ribbon which included the color red in addition to the traditional black and white (black and white were the colors of Prussia, whilst black, white and red were the colors of Germany). The 2nd Class Cross was worn in two different ways: on dress uniforms it was worn mounted alone or as part of a medal bar; in contrast, for everyday use only the ribbon was worn from the second buttonhole of the tunic. In the Second World War, some 4.5 million 2nd Class Crosses were awarded, with 2,362 of these going to Spanish soldiers. The picture shows one of these in its presentation box, mounted on a Spanish medal bar.

1

3

4

2

1. War Merit Cross 1st Class with Swords

This decoration (*Kriegsverdienstkreuz*) was introduced in 1939 as a substitute for the Iron Cross for non-combatants used in previous wars. It had the same grades as the Iron Cross (1st and 2nd Class and Knight's Cross), and to be awarded it the recipient had to have the grade immediately below. There were two variants: with swords, given to soldiers for exceptional service in battle above and beyond the call of duty (but not worthy of an Iron Cross, which was awarded more for bravery), or without swords, for meritorious service behind the lines (also awarded to civilians). The *Kriegsverdienstkreuz* 1st Class was a medal that was worn on the left pocket of the tunic, in the same manner as the Iron Cross 1st Class. The Spanish were awarded sixteen 1st Class Crosses.

2. War Merit Cross 2nd Class with Swords

In the same manner as the Iron Cross 2nd Class, the Kriegsverdienstkreuz 2nd Class with Swords was worn suspended from a ribbon, in this case red-white-black-white-red; meaning that the red and white colors were arranged in the opposite order to that of the ribbon of the Iron Cross 2nd Class. Recipients of the War Merit Cross 2nd Class with Swords wore the crossed swords in miniature on the ribbon when it was on a medal bar. On the everyday uniform the ribbon was worn in the buttonhole of the tunic. 2,200 Spaniards were awarded this decoration.

3. Eastern Winter Campaign Medal (Winterschlacht Im Osten)

This decoration, more commonly known as the "Eastern Front Medal" or the "Frozen Meat Medal", was instituted on May 26, 1942 to mark service on the Eastern Front between November 15, 1941 and April 15, 1942 and to recognize the hardship suffered by German and allied troops, combatant and non-combatant, during the particularly bitter Russian winter of 1941-1942. The colors on the medal ribbon were red, white and black, to symbolize blood, snow and death. This decoration was worn on a medal bar or with a ribbon worn through the buttonhole, in the same manner as the Iron Crosses and the War Merit Cross 2nd Class. Over three million were made and all the Spanish soldiers who fulfilled one of the following conditions was entitled to wear it: fourteen days of active combat within the dates specified, sixty days, non combat, served within the dates specified, wounded in action, killed in action, wounded by frostbite (or any other wound connected to the climate), which was severe enough to warrant being awarded the Wound Badge.

4. Commemorative Medal for Spanish Volunteers in the Fight against Bolshevism

The *Erinnerungsmedaille fur die Spanischen Freiwilligen im Kampfgegen den Bolschewismus* was instituted on January 3, 1944 to honor the 250 *Infanteriedivision*. There are two types of medal, the German made version, made of zinc with bronze plating which often wore off over time (shown here in the picture), and the Spanish made version, which varied considerably in terms of material and quality during the years it was made. As it was a decoration recognized by Spain it was produced in Spain to replace those which had deteriorated or been lost. The ribbon is based on that of the Iron Cross Second Class with the addition of a narrow yellow band in the center, to give the impression of the Spanish flag. This was the only decoration created by the Third Reich to be awarded to foreign allies.

1. Wound Badge in Black

This badge (*Verwundetenabzeichen*) had three classes: black, for those wounded once or twice whilst serving, or for being frost-bitten in the line of duty; silver for being wounded three or four times or for suffering the loss of a hand, a foot or an eye in hostile action or for facial disfigurement or brain damage also in hostile action; and gold, for five or more wounds, total blindness, "loss of manhood", or severe brain damage caused by hostile action. This badge was worn on the lower left breast of the army tunic under any other badges.

2. Infantry Assault Badge in Silver

The silver class of this badge was instituted on December 20, 1939 and awarded to infantry soldiers who met one of the following criteria: having taken part in three or more infantry assaults, participation in three or more infantry counter-attacks, having taken part in three or more armed reconnaissance operations, having been engaged in hand-to-hand combat when attacking a position or having taken part on three separate days in the restitution of combat positions. There is photographic evidence of Spanish soldiers using this badge and the previous badge.

3. Tank Destruction Badge in Silver

The Sonderabzeichen für das Niederkämpfen von Panzerkampfwagen durch Einzelkämpfer im silber was instituted on March 9, 1942 to honor those who destroyed an enemy tank in hand-to-hand combat with explosives; later a gold class was created. The criteria for it being awarded were: silver, the destruction of an enemy tank using light weapons such as a hand grenade, a panzerfaust, an explosive charge, etc.; gold, the destruction of five enemy tanks with the weapons previously mentioned; the anti-tank units were not eligible for this award. Captain Urbano Gómez García, of the Blue Division, appears on the German lists for the destruction of two enemy tanks.

4. Military Merit Cross 1st Class with red emblem

The Order of Military Merit was instituted during the reign of Isabel II, in 1864, to recognize the merit of those in war. The 1937 Regulations for Rewards keeps to the original criteria for awards when it states that, "it will be given to those who distinguish themselves in war operations". Among other heraldic rulings, the regime born at the end of the civil war commanded the crowns on the decorations to be changed, ordering the Republican mural crown to be replaced by an open royal crown; therefore, the crosses awarded to the members of the Division had this new crown, as shown on the cross in the picture. It should be mentioned that there were many variants made of this decoration; the example shown here is that known as the "princess model", and was a little smaller than the others.

5. Medal of Suffering for the Motherland

This medal was created in 1814, originally in order to "Give proof of the appreciation which is due to military personnel, who have had the misfortune of being taken prisoner and were taken to fortresses or enclosures. This was later extended to reward those who had been wounded or injured in active service. The wounded had a red cross embroidered on the medal' s ribbon.

6. Campaign Medal 1936-1939

This was born in the Regulations for Awards in Times of War published in Decree 192 on January 26, 1937 (Official State Gazette No.99), which states that "The campaign Medal will be awarded to those who participated actively in operations or served on the firing line during the minimum time period specified for each sector, with a different ribbon when these are rearguard services". The example shown here is for vanguard services, shown by the black edges of the ribbon; the rearguard variants had green edges.

1. Campaign Medal for the Spanish Division of Volunteers in Russia
This was created by Ministerial Order on November 9, 1943 and was awarded to those who fought with the Blue Division. It consisted of the emblem of the Army in silver with the yoke and arrows, mounted on a German Iron Cross. The ribbon is white with the national colors of Germany and Spain.

2. Spanish volunteers' arm shield
On July 9 1941 the OKH authorized the use of a national shield on the uniform of the Spanish volunteers of the 250 *Infanteriedivision*. This was quite unusual, as only the foreign volunteers enlisted in the Waffen-SS had the right to use a national shield. The example shown here is a type known as "BeVo", after the company which made them, and it was machine sewn. Other models of the shield were printed and yet others manufactured in Spain. The members of the Blue Division wore this shield on the right sleeve, in contrast to the Waffen-SS, who wore it on the left sleeve.

3. Individual Military Medal
The second most important decoration, the Military Medal, originates from the June 29, 1918 Law Setting the Main Guidelines for the Reorganization of the Army. "It is an exemplary and immediate award for marked and highly distinguished actions and services against the enemy." Shown here is one of the fifty-three which were awarded to members of the Blue Division, proven by the fact that "RUSSIA 1941" is written on the medal bar holding the ribbon

4. Medal bar of an ex-member of the division
This magnificent piece gathers together most of the awards which a volunteer of the Blue Division could be awarded; from left to right: Military Merit Medal with red emblem; Campaign Medal 1936-1939; Military Merit Cross (*Kriegsverdienstkreuz*) Second Class with Swords, German; Eastern Winter Campaign Medal (*Winterschlacht Im Osten*), German; Commemorative Medal for Spanish Volunteers in the Fight against Bolshevism, German, and Campaign Medal for the Spanish Division of Volunteers in Russia.

5. Arm badge of the Wallonien Division
This is the arm badge worn by the members of the Wallonien Division of the SS, commanded by Leon Degrelle. A number of Spanish soldiers served in this division when they decided to stay in Germany to fight alongside their German comrades against the Soviet advance.

6. War Cross
This was created in the Regulations for Awards in Times of War published in Decree 192/1937 on January 26. It was awarded "for exceptional merit to those personnel who, distinguishing themselves extraordinarily, do not rise to reach through campaign merit, the Laureate Cross of San Ferdinand or the Military Medal." It should be taken into consideration that many of the Spanish serving in the German Armed Forces were veteran combatants of the Spanish Civil War, and among their number were some who had been decorated with this award. These soldiers wore the 1937 model, whilst those who received the War Cross for actions carried out whilst they were part of the Blue Division or the Blue Legion wore the 1942 model, shown in the picture.

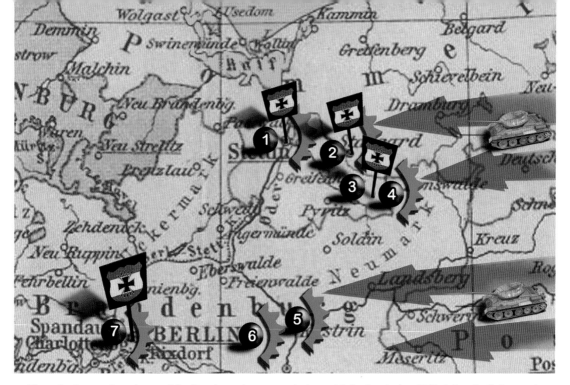

Places in the north and east of Berlin where they were clashes with Soviet during 1945: 1. Stettin, 2. Stargard, 3. Kollin, 4. Arnswalde, 5. Kustrin, 6. Seelow, 7 .Berlin. (1, 2, and 3 Spanish troops in the *Wallonien* Division) (7. Ezquerra Unit in the *Nordland* Division).

The battle in the city of Berlin. Attacking forces (red) and defending forces (black).

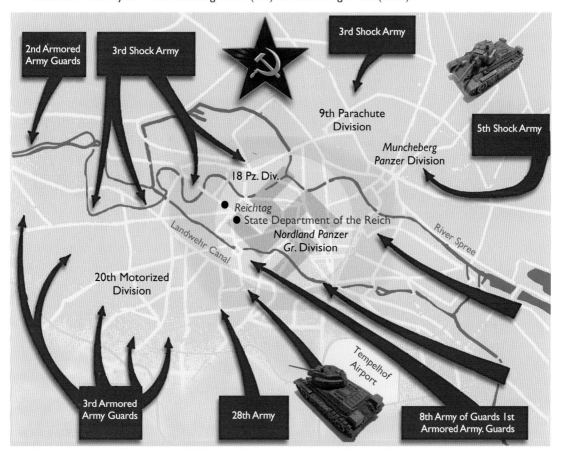

Map of the center of Berlin in 1945 with the locations of the main streets, buildings and places where the Spanish volunteers fought. All of these are mentioned in the next chapter of the book.

0. Reichstag
1. State Department
2. Führerbunker
3. Department of Aviation
4. Hotel Kaiserhof
5. Reichsbank
6. Hotel Adlon

7. Anhalter Bahnhof
8. Möckernbrücke
9. Bahnhof Friedrichstrasse
10. Postdamer Bahnhof
11. Stettiner Bahnhof
12. Lehrter Bahnhof

13 Belle Alliance Platz
14. Potsdamer Platz
15. Leipziger Platz
16. Hans Vogtei Platz
17. Moritz Platz
18. Königs Platz

THE BATTLE OF BERLIN

The Siege Closes In

In January 1945 the Soviet forces had entered Eastern Prussia and their unstoppable advance continued during the first months of this year until the front was temporarily stabilized on the lines of the Rivers Oder and Neisse. The capital of the Reich was at least a hundred kilometers from the front and had become the main target of the eleven armies that made up the 1st Belarusian Front under the command of Marshal Zhukov, who was advancing on the central region of Germany.

However the Germans were able to try to halt their opponents; the place: the hills of Seelow, situated a little more than fifty kilometers from Berlin. This strategic position was made up of some small hills in front of a plain where they waited for the Soviet advance to go by.

In the first hours of April 16 the forces of Zhukov, at the same time as those situated more to the south, corresponding to the seven armies of the 1st Ukrainian Front of Marshal Koniev, started the offensive that had the city of Berlin as its target.

On the other side of the Oder-Neisse line were the German defenses with approximately 400,000 men that were impatiently waiting the attack. These defensive forces were led by General Heinrici (in charge of the Army Group Vistula, which was made up the 9th Army and the 3rd Army Panzer Army) and Field marshal Schörner (commanding the Army Group Centre, which included the 4th Panzer Army). The proportion of men and material favored the attackers; the ratio of men was 5 to 1, 15 to 1 of guns, 5 to 1 of tanks and 3 to 1 in terms of aviation.

At the beginning of the offensive, Zhukov made his 750,000 men and 1,800 tanks advance and open up a path up to the western edge of the River Oder, in the head bridge of Küstrin. There he installed his command post to start the offensive that would arrive at Berlin by the shortest route: the Küstrin-Berlin road. Opposite their positions were the village of Seelow and the hills of the same name. They extended for around forty-five kilometers and made up the strongest point of the German defense system in this area, which was 145 kilometers in total.

At 5:00, Zhukov ordered the flares to be fired that would start the bombardment of the artillery. Close to 17,000 field cannons, mortars and *katyushas* launched a volley that could be heard in the eastern part of Berlin.

The shelling continued for half an hour, destroying trenches and literally crushing the hills of Seelow.

At 5:30 a.m., the 8th Army and the 3rd and 5th assault armies advanced toward German positions, believing that behind the great shower of artillery received, the defenses were being little more than "swallowed up by the ground." In addition, with the aim of making the actions of the survivors more difficult, they used 140 powerful anti-aerial lights to blind them and at the same time make the way easier for the troops. They proved themselves to be of little use, as with the existing dust and smoke they only contributed to making the visibility of the area of the Soviet advance worse.

Finally, when the Soviet vanguard arrived at the first lines of German defense, they found them literally empty, with neither dead or wounded soldiers, which, together with the absence of artillery response made them doubt the real state of the defenders.

In any case, the Soviets continued to advance, leaving the tanks on the roads in order to avoid going onto the swampy plains.

Crouched down along all the hills of Seelow, the Germans waited patiently after having evacuated the first line of defense when faced with the Soviet artillery shelling. The defensive line where the Germans were now waiting corresponded to around fifty-five kilometers approximately from the center of the eastern defense system, which was defended by the most powerful of the three German armies: the 9th Army of General Busse. In spite of this, its real state was way below what it should have been in theory and it had to really hammer down if it wanted to halt the Soviets. On the defensive line was the 9th Parachute Division, previously an elite unit but at that time a second class unit made up of men coming from the *Luftwaffe*. Although the parachutists did not initially find themselves in the first line of fire, the tactical withdrawal of their comrades left them as the first force of the German front in this area, right in the path of the 67th Shock Division of Marshal Chuikov.

The fighting started when the armored units were put under fire by the German artillery, its guns fired, causing significant havoc to the tanks and Soviet vehicles.

At the same time, the 9th Parachute Division opened fire, crushing the Russian infantry men who were in front of its positions, as well as the armored vehicles which had managed to avoid the artillery fire; as a result of the German tactic, the Soviet advance, a priori a military outing for Zhukov, had halted completely.

In any case, the scarce German forces were rendered even weaker due to the numerous losses suffered during the defense of the hills of Seelow.

As previously stated, at the same time Marshal Koniev started his bombardment on a front which extended 390 kilometers to the south of the convergence of the Neisse and the Oder. Using seven armies with a total of around 500,000 men and 1,400 tanks he planned a double assault. The first, led by the 5th Army of the Guard and the 13th Army, with the armored armies of the 3rd and 4th Guard following them, headed toward the Elba and supported Zhukov from the south of Berlin. The second assault, with the 52th Army and the 2nd Polish Army, headed to Dresden.

To confuse the Germans close to his main line of attack, Koniev ordered a dense smokescreen along the whole length of the valley of Neisse to be created.

After fifty minutes of shelling, they installed prefabricated bridges and started the Soviet assault on the dazed German defenses of the 4th Panzer Army. In various areas they were steam rollered, although some points of resistance remained that resisted the initial Soviet push but without managing to stop the advances of Koniev reaching Spremberg, 120 kilometers to the southeast of Berlin.

The Soviet high command was not happy with what had happened, unexpectedly, at this point in the war. Due to the speed of arriving in Berlin (it must be remembered that Koniev had free passage from the south), Zhukov has forgotten about complex strategies, on April 16 he sent his two armies of tanks along roads crammed with vehicles and the remainder went to the 8th Army of the Guard to the left and to the 5th and 3rd

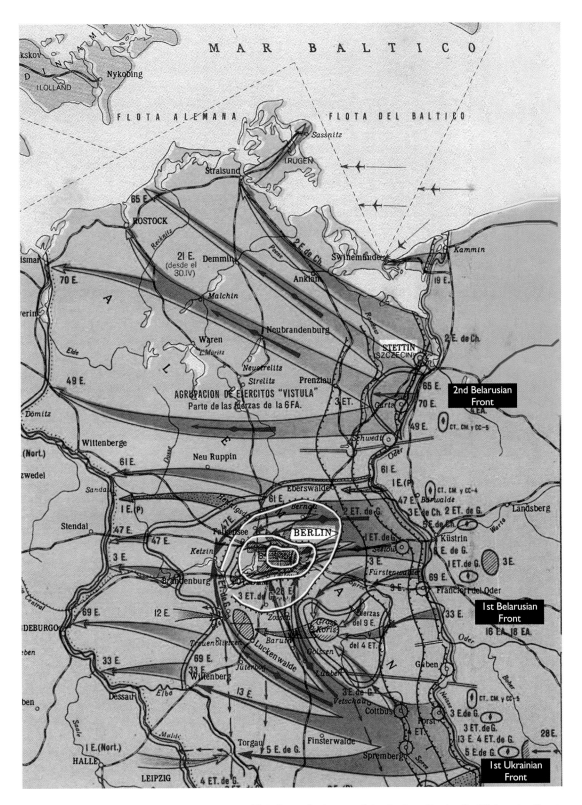

Main lines of advance of the Soviet offensive: 2nd Belarusian Front; 1st Belarusian Front; 1st Ukrainian Front. Maneuver involving these last two on Berlin. Around Berlin are shown the three defensive rings whose locations are detailed in the text of the book.

assault armies in the center and the right respectively.

The two tank armies advanced toward absolute confusion. This part of the Oder Valley which looked out to the hills of Seelow quickly became a gigantic traffic jam of blocked vehicles and soldiers going from one side to another. Only the military units at the head were out of the way of the enormous traffic jams and were able to fight, but in these circumstances the Germans were able to contain them.

At nightfall, the 9th Parachute Division was about to be thrown back. After their first action, the young soldiers fell back to the hills above repelling one intense attack after another. That same night Zhukov had a radio conversation with Stalin who spurred him on with the possibility of heading north with the armored armies of Koniev, to attack Berlin.

The second day of battle began on the hills of Seelow, on April 17. The weakness of the Germans began to be felt whilst the Red Army did not stop contributing units to the fighting, including an army kept in reserve until then (the 47th) which was sent to the vanguard. This continual debilitation required the urgent dispatch of the German reserves from the 56th Panzer Corps to try to maintain the line of fire.

The significant advances of Koniev and the slowing of Zhukov led to Stalin changing Koniev's orders, authorizing him to head for Berlin from the south. This developed into a race between both Soviet marshals to be the first to take Berlin.

During April 8, while Koniev was starting his advance toward the German capital, Zhukov was still stuck in the hills of Seelow. Eventually, his armored vehicles managed to advance fifteen or twenty kilometers toward the southeast of Seelow and to the west of Wriezen, but without being able to open a gap in the German defense.

April 19 finally saw how the German defenses sank when Zhukov's men opened up the sought after gap. The 8th Army of the Guard as well as Chuikov's 1st Armored Army of the Guard opened up a path toward Müncheberg, situated around thirty kilometers to the east of the suburbs of Berlin.

The exact number of losses suffered by both armies in the hills of Seelow is not known, but possibly at least 30,000 Russian soldiers perished, whilst on the German side it could have been around 11,000 losses from among the 18,000 men that were defending the lower hills, with the 3rd Panzer Army decimated by 80,000 soldiers after a week of fighting.

On April 20, Koniev's forces corresponding to the 4th Armored Army of the Guard (under the command of General Leliushenko) advanced some forty-five kilometers to the north, arriving at the city of Luckenwalde, thirty-five kilometers to south of Berlin. For its part, General Ribalko's 3rd Armored Army of the Guard (also integrated into Koniev's forces) took Zossen, thirty kilometers from Berlin.

Meanwhile, during the same day, the 2nd Armored Army of the Guard (belonging to Zhukov's forces) took Bernau, fifteen kilometers to the north east of Berlin, and continued on toward Oranienburg, thirty kilometers to the north of capital.

The left flank of Zhukov's forces penetrated to the southeast until Fürstenwalde, after the destroyed lines of the 9th German Army, a little more than thirty kilometers to the east of Berlin. The fate of the capital of the Third Reich was sealed.

Fighting on the Streets of Berlin

This chapter aims to give an overview of the general events which happened during the Russian attack on Berlin, as well as relating more concretely the various movements of the Spanish volunteers in these final days of the battle for Berlin.

In terms of the general facts, information has been taken from various sources so as to be as certain as possible about the actions which happened on each of those days at the end of April and the beginning of May of 1945. Whilst the participation of the Spanish has been based on the aforementioned scant existing sources. These sources, re-read in the light of the information collected in the most recent studies on the events which happened in the battle of Berlin, lead to the realization that there needs to be a readjustment of the dates which have up to now have been taken as exact in regards to the actions of the members of the *Einheit Ezquerra*, making them coincide more exactly with the events in the city.

The events related here happened in the time elapsed between April 20 and May 2 1945. There is plenty of information on the activity of the Spanish, apart from the period between April 22 and 26, which corresponds to the first days in which there was a Spanish presence in the defensive network of Berlin.

Friday, April 20

After being stationed in Potsdam, not far from the barracks of the 9th Infantry Regiment, the Spanish volunteers transferred to Berlin by order of the *Obergruppenführer* Gottlob Berger, head of recruitment for the *Waffen-SS*. The soldiers were informed of the proximity of the fighting, leaving each of them to make a personal decision whether or not to volunteer for the assigned mission. In principle all the men seemed ready to fight.

The group of Spanish was stationed in two or three companies (more probably in two, with the third in formation with the men who were arriving at the unit's facilities).

The commander (*Sturmbannführer* or *Hauptsturmführer*, according to various sources), Miguel Ezquerra left, after holding talks in Berlin with Ottlob, for Potsdam with the intention of informing his men of these latest orders that he had received. He began by telling the noncommissioned officers of the Spanish contingent: Pedro Zabala Urrutia, Ricardo Botet Moro, Enrique Lafuente Barros, Cipriano Sastre Fraile and Lorenzo Ocañas Serrano.

Saturday, April 21

The 2nd Armored Army of the Guard drew close to the city by the northeast and advanced toward it occupying the territory between the Weissensee (occupied by the 1st Mechanized Corps) and the outskirts of Hohenschönhausen (occupied by the 12th Armored Corps of the Guard). Among them were troops from the 3rd and 5th shock armies at each end.

From the area of Rüdersdorf-Erkner, the troops of the 8th Army of the Guard and the 1st Armored of the Guard also advanced toward the city, carrying out a sweeping maneuver toward the south east with the aim of getting closer to Berlin from the south of the area as well as the area situated to the south east.

The 3rd Armored Army of the Guard reached Königs Wusterhausen, completing the siege of the 9th German Army, rendering them unable to take part in the fighting for the defense of Berlin.

From 11:30, around 500 pieces of heavy artillery, mainly 152 mm, began to hit with their firing not only the suburbs of the capital as previously, but also its center. The enormous quantity of missiles launched affected most of the city, reaching, among other points, the Reichstag, the Brandemburg Bridge, the Royal Palace, Unter den Linden Avenue, etc. Bodies, destroyed vehicles and

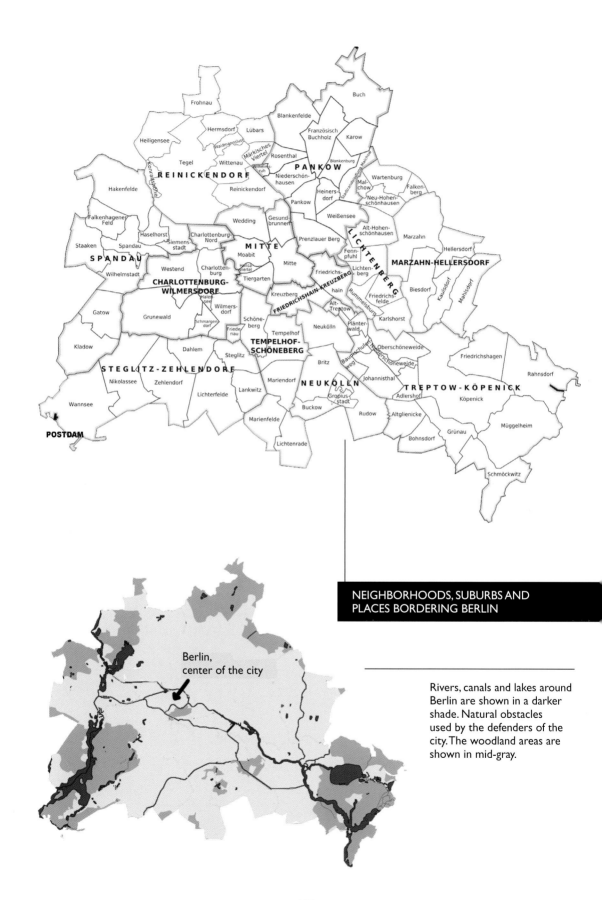

Frohnau

Blankenfelde

Buch

Heiligensee

Hermsdorf Lübars

Französisch
Buchholz Karow

Markisches
Viertel Rosenthal

Tegel Wittenau Wilhelms-
ruh Blankenburg

REINICKENDORF Niederschön-
hausen

PANKOW

Hakenfelde Reinickendorf Heinersdorf Mal-
chow Wartenburg Falken-
berg

Pankow Neu-Hohen-
schönhausen

Falkenhagener
Feld Wedding Gesund-
brunnen Weißensee

Haselhorst Charlottenburg-
Nord Alt-Hohen-
schönhausen Marzahn

Staaken Siemens-
stadt **MITTE** Prenzlauer Berg **LICHTENBERG**

SPANDAU Moabit Fenn-
pfuhl **MARZAHN-HELLERSDORF**

Wilhelmstadt Westend Charlottenburg Mitte Hellersdorf

Hansa-
Viertel Friedrichs- Lichtenberg Biesdorf Kaulsdorf Mahlsdorf

**CHARLOTTENBURG-
WILMERSDORF** Tiergarten **FRIEDRICHSHAIN-KREUZBERG** hain Friedrichs-
felde

Kreuzberg Rummelsburg

Gatow Grunewald Halen-
see Wilmers-
dorf Alt-
Treptow Karlshorst

Schmargen-
dorf Schöne- Neukölln Plänter-
wald

Friede-
nau berg

Kladow Dahlem Tempelhof Oberschöneweide

**TEMPELHOF-
SCHÖNEBERG** Baumschul-
weg Niederschöneweide

Steglitz Britz Friedrichshagen

STEGLITZ-ZEHLENDORF Johannisthal **TREPTOW-KÖPENICK** Rahnsdorf

Nikolassee Zehlendorf Lankwitz Mariendorf **NEUKÖLLN** Adlershof Köpenick

Lichterfelde Gropius-
stadt Müggelheim

Wannsee Buckow Rudow Altglienicke

Marienfelde Bohnsdorf Grünau

POSTDAM

Lichtenrade Schmöckwitz

NEIGHBORHOODS, SUBURBS AND
PLACES BORDERING BERLIN

Berlin,
center of the city

Rivers, canals and lakes around
Berlin are shown in a darker
shade. Natural obstacles
used by the defenders of the
city. The woodland areas are
shown in mid-gray.

other rubble covered the streets, already quite affected by the multiple bombardments of the previous months. The smoke of these explosions and the burning buildings announced the destination of the capital of the Reich: a true inferno of fire, death and devastation was unleashed in the following days.

The point of impact of the artillery fire was much less foreseeable than that of the aerial bombings, which, in some measure, the population of Berlin, just as in other places in Germany, could say they has become used to.

Inside the Berlin *Festung* (fortress), Hitler ordered the arrest of General Weidling and sentenced him to death on suspicion (wrongly) that his troops had withdrawn from the front. The weapons in the anti-aerial towers defending Berlin, responded with their own firing to the intense artillery raid, causing losses for Soviets in the suburb of Marzahn.

The top ministry workers and their organizations left Berlin, whilst the last aerial bombings of the capital were carried out by the U.S.

That same morning the Spanish troops were inspected. (359 men is the number given by F. Vadillo in *Los Irreductibles*). The troops were informed of the new orders anyone who did not want to take part in the difficult undertaking (the defense of Berlin until the last man) was given permission to return to Spain under their own steam, with a little money and safe-conduct out of the German occupied area.

After the address of commander Ezquerra pointing out the causes why many of them had been fighting since the time of the Blue Division: anti-bolshevism, the defense of the West from the Soviet hordes, solidarity with the German people in this terrible war and showing what Spanish soldiers were capable of and how they knew how to fight when the light of victory was shining as well as when the darkness of defeat was visible on the horizon...

After this emotional address, there were thirty-four men who decided not to continue their adventure on the streets of Berlin, opting for the complicated adventure of trying to return to Spain.

The men who decided to stay moved to the centre of Berlin using the most practical means of transport: the Metro (known as the U-Bahn after Unter Bahn, "underground railroad" in German), which was still working.

The journey, had a number of stops at the stations of Krumme Lanke, Toms Hütte, Helene Heim, Dahlen and Hohenzollern, on Line 3 of the U-Bahn; following the route on Line 1 in the direction of the Anhalter area. The Spanish got off the U-Bahn at possibly the closest station to their destination, which would have been Anhalter or the very close Gleisdreieck.

There, following the orders given to Ezquerra, the company in the charge of Pedro Zabala separated from the rest of the men with the order to join the German forces who were trying to regroup in the Alpine redoubt, meeting in this group, according to Ezquerra's version, Martín de Arrizubieta. Following this, the Spanish troops were reduced to two companies.

Regarding the two remaining groups, one stayed under the command of Ezquerra and the other under the orders of second lieutenant Ricardo Botet Moro. This latter contingent was separated from the first, after losing contact during the many skirmishes which took place inside the capital. There were 130 men in total under the direct command of Ezquerra, to them can be added a variable number of soldiers that in one way or another remained temporarily under the command of Ezquerra's unit. In his book he states that around thirty Belgians belonging to the *Wallonien* joined his fighting force; however there is no reference to this in any other source, even bearing in mind that the acts of the Wallonien are well documented.

Route followed, using the Berlin U-Bahn (Metro), by the Ezquerra Unit on April 21, 1945 from Krumme Lanke station, in the area of Potsdam, to the area near to Anhalter station.

When they exited the station and reached the ground, the Spanish were able to see the sad state of the capital: buildings that were blackened and in many cases in ruins, some of them still smoking, destroyed buildings, rubble, barricades. In a word, an inferno ... and the worst was yet to come.

Once in formation, and after Botet had left, Ezquerra's men stayed in an emergency shelter. This was on the ground floor of a half-destroyed building, in what was, in better times, a shoe store. It was near to the State Department, in the area of the ministries.

Ezquerra tells that it was here where, "seventeen French men with the uniform of Doriot's militia, as well as four Belgians of the *SS Wallonie Legion* joined the group." All of them stayed, according to Ezquerra, posted to the unit, but shared out among the Spanish soldiers, not as an independent unit. There is no information that corroborates this, although it is very probable that circumstantially in the clamor of the fighting in the German capital, and at particular moments, men attached to other units, among which could have been French or Belgian men, were temporarily posted in the Spanish unit.

At some point, after arriving in Berlin, the Spanish volunteers were given a significant amount of weapons and munitions. Amongst them were the MP-40 and StG-44 automatic rifles; as well as the feared *panzerfaust*, pistols, hand grenades, MG-42 machine guns, etc. Indispensible weapons for short distance combat against infantry troops as well as armored attack. The great firing capacity provided by these weapons allowed small groups of men to halt, at least temporarily, the advance of the, much superior in number, Soviet troops. In this sense, the MG-42 machine guns and StG-44 assault missile were, together with the dreaded *panzerfaust*, the "stars" of the defense against the Soviets in the streets of Berlin.

The city of Berlin had lost at least two thirds of its buildings as a consequence of the continued "hammering" from the allied bombings, as well as half of the four-million inhabitants it had before the war, many of whom had been forced to leave the capital. The inhabitants that had decided to stay in Berlin had to seek cover in shelters and basements.

As an example of the practical use that was given to any object in the general devastation, the use of the remains of trams and other destroyed or out of action vehicles as barricades can be pointed out, these were then partly filled with rubble to make them stronger as obstacles.

A Berlin semi-ruined by the aerial bombings now prepares for its last defense. Above, wide barricades, reinforced with various vehicles full of the stones taken from the ground of the streets close the main avenues. Under these lines, members of the *Volkssturm* armed with *Panzerfaust* stand guard next to one of the aforementioned barricades.

View of Berlin from one of the towers built in the city for anti-aerial defense, towers that also constituted effective defense fortresses against Soviet land attack. In the foreground, one of the lighter weapons installed on these towers; a quadruple assembly of 20mm model *Flakvierling* 38.

The same rubble from the numerous bombed buildings acted as obstacles at vital times to slow down the advance of the Soviet infantry and its armored elements, whilst creating a terrain of relatively easy defense for men who were well trained and prepared to resist.

Many barricades, strong holds, barriers etc. were created whose mission it was to initially stop the advance of these Soviet troops or at least slow them down. These ranged from the simple pile of rubble and humble sacks, to real fortifications in various buildings (such as that in the Opera House situated in the path of the Soviet advance toward *Reichstag*). Preferably these had machine guns and anti-tank weapons, given the characteristics of combat in the streets of the city.

A special type of "fortification" consisted of the use of tank turrets half buried in various strategic positions in the city, especially the turrets from the Panther tanks half hidden among rubble and located in wide avenues that favored a better control of the terrain and reach of its gun.

As part of the static system of defense of Berlin it was vitally important to have strict control of the bridges that had not been blown up. They were a main defensive elements as anti-tank barriers and obstacles.

However the enormous number of Soviet troops had already tipped the balance long before the assault on the city began. The Soviet army sent a million and a half men supported by vast amount of artillery, tanks and aerial support. Against this force were 45,000 men of the *Wehrmacht* and of the SS, around 2,000 men in the government district and a little over 40,000 men from the *Volkssturm* (armed units with limited training recruited from the civil population), with the armored component being based on around sixty tanks for the defense of the whole city. The ratio was at least 10 to 1 compared to those of the defenders.

The location of the defense forces in Berlin was approximately the following: in the south east was the SS *Nordland* Division; in the south west the 20th *Panzergrenadier* (in a relatively good state); protecting the left flank of the front, to the east, were the remainder of the *Müncheberg* Division; to the north, the remainder of the 9th Parachute Division, and in the center, the 18th *Panzergrenadiers*. Due to the general weakness of these divisions, in all the areas the density of the defensive lines was increased with the support of the poorly prepared men of the *Volkssturm*, the boys of Hitler Youth and the battalions recently created with soldiers scattered from the front, as well as rearguard units. In addition a little support was added by troops of the SS garrison in the capital and lastly by troops from the *Grossdeutschland* Regiment.

In reality, the most numerous of these units which resisted in Berlin was that joined by the men of the *Volkssturm*, with sixty-nine mobilized battalions and another forty-seven that were able to be mobilized, with the problem that in many cases they lacked weapons or had scarce munitions supplies. Also, in Berlin were the remainders of the 503rd SS Battalion of Heavy Tanks, with some *Panzer VI Königstigers*. And it should be remembered that, just like the Spanish unit, the remainder of the French 33rd SS Charlemagne Division and a battalion of the very debilitated Latvian 15th SS Division also took part.

In the capital, the defense forces had only forty-six field cannons and forty-one anti-tank guns, but there were also 270 anti-air-craft guns that could be used in land combat, although their most important proportion was in static positions and therefore did not have the possibility of tactical movement, as was the case of the anti-aerial towers.

Three enormous anti-aerial towers located inside the city provided vital artillery support for the defenders, also serving as excellent observation points in the last days of the war. The first was located in the zoo, the second, in Freidrichshain, and the third in Humboldthain. The towers were situated three kilometers from each other, allowing them to support each other and cover a triangular area in the center of the city with their fire. The maximum horizontal reach of these weapons was 20-22 kilometers, and 14,800 meters for vertical firing. The artillery weapons were mainly made up of 12,8cm, 10,5cm, 8,8cm, and 2cm guns. Their direction of fire was found in other towers situated 350 meters away built for this purpose .

The troops given the task of its garrison mainly belonged to the Luftwaffe and to the Hitler Youth.

Some parts inside these anti-aerial towers were also used as anti-aerial shelters for civilians. Their construction was so robust that they managed to remain practically intact until the end of the war despite being to subjected to punishing intense artillery fire.

The order given on March 6, 1945 to turn Berlin into Fortress Berlin (*Festung* Berlin, in German), with General Reymann in charge of the fortification works, was based on three defensive rings.

The first was a suburban circle (that was placed on top of the route of the circle line of the S-Bahn) that with a perimeter of approximately 234 kilometers circled the whole city. In reality it was based on natural obstacles (lakes, rivers, canals…) and supported in a few defensive positions, mainly consisting of trenches, barricades and anti-tank ditches defended by the *Volkssturm*.

The second was made up of an area covering between the first and the third inner rings, which included the area of government buildings. This second ring was demarcated by the River Spree, to the north, and by the Landwehr canal, to the south; consisting of a perimeter of ninety-six kilometers. It crossed the suburbs of the capital and had a number of defensive elements which in any case were insufficient for what was needed.

The third ring, with a perimeter of forty kilometers, covered the central neighborhoods of Berlin, and was nominally divided into eight defensive sectors plus one central one, each of which was commanded by a colonel and named alphabetically using letters "A" to "H" and using the letter "Z" after "*Zitadelle*" or Citadel for the central sector. In this sector were the most important government buildings such as the *Reichstag*, the State Department and the various State departments; it was the last area of Berlin to fall into Soviet hands.

Sectors A and B (in the north) were garrisoned by the remainder of the 9th Parachute Division with 4,000 men; in sector C (*Neukölln* and *Treptow*) there was the SS *Nordland* Division, with 1,500 men and twenty armored vehicles (mainly *Sturmgeschutz III* and *Panzer V Panther* assault cannons) supported by 2,000 men from the *Volkssturm*, to which the remainder of the 33rd SS *Charlemagne* Division were added after managing to gain access to Berlin on April 24; sector D (*Tempelhof* and *Schöneberg*) was defended by the remainder of the *Müncheberg* Division, consisting of 3,000 men and thirty armored vehicles supported by detachments from the SS, the police, the *Volkssturm* and a SS Latvian battalion; sector E (*Steglitz-Zehlendorf*) was assigned to the 18th Division of *Panzergrenadiers* that posted 3,000 men and some tanks, reinforced by the remains of various *Luftwaffe*, *Volkssturm* and SS units; sector F (*Spandau* and *Charlottenburg*) was mainly defended by 3,000 members of Hitler Youth and members of the RAD (*Reichsarbeitsdienst* – Labor organization of workers employed by the sector); in sectors G and H (neighborhoods in the northeast on the axis of the Frankfurter-Allee) the men of the *Grossdeutschland* Regiment were posted, and finally sector Z or *Zitadelle* was defended by the *Kampfgruppe Mohnke*.

Sunday 22nd to Thursday 26th

There is a lack of information and data showing the activities carried out by the men of the Spanish unit, therefore what is narrated here for these dates concerns the general events of the battle.

Sunday, April 22

The Soviet troops, after difficult clashes, penetrated through the northeast to the suburbs of Blakenburg, Heinersdorf, Buchlolz, Malchow and Biesdorf, the front arriving at the neighborhoods of Weissensee, Lichtenberg and Pankow in heavy rain.

From this day, according to Norling in his book *Raza de Vikingos*, the *Nordland* Division ceased to exist as a military unit, distributing its men in combat groups (*kampfgruppen*, in German) whose troops could have been around 35-45 men. These groups were forced to withdraw to positions in Tiergarten due to the rising pressure of the Soviet machine, which carried on its slow but determined advance on battered Berlin.

Monday, April 23

Despite adverse weather conditions and intense Soviet pressure, some small reinforcements for its defense arrived in the city. In many cases this was soldiers that arrived after days of travelling from their withdrawal from the east. Among them was the *Grossadmiral* Dönitz naval battalion, under the command of Franz Kuhlmann. With this the heterogeneity of the defense troops of Berlin was increased even further.

In the face of the suspected penetration by the Russian troops in the tunnel of the U-Bahn and the S-Bahn (a local train whose lines also crossed the city), the traffic was stopped and barricades put up in many of them.

General Weidling took command of the defense area of Berlin by Hitler's orders. The Russians occupied the suburbs of Berlin, where the defensive siege was weaker. The neighborhoods of Britz, Lichtenfels, Marienfelde, Lichtenberg and Prenzlauer Berg fell one after another.

In the south, the Teltow canal served as a "border line", while to the north the Hohenzollern and Schiffahrts canals (the latter only partially) fulfilled the same mission.

Tuesday, April 24

The 20th Panzergrenadiers Division was forced to withdraw to the Island of Wannsee, with its post on the defensive lines covered by the 18th *Panzergrenadiers* Division, until then the reserve troops. The 9th Parachute Division prepared for the defense of the sectors situated more to the north, being based on the area of the Humboldthain anti-aerial tower; the Panzer *Müncheberg* Division defended the area of Tempelhof airport, and the 11th SS *Panzergrenadiers* Division was responsible for defending the area of Neukölln-Kreuzberg.

On the Soviet side, the 3rd Armored Army of the Guard managed to cross the then "border" Teltow canal, supported by the 6th and 7th Armored Corps of the Guard, the Intense but useless defense ran under the 20th and 18th panzer grenadier divisions supported by a limited armored force made up mainly of PzKfw IV. The 12th Fusiliers Corps of the Guard had already faced Weidling's men who were defending the S-Bahn station and the Humboltdthain anti-aerial tower. The 7th Fusiliers Corps arrived at the Alexanderplatz. The 26th Corps of the Guard and 32nd Fusiliers Corps of the 5th Shock Army arrived at the Schlachthof complex, already in the inner defense ring. The 9th Fusiliers Corps crossed the Spree, causing the withdrawal of members of the 11th SS *Panzergrenadiers* Division assigned to defend the area.

In the south the 3rd Armored Army and the 1st Ukrainian Front joined together.

The day was again rainy, a factor that affected the combatants on both sides.

Wednesday, April 25

The overcast day gave way to a sunny day, but the city was covered by a great cloud of smoke caused by the many fires and explosions.

The Soviet troops consolidated their positions in the various suburbs of the capital, intensifying the clashes with the defenders mainly in the streets of the east and north districts.

The 47thArmy and the 4th Armored Army of the Guard advanced toward Ketzin.; the 125th Fusiliers Corps attacked Spandau and the Gatow aerodrome, although they met with strong resistance. The 2nd Armored Army of the Guard found itself in the outskirts of the suburb of Siemensstadt; the 3rd Shock Army crossed the Hohenzollern canal. The 12th Fusiliers Corps of the Guard advanced toward Moabit, while the 7th Fusiliers Corps was close to the Alexanderplatz. The 5th Shock Army advanced slowly toward the center of the city and the 9th Fusiliers Corps forced the Landwehr canal until arriving close to Görlitzer station. The 8th Army of the Guard, after crossing the Teltow canal, headed toward the area surrounding the Tempelhof airport, where they met with stubborn resistance, given that keeping the airport meant keeping alive the hope of receiving reinforcements and provisions by air.

On this day, Joachim Ziegler, commander in chief of the *Nordland* Division (or, more precisely, of the remainder of its combatants), was called to the State Department, and replaced in his post by the *Brigf* Gustav Krukenberg, recently arrived in the capital of the Reich with the command of a French combat group of the 33rd SS *Charlemagne* Division that possibly, according to Norling, was made up of more that three hundred men.

The 3rd Armored Army of the Guard advanced on the defensive ring marked by the lines of the S-Bahn, progressing from the south to the center zone of the city.

Above the city thousands of miles de pamphlets in German "rained down", printed by the Soviets, directed as much at the soldiers as the civilians resisting in Berlin. The literal translation of these was the following: "To the German soldiers and officers and the population of the city of Berlin. The Red Army is centering its forces on Berlin. Tens of thousands of cannons are being transported to the capital. In the aerodromes thousands of heavy bombers are waiting. We have thousands of tanks. The Red Army has the war power of its allies to deploy its powerful forces. Decisive days are drawing close. The troops of the Red Army are prepared for a definitive assault. If you do not heed our warnings and do not cease your resistance, we will send an incredible cloud of fire and shrapnel against Berlin. We are prepared to annihilate and destroy any point of resistance. People of Berlin, use your brains! Do you wish to die for something that has nothing to do with you, sacrificing yourselves for a handful of ruling Nazis? Disobey their orders! Do not dig any more trenches and abandon your work in the weapons industry! Hide in your shelters! Give food and lodging to the soldiers and officers who do not wish to continue fighting and recognize that you have lost the war! — Soldiers and officers of the German Armies, men of the *Volkssturm*, abandon all resistance, hand yourselves in, go home, go to the shelters! If you disregard our suggestions, you will be guilty of the death of your parents, wives and children, and the loss of all your belongings.

The command of the Red Army guarantees that it will respect the lives and the homes of all those (including members of the National Socialist party) who stop putting up resistance and hand themselves in to the Red Army. The Command of the First Belarusian Front of the Red Army."

Thursday, April 26

During the afternoon the most intense Soviet attacks made the Germans who were defending the north of the capital withdraw to the main railroads of north Berlin.

These attacks were temporarily contained, in the main thanks to the artillery support that the defenders received from the aforementioned anti-aerial defense towers in the north of the city.

The 79th Fusiliers Corps advanced on the Westhafen canal, with only the S-Bahn station of Beusselstrasse resisting, continued toward the station of Görlitzer and pressed on to Kreuzberg. Zhukov's forces invaded Tempelhof airport, whilst other forces progress toward Landwehr canal.

At the end of the day, the 8th Army of the Guard and the 1st Armored Army of the Guard had Potsdamer Strasse to their left and the Heinrich von Kleist park in front of them.

The 18th Panzer Division sent a combat group supported by six tanks and fifteen armored vehicles to try and restore contact with the 20th Division of armored grenadiers, although it met with strong Soviet resistance. The *Müncheberg* Division, meanwhile, took up positions in the area near to the Tempelhof airport, six kilometers from the State Department.

Many of the wounded soldiers remained on the front line despite their circumstances, at times due to the latent fear that a travelling control made up of SS firing squads would detain them and hang or shoot them as deserters.

The facades of some Berlin streets had their walls painted with phrases to inflame the defense of the city such as "Before dawn is when it is the darkest", "Berlin is still German" and "We are withdrawing, but we will win", however, in contrast with the phrases, these streets began to fill up with corpses, of soldiers and civilians, whose bodies remained where they fell after a grenade or rocket explosion.

The city was "strangled", the newspapers stopped being published, in particular, the official newspaper of the party, the Völkischer Beobachter, stopped going to press on April 26 1945 (Vadillo, in *Los Irreductibles*, puts the date as the 24th), being replaced by a new "newspaper" called *Der Panzerbär* (The Armored Bear), which was the vehicle for the defenders of Berlin. The contents of this paper of only 4 pages were dictated by the propaganda machine of the NSDAP (*Nationalsozialistische Deutsche Arbeiterpartei*). Its contents, as well as encouraging the defenders of the city, highlighted the links that united the cause of the NSDAP with European civilization against the "Asian" enemy. The *Panzerbär* was only produced for six days.

On the same day of April 26 the Soviets launched a propaganda newspaper over the capital called *Nachrichten für die truppe*, whose title meant "Berlin has been surrounded", and on its first page appeared phrases such as: "Two thirds of the city have been occupied. – Berlin has been surrounded. –Violent fighting in the entrances to the Metro. –From yesterday evening, Berlin was isolated from the rest of the world. The Soviet Armies have closed the siege around the capital of the Reich and Potsdam. Tank units coming from the north east attacked Ketzin by Nauen, to join with the Soviet forces approaching the ring from the south west, between Potsdam and Brandenburg. In the last few hours of yesterday, Berlin was surrounded by a wide ring of troops. All traces of fronts in the north and the center of Germany have been erased, and the men and the material from these can be directed to the siege around Berlin. Information has been released regarding the involvement of Berlin shortly after the means of propaganda still avai-

Soviet JS-2 tank advancing along the ruined streets of Berlin

lable to the Party let the world know that the Führer led the decisive battle around to Berlin, to therefore feed the myth that National Socialism would heroically to its twilight. However the population of Berlin has not seen the Führer and nor does it expect any message ... – Theater of combat. The 11th Army has been annihilated. – Its commander in chief was General of Artillery Walter Lucht; together with all the staff officers, he has handed himself in to the Anglo-American forces. – The Russians crossed the Elba."

On this date the vital supplies of gas and water to the city stopped.

During these days the Spanish troops patrolled the areas assigned to them in the area corresponding to the second defensive ring, taking up positions to defend it. Life became, despite the number of bombardments that the city was subjected to, relatively routine for those passing time in their lodgings and on the defensive posts. During this time, as had happened in the time of the Blue Division, the volunteers mixed with the civilians. The Spanish received the news of the Soviet advance, and they felt that the long awaited moment had come to face the

Russians and show them how Spanish soldiers fought, loyal to their ideals, not afraid of dying and with the firm intention of not ceding an inch of the terrain they had been assigned to defend.

On 23rd they received news that the Russian had entered Potsdam. There were approximately fifty Spaniards stationed there under the command of a sergeant called Cerezo, most of whom after fighting with extreme courage, even in face to face combat, perished. Cerezo and a few more men managed to survive and cross Russian lines, although the route of these men is lost in the chaos of the last days of the Reich.

On the 24th The Red Army pulled the noose that was strangling Berlin even tighter, but at a cost of suffering a severe loss caused by the defenders of the capital.

In the city, the regular service of the surface railroad and the metro were interrupted.

During these days in which the siege was increasingly choking Berlin, some of the recruited men were able to desert before they were completely under siege, although there is no proof that confirms or denies these desertions.

Friday, April 27

The Soviet troops advanced toward the Potsdamer Platz and Alexanderplatz. The area is bombarded by huge numbers of missiles, especially the dreaded "Katyuska" rocket launchers, also known as the organs of Stalin. After this, the infantry and armored troops attacked. This area next to the "Z" zone, was defended with blood and fire from building to building, doorway to doorway, metro to metro, which did not stop the loss of an indeterminate number of key positions. The intervention of various Tiger II tanks of the 503 SS Battalion managed to temporarily halt the Soviet advance. With a view to stopping the progression of these Russian troops to the center of the city as much as possible, they blew up at least 120 of the 248 bridges in Berlin.

Members of the 2nd Armored Army of the Guard occupied Siemensstadt, drawing close to the bank where the Spree joins with the Havel. The 35th Mechanized Brigade crossed the Spree at Ruhleben.

The 79th Fusiliers Corps advanced toward the district of Moabit.

Leipziger Platz was subjected to powerful artillery fire. The 55th Armored Brigade of the Guard advanced on the area of the Olympic stadium and the sports academy of the Reich. The Soviet vanguard arrived at the areas of the Zoo, Spandau and Gatow. The area of Tempelhof airport also remained under complete Soviet control, negating the possibility of the defenders receiving reinforcements by air.

The 8th Army of the Guard consolidated their positions near to the Landwehr canal. It was rumored that the Russians had blown up the airlocks of this canal, so that the water would begin to run through some railroad and metro tunnels. As these tunnels were used as shelter by many people it is possible that they drowned.

The 3rd Shock Army attacked the Stettiner station, facing the units of the 9th Parachute Division.

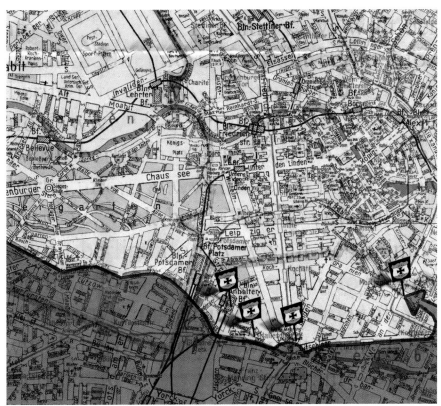

Front line in the battle of Berlin during April 27, 1945 with the various positions of the Spanish volunteers.

At 17:00, after heavy shelling supported by aerial action, the Soviets of the 3rd Armored Army of the Guard broke through both sides of the Hohenzollerndamm.

The air was full of dust and smoke, grenades were going off anywhere, the streets were deserted, full of rubble and craters that would later serve the defenders as places where they could hide to face the advances of the Soviet troops.

The 5th Shock Army progressed slowly toward the area of the Schlesischer railroad station and the Friedrichshain anti-aerial tower.

The Spanish volunteers left their concentration point in the old shoe store after receiving orders, from an air lieutenant colonel who arrived there, to transfer to their new center of operations. This was located in the barracks of the military police (the Reich security service, RSD or *Reichssicherheitsdienst*) quite near to their previous post but much more suited to house troops. A battalion of SS troops was also stationed there.

They were finally given a deployment area in the second ring of the defensive framework of the city.

Their first mission was close, so the men rested and readied their weapons. They knew that within a short time some of them would fall, but even so, the desire to contribute in some small part to the defense of the capital of the Reich could be seen in the strength of their faces and the proud desire to face the enemy as soon as possible.

A liaison arrived at the barracks where the Spanish troops were stationed with the order for commander Ezquerra to appear before the head of the sector: an Engineers lieutenant colonel whose staff officers were in a square close by, that together with its surrounding buildings, who were being submitted to the continual explosions of Russian shells. This chief gave a Ezquerra details of the mission that was being assigned to the

Spanish troops, which would consist of holding back the expected Soviet advance in the area of Moritz Platz.

Upon receiving the orders, Ezquerra passed them on to his men. Their welcomed them with cries and cheers, finally they could release all the tension which had accumulated over the last few days. They would be facing their old Soviet enemies again.

Ezquerra gave the order to leave to the 1st Company, under the command of sergeant Ocañas (previously second lieutenant, or rather, according to the work *Yo, muerto en Russia* with the post of lieutenant of the SS). The unit advanced from the area of the Department of Aviation, protecting themselves behind the wall of the ruined buildings that populated the streets, as well as behind any object which could serve as a shelter from Russian fire. The distance to the Moritz was about two kilometers to the south east, they decided to follow the fastest route, due to the urgency of the situation. This consisted of following Wilhelmstrasse to Stadtmittestrasse and then taking short cuts down the narrower streets to arrive at Oranienstrasse, which had the square at its end.

Making their way between the rubble that covered the streets of the center of Berlin, meant they took around two hours to arrive close to the Moritz Platz. They could already hear the roar of heavy fighting between the German forces and the combined Soviet infantry and armored troops in the area.

There, the Spanish volunteers were witness to the capacity for combat of the youngsters of the Hitler Youth who were defending the metro station. Ezquerra and his men could not help being surprised how these young boys, still of school age, armed largely with anti-tank weapons, hounded the invaders, managing to turn a number of T-34 tanks into scrap. Their attitude encouraged the Spanish even more, if that was at all possible. If some young boys could hold their positions, then why couldn't they, with all their many years of combat experience?

At the end of the street was the small Moritz Platz, which was being advanced upon by the Armored Soviets under protection of its infantry.

To the left of these positions of the Spanish were German troops sheltering in the ruins. As they did not know about the presence of Ezquerra's men, they shot at them, causing them to drop to the ground and respond to friendly fire. When both groups finally identified themselves the shooting stopped. The incident caused the death of three men with another two suffering serious injuries. The reason for the confusion was that the Germans heard voices in a language unknown to them and confused them with Russian troops.

After this event they continued with their advance until they made contact with the enemy, attacking and taking the first barricades behind which the Russians were sheltering, whilst the continual fire of the tanks rang out over the whole area under dispute.

There they waited for the new hordes of men and "Stalin" tanks that were approaching from the south of the square. Crouched down after assuming defensive positions they waited for the order from their chief to shoot against the Soviets. The Russians advanced with caution, although they could not help falling in all the ambushes laid down by the Spanish following Ezquerra' orders.

Shots were raining down on all sides on the Russian infantry, who, when sheltering and falling back, left the way open for the men shooting at the tanks, who managed to finish off four or five of the enormous IS-2 tanks. Losses in the *Einheit Ezquerra* were inevitable, but they managed to halt the advance and cause the withdrawal of the Russians.

After this first clash, the men, on their commander's orders, withdrew slightly to reinforce their positions and take the wounded away. During the confrontation reinforcements of Latvian troops arrived, as well as possibly some other soldiers "on the wrong road" who was attached to the unit temporarily.

The Russians reloaded in less than a quarter of an hour, and the inferno of firing was unleashed again. Yet again, the defenders managed to give a good account of themselves with the armored Soviets, undefended when they were not accompanied by the infantry that knocked down the men crouched down that lay in wait with their anti-tank weapons behind any heap of rubble, holes in the buildings, windows, doorways or at times even approached boldly.

New losses were suffered, on this occasion of at least six men, but they managed to again resist the spearhead of the Soviet advance.

Several hours passed from when they arrived at the square and they were able to see with their own eyes the difficulty of the fighting against the enormous and unstoppable Russian army, which attacked again and again, with seemingly unstoppable reinforcements. Exhaustion was present in all of the defenders, fortunately for them, once the area was stabilized, they were replaced by German SS troops.

This was the first direct contact with the Russian enemy on the streets of Berlin; just an introduction of what would be a coming and going from one area to another in danger, which would lead them to become a real fire fighting unit that tried to halt the fire wherever it occurred.

The Spanish returned to the area near to the Department of Aviation and they prepared to recover their energy after the exhausting clashes they had been in. However the situation in the *Zitadelle* sector was worsening with every second. Men were lacking in each of the gaps that were being opened up by the Russians in the defensive framework and they looked again to the Spanish among other veteran troops. Their mission this time was to try to recover the bridge situated next to the Belle Alliance Platz on the Landwehr canal, which was being attacked by the Russians. Its loss would mean giving free access to the Soviet troops that were advancing from the south on their journey toward the main official buildings of Berlin, headed by the New State Department, in whose bunker Hitler directed, or at least tried to direct, the defense of the capital.

The Spanish advanced via Leipziger Strasse in the direction of Leipziger Platz and from there they won back Wilhelmstrasse, which was under intense artillery fire at that time. Sometimes it was impossible to continue advancing along the street, so the men had to find a way through the buildings by making holes in the walls separating them, as well as through the cellars. Due to the rising difficulty presented by advancing even through the buildings, they decided to direct their route toward Anhalter station. Here, there were many people watching as these soldiers who were carrying a red-yellow-red flag on their arms advanced bravely toward their meeting with the enemy. Although all seemed lost, the character and the good spirits of the Spanish allowed many of the refugees to breathe a slight sigh of relief.

Ezquerra planed to arrive close to the Belle Alliance Platz by means of the metro tunnels leading off from Anhalter station. They found themselves in complete darkness for most of the time, so they advanced with the light of the few torches carried by the officers and two by two so as not to lose contact among the men.

They were to return to the surface via the U-Bahn Möckernbrücke station, so they still had to advance one more kilometer to the east to arrive at their target.

The Belle Alliance Platz was a crossroads which adjoined the Landwehr canal to the south, which was crossed by a bridge already being approached by Soviet advances. The whole area was being subjected to a continuous bombardment, where the cannon fire, high caliber mortars and the deadly "katyuskas" demolish everything. However the defenders, well covered, resisted the strong push from the Russians. From the various streets that led off from the square more and more troops arrived, Germans from the north and Soviets from the south.

The clamor of the fighting was felt by the Spanish, who carefully, but with increasing speed, were approaching the square. They advanced covered by the walls of the buildings of the street that ran parallel to the canal, taking advantage of the heaps of rubble in it and using them as defense against the enemy fire that was growing stronger from the other side. In a few minutes they managed to arrive at their destination, where the fire was stronger. Just a few hundred meters to the south were the Soviets.

The Spanish joined in the defense of the extreme north of the bridge, still in German hands. There they had the possibility of again seeing the courage of the youngsters from Hitler Youth. These boys were in charge of the defense of many of the Berlin bridges.

The Soviet infantry advanced together with the tanks, firing continuously. They were answered with a fire not as heavy but very targeted, as it was concentrated on the area of the bridge they were trying to cross. At least six tanks managed to make their way with their weapons to Wilhelmstrasse.

The Spanish, who were on the left side of the beginning of the bridge, protected by the remains of buildings, started to attack. At the culminating moment of the fighting, by chance, they met another Spaniard posted to a German regiment who eventually became attached to the *Einheit*. He was Ismael Múgica, who became one of Ezquerra' s right hand men, due to his extensive knowledge of combat in

Attackers and defenders.

Above Soviet *Ilyushin Il-2 "Shturmovik"* planes attacking the ground.

To the right, 12,8cm Flak 40 anti-aerial artillery placed in one of the defense towers.

the streets as well as the German language, according to Ezquerra' s version of events.

Three of the tanks that were advancing aimed their positions without stopping their fire. A trio of men: Sastre, Vázquez and Múgica, advanced with their backs to the walls of the buildings followed by another group which included Ezquerra. In this exchange of shots and when nearing the tanks with his *panzerfaust*, Vázquez was wounded. His comrades managed to rescue him, putting their lives in danger under the continual rattling of the Russian automatic weapons.

The final result was positive for the Spanish, thanks to the use of the *panzerfaust*. One of the missiles landed on the first tank, causing an explosion that caused its destruction and killing its occupants. The same happened to three more Russian tanks. The remainder, seeing that they were without the support of the infantry, opted for withdrawal.

The Russians soon returned to the charge with new troops that managed to cross over the bridge thanks to their armored advances. Some of the first houses of the north bank were occupied by the Russians, allowing them to take up positions and make a front on them.

Ezquerra' s men, together with other groups of German soldiers, was assigned the difficult task of clearing them. Ezquerra was hurt in this clash when he fell down a hole into a cellar, which due to the recent explosion of a grenade still had burning embers. With his injured ankle he was taken out by his comrades and evacuated to be looked after at a time when circumstances permitted in the first aid facilities located in the Hotel Excelsior. In the absence of Ezquerra it was lieutenant Múgica who took charge of the Spanish unit.

Meanwhile, the rest of the men from the unit maintained their positions, for a while in some areas they fought hand to hand combat. Hundreds and hundred of Russians conti-

nued their advance despite the many losses they suffered, as these were supplemented by reinforcements. However the German resistance was stubborn which allowed them to stop this new blow, that is, after having lost a significant amount of ground after each Russian attack.

Due to the continual displacement of the line of fire a small number of German troops stayed behind enemy lines; among them were some Spanish and some youngsters from Hitler Youth. They had to fight but not be captured by the, ever growing number of, Russian troops. After intense hand to hand combat, and with some degree of luck, they managed to get back to German controlled territory.

At the end of this, after getting out of this rat trap, they always, according to Ezquerra, counted their losses. Among the deaths and disappearances there were also the cases of bravery: sergeant Carlos Ramos Valdevalles, Eugenio Álvarez Valdecasas, César García Pesquera, Luis Ángel Casado Aspe and Miguel Ramírez Jarama.

The survivors, exhausted after a whole day of tough fighting, subjected continuously to artillery fire that turned the Berlin air into a dark, at times unbreathable, smoke, embarked on their journey back to their barracks.

Again the Spanish volunteers were transferred to new accommodation. From there they would live in some of the Department of Aviation buildings, a large building, modern at the time, that occupied the corner of Leipzig and Wilhelm, close to Leipziger Platz, which in days gone by had had a lively social life and was then turned into a devastated area by the continual bombings.

To avoid civilians being exposed to the hardships brought about by the war, there was an attempt to house them in many shelters, among which the ministry stands out as due to its great size, it was able to give protection to thousands of people.

Saturday, April 28

The fighting grew more intense and constant as the days went by. Exhaustion hit all the combatants, although the defenders kept going as there was no relief for them. Although fighting had been intense in the proceeding days, from the morning of this day the battle reached its climax and would stay at this level until the end.

The 79th Fusiliers Corps continued the advance toward Alt Moabit and had the *Reichstag* in its sights, with the mined and fortified Moltke bridge as its main obstacle. The 2nd Armored Army of the Guard was next to the Landwtheehr canal in the area of Moabit. The 5th Shock Army advanced on the areas of Frankfurter Alle and Lansberger Chausse without managing to take the Friedrichshain anti-aerial tower.

The 26th Fusiliers Corps of the Guard attacked the Alexanderplatz again while the 32nd Fusiliers Corps finished with the last resistance at the Schlesischer railroad station.

The 9th Fusiliers Corps took the Spittelmarkt, a little more than a kilometer from the State Department of the Reich.

The 3rd Armored Army of the Guard and the 8th Army of the Guard carried out an attack to cross the Landwehr canal.

The battle began for Wilhemstrasse, which had for some days been subjected to significant land and aerial bombing and shelling. The permanent fire of the mortars, artillery and of the tanks, together with the enormous number of troops that the Russians presented in combat, forced in many cases the withdrawal of these defending troops in search of new defensive positions.

The Spanish volunteers scattered after many adventures met in the Anhalter Platz where they fought side by side together with their comrades amongst whom were the decimated troops of the *Müncheberg* and *Nordland* divisions, in the area of Alexanderplatz, the Anhalter and Potsdam stations, and Hermann Göring Strasse.

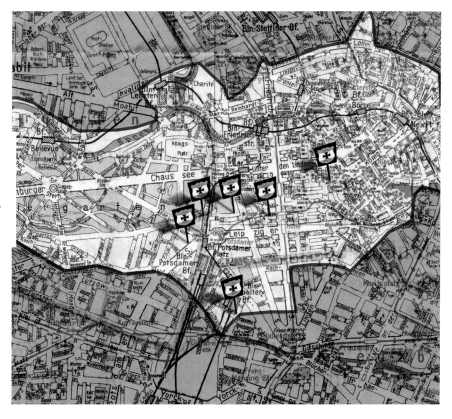

Front line at the battle of Berlin during April 28, 1945 with the various positions of the Spanish volunteers.

There were no orders, simply fight and resist at a given point, until being finally removed from it due to the incessant gun and mortar fire that literally flattened the positions of the defenders. And again on the next corner, the same operation: wait for the armored enemy against a wall in the ruins without firing until the last second, although each time there was less room to fall back.

When possible, the defenders of the city used the few German armored vehicles to move from one side to another. Regarding this, an *SS-Sturmann* Spaniard named Horacio E, left this description: "Whenever possible we got into the tanks so that we didn't have to walk, we were tightly packed together and holding on to one another so as not to fall into potholes. I remember a boy who we called 'the Asturian' who wore a large shield of Spain sewn onto his sleeve who, when going over one of these potholes, slipped to the right side of the tank with the bad luck to get caught up in the chains, let out some terrible cries when his leg was wrenched from his body at the groin, it all happened in a few seconds but to me they seemed eternal, there was nothing we could do for him, he bled to death shortly afterwards."

The Russians continued their relentless advance, arriving with their tanks accompanied by infantry troops on Wilhelmstrasse until they were close to the Department of Aviation. In this area there were defenders together with the troops that had withdrawn from various places on the front. A front that was turning into a closed circle.

The defending troops, subjected to incessant shelling and bombing, were still capable, thanks to their anti-tank cannons, to their *panzerfaust* and, above all, to the heroic and desperate resistance of each and every one of the men, of making the Russians pay dearly for each meter they advanced.

At the end of the day, many bomb craters left the streets of Friedrichstrasse in an impassable state.

When dawn broke, the *Einheit*'s liaison and sergeant and interpreter informed Ezquerra of the recent events. The men were taken by SS troops from the square where they had faced the Soviet advances the previous day. After this, he ordered them to meet again on the cellar of the Department of Aviation.

Once Ezquerra had reunited with his men, and after a short break, he assigned them, together with a Latvian battalion under the command of commander Willi, (or Wallis according to the book *David against Goliath: Latvian volunteers in the Waffen-SS (1941-1945)* by Carlos Caballero) the mission of halting the Soviet advances when they appeared.

Their position was near to the elegant Hotel Excelsior, between the Department of the Army and the State Department, near to the Potsdamer Platz and the rest of the government departments. The hotel was linked by tunnels with Potsdamer station, which, in this situation, favored movement from one place to another avoiding the continuous enemy fire on the streets of Berlin.

The appearance of the Potsdamer Platz was unsettling, covered with destroyed vehicles, mutilated bodies and the wounded who were trying to find cover in the nearby station.

The head of the sector, in telephone contact with commander Willi, gave orders for Ezquerra's men to move to the area of the Kaiserhof Hotel. As it was only a few hundred meters away, the move was not difficult in spite of the intense fire falling on the Zitadelle. When they arrived in the area, the men assumed positions in the hotel and its surroundings.

The Kaiserhof had been one of the best hotels in Berlin, and due to its proximity to the neighborhood of government buildings,

Battery of "Katyuska" rocket launchers opening fire in the streets of Berlin.

Pictures of the side, front, and whole of the German Department of Aviation building. From here many of the units that took part in the defense of the city were organized, among them the unit led by Ezquerra. This building still exists today although with some alterations from that of the Third Reich era. Drawings done by the author with the collaboration of J. Pérez.

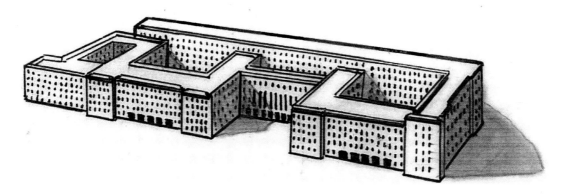

as well as to the various foreign embassies and, of course, it was very close to the State Department, all the important people in the III Reich wanted to stay at the establishment or at least be seen in the salons. For this reason in these elegant times it was common to find the German elite there. Even Hitler, before he was Chancellor, had stayed there, and later, once in power, he had an apartment there.

Ezquerra placed his men at strategic points in the hotel, waiting for the imminent arrival of the Russian advances from the south east. The atmosphere in the building was totally dreamlike. Here there was the same luxury and artificiality that there had been in the already far off time of peace; it was not for nothing that they continued to welcome the same bigwigs, diplomats, journalists and civil servants of high social status, as well as high ranking military men. Of course, there were many elegantly dressed women, artists, cabaret girls, high class call girls as well as food that could not be found, or had never been found, in the larders of most homes in Berlin, including the best French wines and champagnes.

In the microcosm of the hotel they lived each moment as if it was their last. The wild parties were often held in the hotel's cellar, as using the upper floors increased the risks exponentially. It was the kingdom of depravity and luxury, in which some of the men assigned the mission of defending the sector also participated in, as it seemed was the case with some of the men of the *Einheit Ezquerra*, tempted by beautiful women.

Outside of these walls, the Russians drew closer to the area, on this occasion advancing down Kronen Street . They were reconnaissance groups, followed by the tanks, mainly T-34 and the powerful IS-2. The Spanish, French and Belgian soldiers in this area again went to the defense against the Russian incursion, taking up position in the nearby houses with their anti-tank weapons, the MG-42, the

assault rifles and all available weapons. From positions at times practically impossible for the Soviets to find due to the quantity of rubble covering the streets, they were able to give a good account of themselves to the tanks and enemy soldiers.

After finishing off the men of the Russian infantry with intense fire, some men had enough courage to approach the tanks with their *panzerfaust* close up to be able to deal definitive blows aimed at the most unprotected areas: the turret, areas between the wheels, the base, the part next to the driver of the tank ... If they met with a T-34 then it was no easy task, the job became many times more difficult when trying to destroy the monstrous armored forty-six ton tank that was the IS-2. Despite this, after fighting that lasted at least two hours, the result was five tanks out of action, as well as dozens of fatalities and wounded men on both sides.

One of the Spanish, nicknamed "Shorty", on his own managed to turn three tanks into scrap, Múgica finished off another and the fifth was left to sergeant Ferrer.

After this fighting the Russians withdrew again, after having managed to gain some ground from their original position of departure, squeezing ever tighter the grip that was choking Berlin. Once they had been relieved from their positions by relief troops, Ezquerra's men went in the open air to the Hans Vogtei Platz.

During this patrol they could not see any movement from the enemy, and they took up strategic positions to be able to see any likely new Soviet attacks. Hours later the Spanish were again relieved by a German relief battalion, if there was still such a thing as German relief troops in Berlin at that time ... The continual changes in the defensive perimeter that was still being maintained needed a continuous transfer of troops from one street to another, or, what this really meant, from one front to another.

The roar of the shells, the hammering of the fire from the heavy mortars, the rattling of the machine guns, the air bombs launched from the tactical bombers, the cries of wounded or hurt and panicking men and women were what made up the aural landscape of any street in the center of Berlin.

The Spanish, after the latest clash, returned with Ezquerra to the front, toward the Department of Aviation. There, Ezquerra tried to locate Commander Willi to update him on the events of the past few hours, but he was informed that he was in the bunker in the garden of the ministry. Ezquerra, Carranchas, Sergeant García and the unit's interpreter headed toward the door of the bunker, where, after undergoing rigorous security controls they were allowed access. Accompanied by one of the guards they arrived at an inner room where shortly after Willi appeared and after speaking briefly to Ezquerra he led him to another room. Here he found the head of the sector, as well as various generals and other members of the military high command around a table with a map of Berlin showing different colored lines which aimed to represent an up-to-date picture of the various points of advance of the Soviet troops. Ezquerra was introduced to the soldiers, being warmly welcomed by the head of the sector. He then reported on the events which had occurred in the skirmish in the area of Kronen street. Following this, Ezquerra was given new orders, which consisted of defending the area of the government department buildings located between the streets of Herman Göring and Friedrich and Avenue Unter den Linden.

It was not difficult to reach this point, at least in terms of the distance, as each time the moves were shorter and shorter. In spite of this, due to the rubble, ruins, fires and continual attacks from the Russian artillery, it was not going to be an easy trip.

According Ezquerra in his book, at this meeting he was promoted from commander to lieutenant colonel due to his commendable work in combat.

After going back to his men, his first mission was to immediately act with Willi's Latvian soldiers to hold back an incursion by two infantry battalions supported by various tanks which were dangerously approaching the Potsdamer Platz. At that time the forces that resisted the Soviet onslaught in the area were mainly formed of military police troops and were not sufficient to confront the powerful advancing enemy.

Ezquerra's men and the Latvians began to advance in the direction of the aforementioned square, but progress was slowed by the continual bomb explosions of all types and calibers. Surviving this danger, but not without losing at least five men, they managed to access the area surrounding the Potsdamer Platz, where they began to assume positions in semi-ruined buildings. From there the soldiers readied their *panzerfaust* and light weapons against the tanks and infantry, respectively, that had began to occupy the square.

The tactic used consisted of waiting until the target was close enough to be able to give it a welcome worthy of the circumstances, Nobody moved, they kept their fingers on the triggers and on the firers of the *panzerfaust* until the first tank was in a firing position, It was Ezquerra himself who reached the first tank with his *panzerfaust* at the moment that he gave the order to fire at will. A torrent of fire was unleashed from the remains of the buildings on the side of the square onto the Soviets, at the same time finishing off the tanks that were in the vanguard. The infantrymen accompanying them could do little in the face of the incessant fire that they were receiving from each window, hole and heap rubble. Finally, the luckiest managed to withdraw without even being able to respond to Ezquerra's men in an effective manner; many others finished their days there; some others were captured, to avoid the list of victims of the terrible slaughter which had occurred growing longer. Information was obtained from these prisoners without much difficulty, although it could be thought that there was little need, as the latest movements of the enemy could be seen on the next street, corner or square.

As was becoming common practice in those days for the Spanish, after the storm came calm, as once the sector was calmed down they were replaced with a German battalion who occupied their positions.

With this new fire extinguished, the men, visibly exhausted after a long day of continual tension, returned to their accommodation in the Department of Aviation. Night was already falling and they deserved a rest and something warm to eat. But the way back was again under intense artillery fire which the men, who by now were used to it, hardly paid any attention, limiting themselves to completing their journey safely.

After this, according to Ezquerra's version, commander Willi, a colonel of Hitler's personal guard and a noncommissioned officer of the SS, accompanied him to the cellar of the Department of Aviation and from there, moved him by means of tunnels for electricity cables, underground channels and new cellars, in the direction of the Führer's bunker. They continued along these paths, at times lit only by the light of their own torches, until they arrived at a larger cellar in which a SS garrison was posted. There Ezquerra met the main heads of the German government, such as Goebbels, Axmann, Burgdorf, etc.; with Adolf Hitler being present, who presented him personally with the Knight's Cross. These events only appear in Ezquerra's account, and there are no other witnesses, if it is true that there is no proof to corroborate his story then neither is there any evidence to disprove it.

Meanwhile outside the destruction in the city was complete: tumbled down houses, ruins in all the streets and many dead, civilians and soldiers taken by a whirlwind of blood and death that seemed to have no end. Regarding this is this description from Julio Botet's liaison, *SS-Schütze* Julio L.: "I felt hate and rage, ashamed of myself and pleasure when I killed, but above all I felt a terrible panic that I would lose part of my body, all Berlin was a dump of human limbs destroyed by the bombs and shelling.

I remember that there was a German from another unit, I think from the *Luftwaffe*, and me, posted very close to the metro entrance, when we saw a woman holding a child on the other side of the street who was getting ready to cross, the German shouted to her not to move as we were in a area of firing, either she didn't understand or she didn't take any notice of us, but she ran toward us, she hadn't gone more than a couple of step when a grenade exploded in front of her, the deep explosive flung her toward us as if she were a rag doll, she came to us stunned almost naked and bleeding everywhere, the child was decapitated and what was left of the body was a jumble of flesh, the poor women, between cries and wails, began the macabre task of looking for the head of the child, we were indifferent to this, by then nothing bothered us."

Sunday, April 29

During the whole night, Berlin was a true inferno. The smell of decomposing bodies was widespread in areas of the city. The screams of raped women could be heard everywhere.

When day broke the Russians advanced from Grunewald (to the west of the capital), to the outskirts of the *Reichsportsfeld* (the area of the Olympic stadium); from the Anhalter Bahnhof, through the tunnels; from Tiergarten (where there was fighting for the edge occupied by the embassies and the west from the Zoo to Havel), and from the Potsdamer Platz.

At dawn, the 1st Mechanized Corps crossed the existing barriers on the River Spree. The 12th Armored Corps of the Guard made its progress toward the area west of Moabit. The 79th Fusiliers Corps attacked the Moltke bridge after previous intense artillery preparation during the night, encountering however significant points of resistance in the neighboring buildings. A first attack was held back, but a second managed to establish a head bridge in a corner of the diplomatic quarter. Little by little they advanced along Herwarthstrasse. This advance was temporarily contained by the Anhalt Regiment

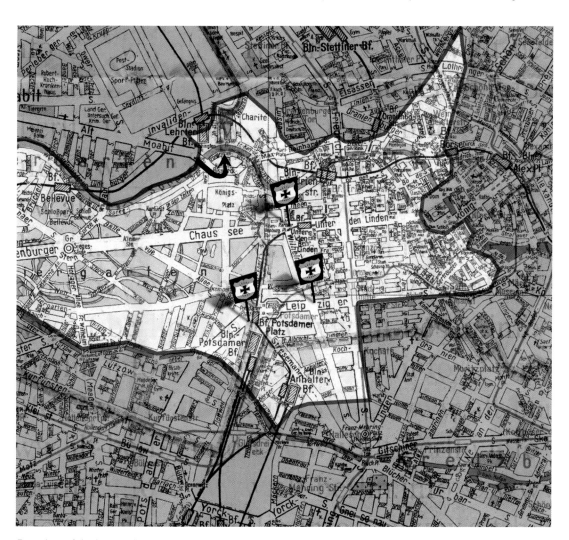

Front line of the battle of Berlin during April 29, 1945, with the various positions of the Spanish volunteers.

with the aid of a group of men from the 9th Parachute Division.

The 3rd Shock Army progressed slowly toward the Stettiner station. The 5th Shock Army advanced toward the Börse (the Stock Exchange) *S-Bahn* station and the *Rotes Rathaus* (town hall), which were in the area defended by members of the *Nordland*. The 32nd Fusiliers Corps captured the Jannowitzbrücke *S-Bahn* station, drawing closer to the Spree. The 8th Army of the Guard began its assault on the Landwehr canal.

Returning to the early hours of that Sunday, four hours after he had separated from his men, and after the supposed encounter with Hitler, Ezquerra returned to the Department of Aviation, where he held talks with his noncommissioned officers.

The orders that had been given to Ezquerra consisted in taking up positions in the area where the *Reichsbank* was. The journey was not very long, although, as previously mentioned, it would need maximum care when the time came to undertake it, as they would have to go over ground, where there was a continuous echo of the roar of the rain of shells which fell unceasingly from the sky, which was still dark, lit only by an orange light coming from the many fires caused by the fighting.

The unit advanced slowly along the sides of the streets, seeking shelter in the remains of the smoking buildings until finally reaching near area near to the *Reichsbank*, where they could see how a Russian company of troops were trying to get near to it.

Inside the bank, in the mixture of defensive troops, were the boys of Hitler Youth; who, on many occasions showed a strength that many men had lost after year of combat.

The men of the *Einheit Ezquerra*, who were still strong despite the few hours spent on resting in last three days, attacked the Russian flank managing to break their line of advance and causing their withdrawal with a number of losses. The action unfolded in a short time, dawn had only just broken.

There was no time for rest, the Spanish were immediately called to the area of the Potsdamer Platz, which was suffering a severe attack by combined infantry and armored forces. They arrived, sheltering themselves in the buildings of the streets leading to the square, and placed themselves in defensive positions which the German troops maintained there.

They stayed in the area for a brief time, soon they were called to another sector in extreme danger of falling under the Russian steamroller. Their new destination, according to Ezquerra, was a few hundred meters to the east, in the area of the Kaiserhof Hotel.

The Spanish volunteers headed toward the agreed area. When they arrived, they found a situation similar to what they had experienced in other sectors: defenders in clearly lower numbers fighting like wild boars, well aware as well that each time there was less room to withdraw to.

In front of them the Russians continued in their continual pursuit, favored by the vast quantities of material making them show their strength. Although their experience of fighting on the streets of Berlin had made them aware of the risk that a single squad could pose, just one man, well positioned and determined to defend the capital until the last drop of his blood had been shed. Also the Russians naturally knew that the fighting would not last long, and therefore perhaps many of them preferred not to risk dying when victory was so close, more than one thought that when the war finished it would be better to be among those celebrating than appearing as one more number on the lists of those killed in battle.

Always men who fought for their country or, in the case of the *Einheit Ezquerra*, for an ideal, they gave much more of themselves

Three pictures taken during the fight for Berlin.

Top: Soviet troops advance covered by
the imposing gun of a JS-2 tank.

Above: the appearance of a Berlin
street after the fighting stopped.

To the right: a couple of officers
next to a building in flames

Soviets supervise the control of a recently
conquered area of the city.

than the Soviet troops, especially when they were launched into combat like true cannon fodder with the aim of saturating the German defenses in order to gain ground.

When they arrived at the Kaiserhof Hotel they began their "cleaning" tasks again, the job of new positions, etc. Due to the darkness in the first hours of the morning they had to use torches to find the enemy. They felt the whistle of bullets on all sides. Here the use of modern automatic weapons carried by many of the men in the unit gave them an excellent fire potential that, when concentrated in small areas, decided the skirmish in their favor again.

Despite this, when it already morning they had not completely expelled the Soviets from their positions.

During the morning, a small group of Spanish commanded by Ezquerra rested for a few minutes in the ruins of the previously majestic Europa cinema. This cinema had a corridor that led out on to the Anhalterplatz that had to be found. Ezquerra gave the order to Lieutenant Lorenzo Ocañas that one of his men should undertake the task of discovering it. The chosen man was Macario Vallejo, who headed for the corridor covered in darkness. Minutes passed, then hours, until they heard shouts in Russian in the distance accompanied by the rattling of machine guns. Fearing the worst, Ocañas ran down the corridor following the steps of Vallejo, when he arrived at the exit he also fell in to the ambush set by the Russians, who managed to capture him. Following the fighting in the area the results for the unit were four dead and one disappeared, Ocañas, who after his capture was taken to the cellar of the Excelsior Hotel, in the power of the Russians, who used it as command post.

After being subjected to intense interrogation, Ocañas managed to stay alive, but stayed as a prisoner in the miserable conditions of the prison camps of the Soviet Union for nine years, before being finally repatriated on the Semíramis ship.

The men, exhausted after long hours of practically uninterrupted combat, returned to their post in the Department of Aviation, where they rested as best they could. They had undergone much fighting, and although they were notably tired, the spirit of these troops and their determination to continue in their resistance against the Russians remained intact.

Throughout that day the German command kept contact with the Russians, after which it was agreed to hold a meeting to talk. Due to the intransigence of both sides, no agreement was reached, as the Russians requested unconditional surrender, which was soundly rejected by the exhausted German troops.

Here, according to Ezquerra in his book, he also participated as a special guest, as he says he was one of the members of the group of Germans sent to negotiate with the Russians. In this case the event is corroborated by the account in Lieutenant Ocañas' book regarding his meeting with Ezquerra when he was already captured, as well Ezquerra's attempt to get to German lines, although without success due to the Soviet enemy.

Monday, April 30

From the first hours after dawn the Russians saturated the German defenses with intense artillery fire. The "Katyushas" launched volleys of rockets one after another, causing destruction in many areas of the reduced defensive perimeter. The roar became deafening, which together with the dust which had risen up and the smoke from the many fires, gave Berlin a ghostly appearance. It was in these conditions that the clashes took place in the streets of the capital.

The Soviets were 300-400 meters from the new State Department. The 79th Fusiliers Corps occupied the Department of the Interior and the western sector of the

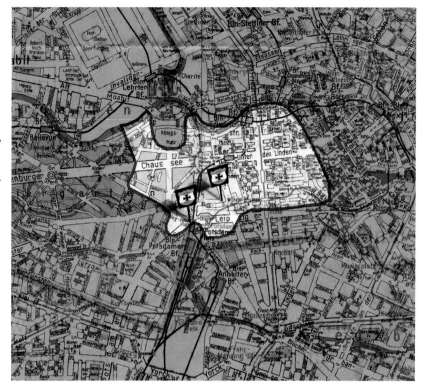

Front line of the battle of Berlin during April 30, 1945, with the various positions of the Spanish volunteers.

diplomatic quarter meeting strong opposition. The 270th Fusiliers Division progressed toward the building of the Kroll Opera, where they met a large German contingent. This then produced the first direct attack on the *Reichstag*, followed by a second, which were repelled partly thanks to the help of the cannons situated in the anti-aerial tower near the Zoo.

The 26th Fusiliers Corps of the Guard attacked the S-Bahn Börse station and the telegraph office again and again.

In the suburbs the neighborhood of Pichelsdorf continued to resist the strong Soviet advance.

General Weidling ordered the transmission of a communiqué in which, due to the extreme nature of the situation, he gave permission to break the circle. This order gave rise to what, in the following hours, produced numerous and mixed attempt to break this grip that was closing tighter and tighter with each minute. There were some who tried to escape by the many tunnels of the capital,

others preferred to escape by swimming by the river surrounding the *Zitadelle*, others preferred to try and find a gap in direct clashes with the Soviets; and all of them with different outcomes.

The escape attempt carried out with more methods was that carried out by the *Nordland* Division, supported by what was left of the armored force of the 503 SS Battallion. This attempt (as happened with that carried out by the *Müncheberg* Division on May 3 over the bridge in the district of Spandau to the northeast of Berlin, called Charlottenbrücke) was finally successful, although at the loss of many of the men who attempted it and of all the armored methods used.

When any German unit managed to break the barrier, immediately hundreds of people, civilians and soldiers, who were waiting in the rearguard, launched themselves at the gap to try and take advantage of the efforts of their countrymen.

The Einheit *Ezquerra* was resisting close to Potsdam Square, protecting themselves in any hole, pile of rubble, abandoned vehicle or object that could be used to cover themselves. With the slogan of "not one step backwards" they resisted advances, but when it made no sense to remain and only at that moment,, Ezquerra authorized the withdrawal through the tunnels of the metro following the men of the *Müncheberg* Division who until then had resisted, and that shortly before had used them to escape the area.

They fled down the dark tunnels at full speed, free for at least a few minutes of exposure to continuous Soviet fire. In the tunnels they met hundreds of civilians who were trying to hide from the Russians, some dead bodies and a heterogeneous mixture of troops that were trying to escape to a station from which escape to the outside would be safer. Although, at this point in the battle, few places, if any at all, would serve as an escape from the continual swipes from the Russian bear.

Some of the Spanish in withdrawal left the Soviet vanguard behind them, moving to Friedrichstrasse, taking up positions near to the State Department, in whose bunker, Adolf Hitler would commit suicide that day at 15:20, his body together with that of Eva Braun was burned there in the garden of the State Department. Some hours later, Reichsleiter Bormann and General Krebs sent a radio message from the High Staff Officers of the Armed Forces to the head of the north sector, Admiral Dönitz, in which they said: "Admiral Dönitz. In place of the former Marshal of the Reich Göring, the Führer has appointed you, Admiral, as his successor. Written authorization is on its way." Likewise, Field marshal Schörner will be supreme chief of the Army and Captain General Jodl, head of Staff Officers of the *Wehrmacht*.

The Soviets, maintaining pressure but without exposing themselves too much as victory was close, tried to continually demoralize the defenders challenging them to surrender.

Tuesday, May 1

During the morning, the Spandau fortress surrendered to the 47th Army; the clashes for the *Reichstag* continued, the building in which the defenders were taking cover was by now severely affected. The 5th Shock Army dedicated itself to the capture of the State Justice Department, the Security Office of the Reich, the State Department and the Department of Communications, in each building it had to face a desperate defense undertaken by men who were already cut off and had no way out. These clashes took a high toll on the defenders, and even higher on the attackers.

The 8th Army of the Guard crossed Bellevuestrasse toward Siegesallee until they definitively captured the Potsdamer Platz station, continuing until they reached close to the Saarlandstrasse U-Bahn station.

The 3rd Armored Army of the Guard advanced along Kurfürstendamm, where it met with the remainder of the Müncheberg Division. In this circumstances, the "pocket" where the last defenders were still resisting was not more than 800 meters wide at any point, although they still almost reached the ring of the S-Bahn in the north as well as the west.

Ezquerra and the few remaining men under his orders, as well as other groups of scattered Spanish soldiers, began the defense of the government quarter in a continuous fight for each building of the limited Berlin territory which was still in the hands of the Germans.

The Russians approached from Wilhelmstrasse and Friedrichstrasse. The defenders clung to each barricade they found, although the intense Russian pressure forced continual withdrawal. Like this, they fought till the bitter end for each doorway. Various tanks were destroyed in this way and hundreds of Russian infantry men were killed, but the incessant volume of men and Soviet weapons did not allow the defenders to rest for a moment.

The remainder of the unit continued on to defend the area of the Department of

Soviet soldier of Mongolian extraction poses armed with a PPSh-41 automatic rifle in a Berlin street.

the Interior, together with the remainder of many other units such as the *Nordland* or *Müncheberg*. The building was defended, as was becoming the norm, meter by meter. Each room was a deadly trap for the Russians, but all these efforts only served to delay the inevitable for a few hours.

The remainder of the *Einheit Ezquerra* met up in the Department of Aviation after a day of continuous fighting and withdrawals. There, Commander Willi gave Ezquerra an order of great importance received shortly before from the *Führerbunker*: form a group with his men and with the rest of the Latvian troops who were still able to fight that would try to break the siege which the Russians had placed around them.

As it was a secret mission, he had to maintain absolute discretion.

Understanding how difficult the situation was, Ezquerra, together with his non-commissioned officers, decided to inform all the men in his unit, including those who were wounded. It was possible that those who could not leave Berlin would inevitably die or be captured by the Soviets, therefore it was necessary to warn all of the men who were able to try and understand the escape attempt as soon as possible. The order was given from one man to another and in a short period of time all of them knew what was happening. They discreetly began leaving their positions and heading toward the Department of Aviation, the agreed meeting point for the group. There the Spanish chose a code word which would allow them be to recognized amongst themselves if they were separated from the main body of the group. The chosen word was, according to Ezquerra, "carajo" (damn), which was unmistakable: anyone shouting this out in the roar of battle could only be a brave Spanish soldier.

There, in the Department of Aviation, Ezquerra confirmed to his men where they were going to advance to and what would be their destination: Stettiner Bahnhof, which was to the north, further on than that the Spree.

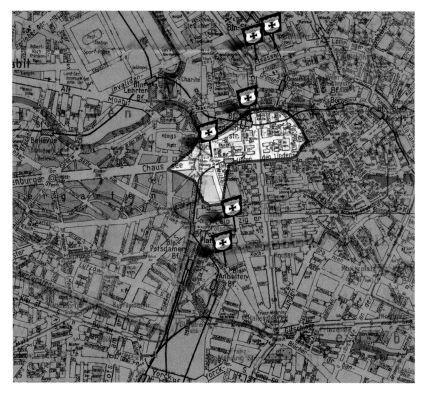

Front line of the battle of Berlin during May 1, 1945, with the various positions of the Spanish volunteers, showing that some groups have managed to cross Soviet lines.

This mission, despite being "secret", would not only affect the Latvians and the Spanish, as other brave troops in the defense of Berlin were also answering the call. All of them, just like the Spanish, had their main aim of crossing the Spree, whose bank was partially occupied by the Soviets, and arriving at the aforementioned Stettiner station.

They left the Department of Aviation by the garage toward the exit, going toward Wilhelm Street. There, they hid among the rubble and the walls of the adjoining buildings, they advanced toward the next metro station, a short distance from the Department. From the station, protected by the metro tunnels, they managed to arrive at the next station of Wilhelmplatz. There, Ezquerra's men, who little by little were mixing with their Latvian comrades, regrouped.

The station was affected by the continual shelling. Inside was completely packed with civilians and soldiers who used it as a place to take shelter.

Finally, an SS colonel managed to go about organizing the various groups of soldiers who were arriving at the station and informing them about the next meeting point: Friedrichstrasse station next to the Spree.

The transfer was again done through the metro tunnels to avoid the many risks on the ground. Due to the darkness of the underground tunnels the soldiers had to use their torches, also walking in single file to avoid losing contact with each other. During the long walk they went around various obstacles in the tunnels, and they also found some dead bodies of the unfortunate people who had ended their days there. Eventually they arrived at Friedrichstrasse station where they found a similar sight to that in the previous station. Thousands of people piled up with their few possessions, many of them wounded and in some cases surgically operated on right there in conditions that were very dangerous.

Again it was necessary to regroup the men that were arriving little by little by the tunnels and without wasting time they prepared themselves to reach the surface after leaving the safety of the underground metro tunnels.

In the street, the roar of the bombs that crushed the center of Berlin were deafening, and even more so there, due to the proximity of the station to the Weidendamm bridge, whose edge marked the north front line of Berlin and which had to be crossed to arrive at the group's final destination: the Stettiner Bahnhof. As the Russians knew that this bridge was one of the possible escape routes of the surrounded German troops, they had posted infantry troops and tanks on the bank north of the Spree.

The Weidendamm bridge had obstacles put up as anti-tank barriers by the defenders, as well as the bodies, in many cases completely mutilated, of people who had tried to cross it unsuccessfully under the heavy enemy fire on previous rash attempts.

The Soviet troops fired on anyone who got close to the bridge, as well as the groups of enemy troops who were able to form on the south bank. For this reason, Ezquerra's remaining men, as well as the Latvians who accompanied them, studied the situation in order to cross the bridge in the most suitable manner.

Obviously, it was not only the Spanish who tried to challenge the Russian defensive line, other German troops formed part of the group and used the scant remains of the armored weapons still in working order to support the mission.

Ezquerra warned that the only feasible way to succeed was to advance with maximum caution and speed, and above all... with a lot of luck, the same good fortune that had accompanied the survivors of the group up until then.

It was possibly during one of the attempts to force the crossing by the German troops, when Willi and Ezquerra gave their men the order to advance. They began to cross the bridge, but the amalgam of the dead bodies that they saw in front of their eyes meant that most of them fell behind and decided not to follow their leaders, frightened by the horrific scene. Of the Spanish only the hardened sergeants Roberto Gracia and Juan Pinar, as well as corporal Carranchas managed to cross. The rest of the men who did not have the strength to try remained on the south bank of the river, possibly fighting until the end.

The four Spanish, not without a dose of good luck, managed to cross the bridge to immediately take cover in the first house they found to their left.

Covered from enemy fire in the ruins they were able to rest for at least a few seconds. Many men lost their lives attempting the deadly crossing of the Spree under enemy fire.

According to Ezquerra, he and the corporal, armed with panzerfaust, tried to finish off the tanks that were protecting the Weidendamm bridge, whilst the two sergeants and Willi covered them with their automatic weapons from the high floors of the building. They advanced crouching down among the rubble after leaving the doorway, drawing near to two of the three armored vehicle posted close by. When they were within firing distance, they fired their weapons, managing to reach one each, whilst the third bore down on them rapidly with its roaring engine turning round to finish off the danger that a few seconds before had been the cause of the destruction of their two comrades ... only to receive another on target shot from a third *panzerfaust*. The Russian infantry men riddled the area where the two men were, a rain of fire and shrapnel literally rained down on top of them. Confronted with this situation, and constantly covered behind objects, they ran at full speed toward the protection of the building from where their comrades did their best to protect them. They managed, but then the Russians were concentrating their fire on the house. The defenders responded, but they could not

maintain their position on the high floor for long. They quickly assessed the positions of the Soviets that were firing at them and went down toward the doorway to get out as soon as possible. However the Russians challenged the men' s attempt to leave and concentrated their fire on the doorway seriously wounding Willi in his right leg and causing the withdrawal of the group of men toward the ever lessening safety offered by the walls of the battered building. They managed drag the wounded man inside the house, where they staunched the wound that was bleeding heavily. However this was only a temporary solution, as they lacked the means and the time to adequately treat the wound. Willi, at his own request, and so as not to compromise the escape attempt of his comrades, would stay there with his weapons to defend himself until the Russians arrived at the house.

As exiting by the doorway was far too dangerous the four Spaniards decided to give it their all and use the remaining *panzerfaust* to destroy the positions where the Russians were as much as possible.

Meanwhile, on the other side of the bridge, many men who had seen the explosion of the tanks, and the intense fighting taking place on the north side, had decided to try and cross it. The soldiers of the Kriegsmarine were the first to cross it, and afterwards many others took advantage of the situation, possibly also some of the Spanish who had not crossed at the first opportunity.

Faced with this avalanche of disorganized troops crossing the Spree the Russians withdrew a few meters without stopping those who were crossing while new Soviet troops led by new tanks arrived from Karlstrasse.

In the inferno of fire that was being unleashed, Ezquerra and Sergeant Pinar got separated from Sergeant Gracia and Corporal Carranchas. They did not find each other again leaving the *Einheit Ezquerra* now made up of only Ezquerra himself and his loyal ser-

The German *Panzerkampfwagen VI Ausf.B "Königstiger"* tank was a deadly rival for any allied tank, but the situation in Germany in the last years of the war stopped mass production. Some of these tanks, such as that shown here, fought in Berlin, but there was not enough to be able to halt the Soviet invader.

geant. Some men from different units joined them to try and reach their common aim: the so near and yet so far Stettiner Bahnhof.

Due to the power of the fire from automatic weapons and Russians grenades that was raining down, the street they were on was completely battered, they decided to approach their target through the inside of the houses. Using the *panzerfaust* again they managed to make holes in the walls separating the buildings that were large enough to get through. With this process, often used in the battle of Berlin by both sides, they arrived, without being detected by the enemy at Elsastrasse, where they exited again. And from there, after covering a few meters they managed to arrive at their target. The last order received by the *Einheit Ezquerra* had been carried out, despite all the men having perished or disappeared with the exception of their leader and Pinar.

However the Stettiner Bahnhof was no more than a carbon copy of other stations where many civilians were taking cover, as well as soldiers who had discarded their uniforms before their imminent capture by the Soviets.

Once they arrived, Ezquerra, Pinar and the group of men accompanying them decided to carry on with their endeavor and try to continue their escape from Berlin. For this they decided to return to the dark metro tunnels to continue their flight from the Russians. However as this area of Berlin was a territory that was already occupied by the Soviets, they met with enemy force that opened fire, stopping them from advancing by the train tunnels. This forced them to think through the situation again and they decided to retrace their steps, but not without having suffered a number of losses in this encounter.

They decided to risk going to the outside and continue their advance toward the north. They formed two lines of men, and with their backs to the walls of the buildings each of them progressed along the pavement. They advanced without knowing what awaiting them. Where were the Soviets posted? Would they have contact with other groups of men to jump over this noose that was choking Berlin? Although, obviously, after so many fights and subsequent withdrawals of the recent hours, without any rest, moral was not good, the idea of some of them achieving their task or the simple fight for survival of many others, kept these men still united in such a difficult undertaking.

They managed to arrived at the bunker of the Stettiner Bahnhof, where they met German troops, there, after contacting their commanders, they asked to join the unit. However they could do little together with the new group, the fighting capacity of the German soldiers had disappeared and it was there where they were finally captured by the Russians without having been able to try to cross the ever denser Russian lines again. At this point Ezquerra and Pinar were separated, and they did not see each other again.

After being freed by the Soviets in December 1955; Pinar recounted in his memoires that he took part in the defense of Berlin (as narrated by Ezquerra in his book) and even having seen a destroyed tank inside which he recognized Martin Bormann.

After the Russians arrived Ezquerra was captured, together with the soldiers who were in the bunker. Nobody resisted. Taken outside, they formed a line to be transferred under armed guard to the gathering area for prisoners of war. They formed endless line of prisoners that walked through the destroyed streets of Berlin, exhausted after suffering so many indignities.

Ezquerra, for his part, after being held captive for several days, managed to escape a poorly guarded group of prisoners. After many ups and downs and disguising himself as one of the thousand of forced workers that the Germans had used in their territory, he arrived in Spain via the Pyrenees.

Wednesday, May 2

An hour after midnight, Colonel von Dufving was sent as a German negotiator to cross the Soviet lines to try and negotiate surrender. The meeting with the Soviet negotiator General Chuikov, in Schulenburgring, concluded with the unconditional surrender of the German troops stationed in Berlin.

Whilst these negotiations were taking place the Soviet troops were carrying out the final assault on the *Reichstag*. The 9th Fusiliers Corps, finally finished off the resistance of small groups of armed determined men who fought to the end making strongholds forts in some buildings. Finally the Soviet flag was placed on the roof of the building.

The Germans also stopped using the metro tunnels to halt the advance of the Soviets. The north-south axis of the U-Bahn lines was flooded (the floods affected the part of the line between the BHF Wedding station until beyond Mehringdamm station, on line 6, and even Südstern, on line 7), although it also affected the east-west axis (from Potsdamer Platz to Frankfurter Allee on line 5 and to Rosenthaler Platz on line 8). There were also other stations and railroad lines flooded in different place of the Berlin underground system.

It seems it was troops belonging to the Waffen-SS who were responsible for this action, and if on the one hand it achieved their aim of halting the Soviet advance, it also caused losses among those who were sheltering in the metro stations.

During this day, most of the men from the unit had fallen in combat. Some of them still resisting belonged to the mix of units defending Berlin, amongst whom were the remainder of the Latvian fusilier battalions who defended the area of the Department of Aviation and who unsuccessfully tried to cross the enemy lines, or the extremely battered survivors of the Müncheberg Division, the Nordland Division, the 9th Parachute

Young German soldiers, most of whom came from the *Hitlerjugend*, in prisoner lines, confused by a defeat that their intense national-socialist indoctrination would not admit.

Division and the 18th Armored Infantry, launched an assault from the bridge on the Havel in Spandau-Oeste (called Charlottenbrücke) to escape the siege.

With them were civilians who saw the last opportunity to escape the city by crossing this bridge, which was still defended by some detachments of the Hitler Youth, in any way possible.

This break of the siege was carried out under the incessant artillery fire of the 47th Soviet Army posted on the other bank, which produced terrible carnage. Despite this, the urgent desire of those under siege meant they managed to expel the Soviet soldiers from the positions where they were posted on the western edge of Charlottenbrücke.

Resistance in Berlin was officially terminated around 13:00, but some groups of men continued fighting until they were finally crushed by the Soviets. Some, not many, were lucky and managed to slip though the Russian lines and managed to escape the city.

At midday, Marshal Zhukov ordered the ceasefire. The cannons stopped firing among the ruins, soon leaving the capital immersed in a "deafening" silence. The battle of Berlin had finished.

Stalin closed the day by letting the whole Red Army know that Berlin had fallen, with these words: "Today, May 2, 1945 at 23.30, the capital of our country, Moscow, salutes the First Belarusian Front and the First Ukrainian Front with a twenty-four-gun salute from 323 cannons to honor its great success in capturing Berlin."

In the end only a few managed to arrive at the "safety " of the territory occupied by the western allies, most of them died in the attempt and many survivors were captured by the Soviets. The latter suffered the living death of being a prisoner in the gulags, where, despite the threats, torture, killings, hunger and many punishments, the Spanish, led by Captains Teodoro Palacios Cueto and Gerardo Oroquieta Arbiol, managed to keep morale high during the nine years they were kept prisoners.

Ezquerra' s case was very particular, in that he managed to escape such a brutal battle alive and escape from Spain after tricking the Soviet captors.

For the unfortunate "illegal" volunteers who were able to return to their country, their only choice was to try and stay anonymous or, as happened in the case of some, run the risk of being subject to a war council for "abandonment of destination" as a consequence of the disobedience of the rules issued by the Spanish government in this respect. Although this man managed to be absolved a couple of years later.

Thursday, May 3

On May 3 the Soviets distributed an information sheet among the population written in German which started thus: "Berlin has been taken.- The troops of the First Belarusian Front (under the command of Marshal Zhukov), together with those of the Second Ukrainian Front (under the command of Marshal Koniev), have defeated the Berlin groups of defenders, capital of Germany, center of imperialist German and source of German aggression. The city resisted until 15:00 May 2, when the head of the defense of Berlin (General of Artillery Weidling and his staff officers) were taken prisoner. Until 21:00 of the same day, the Soviet troops had taken more than 70,000 prisoners …"

Despite the defeat, some groups of soldiers still continued fighting the Soviets in small pockets of resistance in the city. The cost of human lives in the battle was huge, for the defenders and civilians as well as the Soviets, who from April 16 to May 8 recorded the following losses: 70,000 dead and 280,000 disappeared, wounded and sick. To that was added the loss of around 2,000 tanks and 500 planes. Possibly the actual losses during this period were even higher.

REPATRIATION

The process of returning home was, understandably, extremely complicated. The circumstances of the occupation of the old Reich both by the Soviet and the western allies, as well as the destruction of the majority of its infrastructures did not allow for easy movement through their territory at all.

The first phase of the return of the surviving men from the Ezquerra unit was to go from the area occupied by the Soviets to escape to that controlled by the western allies. Belonging to the SS was a negative factor for the Spanish in the western sector, but it could mean immediate execution if they were captured in the eastern sector. From shortly before the surrender various Spanish (among which, according to Ezquerra, were about 30 members of his unit) managed to leave Berlin, and later Germany, thanks to the help of the Spanish consulate in the German capital. Other groups of Spanish (possibly those who stayed in the area of the Alps), after having renounced their oath of loyalty to Hitler, received passports to neutral Switzerland, where they remained imprisoned in the camps of Oerlikon-Zurich and Laplaine-Ginebra. These men, after the relevant authorizations and with the intervention of the Spanish government, managed to embark on their return in a train that left from Berne and arrived at the French station of Chambery on June 17, but at this station, the train was attacked by forces from the old maquis, and had to return to Switzerland with the Spanish again imprisoned in the camps of Laplaine-Ginebra and Bühler-Apenzell. They had to wait until December 3, when after going through France, they managed to return to Spain by boat on board the Plus Ultra.

Another group of Spanish, after being captured by the Western allies, passed through some concentration camps before finally being freed. This is what happened to some of the men who had served under the orders of Lieutenant Ortiz (who belonged to the 102nd) and had remained in the mountains of north Italy without therefore going through Stockerau, such as Antonio Pardo (who became a prisoner in Udine and was detained until October 1948) or Federico Martínez (captured in Gorizia and detained in Rimini until July 1949, from where he fled, returning to Spain clandestinely through Puigcerdá). Other men who served in the Wehrmacht managed to get to Rome (with the collusion of the Italian population) and from there they managed to be repatriated to Spain.

However, many Spanish remained prisoners of the Soviets. In the gulags they had to survive for long and difficult years, subjected to all types of trials and tribulations.

After the death of Stalin in March 1953 the living conditions of the prisoners improved and rumors began to circulate of possible repatriation. A year later the prisoners were gathered at the port of Odessa. Of them eighteen decided to remain in the USSR together with sixty-five deserters, who out of fear at being subject to military trial, did not return to their country either.

On board the Semíramis the impatient Spanish wanting to set foot on their country's soil after years of imprisonment. Their return was experienced first hand by thousands of people at the port of Barcelona.

Emotion overwhelms the repatriated men on board the Semíramis.

Photograph courtesy of Luis E. Togores.

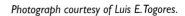

Muñoz Grandes during the reception given for the repatriated men from the Semíramis at the War Department.
Photographs courtesy of Luis E. Togores.

Left:
Another picture of the reception held from the repatriated men on the Semíramis at the War Department in 1954.

Below:
Former members of the SDV on parade in Palma de Mallorca in the 1970s.

Opposite page.

Burial with military honors of Captain General Muñoz Grandes, who died on July 11, 1970.

Another picture of the funeral of Muñoz Grandes. The Civil Guard, in full uniform, march in procession with arms at the funeral of the Captain General from Madrid on Paseo of the Castellana.

Photographs courtesy of Luis E. Togores

On Friday April 2, 1954 the Spanish prisoners of war after having been imprisoned for ten or twelve years in the Soviet gulags, returned to Spain as a result of the negotiations between the Soviet and Spanish governments. This long-awaited return was carried out on board the Greek ship Semíramis flying under the Liberian flag, chartered by Spain under the Red Cross, that left from the port of Odessa and docked at the port of Barcelona with 286 people.

They were distributed according to their origin, in the following manner:

A contingent of prisoners of war made up of 248 men divided thus: 219 belonging to the Spanish Division of Volunteers, seven from the Spanish Legion of Volunteers, twenty-one from Waffen-SS troops and one from the Blue Squad.

The remaining contingent of thirty-eight people was divided up thus: four "war children" and thirty-four prisoners; these in their turn had the following origins: nineteen marines, most of whom were crew members of the motor ship Corporal San Agustín, a ship that transported shipments of gold from the Bank of Spain to Odessa, and the others, marines of the Republican fleet that had found themselves in Soviet territory when the Spanish Civil War finished; twelve men that had been students of the Kirovavad air academy and after the Spanish Civil War did not renounce Spanish citizenship, being declared dissidents because of this and imprisoned in camps, and three workers arrested in Germany at the end of the Second World War. (facts obtained from article of the excellent *Revista Española de la Historia Militar* (*Spanish Journal of Military History*) with the title "Semíramis, 1954: El regreso de los cautivos de la División Azul" (*Semíramis, 1954: The Return of the Prisoners of the Blue Division*).

At 17:35 on April 2 1954 the boat docked at the port, the men who disembarked were thin and emaciated after a long imprisonment, thus concluding the "adventure" of many of them in their fight against the Soviets.

They were received there by a great crowd of people among whom were family members and other close friends. In the name of the Head of State, the Secretary General of the Movement, Raimundo Fernández Cuesta, and from the Army, Lieutenant General Muñoz Grandes (first head of the Blue Division), went on board to welcome them, accompanied by Agustín Aznar, national delegate for Health. In the basilica of the Merced a thanksgiving was held, in the presence of the Archbishop of Barcelona, Modrego.

However the Semíramis did not repatriate all the prisoners who had remained in the USSR, as in 1955 it came to be known that there was still an undetermined number of Spanish there. In fact, one of them was a man who fought in the Ezquerra unit in the battle of Berlin, Juan Pinar, who was freed on December 1955.

Despite the bad relationship between the Soviet and Spanish governments, thanks to the intervention of the Red Cross, 2,500 Spanish were repatriated in seven "journeys" between September 1956 and May 1959 (in the months of September, October, November and December 1956; January and May 1957, and May 1959), journeys that in the main were undertaken by the Crimea ship with the port of Castellón as its destination. However, the Spanish government thought it advisable that these repatriations, due to the delicate situation of these international relations, went almost unnoticed in the newspapers and reports of the time.

Among these last repatriated men there were a few belonging to the SDV, with one who, belonging to the Waffen-SS, had been captured in Yugoslavia, possibly a member of the 102nd Company.

UNIFORMS, WEAPONS, AND TACTICS

Uniforms

The uniforms worn by the Spanish volunteers, as a result of the situation in Germany in this period, were very diverse. The organization of supplies was affected by the war on the many fronts, therefore in the ranks of the *Einheit Ezquerra* there were "green" uniforms of the SS mixed with the camouflage uniforms of various types and even some of the *Wehrmacht*.

In any case, the Spanish were supplied with mottled camouflage M44 uniforms in Potsdam, which consisted of a army jacket with four pockets very similar to the Feldbluse M43 and fitted pants, both made of rayon printed in five colors (different shades of green and brown).

Some men still kept their blue shirts, which by then were used as everyday wear, under their German uniforms, among the men who joined the Blue Division. This shirt was the distinctive clothing of the Spanish Falange of the JONS and used continuously despite not complying with the increasingly less strict rules for military uniforms, There are also texts that talk about the use of some elements of the uniform of the Spanish Army. As for footwear, apart from the case of some volunteers who kept their high boots, the most commonly used at this point of the conflict were short boots with gaiters.

The belts used were mainly regulation SS issue, although *Wehrmacht* issued belts were also possibly used. There are also reports of legionnaires of the Tercio who continued used their belts with the harquebus and crossbow, as well as leather wristbands.

The headgear which was used was either the 35/40 and 42 model helmets, with or without badge, or the peaked cap introduced in 1943 for its improved comfort.

Although it is true that there are no known photographs in existence of the Spanish in the battle of Berlin, their uniform is known from the accounts related by the survivors and witnesses. It is logical to think that, along with the other formations of foreigners who fought as part of the German Armed Forces, they wore the uniforms used by the other German soldiers, and more precisely similar to those belonging to the *Waffen-SS* units that were fighting in Berlin, such as the men of the *33.Waffen-grenadier Division der SS (Französische No.1) Charlemagne*.

The characteristics of the Spanish uniform were the shield on the left sleeve (as was regulation in the *Waffen-SS*) with the national colors and the word "Spain" on the upper part.

Possibly, not all the men wore this, given the different origins of the troop of the Ezquerra unit, but those that did were mainly those who had served in the Division or the Blue Legion. In many cases this shield was fixed to the uniform simply by pins without sewing, and sometimes it was placed on the right sleeve, contravening the established order. There were variations within the design of this shield, a yoke with the arrows could have been embroidered, an Iron Cross or a swastika.

On the sleeve, above the shield, there should have been the regulation eagle of the *Waffen-SS*, into which the Spanish unit was integrated. Other decorations that could be seen on the uniforms were bands on the right arm indicating having destroyed an armored vehicle in combat; as well as Spanish or German decorations (the former in the case of former members of the Division or the Blue Legion) or emblems of the Falange or the SEU (Spanish University Union of the Falange).

Decorations

It should be taken into consideration that many of the volunteers had already taken part in a great deal of combat, either in units under Spanish or German command during the Second World War, and even during the Spanish Civil War, which is why it was possible that they wore decorations obtained during these periods of service on their uniforms.

As a point of interest the number of medals obtained by the members of the Blue Division should be remembered, as some of them formed part of the Ezquerra unit. They were: a Knight's Cross with Oak Leaves, a Knight's Cross, two German Crosses in Gold, 2,497 Iron Crosses (of these 138 were First Class), 2,216 Crosses of Military Merit with Swords (of these sixteen were First Class).

In addition it seems that most of the men who took part in the defense of Berlin, earned the right to have the Iron Cross Second Class for their participation. Regarding the Knight's Cross, only Ezquerra said that he received it from the Führer himself, although as stated previously there is no proof or witnesses to this event (the only Spanish who received it officially were the two Chief Generals of the Blue Division).

The Iron Cross Second Class was generally awarded for merit in combat, to be awarded this required a brave act against the enemy or for actions beyond the call of duty.

Normally the ribbon was used on the uniform, fixed in the second buttonhole of the army jacket.

The Iron Cross First Class was awarded for three or four acts of courage, meaning higher honor for the recipient.

The Knight's Cross. The recipient had to be in possession of the Iron Cross First Class, as well as bravery and excellence for outstanding actions in combat beyond the normal call of duty.

The Cross of War Merit Second Class with Swords recognized those soldiers whose acts of valor were beyond the call of duty, although without the criteria needed for the Iron Cross. These acts could correspond to acts of valor without being under enemy fire or for the planning or leading of operations of combat. The Cross without swords was generally awarded for actions of merit in general.

The Spanish Decoration for the members of the Division and the German Decoration for members of the Division, were awarded respectively by the Spanish and German governments to the members of the Spanish divisionary corps who took part in the fight against Bolshevism in Russia.

The Medal of the East, was awarded to those who fulfilled the following criteria on the front: fourteen days of participation in combat or sixty days of service in a combat zone (even without having to have taken part in combat) or been wounded or has severe frost bite to receive the emblem of wounded in combat.

The wounded in combat emblems were awarded in three grades: black, silver and gold. The version depended on the number of wounds received in hostile action or for serious wounds. The first was given for one or two wounds in hostile action, the silver for three or four times and the gold for five times or more.

Badge for having taken part in an attack, which was given for taking part in three attacks on different days. In the case of more than three attacks, it had a number in gold in the lower part indicating the number of attacks.

The bands for destruction of tanks existed in two grades: silver, for having individually destroyed an enemy tank using a portable weapon, and gold, that was given for having destroyed five enemy tanks using a portable weapon.

This decoration was not given to troops in anti-tank units.

Light Armament

In the confusion of the last days of the Reich, the weapon given to the troops varied more according to availability than to necessity. For this reason, it was difficult, if not impossible, to say with certainty which weapons that the Spanish contingent used in the fighting. Apparently the unit had a quite good provision of weapons in Potsdam, given the circumstances. Among them were the assault rifles StG-44 or MP-44, of great use in the street fights of Berlin due to their high rate of fire and their greater reliability for short and medium distances. It was therefore an ideal weapon for a limited number of defenders to try to contain the enormous mass of Soviet soldiers flooding Berlin.

The other main weapon used by the Spanish was the *panzerfaust*, which gained a fearsome reputation among the crew of the Armored Soviets, who again and again suffered its effects on the Berlin streets. As it was best used for short and medium distances it was could be used by soldiers hidden in the rubble and ruins that filled the streets.

Perhaps, what stands out the most in the fighting was the abundance of weapons carried by Spanish, it was not uncommon for many of the men to carry one or two pistols and they were mainly equipped with automatic weapons and grenade launchers, reducing the rest of the load of its equipment to the minimum.

StG 44

The MP-43, MP-44 and StG-44 can be considered the first modern assault rifles. They originated due to the need to increase the fire power of the infantry troops, already apparent even from the time of the First World War. The weapon possess a gas canister that acted on a cap situated in a cylinder on the cannon. Its first name was MP-43, after 1943, the year of its "birth"; in 1944 the name changed to MP-44, seemingly in line with the change of year, and finally it was given the name of Sturmgewehr which means assault rifle (it seems that this name was given to it by Adolf Hitler). This rifle has had a significant influence on the infantry weapons developed after the war.

Among its specifications are:

Length:	940mm
Weight:	5,12kg
Barrel:	420mm
Caliber:	7,92mm Kurz
Rifling:	4 Grooves/Dextrorsum
Action:	Gas Operated
Feed System:	30-Round Detachable Box Magazine
Rear Sight Sliding:	Up To 800m
Initial Speed:	647m/s
Rate Of Fire:	500rpm
Firing:	Shot by Shot and Machine Gun

MP-40

The MP-40 (and its variations MP-38, MP-38/40, MP-40/2 and MP-41) was a weapon tried and tested efficiency during war, making it "very sought after" by both the German and Soviet sides. By the end of the war approximately 1.047,000 units had been manufactured. This made it one of the most famous weapons of the Second World War. It had great precision even between 50-100 m. Its strong points were its easy maintenance, durability and lightness.

Among its specifications are:

Caliber:	9mm Parabellum
Selector:	Automatic
Feed System:	32-Cartridge Straight magazine
Empty Weight:	4,03kg
Loaded Weight:	4,7kg
Length:	833mm
Rifling:	6 Grooves/Dextrorsum
Rear Sight Leaf:	100-200m
Rate Of Fire:	450 A 550rpm.
Initial Speed:	381m/s
Effective Range:	200m

Walther P38

Pistol manufactured to replace the very well-known P08 Luger, obtaining a robust weapon characterized by handling and maintenance which was quite improved with respect to its predecessor. Another of its advantages was the lower cost and its faster production. Due to its qualities it soon became a very popular weapon that spread to the various branches of the German Army and the SS.

The "life" of this weapon did not end when the world war finished, as it was manu-factured freely in France and Turkey, conti-nuing to be produced at a date as late as 1957 as the chosen weapon of the *Bundeswehr*.

Among its specifications are:

Caliber:	9mm Parabellum
Total Length:	214mm
Barrel Length:	125mm
Weight With Empty Magazine:	950gr
Weight With Full Magazine:	1,050gr
Feed System:	magazine of eight cartridges

Kar 98k

This was the rifle commonly used in the German Army all throughout the war. It came about because of the need to have a more manageable rifle than the Mauser Gewehr 98, used in Germany for many years. They were reliable and manageable rifles, although during the war (and even more so in the last period) it became obvious that it had limited fire power when faced with the new automatic and semi-automatic weapons that were being produced. Despite this, its production continued until the last year of the war (the last of them were manufactured at least a month before the end of the conflict), totaling more than 11 million and a half models produced in their different variants).

At the beginning of the war there was a beautiful design, although afterwards some of its pieces were replaced with other cheaper substitutes and with materials of less strategic interest, although this did not alter its tried and tested efficiency for use.

Among its characteristics are:

Caliber:	7,92mm
Total Length:	1,110mm
Barrel Length:	600mm
Unloaded Weight:	3,8kg
Weight With Full Magazine:	3,94kg
Feed System:	magazines of five cartridges

Gewehr 43

The German authorities, after obtaining models of Soviet semi-automatic Tokarev SVT 40 weapons, felt the need to provide a weapon with similar characteristics for its Army, as faced with the imposing superior number of Russians in its counterattacks it was necessary to provide the defending troops with a better volume of fire than its weapons were capable of offering at that time.

It was the only semi-automatic rifle that was produced in significant quantities during the Second World War in Germany. Its main characteristics were its robustness, its precision and high level of reliability. The fact that it had not arrived in large quantities to the troops of the first line was due to, more than its possible limitations, its coexistence with the weapons known as assault rifles, less powerful but more practical to use and with more fire power.

Among its characteristics are:

Caliber:	7,92mm
Type:	Semi-Automatic Gas Powered
Operation:	Semi-Automatic
Total Length:	1.117mm
Barrel Length:	545mm
Unloaded Weight:	4,3kg
Feed System:	Magazine extractible with capacity for ten cartridges
Rifling:	4 Grooves/Dextrorsum

MG34

It was the first machine gun in the world capable of maintaining a high volume of fire without losing its characteristics of speed of movement or its flexibility of tactical use. It had a high rate of fire, which together with its easy maintenance even in adverse conditions, gave it great importance in the "light" arsenal of the German Army. Its main drawback was its high production costs, which, due to its great effectiveness, did not stop it being produced throughout the whole war. It was also used on armored vehicles and tanks.

Among its specifications are:

Caliber:	7,92mm
Munition:	Tracer, anti-armament, incendiary, cartridge
Selector:	Automatic and semi-automatic
Weight:	12,11kg
Firing Speed:	800 to 900 projectiles/minute
Exit Speed:	762m/s
Range:	800 meters with bipod, 3,000 meters with tripod and telescopic sight
Action:	Recoil
Feed Supply:	By belt

MG42

Despite these excellent predecessors of the MG34, the advance of the war showed the German authorities that a new machine gun that could be manufactured easily in large quantities was necessary. Thanks to this need the MG42 was born, which, although similar in many aspects to the MG34, has a design which sought to improve easy handling and maintenance even in the most extreme conditions such as mud, snow, dust and water. In addition it had a rate of fire of between 300 y 400 shots per minute more than the MG34, turning it into a weapon of devastating effect. It was also used as an auxiliary weapon in various types of vehicles and tanks.

Its good design and easy construction mean that the MG42 as well as its varieties have continued to be used in various armed forces up to and including today.

Among its specifications are:

Caliber:	7,92mm
Type:	Automatic machine gun
Length:	1,2m
Weight	11,56kg
Firing Speed:	1,200 projectiles/minute
Exit Speed:	762m/s
Range:	800m with bipod; 3,000m with tripod and telescopic sight
Action:	Recoil

Panzerfaust

The *panzerfaust* was the first anti-tank weapon of easy production and tried and tested efficiency. It was in fact a cannon without recoil made of a steel tube with a firing mechanism inside which the grenade and a cartridge of black dust were placed. The grenade was loaded empty and had a wooden tail with four steel wings.

It was used by lifting the rear sight and cocking the firing mechanism, squeezing the trigger and the gunpowder charge fires the grenade. It was a weapon that was easy to use and shoot, as it was cheaper to made a new one than go back to arm the empty tubes. It was able to have a devastating effect in expert hands, as well as disciplined users. Its ease of use meant that it was widely used by the men of the *Volkssturm*,

mainly made up of older people and children. To facilitate its use, all the *panzerfaust* had a label stuck on its "head" with illustrations and instructions for how to use it.

It was greatly feared by the Soviet armored forces in general and even more in urban land combat, which became the ideal places for its use in skirmishes and ambushes. In addition the Soviets made good use of weapons captured during the battle of Berlin. Its characteristics varied according to the various models what were made. Among the different types are:

	Pzf Klein 30	Pzf 60	Pzf 100	Pzf 150
Date of manufacture	Aug.43	Aug.43	Nov.44	Mar.45
Diameter of the tube	15cm	10cm	6cm	6cm
Range	30m	60m	100-150m	150m
Propellant	300gr	190gr	139gr	139gr
Penetration	140mm	200mm	200mm	+200mm
Weight	3,2kg	6,1kg	6,8kg	6,7kg

Stielhandgranate (stick hand grenade)

The classic German stick grenade, omnipresent on all the fronts during la war. They were popularly known as "potato mashers" and were easy to carry in belts and the legs of boots, although they were cumbersome in comparison with the "egg" type grenades. They had a hollow wooden handle joined to a metal head which contained a high explosive charge. Their main capability was the damage that the explosion was able to inflict, rather than its power of fragmentation of shards of metal. In later versions a better fragmentation effect was achieved by adding rings of shrapnel (Splitterringe).

The grenade was started by unscrewing the bottom and removing the detonation cord which was inside the wooden stick on which the explosive charge sat.

There were various models, with the most common being the StiGr 24 and StiGr39.

	StiGr 24	StiGr 39
Diameter	70mm	70mm
Weight	595 gr	624 gr
Length	356mm	406mm
Charge	TNT	TNT
Delay	4-5 sec.	4-5 sec.

Eihandgranate 39

This "egg" type grenade was a compromise between size and explosive capacity. Its main advantage was the ease with which it could be stored and transported, while its main defect was its lack of deadly effect compared with the stick grenades (in comparison with the StiGr 24, it carried a 112gr of explosive compared to 165gr). It was made of two halves, with the fuse between them.

There were various models from the original grenade, like those that used cement, metal fragments or small quantities of explosives, but in most cases, these grenades were too fragile, and were less effective than the usual ones.

Weight:	230gr
Length:	7,6cm
Explosive Content:	112gr

As well as German made weapons, many weapons from other places were used, mainly seized from enemy armies. Among these was the use by German soldiers who fought on the eastern front in the last years of the war of the automatic rifle PPSh 43 of 7,62mm, greatly liked due to its low maintenance, as well as its impressive firing capacity.

Armoured Forces

The main elements in the advance that the Soviets carried out on the eastern front and specifically in the battle of Berlin, were their aerial superiority, artillery, armored force and enormous number of men. Faced with this deployment of material and human means, the only thing the defending troops could do was withdraw to a greater or lesser extent from the inevitable Soviet advance.

In terms of the armored forces the main force were the tank, models T 34/76, T 34/85, M 4 Sherman, JS-IA, JS-IB, JS-II and JS-III. In front of these armored beasts the defenders of Berlin and mainly the shock units, among whom were the Spanish posted in the *Waffen-SS* risked their lives. Obviously, the various models of the JS were the jewel in the crown of these armored forces, which continued on and served as a basis for the armored soviet force of the postwar. Likewise, the self-propelled artillery played an important role in supporting the infantry troops, with the ISU-152 being their main and most powerful representative.

The main characteristics of the tanks faced by the Spanish post in the Ezquerra unit and their German comrades are described here.

M 4 Sherman

Weight:	30,5tn.
Length:	6,23m.
Width:	2,67m.
Height:	2,96m.
Armor:	105mm.
Engine Power:	450 Cv.
Speed:	42km/H.
Range:	161km.
Crew:	5
Armament:	1 gun of 76,2mm or of 75mm

T-34/76

Weight:	30t.
Length:	6,07m.
Width:	2,95m.
Height:	2,65m.
Armor:	60-75mm.
Engine Power:	500 Cv.
Speed:	50km/H.

Range:	300km.
Crew:	4
Armament:	1 gun of 85mm + 2 machine guns of 7,6mm

T-34/85

Weight:	2t.
Length:	6,07m.
Width:	2,95m.
Height:	2,72m.
Armor:	60-75mm.
Engine Power:	550 Cv.
Speed:	37km/H.
Range:	150km.
Crew:	4
Armament:	1 gun of 85mm + 3 machine guns of 7,6mm

JS-IA

Weight:	44t.
Length:	6,77m.
Width:	3,07m.
Height:	2,73m.
Armor:	100-160mm.
Engine Power:	500 Cv.

Speed:	53km/H.
Range:	400km.
Crew:	4
Armament:	1 gun of 76,2mm + 2 machine guns of 7,6mm

JS-IB

Weight:	45t.
Length:	6,77m.
Width:	3,07m.
Height:	2,75m.
Armor:	100-160mm.
Engine Power:	550 Cv.
Speed:	37km/H.
Range:	150km.
Crew:	4
Armament:	1 gun of 122mm + 3 machine guns of: 7,6mm

JS-II

Weight:	46t.
Length:	6,77m.
Width:	3,07m.
Height:	2,75m.
Armor:	100-160mm.
Engine Power:	550 Cv.
Speed:	43km/H.
Range:	190km.
Crew:	4
Armament:	1 gun of 122mm + 3 machine guns of: 7,6mm + 1 machine gun of 12,7mm

JS-III

Weight:	45,8t.
Length:	6,67m.
Width:	3,20m.
Height:	2,44m.
Armor:	120-200mm.
Engine Power:	550 Cv.
Speed:	40km/H.
Range:	190km.
Crew:	4
Armament:	1 gun of 122mm + 1 machine gun of 7,6mm + 1 machine gun of 12,7mm

Isu-152

Weight:	45,5t.
Length:	9,8m.
Width:	3,56m.
Height:	2,52m.
Armor:	35-100mm.
Engine Power:	520 Cv.
Speed:	37km/H.
Range:	180km.
Crew:	5
Armament:	1 gun-howitzer of 152mm + 1 machine gun of 12,7mm

Faced with the enormous amount of armored Soviet material, the Germans could only put up a few armored units, its armored divisions having already been destroyed by the continual defensive fights which had been taking place over the previous months. These units corresponded, as stated previously, to the remainder of the 503rd SS Battallion of Heavy Tanks (*503rd Schwere Panzer Abteilung*), with some twenty *Panzer VI Königstiger* of the SS *Nordland* Division and the remainder of the *Müncheberg* Division with around thirty tanks (mainly *Sturmgeschütz III, Panzer IV* and *Panzer V Panther* assault cannons). As well as those mentioned, less often, other armored vehicles were found in the defense of Berlin, such as the *Borgward Ausf.B Panzerjäger Wanze* (SdKfz.301) (an armored vehicle based on the chassis of the *Panzer I Ausf.B* with anti-tank grenade launchers), *Opel "Maultier"15 cm Panzerwerfer 42 auf Selbstfahrlafette SdKfz.4/1* (armored vehicle with rocket artillery launcher similar in use to the Soviet "Katyuska") or the *Panzerjager Pak 43/3* with 88 mm gun, as examples. The defenders also used Panther tanks in a bad or deteriorated state (although with full artillery capacity) as static defenses, half-buried in the Berlin streets or partially covered by rubble. They put them in streets that allowed for a wide range of fire, taking advantage of their lesser exposure to enemy fire and their privileged position.

The last armored element with a notable presence in the Berlin defense to be mentioned here is the SdKfz.251 armored transport for troops and its different variations.

Sturmgeschütz III (G model)

Weight:	24,1t.
Length:	6,77m.
Width:	2,95m.
Height:	2,16m.
Armor:	16-80mm.
Engine Power:	300 CV.
Speed:	40km/h.
Range:	155km.
Crew:	4
Armament:	1 gun of 75mm + 1 machine gun of 7,92mm

Panzer IV (H model)

Weight:	25t.
Length:	5,89m.
Width:	3,29m.
Height:	2,68m.
Armor:	80mm.
Engine Power:	300 CV.
Speed:	38km/h.
Range:	200km.
Crew:	5
Armament:	1 gun of 75mm + 2/3 machine guns of 7,92mm

Panzer V Panther

Weight:	44,8t.
Length:	6,88m.
Width:	3,44m.
Height:	3.00m.
Armor:	80-120mm.
Engine Power:	700 CV.
Speed:	46km/h.
Range:	177km.
Crew:	5
Armament:	1 gun of 75mm + 2 machine guns of 7,92mm

Panzer VI Ausf.A Tiger

Weight:	56.9 or 62.72t.
Length:	6.28m.
Width:	3.55m.
Height:	3m.
Armor:	25-120mm.
Engine Power:	700 CV.
Speed:	38km/h.
Range:	110km.
Crew:	5
Armament:	1 gun of 88mm + 2 machine guns of 7,92mm

Panzer VI Ausf.B Königstiger

Weight:	69,7t.
Length:	7,26m.
Width:	3,75m.
Height:	3,09m.
Armor:	150-185mm.
Engine Power:	700 CV.
Speed:	38km/h.
Range:	110km.
Crew:	5
Armament:	1 gun of 88mm + 3 machine guns of 7,92mm

SdKfz.251/1

Weight:	7,81t.
Length:	5,8m.
Width:	2,1m.
Height:	1,75m.
Armor:	6-14,5mm.
Engine Power:	100 CV.
Speed:	52,5km/h.
Range:	300km.
Crew:	2 + 10
Armament:	2 machine guns of 7,92mm

This armored force was used precise way in most cases to tactically support the defending troops. Possibly the Spanish from the Ezquerra unit met with some of these armored vehicles in their comings and goings on the Berlin streets. The last use of the Germen tanks was to support the various escape attempts of the troops surrounded by the bridges that marked the *Zitadelle* sector.

Soviet Troops

The Soviet forces that took part in the attack on Berlin belonged to the First Belarusian Front of Marshal Zhukov and to the First Ukrainian Front of Marshal Koniev. The forces of the former surrounded the capital from the north, east and west, whilst the latter came from the south, east and west.

In the clashes which took place on April 27 in the area of Belle Allianze Platz, the Spanish came up against the troops of the 8th Army of the Guard of Colonel General Chuikov; in the Möritz Platz they faced the men of the 9th Fusiliers Corps (part of the 5th Shock Army of Colonel General Berzarin).

When they were defending the area of Anhalter station on April 28 they again clashed with the "old" enemies of the 8th Army of the Guard.

On April 29 they met the Soviet advances of the 26th Fusiliers Corps of the Guard (part of the 5th Shock Army) in the area of the Reichsbank. When returning through the Anhalter area, the men of the unit clashed with the men of the 8th Army of the Guard and the 92nd Armored Regiment of the Guard.

Later, the general disorder, prevailing chaos and collapse of the defense, determined the fragmentation of the members of the unit, although possibly they continued to fight against these same Soviet units that were advancing on the streets of central Berlin.

In the last chapter of the history of the Ezquerra Unit, when the remainder of the unit were trying to reach the Stettiner station, they met with Soviet forces belonging to the 3rd Shock Army of Colonel General Kutznetsov.

The human composition of these Soviet troops was quite disparate, as they came from the many republics that made up the USSR, and apart from mainly the elite regiments of the Guard, they could be very different in their appearance, both in language and clothing. Among them were Russian, Belarusians, Ukrainians, Karelians, Azerbaijanis, Armenians, Azeries, Georgians, Tatars, Uzbeks, Kazakhs, Bashkirs, Mongols, Cossacks, Siberians, etc.

The uniforms, similarly to what happened with the German side, were also quite varied. Therefore, along with the main dark brown uniform there was also another khaki colored one. Headgear ranged from a metal helmet to a leather helmet with earflaps, leather caps, khaki caps, all in various states of repair after the many months that the troops has spent on the front.

Tactics

A battle on urban ground confers very specific characteristics on the tactics used by the troops, both defending and attacking sides. This fact, together with the decision taken by Hitler to turn Berlin into a fortress that had to be defended down to the very last meter, gave rise to a cruel battle in which the powerful Soviet Army could still be momentarily detained for a few days despite the "theoretical" limited fighting value of most of the defending troops.

Throughout history urban terrains have been witness to the way in which small forces with limited preparation can put a halt to, or even force a withdrawal from, large regular armies. In Berlin something similar occurred, but the heterogeneous defending forces, in which elderly men were posted in *Volkssturm*, boys of the Hitler Youth, women, as well as diverse and decimated regular troops, despite causing numerous losses for the Soviets could not contain forces that were so astonishingly superior both in terms of armament and number.

It should be remembered that a highly motivated defender can be a hard nut to crack due to knowledge of the terrain and unbending desire to protect his territory from invading soldiers, who in the case of

JS-II tanks on the streets of Berlin.

the Soviet had a double handicap: a lack of knowledge of the terrain and knowing that the end of the war was approaching which increased fear of falling so close to a victorious return home.

All these factors influence the fighting that took place between the end of April and the beginning of May 1945 in the capital of the Reich, although on a practical level these were not determining factors in the result due to the previously mentioned Soviet superiority in all aspects.

The tactics of the Germans in the urban fight were based on the knowledge acquired over many years of war and on the physical characteristics of a city with a large number of bridges and waterways. Most of the central districts of the city had blocks of buildings,

some of them with interior patios, built on streets which were more or less straight and peppered with canals, parks and railroad tracks. Height did not offer a significant advantage in these fights (apart from, of course, those fabulous anti-aerial defense towers which were in the city), as the city was completely flat and its small variations were of no account.

The Soviet tactics did not recommend that tank units were sent inside a city in enemy hands, as their movements would be very limited due to the urban layout, which at the same time was a perfect terrain for the creation of barricades and anti-tank obstacles that further "channeled" the direction of the advance of the tanks. Another important factor was that any building could be turned into a fiercely defended redoubt which would inevitably produce a high number of losses.

In the case of the battle for Berlin, the Soviets organized attack detachments where they combined a battalion of tanks, one of snipers, one of artillery, a squad or company of engineers and a squad of flamethrowers.

The advance of the Soviet tanks however was not restricted to the areas on the outskirts of the capital due to the high number of parks, gardens, etc.,which allowed them to go past the possible points of German resistance and attack them on its various flanks. However, going deeper into the city, the high density of buildings and the increased narrowness of the streets significantly reduced the possibilities of movement for the tanks. The only areas that allowed a higher degree of freedom were the wide avenues which were to be found in Berlin, although many anti-tank obstacles and various strong points of resistance has been put in place on them.

The tanks in the central areas mainly took on the role of supporting the infantry forces. This was the same infantry that has to previously eliminate any resistance in the adjoining buildings in order to allow the safe advance of the tanks, that is to say a combined attack of troops on foot and tanks, who were able to advance when they had their flanks protected. Therefore, when there was a point of resistance, the engineers and infantry were given the task of attacking it with support from the artillery and soldiers with flamethrowers.

The SS troops did not usually make barricades near to the corners of streets which were straight because they could be attacked by artillery fire from high positions in other buildings, creating a very dangerous disadvantageous situation.

Instead of this, they put snipers and men with machine guns on roofs and high floors of the buildings, who as well as covering their advance remained safe, in most cases, from the guns of the Soviet guns that could not manage to get enough height to shoot at them. In the same manner, men with *panzerfaust* or *panzerschrek* situated in lowdown positions, such as the rubble at the foot of buildings or cellar windows, could "close down" all the defensive system designed to trap the Soviet tanks and soldiers.

Understandably, these tactics were imitated in Berlin by other defensive troops, belonging to the *Wehrmacht*, *Volkssturm* or boys of the Hitler Youth; obviously, not with the same expertise that troops as experienced as the SS could demonstrate, although not with any less bravery.

The Soviet attackers did not apply the same tactic in each and every one of the strong points that they encountered. Sometimes the initiative was taken by the tanks, who were able to advance along two three streets allowing an improved degree of mobility for the attacking troops, although remaining unprotected given the scant number of infantry men that were able to accompany them. However a win of the agreed terrain proceeded to establish the front line with the taking up of strategic positions by the attacking troops .

The Soviets stressed the importance of not scattering the attacking troops too much in order to avoid them being attacked whilst in a position of disadvantage, therefore, they used to attack on a relatively narrow front with each attacking group.

As mentioned previously, there were many ambushes against Soviet tanks and troops, and to counteract the cost of so many vehicles and men, the Soviets began to put men armed with automatic rifles on the tanks with the task of raining down a shower of lead on the doors and windows where the defenders were fighting from. Another solution was to take advantage of the superiority of aviation and artillery attack so that it was

Destroyed Soviet tanks in front of one of the imposing anti-aerial defense towers whose guns temporarily stopped the Soviet advance in some areas of Berlin.

the aerial bombs and the shells that literally "crushed" the prepared defenses in any building of any street in Berlin.

The Soviet infantry started to move from house to house instead of advancing in a straight line down the streets. Their movements were carried out as a consequence of the conditions of the terrain.

Attackers and defenders often avoided going out onto the street by going from one building to another, the number of *panzerfaust* (on the Soviet as well as the German side as they had captured supplies of the weapon) allowed for the creation of "corridors" to be opened up between the buildings parallel to the streets which were much safer than them. Whilst some troops marched at ground level, other men took the high floors

of the buildings to also be able to use the attics as a link between some buildings and others.

Despite the theoretical correctness of these tactics, the reality was that the Soviets had to confront hundreds of ambushes that cost a high number of losses of tanks as well as men.

In terms of the case of the Spanish troops who took part in the defense of Berlin, their activity was that of what has come to be called a "firefighting unit"; that is, powerfully armed units that were sent to one or another sector of the front that found itself in danger of being broken by part of the enemy troops.

At this point in the conflict, and due to the lamentable state of the Berlin streets, movements had to be carried out on foot on streets full of craters and rubble under enemy fire or through the metro tunnels.

In the first case the advance had to be carried out by trying to stay with their backs against the walls of the buildings (or what was left of them) as much as possible so as to be walking uncovered for the least time possible, and always, as Ezquerra tells in his book, moving in single or double fire, giving the least possible front to the enemy.

Although when advancing along the streets inside the defensive German perimeter the powerful Russian artillery fire was capable of causing numerous losses, and due to the incessant "hammering" of the artillery, in some cases it was necessary to abandon the route on the ground, faster and more direct, in order to advance through the tunnel system of the Berlin metro. The area the Spanish were fighting in had a healthy metro network with different stations which served as entrances down into it. Moving around these tunnels was complicated on occasions by various obstacles, the darkness and the crowds of people that were sheltering in the stations. It was necessary to use torches and for the men to walk single file, as close as possible to each other, through the tunnels. Once they had arrived in the deployment area, it was fundamental to know the position of the neighboring friendly units, as well as the direction of the advance of the enemy troops.

The advances of the Soviet enemy were made up of infantry and armored forces, therefore the defensive priority was to gun down the infantry with the aim of leaving the tanks unprotected, when the moment could be capitalized on for their destruction.

The men took advantage of craters and rubble that could offer protection, as well as the walls, windows, terraces and any place that could offer protection in the buildings from where they could fire their weapons. The Spanish, with rifles, assault rifles, machine guns, etc., generated a powerful volume of fire concentrated on the small areas where the Soviets were advancing. This fire allowed for a number of infantry men to be shot down, at the same time that it forced many others to seek cover or withdraw. Right at that the men armed with *panzerfaust*, up till then sheltered behind any protection, went out defenseless to get as close as possible so as not to make a mistake when firing on the monstrous tanks. Obviously, to achieve the destruction of the tank it was necessary to reach the weakest areas of its armor.

All this process was carried out under cover of fire of their comrades, which continued whilst the soldier that was attacking the Soviet tanks returned to his original position.

The fragile defensive lines made up by these groups of men, were still able to halt the Soviet attacks, they had to be flexible and be ready at the right moment to withdraw on demand, and return again to organize themselves a few meters back to face the enemy. The tactical withdrawal was a significant aspect, within these combat maneuvers.

On certain occasions in which, despite the defensive effort of the Soviets, they managed to cross the lines, some of the men were able to stay in the enemy rearguard with the subsequent risk of being captured or shot down. Faced with this situation, the solution was to try to return to their own lines by force (more feasible when the number of men involved was high) or do it after waiting for the right moment to cautiously cross the enemy lines, preferably during the night. (A more practical method when the men were alone or in small groups).

After the fighting, once the enemy advance was halted and the front lines reestablished, the men were relieved from their positions by other regular army units to then wait to be directed to another area of the front at risk.

SHORT BIOGRAPHY OF MIGUEL EZQUERRA SÁNCHEZ

Born in Huesca possibly in 1903, Miguel Ezquerra Sánchez was, in the middle of the 1930s a teacher affiliated to the Spanish Falange. When the Civil War was declared after the raising of arms of the troops in Africa on July 18, 1936, he joined up with his Falangist comrades to later go to a recruitment centre. During the conflict he was posted to the 7th *Bandera de Falange*. He participated in combat on the fronts of Madrid, Aragon and Extremadura, reaching the post of provisional lieutenant. At the end of the war he headed to Malaga with the company that was sent there, where he received his discharge after requesting it to return to carry out his profession of teacher in state schools. He started a new married life with Consuelo, with whom he had two daughters: Consuelo y Pilar.

Later, and through the State Department, he was sent in 1940 as a Spanish teacher to the French city of Bayona. After the invasion of Russia by Germany, Ezquerra returned to Spain with the intention of enlisting in the Blue Division, although he did not manage it on his first attempt, as there were many volunteers to fill the available places to form the unit.

It was at the end of 1942 when with the necessary change in the Division he was able to take advantage of his opportunity. Firstly he enlisted as a soldier, although eventually he was able to leave with his former grade of lieutenant in the battalion of commander Millán, leaving his wife and children in Seville.

He served in an anti-tank unit in the area of Leningrad, where he would be decorated in 1943 with the Medal of Merit of War Second Class. His long journey as member of the Division ended on October 7, 1943, the date on which they received the order to return to Spain.

After being repatriated he joined the Tercio. During 1943 and part of 1944 he passed time in the company of his wife and two daughters, fully dedicating himself to family life. However Ezquerra did not consider his participation in the Second World War to be over yet, as he felt a deep yearning for his time in Russia fighting against communism, which is why he secretly prepared to leave Spain for the German Reich.

On April 2, 1944 he secretly crossed the border of the Pyrenees as part of a group of men who shared his goal. For this it was necessary to hold up a civil border guard with his pistol and even shoot into the air a few times before managing to get to France.

The shots also alerted the German soldiers who were on guard on the French side of the border, who immediately found them and held them up at gunpoint . After taking out their weapons and with their arms up they surrendered themselves to the German soldiers, who took them to a nearby Gestapo barracks. With their military past investigated and confirmed and their intentions to join the German army known, Ezquerra and his comrades were sent to San Juan de Luz (Ezquerra was contacted by the SS for the first time here), to Biarritz, and later to Versailles (to the Reina barracks), where they spent three weeks training.

In contrast to other Spaniards who could not "validate" their prior performance in the Division or in the Blue Legion, Ezquerra was able to make the Germans let him wear the decorations of a lieutenant (he talks about this in his interview in Interviú No.339, Madrid, November 1982, where he was registered as Captain Kronos).

After Versailles he was transferred to Stablack Süd, (Eastern Prussia) where he joined the Spanish being trained there. En Stablack he met men like Ricardo Botet Moro and Rufino Luis García Valdajos, who would be future comrades in the defense of the city of Berlin.

Ezquerra, now working for the SD, received the mission to be under orders of the *Sonderstab F* in the south of France, from where Cauterets was given the mission of channeling the Spanish that crossed the border to Stablack with the aim of creating a unit of Spanish volunteers. Shortly afterwards, possibly at the end of May 1944, he was transferred to Paris to do a training course for the officers of the *Abwehr* (the same one that García Valdajos had done shortly before).

Not many days had gone past when the Normandy landing happened, and Ezquerra was given the task of organizing a company of Spanish to act between enemy lines in sabotage tasks. This company, formed from the second half of June, which did not have many men, came from various units (Mountain troops from Hall im Tirol, volunteers recently arrived to the *Brandenburg* from the 102nd and other units where there were Spanish). These soldiers knew English and dressed as fellow countrymen with the aim of going unnoticed. According to the interview given in Interviú, Ezquerra commanded a unit of around eighty to ninety Spanish to whom some French Nazi sympathizers from Doriot's party and some Russians were added (Ezquerra was not positive about the latter, as he considered them cowards).

The unit stayed attached to a superior unit of the SS (the identity of which is unknown) and from June 27 they carried out incursions into occupied territory. Putting down mines, changing the directions of the traffic lights, blocking roads, all this to try and slow down the allied advance. But sooner or later they were discovered and the unit suffered an intense artillery and even aerial attack, after which the hunt started for the Spanish, but they, after more than 20 hours of bother, managed to finally make contact with German troops.

When they headed back to the rearguard they were again "reclaimed" to join a *Waffen-SS* battalion (of which they are not any details either) that resisted an allied attack. Again they took part in guerrilla missions, blowing up a fuel store and destroying positions that could serve the allied forces as strong holds.

A week later they were attached to the *Brandenburg* Division and received a new group of Spanish who were possibly stationed in Versailles as reinforcements. Totaling by now more than 150 men, they continued their "tasks" on the Normandy front. However, the losses during the service were very significant, with the unit, that was redeployed to Paris, finally being out of combat.

On August 25, 1944, when the allied troops were entering the French capital, Ezquerra and some other Spanish tried to leave the city in a car, not without receiving shots from the French resistance near the Opera and the Place de la Concorde that destroyed the tires of the vehicle forcing them to continue on foot. Finally they left the city even after having seen the allied troops on the Paris streets, troops which included the tanks of the Division of general Leclerc which the exiled Spanish republicans served in after the Civil War.

After leaving Paris, Miguel Ezquerra first went to Vienna and then to a *Luftwaffe* barracks in the Czech town of Wutweiss. Later he was called to Berlin to lead a secret mission in South America which he did not carry out, as he was given the command of a unit of Spanish commandos that took part in the beginning of the offensive of the Ardennes in the "brandenburgueses" (special operations unit of the German Army), that had been included from then on inside the *SS Jagdverband* of Otto Skorzeny.

The offensive of the Ardennes began on December 16, 1944. The men commanded by Ezquerra found U.S. infantry troops with artillery support in the wood of the Ardennes. Ezquerra divided the Spanish into two groups and launched the attack. The first group blew up the American munitions by surprise causing chaos, whilst the second group attacked the campaign tents. When the Americans came out from their hideouts the Spanish were firing on them, until they were all taken down. The strike by Ezquerra's unit cost them at least three dead and two wounded, but the Americans suffered 300 losses, the majority of which were prisoners, and the loss of a munitions store for an entire Division.

It was a great victory for the reduced group of Spanish, although it did little good, as the attack of the Ardennes finally was headed for stagnation and a withdrawal on the lines of the beginning of the offensive. During these actions Ezquerra suffered frostbite in his foot and an infection, which is why he was transferred to Wiesbaden, in Germany, for an operation. When he had recovered, he was sent to what would be his new destination: Berlin.

Between February and March 1945 he was given the task, on orders of General Faupel, through the Instituto IberoAmericano, to form a unit for the *Waffen-SS* made up of the Spanish who he had to convince to join

it. Faupel may have helped Ezquerra economically to facilitate his recruitment work. Among the volunteers there were veteran survivors of the *Wallonien*, students and some workers from the Todt Organization; there could even have been some of those who had been "captured" who had pending sentences with the German justice system. Ezquerra, in his interview in Interviú, states that he had signed authorization from Heinrich Himmler, head of the SS. With all of these he formed a unit which was given the name of its leader: *Einheit Ezquerra*.

At the same time that Ezquerra was doing his "gathering" of men to increase the numbers in his unit, there was another Spaniard in Berlin undertaking a similar activity, although with a very different outcome. His name was Gonzalo Rodríguez del Castillo, a journalist and the last Spanish diplomatic representative in Berlin. Really, the Spanish Diplomatic Corps should have been under the command of Diego Bohigas, who was the ambassador for the Spanish diplomatic mission, but he had received the order that the legation would be moved on March 30, 1945 to Bregenz, next to Lake Constantine, in neutral Switzerland, where due to the events of the war the new ambassador of Spain in Germany would reside.

In this very critical situation which the city found itself in the spring of 1945, Bohigas offered Rodríguez del Castillo the chance of joining this caravan that was moving most of the Spanish delegation, but he refused, remaining to all intents and purposes the last Spanish diplomatic representative in Berlin.

In recent times Rodríguez del Castillo had undertaken many negotiations with the Todt Organization and with the German Labor Front (DAF) to obtain safe-conducts, train tickets and food coupons for the Spanish who belonged to these organizations. According to the book by Fernando

Vadillo, *Los irreductibles*, just between April 12 and 16, 1945, 200 Spanish workers travelled by train to be repatriated.

Obviously, this task clashed full on with that of Ezquerra, whose intention it was to recruit the men "protected" by Rodríguez del Castillo.

Again, according to Vadillo, at a face to face meeting between Ezquerra and the diplomat, they were on the verge of coming to blows.

With the unit that bore the name of its commander, as was customary in German military organizations during this period of the conflict, made up of two companies with light armament, he participated in the swan song of the capital of the Reich, reaching the post of Lieutenant Colonel of the *Waffen-SS*. A third company, or what could be organized of it, could have been sent to the Alps to form part of the defense of the "alpine fortress."

Ezquerra, again in his interview, states that with his unit (it must have still been in formation) he participated in the fighting that took place in Stettin, where for some days he defended a head bridge that the Germans had on the Oder; there, "the fighting against the Russian tanks was terrible and served to acclimatize my soldiers", according to the then commander of the *SS Ezquerra*.

After this fighting they were sent to Berlin and posted to the *Nordland* Division and after various actions against the armed Soviet forces they were "converted" into a reserve unit and directed to the cellars of the Department of Aviation.

Miguel Ezquerra received recognition for his valor in combat, obtaining the distinction of the Knight of the Iron Cross and German nationality personally granted by Adolf Hitler, according to Ezquerra in Interviú.

He had to surrender to the Russians in Stettiner Banhof, after they had stolen his watch and broken some teeth, the Soviet soldiers ordered him to fall in with the column of prisoners being taken to the east in which there were various Spanish comrades.

Once in Poland they were put in an abandoned concentration camp. There, Ezquerra and his comrades (two Spaniards and two French men) robbed a backpack of supplies from a German prison officer and got hold of a file. When night fell, Ezquerra went up to the only Russian guard watching the area to speak to him, and at that moment one of the French stabbed him. Later, the five of them escaped the camp and were then free in Poland.

Ezquerra and his comrades met thousands of prisoners freed by the Russians on the way. Among them they met a Jew who had been in a German concentration camp; he joined the group and even found food for them. In a village, in occupied Germany, Ezquerra and his comrades gave the Jew the slip, as Ezquerra did not know where he came from and suspected that he may betray them if discovered.

Again on the move they met French soldiers who had been prisoners of the Germans; the two French who were with Ezquerra lied and said that they had also been prisoners of the Germans, and that their Spanish companions had been forced laborers.

The French, fed and transported the former SS in their truck to the outskirts of Berlin, there the group of escapees separated: the two French managed to get a pass to return to France, the two Spaniards decided to carry on under their own steam and Miguel Ezquerra, now on his own, returned to Berlin.

He was hidden there by a friendly family and obtained documents at the Instituto IberoAmericano which enabled him to pass for Argentinean. At the end of May Ezquerra was transported to Magdeburg in Russian trucks together with a group of people, some of whom were supposedly being repatriated to Argentina. On the border of the Soviet and British areas some English soldiers did not allow those with Argentinean nationality to cross, however, some British ex-prisoners who had made friends with Ezquerra during the journey, intervened for him and finally he was allowed to cross.

In Magdeburg, some American journalists asked the Spanish if they knew a certain Miguel Ezquerra, to which they answered that they did not, suspecting a possible trap to capture him.

After various adventures he managed to reach Brussels, where he separated from his comrades.

In the Belgian capital he made contact with Spanish republicans who were unhappy with communism. Ezquerra, trying to formalize his situation, made for the Argentinean embassy to relate his uncomfortable and dangerous situation, to later be sent to Spain.

At that time, not all of the embassy staff were prepared to take the risk of helping a fugitive, and no-one would do much to help him, although he finally managed to at least get them to give him a new identity as a Spanish Republican freed from a concentration camp. (This version, taken from his book, differs from that remembered in his interview to Interviú, according to which he obtained the documentation by making it himself with ink pads and official paper in the Instituto IberoAmericano, these documents identified him as Fernando Reyes Calvo, of Argentinean nationality).

On his "escape", Ezquerra warned that an Argentinean nationality was perhaps not the best one that he could have adopted, as Perón's government was considered to be fascist by the Soviets. In spite of this, he joined some American and British ex-prisoners of war who were going to be sent to the north of Germany, in the area of U.S. control. Everything was going well with his new comrades until a couple of British soldiers had suspicions about Ezquerra, however they did not report him (Ezquerra states that they also professed a certain degree of hatred for the Soviets due to the many outrages that they had committed against German civilians), and he reached the Belgian city of Liege with his secret unnoticed.

On one occasion he met some Spanish communists who came into a restaurant that Ezquerra was in. Upon being discovered, and to avoid anything worse happening, he fled Belgium for Paris, a city he already knew, on this occasion he assumed the identity of a refugee.

In Paris, some Spanish friends, some of whom were ex-Republicans, gave him a free pass for the whole of France (according to his interview in Interviú, it was a Spaniard called Ricardo Bruguera who gave him his own documents, something that really would have been strange but for the fact that the identity of Ricardo Bruguera was also false).

In spite of this, he was not much safer in France, as all suspects were routinely arrested and interrogated. (Ezquerra tells in his story how he was the first on the most wanted list, the truth of this can be viewed with some suspicion).

With the help of villagers me met on the way he continued to advance toward the Spanish border hiding in the corners of the roads, woods and areas with little traffic. In this manner he arrived in Dax, where he worked in a sawmill, until one day he decided to steal a bicycle with which he reached the outskirts of Hendaya, where he abandoned the vehicle and got across crossed the border via the Pyrenees. Again in his interview, conducted 40 years later, Ezquerra gives a different version in which he tells that for his final border crossing he had to hold up two gendarmes at gunpoint, who he then forced to guide him to the border after disarming them (something similar happened when he left Spain, which seems more credible). When he finally arrived at the border, the Civil Guard came to his aid and then he finally entered Spain.

Due to the law that was in place regarding the Spanish who worked for the German Army once the Blue Legion was withdrawn by the Spanish government, Miguel Ezquerra had lost his Spanish nationality, so he decided to head for Portugal, where he would publish the book about his experiences in the conflict, *Berlin a vida o muerte*.

Once in Spain, according to Ezquerra's own version, he worked for the Spanish secret service and then enlisted in the French Foreign Legion in the information services when he joined the Bureau of Territory Security, ending up working as a double agent for the Spanish in Argel (as Ezquerra states, "the Spanish consul in Orán was a fellow commander of the Blue Division", so collaboration with him was easy).

Later, as a French legionnaire, he took part in the Indochina war, where, according to him, he was in conditions of "heavy" combat for nearly a year between the delta of the Mekong and the Red River. Then he managed to return to Algeria, where, now as sergeant, after a year he was discharged from the French Foreign Legion.

He was contacted again by the Bureau of Territory Security to continue working for them, but Ezquerra refused. He went to Casablanca, where he was arrested by the Bureau of Territory Security at the entrance to the Spanish consulate. He spent ninety days in a jail that he describes as disease-ridden, sharing five square meters with a dozen prisoners. Eventually, after these three months of imprisonment, he was transferred in a truck to the Spanish area of the Protectorate, his destination was Ceuta jail.

From there he went to mainland Spain, although only to continue to be imprisoned, in this case in Carabanchel. Finally, shortly afterwards he obtained his freedom due to, an undisclosed, crime (Ezquerra again states in his interview that the cause of his imprisonment was in relation to "things in the secret services which it is better not to enter into detail about").

His next steps took him from Madrid (where he only stayed for a short time) to the Caribbean, after being contracted to form a Caribbean Anti-communist Legion in the service of the dictator of the Dominican Republic, Leonidas Trujillo, an idea that at first satisfied Ezquerra. But the reality did not convince him, so as soon as he could, after some incidents the details of which he did not disclose, he left the Dominican Republic for neighboring Haiti.

Afterwards he went to Venezuela to complete his long journey in Brazil, where he was able to settle thanks to his contact with exiled Germans (very possibly ex-SS settled in the South American country) living in Santa Catarina, on the borders of Paraguay and Brazil.

Santa Catarina was a large forestry colony which was isolated from the rest of the world thanks to the leafy jungle surrounding it. It could only be accessed by people that had been guaranteed either by one of the residents or by people who reliably confirmed their real identity during the Second World War.

According to Ezquerra and the myths that were created at the end of the war, many of the German leaders who escaped after Germany's defeat settled there (among them, he states in his interview en Interviú, was Martin Borman, who he also recalls having seen during his escape from Berlin, and Doctor Mengele). Ezquerra did not spend a long time there, as thanks to his contact with the Spanish ambassador in

Asuncion (Paraguay), Giménez Caballero, he obtained a timber concession in Alto Paraná (in the Strössner colony). He stayed there for a couple of years, but it was not worth while, mainly due to the constant fight with the jungle and the worst red tape he had encountered. After leaving there he lived for a few years in Argentina and Chile, returning permanently to Spain.

When he was back in his country he joined CEDADE (Spanish Circle of Friends of Europe), taking part in a congress in Madrid in 1973, where he wore his decorations obtained in the world war.

He died in October 1984, and was buried in the Almudena cemetery in Madrid, together with his comrades, in the vault of the Blue Division.

He was a man with a surprising and very intense life, and if his biography, debated by many, shows various facts that can not be verified, his word as a soldier and a Spaniard deserves at least some degree of trust.

Various countries that Miguel Ezquerra passed through, both during the period of the Second World War (dark gray), and the post-war period (lighter gray).

Below left: Death notice of Miguel Ezquerra Sánchez.

The only known photograph of Miguel Ezquerra, taken in 1982 in an interview for *Interviú* magazine. Image kindly granted by *Interviú* magazine by its chief editor Aitor Marín for publication in this book.

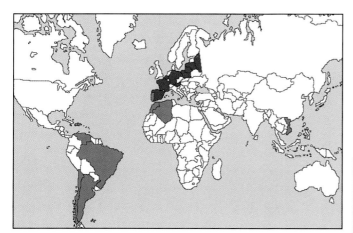

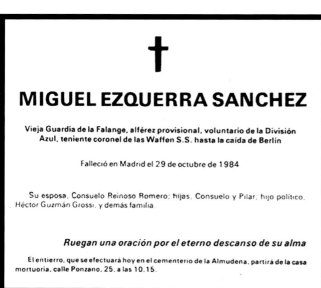

†

MIGUEL EZQUERRA SANCHEZ

Vieja Guardia de la Falange, alférez provisional, voluntario de la División Azul, teniente coronel de las Waffen S.S. hasta la caída de Berlín

Falleció en Madrid el 29 de octubre de 1984

Su esposa, Consuelo Reinoso Romero; hijas, Consuelo y Pilar; hijo político, Héctor Guzmán Grossi, y demás familia.

Ruegan una oración por el eterno descanso de su alma

El entierro, que se efectuará hoy en el cementerio de la Almudena, partirá de la casa mortuoria, calle Ponzano, 25, a las 10.15.

POLITICAL RELATIONS BETWEEN SPAIN AND GERMANY DURING THE SECOND WORLD WAR

To find out more about this subject in depth I recommend reading the interesting articles by María Soledad Gómez and Esther Sacristán, on which this part of the book is based (*see bibliography*).

When the Spanish Civil War ended, Francisco Franco became head of the Spanish state. The significant help that he received from Germany and Italy for the Spanish regime during this conflict made it very "close" to both countries, which could be considered the best examples of the new authoritarian system in Europe, whose power was growing day by day. Franco had a large debt, not only moral, with Hitler's Germany and Mussolini's Italy, and its payment was duly claimed. The sum total of the debts that Spain had with the Italian government ran to more than 7,000 million Lira, reduced to 5,000 million by Benito Mussolini in exchange for economic advantages in its trade with Spain. After the corresponding diplomatic meeting, a repayment schedule was established with a repayment plan which covered the period between 1942 and 1967. With respect to its debt to Germany, Spain was obliged to allow the entrance of German businesses into the Spanish economy. With respect to the financial debt incurred, there were diplomatic meetings which extended the repayment period. At the end of the Second World War, Spain, after having made very few payments, unilaterally cancelled this obligation in 1945.

The new Spanish State born out of the Civil War looked to be recognized at world level at the same time as showing its political leanings. A friendship treaty was signed with Portugal, knowing full well the pro-British leanings of this country and in March 1939 a friendship treaty was signed with Germany that left Spain in an inferior situation to Germany, with whom it stayed linked. In addition, Spain adhered to the Antikomintern Pact, focused on opposing Soviet communism, with unspecific obligations to be fulfilled. On May 8, the Spanish government withdrew officially from the Geneva League of Nations.

With the beginning of the Second World War a new era was opened up in Spain's international relations. When, on September 3, 1939, Great Britain and France declared war on Germany, Franco, in the name of the Spanish government made a public appeal to reconsider the situation and restart negotiations. The situation was complex, as there really was a great political and ideological affinity between the powers of the Axis, but the western allied powers, especially France, were closer to Spain and its North African territories, with the consequent risk of a severe "blockade" that, by sea, would be led by Great Britain. These facts, together with the disastrous state of Spain after the recent Civil war and with the obvious depletion of the population, determined that the Spanish government decide on a neutral stand in the world conflict, a position it also maintained during the Great War. On September 4, 1939 a Decree officially proclaimed neutrality: "Officially confirming the state of war that, unfortunately, exists between England, France and Poland, on one side, and Germany, on the other, I order by the present Decree the strictest state of neutrality, of Spanish subject, in accordance with the laws in force and the principles of public international Law .

Delivered in Burgos, September 4, 1939. Year of Victory. — Francisco Franco — The Secretary of State, Juan Beigbeder y Atienza."

In this fashion, the atmosphere of disquiet of the Spanish came to an end.

The editorial of ABC on this day said, amongst other things: "This attitude represents, on one hand, the magnificent beginning of an international policy based on the strictest independence, and on the other, the logical consequence of impetus to rebuilding currently at work in Spain."

In terms of the real possibilities of Spain and the case of military intervention, the Spanish Army, although "tired" and with an armament that would quickly become obsolete, was significant numerically speaking and with great experience in combat. Actually, the armament that Italy and Germany had supplied to the Francoist army was very advanced but it was becoming out-of-date very rapidly.

It should be remembered that the most modern armored vehicles of the Spanish army were the T -26 tank of Soviet origin and the PzKw I tank of German origin, already old-fashioned in 1940.

This declaration of neutrality by Spain allowed the Germans to act safe in the knowledge that the Iberian peninsula would not serve as an area of operations for the western allies. On the other hand, the powerful German Army, secure in its superiority, would not need the depleted Spanish Army for any offensive operation in Europe, it was enough to have it as a "friend."

Between the months of May and June 1940 France was crushed by the unstoppable German advance. The Spanish government watched the events with admiration, pro-German feeling ever increasing in Spain. This admiration changed the direction of the Spanish Government to a certain extent, as up till then it had held Italy more as its reference. On June 3, 1940, Francisco Franco had sent a missive to Adolf Hitler in which he confirmed that he was prepared to offer Germany the services that it considered most necessary.

In the middle of June 1940 the highest Spanish political and military requests tried to get on the bandwagon. In this whirl of enthusiasm the idea was put forward to form part of the new victorious order and to revive the old crowns of the Spanish empire in North East Africa. Days before the French surrender to Germany, Spain modified its neutral status to that of no belligerence; this new position allowed the French Government to show its support for the powers of the Axis.

Relations began to be established between Madrid and Berlin with purely militaristic aims, so that strong men like Ramón Serrano Súñer, Dionisio Ridruejo and Antonio Tovar (the latter two linked to the Francoist regime' s propaganda system) negotiated the use of Spain as a base of action for so-called Operation Félix, with which the occupation of the enclave of Gibraltar was planned, stopping the hegemony that the British had at an aerial and naval level in Mediterranean waters. In the same manner a new front would be opened for the carrying out of military operations in North Africa.

The Spanish goals if they entered into war with the Axis were very clear, Gibraltar would continue to be under Spanish sovereignty, as well as the territories that would be taken in North Africa, in Algeria and in

French Morocco. Also the Spanish expansion would happen toward the territory in the Gold River and the Golf of Guinea.

These matters between Spain and Germany required a strong impulse, which is why it was decided to have a meeting between the two high commands of the respective countries. Therefore, after a visit to Madrid by Himmler, head of the Gestapo, and the visit, on September 13, 1940, by Serrano Súñer as Secretary of State and the Government to Berlin to talk to Hitler, and later on 16th with von Ribbentrop (who came to welcome him at Anhalter station), it was agreed that a summit meeting was needed.

This took place on October 23, 1940. In the meeting at Hendaya between Francisco Franco and Adolf Hitler, accompanied by their respective Secretaries of State, a protocol was drawn up (Hendaya Protocol), where the participation of Spain in the war in exchange for the aforementioned compensation of territories was given consideration.

Among Hitler's doubts about Spain's possible support in the war, were the Spanish requests regarding North African territories which clashed with the interests of the Vichy France (German ally) and the situation created in the Balkans due to the defeat of the Italian army in Greece in October 1940. In the end Spain did not take the step of becoming Germany's ally. Despite this the aforementioned Hendaya Protocol was signed, in which Spain promised to enter into war together with Germany when the demands regarding territories in North Africa and the necessary military help had been met.

Lastly, the only Spanish territory that was occupied during the conflict was the city of Tangiers, in 1940, with the argument that after the fall of France this city had become ungovernable. In 1945 Spain left the city, declaring it again an open city.

On November 19, 1940, Hitler, in a meeting with Serrano Súñer held in Berlin, requested a date for Spain's entry in the war and the beginning of the siege of Gibraltar. The Spaniard emphasized the significant Spanish logistical problems in embarking on this campaign.

Due to Spain's delay in intervening to intervene, Germany asked permission for troops to pass through Spanish territory with the aim of attacking Gibraltar. On December 11, 1940 Spain rejected the request putting forth the argument of the impossibility for Spain to maintain sovereignty over Spanish Guinea and the Canary Islands if there was an English attack. In addition, it also put forward the excuse of the Spanish army's lack of materials, as well as the need to receive significant amounts of transport and grain. Further meetings of Franco with the leaders of Italy and Vichy France – with Mussolini in Bordighera and with Petain in Montpellier, in February 1941 – did not change Spain's position in the conflict in any way.

On June 22, 1941 German troops carried out a surprise attack on the Soviet Union, causing in most of Europe a feeling of euphoria. In Spain, the regime's leaders identified with Germany, it was not for nothing that the Soviet Union had been the main support of the Republican Army during the Spanish Civil War. In Spain there were discussions and meetings asking for participation in the fight again communism, embodied by the Soviet enemy, which it considered largely guilty for the Spanish Civil War. The Spanish government listened to the clamor of the people and allowed the organization of companies of volunteers (mainly Falangists) to support Germany on the Eastern Front.

Lastly the Spanish Division of Volunteers, which under the command of general Agustín Muñoz Grandes left for the Russian front in August 1941.

However the war began to show significant setbacks for the German Army: the summer offensive was halted in Caucasus at the end of September, the terrible slaughter of Stalingrad started, and there was the allied landing in Casablanca in November 1942.

On February 17 there was a meeting in Seville between Franco and Oliveira Salazar where the Iberian Pact was signed, which assumed a rapprochement to Portugal that in spite of its dictatorial regime continued to maintain close relations with the United Kingdom. On November 8, 1942, the U.S. ambassador gave a letter to Franco from Roosevelt which informed him of the occupation of the French territories in North Africa and guaranteed the neutrality and integrity of Spanish territory.

Franco received a significant amount of allied pressure forcing Spanish foreign policy to maintain an ambiguous balance to keep both sides "happy" as much as possible, causing on September 3, 1942 Serrano Súñer to be replaced in the State Department by Francisco Gómez Jordana, considered as being closer to the western allies than his predecessor.

The supplies provided for Spanish territory were limited to Italian and German planes and boats, but on the other hand agreements were signed to send supplies and raw materials to the Third Reich.

In 1943 the decline of German power in Europe and North Africa continued, a situation that did not help the balanced position maintained by the Spanish government, therefore it accepted the only way out that remained under English and North American pressure to its initial neutral position, making this effective on October 3 (some sources says the 1st) 1943. The members of the Spanish Division of Volunteers also began to be repatriated from December of that year.

Spain, or rather, Francoist policy, continued debating between the pressures of the allied forces and its pro-German stance. Supplies and raw material, above all wolfram (essential for advanced precision engineering and the production of weapons), iron, zinc, lead and mercury continued to be sent to Germany. On October 25, 1943 the United States Government demanded that Spain totally cease the export of wolfram to the Axis under threat of cutting petrol supplies, temporarily suspending the dispatch of petrol to Spain in January 1944. This situation led to the collapse of the Spanish State, therefore on May 2, 1944 they finished exporting wolfram to Germany (although possibly a very small quantity until August of that year), German agents were sent away from Tangiers, the Japanese mission was closed in Spain and a promise of collaboration with the U.S. and Great Britain was obtained for military affairs. Some months later, planes from North American Air Transport Command received authorization to refuel on Spanish territory.

On April 12, 1945, with the war in Europe almost finished, Spain broke diplomatic relations with Japan. At the end of the world conflict, Spain found itself in a difficult situation, as the winners continued to see its government as having clear fascist leanings. A period of isolation began which only had an end in sight when the western powers considered it necessary to put military bases in Spain during the cold war. Although all of this is part of another story.

RANK EQUIVALENTS IN THE WAFFEN-SS, WEHRMACHT, AND SPANISH ARMY[1]

WAFFEN SS	WEHRMACHT	EJ. ESPAÑOL
SS-Grenadier	Schütze	Soldado
SS-Obergrenadier	Oberschütze	Soldado de 1ª
SS-Sturmann (SS-Strm)	—	Cabo
SS-Rottenführer (SS-Rttf)	Gefreiter	Cabo 1º
SS-Unterscharführer (SS-Uscha)	Obergefreiter	Sargento
SS-Scharführer (SS-Scha)	Unteroffizier	Sargento 1º
SS-Oberscharführer (SS-Oscha)	Unterfeldwebel Feldwebel	Brigada Sin equivalencia
SS-Hauptscharführer (SS-Hascha)	Oberfeldwebel Hauptfeldwebel	Subteniente Sin equivalencia
SS-Sturmscharführer (SS-Stscha)	Stabsfeldwebel	Suboficial Mayor
SS-Untersturmführer (SS-Ustuf)	Leutnant	Alférez
SS-Obersturmführer (SS-Ostuf)	Oberleutnant	Teniente
SS-Hauptsturmführer (SS-Hstuf)	Hauptmann	Capitán
SS-Sturmbannführer (SS-Stubaf)	Major	Comandante
SS-Obersturmbannführer (SS-Ostubaf)	Oberstleutnant	Teniente Coronel
SS-Standartenführer (SS-Staf)	Oberst	Coronel
SS-Oberführer (SS-Obf)	—	Sin equivalencia
SS-Brigadeführer und Generalmajor der Waffen SS (SS-Brif)	Generalmajor	General de Brigada
SS-Grupenführer und Generalleutnat der Waffen SS (SS-Gruf)	Generalleutnant	General de División
SS-Obergruppenführer und General der Waffen SS (SS-Ogruf)	General der Infanterie, Kavallerie, etc.	Teniente General
SS-Oberstgruppenführer und Generaloberst der Waffen SS (SS-Obgruf)	Generaloberst	Capitán General
—	Generalfeldmarschall	Sin equivalencia
SS-Reichsführer SS[2]	—	Sin equivalencia

1 Some ranks are not direct equivalents to those in the present day Spanish Army
2 This post was only undertaken by Heinrich Himmler.

SS troops. Emblems of rank worn on the neck of the SS troops army jackets.

Reichsführer-SS			SS-Obersturmführer		
SS-Oberstgruppenführer			SS-Untersturmführer		
SS-Obergruppenführer			SS-Sturmscharführer		
SS-Gruppenführer			SS-Hauptscharführer		
SS-Brigadeführer			SS-Oberscharführer		
SS-Oberführer			SS-Scharführer		
SS-Standartenführer			SS-Unterscharführer		
SS-Obersturmbannführer			SS-Rottenführer		
SS-Sturmbannführer			SS-Sturmmann		
SS-Hauptsturmführer			SS-Schütze/SS-Oberschütze		

Goebbels congratulating a very young soldier innocently determined to confront the enemy. Lauban, March 1945.

BIOGRAPHIES

Ion Antonescu

Romanian soldier and statesman, born in Pitesti in 1882 and died in Jilava in 1946. From September 1940 to August 23, 1944 he was Romanian Prime Minister and later head of State.

Born into a traditionally bourgeoisie military family, he went to military schools and later entered the French military academy in Saint-Cyr, where in 1911 he became head of promotion. As lieutenant, Antonescu took part in the suppression of the peasants revolt in Galati in 1907; in 1913 he took part in the Balkan War, where he received the highest Romanian decoration for his commendable work. In the First World War Mundial Antonescu was head of Staff Officers of Marshal Prezan.

As Prime Minister he made the decision about Romania's incorporation into the

Second World War on the side of the Axis, given that they offered guarantees to Romania for the return of land annexed by the Soviet Union in 1940. After the defeat of Stalingrad, Antonescu thought that the war was lost, and therefore tried to find a way to get out. Therefore, throughout 1943, in the name of the Romanian Government his diplomats maintained contact with representatives of the allied forces with the aim of signing a separate peace accord.

The opposition against Antonescu's government grew day by day, leading to the conception of a coup d'état which finally took place on August 23, 1944, when the Romanian King Mihail, supported by the main politicians, removed Antonescu from office and arrested him. After his arrest, he was handed over to the Soviets, who detained him for two years before sending him back to his country to be judged and an "example" made of him. Sentenced to death by the "People's Court", on June 1 1946 he was executed in Jilava together with his closest collaborators.

Martín De Arrizubieta Larrinaga

The story of this controversial personality is mainly known thanks to the magnificent article written about him by Núñez Xeitas (*see bibliography*), with some interesting information about him to be found also on the internet, on the webpage: http://wikanda.cordobapedia.es.

Martín de Arrizubieta Larrinaga was born in Mundaca (Vizcaya) in 1908. The only child of a Basque couple, Martín studied for an ecclesiastical career with the Jesuits, moving later to the secular clergy.

At the beginning of the Civil War, being a militant of Basque nationalism he enlisted as a volunteer in the Gudaris Battalion. The fall of the north front into the power of the nationals made Arrizubieta their prisoner. Using his priesthood, he convinced his captors that in reality he was being forced to fight for the Republicans. He achieved his goal of being released from prison, but he was posted to a battalion of requêtes, where he was given the grade of lieutenant. He did not spend long with the requêtes, as some months later he managed to obtain a permit that allowed him to leave and return to France.

He lived peacefully in the south of France, in the area of San Juan de Luz, with the help of the French-Basque separatists, but at the beginning of the Second World War he was urged to join one of the levies being carried out the French Army. Eventually, and despite his opposition, he was integrated into a battalion of the Foreign Legion, which in a short time left southern Marseilles to go to the front.

The unstoppable German advance finished with the Arrizubieta company being captured by the Germans on the outskirts of Verdun in 1940. From there he went from one prison camp to another in Germany, disguising himself as a French priest until in one of them, Heinkel, in Rostock, he deception was discovered by Petainist prisoners who denounced him to the Gestapo.

In the end he managed to finally avoid execution and was taken to a factory in April 1942. Again he had problems with other pro-German workers, leading him to decide to a supporter of Germany, as it was showing a more "placid" situation at that time. Arrizubieta even invented that he was really a Francoist spy trying again to make things even more complicated in his long career of identity switching.

In November 1943 he was lucky enough to meet a Jesuit friend who visited him in the work farm where he had been for some time, by the name of Francisco de Echevarría, lecturer at the University of Comillas. Echevarría managed through his influence to get Arrizubieta "sent" to Stettin in January 1944. But Echevarría wanted something better for his friend, so the von Faupel, who was head of the Berlin *Instituto IberoAmericano* interceded for him. General von Faupel finally reclaimed him in September 1944, managing to get him freed and then finding him a post working for him at the aforementioned institute.

There he became one of the important men at the Institute to be given the task of going back to a revive the previous importance of one of the publications that the institute produced in Spanish, the weekly magazine directed at Spanish workers called *Enlace*.

In this manner, in a few months Arrizubieta went from being forced labor to being the person responsible for a publication which most of the Spanish living in the Reich had access to. He then became the head and editor of the main magazine of Nazi propaganda in Spanish. From this magazine, as well as underlining the European character of the fight against communism, he managed to report on the invasion of Spain by the German army, the overthrow of General Franco and his replacement by a genuinely national socialist Spanish regime, the "liberation of Euskadi" and the establishment of another similar regime.

Obviously, the magazine abandoned its pro-Falangist origins (not for nothing was it originally controlled by the attitudes of the FET-JONS local office for Germany) to "mutate" into a Spanish national socialist direction in which the permanent union between nationalism and socialism was praised. The weekly magazine insisted that "the salvation of humanity lies with us, the defenders of the New European Order" and Arrizubieta himself declared that "if Germany wins the war, it will not respect the Spanish border."

The nationalist direction acquired by Enlace, obviously was not at all liked by the Spanish diplomatic corps, causing a certain degree of confusion among the Spanish community still living in Germany. This community, as mentioned previously, was made up of two columns: workers and Spanish soldiers serving in Germany.

At the *Instituto IberoAmericano* he had a comfortable situation, but the events of the conflict were leading toward a progressive deterioration of Germany's situation. General von Faupel asked Miguel Ezquerra to post Martín de Arrizubieta in the unit that was being formed under his command on the outskirts of Berlin in April 1945 (according to Miguel Ezquerra in his book).

He therefore ended up being incorporated into a military unit with the rank of second lieutenant, although fortune again was in his favor, as he belonged to the company that was leaving for the Tyrol, escaping the destination of his comrades who would give their lives in the Berlin streets.

In the end Arrizubieta's company was not able to arrive at its destination due to the situation of the conflict on German territory, meaning they were scattered all over the lands of the Reich.

Ezquerra tells in his book that Arrizubieta managed to make contact with Yugoslavian forces under the command of Marshal Tito, finishing up joining his staff officers. Ezquerra also said that Arrizubieta formed part of the commission that the Yugoslavians sent to the Holy See to make contact (this idea seems quite bizarre due to the complicated nature of the story, but it should be remembered that Arrizubieta's life had many twists and turns, making it seemingly impossible that everything happened in the way that it has been told).

The most reliable version, based on that told by Núñez Xeitas, is that Arrizubieta left Berlin in the second half of March 1945 with the group of Spanish that were heading toward the Alps. When they arrived in North Italy they disbanded and Arrizubieta went to Tarvisio, later going to Porderone, arriving there on April 10. He stayed there temporarily working in a silk factory.

In 1946 he returned to carry out his most political undertaking, getting close to the Basque nationalist circles by meeting leaders close to the Basque Nationalist Party in Rome. This contact with members of the Basque party was based on its progressive rapprochement toward Basque nationalist theories with the final aim of forming a "confederation of Iberian nationalities under the sign of a Spanish republic."

He tried to obtain, without success, through his contact from the Basque Nationalist Party, passage as an exile to Mexico, selling his time in Berlin as a simple trick to cause differences and divisions within the Falangist camp.

Whilst waiting for his passage to Mexico, Arrizubieta moved to the French Basque Country to be nearer to his native land with a view to later negotiations with the BNP. However these broke up and after staying there for some time he made the "jump" over the Pyrenees to return to what were then Vascongadas Provinces.

When he returned to Spain he told of how he had remained in various concentration camps during the world war, under he was freed and could return to his country. But he had left Spain as a deserter, and therefore had to undergo a war council where he was sentenced to death and later pardoned and his punishment commuted for exile in Cordoba, where he arrived at the end of 1947 after the intervention by his uncle, the Dominican priest Larrinaga, who "recommended" him to the Bishop of Cordoba Menéndez Raigada, making him director of the parish of San Andrés, later being called parish of Santa Marina in the period between 1954 and 1983.

During the 1950s and 1960s, according to Núñez Xeitas, he entered the orbit of the

Spanish Communist Party, in contact with opponents in Cordoba of the Francoist regime, particularly those grouped around the magazine "Praxis. Magazine of Mental Hygiene Mental for Society", led by the psychiatrists Carlos Castilla del Pino and José Aumente Baena and promoted by progressive Christian sectors who had Marxist leanings.

On a number of occasions he supported activists against Franco's regime, who received shelter and protection in his church. In addition he also had links with the Popular Liberation Front at the beginning of the 1960s, where he was active with the nickname of "The Ogre." The PLF, popularly known as "Felipe", was an illegal anti-Francoist political organization which was active in the period between 1958 and 1969, based on the failure of implementing leftist political formations due to the repression that they suffered during the era of Franco. In 1966 Arrizubieta organized together with a large group of neighbors of the neighborhood of Santa Marina the creation of an Association of the Heads of the Family, according to the new law of Associations.

In the 1970s he began to extend his stays in his native land, establishing links with some opponents of the regime from the Basque Country, such as the poet Gabriel Aresti and the Sastre-Forest couple, radicalizing their nationalist position. In 1983 he retired, retuning to his native country permanently and to his country house in Mundaca; but without finding his place in the intellectual and political panorama. He returned again to Cordoba, where he died on September 1, 1988.

Arthur Axmann

Head of the Hitler Youth from 1940 to 1945. Born in 1913 and died in 1996. When he was fifteen years old he requested entrance to the *Schülerbund* of the Hitler Youth, which he was a member of until he finished his degree in 1931. In 1932 he was named *Gebietsführer* and leader of the *Soziales Amt*

Reichsjugendführer
ARTHUR AXMANN

der Reichsjugendführung, branch of the social service of the Hitler Youth.

During the Second World War he signed up as a volunteer of the *Wehrmacht*, and was retired from service on the front after he had to have his right arm amputated. In 1940 he replaced Baldur von Schirach as leader of the Hitler Youth, a post he would keep until the war finished.

At the end of the war he was a "tenant" in Hitler's bunker, from where he was able to escape as soon as the Führer took the decision to commit suicide. He managed to leave the bunker with Hitler's private secretary, Martin Bormann, and the Führer's private doctor, Stumpfegger.

Although he managed to avoid capture for some months, he was finally captured by the allied secret services, who after interrogating him on a number of occasions freed him in 1946. In 1947 he was imprisoned again and in 1949 he was tried and sentenced to three years and three months of civil service. He was imprisoned again in 1958. He escaped from prison helped by the Israeli secret service in exchange for giving information which helped to locate the former officers of the SS responsible for the Nazi extermination camps. After a long period in Spain, he died in Berlin in 1996.

Gottlob Berger

Soldier and politician, born in 1896 and died in 1975. He belonged to the German Army during the First World War, reaching the rank of first lieutenant of the infantry when the war ended, where he obtained the Iron Cross First and Second Class. In 1922 he joined the Nazi Party, forming part of the SA and later, from 1936, the SS.

During la Second World War, from 1940 he was head of the Staff for the military branch of the SS, in charge of matters related to the territories of the east. In August 1944 he was sent to Slovakia to suppress the upri-

sing there, After this, he was given the task of controlling all the prisoner of war camps.

At the end of the war he was arrested and put on trial, being sentenced to twenty-five years in prison for his connection to the genocide of the Jews, with this sentence later being reduced to ten years.

After he was freed, he collaborated with the ultra right publication *Nation Europe*.

Martin Bormann

German politician. Born in 1900 and died in 1945. During la First World War he served in the Army for a short time. In 1929 he married the daughter of a close collaborator of Adolf Hitler, with whom he would have a close relationship with for the rest of his life. His loyalty to Hitler led to him being a trusted man. His high position as head of the State Department and director of the NSDAP allowed him to reach a strong position which let him conspire against other important people in the Reich such as Dönitz, Rommel and Göring. He aspired to be Adolf Hitler' s successor, although it was Dönitz

who was chosen. It presumed that he died in Berlin when trying to escape the *Führerbunker* after the capital was taken by the Soviets.

Ricardo Botet Moro

Possibly born in 1920, at an early age he felt drawn to the military life, when he was sixteen years old he joined the ranks of the national army in the Spanish Civil War. After this little is known about him until he enlisted in the Blue Division, in which he served between 1941-1942 posted to the II/269th Infantry Regiment. There he obtained the decorations of sergeant, the Iron Cross and the Assault Plaque. Later he was one of the few Spaniards who stayed after the repatriation of the Division, in the Blue Legion.

When the Legion was repatriated in its turn, Sergeant Ricardo Botet Moro, together with Rufino Luis García Valdajos and other comrades, decided on April 5 to jump on the train headed for Spain on the outs-

kirts of Hanau, finally being sent together with other Spanish to the Reina barracks in Versailles.

Possibly around April 15, 1944, he was sent together with García Valdajos, to Stablack Süd. Although there is no information, he may have followed the steps of García Valdajos and joined the SD, as shortly afterwards there was news of both of them taking part on French territory in an unsuccessful special operation to capture a North American officer who supported the maquis.

At the end of October 1944 he took part as an interpreter for García Valdajos, thanks to his knowledge of French, in the meeting held with Leon Degrelle in the Adlon Hotel in Berlin with the aim of incorporating new men into his recently created Walloon SS Division.

Botet was one of the heads of section of the Spanish company incorporated into the *Wallonien* with the rank of *SS-Oscha* (first sergeant) under the command of García Valdajos; later it would be called 3rd Comp./I Battalion of the 70 SS Reg. of the 28.SS-*FreiwilligenPanzergrenadier-Division Wallonien*. He took part in the fighting at Stargard and Stettin (February and March 1945), later rising to the rank of *SS-Ustuf.* (second lieutenant).

He obtained the Iron Cross 2nd Class, on the Voljov front during his time with the Blue Division (1941-1942), and the Iron Cross 1st Class, on the Pomerania front (1945) when he commanded one of the sections of the aforementioned 3rd Company.

After being withdrawn from the Walloon Division he was stationed at Potsdam, where he stayed as part of the unit commanded by Miguel Ezquerra.

With the Ezquerra unit he took part in the defensive fighting of the city during the end of April and beginning of May 1945. He managed to escape from the Soviets, wandering from then on to Germany disguising himself as force labor until he was finally captured by British troops, in the area controlled by the allied forces. He spent a year as prisoner of the British and in 1946 he returned to Spain.

Wilhelm Burgdorf

German soldier. Born in 1895 and died in 1945. After commanding an infantry regiment, in May 1942 he was named sub director of the Personnel Department of the Army and was promoted to head of the department in October 1944. During this final period he combined these tasks with being main aide of Adolf Hitler. In the last days of the war he stayed with Hitler in the *Führerbunker*, where he committed suicide on May 1, 1945 when he was faced with it falling into Soviet hands.

Vasily Ivánovich Chuikov

Soviet soldier. Born in 1900, died in 1982. He joined the Red Army during the Russian Revolution, later joining the Frunze military academy. During the Second World War he took part in the Soviet occupation of eastern Poland oriental in 1939 and in the Winter War of 1940.

He took part in the defense of Stalingrad at the front of the 62nd Army, promoted after the victory in Stalingrad, to the 8th Army of the Guard due to his performance in battle. Despite being one of the people responsible for this victory and being considered as the top specialist in urban attacks, all the glory went to Marshal Zhukov, with whom relations went from bad to worse. During the final attack on the Reich he led the advance on Poland, driving the 8th Army of the Guard in the 1st Belorussian Front under the command de Zhukov. He took part in the Soviet offensive that captured Berlin. In 1955 he was promoted to Marshal of the Soviet Union, and between 1960 and 1964 he was commander in chief of the Land Forces of the Army. From 1961 until his death he was a member of the Central Committee of the Communist Party of the Soviet Union.

Leon Joseph Marie Ignace Degrelle

Belgian politician and soldier. Born in Bouillon in 1906 and died in Malaga in 1994. During his youth he complemented his studies in Law with various travels around the world. At twenty years old he had already published various books and soon after he began to run a newspaper and publishing house, founded by a Catholic and conservative political party called Christus Rex. In the elections of 1936

Waffen-SS, where they served Spaniards. After the defeat of the Reich, he left for Norway, from where he managed to escape by air to the north of Spain. Wounded in the crashed plane landing, he obtained political asylum in Spain, where he finally settled.

Despite the death sentence hanging over his head in his native country (he was tried in absentia, and in December 1945 his Belgian nationality was withdrawn, and he was sentenced to death for collaborating with the Nazi invaders), this could not be carried out thanks to the protection that Degrelle received in Spain. At the beginning of the 1970s he was one of the main promoters of CEDADE, dedicating his last years to writing fascist propaganda, as well as publishing various books.

In 1954 he was granted Spanish nationality, adopting the name José León Ramírez Reina which saved him from being extradited after the death of Francisco Franco.

Karl Dönitz

German soldier and president of the Reich. Born in 1891 and died in 1980. He entered the Imperial Navy in 1910 as a cadet. He took part in the First World War as a member of the crew of the cruiser Breslau. In 1916 he requested a transfer to the submarine force, which accepted him in October of that year. In 1918 he was captured by the British, remaining in a prison camp until 1920. In the post war period he formed part of the Reichswehr, reaching the rank of 1935 of Naval Captain of the rebuilt Kriegsmarine in 1935, taking the command of the 1st Fleet of Submersibles. In 1936 he was named commander in chief of the submarines. At the end of the Second World War Mundial, Dönitz was granted the rank of Commodore, and in October 1939 that of Rear Admiral.

He commanded the Kriegsmarine bet-

it managed twelve senators and twenty-one representatives even managing a Secretary. The political changes happening in different countries during this decade and the beginning of the world conflict led him to a closer ideological affiliation to fascism, as well as developing an independent Walloon movement. When war broke out he was detained in a concentration camp due to his national socialist leanings.

Free thanks to the German invasion of Belgium and France, he fought together with the forces of the Axis in the Walloon Legion (*Legion Wallonie*) which was posted to the *Wehrmacht*. Despite having enlisted as a simple soldier, in 1943, when his unit stayed attached to the Waffen-SS, he now took on the rank of lieutenant.

He rose to command the staff officers, of the then *SS-Sturmbrigade Wallonien*. He participated in 1944 in the battle of the Korsun-Chercassy pocket, where the bravery of the Walloon forces that were under the command of Degrelle were clearly evident .

In October of that year, the unit went back to again form the 28th Division of the ween January 30, 1943 until the end of the war with the rank of Admiral. He was named as Hitler's successor by the Führer himself, a post that he held for twenty-three days, between April 30 and May 23, 1945.

He was arrested by allied troops and tried for war crimes in Nüremberg. Found guilty and sentenced to ten years in prison, he was freed in 1956 and retired completely from public life, during which time he wrote two books about his experiences as a sailor and short-lived head of State. He died at the age of eighty-nine.

Jacques Doriot

French politician. Born in 1898, died in 1945. Metal worker, he was secretary general of the Young Communists of France. He was expelled from the French Communist Party in 1934 for having wanted to organize the Popular Front. He founded the *Parti Populaire Français* (French Popular Party, FPP) and the newspaper *La Liberté* in 1936. During the Second World War, after the fall of France, he was a supporter of collaboration with Germany, taking part in the founding of the French Legion of Volunteers against Bolshevism (FLV), in which he enlisted, fighting on the Russian front together with the Germans. After the allied landing in Normandy in 1944 he fled to Germany. He died when his vehicle was machine gunned by two planes, possibly Germans.

Emilio Esteban Infantes y Martín

Spanish soldier. Born in 1892, died in 1966. He entered the Toledo Infantry Academy, where he was a colleague of Francisco Franco and Juan Yagüe. He took part in the Civil War on the Francoist side and later in the Second World War as head of the Blue Division, replacing the command of Muñoz Grandes. He was awarded the Knight's Cross of the Iron Cross, returning with the Blue Division to Spain in 1943. He continued with his military career, dying in 1966.

Wilhelm Von Faupel

German soldier and director of the *Instituto IberoAmericano* in Berlin. He was born in 1870 in Berlin and died in 1945. He had a military career, taking part in 1901 in the German expedition against the Chinese insurrection of the boxer. Later, from 1904 to 1907 he was sent in the German protectorate of southeast Africa, to serve next as instructor of the Argentine forces. In 1911 he joined the academic body of the War College of Argentina in Buenos Aires.

At the beginning of the First World War he returned to his country, where he was sent with the staff officer to the western front, ending the war with the rank of lieutenant colonel. After the war he went on to serve in the French corps that proliferated in Germany, afterwards returning to Argentina, where from 1921 to 1926 he acted as military adviser for the army. In 1926 he obtained a high post in Brazilian Army and from 1927 to 1930 he served the State of Peru as inspector general of its Army.

He returned to his country in 1931, where thanks to his contact with the NSDAP, in 1934 Adolf Hitler called him to the State Department, naming him as director of the *Instituto IberoAmericano* in Berlin, which under his control he turned into an organ of propaganda and dissemination of national socialism in the Spanish speaking countries. This first period of the leadership of the institute of relations with Spanish speaking countries lasted from 1934 to 1936.

In November 1936, Hitler named him first ambassador of the general barracks of Franco in Salamanca, in charge of Reich business in Spain. Despite having received precise instructions from the State Secretary of the III Reich, von Neurath, not to meddle in Spanish political affairs, he became involved alongside his wife Edith in political intrigue supporting dissident sectors of the Falangist Party, particularly the *hedillista* faction. Faupel saw with great displeasure how, according to him, the real revolutionary fascism that he saw in the Spanish Falangists Spanish was becoming more and more orientated toward a conservative and Catholic clericalism. During this period, Faupel maintained close relations with some Falangists, trying to instill in them the authentic national socialist spirit, later taking some of them to Berlin as translators and journalists.

All of these "activities" led Francisco Franco, with whom he had initially maintained a good relationship, to consider him unworthy as a representative of the Reich, forcing him to step down in the summer of 1937, and he was replaced by the more conservative Eberhard von Stohrer.

Returning to Germany he was reinstated to the leadership of the *Instituto IberoAmericano*, replacing Albrecht Reinecke, where he completed a second cycle from 1938 to 1945. It was in this second period when he developed a close relationship with men such as Martín de Arrizubieta and when he helped the formation of the unit under the command of Miguel Ezquerra.

The *Instituto IberoAmericano*, from its creation in Berlin in January 1930, had been a center of scientific investigation and cultural exchange between Germany and Spanish speaking countries. In commemoration of the "beginning of the relationship between the New and Old Worlds", the opening ceremony took place on October 12, the day of the discovery of America by Columbus, also called "Día de la Raza."

Prior to the arrival of Faupel, the cultural life of the institute was quite modest due to the low budget received by the State. Under the direction of Faupel, the institute did not only fulfill its cultural mission, but also opened up its range of interests joining them to those of the Reich's foreign policy. From being an institution that concentrated on Hispanic studies, it became an important organ of propaganda and national socialist dissemination in the Spanish speaking countries. From there, Faupel organized the publication of three magazines on Ibero-American subjects, two of them in Spanish (the interdisciplinary magazine *Ibero-Amerikanisches Archiv*, from 1930, and from 1939 *Ensayos and Estudios*, a magazine about culture and philosophy in Spanish and Portuguese). From 1944 he edited a new publication called Enlace, a weekly publication aimed at Spanish workers in Germany. This last publication was controlled in the beginning by the FET-JONS organization in Germany.

The weight of the weekly publication *Enlace* was carried by Martín de Arrizubieta and from it announcements were launched in favor of a new order led by Germany, with Spain remaining led by Franco in a sorry state, which caused various protests by the Spanish diplomatic corps.

From his privileged position at the *Instituto IberoAmericano*, Faupel established a good relationship with the SS and with the SD. From 1942 he threw himself into helping Latin American and Spanish students with everything allowed by his post, as well as the members of the Spanish Division of Volunteers and the more than ten thousand Spanish workers recruited from 1941 who worked in the Reich, for whom he managed to obtain more than 800 subsidies and grants.

A final assignment of the institute was to serve as a point of reference and meeting point of the Spanish that after February 1944 wanted help with such things as maintaining links with other Spanish and contacting the *Waffen-SS* in order to join them. At the same time it helped to increase as much as possible the moral of these men who had fought and died so far from home.

The publication *Enlace* had a chapter entitled "Soldiers of an ideal" that provided information about and for the Spanish volunteers that were fighting for Germany. Here, many combatants saw their letters published, mainly from the front or the answers that they received. In terms of the people who acted as journalists for this publication, Sourd says that they used German uniforms, both of the SS as well as the *Heer* according to the case of each of them and bearing in mind that many were veterans of the Spanish Division of Volunteers. Regarding the people involved apart from the incomparable Martín Arrizubieta, Sourd mentions Juan Ximénez, Ramón Farré, José Salazar, Eduardo Pérez, Eugenio Pinero and R. Monzón, the latter was from Central America, whereas the rest were Spanish by birth.

The situation of the conflict in Europe in its dying moments obviously limited the cultural activities of the institute, as the staff had been greatly reduced. The same was not the case for political and military subjects, as the help Faupel gave to Miguel Ezquerra was seen as decisive in the formation of the Spanish unit that under the Nazis defended the streets of Berlin from the Soviet avalanche.

The Faupel couple committed suicide when the Russians arrived in the capital of the Reich for fear of being captured alive.

Antonio García Navarro

Spanish soldier. Born in Pamplona in 1890. He entered the Toledo Infantry Academy in 1909 and took part in the Morocco campaign in 1926, later going on to serve in the Canary Islands.

During the Civil War in Spain he joined the uprising from his military destination in La Coruña, arriving during the war to command the 61st Division. In May 1943 he joined the SDV, taking command of the Staff Officers of the Division, going on to later be named head, with the rank of colonel, of the SLV, posted to the 121st German Infantry Division.

After the world conflict finished he was

promoted in 1946 to Brigade General and in 1952 to General of Division, to step down in 1974 with the honorary rank of lieutenant.

Abel García Olivas
Spanish soldier. Born in Aranjuez in 1917 (other sources say it was in 1913) and died in Germany in 1967. His story has been one of the most controversial among those of the many Spanish who fought in the Second World War on the German side, with it being quite difficult to know what was true and what was not. The following compilation of information about his life is based on the magnificent study by Sourd.

According to his declarations made in Germany, in 1934, he left the Spanish military academy as a medical officer (although, as will be seen, this is rather debatable). During the Civil War he was captured by the Republican side on July 26, 1936, managing to escape and going on to Franco's army on July 25, 1938 (although according to other sources he was in prison camps during the whole armed conflict). He served in this army until the end of the war, receiving three war wounds and six decorations (again according to his declaration given in Germany).

After starting Operation *Barbarroja* he decided to enlist in the SDV, which he would join on October 15, 1941 as a simple soldier, as there were no officer posts. He was promoted, and in November 1942 became nursing sergeant and went to the hospitals of Grigorow and Gattschina. There (according to his version told to the Germans) he was given the rank of lieutenant, serving with this rank in the II Artillery Group and in the III Battalion of the 269th Regiment, as well as, possibly, in a 5th Health Group of the SDV.

According to the documentation of the Health Group, García Olivas said he was a doctor, and not a medical officer. In August 1943 he had accumulated enough time in service to be named provisional medical officer. In November 1943, with the dissolution of the SDV, second lieutenant García Olivas stayed with the SLV attached to the hospital in Riga and finally in Königsberg, as a member of the only Spanish Health Corps remaining in Russia (according to his version). Lastly he says that in January 1944 he reached the rank of medical commander.

The dark side of all of this career lies in his most likely false medical license. According to some theories about his life, he could have passed as a doctor quite easily due to the need for health care staff in the various units. Once inside the military health services, due to his knowledge of French he looked for work as medical liaison, avoiding direct "contact" with the patients.

In June 1944 he finally left for Spain during a pass, where he stayed for two months, as on August 15, 1944 he crossed, in this case illegally, the French border to arrive in Berlin, where the Waffen-SS accepted him with the rank of *Waffen Hauptsturmführer der SS* (on November 11, 1944) and he was sent to the *Amtsgruppe D* of the SS FHA.

The thread of his story is lost during the last period of the conflict, although there are suspicions that his deception was discovered by the German authorities, as Manuel Espinosa Rodríguez, at that time Spanish naval attaché in Berlin, recounted the following event in one of his books: "Three SS officers, correctly dressed with impeccable street uniforms, appeared in my office at the Embassy. A commander and two captains. The three of them with emblems of the Military Health Corps (...) They brought me a medical captain – the best dressed of the three – so that we would do the most appropriate thing with him: repatriate him, imprison him, etc. He was Spanish and they had discovered that he was not a doctor as he kept on insisting. They came from the Russian front where, of course, the now condemned man had shown unquestionable bravery but not practical medical knowledge."

Although there are no names, the profile perfectly fits the case of García Olivas, so the mystery remains, but the suspicions are more than founded.

It is known that he was captured by the Americans at the end of the war due to the existence of a report of the interrogation of García Olivas carried out by the Americans during this period.

After the war he stayed in Germany, where it seems that he dedicated himself to a number of activities between 1945 and 1964, including jobs in various industrial firms, in a travel agency and a poultry farm, without being involved again with medical tasks, as would have been logical. This fact makes the story created by García Olivas regarding his life even more suspicious.

He made a few visits to Spain from his "exile" in Germany. In one of these he managed to obtained, through the Ex-prisoners office of FET-JONS in Madrid, an ID card of an ex-prisoner dated 1951 in which García Olivas appears in the photograph with the uniform of medical captain. During another visit undertaken in 1953 he managed to make the Catholic Youth Action of the Diocese of Madrid name him correspondent of their magazine for Europe, with its corresponding editions in Spanish, German and French.

He married a German in 1953, separating shortly afterwards. He died some years later, in 1967.

Rufino Luis García Valdajos*

Born on May 4, 1918 in Tordesillas (Valladolid) to a middle class Catholic family. When he was five years old he moved with his family to Madrid. In 1936 he began his studies in Law finding himself on vacation in Valladolid at the beginning of the National Uprising on July 18 of the same year. As a Falangist, he enlisted as a volunteer for the Civil Guard. At the end of August he entered the Falange militia, going on to serve in a *Bandera de Castilla*. He fought on the Madrid front, in the sector of the Rozas. On January 11, 1937 he was chosen to take part in a training course for provisional second lieutenant that took place in the city of Granada. Later he started to serve with his new post in the B Battalion Hunters of Serrallo No.8, belonging to the 11th Division, with which he participated in

---

* Photo courtesy of Erik Norling

fighting on the Extremadura front and later on the Madrid front until the end of the Civil War. He was rewarded during the conflict with various medals.

By July 1939 he had risen to the rank of provisional lieutenant, and was posted to the 1st Regiment, that was sent to the capital, where he was in service for the following three years.

García Valdajos requested to enlist in the Blue Division in June 1941, but without success. He tried again unsuccessfully in the summer of 1942, finally managing in September 1942, when he could not keep his post from the Spanish army but accepted his entrance as a soldier.

On September 12, 1942 he arrived in the city of Logroño, where he met his replacement battalion, where he managed to rise to corporal. Later, on November 22, 1942 his train crossed the French border transporting the 18th Marching Battalion, where he was incorporated. Its destination was the Leningrad front, after arriving there he was posted to the 11th Company of the 2nd Battallion of the 269th Regiment. For a year he took part in various clashes against the Soviets, above all in the battle of Krasny Bor, accumulating experience in combat which would greatly be worthwhile in the future. In the Blue Division he also served in the cartography section of the staff officers of colonel Rubio.

In November 1943 the Blue Division was withdrawn from the front and repatriated to Spain, with the Blue Legion staying in Germany. When the Division was dissolved García Valdajos put himself forward as a volunteer for the Legion, being posted as a sub officer until its dissolution. When the Legion was repatriated García Valdajos and other comrades, among whom were Sergeant Ricardo Botet Moro, decided to stay in Germany. A report in Madrid dated June 3, 1944 informed the fifty-two legionnaires they were considered deserters from May 1 of that year.

After jumping the train which was traveling to Spain on April 5, on the outskirts of Hanau, he headed toward the nearest Wehrmacht post, from where he was sent to the Reina barracks in Versailles, where the Spanish who had crossed the border to join the German forces were waiting together.

From there, on April 15, 1944, García Valdajos and forty other comrades were sent to Stablack Süd (Prussia), arriving on the 20th of the same month. García Valdajos was given for the first time the rank of lieutenant (*Oberleutnant*), of the Spanish Army, and was contacted by the SD, which offered to enlist him in a special unit that was fighting against exiled Spanish who were acting as terrorists in France.

On June 7, 1944 he moved to Paris to undertake a two-week course for officers of the SD for fighting against the maquis (with one of the sections of the Abwehr), where he learned code techniques, how to use radio transmitters, explosive making, use of various types of vehicles and weapons, etc., for which he received a high qualification at the end of the course.

When he had been adequately trained he undertook anti-maquis activities in the rearguard of the Normandy front from June 23 to September 16. The men that he led came probably partly came from those posted in the anti-maquis service in the area of France belonging to the *Brandemburg* Division. García Valdajos, after being in service in the north, went on to have his operations camp in the center and south of France.

There he "controlled" and acted against the ever more numerous French resistance groups. Together with Ricardo Botet, he took part in a special capture mission of a North American officer who was serving in the ranks of the maquis.

Later he was called to Berlin, where he was congratulated for his magnificent accomplishment of the missions assigned to him, and was invited to a training course for officers.

On October 4, 1944 García Valdajos was in Berlin waiting for a new mission and possibly was attaché to the *Instituto IberoAmericano* headed by General Wilhem von Faupel, former ambassador of the Reich German in Spain. From there he coordinated the activities of the Spanish who lived and worked in Germany.

In Berlin, Ricardo Botet convinced García Valdajos of the importance of making contact with Leon Degrelle, Rexist leader that at that time was in the capital of the Reich recruiting men for his recently created SS Division Valona.

He finally met with Degrelle at the end of October 1944 in the Adlon Hotel in Berlin, with Botet acting as interpreter, as he spoke German and French. A version of the events exists which confirms the possibility that also present at the meeting were Alfonso Van Horembeke, a Belgian citizen who had obtained Spanish nationality fighting in the Civil War. In any case the wishes were granted both of the Walloons of finding new men for the unit, and of the Spanish, who wanted to enter in combat formations. Leon Degrelle, after having reached an agreement with García Valdajos, named him head of the Spanish soldiers posted in the Walloon Division.

Once the agreement was "signed", the Spanish, with García Valdajos at the front, were sent to Breslau on November 1, 1944, where the reserve unit of the Belgian Division was located.

The men who initially arrived in the unit mainly came from two different places: on one hand, from the Spanish training battalion in Soldbald, in Hall im Tirol, and on the other from the recruitment of Spanish workers in Germany.

Just a week later they were transferred to the west, to Alfed-Leine, near to Hannover. García Valdajos was organizing his company

and named as heads of section Ricardo Botet and other former officers of the Blue Division, such as Lorenzo Ocañas and Rafael Lafuente, to whom he gave the higher rank of non-commissioned officers, *SS-Oberscharfürer*. The unit consisted of at least 100 men, or may have reached up to 240 according to other sources.

A little later, toward the middle of November, they were transferred to the training camp at Hemmendorf/Aldendorf, also near to Hannover, with García Valdajos needed in Berlin to undertake administrative tasks.

Due to the offensive at Ardennes, on December 25 the Spanish company, just like the rest of the Walloon Division, went from a pre-warning situation due to the possibility of having to advance on Belgian territory. A returned García Valdajos and members of his unit accompanied Leon Degrelle in a reconnaissance of the area of action to see if the situation necessitated the deployment of the *Wallonien* in Belgium.

On January 7 the offensive stopped and the reconnaissance group returned to their barracks, and García Valdajos returned to Berlin to assess the state of the situation.

It was at the end of January 1945 when, after the blazing advance of the Soviet troops north of the Reich, a combat group was formed of the 69th and 70th regiments of the *Wallonien*, as well as the 28th SS Artillery Detachment. This combat group was immediately sent to Pomerania to try and halt the powerful offensive of the Red Army. The Spanish unit was permanently formed of the 3rd Company of the 1st Battalion of the 70th Grenadiers Regiment. This regiment was under the orders of the *SS-Obersturmführer* Robert Denie, whilst the Spanish company was commanded by the *SS-Untersturmführer* Rudi Bal, a Belgian officer who was born in Argentina and spoke Spanish, due to the absence of García Valdajos, who had stayed in Berlin, where he was going to marry a

German woman called Ursula Jutta-Maria Turcke and had to complete all the red tape needed by all SS officers to carry out this act (his request was registered on February 2).

The fighting that followed was very intense, resulting in many losses on both sides, one of them being Rudi Bal on March 6. He was possibly replaced as commander by the SS-Ustuf Albert Steiver, also of Walloon origin, who later remembered in his memoires that he had commanded the "Spanish company" in the fighting around Stargard.

It was February before García Valdajos rejoined his unit again after his time in Berlin, during the fighting in the sector of Arnswalde. Few Spanish survived the fighting or avoided being captured. Around sixty men were withdrawn from the front to be reorganized, among them was García Valdajos.

On March 16 Valdajos arrived at the "Alfred-Leine" barracks of the Walloon unit ordered the Spanish who were in Potsdam to await new orders. In the middle of March 1945 the Spanish separated from the *Wallonien*.

Between 100 and 150 Spanish were gathered in Potsdam after the management of García Valdajos, these men remained under the command of Miguel Ezquerra Sánchez, with García Valdajos as the Spanish liaison officer with the main officers of the SS. Although by the end of April García Valdajos was back with the troops commanded by Ezquerra for the defense of Berlin.

He survived the fighting, and after the city was taken by the Soviets he managed to hide from May 9, 1945, on which day he requested shelter in the Spanish embassy. He did not find any help there, as it was close to being controlled by Spanish communists. He left the embassy on May 13, 1945 to hide on the destroyed streets of Berlin until June 8 when he managed to cross a Soviet check point and flee the capital.

Disguising himself as a ex-forced labor he headed for Stendal, in the Russian area. He managed in November 1945 to contact the general barracks of the British forces in Berlin, where they took him in and listened to his fictitious story. He managed to pass as a displaced person, going through various refugee camps in Germany, Holland, Belgium and finally France.

On December 14, 1945, after he arrived at the Spanish-French border of Irun, he managed to cross the bridge separating the two countries. Once he was in his home country, five days later he arrived at his former barracks. Because of his desertion he was subject to a war council, after which he was not jailed, being granted complete freedom on March 1, 1947.

After this period, little is known about the life of this Spaniard who experience first hand the organization of various Spanish units posted in the forces of the Reich after the return of the Blue Legion. Erik Norling wrote a very interesting book about this important character who served as a basis for this biographical sketch.

Paul Joseph Goebbels

German politician and Minister of Propaganda of the Reich. He was born in 1897 and died in 1945. When he was four years old he suffered from osteomyelitis that withered his right calf and left him with a slight limp. He studied philosophy, history, literature, art and classical languages. Goebbels put himself forward as a volunteer for the German Army in the First World War, but was rejected due to his limp.

He joined the Nazi Party in 1922 and in 1926 was named Gauleiter of Berlin. Head of propaganda of the NSDAP in 1930, when the Nazis rose to power in 1933 he was named Minister of Propaganda and Popular Illustration. At the beginning of the Second World War, Goebbels permanently banned any type of information from outside Germany, encouraging the belief of the German people in the final victory.

Goebbels has been attributed with great influence over modern propaganda. He managed to made the Germans believe that victory was finally arriving despite the many blows that, with the conflict already advanced, the Reich received.

Loyal to Hitler, on April 22, 1945 Goebbels and his family decided to stay in the *Führerbunker*, where, after killing his children, Goebbels and his wife committed suicide, to avoid being captured by Soviet troops.

Manuel Hedilla Larrey

Spanish politician. Born in Santander in 1902 and died in Palma de Mallorca in 1970. He was a militant of the Spanish Falange of the JONS from 1934, being chosen the following year as head of the party in his native province and national advisor. He took part in July 1936 in the military uprising that gave rise to the Spanish Civil War, playing a leading role in the uprising of La Coruña and Vigo. In September 1936 he was chosen as national head of the Provisional Command Junta of the Spanish Falange of the JONS.

On April 15, 1937 he called an extraordinary meeting of the National Council of the Spanish Falange with the aim of solving the, "… acute crisis of authority, discipline and relaxation of the national union principles, caused by the provisional character of the regime of the Command Junta." The following day Agustín Aznar, José Moreno, Jesús Muro, Sancho Dávila and Rafael Garcerán drew up a list of charges against Manuel Hedilla and then they agreed to remove him from his post, dissolve the Provisional Command Junta, institute a triumvirate composed of Aznar, Dávila and Moreno who took charge from that moment of the national leadership and called a national council. Finally, on the 18th, after a meeting of the national council, Manuel Hedilla was chosen national head of the Spanish Falange of the JONS, which immediately notified the head of State, General Franco, of his election.

On April 19, 1937 the Decree of the Unification of the Falange took place with the traditionalists under the leadership of Franco. This fusion, although it achieved political tranquility in the nationalist zone, supposed the practical disappearance of the Spanish Falange as it was conceived of by Hedilla. Clearly upset, he did not accept the leadership of the Political Junta of the FET and of the JONS that had been granted by decree on April 25 by Francisco Franco.

He was arrested on April 25, 1937 under the accusation of having conspired against Franco, and was condemned to death. The sentence was commuted, and after being imprisoned in the Canary Islands he was transferred to Mallorca until he regained his freedom in 1947. He did not return to political life, dying in 1970.

Alfred Jodl

German soldier. Born in 1890 and died in 1946. During the First World War, as an

artillery officer he took part in fighting on the western and eastern fronts, being wounded on two occasions. He continued with his military career, meeting Adolf Hitler in 1923 and worked alongside with him. In 1935 he was named head of National Defense of the *Wehrmacht*. On August 26, 1939 he was promoted to General. During the Second World War he was head of the Department of Command and Operations in the OKW, as Hitler's strategic advisor. When he died he was named head of Staff Officers of Karl Dönitz, signing the unconditional surrender of Germany in Reims on May 7, 1945.

He was arrested by the British army in May 1945, interned in the prison camp of Flensburg and sentenced by the Nüremberg court for war crimes, crimes against peace and crimes against humanity, and was executed by hanging on October 16, 1946.

Iván Stepánovich Koniev

Soviet soldier. Born in 1897 and died in 1973. He took part in the First World War and later joined the Bolshevik Party and the Red Army, where he served as artillery. He entered the Frunze military academy, climbing the military ladder during the period between wars. In 1937 he became a representative of the Soviet Supreme, and two years later a member of the Party Central Committee.

During the Second World War he took part in many battles, from the defensive battles of Moscow and Smolensk, to Kursk and the Soviet offensives between 1944 and 1945. He commanded the Ukrainian Front, that would eventually be called the 1st Ukrainian Front, until the end of the war. In 1945 Koniev and Zhukov forced the front at the Oder and advanced to Berlin; however, Koniev had to deviate to the south east because Stalin gave the order that it would be Zhukov who would take Berlin. Koniev met the North Americans in Torgau and then went to Prague, later occupying it.

Hans Krebs

In the post war period he reached the rank of commander of the land forces of the Soviet Union. In 1956 he became commander in chief of the Armed Forces of the Warsaw Pact. Later he carried out the role of commander of the Armed Forces of Eastern Germany, and was later named Inspector General of the Department of Defense.

Hans Krebs

German soldier. Born in 1898 and died in 1945. During the First World War he put himself forward as a volunteer in the Imperial German Army, where he became lieutenant. Following his military career he took on the role of head of various army groups until he was made infantry general. In the Second World War he took on the leadership of the OKH until the end of the conflict. During the battle of Berlin, Hans Krebs moved to the *Führerbunker* until, surrounded by the Soviet troops, he eventually opted for suicide.

Wilhelm Mohnke

SS Brigadeführer. Born in 1911 and died in 2001. On September 1, 1931 he joined the National Socialist Party and two months later he was asked to join the SS. He was one of the 120 original members of Hitler' s guard corps, known as the *Stabswache Berlin*, formed in 1933. Mohnke was one of the generals who was with Adolf Hitler until the end.

During the Second World War he served as commander of the 5th Company of the *SS-Leibstandarte* in the Polish campaign, obtaining the Iron Cross First Class. He took part in the French and the Balkan campaigns, where he was wounded.

After various failed attempts to introduce an armored brigade into the *Leibstandarte*, he was transferred to a replacement battalion until he was given the command of a regiment in the *12.SS Panzer Division Hitlerjugend*.

He took part in the fighting at Normandy, where he received the Knight' s Cross; the

Falaise pocket; the *Operation Wacht am Rhein*, and the battle of Berlin, where he found himself in charge of the defense of the government quarter of the capital of the Reich.

He was captured by the Russians whilst trying to escape the *Führerbunker*, and was subjected to imprisonment and intense interrogation until 1949, when he was transferred to the camp in Woikowo, where he remained until October 10, 1955. After he was freed he was still tried a number of times for events which happened during the French campaign and for the Malmedy massacre, without being found guilty.

Agustín Muñoz Grandes

Spanish soldier. Born in 1896 and died in 1970. As an young man he entered the Toledo infantry academy. Two years after his graduation, in 1915, he served in North Morocco with the Spanish Army. He took part in the Alhucemas landing, where he was wounded.

With the Republican government, in 1931 he climbed the military ladder and was named second head of the Assault Guard. From 1933 until 1935 he was head of the police of the Republic.

A pro-Falangist soldier, at the beginning of the Civil War in Spain he tried to flee from the territory controlled by the Republic, although without success, and was imprisoned in the Modelo prison in Madrid. In 1937 he was in Francoist territory commanding the IV Navarra Brigade. Later he was promoted to general, leading the Moroccan Army Corps.

He was a member of the post war cabinet as Department Secretary General of the FET and of the JONS, later being named military governor of the Gibraltar Camp.

When the Second World War broke out and coinciding with the German occupation of the USSR, Franco put him on the front of the Spanish volunteers unit, known as the

Blue Division. He maintained good relations with the high commands of the German Government. Adolf Hitler, awarded him the Knight' s Cross of the Iron Cross and Oak Leaves.

After he returned to Spain in 1943 he was promoted to lieutenant general and named head of the military house of the Generalísimo. This post meant that Muñoz Grandes no longer had command of troops, which is why this promotion has been interpreted as a strategy by Franco to decrease the growing power of Muñoz Grandes after his time on the Russian front and his close contact with Adolf Hitler. Years later he reached the post of Army minister and rose to captain general. In 1962 he was named vice-president of the government. He died in 1970.

Lorenzo Ocañas Serrano

Born in April 1915 in Montoro (Cordoba). During the Spanish Civil War he enlisted in a *Bandera de Falange*, finishing the conflict with the rank of second lieutenant. He later decided to enlist in the Spanish Division of Volunteers through the militia in Castellón, and joined it in July 1941. In December 1941 he was wounded in Possad, on the Russian front. During the period of service in Russia, Lorenzo Ocañas became hardened in the tough fighting which the German forces had against the Soviets. After his return to Spain, his anti-communist ideals led him toward the path that others had opened up: the return to Germany to follow the fight against communism. In July 1944 he met four other officers who had also served in the SDV in a café in Madrid and decided to return to Germany.

On August 1, 1944 in Barcelona they discussed whether to cross the border on the 4th or 5th of the same month. In the end this last date was chosen, and at 7:00 in the morning, in the company of La Puente, also a second lieutenant, he crossed the border at Port Bou. After passing through Cerbéres and Banyuls they arrived in Perpignan. Next they headed to Innsbruck, to

arrive at the Spanish training camp in Hall im Tirol.

In November 1944 they were sent to the *Wallonien* Division, arriving in Cologne, where a company had been formed with Spanish soldiers; with Ocañas as head of a section. He took part in the intense fighting that the *Wallonien* had on the outskirts of Sttetin, until in February 1945 he was sent to Potsdam, where he joined the unit under the command of Miguel Ezquerra. On April 28, 1945, taking part in combat against the Russians, according to his own version in command of a section and with the rank of SS lieutenant, near to the Berlin Excelsior Hotel, he was captured by the Soviets. He was a prisoner from then on, passing through various gulags until he finally returned to Spain on April 2, 1954 in the Semíramis.

Upon his return to Spain he was put on trial. The interrogation was led by colonel Joaquín Huidobro. After deciding not to pay the 163,315 pesetas owed to him for services rendered, he declared the case dismissed. Colonel Castillo discussed with the minister whether the backdated pay could be paid. The answer was again negative.

Ocañas was excluded from the reception given for the prisoners from Cordoba from the Blue Division when he arrived in Cordoba.

He requested to be allowed to rejoin the armed forces, something which had been denied him by this "predecessors" in the final period of the world war.

He found work in the Bank of Spain at its branch in Cordoba. He lived there in the neighborhood of Lepanto. He married, was widowed and was remarried and did not have any children.

He died in the hospital of los Morales in Cordoba from a chronic pulmonary illness (a result of his time in Russia).

His remains are in the cemetery of San Rafael, where Martín de Arrizubieta is also buried.

José Ortiz Fernández

There is no information about Ortiz Fernández before the Civil War, during which he reached the rank of lieutenant in the Legion.

Later, he enlisted in the Blue Division and once he was dismissed he decided to accept an offer to work in film dubbing in the UFA studios in Berlin. But on the way to the capital of the Reich he met an officer of the *Abwehr*, beginning to cooperate with this organization on the mission to discover the heads of the maquis who were in Boulogne together with Spanish refugees.

Together with a certain Arroyo he managed to attached himself to a group of guerrillas mostly made up of Spanish. After these activities in the area of Boulogne both Spanish were finally incorporated into the *Karstjäger* in December 1944, when the troops of this brigade under the command of the *Sturmbannfuhrer* Werner Hahn were being completed by the arrival of volunteers of different nationalities (Italian, Slovenian and Yugoslavians of German origin). In September 1944, when the *Abwehr* was absorbed by the SS, the Italian-Spanish detachment were reorganized in Ivrea, north of Turin. There they found out they had been incorporated into the *Waffen-SS*. According to his testimony, José Ortiz was sent to Solbad Hall im Tirol to take part in a course which would train him as an officer of the Waffen-SS, and then he went as a recruiter to various prison camps around Vienna in which Spanish workers who had left their factories and places of work were incarcerated. Ortiz convinced a hundred of them, which he organized into a company in October 1944 of which he was named commander with the post of *Untersturmführer*.

The Spanish company was posted to the 59th *Gebirgsjäger-Regiment* of the *24. WaffenGebirgs-(Karstjäger)-Division der SS del Sturmbannführer Werner Hahn* and began to operate in the region of the Alps where the borders of Germany, Italy and Yugoslavia met. The *Untersturmführer* Ortiz Fernández and his men were stationed in Villach and in Pontebba, ready to fight the allied forces that were advancing from the south, although in practice they were basically given the task of fighting against the Italian and Yugoslavian partisans who were attacking the German rearguard. From there they went to Tolmezzo, where the well-known Garibaldi Partisan Division operated, and from there, there are no more reports of Ortiz Fernández.

Information about some of these activities of the Spanish posted in the SS and stationed in Italy comes from the great work by Gregorio Towers.

Ferdinand Schörner

German soldier. Born in München in 1892 and died in 1973. During the First World War he was an instructor, obtaining the decoration

"Max Blue" (*Der Blaue Max*, the prestigious decoration officially called *Pour le Mérite*). In the period between wars, he joined the Nazi Party, and played an important role in the creation of the *Waffen-SS*. He took part in the invasions of Poland and the Balkans, Operation *Barbarroja* and various operations on the eastern front.

In 1944 Generalfeldmarschall Schörner was made commander of the Group of North Armies until January 1945, when he was named commander of the Group of Center Armies. He was designated commander in chief of the Army by Hitler in his political testament, although the end of the conflict stopped this testament from coming to fruition.

At the end of the war, now a prisoner, he was handed over to the Soviet Union. He was sentenced to twenty-five years in prison, of which he only served ten. He was freed in 1955, again being tried for crimes committed during the war and being imprisoned in 1957, to be permanently freed in 1963.

Ramón Serrano Súñer

Lawyer and Spanish politician. He was born in 1901 and died in 2003. He studied a degree in Law, graduating with honors in 1923. He was president of the Professional Association of Students, where he met José Antonio Primo de Rivera, secretary of the same student association. He married Francisco Franco' s sister-in-law in 1932.

Continuing his political career, he became member of parliament. When the Civil War began he was in Madrid, where he was arrested and imprisoned in the Modelo prison by the Republican authorities without any trial or charge against him. He finally managed to escape and arrived in Salamanca via Alicante and Marseille. Francisco Franco named him president of the Political Junta of FE. He drew up the unification decree that joined the Falange and the *Comunión Tradicionalista* into a single party called the *Falange Española Tradicionalista* and of the JONS. He was the main author of the Code of Work promulgated in 1938, which was the first of the Fundamental Laws that constituted the Francoist State.

During the Second World War Serrano Súñer was the main promoter of the pro-German feeling in the Spanish government, leading to the alliance with Nazi Germany reaching its high point in the first years of the war. In September 1940 he went to Berlin as special envoy of the Spanish Government. A month later he prepared the meeting that Franco and Hitler had in Hendaya with the aim of negotiating Spain's possible entrance in the war on the side of the Axis.

In 1941 Serrano Súñer suggested the organization of the Blue Division to Franco after the beginning of the invasion of the Soviet Union.

In this manner Francoist Spain returned the support that Hitler has given in the Civil War without becoming belligerent in the Second World War. The change of sign in the conflict meant Serrano Súñer was losing influence until he was removed from his post at the end of 1942.

He later dedicated himself to being a lawyer, as well as being attorney in the Francoist courts in 1957. He died in Madrid at the age of 101.

Otto Skorzeny

Austrian engineer, *Obersturmbannführer* of the *Waffen-SS*, specialist in special opera-

tions. During the Second World War his name was linked to the most important special operations carried out by the Nazi regime. He was the head of the commandos that freed Benito Mussolini from his imprisonment in Gran Sasso. This fact, and the fame it brought him, meant that he was considered the most dangerous man in Europe by the allies.

He intervened in many missions in various places in Europe, from the eastern front to the battle of Ardennes, where some Spanish served under him.

At the end of the war he was captured and tried for presumed war crimes, which he was absolved of; however, he was put in denazification camp until he escaped, thanks to the help of three former SS officers disguised as North American soldiers. He arrived in Spain, where he remained until his death. It is believed that he was one of the main founders of the ODESSA organization, by means of which former German SS were able to escape allied persecution, by means of them being moved to different papers and the creation of false identities.

He published his memoires in two books entitled *Vive peligrosamente* and *Luchamos y perdimos*.

Felix Martin Steiner

German soldier and politician. He was born in 1896 in Nesterow and died in 1966 in Münich. During the First World War he took part in combat on both the eastern and western fronts.

After the Great War he was posted to the *Reichswehr* until he decided to move over to the recently formed *SS-Verfügungstruppe* (precursor of the Waffen-SS). In the Second World War, in 1940 he participated in the French campaign as commander of the *Deutschland* Regiment of the SS, receiving the Knight's Cross of the Iron Cross. In 1940, Steiner was promoted to the rank of general and he was given the command of a new unit, which would be the precursor of the future *Wiking* Division.

With the Wiking he took part in many actions on the eastern front: in the southern sector from June 1941 and during the actions of 1942. In December 1942 he was awarded the Oak Leaves for his Knight's Cross.

In 1943 the Wiking was active in the area of the River Don against the ever more powerful Soviet attacks. Later, also in the first months of 1943, he was given the command of the III *Panzer* SS Army Corps, which he commanded until October 1944, during which period he was promoted to the rank of *SS Obergruppenführer* and in August 1944 he was awarded the Swords for the Knight's Cross of the Iron Cross. At the beginning of 1945 he was given the command of the XI SS *Panzer* Army in the Pomerania sector, where he fought until the end only managing to halt on a local level the permanent blows that the Soviet Army was inflicting on an already dying Reich.

In May 1945, after the German surrender, he was captured by the allies, and was later freed by the British. In the post war period, Steiner maintained important contacts with other SS veterans. He died in Munich in 1966.

Josip Broz, "Tito"

Yugoslavian soldier and politician. He was born in 1892 in Kumrovec (present day Croatia and at that time part of the Austro-Hungarian empire) and died in Ljubjana in 1980 (present day Slovenia, previously Yugoslavia).

After he left home he worked as a locksmith's apprentice, beginning to show interest in the workers movement. In 1910 he joined the Metalworkers Union and the Social Democratic Party of Croatia and Slovenia. He worked for other companies as a laborer, a period during which he became militant in the trade union world.

During the First World War he served in the Austro-Hungarian army, although he was arrested for carrying out anti-war propaganda. In 1915 he was wounded on the Russian front, and was finally captured with his battalion. He immediately went to a concentration camp in the Urales, to eventually escape and enlist in the new Red Army and

join the Russian Socialdemocratic Workers Party, which later became the Communist Party of the Soviet Union.

After carrying out his political activities in the period between wars, in 1937 he became secretary general of the Communist Party of Yugoslavia.

During the Second World War, and after the invasion of his country by the troops of the Axis, together with the Yugoslavian communists they organized a resistance movement against the invaders, with Tito as head of the Military Committee of the Communist Party of Yugoslavia and later as marshal of Yugoslavia. His strong ties with the Soviet leader Stalin meant that he could exert great influence on the armies of the allied United States and British.

At the end of the war and with other rival partisan groups eliminated, the country stayed unified under the control of Tito' s Government, establishing itself as a Socialist Republic. It gradually managed to separate itself from the orbit of Soviet influence that was omnipresent in the post-war period all over Europe. Years later, and as president of the Federal Socialist Republic of Yugoslavia, together with other African and Asian countries, he joined the group of non-aligned countries.

Alphonse Van Horembeke

Of Walloon origin, he served during the Spanish Civil War in the IV *Bandera del Tercio* and afterwards in the 67th Company of the *XVII Bandera*, taking part in the fighting of the Bielsa pocket.

In 1940 he worked for the railroad of the German Reich (*Deutsche Reichsbahn*), going to his country to enlist in August 1941 in the Legion Wallonie, in which he served until he was demobilized after the Cáucaso campaign.

Later he served with the SD in Liege and Ghent. In 1944 he was secretary of the Youth Front in Vizcaya. There he was given the mission of enlisting in the German Armed

Forces a group of members of the young Falangists who had this intention. Therefore, Van Horembeke tried to get in contact with friends to ensure that these volunteers were integrated into the ranks of the Flemish *Langemarck Brigade* (after *27.SS-Frw.Gr.Div. Langemarck*), part of the SS. The reason for choosing this unit was that he had shared room on the front with the SDV in the area of Leningrad from 1941 to 1943.

Together with Van Horembeke was Juan Beltrán de Guevara, in charge in Versailles, where the latter abandoned the former to join a group of German soldiers and Romanians who left for the eastern front.

Despite the problem that this abandonment caused to the mission, Van Horembeke continued with it. He left for Lichterfelde West/Berlin where he knew that he would be stationed with the reinforcement battalion of the *Langemarck*. Van Horembeke did not speak Flemish or German, which meant there was a lack of Flemish interest in the idea put before them by the Walloon, so that from the *Langemarck* he headed toward the *Wallonien* barracks, where, obviously, he could be understood and possibly helped.

In July 1944, in the Heidelager camp in Poland, Van Horembeke met an old friend called Paul Kehren whom he had met in the Tercio. After telling him about his mission, the two of them finally were able to contact Leon Degrelle. The latter, always in need of troops for his unit, gave the go-ahead to the task of incorporating Spanish into the *Wallonien*. Kehren y Van Horembeke began their "fishing" in the Stockerau barracks, where he had had news that there were Spanish soldiers.

When they arrived there they met Juan Beltrán de Guevara, the other emissary that had left Spain together with Van Horembeke. They threw themselves into the task, managing to convince some of the Spanish there (possibly around thirty-six) of the advantage they would have if they belonged to a prestigious unit like the *Wallonien*. He followed his route, now accompanied again by Beltrán, to recruit more men from the various industries of different places in the Reich where Spanish were to be found.

In this period Van Horembeke made contact with the *SS-Ostuf.* Luis García Valdajos, due to the latter's knowledge of the whereabouts of Spanish in the German Armed Forces. Together with him, in October 1944, he had a had a meeting in the Hotel Adlon in Berlin with Leon Degrelle which Ricardo Botet also attended.

After he had finished his recruitment tasks he joined active military service in the hard fighting of the Wallonien in Pomerania. When the Spanish left for Potsdam to be posted to a new unit under the command of Miguel Ezquerra he joined them and fought alongside them in the defense of Berlin against the Soviet troops, until he was eventually captured.

Having seen that one of his Spanish comrades who had been captured had been executed just for being Spanish, he declared himself Belgian. His destiny led him to be in many prisoner of war camps until he arrived in Kovno, where he had the fortune to be handed over to the allied commission which repatriated him to Belgium. There his "record" catapulted him immediately toward a punishment of twenty years in prison. At the beginning of the 1950s he was permanently freed, returning to his second native country, Spain, where he obtained nationality.

For any information about the Wallonien and its members, among whom were a number of Spanish, reference can be made to the excellent study on this unit written by Erik Norling.

Ulrich Friedrich Wilhelm Joachim Von Ribbentrop

Politician, soldier and Secretary of State of Germany from 1938 to 1945. He was born in 1893 and died in 1946. During the First

World War he joined the Army fighting on the eastern front and in Constantinople, reaching the rank of lieutenant and obtaining the Iron Cross.

In the period between wars he dedicated himself to business activities, and was considered an apolitical man buried in his work.

In 1930 he met Adolf Hitler and two years later he joined the German National Socialist Workers Party (NSDAP). He acted as adviser for Adolf Hitler on matters of foreign policy. In February 1938 was named Secretary of State of the Reich. He signed the Molotov-Ribbentrop Pact with the USSR to ensure the stability of the eastern front in a hypothetical war in Europe. It was the instigator of the alliance between Italy, Germany and Japan to form the Axis.

After the war finished he was arrested by the British army and taken to trial at Nüremberg, where he was accused of war crimes, crime against peace and genocide because he was the person responsible of convincing the countries around the Reich to deport the Jews to Germany to be exterminated. He was the first Nazi leader to be executed by hanging in the early hours of October 16, 1946.

Helmuth Weidling

German soldier. Born in 1891 and died in 1955. During the Second World War he took part in the invasion of Poland, in the battle of France and the fight on the eastern front.

In 1942 he reached the rank of Major General, moving up to Lieutenant General in January of the following year. In October 1943 he was made commander of the XLI *Panzer* Corps, and two months later he was promoted to General of Artillery.

He was made commander to direct the defense of the capital of the Reich during the battle of Berlin after having corrected the error which led to him being sentenced to death for cowardice when he commanded the LVI *Panzerkorps*.

Decorated with the Knight's Cross with Oak Leaves and Swords, he gave up the city on May 2 to the Soviet troops despite his orders not to surrender. He was imprisoned by the Soviets, dying as their prisoner in 1955.

Walter Wenck

German soldier. He was born in 1900 in Wittenberg and died in 1982. He signed up for the Army from a young age, becoming a professional soldier. During the Second World War, in 1942 he gave classes in the military academy, and during the same year he was named head of the Staff Officers of the 57th Armored Corps. Other posts that he held during the conflict led to him being head of the Staff Officers of the 1st Armored Army,

head of operations of the OKH and head of the directive group of the OKH. In 1945 and with the rank of general, he was named head of the 12th Army, in which Adolf Hitler had put his hopes of raising the site of Berlin, a maneuver which he was unable to carry out in the end.

Georgui Konstantínovich Zhukov

He was born in 1896 and he died in 1974. Politician and marshal of the Soviet Union, he was considered as the most famous and successful of the commanders of the Soviet Army during the Second World War.

During the First World War he served as a soldier in a regiment of dragoons, and was decorated twice with the St. George Cross for his performance.

He fought in the Russian Civil War of 1918-1920 against the white Russians, receiving the Order of the *Bandera Roja*.

He took part in a great deal of combat against the forces of the Axis over the Second World War, such as for example the battle of Moscow, the siege of Leningrad, the Bagration Operation and finally the battle of Berlin.

Photograph of a *SS-Rottenführer* whose identity and posting are unknown. The curiosity regarding where he comes from are increased by the fact that on the pocket of his army jacket the emblem of the yoke and arrows of the Spanish Falange of the JONS is visible.

GLOSSARY

Abwehr

The *Abwehr* (*Amt Auslandsnachrichten und Abwehr*), in English, Foreign Information and Counterespionage Service, was the organization in charge of gathering information for the OKW.

In 1935, the navy officer Wilhelm Canaris was named head of the Abwehr, and was promoted to Rear Admiral a year later. Canaris has to confront the anxieties of control of Heydrich and the SD, who wanted to exert absolute control over the information activities of the whole German Army.

On 18 February 1944 Himmler convinced Hitler to remove Canaris and incorporate the information services to the RSHA (*Reichssicherheitshauptamt*, Central Administration of the Security of the Reich), which meant the "literal" disappearance of the *Abwehr*.

CEDADE

Abbreviation of the *Círculo Español de Amigos de Europa* (Spanish Circle of Friends of Europe). National socialist style organization no longer in existence.

DAF

Abbreviation of the German Workers Front (in German, *Deutsche Arbeitsfront*). It was created in 1933, and during its existence, under the command of Robert Ley, it replaced all the trade unions up to then in Germany as an organization to represent workers. It had more than twenty-five million members which turned it into one of the most powerful organizations within the national socialist regimes.

Freikorps

The name *freikorps* (whose literal meaning is "free corps", "body" being understood as organization was originally applied to German military or paramilitary units.

Their origin can be found in the movements of the veterans of the First World War who felt completely disconnected from civilian life and unhappy with the conditions which produced Germany' s defeat in the war.

In these formations there were also who had returned to active military service, as various freikorps fought in the Baltic, Prussia and Silesia from the end of the First World War, at times with significant success against regular troops. And although they were officially dissolved in 1920, its former members took part in the failed attempted coup d' état in 1923 known as the "*putsch de Munich.*" A number of its members became important personalities in the political structure of German National socialism.

Gestapo

Abbreviation of *Geheime Staatspolizei*, in English, Secret State Police. The Gestapo had its origins in the Prussian Secret Police organized by Hermann Göring in 1933.

Its first head Diels, was succeeded by Heinrich Himmler when the German police forces were reorganized in 1936, it became specialized in political crimes in the Sipo (Security Police of the Reich). In 1939 it stayed integrated as a department of the Main Office of the Security of the Reich, working in close collaboration with the SD.

It came to have a network of around twenty thousand agents and more than one hundred thousand informants spread across the world. In the trials which took place in the city of Nüremberg it was declared to be a criminal organization.

Gulag

Gulag is the name given to the State Soviet forced labor camp systems, used for incarcerating political prisoners.

The Hitler Youth

The Hitler Youth (known in German as *Hitlerjugend*, or abbreviated to HJ), was born in 1922 from the appearance in the *Völkischer Beobachter* newspaper of the notice of a special group designed for boys between fourteen and eighteen years old protected by the NSDAP. The pillars which held up the HJ were nationalism, physical activity, camaraderie and life in the fresh air, as well as the formation of new leaders for the State and the Army. The organization remained supervised by the SA and was initially headed by Adolf Lenk.

In 1928 the HJ expanded, adding a section for boys between ten and fourteen years old initially called *Deutsche Knaben-schaft*, which changed its name in 1931 to *Deutsches Jungvolk in der Hitler-Jugend*. Later the organization expanded to add a female section for girls between the ages of fourteen and eighteen called *Schwesternschaft der Hitler-Jugend*, and from 1930 it was called *Bund Deutscher Mädel* (BDM). In 1931 the age range was increased adding a section for younger girls called *Jungmädelgruppe*. In the same year Baldur von Schirach took control of these Hitler Youth groups, making them independent a year later from the SA and with both groups abolished by the Weimar Government in June.

When Adolf Hitler came to power, the HJ absorbed other small right wing youth organizations, making it obligatory from 1939 for young people over the age of seventeen to belong to the HJ, and for all children from ten years old in 1941. Baldur von Schirach was replaced as leader by Arthur Axmann in 1940.

The boys of the HJ carried out certain adult missions in support of the armed forces, especially for anti-aerial defense and, as the conflict was advancing, the organization produced many new soldiers, especially for the SS, fundamentally the 12th SS *Panzer* Division, which was mainly formed of former HJ.

In the final months of the war younger and younger members of the HJ enlisted, many of them integrated in the *Volkssturm*.

Kampfgruppe

German term that translates into English as "combat group." It refers to the temporary grouping of different small or large units in the German Armed Forces. These groups stayed under a single command during for the duration of the mission or watch of the order for which they were created. There were many of them during the last stage of the Second World War, characterized by the name of the military leader who was in command.

Kriegsmarine

This is the German name given to the German War Navy under the Third Reich. It was created in 1935 and ceased to exist in 1945. From 1943 its commander in chief was the Admiral Dönitz.

The German War Navy during the Second World War played an important role, both in the use of its surface boats and its submarine arm.

NSDAP

This corresponds to the abbreviation for *Nationalsozialistische Deutsche Arbeiterpartei,* which in English translates as German National Socialist Workers Party.

It was created by Adolf Hitler and some collaborators in September 1920. In 1923 they failed in their attempt to launch a coup d' état in the so-called "putsch de Munich." After the attempt the party was banned, although it became legal again in 1925. It was in 1933 when Adolf Hitler, leading his party, victorious in the elections, reached the State Department. A few months later the other political parties were abolished, leaving the NSDAP as the only party until the end of the Second World War. Afterwards, its leaders were persecuted by law.

OKW

This is the abbreviation for what was known as the *Oberkommando der Wehrmacht* (High Command of the Wehrmacht). It was theoretically the Staff Officers of the army during the period of National socialist Germany, coordinating the efforts of the Army (*Heer*), the Air Force (*Luftwaffe*) and the Navy (*Kriegs-marine*), under the direct command of Adolf Hitler via Field marshal Keitel and General Jodl. Although at the beginning of the world war it still did not exercise excessive control over the German Armed Forces, as it was progressing the OKW began to issue more direct orders to the military units, mainly to the deployed forces on the western front, so that in 1942 the OKW controlled the German Armed Forces on this front, whilst the *Oberkommando des Heeres* (OKH, High Command of the Land Army) carried out the same mission for the troops on the eastern front.

OKH

This is the abbreviation for the Oberkommando des Heeres or High Command of the Land Army. It was the administrative office in charge of organizing and coordinating all that relating to the German land army, including its participation in war operations. Its leadership was assumed by General Brauchitsch after Von Fritsch was forced to leave the post in February 1938. Hitler personally led this department from December 19 1941 until the end of the war.

O.S.S.

The Office of Strategic Services was created by the United States president, Franklin D. Roosevelt in July 1942 to replace the previous US intelligence service, the Office of Coordination of Information, which had been considered not very effective.

It had the responsibility of collecting and analyzing all types of information about the various countries at war with the United States. In the same manner it helped in the formation and with various materials to organize guerrillas, sabotage and espionage activities in different countries .

In October 1945 the organization disbanded, with a new organization called the Central Intelligence Agency, more commonly known as the CIA, being in charge of these activities.

SD

This is the abbreviation by which the Sicherheitsdienst (Security Service) was known, and it corresponds to the intelligence service of the SS. It was created in 1932 under the command of Reinhard Heydrich with the mission of serving as protection for the leaders of the NSDAP from possible enemies both within the Party and outside. In 1938 its responsibilities increased, as its new camp of operations was not only the NSDAP, but the whole German State supporting the Gestapo. During the period of 1933-1939 the SD was under the authority of the Sicherheitspolizei, passing from 1939 to be under the authority of the Reichssicherheits-hauptamt.

The SD wove a dense network of agents and informants both inside the borders of the Reich and in the occupied countries, obtaining all types of information from the different strata of society, including of course its own German Armed Forces. This information, after having been sifted and suitably prepared, was sent to the Kriminalpolizei (Criminal Police), commonly known as Kripo, and to the Gestapo; which took charge of the tasks carried out by the political police system

SS

This corresponds to the abbreviation of the German Schutzstaffeln, which in English translates as "Protection Squads." It was a military and security organization of the NSDAP which from 1929 to the end of the world conflict was led by Heinrich Himmler. It was established as Adolf Hitler's personal guard in 1925, going on to gradually have a larger number of members and functions within the military-political framework of Germany both in the pre-war period and during the war, becoming one of the most important organizations in the Third Reich. The SD and the Gestapo were established under its tutelage.

Military Units of the SS and Usual Rank of the Commanders

Gruppe: This corresponds to a squad. Its number ranged between nine and twelve men. Its command was given to a *SS-Unterscharführer*, although depending on the losses suffered and the criteria of the situation the combat the command could even be held by a SS-Schütze.

Zug: This corresponds to an integrated section of around fifty men. Generally, one of the *Zug* of the *Kompanie* was under the command of a *SS-Untersturmführer*, whilst the other two were commanded by a *SS-Oberscharführer* or a *SS-Hauptscharführer*. Also, the demands of the situation of the combat and the existing losses could determine that all the *Zug* were commanded by noncommissioned officers or even by *SS-Sturmscharführer*.

Kompanie: This corresponds to a company. Its number of men varied between 150 and 201. Generally it was under the command of a *Obersturmführer* or a *Hauptsturmführer*. The officer that had permanent command was called *Kompanie Chef* (company chief), whilst the officer that had temporary command was called *Kompanie Führer*. Again due to the requirements of combat, and due to the losses, a *Untersturmführer* could find himself commanding a company.

Bataillon: This corresponds to a battalion. Its number ranged between 500 and 861 men. Generally the command was under a *Sturmbannführer* or a *Obersturmbannführer*.

Völkischer Beobachter

The translation of this into English would be Popular Observer. This German newspaper was the official organ of the NSDAP from 1920. Its origins were the *Münchner Beobachter* (Munich Observer), which was acquired in 1918 by the Thule Society and in August 1919 was given the name *Völkischer Beobachter*. Although it was originally published weekly, in 1923 it became a daily. On its front page, added to its name was the slogan "Combat Newspaper of the National Socialist Movement of Great Germany." Its last edition varied in date, in the territories of the north of the Reich: April 27 1945, or in the territories of the south of the Reich: April 30 1945.

Volkssturm

The *Volkssturm* (this can be translated as "attack of the people") was the popular army that was created by the decree of the Führer on September 25, 1944. With this decree it was established that all the men between sixteen and sixty year old who were able to hold a weapon, were conscripts and integrated into the country's defense plan against the advance of the Soviet Army in the east and the western allied troops in the west and in the south.

Three categories were established for the recruitment of the members of the *Volkssturm*:

a.) Men suitable for combat, born between 1884 and 1924; that is, who were between twenty and sixty years old, most of whom had served in the armed forces during the First World War.

b.) Men born between 1884 and 1924 who, because they were carrying out specialized work, were not already in military service.

c.) Men born between 1925 and 1928, from sixteen to nineteen years old, who were not yet doing military service.

From January 1945 the units of the *Volkssturm* were attached to the military units that were fighting on their respective sectors on the front.

Their effectiveness in war in general was low, although in some cases they managed to checkmate the enemy troops.

Waffen-SS

This was the combat corps of the *Schutzstaffeln* (SS). Although at the beginning it was just a protection unit for the leaders of the NSDAP, it became a very powerful combat force with close to a million men of very diverse nationalities who, in many cases, acted completely on the edge of the *Wehrmacht* on the various battle fronts during the Second World War. They were led by the *Reichsführer-SS* Heinrich Himmler.

At the end of the war, many of its members were subject to trial at Nüremberg for their participation in different atrocities and war crimes.

BIBLIOGRAPHY

Ailsby, C., *Hell on the Eastern Front, The Waffen-SS War in Russia. 1941-1945*, Brown Packaging Books Ltd., 1998.

Alcaide, J.A., "Berlín a muerte", *Revista Española de Historia Militar*, N°10, Quirón Ediciones, 2001.

Antill, P., *Berlin 1945, End of the Thousand Year Reich*, Osprey Publishing, 2005.

Archivos del Min. de Asuntos Exteriores.

"Bajo las banderas del III Reich alemán. Españoles en Rusia, 1941-1945", *Revista Defensa*, Mayo 1999.

Beevor, A., *Berlín 1945, La caída*, Memoria Crítica, 2002.

"Berlin 1945", *Magazine 39-45* n° 82 y 83, Hors-Série Historica, 2005.

Biddiscombe, P., *Los últimos Nazis, El movimiento de resistencia alemán 1944-1947*, Inédita Ediciones, 2008.

Bishop, C., *Hitler's Foreign Divisions, Foreign Volunteers in the Waffen-SS 1940-1945*, Amber Books Ltd., 2005.

Bowen, Wayne H., "The Ghost Battalion: Spaniards in the Waffen-SS, 1944-1945", *The Historian*, vol. 63, 2001.

Boyle D., *La II guerra mundial en imagines*, EDIMAT Libros S.A., 2000.

Bueno, J.M., *La división y la escuadrilla azul, Su organización y sus uniformes*, Aldaba, 2003.

Caballero, C., *Carlomagno, Voluntarios franceses en la Waffen-SS*, García Hispán, 2003.

– *Morir en Rusia, La División Azul en la batalla de Krasny Bor*, Quirón Ediciones, 2004.

– *El batallón fantasma, Españoles en la Wehrmacht y Waffen-SS, 1944-45*, CEHRE y ACTV, Alicante-Valencia, 1987.

– "Los últimos de los últimos, El batallón fantasma", *Revista Defensa*, Extra n°53.

– "Waffen-SS, Los centuriones del III Reich," *Revista Defensa*, Extra n°21.

– y Guillén, S. *Las escuadrillas azules en Rusia*. Almena. 1999.

Cardona. G., *El gigante descalzo*, Aguilar, 2003.

Darman, P., *Uniforms of World War II*, Blitz Editions, 1998.

Davis, B.L., *German Army, Uniforms and Insignia, 1933-1945*, Brockhamptom Press, 1992.

Escuadra, A., *Bajo las banderas de la Kriegsmarine, Marinos españoles en la Armada alemana*, Fundación Don Rodrigo, 1998.

Ezquerra, M., *Berlín a vida o muerte*, García Hispán, 1999.

Fernández, F., *Carros de combate y vehículos acorazados alemanes*, Servicio de publicaciones del EME, 1988.

Fey, W., *Armor Battles of the Waffen-SS, 1943-45*, Stackpole Books, 2003.

García, A.M., "Galubaya Divisia," *Crónica de la División Azul*, Fondo de Estudios Sociales, 2001.

García, M., "Semíramis, 1954: El regreso de los cautivos de la División Azul," *Revista Española de Historia Militar* Nº46.

Gómez, M.S., "España y Portugal ante la Segunda Guerra Mundial desde 1939 hasta 1942," *Espacio, Tiempo y Forma*, Serie V. Historia Contemporánea, t 7, 1994.

– y Sacristán, E., "España y Portugal durante la Segunda Guerra Mundial," *Espacio, Tiempo y Forma*, Serie V, Historia, Contemporánea, nº2, 1989.

Heiber, H., *Hitler y sus generals*, Memoria Crítica, 2005.

Holzträger, H., *In a Raging Inferno, Combat Units of the Hitler Youth, 1944-45*, Helion. 2000.

Jacobsen, H.A. y Dollinger, H., *La Segunda Guerra Mundial*, Volumen octavo, Plaza & Janés Editores S.A., 1989.

Keegan, J., *Waffen-SS. Los soldados del asfalto*, Editorial San Martín, 1979.

Kent, C., Wolber, T., y Hewitt, C., *The Lion and the Eagle: German-Spanish Relations Over the Centuries; an Interdisciplinary Approach*, Berghahn Books, 1999.

Kleinfeld, G. y Tambs, L., *La división española de Hitler, La División Azul en Rusia*, Editorial San Martín, 1983.

Kurowski, F., *Hitler's Last Bastion. The Final Battles for the Reich, 1944-1945*, Schiffer Military History, 1998.

"L´agonie du III Reich, 1945, Berlin." *Batailles & Blindés*, Hors-Serie nº1, 2005.

Lagarde, J., *German Soldiers of World War Two*, Histoire & Collection, 2005.

Lehmann, A., *En el búnker de Hitler, Testimonio de un niño soldado que vivió los últimos días del Führer*, Editorial El Ateneo, 2005.

Loringhoven, B.F., *En el búnker con Hitler*, Booket, 2007.

Lumsden, R., *SS Regalia*, Grange Books, 1995.

Mabire, J., *Los Waffen-SS franceses, Los últimos defensores de Hitler*, Biblioteca Nacionalsocialista Iberoamericana Volumen V., 2003.

Mitcham, S.W., *German Order of Battle*, Volume two, Stackpole Military History Series, 2007.

Mollo, A., *The Armed Forces of World War II, Uniforms, Insignia & Organization*, Greenwich Editions, 2000.

Morales, G. y Togores, L.E., *Las fotografías de una historia, La División Azul*, La Esfera de los Libros, 2008.

Moreno, X., *La División Azul, Sangre española en Rusia, 1941-1945*, Booket, 2006.

Muñoz, A., *Göring´s Grenadiers, The Luftwaffe Field Divisions 1942-1945*, Axis Europa Books, 2002.

Nart, J., "El Jefe español de las SS," *Interviú núm*, 339, Madrid, noviembre de 1982.

Norling, S.E., *Guerreros de Borgoña*, García Hispán Editor, 2008.

– *Raza de Vikingos, La División SS Nordland (1943-1945)*, García Hispán Editor, Segunda Edición.

– "The story of a Spanish Waffen-SS-Officer, SS-Obersturmführer R. Luis García Valdajos," *Siegrunen 79.*

Núñez Seixas, XM, "¿Un nazismo colaboracionista español? Martín de Arrizubieta, Wilhelm Faupel y los últimos de Berlín (1944-45)," *Historia Social* 51, (2005).

Pallud, J.P., Parker, D. y Volstad, R., *Ardenas 1944: Peiper y Skorzeny*, Ediciones del Prado, 1994.

Pérez, C.A., *Españoles en la Segunda Guerra Mundial (I) Combatiendo por el III Reich*, 2006 (text on the internet).

Peterson, D., *Waffen-SS Camouflage Uniforms & Post-War Derivates*, Windrow & Green Ltd., 1995.

Puente, M. Yo, *muerto en Rusia, Memorias del Alférez Ocañas de la División Azul*, Editorial San Martín, 2003.

Recio, R., *Españoles en la segunda guerra mundial (el frente del este)*, Vandalia, 1999.

– y González, A., *Uniformes del ejército de tierra alemán, Heer 1933-1945*, Euro Uniformes.

– *Das Heer, Uniformes y distintivos*, Agualarga, 1996.

Ryan, C., *La última batalla, La caída de Berlín y la derrota del nazismo*, Salvat, 2003.

Simons, G., *La Segunda Guerra Mundial*, "Victoria en Europa I," Time Life Folio, 1995.

Sourd, Jean-Pierre, *True Believers, Spanish Volunteers in the Heer and Waffen-SS, 1944-1945*, Europa Books, 2004.

– *Croisés d´un ideal*, Dualpha, 2007.

Torres, G., *Diccionario del Tercer Reich*, Tikal, 2009.

– "Españoles en las Waffen-SS, Italia, 1945", *Revista Española de Historia Militar*, nº10, 2001.

Trevor, H.R., *Los últimos días de Hitler*, José Janés Editor, 1949.

Tusell, J., *Gran Crónica de la Segunda Guerra Mundial*, Volumen 16, Edilibro, 1945.

Vadillo, F., *Los irreductibles*, García Hispán, 1993.

Westwell, I., *Brandenburgers, The Third Reich's Special Forces*, Ian Allan Publishing, 2003.

Williamson, G., *Las SS: Instrumento de terror de Hitler*, Ágata, 2002.

– y Andrew, S., *The Waffen-SS (4). 24 to 38 Divisions & Volunteer Legions*, Osprey Publishing, 2004.

Ziemke, E.F., *La batalla de Berlín, Fin del Tercer Reich*, San Martín, 1982.